People® weekly

MAGAZINE
GUIDE TO MOVIES
ON VIDEO

People weekly ®

MAGAZINE
GUIDE TO MOVIES ON VIDEO

Edited by
RALPH NOVAK
and
PETER TRAVERS

Collier Books
Macmillan Publishing Company
New York

Collier Macmillan Publishers
London

Macmillan Publishing Company
866 Third Avenue, New York, N.Y. 10022
Collier Macmillan Canada, Inc.

Library of Congress Cataloging-in-Publication Data

People magazine guide to movies on video.

  Includes index.
  1. Video recordings—Reviews.   2. Moving-pictures—
Reviews.   I. Novak, Ralph.   II. Travers, Peter.
III. People magazine (New York, N.Y.)
PN1992.945.P46   1987   791.43'75   87-9420
ISBN 0-02-029862-5

Macmillan books are available at special discounts for bulk purchases for sales promotions, premiums, fund-raising, or educational use. For details, contact:

> Special Sales Director
> Macmillan Publishing Company
> 866 Third Avenue
> New York, N.Y. 10022

10 9 8 7 6 5 4

Printed in the United States of America

Designed by Claudia DePolo

To Robyn, Alex, David, and Jenny—for understanding

P. T.

To my parents, Florence and John Novak,
with love and thanks for all those trips
to the Tiffin and the Roundup

R. N.

Contents

Acknowledgments

People began publishing movie reviews in 1977. Since these reviews ran without bylines until 1984, the names of a few of the writers are lost to history, but we would like to thank Scot Haller, Jim Calio, Tom Cunneff, Ira Hellman, Jim Jerome, David Hiltbrand, Irma Velasco, Cornelia Kennedy, Jeff Jarvis, Susan Champlin, Claudia Dowling, Lee Aitken, Mark Donovan, David Hutchings, Eric Levin, Arthur Lubow, Thaddeus Novak, and Jim Seymore. Their wit and insight helped make editing this book much more of a pleasure than a job.

Our gratitude also goes to Pat Ryan, *People*'s managing editor during the beginning of this project, for endorsing it and our participation. Deborah Himmelfarb and Jill Picariello of the *People* promotion department had the original idea for the book and the energy to push it (and us) along. Nancy Eils, Diane Kelley Giles, and Nelida Granado handled the organization and typing with diligence and patience, and we could not have asked for a more efficient, cheerful photo researcher than Joyce Campbell Seymore. Rose Ann Ferrick copyedited the manuscript with remarkable perseverance and attention to detail.

Whenever possible, at the end of each review we have noted which videotape distributor handles the movie. In cases where a film is too recent or too obscure to be available on tape, or we just couldn't find it, we have used "N/A" for not available. (In some few cases, such as the old *King Solomon's Mines* or *The Buddy Holly Story,* films have been withheld from videotape for various legal reasons.)

As for mistakes, we'll accept full responsibility, then blame each other.

People weekly®

MAGAZINE
GUIDE TO MOVIES
ON VIDEO

MOVIE REVIEWS

A

▲ ABOUT LAST NIGHT . . .

It's not a good idea to make a love story about two people who are so self-absorbed, sniveling, and bad-tempered that the audience wants them to end up in a dumpster, not living happily ever after. It's not a good idea to make a social satire about single people when they are already so inconsequential and empty that the effect resembles trying to puncture a deflated balloon. That doesn't leave much for this movie to do other than show off how handsome Rob (*Youngblood*) Lowe is and how charming Demi (*St. Elmo's Fire*) Moore can be. They play the couple in question, a restaurant supply salesman and an advertising agency artist, but they're not really to blame for the ill will their characters generate. Nor are Jim (*The Man with One Red Shoe*) Belushi and newcomer Elizabeth Perkins. Belushi plays Lowe's best friend, a relentless male chauvinist boor who keeps saying things like "You never call a broad more than once a week"; his lines are never any funnier than that, but they're usually a lot more obscene. Perkins is Moore's best friend, an all-time sourpuss who won't stop trying to sabotage the Lowe-Moore relationship. All four of these tiresome malcontents spend most of the movie griping about one another. They're also so shallow that Lowe's and Moore's idea of a tragic problem is whether to have ham or turkey for Thanksgiving. The film was the first feature by Emmy-winning director Edward Zwick. It was adapted from David Mamet's play, *Sexual Perversity in Chicago,* by Tim Kazurinsky and Denise De Clue, who had never had a screenplay produced before and whose talents would seem more appropriate for writing tomato paste can labels. When Belushi tells Lowe he's so good-looking that "the best thing that could happen to you would be an industrial accident," the film's high point in humor has been reached. The film was shot mostly in Chicago, which is portrayed as a beautiful city inhabited only by small-minded people who are always in a bad mood; its citizens should have sued for defamation of character.
R / 1986 / RCA/Columbia

▲ ABSENCE OF MALICE

As a mobster's son who runs a clean wholesale liquor business and an ambitious Miami newspaperwoman who wrongly links him to a murder, Paul Newman and Sally Field are great to look at. Furthermore, reporter-turned-screenwriter Kurk Luedtke and director Sydney (*The Way We Were*) Pollack raise an interesting question: What happens when an innocent citizen is bullied by a zealous news organization? There is, however, no plausible answer forthcoming. The plot is packed with glaring flaws. For one, Field never tries to get Newman's side of the story, an unlikely gaffe for a big-city journalist. More seriously, Newman's suffering seems trivial. The suicide of his friend, nicely acted by Oscar nominee Melinda Dillon, comes off as a blatant plot contrivance to raise the film's emotional ante. Even when he and Field become involved (of course), their showdowns ring false. When Field asks Newman if he's heard of women's liberation, he blithely snaps, "Most of them are ugly." Her feminism is so caricatured that after offering to buy his dinner, she teases, "Unless that'll make you impotent." Newman is just fine and picked up his fifth Oscar nomination as Best Actor (he lost to Henry Fonda in *On Golden*

1

Pond). It's this morally muddled, tediously self-righteous film that goes limp.
PG / 1981 / RCA/Columbia

▲ THE ADVENTURES OF BUCKAROO BANZAI

A comedy that became a minor cult classic, this movie is about as wacky as they come—and about as incoherent. Peter Weller plays sci-fi hero Buckaroo Banzai, a futuristic Renaissance man—brain surgeon, scientist, and rock performer. With the help of something called an Oscillation Overthruster, Buckaroo has broken through the dreaded eighth dimension; that is, he can travel through solid matter in his jet-powered pickup truck. But that trick unleashes some weirdos from outer space; they are so bizarre they keep turning up in business suits, looking like the CIA. John Lithgow plays a crazed alien inhabiting the body of the Italian scientist who invented the first Overthruster; his performance, highlighted by his blackened gums, lowers dementia to new depths. Ellen Barkin plays Buckaroo's girlfriend. In one inspired bit of black humor she tries to commit suicide in a club where Buckaroo is performing; when someone accidentally bumps her gun and the shot goes into the ceiling, the boys in the band instantly draw their guns, suspecting an ambush. Jeff Goldblum adds more quirkiness as a surgeon recruited for the Banzai gang when it takes out after the evil aliens. Weller's absolutely straight performance makes his character seem even loonier than he sounds. He lives with the gang in what looks like a run-down warehouse while the alien spaceships look like caves littered with junk food wrappers. And you've got to love the credits at the end, when the cast struts down a street dressed in outlandish outfits. Directed by W. D. Richter, who wrote *Invasion of the Body Snatchers* and *Brubaker,* the film is like *Blade Runner* with a sense of humor. It's high-tech seedy, the kind of movie you laugh at out loud, sometimes without even knowing why.
PG / 1984 / Vestron

▲ AFTER HOURS

Dante had nothing on director Martin Scorsese, who sees evening romance in the Big Apple as only slightly less terrifying than an express run through the nine circles of hell. Scorsese's Inferno, a poison valentine to New York City, is a comedy of startling originality, a racy, raucous ride through the night, bound to leave viewers reeling with laughter. The film's coproducer, Griffin Dunne, stars as a bachelor bored with his job as a word processor operator and with evenings alone in his apartment, switching cable TV channels. One night, reading Henry Miller's *Tropic of Cancer* in a dreary coffee shop, Dunne strikes up a conversation with appealingly available Rosanna Arquette, who invites him over to her friend's loft in the artsy Manhattan enclave of SoHo. And so begins Dunne's waking nightmare—murder for him, mirthful for us. Scorsese, working with Fassbinder's master cameraman Michael Ballhaus, finds eerie beauty in SoHo's industrial lighting and rain-splattered streets, and fun in such details as the cannonball velocity of keys thrown from a loft window. A small but superbly crafted film, *After Hours* is expertly edited by Thelma Schoonmaker and written by Joseph Minion, who created it as a part of his course work at Columbia University's Graduate Film Division. Arquette's monologue about her husband, a *Wizard of Oz* freak who can't reach orgasm without shouting "Surrender, Dorothy," is a particular gem. The acting, even in the smallest roles, is uniformly splendid. Besides Arquette and Dunne, standouts include Teri Garr as a sex-starved waitress trapped in a '60s beehive hairdo; Catherine O'Hara, who tries to run down Dunne with her Mister Softee truck; Cheech and Chong as bickering thieves; and especially sexy Linda Fiorentino, a scene stealer as a kinky sculptress who involves Dunne in S&M, a suicide, and a narrow escape from his own death. It's not that they don't make comedies like *After Hours* anymore. The fact is there's never been a comedy quite like this one.
R / 1985 / Warner

▲ AFTER THE REHEARSAL

Ingmar Bergman said that *Fanny and Alexander,* 1984's Oscar winner for best foreign film, would be his last movie. *After the Rehearsal,* a brilliant fragment, 72 minutes long and filmed after *Fanny and Alexander,* was originally shown on Swedish television, but it's powerful on the big screen as well. Set on a stage after rehearsal, the plot concerns a theater director, played by Erland

Josephson, who bears a remarkable resemblance to Bergman. He's directing a young, beautiful actress who will do anything to further her career and an aging star who may have had an affair with the director. In fact, the relationships among the three—past and present—are confusing. The young actress, played by Lena Olin in her first major role, seems at times to be the director's daughter from a liaison with the older woman, played by Ingrid Thulin. At one point Josephson and Olin act out what would happen if they had an affair, right there on the stage, as if they were reading for a play. It's a tribute to Bergman's genius that he can control such scenes and keep his camera on his actor's faces in extreme close-up for much of the film without being boring. He did it in such movies as *Scenes from a Marriage* and *Face to Face,* and it works here, too, thanks in part to his longtime cinematographer, Sven Nyukvist. It's hard not to read this bitter portrait of an exploitive, cold man as a scathing self-indictment by Bergman. But then, he never spared anyone, including himself. (In Swedish with subtitles.)
R / 1984 / RCA/Columbia

▲ AGAINST ALL ODDS

The odds are decidedly not in favor of this movie comparing favorably with *Out of the Past,* the 1947 film noir classic on which it is based. Robert Mitchum, Kirk Douglas, and Jane Greer made up the romantic triangle in that movie, in which director Jacques Tourneur told the story of a tough dame who ruins two men. This needlessly complicated update, directed by Taylor Hackford, just limps along. Still, if you like colorful atmosphere (Mexico looks luscious), great bodies (courtesy of Rachel Ward and Jeff Bridges), and campy dialogue, it could be diverting. Bridges, exuding matinee-idol panache, is terrific as a football star on the skids who takes on a gumshoe job for an L.A. club owner, played with shifty authority by James Woods. Ward has run off to Mexico with $50,000 of Woods's ill-won money, and he wants to find her. Ward plays a spoiled woman whose mom (the very same Jane Greer from the Tourneur film) owns Bridges's football team. Meanwhile, Mom and her boyfriend (Richard Widmark), involved in a real estate scheme that leads to murder, set up Bridges as a patsy. Okay, it wasn't easy to understand the first version

either. But that one had that no-nonsense bad-girl performance from Greer. Ward is pallid by contrast. Though she was smashingly sexy in *Sharky's Machine* and sweetly appealing in TV's *The Thorn Birds,* the vital spark is missing in this case. Greer's bitchy, all-stops-out cameo only reminds us of what's missing. *Out of the Past* had the texture of cold steel; *Against All Odds,* with its pretty colors and upbeat ending, seems made of marshmallow.
R / 1984 / RCA/Columbia

▲ AGATHA

Dustin Hoffman was distressed that First Artists denied him his contracted final cut (he disowned any producer credit). But *Agatha* seems to have gotten along very well without his editing. Based on Agatha Christie's actual eleven-day disappearance in 1926, the movie is billed as "a fictional solution to a real mystery." Vanessa Redgrave plays the overwrought mystery writer who discovers that her husband is dallying with his secretary. She escapes to Harrogate (a once posh British spa exquisitely refitted for the film) and plots a solution to her problem. Hoffman, an American gossip columnist, tracks her down, falls in love with her, and saves her life. Redgrave, with her gently aristocratic face, is perfect for the role; she and the much shorter Hoffman make an engaging, if odd, couple. Timothy Dalton, who later became the fourth James Bond, also stands out as Agatha's cheating husband. And Kathleen Tynan, who wrote the book the movie is based on and coauthored the screenplay, concocted a solution to the gap in Christie's life worthy of a Poirot.
PG / 1979 / Warner

▲ AGNES OF GOD

As an event in the Broadway theater, *Agnes of God* was compelling drama. In a face-off between spirituality and psychiatry, three women form an unholy trinity of obsession: Agnes, a young nun with arcane ideas about sin and sex, apparently has strangled her baby after giving birth in a convent. In the legal proceeding that follows, her mother superior and her court-appointed psychiatrist battle over Agnes's welfare. "I know what you are," says the mother superior to the shrink.

"I don't want that mind cut open." Even Agnes tells the woman, "You want to take God away from me." It's *Equus* in skirts, but onstage the vivid performances of Elizabeth Ashley, Geraldine Page, and Amanda Plummer camouflaged the drama's secondhand sensibility. In converting his play to the screen, writer John Pielmeier has set the story in Quebec and spoiled the cloisterphobia of his work with exterior scenes. Thus transformed, *Agnes of God* proves occasionally hypnotic, but as a movie it lacks what is a necessity for this kind of drama: a smokescreen of bravura acting. Surprisingly, the most unoriginal sins are committed by Jane Fonda, who never invests the shrink role with the intensity it demands. With her movie-star-plays-career-woman outfits and coifs, Fonda prizes her composure too much to play this obsessive woman. She lets Pielmeier's one telltale bit of business—the doctor is a chain-smoker—do all the work. Consequently, while watching *Agnes* you recast her role with, say, Vanessa Redgrave or the young Barbara Stanwyck—actresses who might have brought an inherent passion to the part. As the mother superior, Anne Bancroft doesn't conjure up much fervor either (her nomination as Best Actress is a bigger mystery than any in the film). So the entire emotional geometry of the movie is thrown off. Yet Meg Tilly makes Agnes a mesmerizing figure. As determined in the secular world as she is ethereal, she embodies all the ambivalence that the script revolves around. She seems a woman of singular conviction whose conscience is worth the fight that Bancroft and Fonda wage over it. Still, that's hardly enough to sustain the film. *Agnes* needed a director with a flair for the daring, but instead it was reined in by a master of the middlebrow, Norman Jewison. *Agnes of God* should ask for the audience's absolution.

R / 1985 / RCA/Columbia

▲ AGUIRRE: THE WRATH OF GOD

Whither El Dorado, mythical city of the Incas? Nowhere, archeologists now seem sure. But Lope de Aguirre, a real-life 16th-century Spanish conquistador, and his band of explorers learned that the hard way—by two months of rafting through an Amazon River jungle, dodging cannibals and poisoned arrows. Brilliantly directed by Werner Herzog, the trip is the stuff of which myths are made. Klaus Kinski's quietly flipped-out, Queeg-like performance as Aguirre made this German film a contender for the cult-film status it has now indelibly achieved.

Unrated / 1972 / Continental

▲ AIRPLANE!

From takeoff to landing, this whacked-out parody is a loopy flight of fancy. Fly the flaky skies of "Trans American," and your ticket for the smoking section is literally smoldering; your coffee, tea, or me is served *before* dinner; and the in-flight movie shows a terrible airplane crash. Up in the cockpit, Kareem Abdul-Jabbar is moonlighting as the copilot, and a plastic Jesus sits reassuringly atop the instrument panel. Among the passengers, a nun reads *Boy's Life,* while a boy peruses *Nun's Life.* It's that kind of film, a cheerfully slapdash send-up of everything from the *Airport* movies to *Jaws* to *Saturday Night Fever,* written and directed by Jim Abrahams, David and Jerry Zucker, who had had a cult success with *The Kentucky Fried Movie.* Not every joke works, to be sure, but they come along with such zingy regularity that it doesn't much matter. Veterans Lloyd Bridges, Peter Graves, Leslie Nielsen, and Robert Stack get their laughs simply by playing it straight.

PG / 1980 / Paramount

▲ AIRPLANE II: THE SEQUEL

It could well have been just another crass, exploitative sequel, but *Airplane II* is an amiable, fresh comedy. The strange, surprising success of 1980's *Airplane!,* which cost about $3.5 million and grossed more than $150 million, would be hard to duplicate. This film includes basically the same cast and crew but without the writing-directing team of Jim Abrahams and David and Jerry Zucker, who were responsible for the original's relentless black humor. They gave way to the relatively unknown Ken Finkleman, making his directorial debut. (He wrote the screenplay for *Grease 2.*) The plot has to do with the launching of the first commercial shuttle to a moon colony. Sight gags and non sequiturs tumble all over one another. Fans of the original will be pleased that Robert Hays and Julie Hagerty return as the love-crossed stars. Lloyd Bridges is back as the chain-smoking air traffic controller; so are

Peter Graves as the pederastic pilot and Stephen Stucker as the wisecracking gay at Mission Control. Both Leslie Nielsen, who followed Abrahams, Zucker, and Zucker to the undeservedly short-lived TV comedy "Police Squad!" and Robert Stack have been replaced. Instead, *Airplane II* boasts William Shatner as an energetic lunar base commander and Chuck Connors as the gruff Sarge at the launch site. Sonny Bono also appears as an impotent bomber who has purchased his explosive device in the airport gift shop; Chad Everett is a conniving crew member; Raymond Burr is a judge; and game show host Art Fleming has a cameo as himself. Don't expect overwhelming amounts of common sense; just expect to laugh. *Airplane II* not only manages to lumber down the runway, it even flies under its own power, a rare accomplishment for a sequel.
PC / 1983 / Paramount

▲ AIRPORT '77

Oscar winner Jack Lemmon hid behind a black moustache but otherwise looked unashamed of selling out his talent for this second and tackiest sequel to 1970's box-office hit, *Airport.* He turned up as the stereotypic captain-in-command whose hijacked 747, loaded with booty and ancient stars, crashes and sinks in the Bermuda Triangle. Despite admirable special effects, those given to realism may be surprised when the plane stays in one airtight piece. The film itself sinks fathoms below *The Poseidon Adventure* and only rarely rises above *The Hindenburg.*
PG / 1977 / MCA

▲ ALAMO BAY

Maybe it looked good on paper. The story does have the immediacy of a newspaper headline: It was inspired by a 1980 *New York Times Magazine* article about the outbreak of violence between Texas shrimp fishermen and the Vietnamese refugees they believed were encroaching on their territory. Director Louis Malle, a Frenchman who has lived in America since 1977, saw the possibilities of drama in the difficulty of assimilation. More than one hundred thousand Vietnamese settled in Texas after the Vietnam War ended in 1975. They lived apart, working tirelessly, showing little interest in learning English, and ignoring

the local fishing laws. A blowup was all but inevitable. Goaded by the Ku Klux Klan, the Anglos began firebombing Vietnamese boats and house trailers. Malle said this modern variation on the battle of the Alamo represented "a terrific setting for a film. We just needed great characters and a great story." He didn't get either. Alice Arten's screenplay is primarily a study in stereotypes. Ed Harris, playing a Texas shrimper, might as well go around wearing a badge that reads "bigot." Harris is supposed to elicit sympathy, since the bank won't give him an extension on his loan and foreigners are fishing his waters. But the man is at heart an inflexible slug who beats the wife he cheats on and who is not above a little gook-baiting either. In contrast, Ho Nguyen, then a Vietnamese medical student at Houston University with no previous acting experience, is shy and near saintly as a struggling refugee. Malle tries to balance the ledger by casting Amy Madigan as a local girl who helps her sick father (Donald Moffat) run a fish-processing factory while carrying on with Harris. It is Madigan who comes to recognize the injustice being done to the Vietnamese. Madigan and Harris (who met and married when they co-starred in *Places in the Heart*) are intelligent, forceful actors, and they generate real heat in a dance sequence that seems to belong to another film. Yet their characters remain cardboard figures in a supercharged landscape that Malle fails to activate. Malle's dedication to this project is unquestioned. But he has made a dry, airless package of a movie in which everything comes too neatly labeled: Search for human drama at your peril. You'll come away empty.
R / 1985 / RCA/Columbia

▲ ALIEN

To the list of classic sci-horror films that includes Lugosi's *Dracula*, both versions of *Invasion of the Body Snatchers*, *The Exorcist*, and *Night of the Living Dead*, add this wonderfully unsettling tale about blobs that breathe and live in dank holes on some unknown planet. Seven astronauts—including Tom Skerritt, Sigourney Weaver, John Hurt, and the versatile Yaphet Kotto—are the human protagonists, the crew of a cargo-carrying spaceship that is diverted into a lot of trouble. Only creature-feature fans with strong stomachs will root for the shape-changing aliens, rendered with the best effects since *Star Wars.*

Director Ridley Scott doesn't shortchange his actors though. Weaver is particularly impressive in the aggressive role she reprised in *Aliens* in 1986. Overall, this film is enough to restore one's faith in monsterkind.
R / 1979 / CBS/Fox

▲ ALIENS

So much for the theory that sequels never equal the original. Director James (*The Terminator*) Cameron expanded and improved on Ridley Scott's 1979 smash, *Alien*. Guaranteed to knock the wind and wits out of you, his follow-up is more than just scary. Try stylish, rousing, and amusing for starters. Sigourney Weaver, a warrant officer on the first trip of the spacecraft *Nostromo,* is the only cast member to return. She and her cat were the only survivors of an alien attack on the ship's crew, which included Tom Skeritt, Veronica Cartwright, and John Hurt. Most people remember Hurt best since the alien burst angrily out of his stomach to wreak bloody carnage. Be warned that Cameron repeats that effect and takes it a few steps further. Effects expert Stan Winston, who worked with Cameron on *The Terminator,* designed the meanest, mangiest, slime-drippingest creatures to ever inhabit a viewer's nightmares. But to reveal more would spoil the fun (yes, these stomach-churners are a hoot for some of us). Let's just say that Weaver has made it home after fifty-seven years. Don't worry, she still looks gorgeous, having whiled away the years in suspended animation. She returns to the alien-infested planet of Acheron because sneaky Paul (*Diner*) Reiser tells her that families have moved there with no idea of the danger. So Weaver (sans cat) jumps on board with a new crew, who carry sophisticated weapons but trade the kind of quips you hear in old Westerns and WWII combat films. "Saddle up," says one. There's a love interest for Weaver in the personable Michael Biehn, also from *The Terminator,* and a charmer of an abandoned child (Carrie Henn) for Weaver to mother. Nothing new here except the clever way Cameron uses humor and heartbreak to get the audience rooting for Weaver. Despite the competition from the hardware, Weaver (Oscar-nominated as Best Actress) comes through with a spirited, knockout performance that dominates the film. Her final duel with the alien queen would shame Rambo. If you want your juices

stirred by experts, leave Aunt Nellie home and check out *Aliens*—a sure bet to be the class-act thriller for a long time to come.
R / 1986 / CBS/Fox

▲ ALLIGATOR

Everyone has heard tell of pet baby alligators being flushed down the toilet and thereafter roaming the sewers. With wit and satirical invention, screenwriter John (*Return of the Secaucus Seven*) Sayles transforms that old story into a humdinger horror film that delivers thrills without letting up on the funny bone. In a prologue, no sooner does a little girl dub her pet Ramon than her irate daddy flushes the reptile into a watery oblivion—temporarily. The child grows up to be an adult herpetologist (played by Robin Riker) called in by the police to investigate a bizarre series of sewer murders. The only clues are chewed-up body parts. Cop Robert Forster is the first to see the fully grown Ramon (now thirty-six feet long) just after the gator has dined on his partner. Nobody believes Forster until the monster hits the city streets. Ramon even shows his social conscience by attacking a lawn party thrown by a vivisectionist. Director Lewis (*The Lady in Red*) Teague keeps the movie moving briskly; special effects wizards do the same for Ramon.
R / 1981 / TL

▲ ALL NIGHT LONG

"Night is the new frontier," Barbra Streisand tells Gene Hackman encouragingly after a row with his boss has reduced him to running an all-night drugstore inhabited by customers resembling the zombies in *Dawn of the Dead.* Everyone in this sodden comedy seems similarly lobotomized. Hackman's wife (Diane Ladd) pads about listlessly. His dull-witted teenage son (Dennis Quaid) calls a cerebral hemorrhage a brain hemorrhoid. And Hackman's ditzy girlfriend (Streisand), a nymphomaniac married to his wife's cousin, is bedding Quaid on the side. Ending up as a singing waiter in an Italian restaurant, Hackman tries hard to make sense of his surroundings, but nobody could manage that. Streisand replaced the sacked Lisa (*Yanks*) Eichhorn as a favor to her pal (and then agent) Sue Mengers, the wife of the film's director, Jean-Claude Tramont. But Barbra seems to be doing an im-

personation of Goldie Hawn on Quaaludes. Her attempt to play a character other than herself is praiseworthy, but a stupefied Streisand is worse than no Streisand at all. Miscast as an untalented country singer, she bleats about a heart "carelessly tossed from a speeding car onto the hard-luck pavement of life." After just a little of this off-key offal, one wishes the lights would go out.
R / 1981 / MCA

▲ ALL OF ME

Hollywood has never quite known what to do with Lily Tomlin and Steve Martin. Like Bill Murray, the two comedians are mainly adroit at striking attitudes; their performances usually comment on the action as much as carry it out. Consequently, Tomlin and Martin often defy assimilation: It's no laughing matter trying to find a script that can accommodate the comic sensibilities of either. *All of Me* does it for both—because it is a comedy mainly about attitudes. Directed by Carl Reiner, *All of Me* is a slapstick, hipster hybrid of *Heaven Can Wait* and *Tootsie*. Martin plays a malcontent lawyer presiding over the last hours of a rich, bedridden spinster. The spinster is Tomlin, performing with great glee like a wicked witch of Beverly Hills. At the moment of her demise, Tomlin tries to use an Eastern mystic's technique to trade places with her servant's pretty daughter, Victoria Tennant. But the experiment goes awry, and Martin finds himself a stranger in his own body, with Tomlin controlling his right side while he controls his left. Phil Alden Robinson's script has its contrivances, but in this case the stars' stand-back-from-it-all styles neutralize those troubles. With his herky-jerky physical comedy this time integrated into the script, Martin was voted the year's Best Actor by the New York Film Critics Circle. And while Tomlin gets the short end of the shtick, she is no less funny as a disembodied voice than as a disgruntled shrew. *All of Me* shows a fine appreciation for the little weirdnesses of life and provides some gratifying shenanigans.
PG / 1984 / Thorn/EMI

▲ ALL THAT JAZZ

Explaining the theme is easy. A self-pitying musical-comedy director is preoccupied with death. But it's harder explaining how Bob Fosse made that maudlin quasi-autobiographical notion into one terrific movie. Absorbing and profound, *All That Jazz* brims with the nervous energy of fear, self-mocking irony, desperation, and an insane kind of hope. One key reason is a spectacular starring performance by Roy Schneider, who in a Vandyke beard resembles Fosse. The director uses the hypnotic close-ups and vivid settings of his earlier Oscar winner, *Cabaret*, but here blends them with fantasy sequences. His choreography hasn't suffered either. One smoky, shadowy ensemble dance is as erotic as any ever filmed. Ann Reinking, Fosse's onetime real-life companion, lives with the film's hero. Leland Palmer plays a dancer who's his sometime wife (Fosse was married to Gwen Verdon). Erzsebet Fold, 13, is the daughter. All the actors profit from Fosse's choreographic ingenuity. The film creates its own universe so well that even footage of open-heart surgery (which Fosse went through in 1975) isn't out of place. Is this neo–musical comedy? Melo-musical? Call it superb and leave it at that.
R / 1979 / CBS/Fox

▲ ALL THE RIGHT MOVES

Here's presumption in movie titles. Except for the casting of then new star Tom Cruise, first-time director Michael Chapman made hardly any right moves in this turgid teen drama about coming-of-age in a Pennsylvania steel town. Cinematographer Jan DeBont gives the film the gritty look of *The Deer Hunter*, but the script by Michael Kane (from a *Geo* article by Pat Jordan) has the mushy feel of a TV movie. Cruise and pals Paul Carafotes and Christopher Penn (yes, he is Sean's brother and a beefier version of same) see college football scholarships as their only escape from a bleak future. The trouble is, the filmmakers rarely make the kids' lives seem all that bleak. The guys boogie in the locker room to a rock sound track, make out with cheerleaders, and have time for hijinks involving jockstraps. For a while, it's *Porkys* meets *Flashdance*. Then, suddenly, Penn's girl is pregnant, and he must forget football for marriage, while Carafotes—whose poor grades put him out of scholarship contention—turns to a life of crime. Cruise almost blows his chances for the scholarship by mouthing off to the coach, played in the lovable-lout tradition by *Poltergeist*'s Craig T. Nelson. Nelson wants to blow town as much as Cruise,

and these two actors are good enough to make a cliché-ridden conflict seem momentarily compelling. But Chapman, deservedly praised for his cinematography on *Taxi Driver* and *Raging Bull,* won't settle for a small, simple story. He shoots the football scenes in slogging slow motion, reveling in the mud-and-macho lyricism. And he treats Cruise and girlfriend Lea Thompson like a modern Romeo and Juliet. Chapman doesn't use the score of *West Side Story* to hype their sexual encounters, but by throwing in everything else, he ends up sacking himself.
R / 1983 / CBS/Fox

▲ AN ALMOST PERFECT AFFAIR

A good argument can be made that this is director Michael Ritchie's worst movie—his others include *The Candidate, Smile,* and *Semi-Tough.* A young producer (Keith Carradine) goes to the Cannes Film Festival, tries to peddle his low-budget movie about Gary Gilmore on death row, and falls in love with a married woman (Monica Vitti). Cameos by Farrah Fawcett, George Peppard, and Brooke Shields (shot at 1978's festival) supply a little cinema verité. Surprisingly, Ritchie handles his foreign actors better than Carradine, who seems mainly puzzled. Vitti is marvelously vulnerable as the older woman, and veteran Raf Vallone is reassuringly dignified as her producer husband. The final scene, lifted straight from *Casablanca,* features Carradine and a pal strolling down a misty airport runway. Perhaps conceived in homage, the idea looks more like a rip-off. Ritchie, often a director of great originality, should have known better.
PG / 1979 / Paramount

▲ ALMOST YOU

Almost You is almost a movie. What it is instead is a fluffy puff of intelligence spread very thinly over 96 minutes. It stars Brooke Adams and was, curiously enough, written and directed by newcomer Adam Brooks. The movie aspires to be a quiet little romantic comedy, focusing on a rocky marriage between Adams, as a New York freelance illustrator, and her unsatisfied husband, Griffin Dunne, who is inheriting the family clothing business. When Adams is hit by a taxi, the accident incapacitates her and briefly liberates the philanderer in Dunne. Adams is coolly attractive, and Dunne, though he is discomfitingly similar to Dudley Moore, radiates nervous energy. The bright spot is filled by Karen Young, playing a therapist who starts out working on Adams's hip and ends up working on her husband. Young has an alluring kind of weary charm; she looks as if she ought to be in an Ingmar Bergman film. Josh Mostel also makes a notable contribution as a jolly friend who wisecracks through a dinner party given by Adams and Dunne. The humor is cynical: "Any idiot can have a long-term relationship; all you have to do is smile a lot." There's not enough of the humor in any case. The plot seems to fade, leaving the kind of feeling that might be derived from watching an interesting band tune up for a while and then go home without playing anything.
R / 1985 / Key

▲ ALPHABET CITY

A is for atrocious, B is for banal, C is for crummy. . . . The title actually refers to several avenues, designated by letters, in a section of Manhattan favored by addicts, derelicts, and struggling artists—but no one quite like the character played by Vincent Spano in this movie. He is already the neighborhood crime boss—and a busy boss at that. In one night he rescues his sister from a prostitution ring, shakes down the owner of a disco, makes a daring escape from the police, murders a bunch of gangsters, ponders torching his parents' apartment building, and makes love to his girlfriend. He remembers to bring disposable diapers for his baby too. Director Amos Poe, who had built an underground reputation of sorts, seems to think an absurd plot, clichéd dialogue, and cartoony characters can make a commercial hit. W is for wrong.
R / 1984 / CBS/Fox

▲ ALTERED STATES

As a filmmaker, Ken Russell does not believe in half measures. Why go partway when one can just as easily go too far? So it comes as no surprise that his adaptation of Paddy Chayefsky's 1978 novel about altered states of consciousness is as pretentious, excessive, bizarre, and (occasionally) awe-inspiring as any movie in recent

years. (A horrified Chayefsky took his name off the picture.) The story concerns a faculty member (William Hurt) at Harvard Medical School who subjects himself to increasingly dangerous experiments with psychedelic drugs. Russell's visual effects make *2001* (from which he borrows freely) look like Mickey Mouse, and in the best scene the professor, transformed into a primitive man, runs wild through the streets of Boston. No character—including the undeniably talented Hurt in his movie debut—is even vaguely likable, and the mawkish ending is a laugh. In the Russell tradition, there are brilliant flashes on an overwrought trip to nowhere.
R / 1980 / Warner

▲ ALWAYS

If this movie were a horse, you'd shoot it to put it out of its misery. Directed by Henry (*Can She Bake a Cherry Pie?*) Jaglom, who developed a cult reputation for making personal films, this one is so personal that only Jaglom would want to see it. It is based on his real-life divorce from wife Patrice Townsend, and they play themselves. Townsend is a bright, gorgeous, touching actress; for her to have been stuck in Jaglom films is roughly equivalent to baseball Hall of Famer Ernie Banks having toiled away throughout his career with the futile Chicago Cubs. Jaglom is another story. He portrays himself as a sniveling, self-pitying jerk nobody would want to spend thirty seconds with, and he's totally convincing. The plot centers on Jaglom's attempt to lure Townsend back into marriage after a two-year separation. (If he really whined about it this much in real life, it's no wonder she went through with the divorce.) A party ensues, at which the only people who aren't foolish and/or loathsome are Melissa ("All My Children") Leo, as Townsend's sister, and Jonathan Kaufer (he directed *Soup for One*), as the sister's boyfriend. Not since the beginning of recorded time have 105 minutes passed so slowly.
R / 1985 / Vestron

▲ AMADEUS

Director Milos Forman, riding on waves of Mozart's incomparable music, makes something undeniably thrilling out of Peter Shaffer's 1980 Broadway smash. It won the 1984 Best Picture Oscar, plus individual awards for Forman and F. Murray Abraham (as Best Actor). But admirers of the show about a fictional battle between God and 18th-century Italian composer Antonio Salieri over a prodigy named Wolfgang Amadeus Mozart must be prepared to make some adjustments for the film version. The play, turning on the conflict between Salieri's mediocrity and Mozart's then unrecognized genius, was faster, funnier, and innately more theatrical. Shaffer hasn't simply adapted his work for the screen, he has rigorously rethought it. There's a new central character: the voice of God in the form of Mozart's music. Onstage, the music was an afterthought piped through tinny theater speakers. Onscreen, music coordinator John Strauss and conductor Neville Marriner make the Mozart melodies speak more eloquently than any of the characters. The result is a trade-off: a feast for the ear that wreaks havoc with dramatic flow. Forman doesn't help the pace, using a musty flashback technique to frame the film. But once the story begins in earnest, with court composer Salieri's first meeting with Mozart in Vienna, Forman guns his engines with all the brio he deployed in *One Flew Over the Cuckoo's Nest*. The location work in Prague pays off not just in beauty but also as inspiration for the actors. Though Shaffer and Forman sometimes use irritatingly anachronistic dialogue ("Show me your stuff") and mixed accents, the film is cunningly cast without star names. Jeffrey Jones is wickedly splendid as Emperor Joseph II, Elizabeth Berridge brings surprising strength to the one-dimensional role of Mozart's scheming wife, and stage actor Roy Dotrice is a mix of fire and ice as Mozart's ramrod father. But Amadeus centers—as it must—on Tom Hulce and Abraham, two American actors rising marvelously to the challenge of their careers. Abraham's Salieri moves from unholy glee at sabotaging God's "obscene creature" to racking guilt. Hulce, the nerd in *National Lampoon's Animal House*, is Mozart. His flat voice and open face are as American as the Nebraska prairie, and the way he exaggerates Mozart's hyena laugh and childish gestures sometimes ties a tin can to his performance. But Hulce grows in the part. His deathbed scene, as he dictates the *Requiem* to Salieri, was the screen's most successful attempt to date at depicting genius. With Mozart's magical music swirling around them, Hulce and Abraham share a duel triumph in a film that

Amadeus: F. Murray Abraham and Tom Hulce explore the intricacies and excesses of the creative mind in Milos Forman's film about Wolfgang Amadeus Mozart and his admirer-rival, Antonio Salieri.

stands as a provocative and prodigious achievement.

PG / 1984 / Thorn/EMI

▲ THE AMATEUR

If its story line wasn't so improbable and so similar to *Three Days of the Condor,* this would be a far more enjoyable spy thriller. The actors—mainly John Savage, Christopher Plummer, and Marthe Keller—are appealing, as are the Toronto, Vienna, and Munich locations. Try, however, to swallow this chain of events: International terrorists take over an American consulate in Munich. They kill a hostage, a journalist who is Savage's girlfriend. He is a civilian employee for the CIA back in Virginia. When, for political reasons, the agency refuses to pursue the terrorists, Savage blackmails a CIA official into teaching him to be an agent; then, after the equivalent of a cram course in assassination, he chases the terrorists to Czechoslovakia. There he meets friendly Keller and not-so-friendly Plummer, a Czech spy who's also a Shakespearean scholar. It all strains credibility. Director Charles (*Anne of a Thousand Days*) Jarrott seems to have forgotten Robert Redford and Faye Dunaway went through most of this in *Condor,* which may not have been more realistic than this movie but did at least get there first.

R / 1982 / CBS/Fox

▲ AMAZING GRACE AND CHUCK

In its many moments of horrendous naiveté and egregious sentimentality, this antiwar fable seems like the *Love Story* of nuclear politics: Love means never having to say you blew the world to pieces. The premise is the very definition of wishful thinking. A 12-year-old Montana boy, terrified by what he sees during a tour of a missile silo, decides to stop playing baseball until nuclear weapons have been eliminated. That inspires a pro basketball star to copy him, which sets off a chain reaction among athletes and then children all over the world. Preposterous? Yes. And yet

this is a touching, winning film that finally makes its stubborn innocence seem as much genius as folly. This success is largely due to an astonishingly good cast. There are affecting scenes between somber Joshua Zuehlke, 12, as the boy and William L. Petersen as his father, an Air Force Reserve fighter pilot who is torn between love for his son and fear that all his beliefs are under attack. Gregory Peck, as President of the United States, masterfully creates a complex character. Jamie Lee Curtis plays the basketball player's financial manager with a bright, wisecracking manner that relieves a lot of the movie's self-importance. Most impressive is NBA star Alex English, who plays Amazing Grace Smith, the thoughtful jock who follows in Zuehlke's footsteps because he too is desperate to do something—anything—about a seemingly hopeless problem. Pro basketball's 1983 scoring champion (and a published poet), the 6-foot, 7-inch English displays an exacting combination of strength and gentleness, and his performance would be a triumph for a seasoned actor. The cast and director Mike Newell had to be near perfect, because the script by producer David Field seems desperate. A subplot, for instance, brings in a sinister character who sounds like a reject James Bond villain to try to stop the antiwar movement. The lines are not only of the "But wouldn't it be nice . . ." school, they actually include that phrase. The ending is both corny and foolish. Crackpot stuff, this. But there are worse ways to go crackpot than by calling attention to the implications of nuclear weapons.
PG / 1987 / N/A

▲ AMERICAN ANTHEM

There hadn't been this much raw energy in a film since *Rocky*. On the other hand, all that kinetic force is totally unfocused, leaving a pastiche of undirected elements that never forms a convincing whole. Olympic gold medal gymnast Mitch Gaylord debuts as a small-town boy who forsakes a college football scholarship to make motorcycles, though his real love is (surprise) gymnastics. Lucky thing his Arizona town is big enough for a cycle shop and a championship-level gymnastics training center, complete with a Russian coach. His home life is a poor man's *Great Santini,* as he watches his family fall apart in between feuds with his unemployed father, TV

actor John Aprea. His mother, played by ex-"Mama" Michelle Phillips, says such things as, "You've gotta pull it together now, Steve. Pull it together for yourself." But the film isn't just about Gaylord. There's Janet (*A Chorus Line*) Jones as an imported New York gymnast who can't cope with the strictures of training for the Big Meet. There are a couple of teammates (Stacey Maloney and Maria Anz) who get nary a glance until the finale. Gaylord doesn't sound half as intense as he looks—and that's the problem with the film. It tries so hard to distance itself from the teen-shlock genre, it ends up confused. Motivation is only hinted at. And we never really learn what's inside the film's most intriguing character (played with zest by Andrew White), Jones's angst-filled cousin, who turned to composing music following the auto accident that killed his parents and left him handicapped. Director Albert (*Purple Rain*) Magnoli incorporates a pop sound track and uses some slick gymnastics scenes well. He also takes on too much in what amounts to an underdeveloped statement on the pressures of small-town life. It's like trying to master the parallel bars, rings, and side horse before leaning to stretch.
PG-13 / 1986 / Karl-Lorimar

▲ AMERICAN DREAMER

With some movies you have to check your brain at the door of the video rental store. With *American Dreamer,* you'd better check your calendar too. This romantic comedy comes on like the most lighthearted lark of 1954. It shamelessly embraces the values (production, moral, and other) of Eisenhower-era filmmaking: It's an American-in-Paris story featuring the fulfillment of housewife fantasies, amnesia, and a parade of costume changes approaching a fashion show. About the only things missing are Thelma Ritter and a Doris Day song on the sound track. Borrowing its opening from *Romancing the Stone* (which itself shoplifted from the classic *Sullivan's Travels*), the movie begins with a murder-on-a-train sequence that is really a figment of heroine JoBeth Williams' imagination. Displaying little of her usual panache, she is a shlumpy Ohio housewife who turns her daydreams into the winning entry in a romance-novel contest. She wins a trip to Paris, which she takes solo against the wishes of her overbearing husband. Knocked unconscious in a car accident, Williams awakens to the belief that she is a romance-novel heroine who is everything her real self is not. Through a series of misunderstandings that would challenge even the credulity of Lucy Ricardo, Williams winds up with Tom Conti, an Englishman living in Paris. Conti doesn't have much of a part; it's the befuddled Dudley Moore role without the obligatory piano sequence. Director Rick Rosenthal takes the '50s sitcom idiocies of the script and italicizes them—when sabotage would serve him better. Did he really think he could pass this off as '80s sophistication when any old episode of "Dynasty" outglosses, outwits, and outsexes this film? *American Dreamer* is the sort of Ross Hunter dream-come-true escapade that became obsolete the moment feminists went into the streets and Paris went condo.

PG / 1984 / CBS/Fox

▲ THE AMERICAN FRIEND

When he's off, Dennis Hopper can well be an atrocious actor—and this turkey more than matches his wretched performance. Bruno Ganz is persuaded to murder a total stranger in a Paris Metro station, but the reasons (and Hopper's presence) are as murky as the plot. Blame for this fiasco must rest with Wim Wenders, the German director, who slips badly here.

Unrated / 1977 / Pacific Arts

▲ AMERICAN GIGOLO

Director Paul Schrader has always had a fascination with the world of sleaze. He explored the sexual exploitation of females in *Hardcore,* so perhaps it was the concept of equal time that made him turn to men here. (Indeed, in this film he has even included a furtive shot of male frontal nudity, a rarity for mainstream movies in chauvinist Hollywood.) There is nothing tacky about the milieu of gigolo hero Richard Gere, though. He is clothed by Giorgio Armani, fed in L.A.'s chichi Polo Lounge, and driven about in a fleet of limos. All this is lovingly framed and photographed by cinematographer John Bailey (a cameraman on *Days of Heaven*). The heretofore gifted Gere, who took over the role when John Travolta dropped out, seems unable to act his way out of a Vuitton bag this time, but it is

not crucial—he *looks* spectacular. Supermodel Lauren Hutton, on the other hand, appears a trifle worn, but she performs well. Theirs is a love story set in a big-money, murder-mystery format that seems both unlikely and plodding. Nobody is going very far. But what slides of the trip!

R / 1980 / Paramount

▲ AMERICAN HOT WAX

The medium and the message are one and the same: Long live rock 'n' roll. The movie is a romanticized week in the life of Alan Freed, a deejay who made the airwaves do-wop in the late '50s before being ruined by a variety of accusations including taking payola and glamorizing loose morals for his youthful following. Tim McIntire plays Freed—it was his first major role, and he put it on marvelously, down to the garish plaid sport coat. Laraine Newman is a songwriter whose quartet needs a break. Loosely modeled on Danny and the Juniors, the group gets its shot in a be-there-or-be-square concert featuring the real Jerry Lee Lewis and Chuck Berry, after twenty years. As flashbacks go, this flick has it, as the saying went, made in the shade.

R / 1978 / Paramount

▲ AMERICAN POP

With his saucy *Fritz the Cat,* explicit *Heavy Traffic,* and racially controversial *Coonskin,* Ralph Bakshi showed that he is to Walt Disney what Mick Jagger is to Perry Como. In a genre populated with cuddly forest creatures, he introduced unkempt, foul-mouthed, and street-wise antiheroes. His latest project portrays a family's obsession with music through four generations. The saga begins with an immigrant kid who starts working in burlesque houses, and traces his progeny through the birth of rock 'n' roll all the way up to the punk/new wave ruckus of the '80s. But the movie is really about ambition and freedom; pop music is a vehicle because the stakes are high. Scenes of glitzy performances are, for example, interspersed with bloody war shots. The script by Ronni Kern has some surprising twists and fine dialogue. The sound track notably avoids the chestnuts one might expect. Why, though, include the Sex Pistols in a movie about American pop? And if them, why not the Beatles? Other-

wise, *American Pop* is a vivid addition to our visual culture and yet another innovative triumph for Bakshi.
R / 1981 / N/A

▲ AN AMERICAN WEREWOLF IN LONDON

"Is that you, Harry?" may sound like an innocuous line, but it's one of the many howlers in this hip horror flick from *Animal House* director John Landis. Like *The Howling*, this film has a fast, funny script and stunning visual effects. It stars that onetime Dr. Pepper plugger David Naughton—no, he doesn't sing "I'm a werewolf, he's a werewolf, she's a werewolf; wouldn't you like to be a werewolf too?" He and then newcomer Griffin Dunne (author John Gregory Dunne's nephew) are innocents abroad who encounter a man-eating monster on the moors. Dunne is undone. Naughton survives only to find he has bitten off more than he can chew. The sound track is laced with amusingly apropos tunes like "Blue Moon," "Moondance," and "Bad Moon Rising." (But where, oh where is Warren Zevon's "Werewolves of London"?) Naughton is appropriately all-American, while Dunne displays a deft comic touch despite an increasingly unsettling appearance. Landis maintains the delicate balance between horror and humor until the final scene's gratuitous series of car crashes, a curse left over from Landis's *The Blues Brothers*. Be advised to catch this one before the next full moon.
R / 1981 / MCA

▲ AMITYVILLE II: THE POSSESSION

The first night the family moves into their new home, the walls quake, things start to fly around, and a couple of paint brushes up and write "dishonor thy father" and "pigs" on the walls. Later, fires break out, the electricity goes off and on, pipes burst, and the family members start beating one another up and having incestuous relationships. This, obviously, is nobody's dream house. Most people in this situation would ask for a refund, put the place back on the market, or at least call in an aluminum-siding salesman. But Burt (*Rocky*) Young and wife, Rutanya (*The Deer Hunter*) Alda, try to brazen it out, even when it's

obvious that their son, played by Jack Magner, has become possessed and that their Long Island colonial is the house that became the Amityville Horror in the 1979 film—of which this gruesome, tedious sequel is actually a prequel. The demon doing the mischief is brutal, yet has a sense of decorum. When James Olson shows up as a priest wanting to do an exorcism, the demon tells him, "You can't do that; you aren't authorized." Olson has some success—his crucifix seems to be of a higher caliber than those wielded by clergymen in most recent horror films—but then, maybe the demon was only possessing at half-throttle, saving up his good stuff for Margot Kidder in the '79 film. The movie was Italian director Damiano Damiani's first in English; few breathlessly awaited his second.
R / 1982 / Embassy

▲ THE AMSTERDAM KILL

Unbridled loyalty to Robert Mitchum is the only reason to see this story of heroin high jinks apparently made to employ hordes of out-of-work Chinese actors. As a good cop gone bad (and now good again), Mitchum shuttles between Amsterdam and Hong Kong, wondering who's crossing him. Is it Richard Egan? Bradford Dillman? Leslie Nielson? More likely, it was Mitchum's agent or whoever talked him into this property. There is plenty of violence but no real menace. Excepting Mitchum's pleasantly understated performance, the movie is like one of those boats bobbing up and down in Hong Kong harbor—junk.
R / 1978 / RCA/Columbia

▲ AND THE SHIP SAILS ON

Like a painting by Dali or Magritte, this film by Federico Fellini is full of fascinating images that almost, but never quite, reflect reality. Fellini had made impressionistic films before, of course. *Amarcord* or *Fellini's Roma* had the unifying quality of seeming to relate to the director's own life, but what this movie relates to is anyone's guess. It is, for one thing, a tribute to artifice. It begins in archaic-looking black and white. After a few minutes, there is an apparently random change to color film. The characters address the camera directly throughout, the sets are obviously

sets, and at the end of the film the camera pulls back to show the whole studio setup, including Fellini himself, being dollied around by his crew. As for the story: A group of opera lovers and performers seems to have chartered an ocean liner to take the body of a just-deceased diva to her favorite island for burial. The time is just before World War I and a group of Serbian refugees shows up. So does a gunboat. So do an out-of-sorts rhinoceros and a Russian who hypnotizes chickens. There is a pudgy young duke who looks more like a woman than most of the women. Impromptu arias sprout up everywhere, including in the ship's boiler room. (The music is Verdi and Rossini, with new librettos.) The ship's passengers are not, by Fellini standards, an especially garish lot, but they're not your typical Burger King crowd either. The most familiar face is that of Englishman Freddie Jones. Nobody should watch this film expecting a nice clear-cut story with heroes and villains. Even Fellini admitted, "Now that *And the Ship Sails On* is finished, I can no longer say what was the original intention." But it is, like nearly all Fellini's work, visually stunning. And for people who don't mind being exasperated by intriguing puzzles, it's more than worthwhile. (In Italian with subtitles.)
PG / 1984 / RCA/Columbia

▲ ANDY WARHOL'S BAD

The title said it all. This mess wasn't even famous for fifteen minutes. Carroll Baker plays the madam of a murder-for-rent ring operating out of her electrolysis salon in Queens. Recommended only for terminally desensitized TV-violence freaks.
X / 1977 / Embassy

▲ ANGEL

Imagine a cook who dumps caviar, lobster, truffles, and champagne into a pot and boils them into a stew. That's what first-time director Robert Vincent O'Neil did with this film. He had the ingredients. His setting is the wonderfully sleazy, scary, hyperintense world of Los Angeles's Hollywood Boulevard. His plot involves a teenage girl who is putting herself through prep school by streetwalking at night. His cast includes such idiosyncratic actors as Cliff Gorman, the late

Dick Shawn, and Susan Tyrrell. Donna Wilkes, formerly McLean Stevenson's cutesy daughter on TV's "Hello, Larry," was still, at 22, young enough to pull off the title role. The old cowboy star Rory Calhoun shows up playing an old cowboy star; he hangs out on the Strip chatting about Tom Mix and John Wayne. O'Neil makes a mess of all these possibilities, taking the easiest way out of every situation. Gorman, who plays a homicide cop, Shawn a transvestite, and Tyrell a cigar-smoking lesbian, madly overact their overdrawn characters. Wilkes is appealing but ends up in a preposterous chase scene, trying to gun down a rapist-murderer. Played by John Diehl with a fierceness that would make Robert De Niro seem casual, he is described as "necro(philiac), bisexual, and impotent." He also eats a raw egg, shell and all, then slobbers a kiss on a picture of his mother. This guy is obviously not a prime candidate for Congress. The violence is gratuitous and exploitive. The nudity is gratuitous and exploitive. The movie is gratuitous and exploitive, just another squandered opportunity.
R / 1984 / Thom/EMI

▲ ANGELO MY LOVE

Robert Duvall, Oscar winner for *Tender Mercies,* has recorded as many memorable performances as any actor around. But as a director, he has a way to go. Not that this movie is all bad—it's just chaotic. The plot is slight: A drunken old gypsy is accused by a young gypsy boy of stealing his ring, an heirloom. The older man is acquitted at a gypsy trial, but the young boy and his brother spend most of the movie trying to prove that the verdict is wrong. That's not the worst premise in history. The problem is that we can never really tell whether this movie is a documentary or fiction—and things get even more confusing when real-life gypsies seem to be playing themselves. The movie really boils down to a showcase for the kid, Angelo Evans, a Duvall find from the streets of New York. He's something of a little bully, hollering and shouting at everyone in sight, but engaging nonetheless. And the glimpses into the gypsy community are truly astounding, the best since the slicker if less authentic *King of the Gypsies* in 1978. There's the drama of the community trial of the old gypsy and a stunning look at a feast day in Canada. In fact, the old man "defendant," played by a gypsy named Steve

"Patalay" Tsigonoff, is the most interesting character on the screen, a potential movie all by himself. But the action around him just doesn't hold together. There's motion without direction, too much good intention, and not enough execution.

R / 1983 / RCA/Columbia

▲ ANNIE

Director John Huston, best known for such dark films as *The Treasure of Sierra Madre, The Misfits,* and *Prizzi's Honor,* in his first musical, turned the Broadway show derived from "Little Orphan Annie" into a bright, happily sentimental extravaganza. He was helped by choreographer Arlene Phillips, best known for her Dr. Pepper commercials, and cinematographer Richard Moore, and he was blessed by his cast. Aileen Quinn, who was 9 when the film was shot, sings appealingly, and she manages to be cute without being coy. Carol Burnett, as the tipsy orphanage director whom Annie escapes, displays her considerable comic repertoire of double takes and pratfalls. As a Briton, Albert Finney was a strange choice to play the quintessential American capitalist Daddy Warbucks—but he is effectively bluff, with nicely reluctant warmhearted impulses. Ann Reinking, as the secretary who talks Warbucks into temporarily adopting Annie, is slyly charming and, of course, a peerless dancer. Bernadette Peters and Tim (*The Rocky Horror Show*) Curry, as a ruthless couple who pretend to be Annie's parents to get Warbucks' reward, are ideal, while Geoffrey Holder as the factotum Punjab and Edward Herrmann as FDR are endearing. Huston inexplicably lets clips from Greta Garbo's *Camille* run on at great length, and those familiar with the original Broadway score will miss some edited-out songs. But family audiences are advised to forget the critical carping and go rent this film now; you won't want to wait until *Tomorrow.*

PG / 1982 / RCA/Columbia

▲ ANNIE HALL

Still the best film of Woody Allen's consistently dazzling career. Allen and his sidekick Diane Keaton portray a contemporary urban couple afflicted with all his familiar obsessions—death, movies, sex, analysis, and obsession itself. If this is all déjà vu, it's also proven funny, and Allen has a smashing backup cast including Shelley Duvall, Paul Simon, Tony Roberts, Colleen Dewhurst, and then newcomer Christopher Walken as Keaton's crazy brother. Marshall McLuhan appears briefly as a lukewarm medium for a message about intellectual snobbery. Keaton won the Academy Award as Best Actress and Woody failed to show up in his hated Hollywood to collect well-deserved Oscars for direction, screenplay (co-written with Marshall Brickman) and—in the year of *Stars Wars,* yet—Best Picture.

PG / 1977 / CBS/Fox

▲ ANOTHER COUNTRY

With his first feature, Polish director Marek Kanievska proved himself a magician. He transformed an oblique London stage hit into an absorbing, accessible movie that bedevils the mind with memorable images, even if there is less to it than meets the eye. Adapted by Julian Mitchell, who wrote the play, this class-conscious drama is a meditation on the motives of Guy Burgess, the proper English diplomat who turned traitor and defected to the Soviet Union in 1951. Here he is called Guy Bennett. As a teenager in 1932, he is one of his prestigious boarding school's best and brightest students. Within the institution's baroque social system, which is the movie's real villain, the openly ambitious and homosexual young man seems assured of membership in the school's elite ranks. But when his infatuation with a fellow student turns into an affair and his sexual orientation proves more than a phase, the social system turns against him. Kanievska, who previously directed for English and Australian television, artfully captures the hypocrisy of the academic hierarchy. As Bennett, spindly Rupert Everett, who created the role in London, gives a first-class performance. And as the school's would-be socialist, Colin Firth capably etches the friend who fuels Bennett's betrayal of the Empire. But poignant performances and the wise adaptation cannot camouflage the speciousness of playwright Mitchell's conceit. Are we really to believe that social slights make someone a spy? Despite the appeal of his diversionary tactics, Kanievska never makes Mitchell's case completely persuasive. Like its hero, *Another Country* is essentially a sham, but an elegant one.

PG / 1984 / Embassy

▲ ANOTHER MAN, ANOTHER CHANCE

Imagine the director of the Oscar-winning *A Man and a Woman* changing his hero and heroine into James Caan and Genevieve Bujold and moving the story to the American West in frontier days. If you're having trouble, so did French director Claude Lelouch. Caan plays a veterinarian whose wife is raped and killed; Bujold is a French immigrant whose photographer husband meets a violent end. Lelouch's scenes are often stunningly beautiful, but this is a thin, warmed-over ragout.
PG / 1977 / N/A

▲ ANY WHICH WAY YOU CAN

It would take a pretty sharp moviegoer to detect any difference between this unpretentious sequel and the ditzy original, *Every Which Way but Loose*. Sure, Glen Campbell croons the title tune instead of Eddie Rabbitt, but apart from that the two screenplays are practically interchangeable. Clint Eastwood is the same easygoing fellow he was in *Every Which Way*, likably laconic but quick with his fists. Sondra Locke (Clint's real-life lady love) still can't sing worth a darn, and the late Ruth Gordon substitutes vulgarity for humor. If Clyde, the other star, gets a little more screen time, that's just dandy because he's an eminently agreeable orangutan. Director Buddy Van Horn ties up all the loose ends from the 1978 work and stages a vigorous bare-knuckle brawl to conclude the action. It's hardly memorable now to anyone but Eastwood, who's probably still counting the profits.
PG / 1980 / Warner

▲ THE APPLE DUMPLING GANG RIDES AGAIN

It's hard to be unhappy with such a cheerfully inane Disney film, even when it's a sequel to an already tired plot. Harry Morgan is still in dubious command at Fort Concho; bungling outlaws Tim Conway and Don Knotts are still failing to terrorize the countryside; and Kenneth Mars, as Sheriff Woolly Bill Hitchcock, is still vaingloriously upholding lawlessness and disorder. Conway and Knotts could do these kinds of pratfalls and double takes in their sleep. But Mars's excesses of zeal and frustration are what make this passable adult fare instead of just a half-baked kids' film.
G / 1979 / Disney

▲ APRIL FOOL'S DAY

This is another semiholiday film in which a bunch of college kids gets marooned on an island with a slasher. The movie does have a few relatively entertaining things going for it, though. One is that director Fred (*When a Stranger Calls*) Walton and screenwriter Danilo Bach have senses of humor. They don't get carried away with the blood and guts and incorporate a subtheme of silly April Fool's Day practical jokes into the more surgical parts of the script. The cast, mostly newcomers, is attractive and can act; they're like a bunch of soap opera performers making a suitable amount of ado about nothing. Amy Steel, Ken Olandt, and Deborah Goodrich especially are impressive. While he spends most of the film as a corpse, Griffin O'Neal—right, the guy who is the brother-in-law of John McEnroe—acquits himself nicely. And fans of Deborah Foreman undoubtedly will be pleased to have a chance to see her greatest performance other than *My Chauffeur*. Foreman plays a spoiled, slightly spaced-out coed who invites some friends to her family's island hideaway (in what is actually British Columbia). What happens after that adds nothing very revolutionary to cinematic literature, but there are a couple of zippy twists at the end. Anyway, it's not as if they used up a really good horror movie holiday, like Rat-Catcher's Day (July 22) or World's End Day (October 22).
R / 1986 / Paramount

▲ ARMED AND DANGEROUS

Calling all cars: be on the lookout for an overweight, underappreciated comedian in search of a vehicle. Although he's one of the funniest performers around, John Candy has had a floundering career in films. Since he isn't leading-man material like Tom Hanks or a consistent caricature like the late John Belushi, Hollywood has never gotten a handle on him (except as the second banana in *Splash* and *Volunteers*). Admittedly, he's not the easiest comic to market. There's something fundamentally frightening and mean-spirited about him (which would have made Candy

ideal in Danny De Vito's role in *Ruthless People*). In this makeshift comedy about a security guard on the loose in L.A., Candy is merchandised as a one-man *Police Academy*. But once again he's playing situations, not playing a character. Even his former SCTV pal Eugene Levy, who has also suffered from movie miscasting, fares better. As a lawyer moonlighting among misfit guards, Levy funneled his frustrated dope shtick into a workable role. There is, however, an unexpected pleasure: Meg Ryan, an up-and-comer who was also in *Top Gun* as Anthony Edwards's ditsy wife. She plays the daughter of a crooked businessman, and the movie suddenly acquires a heart whenever she appears. Giddy but guileless, Ryan displays a disarming vulnerability. It may be only petty larceny to steal a clinker like this, but Ryan makes it something more than a moving violation.
PG-13 / 1986 / RCA/Columbia

▲ AROUND THE WORLD IN 80 DAYS

Don't get your hopes up about this 1956 film that won five Oscars, including Best Picture. Its reissue showed that time had not been kind to late producer Mike Todd's version of the 1873 Jules Verne classic about proper Britisher Phileas Fogg, who wagers that he can circle the globe in eighty days. The movie just slogs along, despite an elegant performance by David Niven as Fogg and a warmly humorous one by the Mexican comic Cantinflas as Fogg's valet, Passepartout. What hurts the film today is the very thing that helped make it big office then: its size. One of the pioneers in wide screen as a weapon against television, Todd used a 65-mm process that with typical modesty he labeled Todd-AO. But like a kid with a new toy, Todd didn't know when to stop with the darn thing. At 178 minutes, the film doesn't so much utilize its many locations, including London, Paris, and Madrid, as exhaust them. For Todd a handful of stars wasn't enough, either. He used forty-four names in bit roles (first called "cameos" by Todd). A novelty then, overuse has made it an irritation by now. For every star on the order of a Sinatra or Dietrich, there's a satellite such as Caesar Romero, Jack Oakie, and Andy Devine. Todd wasn't above putting a few things over on the audience—he was a salesman as much as a showman, and in this flaccid film his is the only real energy. So how to explain that *Around the World* took the Oscar in the year of *Giant*, the *Ten Commandments*, and *The King and I?* Todd's reputed idol, P.T. Barnum, had an answer: There's one born every minute.
G / 1984 / Warner

▲ ARTHUR

Dudley Moore has the angelic yet decadent look of a choirboy gone to seed. In this, his most brilliantly crazed performance, the five-foot two-inch actor proves that he can be a giant when it comes to comedy. As Arthur, a poor little rich boy with a tendency to tipple, Moore is faced with a horrible decision—stick with the lady he loves (Liza Minnelli) and lose a $750 million inheritance, or marry the incredibly insipid choice of his parents, Jill Eikenberry, and be rich and miserable. Though he speaks bravely of riding the subway ("Where is the subway?" he asks), eating tunafish sandwiches, and even getting a job, Arthur just isn't cut out to be poor. Writer and director Steve Gordon, a veteran of such TV sitcoms as "The Dick Van Dyke Show" and "Barney Miller," made a smashing big-screen directing debut. His hilarious screenplay is a minefield of laughs. (Sadly, Gordon died shortly after the film's release.) If anyone could steal any of Moore's thunder, it's Sir John Gielgud, who gives a deliciously dry performance as Arthur's unflappable manservant and won a Best Supporting Actor Oscar in the bargain. An Oscar also went to the film's lyrical theme song. One small quibble: Moore spends almost half the film acting drunk; he's very good at it, but it does begin to get tiresome. Never mind. This is a funny movie.
PG / 1981 / Warner

▲ ASSASSINATION

. . . as in character, plot, career. Maybe this sorry Charles Bronson vehicle didn't hurt his future as a box-office draw, but it didn't help. He plays a veteran Secret Service man assigned to protect a post–Nancy Reagan First Lady from an implausible assassination plot based on—get this—the President's impotence. Bronson simply goes through the motions, foiling attempt after pedestrian attempt with quicksilver reflexes and a tired stare. There is plenty of character nondevelopment as Bronson travels cross-country trading insults with the First Lady, bitchily played by

Arthur: Dudley Moore won a well-deserved Oscar nomination for playing a constantly inebriated millionaire playboy in a comedy that seems richer and more hilarious with repeated viewings.

Bronson's real-life wife Jill Ireland, who struggles vainly to conceal her British accent. Along for the ride are Jan Gan Boyd, as a seductive agent who is perkier than Mary ("Entertainment Tonight") Hart, and veteran character actor Michael Ansara, as a slimy senator orchestrating the murder plot. Director Peter Hunt, who edited the first five James Bond films before directing *On Her Majesty's Secret Service* (1969), does little with screenwriter Richard Sale's script (based on Sale's novel *My Affair with the President's Wife*). Bronson fans in search of espionage won't find anything here remotely like 1977's tense *Telefon*.

PG-13 / 1987 / N/A

▲ AT CLOSE RANGE

Stick this movie out. The rewards are worth wading through the muck, especially thick in the first fifteen minutes. That's when director James (*Reckless*) Foley puts the hard sell on his star, Sean Penn. To play a dirt-poor tough in rural Pennsylvania (the film was shot in Tennessee), Penn has peroxided his hair and, with the help of trainer Ray Kybartas, pumped up his biceps and chest to near Rambo size. Foley's camera hovers in rapt adoration: See Sean booze and brawl with his low-life buddies. See Sean flirt with his girl, played by Mary Stuart Masterson. See Sean nibble his toenails (no kidding, he does). Then, just when you're dismissing the whole enterprise as a Mr. Madonna movie, something astonishing happens: Christopher (*The Deer Hunter*) Walken comes on as the adored gangster father who abandoned Penn as a child, and the story takes hold. With his fast cars, easy money, and easier charm, Walken offers a life Penn can't get by sitting on the front porch with the folks. Mom is sharply etched by Millie (*The Diary of Anne Frank*) Perkins, and as grandma and half-brother, respectively, Penn's real mother, Eileen Ryan, and real brother, Christopher Penn, are especially effective. (No, Sean's real bride doesn't show up, though she does sing the film's theme song.) Inspired by Walken, who has never been better, Penn stops preening and gives the least

tricky, most heartfelt performance of his then seven-movie career. A hellish seduction ensues after father lures son into the family business. Thieving, Penn thinks, will bring him closer to his father and the new life he craves. One moonlit night he learns the error of that notion. Accompanying Dad and his gang to a swamp, Penn watches in horror as they casually drown a harmless informer. Raising a silencing finger to his grinning mouth, Walken asks his son's complicity in evil. It's an image that ranks with the most chilling in film memory. Later, when Penn rebels, the father cold-bloodedly tries to arrange his son's murder. What happens will not be revealed here, but Nicholas Kazan's screenplay was inspired by the real-life 1978 Johnston family murders in Pennsylvania. Details are exaggerated, but the heart of the case is not. As the son who is trying to rise above the dark impulses he shares with his father, Penn is shattering. But it's Walken's performance that makes the movie. Not since Robert Mitchum in 1955's *The Night of the Hunter* had there been such a convincing demon prowling the screen. *At Close Range* should come with a warning label: movie dynamite.
R / 1986 / Vestron

▲ ATLANTIC CITY

"Rackets, whoring, guns—it used to be beautiful," sighs retired hood Burt Lancaster, recalling the good old days of this New Jersey resort town. Then came legalized gambling in 1976. Out of the rebirth of rundown Atlantic City, French director Louis (*Pretty Baby*) Malle and playwright-turned-screenwriter John (*The House of Blue Leaves*) Guare have fashioned a compassionate, mournfully funny saga of dreamers taking one last jump for the jackpot. Lancaster has been reduced to running numbers, caring for a shrewish invalid widow (Kate Reid), and peeping at neighbor Susan Sarandon, who stands naked at a window washing her body with lemon juice to get out the stink of the oyster bar where she works. When Sarandon's sleazy ex-husband (Robert Joy) gets rubbed out by the Mafia while trying to sell his cocaine stash, the fishwife and hood seize the drugs and their chance. Their love scenes are remarkably poignant, thanks to Sarandon's sizzle and Lancaster's lovely etching of an old man rejuvenated by a young woman's passion. The bubble soon bursts, but Malle touches the exhilaration that comes when, however fleetingly, new life rises from the ruins. Lancaster lost the Best Actor Oscar to Henry Fonda in *On Golden Pond*, but his performance here is the most moving and memorable of his screen career. The film itself remains one of the few authentic masterworks of the decade.
R / 1981 / Paramount

▲ AUDREY ROSE

Cashing in on a hot topic of the time, this reincarnation flick resurrected themes of *The Exorcist*, *The Omen*, and even an old laugher, *The She Creature*. Anthony (*The Elephant Man*) Hopkins creates a few tense moments as an anguished father who tells Marsha Mason and John Beck that their little girl is really his daughter returned to life. (Hopkins later co-starred with that famed trans-channeler Shirley MacLaine in *A Change of Seasons* so maybe he was on to something.) The movie itself seldom seems to know where it's going. Note to parents tempted by the PG rating to let the tots watch: There is an ugly insistence on replaying a scene in which a child is trapped inside a burning car.
PG / 1977 / MGM/UA

▲ AUTHOR! AUTHOR!

If anyone yells out the title of this film after seeing it, screenwriter Israel Horovitz may want to think twice before 'fessing up. It's about a New York playwright, Al Pacino, who simultaneously faces a Broadway opening and desertion by his wife, leaving him alone with five young children. Pacino, moaning about how depressed he is on the one hand and flaunting his warm feelings toward the kids on the other, practically oozes lovability. The children, led by the wise beyond his (or anyone else's) years teenager Eric Gurry, rattle off sarcastic comments nonstop. There's a nicely understated performance by Tuesday Weld as the wife. Dyan Cannon, as his play's—and, briefly, his personal—leading lady, is beguilingly showbiz. Bob (Elliott) and Ray (Goulding), as a lawyer-accountant brother team, and Judy Graubart, as a browbeaten secretary, do nice bits. Pacino, though, is oppressively downcast. And director Arthur (*Making Love*) Hiller mostly just drops punch lines and demands laughs.

At one point Pacino's character says his play is serious but written "in a comedy mode." This is a comedy written in a whining mode.
PG / 1982 / CBS/Fox

▲ AUTUMN SONATA

Since the best of Swedish director Ingmar Bergman's films so often seem agonizing, it's something of a mystery why anyone should willingly sit through them. One answer is that there's a catharsis involved in sharing the pain. In this case, though, there are two other reasons: Ingrid Bergman and Liv Ullmann. Ingrid (no relation to Ingmar) never gave a greater performance and looked stunning at 63. She plays an internationally successful pianist. Ullmann, purposely frumped up for the part, is her underachieving housewife daughter. (Linn Ullmann, daughter of Liv and the director, plays Liv as a girl in flashbacks.) The film penetrates the mother-daughter relationship the way *Scenes from a Marriage* probed husbands and wives—the insights into noncommunication and self-deception are devastating. Ingrid and Liv respond to each other, clashing and reconciling with looks and gestures, throughout the film. And when director Bergman fills the screen with close-ups of those two lovely, expressive faces, the film is as moving as any ever made. Ingrid won an Oscar nomination for what would be her last feature film (she died in 1982); it was a fitting conclusion to an extraordinary career.
PG / 1978 / CBS/Fox

▲ AVALANCHE

This used up just about the last possible disaster film theme, except perhaps for the potato famine. (Editor's note: We were wrong. The next year *The China Syndrome* began Hollywood's continuing concern with nuclear holocaust.) The only intriguing aspect of the movie, in fact, is watching Rock Hudson in one of his last feature films before his AIDS-related death in 1986. Too bad the film is far from this underrated actor's best. Here we have Hudson gone amok; normally resourceful and, at the very least, dignified, he is allowed by director Corey (*Cry Rape*) Allen to become a loud-talking, wildly gesturing stranger. He's built a new ski resort, ignoring environmentalists, and all but asks for a you-know-what. As his divorced but still loving wife, Mia Farrow looks less wan than usual. Four years later she had the great good luck to team up with Woody Allen, a director who knew how to bring out her loveliness and varied talents as an actress. But here she has an impossible role, including the line, "You stifle me; I need some space." Even the avalanche itself—a mix of special effects, stock footage, and what seem to be large clumps of laundry starch falling on people—is ho-hum, and lovely scenery at the Durango, Colorado, location is wasted on overexposed film. It is, in short, a snow job.
PG / 1978 / Embassy

▲ AVENGING ANGEL

Angel, the teenage L.A. hooker who became a hooker emeritus-vigilante, then a prelaw student-vigilante, may turn into one of those classic female roles (like Lady Macbeth, Blanche du Bois, or Lassie) that can be portrayed by a succession of performers. In this sequel to the 1984 box-office smash, the title role passes to Betsy Russell, granddaughter of columnist Max Lerner and co-star of *Private School*. She is also someone who, the film's press agents said, "firmly believes the body is a temple and should not be abused." In this film she is out to get even with some villains after they kill a cop who befriended her. To this end she hits the streets with a trunkful of miniskirt outfits and a wagonload of weapons and ammunition. Like the original *Angel*, starring Donna Wilkes, this film seems so cheaply made you wonder if the actors were paid with surplus cheese. Old-time cowboy Rory Calhoun and Susan Tyrrell are in the cast again. The esteemed Ossie Davis halfheartedly portrays a police captain. Director Robert Vincent O'Neil, whose credits included *Blood Mania* before he got into the *Angel* business, maintains an amazingly consistent sense of tedium. Never suspenseful, funny, or clever, the movie doesn't even begin to even muster enough violence or sex to satisfy fans of such things. Never mind, *Angel Joins the Supreme Court* has a nice ring to it.
R / 1985 / New World

▲ THE AWAKENING

Back in the old horror film days, dealing with a mummy was easy. Whenever an archeologist was rash enough to unearth an old Egyptian pharaoh, somebody would boil up a pot or two of tana leaf juice and mumble some pig Latin. Then out would pop Lon Chaney, Jr., who would limp about and make curses come true. In more modern chillers, things are no longer so simple—or so entertaining. When Charlton Heston sets to digging about in the Nile Valley and finds a tomb the size of Delaware, he has to deal with Egyptian nationalism and computer analysis. Then, too, there's a love pentangle including him, his first wife (Jill Townsend), his assistant and second wife (Susannah York), his daughter (Stephanie Zimbalist), and an older woman, Queen Kara, who's 3,700 if she's a day. The film is directed by British TV veteran Mike Newell in a herky-jerky way. Heston, supposedly enthralled with the idea of bringing the wicked Kara back to life, comes close to losing his dignity. The plot, from a story by *Dracula* author Bram Stoker, seems like a feminized version of the nouveau devil stories. Only the Egyptian locations maintain their reputation. Heston, after dabbling in incest, finds that ultimately daughter's heart belongs to mummy.
R / 1980 / Warner

B

▲ BABY IT'S YOU

We could have done without any more movies about high school kids in the '50s and '60s. But this one is, against all odds, a moving little film. Directed by John (*Lianna*) Sayles, the story (also by Sayles) focuses on a troublesome, bizarre boy's crush on his school's wholesomest coed. The plot has murky moments, but the leads are appealing and resourceful. Rosanna Arquette, as the high school golden girl encountering the complications of growing up, shades her performance with wonderful touches of surprise and puzzlement; her drunk scene when she starts college and wants to impress her classmates with her worldliness is a marvel of mounting hysteria. The boy, who idolizes Frank Sinatra and is such an operator he is nicknamed for the brand of contraceptive he uses, is played by Vincent (*The Black Stallion Returns*) Spano with a subtle mix of charm, vulnerability, and frustration. Sayles includes some telling moments—the pedantic teacher warning girls about skirt lengths before the prom, the worldly dorm mate taking Arquette under her wing (the role is nicely underplayed by Tracy Pollan). And Sayles lends a bittersweet quality to the students' lives by accentuating their obsession with illusions. Spano, for instance, ends up with a nightclub act in which he lipsyncs to Sinatra records. This is the kind of film that frequently rewards viewers with quiet glimpses of truth.
R / 1983 / Paramount

▲ BACHELOR PARTY

Directed and co-written by Neal Israel, this alleged comedy is notable for lack of taste as well as lack of laughs; the best thing to be said for it is that this is equal-opportunity boredom. (There are some penis jokes mixed in with the breast jokes.) Tom Hanks plays a lovably shiftless school bus driver. You can tell he's a real rascal when he uses a blowtorch to cook his dinner. He's engaged to newcomer Tawny Kitaen, a debutante whose father, George Grizzard, wishes she would marry someone more couth. Hanks is given a bachelor party by his buddies, who have a lot in common, mostly a penchant for overacting. (Adrian Zmed is the most familiar face.) The obvious complications ensue, centering on Hanks's promise to Kitaen that he won't dabble among the hookers invited to the party. The film's best joke comes when one of the buddies, despondent about his own marriage, tries to slit his wrist with an

electric razor. Every other time they were stuck for a punch line, it would seem, Israel and co-writer Pat Proft decided to toss in an obscenity.
R / 1984 / CBS/Fox

▲ BACK ROADS

"Darlin'," drawls Tommy Lee Jones to Sally Field a few minutes into this movie, "we're traveling on wit and grit." Wit and grit, it turns out, are no substitutes for a script. Martin Ritt, after directing Field to an Oscar in *Norma Rae,* seemed to have set out to make a film with absolutely no social conscience. If so, he succeeded. Field plays a hard-luck whore and Jones a down-and-out boxer; they team up for a cross-country ramble from Alabama to California and encounter a solicitous sailor, David Keith. Field and Jones are immensely likable, but all they do is hitchhike, go honky-tonking, fight, and make up. It's just a matter of time before they realize, inevitably, that they were made for each other—94 draggy minutes, to be exact.
R / 1981 / CBS/Fox

▲ BACK TO SCHOOL

This film represented a perilous time for American culture. Rodney Dangerfield had become convinced that he could act. Maybe it was the box-office success of his films *Caddy Shack* and *Easy Money.* Maybe it was the director of this movie, Alan Metter, whose biggest prevous credit was a Dangerfield music video. In any case, Dangerfield doesn't just do his goggle-eyed, collar-pulling shtick in *Back to School;* he emotes. He plays serious scenes involving paternal pride, social-class differences, bitterness. He seduces Sally Kellerman. He even, heaven help us, quotes from Dylan Thomas. Donald Duck would have about as much chance of pulling off "Do not go gentle into that good night" as Dangerfield does, and Don is easily the better actor. Thankfully, most of the film is played for laughs. Dangerfield does his self-deprecating bit as a prosperous businessman who goes to college to set a good example for his son, an aspiring dropout. A squad of writers including Harold (*Ghostbusters*) Ramis provided Dangerfield with volleys of punch lines.

A few hit, such as one about Dangerfield's wife (played by Adrienne Barbeau in a surly fashion). The wife, Dangerfield says, is so self-involved "when we make love, she calls out her own name." Most of the jokes, though, are older than the sacks under Rodney's eyes. He says, for instance, that he used to date an English teacher: "I wrote her love letters, and she corrected them." Though Dangerfield's lusting after coeds pushes the bounds of good taste (he ends up with Kellerman, one of his professors), this is hardly the most offensive campus comedy of all time. Keith (*Christine*) Gordon as Dangerfield's son and newcomer Terry Farrell as the son's dream girl are appealing. Ned Beatty has a great time portraying the college's unprincipled administrator, "Dean Martin." Still, this is at best a fly-weight movie. It is not—repeat not—Rodney, a warm-up for *King Lear.*
PG-13 / 1986 / HBO/Cannon

▲ BACK TO THE FUTURE

At a time when the very idea of another teen sci-fi saga could cloud the eyes and dull the senses, along came *Back to the Future* to prove there's plenty of juice left in this kind of movie. Consistently compelling, witty, and imaginative, this time-travel fantasy offers more rapturous fun than a gaggle of goonies. Michael J. Fox, already a star on TV's "Family Ties," made a career breakthrough as Marty McFly—a hip California high schooler with a boozer mom, a wimpy dad, and two slugs for siblings. McFly finds solace in his guitar, his pretty girlfriend (Claudia Wells), and a Rube Goldberg–type scientist (beautifully overcooked by Christopher Lloyd) who has turned a De Lorean car into a time machine with the help of plutonium stolen from a group of Libyan terrorists. McFly is zapped back thirty years in this contraption. It's the same small town, but McFly hasn't been born yet. This time his parents are the 17-year-olds. McFly's mother, played with Ann-Margret oomph at 17 and 47 by Lea Thompson (she was 24), develops a crush on the boy she doesn't know is her son. McFly must divert his mom's amorous attentions to his dad or risk changing history. It's a tribute to director Robert Zemeckis that this situation never veers into the vulgar. The film, written by Zemeckis and Bob Gale, is alternately hilarious (as McFly

tries to deal with a world before rock, video, and men's purple underwear) and heartfelt (as the son teaches his father how to be a man). The period props, from Davy Crockett posters to the Four Aces warbling "Mr. Sandman," are also first-rate. Jacked-up technology takes a backseat to charm here, and the film is better for it. In a role he took over early in production from Eric Stoltz, Fox is smashing. He can reduce an audience to convulsive laughter simply by trying to convince a nonplussed citizen of the '50s that Ronald Reagan occupied the White House in 1985. And Crispin Glover is his match, turning McFly's father in both periods into a figure of dignity as well as fun. Revealing more of the surprises would be dirty pool. Just sign on for the trip. *Back to the Future* offers a most dazzling joyride.
PG / 1985 / MCA

▲ BAD BOYS

This brutal, preposterously plotted melodrama pretends to be imbued with a social-conscience about the conditions inside today's juvenile correctional facilities. In fact, director Rick Rosenthal uses a potentially explosive subject to trot out every prison movie cliché this side of tin-cup rattling. Then he added R-rated sadism and sex. Sean Penn plays—and superbly—a 16-year-old thug put away after running down a Puerto Rican boy while making his getaway from a robbery. The dead kid's brother, Esai Morales, retaliates by raping Penn's girl, Ally Sheedy, and gets tossed in the clink himself. How do two known natural enemies happen to be housed together? "There was a logjam in admissions," says prison official Reni Santoni in what must stand as a classic of lame excuses. Santoni should have simply admitted there'd be no story otherwise. Penn's performance is the film's only attraction. He was good enough in the small role of Timothy Hutton's cadet pal in *Taps* to inspire one to seek out his name in the credits and remember it. Then, in 1982's *Fast Times at Ridgemont High,* he was a comic howl as a zonked-out surfer who challenged each wave with a jaunty, "Hey, Bud, let's party." In this, his first starring role, Penn takes the screen like a young Jimmy Cagney and at least fights the script to a draw against near-insurmountable odds.
R / 1983 / Thorn/Emi

▲ THE BAD NEWS BEARS IN BREAKING TRAINING

Will the sandlotters make it to their play-off game in the Houston Astrodome? Will they outrazz a team of Texas roughnecks? This sequel to *The Bad News Bears* had to score without Tatum O'Neal and Walter Matthau and turned into the equivalent of a .500 ball club. William Devane, as father to the rebellious left fielder he abandoned eight years ago, does a nice turn as the conscripted coach, and the tykes are as endearingly anarchic as ever. For those parents worried about the locker room language of the original, Chris Barnes, who steals the show as Tanner Boyle, has had his mouth scrubbed.
PG / 1977 / Paramount

▲ BAD TIMING/A SENSUAL OBSESSION

Such Nicholas Roeg films as *The Man Who Fell to Earth* and *Don't Look Now* won him cult appreciation, but this one is a little more accessible. Art Garfunkel, who hadn't appeared in a movie role since *Carnal Knowledge* in 1971, plays an American psychoanalyst teaching in Vienna. At a cocktail party he meets Theresa Russell, another American living abroad, and it's lust at first sight. They make love, quarrel, and finally break up. Russell then tries to commit suicide, and the race to save her life provides the drama of the film. As the unhibited, hedonistic girlfriend, Russell is sensational. Garfunkel, her cool, seemingly rational lover, provides a perfect counterpoint until he is consumed by jealousy. Harvey Keitel plays an unlikely police inspector checking for foul play. Roeg's easy manipulation of time may confuse some; he thinks nothing of flashing forward, back, and sideways almost simultaneously. And the steamy sex scenes got it an X rating.
X / 1980 / N/A

▲ THE BALLAD OF GREGORIO CORTEZ

The first major movie to spring from Robert Redford's Sundance institute in Provo, Utah—a workshop for independent filmmakers—is set in turn-of-the century Texas. Directed by Robert (*Short Eyes*) Young, it is based on the true story

of a Mexican tenant farmer who unwittingly became an outlaw when he killed a sheriff in a tragic misunderstanding. He then eluded posses who tracked him for four hundred fifty miles and eleven days across the Rio Grande Valley before finally arresting him. The star is Edward James Olmos, later to win fame on TV's "Miami Vice," who portrays Cortez with a soulful humanity. Director Young records the chase and subsequent trial from two points of view, showing the cruel capriciousness of frontier justice. The supporting cast is first-rate, with exceptional performances by Bruce (*Animal House*) McGill as a low-key reporter, Rosana (*Cannery Row*) De Soto as a compassionate interpreter, James (*Urban Cowboy*) Gammon as the tough but principled Texas Ranger who saves Cortez from a lynch mob, and Barry (*War Games*) Corbin as the court-appointed attorney who defends the Mexican. The movie, shot by cinematographer Ray Villalobos, makes the most of the striking vistas of Texas, New Mexico, and Colorado. Brought in at a dimestore price of $1.5 million, it is the American equivalent of Australia's *Breaker Morant*. Redford and everyone else concerned with the film should be proud of their achievement.
PG / 1983 / Embassy

▲ THE BALTIMORE BULLET

From the opening break, this movie about pool players is behind the eight ball, thanks to the inescapable comparisons to *The Hustler* and *The Color of Money*. Well, it's not either of them, but it's not terrible either. James Coburn and Bruce Boxleitner star as pool-shark partners who never play against each other. In one funny scene they masquerade as mechanics in a small town and work a pool-hall scam until the locals catch on. Only a Hollywood scriptwriter, though, could have concocted what happens in their inevitable showdown. Director Robert Ellis Miller also gets carried away with messy subplots, but he shrewdly cast ten real-life pool professionals in supporting roles. They aren't actors but do put on a dazzling display of trick shots when they let their cues do the talking. Also chalk up pleasant performances by Coburn, Boxleitner, and Omar Sharif, as a consummate gambler; Ronee Blakley could have been scratched, however. The movie's best line goes to Coburn, who cautions his protégé before

the big match: "Remember, kid, I taught you everything you know, but I didn't teach you everything *I* know."
PG / 1980 / CBS/Fox

▲ BARBAROSA

All right, pay attention: While this Western about a red-haired outlaw stars country singer Willie Nelson, and he had long been planning to make a film based on his album "Red Headed Stranger," this is not that film. And guess who directed this movie, set mostly in Mexico but shot mostly in Texas: an Australian, Fred (*The Chant of Jimmie Blacksmith*) Schepisi. It might have been possible for a good movie to come out of all that confusion. One didn't. This is just a ponderous and preposterous tale about a clever gunman who is involved in a vendetta with a Mexican family for reasons that are never clear. He stumbles across a clumsy farm boy—a corpulent Gary (*The Buddy Holly Story*) Busey—who is also on the lam, having inadvertently murdered his brother-in-law. They team up. Nelson is a natural, relaxed actor, and Busey is a good one, too, if more self-conscious. But this film has a script so forlorn and humorless, so hazy and unlikely, that they can't do much other than look weathered and naive, respectively. The only thing that saves the ending from seeming especially impossible is that the rest of the movie seems that way too.
PG / 1982 / CBS/Fox

▲ THE BATTLE OF CHILE

As documentaries go, this is a small masterpiece. Shot in black and white, it chronicles six months of chaos leading up to the overthrow of Chile's President Salvador Allende in 1973. While the slant is decidedly anti-U.S., the footage is often brilliant. In one chilling scene, the camera focuses on a soldier aiming his gun right at the lens; suddenly the picture goes wildly out of control, and we realize the cameraman has been shot. He died, and the rest of the Chilean camera crew fled the country shortly after the bloody coup. Though more than 3 hours in length, *The Battle of Chile* is a riveting film. (In Spanish with subtitles.)
Unrated / 1978 / N/A

▲ THE BEASTMASTER

If he could really talk to the animals, Marc (*79 Park Avenue*) Singer—star of this swords-and-sorcery epic—should have told them to hold out for better parts in the future. This film, directed by Don (*Phantasm*) Coscarelli, is occasionally bad enough to be funny, but more often it just seems interminable. Singer plays a warrior whose mythical village is wiped out by a marauding band. He seeks revenge using powers that just come naturally to a man who was given birth to by a cow (yes, that's one of the parts bad enough to be funny). Because he is able to communicate with animals, he enlists the aid of an eagle, two ferrets, and a panther. Later Singer hooks up with John Amos, once of TV's "Good Times," done up here in a leather outfit that might have come from Frederick's of Hollywood. Another ally is Tanya Roberts, perhaps the sixth best actress ever to play one of "Charlie's Angels." She gets to show a lot more in this film than she ever did on ABC, but none of it has to do with acting ability. When the main villain, Rip Torn, evil priest of the god Ar (or is it "R" or "Are" or "Arrrgh"?), tries to make a human sacrifice of her, he immediately gains the audience's sympathy, even though he has black teeth, stringy hair, and barrettes that look like human skulls. There is a lot of fire, magic, and impaling in this one, as well as much mincing, dicing, slicing, chopping, and trimming with swords. The film was photographed by John Alcott, who has often worked with Stanley Kubrick and won an Oscar for *Barry Lyndon*. He deserved another this time for resisting what must have been a temptation to cap his lenses and go home.
PG / 1982 / N/A

▲ BEATLEMANIA—THE MOVIE

Resurrection is rarely successful, except in show business. Various Elvis imitators, who often sound like death warmed over, have nevertheless prospered. In four years on Broadway and on tour, *Beatlemania* grossed more than $40 million, and as a movie collected some more of what can't buy you love. Like the stage show, the movie is a simulated Beatles' concert and multimedia show in which four young actor musicians impersonate the Fab Four. John Lennon is played by David Leon, Paul McCartney by Mitch Weissman, George Harrison by Tom Teeley, and Ringo Starr by Ralph Castelli. (Only Weissman was in the original quartet that opened the show on Broadway in 1977.) Both visually and musically, their impersonation is eerily realistic; at times the resemblance even overshadows the performance. The real stars of Beatlemania, though, are thirty Beatles songs. Much less effective is the film's attempt to sketch the social evolution of the era between Camelot and Woodstock. The songs are backed by film clips and streamer headlines (LT. CALLEY CHARGED WITH MY LAI MURDERS) that recall Vietnam, drugs, civil rights, and the Generation Gap. Film clips and songs are sometimes mordantly combined; LBJ is shown onscreen while the foursome sings "Nowhere Man." More often the parallels are cute or limp. Hard-core buffs will regard the show as a ghoulish rip-off. Younger fans may more uncritically relish this as the next best thing to having been there.
PG / 1981 / USA

▲ BEAT STREET

Coproduced by Harry Belafonte and shot on location in New York, this break dancing film wonderfully fuses the virtues of its predecessors—refining the gritty street scenes and realistic passion of 1983's low-budget *Wild Style* while better developing a plot similar to *Breakin'*. The movie's intentions are overt: to spread the word that a little talent, intelligence, and guile can propel ambitious kids out of the ghetto. Guy Davis, the son of Ossie Davis and Ruby Dee, is insightful as a young deejay whose only escape from the South Bronx is through his music. Rae Dawn Chong is both forceful and endearing as a sophisticated modern-dance director. Jon Chardiet is strong, too, as a graffiti artist who must choose between his art and the responsibility of raising a family. At times the film shies away from real violence in favor of dance fights between the New York City Breakers and the Rock Steady Crew—shades of *West Side Story*. But there is a vividly energetic finale, the funk equivalent of a vaudeville extravaganza. Director Stan Lathan made this a film that does for break dancing what *Saturday Night Fever* did for disco.
PG / 1984 / Vestron

▲ BEAU PÈRE

It's not exactly *Lolita* and it has a French accent, but this movie is the story of a 30ish man with a seductive 14-year-old stepdaughter on his hands. (The title is a pun, since "beau père" in French means "handsome father" as well as "step-father.") After the sudden death of the girl's mother, Patrick Dewaere, who plays on out-of-work musician, finds himself stuck at home alone with the nymphette. She is the coolly sexy Ariel Besse. One thing leads to another, and they fall in love, slowly but convincingly and quite touchingly. The film works, thanks to some fine understated acting by all and a smooth, convincing directorial effort by Bertrand Blier, who won an Oscar in 1978 with the comedy *Get Out Your Handkerchiefs,* another story of manners and mores in contemporary France. You'd think that a story about an older man who is seduced by a teenage girl would be material for a porno movie house, but in Blier's capable hands, it's not. In fact, the scenes leading up to the moment they hit the sack together are so funny they have the effect of disarming almost anyone who could be getting uncomfortable with such a theme. (In French with subtitles.)
Unrated / 1981 / Media

▲ THE BEDROOM WINDOW

Welcome to Hitchcock territory. The daring is missing, ditto the moral ambiguity that can lift a suspense picture to the rarefied level of art—Master Alfred's *Rear Window,* for example. But why kick? Writer-director Curtis Hanson came up with a sexy thriller sure to hold an audience in thrall. Hanson uses real characters to draw you in, instead of gore tactics and grating music. Steve Guttenberg plays an open-faced Baltimore executive who lucks out with the boss's sultry French wife (Isabelle Huppert) at an office party. Back at his apartment, the two put real heat into their lovemaking. The scene evokes the opening of *Psycho,* in which lover John Gavin plays with Leigh's bra (Huppert doesn't wear a bra, but Guttenberg plays anyway). Later, while Guttenberg is in the shower, Huppert gazes out the window to see a brutal attack on a young woman (Elizabeth McGovern), who barely escapes alive.

Huppert, fearing her jealous husband, refuses to be a witness. Conscience-ridden, Guttenberg pretends that her description of the would-be rapist-murderer is his own. When a shrewd lawyer, performed with snit and polish by Wallace Shawn, trips him up in court, Guttenberg finds himself the prime suspect. In true Hitchcock fashion, the innocent man must prove his innocence. Amazingly, the familiar is still fun, especially with Hanson's new twists. Guttenberg, finding the heart in his shallow yuppie hero, has never been more appealing. When he teams with the enchanting McGovern to trap the killer, romance flourishes, with charm filling in most of the credibility gaps. But the movie's sizzle comes from Huppert, a wow in or out of her fancy wardrobe, who can move from torrid ardor to cool bitchery in a second. This may be the star-making role she thought she had in *Heaven's Gate. The Bedroom Window* adroitly fulfills the condition essential to a good thriller. Just when you think you've seen it all, you haven't.
R / 1987 / Karl-Lorimar

▲ BEING THERE

Peter Sellers was always very funny, and sometimes brilliant, as Inspector Clouseau in the Pink Panther movies. As fans of old late-show British comedies know, however, he is equally talented at more subtle kinds of humor. Here he plays a mentally deficient gardener who is literally forced onto the street after his employer dies. He is taken in by a rich businessman and his wife, who find his simplemindedness quite charming. One thing leads to another and Sellers soon finds himself meeting the President of the United States and dispensing economic advice. The story, based on Jerzy Kosinski's satirical novel, looks at the world through the eyes of someone not as sophisticated—or jaded—as everyone else. That the Sellers character can become an overnight media sensation simply by describing his formula for growing plants is a pointed comment on America's celebrity-worshiping gullibility. Shirley MacLaine is drolly enchanting as the businessman's wife; Melvyn Douglas was affecting enough as the dying millionaire to earn a Best Supporting Actor Oscar, and Jack Warden's President is just the right blend of bluster and foolishness. But the movie's main effect is to confirm how versatile Sellers was.

PG / 1979 / CBS/Fox

▲ THE BELIEVERS

This god-awful garbage is the misbegotten result of a collaboration between a good cast (Martin Sheen, Helen Shaver, Jimmy Smits), a great director (John Schlesinger), and a great cinematographer (Robby Müller). Occult-film fans who relished the spray of chicken blood in *Angel Heart* will no doubt delight in the even more graphic gore included here. Schlesinger offers an electrocution before the credits as a warm-up, then moves on to bleeding chickens, exploding bodies, and the sickening mutilation of young boys. Schlesinger, the distinguished director of *Midnight Cowboy, Darling,* and *Far From the Madding Crowd,* didn't even have the honesty to admit he's out to make a buck in the exploitation market after a series of box-office flops (*Honky Tonk Freeway, Yanks, The Falcon and the Snowman*). In interviews he pompously maintained that he's interested in the corruption of the Santeria religion, a faith whose origins date back to the African slave trade. Sure, and *The Texas Chainsaw Massacre* was really a cautionary docudrama about the misuse of power tools. The story here focuses on Sheen, a recently widowed police psychologist who moves to Manhattan with his young son, played by Harley Cross. Shocked by a series of grisly ritual murders, Sheen finds his family, his sexy landlady (Shaver), his friends (Elizabeth Wilson, Lee Richardson), a no-bull cop (Robert Loggia), and a shifty-eyed millionaire (Harris Yulin) embroiled in Santerian rites. Since an estimated three million Americans practice Santeria today, and since its believers insist that they summon supernatural forces for benevolent reasons, a fascinating film might have been made. Schlesinger, however, is concerned with an aberration of Santeria that he and screenwriter Mark Frost, of television's "Hill Street Blues," have conjured up from a compendium of horror flick clichés. One of the film's saddest sights is Malick Bowens, the actor who brought such dignity and compassion to his role as Meryl Streep's servant in *Out of Africa,* prancing about maniacally like something out of *Abbott & Costello Meet the Voodoo Vampire.* For all its claims to authenticity, *The Believers* plays like what it is: claptrap.

R / 1987 / N/A

▲ THE BELL JAR

Sylvia Plath was a minor confessional American poet when she killed herself on a cold February day in 1963 in London. She subsequently became a cult heroine, and her autobiographical novel, *The Bell Jar,* became a rite of passage for young women. The film picks up the Plath character's life in 1953 when she is a scrubbed golden girl at Smith College, then follows her through a summer as a guest editor of *Ladies' Day* (in real life *Mademoiselle*), a gruesome suicide attempt, and a nervous breakdown. Marilyn Hassett plays the antiheroine and hits as many highs and lows in acting as Plath did in life. Her performance is at times embarrassingly amateurish, at others beautifully sensitive. Julie Harris, as Plath's well-intentioned mother, adds some class, and Robert Klein is effective in a cameo as a disc jockey, but the best thing about the film is Donna Mitchell as Plath's self-destructive best friend. (In 1987, Harvard psychiatrist Jane V. Anderson won a $150,000 settlement of her suit charging that Mitchell's character had defamed her.) Otherwise, *The Bell Jar* suffers from maudlin lapses, and director Larry Peerce fixates on screaming scenes. Plath deserved better.

R / 1979 / Vestron

▲ BEST DEFENSE

Surprisingly, for a comedy about the weapons trade, *Best Defense* did not keep its eye on its targets. This is a tale about a little tank that couldn't shoot. But director Willard Huyck, who co-wrote the script with his wife, Gloria Katz, indiscriminately aims for whatever passes in front of his lens—without hitting a laugh. Seeking sanctuary in lowest-common-denominator humor, this noisy comedy turns into a celebration of sexism in the workplace and racism in the field. Huyck's unfocused direction leaves the actors stranded. As the down-and-out engineer who stumbles upon plans for a top-rank tank, Dudley Moore drifts through the movie. His character is a cad, and Moore doesn't even bother to soften

him, as he did in *"10"* and *Arthur.* In the role of his sexy and lascivious supervisor, Helen Shaver only promotes the stereotype of the predatory woman. The movie's major miscalculation is Eddie Murphy, who is billed as "strategic guest star." Playing an Army lieutenant manning Moore's tank in Kuwait, Murphy cannot unleash his put-upon-black routine. This time he's not the victim of discrimination; those humiliations are relegated to his two Middle Eastern trainees cum lackeys, who could be Arab descendants of the Three Stooges. Without a plot that suits his persona, Murphy looks lost. This misbegotten movie's moral seems to be that the best defense is constant offensiveness.
R / 1984 / Paramount

▲ BEST FRIENDS

So testy is the tone of this semi-romantic semi-comedy, and so petulant and unlikable are the characters they play, that Goldie Hawn and Burt Reynolds need all the charm and goodwill they can muster just to keep it from becoming a disaster. They are two Hollywood screenwriters who, having lived together for three years, decide to get married. The mere idea of taking this step and meeting their in-laws sends both of them into such paroxysms of anxiety they become instant boors, snarly and insufferable. He fumes when they go to Buffalo to meet her folks because it's cold; she fumes in Virginia because his mother expects her to serve coffee. It may not sound that serious, but Hawn and Reynolds begin to act as if they'd just discovered that they've married someone who has the black plague, mass-murderer tendencies, and a wig (no offense, Burt). Director Norman (*In the Heat of the Night*) Jewison and writers Barry Levinson (pre-*Diner*) and Valerie Curtin (they collaborated on Jewison's *And Justice for All*) had in mind something about "the perils of modern marriage," according to the film's publicity. What sort of marital wreckage have they been prowling around in lately? This film only trivializes real problems, gaining few laughs in the process. While there are spotty triumphs by the supporting cast—notably Jessica Tandy and Audra Lindley as the mothers—the film seems contrived and mean-spirited. Its elements represent a match made not

in heaven but in the doghouse. One sterling compensation: a meltingly romantic theme ballad, "How Do You Keep the Music Playing?" by Michel Le Grand and Alan and Marilyn Bergman. Recorded by such greats as Sinatra and Susannah McCorkle, the song is already a near standard sure to survive the second-rate film it graces.
PG / 1982 / Warner

▲ THE BEST LITTLE WHOREHOUSE IN TEXAS

Well, gosh durn it if this movie ain't lower 'n an armadillo's snout an' twice as filthy. The film version of the Larry King–Peter Masterson Broadway musical, by King, Masterson, and director Colin (*Foul Play*) Higgins, seems devoted mainly to squeezing as many gratuitous cuss words as possible into 118 minutes. (King himself called the adaptation a "mess" at one point.) It's a shame, because the childishness of the script overshadows a marvelous performance by Dolly Parton as the madam of the house in question. She sings wonderfully, and the movie supplements Carol Hall's tuneful score with two of Parton's own songs, "Sneakin' Around" and "I Will Always Love You." Dolly looks lovely, which isn't easy when she's gussied up even more than usual to fit the role; the best thing Higgins does, in fact, is use her in close-up a lot so that her face, not her body, is the focus. She acts with a winsome sense of humor. And she strikes up some convincing chemistry with Burt Reynolds, who through no fault of his own is upstaged as the sheriff of the town where Dolly does business. (He sings one duet with her, doing no noticeable damage.) There's a lot of running around by scantily clad, buxom young ladies, slightly less by scantily clad, muscular young men. Jim Nabors, Dom De Luise (who's feeble as a TV consumer reporter cracking down on Dolly's house), and Lois Nettleton have supporting roles that are embarrassing in varying degrees. Charles Durning, though, does a nifty turn as a side-stepping pol and danced off with an Oscar nomination. But what can you do about a movie with laugh lines such as "We can't just sit around here waiting to grow tits" or "He's gonna kick that boy's ass"? Your call.
R / 1982 / MCA

▲ THE BEST OF TIMES

Robin (*Moscow on the Hudson*) Williams and Kurt (*Silkwood*) Russell make such a likable team they obscure most of the excesses of this movie. Williams plays a young bank executive who has never been able to live down the fact that he dropped a crucial pass in the Big Game of his high school career; Russell, who threw the pass, is better adjusted, though his wife is leaving him and his business is floundering (he paints designs on vans—for example, Princess Di surrounded by sharks). When Williams arranges a rematch of the football game, it sets in motion a series of events that won't be unfamiliar to anyone who has seen *The Longest Year, M*A*S*H*, or *The Bad News Bears*. The game itself is flat, though the movie was written by Ron (*Under Fire*) Shelton, a former minor league baseball player who might have been expected to have a livelier sense of athletic drama and comedy. Director Roger Spottiswoode, so effective in *Under Fire,* knuckles under to sappiness here. But Williams does such an engaging Everyman it's impossible not to root for him, and Russell plays straight man without being upstaged. Pamela (*Clan of the Cave Bear*) Reed, as Russell's wife, and Holly (*Under Fire*) Palance, as Williams', are appealing too. Football widows will understand Palance's dictum that under no circumstances will the words ''Dick Butkus'' be allowed at the dinner table. Margaret (*Love Child*) Whitton adds a nice bit as the massage parlor hussy who gives Williams the idea for replaying the game. Things too often get silly without being compensatingly funny, but there is a kind of neo-Capra charm to the fantasy of being able to do something about those daydreams that start off, ''If only I had. . . .''
PG-13 / 1986 / Embassy

▲ BETRAYAL

When a London publisher learns his literary agent friend is having an affair with his wife, it sounds like the eternal triangle, by now a bit of a bore. Well, *Betrayal,* adapted by Harold Pinter from his 1978 play, is a live wire. As always, Pinter crafts his dialogue to detonate. Ditto his silences. He tells his story backward—starting with the end of the affair and ending nine years before on the day it began. This can seem gimmicky, as it did in the 1980 Broadway production, which was not helped by the miscasting of Roy Scheider and Raul Julia. But Pinter and first-time feature director David Jones cast the film just right. As the fastidious publisher, Ben Kingsley proved his stunning debut in *Gandhi* was no fluke. Holding his body rigid, Kingsley, with darting eyes and a wounding wit, reveals the cuckolded husband squirming inside. This is remarkable, richly suggestive acting. Jeremy (*The French Lieutenant's Woman*) Irons also delivers a finely calibrated performance portraying the false friend. One long Kinglsey-Irons restaurant scene in which neither speaks directly to the other is tension-charged and beautifully managed. Only British TV actress Patricia Hodge disappoints; as Kingsley's wife, she can handle Pinter's language but lacks the seductiveness the role requires. (Blythe Danner filled both requirements gloriously on Broadway.) No matter. *Betrayal* is Pinter at his wicked best, having us on with his verbal pyrotechnics until the emotional truth explodes in our faces.
R / 1983 / CBS/Fox

▲ THE BETSY

The Betsy is a car that aging automotive mogul Laurence Olivier and young ambitious race driver Tommy Lee Jones want to develop. By all rights the sixty-miles-per-gallon comer of a car should be the hero of this Harold Robbins saga, something to make the murder, intrigue, and impossibly trite dialogue worthwhile. Unfortunately, we soon lose sight of the Betsy altogether, while illicit sex (Olivier and daughter-in-law, Jones and his boss's mistress and daughter) blossom amid heavy-handed pop psych flashbacks. Lesley-Anne Down is gorgeous as the girlfriend, but she and the rest of the cast—especially Olivier and Robert Duvall—should have been embarrassed about having appeared in this lemon.
R / 1978 / CBS/Fox

▲ BETTER OFF DEAD

The temptation is to write off this loud and loutish teenage comedy as just another nail in the coffin of a tired genre. But *Better Off Dead* deserves special condemnation. Viewers are encouraged

to demand refunds, form citizen awareness groups, and expose the culprits. Start with producer Michael Jaffe, who backed newcomer Steve Holland as writer and director. What went through Jaffe's mind when he read Holland's script about a nerdy high schooler who makes "fun" attempts at suicide when his girl leaves him? What appealed to Jaffe most? The total absence of wit? The jokes about obesity, nausea, and defecation? The chance to humiliate some hitherto fine actors? John Cusack, who made a striking impression in *The Sure Thing,* here is a singularly unappealing teen hero. Only Kim Darby (remember her, please, as the courageous sprite in 1969's *True Grit*) has it worse. Playing Cusack's mother (she keeps spooning out globs of purplish food and watching her family turn green), she delivers a sadly desperate performance. Still, the actors are more to be pitied than pummeled. Save the volleys for Holland—"Savage Steve" to his bosses who with misguided pride labeled this film as a Savage Steve Holland Production. "Savage" (a nickname from his apparently ongoing adolescence) was, at 25, able to get a studio to put him in charge of a major motion picture. Any more questions about what's wrong with Hollywood?
PG / 1985 / Key

▲ BETWEEN THE LINES

A gently funny, gently sexy, and sometimes gently dumb film about an underground newspaper in Boston about to be sucked up by a publishing tycoon of the Rupert Murdock ilk. Director Joan Silver (who did *Hester Street*) rounded up an extraordinarily attractive cast of young actors, then unknowns, including Lindsay Crouse (*Slap Shot*), Gwen Welles (the reluctant stripper in *Nashville*), Jill Eikenberry (now a staple on TV's "L.A. Law"), Jeff Goldblum (star of *The Fly*), and John (*The Trip to Bountiful*) Heard, a stage veteran making an impressive movie debut.
R / 1977 / Vestron

▲ BEVERLY HILLS COP

Dirtier and hotter than Harry, Eddie Murphy is also the funniest screen cop since the Keystones. From the moment he flashes his radiantly lewd grin, this comedy caper is off and running. Mur-

phy plays a Young Turk on the Detroit force who horns in on Beverly Hills police turf to nose out the killer of his buddy. Furst he snags a suite at a chic hotel by pretending to be a reporter on a Michael Jackson story ("If Michael calls, tell him I'll catch him later"). At a swank art gallery, he talks his way past an espresso-sipping sleazo—in a sidesplitting cameo by Bronson Pinchot—to find the manager, a childhood friend whose employer might hold the key to the murder. That's when Murphy meets the B.H.P.D. Dressed like bank tellers, with manners to match ("Please put your hands up, sir"), these Beverly Hills officers—from Ronny Cox's chief to Judge Reinhold and John Ashton's subordinates—are hopeless bunglers. Plausibility inevitably takes a backseat to fun, but a more incisive comic approach to police methods would have been welcome. Still, director Martin Brest has a quirky camera eye and a knack for details. Murphy has never been more likable. He had star help in his first two movies (Nick Nolte in *48 Hrs.* and Dan Aykroyd in *Trading Places*), but he is king of his own hill this time. Even when the plot misfires, Murphy comes out shooting from the funny bone—and it's bull's-eyes all the way.
R / 1985 / Paramount

▲ BEVERLY HILLS COP II

In 1984, Eddie Murphy coupled his comic and acting talents and made a real crowd pleaser ($294 million) out of a patchwork plot about a Detroit cop invading Beverly Hills to avenge a buddy's murder. No reason this sequel shouldn't be as entertaining. Just don't look too closely. Between the shoot-outs, scatology and misogynist sex jokes, you might notice that Murphy has turned into one slick Hollywood package. He's not acting this time, he's doing stand-up. The story for part *II,* credited to Murphy and his manager Robert Wachs, is obvious in its purpose: to show off Murphy showing off. He does character impressions (reggae psychic, delivery boy, pool cleaner at the Playboy mansion), Hums "The Dating Game" theme and laughs louder than anyone at his own street-smart savvy. Every move is so calculated, the spontaneity goes out of the picture. Murphy had earned our good will in the past (*48 Hrs., Trading Places*). Here he was merely trading on it. The supporting cast, including Judge Reinhold, John Ashton and Ronny

Cox, does little more than play stooges to Murphy's Mr. Cool. No one steals scenes from the star the way Bronson Pinchot—as Serge the art dealer—did in the original. Blond bombshell Brigitte Nielsen (Mrs. Sly Stallone) gives it a game go. Gorgeously long of leg (she's 6½), Nielsen is ideally cast as the Ms. Big of Crime, but she's never allowed to develop her character above the hemline. Director Tony Scott, following his pattern with Catherine Deneuve's chic vampire in *The Hunger* and Kelly McGillis' sexpot pilot trainer in *Top Gun*, treats women as soulless mannequins. The snickers Murphy gets at Nielsen's expense (''God, that's a big bitch'') leave a nasty aftertaste. So does too much of this hard-sell sequel. Murphy may still be a sure thing at the box office, but this time he shortchanged himself and his fans.
R / 1987 / Paramount

▲ BEYOND AND BACK

You'll remember the Sunn Classics film folks. They're the ones who ran computer searches to find out what subjects people were interested in and made movies slavishly following the results, which they then promoted like the devil on TV. *In Search of Noah's Ark* and *The Life and Times of Grizzly Adams* were their most lucrative earlier printouts, and in this film they latch onto the life-after-death craze, fed by the reports that people clinically dead have experienced various sensations suggesting an afterlife. The film uses a mongrel form Sunn calls ''docu-drama'' that grates pretentiously on the nerves. The cast, if they are not amateurs, sure act like it. People lose consciousness, see flashing white lights, and perceive various spiritual presences, then revive. About this time a viewer wakes up, too, now uncertain even if there is life after the opening credits.
G / 1978 / United

▲ BEYOND THE LIMIT

Richard Gere found a role he's perfectly suited to in this grim, moody drama based on the Graham Greene novel *The Honorary Consul*. Gere's screen image is of superficiality and lack of connection; adroit at displaying lust, he has almost no ability to convey passion. In this film he plays a half-Paraguayan, half-English doctor practicing in a small Argentinian town. Despite his lack of ideals or principles, he becomes swept up in a plot by Paraguayan rebels to kidnap an American diplomat. Gere is convincingly cynical, exploitive, cold. He doesn't turn out to have a heart of gold—or any kind of heart. He has an emotionless affair with the ex-hooker wife of his friend, the alcoholic British consul, played with subtle modulation by Michael Caine. (The wife is Mexican actress Elpidia Carrillo, who is called on mainly to be sensual.) By the time Caine becomes involved in the kidnap plot, it's clear that Gere's inability to commit himself is chronic. He's eventually given up as a hopeless case even by his friend, the local Argentinian police colonel, played by Bob (*Mona Lisa*) Hoskins. The film is mostly heavy going. The Argentina and Paraguay governments are both brutally repressive, and the rebels are ruthless; nobody believes in anything but survival. But Greene's story, adapted by Christopher Hampton and directed by John (*The Long Good Friday*) Mackenzie, keeps most of the attention on the three principals. Even if you don't like them, you want to find out what's going to happen to them next.
R / 1983 / Paramount

▲ BEYOND THE POSEIDON ADVENTURE

Irwin Allen might have invented a dictum that the disaster is never over until the last gross is out, and the *Poseidon Adventure* grossed $42 million. The faces in this sequel, however, were changed: Everyone in the original's cast was either rescued or killed off, so this time Michael Caine plays a crusty tugboat captain. How a harbor tug happens to be in the middle of the ocean is never sufficiently explained, but the *Jenny*'s crew (including Sally Field, reverting to her supercute *Flying Nun* persona) finds the wreck of the *Poseidon* and decides to go aboard for salvage. They meet another scavenger (Telly Savalas) and some more medium-level star survivors, trapped in the still-flooding, upside-down wreck. Nobody should be blamed for trying to escape. One consolation (aside from the unintentionally hilarious script) is that the liner blows up in the last scene, signaling the end of the Poseidon Adventures, unless a couple of survivors are still out there floating around, waiting for *The Poseidon Flotsam and Jetsam*.

PG / 1979 / N/A

▲ THE BIG CHILL

Writer-director Lawrence Kasdan, borrowing from comic books, made high camp hoot out of *Raiders of the Lost Ark* and *The Empire Strikes Back*. Borrowing from '40s crime dramas like *Double Indemnity*, he wrote and directed 1981's *Body Heat*. In this film, borrowing the basic theme of '60s-activists-adrift-in-the-'80s from John Sayles' low-budget gem *Return of the Secaucus Seven*, Kasdan co-wrote (with Barbara Benedek) and directed an enormously popular movie. Though it's intelligent, quick-witted, and slickly produced, there's no escaping the ponderous philosophizing that keeps spoiling the fun. A group of seven old friends reunite for the funeral of Alex, one of their pals, who has committed suicide. Chilled by this intimation of their own mortality, each begins to question his or her life. Kevin Kline, eschewing protest, has become a running-shoe magnate; his wife, Glenn Close, is a successful doctor. JoBeth Williams has sold out for security as the wife of an ad man; Mary Kay Place is a lawyer who no longer defends the poor; ex-radical Tom Berenger has parlayed his looks into a starring role in a "Magnum P.I."-type TV series; Jeff Goldblum has stopped writing political tracts to work for *People* magazine; and William Hurt, a disillusioned and impotent Vietnam vet, has stopped doing anything but drugs. The acting ranges from first-rate (Hurt) to fatuous (Meg Tilly, as Alex's young girlfriend). Goldblum gets the most laughs, but Berenger goes deeper by providing his TV hunk with a surprising measure of dignity. While the women's roles are conceived on more conventional lines, Close (so fine as the mother in *The World According to Garp*) copped the film's only acting Oscar nomination. Sadly, Kasdan sets forth these characters with a patronizing patness notably absent from Sayles' film. Alex, who is never seen, becomes the most interesting by default. He represents the spirit of the '60s, as does the superb soundtrack (Stones, Three Dog Night, Marvin Gaye) that Kasdan uses like an open faucet of nostalgia. He also uses cheap TV movie plot devices, like Place's beat-the-biological-clock search for in-semination. Too bad. Because it's really the talk, when it's simple and direct (plus the little shocks of recognition), that makes *The Big Chill* the close-to-the-bone movie for the baby-boom generation.

R / 1983 / RCA/Columbia

▲ THE BIG FIX

Flush from his Oscar win as Best Actor for 1977's *The Goodbye Girl*, Richard Dreyfuss made himself coproducer and star of this picture. His co-star is a bygone era: the revolutionary '60s. Dreyfuss plays a '70s private eye with two kids, an ex-wife (who is into a mind-shaping cult called BEST), and a bad case of Berkeley nostalgia. When an old girlfriend (Susan Anspach) asks him to check into an election campaign smear, he is less than consumed by the case until she turns up dead. His search for the killer raises the question of where the radicals of yesteryear are—and answers it, hilariously. Dreyfuss is good, if a trifle cutesy, as the gumshoe. But it's F. Murray Abraham, 1985 Oscar winner for *Amadeus*, who steals the show as an Abbie Hoffmanesque rad-turned-ad-game-hustler. Too bad Jeremy Paul (*Heroes*) Kagan's direction tends to dull rather than develop an intelligently complex plot from Roger L. Simon (who also wrote the 1973 novel the film comes from).

PG / 1978 / MCA

▲ THE BIG RED ONE

Sam Fuller was long the darling of the sometimes perverse cahiers du cinema crowd for churning out unpretentious potboilers like *I Shot Jesse James*, *Forty Guns*, and *Shock Corridor* on starved budgets and shrunken shooting schedules. At 68, the cigar-chomping maverick went big-studio legit with this epic and box-office stars Lee Marvin and Mark Hamill. He tells a semiautobiographical tale of a rifleman's World War II experiences in the Army's First Infantry Division. (Known as the "Big Red One" for its insignia, it later fought in Vietnam.) The film's vast scope blurs Fuller's trademarked close-up intensity, and he still doesn't write dialogue but rather tabloid teaser. For example, Marvin, as a tough sergeant, snarls at dogface Hamill: "We don't murder, we kill."

That moral distinction and the script's attempts at profundity are foolish, but thanks to Fuller's dime-novel heart and B-picture instinct, the film has the exuberant kick of first-rate trash.
PG / 1980 / CBS/Fox

▲ THE BIG SLEEP

Bogie played the cynical private eye Philip Marlowe in the '46 version. Robert Mitchum (at 61) boldly followed that act in this remake purporting to be a more faithful rendering of Raymond Chandler's novel. In a wonderful opening sequence, the camera is behind the wheel as Mitchum's Mercedes roars down a winding English road toward the estate of an aging general (James Stewart) who has two wild daughters, a gambler (Sarah Miles in the old Bacall role) and a nymphomaniac (Candy Clark). Blackmail is the general's immediate problem, and Mitchum discovers others: a vanished son-in-law and a chain reaction of murders. Though the plot is intricate, a combination of weighty performances, light porn, poison, and a blizzard of bullets makes *The Big Sleep* positively rousing.
R / 1978 / CBS/Fox

▲ BIG TROUBLE

If director John (*Love Streams*) Cassavetes offered his viewers pretzels and a glass of beer with this home movie, he might be forgiven. As it is, anyone paying even the price of an overnight video rental is paying too much. The film features a lot of estimable actors, such as Peter Falk, Alan Arkin, Robert Stack, Beverly D'Angelo, and Charles Durning. Many of them are Cassavetes's friends, or at least they were until he roped them into this sloppy, tedious comedy about a con man (Falk) who tries to bilk an insurance company by faking his own death. Arkin, an insurance salesman, gets involved in the scam because he's desperate for money to send his triplets to Yale. That part of the plot is introduced immediately, setting a who-cares tone that is maintained throughout as terrorists, insanity, and death meander in and out of the frame. One of Falk's big scenes has him trying to get laughs out of the facial contortions displayed by someone undergoing a heart attack. Anyone who has the choice should opt for his Uncle Ziggy's films of his trip to Wyoming.
R / 1986 / CBS/Fox

▲ BIG TROUBLE IN LITTLE CHINA

Mix a screwball adventure comedy with martial arts film. Add a heavy dose of special effects. Bake for 100 minutes. What you get is this sorry mess. Director John (*Starman*) Carpenter's movie is peppered with cliché after cliché that, instead of being sent up, just lie there like lumps. Kung-fu action sequences seem to be thrown in to keep the audience awake. The out-of-place Kurt (*Silkwood*) Russell plays a truck driver whose friend Dennis (*Year of the Dragon*) Dun has his fiancée stolen by an evil spirit embodied by James (*Missing in Action*) Hong. Dun and Russell are aided in their rescue attempt by a local attorney, Kim (*Police Academy*) Cattrall. Russell carries a knife in his teeth a lot, while Dun does all the fighting. The film has a workable campiness at times, and the special effects by Richard (*Star Wars*) Edlund are terrific. But they aren't reasons enough to see this film. There's more mystery and excitement in a fortune cookie.
PG-13 / 1986 / CBS/Fox

▲ BILLY GALVIN

"You gotta have something to point to," construction worker Jack Galvin tells his college-age son, Billy. For Jack, that something is both tangible, the Boston skyscrapers he's worked on, and intangible, the chance for Billy to make more of himself than his blue-collar father. Problem is, Billy wants to follow in the old man's footsteps. That rift is at the heart of this unpretentious domestic drama. Billy, solidly played by Lenny Von Dohlen, wants to bridge the gap between himself and his father (Karl Malden in his first big-screen role since 1983). "I thought you said you love me," he says to Malden, who replies, "You've got convenient hearing." Von Dohlen is appropriately angst-filled, and Malden is a bundle of idiosyncrasies, calling everyone "yardbird" and having door-slamming contests with his understanding wife, played by Joyce Van Patten. Toni Kalem rounds out the strong cast as Von Dohlen's girlfriend. The proportions are hardly epic, but director John Gray's knack for detail provides a bittersweet slice of real life.

PG-13 / 1987 / N/A

▲ BLACK AND WHITE IN COLOR

As a story about an absurd World War I skirmish between two motley groups of Frenchmen and Germans in West Africa, this European-African production was absorbing enough to upset *Cousin, Cousine* and *Seven Beauties* for the best foreign film Oscar. As a satire on colonialism, it is devastating, and never more so than when two French missionaries, after collecting local ceremonial statues as trade-ins on crucifixes and sacred hearts, mockingly burn all the pagan idols —except the ones they can sell to art collectors. Director Jean-Jacques Annaud would later score with *Quest for Fire* and falter with his murky filming of Umberto Eco's *The Name of the Rose*. (In French with subtitles.)

PG / 1977 / N/A

▲ THE BLACK HOLE

Here is a perfectly standard Walt Disney adventure yarn set in outer space, apparently as an excuse to disburse $20 million on special effects: Though perhaps fiercely complicated to execute, they seem almost commonplace by now. The mysterious phenomenon of the title looms intriguingly throughout the movie, but proves disappointing when finally explored. There is, however, one spectacular moment during a meteor storm; and John Barry's score is a welcome change from John Williams's overorchestrated *Star Wars* space sonatas. The screenplay is strictly comic-book stuff, and the only decent dialogue is assigned to a pair of winning (but familiar) robots named Vincent and Bob. Maximilian Schell is appropriately sinister as the mad scientist (at one point he even says, "The ends justify the means") determined to plumb the depths of the black hole. But even accomplished actors like Anthony Perkins and Ernest Borgnine appear lost in space under the pedestrian direction of Gary (*Freaky Friday*) Nelson.

PG / 1980 / Disney

▲ THE BLACK MARBLE

Joseph Wambaugh, the bittersweet dramatist of police life, took a shot at romantic comedy this time and misfires. The plot consists of two independent stories that occasionally meet but rarely fuse. In one, a professional dog trainer (Harry Dean Stanton) kidnaps a prize schnauzer for ransom money to pay off his gambling debts. In the other, a broken-down detective who has taken to drink (Robert Foxworth) is paired with a hardboiled policewoman (Paula Prentiss). The department wants her to straighten him out, but she's not interested ("He's a candidate for the canvas blazer with wraparound arms," she snaps). Foxworth, as a Russian-American who gets misty over balalaika music and wipes his eyes with his tie, is a likable lummox, but Prentiss, with her tough veneer, is at best brittle. The boredom of watching the pair fall inevitably for each other makes the jittery appearances of Stanton, as the desperate dognapper, richly welcome. When he and Foxworth tussle in a kennel, the jostled mutts start baying in protest, which would be an appropriate response to the movie in general.

PG / 1980 / CBS/Fox

▲ BLACK MOON RISING

This crime caper has about as much redeeming social value as a vat of corn chips. But it is close to the quintessential Grade-B movie—fast, funny, sexy, and thoroughly diverting. Tommy Lee (*The Executioner's Song*) Jones plays a professional thief hired to steal a computer tape needed to prosecute a tax case. Fleeing with the tape, he is forced to hide it in an experimental car that's making a gas station stop. When the car is in turn stolen by Linda (*The Terminator*) Hamilton, an operative for an auto-theft ring, Jones finds himself on a life-or-death quest. Jones, grittily amusing, and Hamilton, sly and sensuous, are backed up by a veteran cast that strikes just the right semiserious tone. Robert Vaughn's officiously nasty mode was first brought out in *Bullitt*, and he has been recycling it ever since. It fits exactly in this case with his role as the head of a car-theft ring, which is run with such corporate efficiency it looks as if it must have a pension plan. Richard Jaeckel affects an air of nerdy determination as the ex-NASA scientist who designed the experimental car, which is supposed to be hydrogen-powered and go 350 mph (the car is portrayed by a real thirty-six-inch-high show car, the Concordia II, designed at Concordia University in Montreal as an aerodynamics project). Former jock Bubba Smith, who plays a government agent, dispenses with his usual buffoonery: He doesn't have to do a lot of acting to seem big and tough. Rock singer Lee Ving of Fear snarls convincingly as an enforcer for the tax dodgers. Nothing is overdone. Jones is clearly a good guy, but when he gets beaten to a pulp he doesn't get instantly revitalized the way most movie heroes do; he spends the rest of the film moaning about his injuries. John Carpenter, who directed such films as *Halloween* and *Escape from New York,* co-wrote this one from his own idea. It was directed by Harley Cokliss, whose most impressive previous credit was as the second unit director for *The Empire Strikes Back.* He shows admirable restraint, knowing just how long to let his chases, fights, and love scenes go on. While the ending forces viewers to suspend their disbelief from here just about to Bora Bora, Cokliss never really insults anyone's intelligence. It's as if he's saying, "All right: If we're going to look for escape, let's escape in style."

R / 1986 / New World

▲ THE BLACK PEARL

One has to respect a movie whose star was discovered while making deliveries for a New York supermarket. And Mario Custodio, 18 when the film was shot, is agreeable enough as a young man learning to dive for pearls off the coast of Mexico. It's also a pleasant surprise when Gilbert Roland, looking younger than his 73 years, shows up as the diver's mentor. Apart from some lovely underwater photography, however, there is little to recommend this adventure flick. Certainly not the allegedly deadly *mania diablo,* a flying manta ray, rendered laughably unterrifying by the shoddy special effects. Worst of all is the Ahab-lashed-to-the-whale ending lifted straight from Moby Dick. It's a lesson from Mario, anyway: One minute the world is your oyster, the next minute you're in the stew.

PG / 1978 / N/A

▲ THE BLACK STALLION RETURNS

"You are courageous to have come so far," the Berber chief tells teenager Kelly Reno. True enough. The boy has, after all, jumped onto a speeding truck driven by stallion-napping Arabs, stowed away on a plane from New York to Casablanca, nearly died of thirst, and trudged across miles of Sahara to catch up with the steed he starred with in the dark-horse movie success of 1979. This sequel is preposterous and slow but beautiful to look at. Director of photography Carlo De Palma made the most of the Algerian, Italian, and Moroccan locations, and a climactic inter-tribal race is a classic hoof-pounder. Most adults will have to rely on the visuals for entertainment, though. Reno, then 16, was less cuddly than he was in the original. Teri Garr returns as Reno's mother, but she has only about a minute of onscreen time. Vincent Spano, as an Arab who befriends Reno, manages some warmth. And Cass Ole, who has the title role, is a performer of a different color, of course. He is a wonderfully photogenic animal, at least as expressive as a lot of actors these days. In his big race scene, it would be unfair to reveal who wins. Just remember what great riders kids can be when the fates and scriptwriters are on their side.

PG / 1983 / CBS/Fox

▲ BLACK SUNDAY

An Israeli commando, played by stalwart character actor Robert (*Jaws*) Shaw (he died a year later), outwits Marthe Keller, an unflinching Arab terrorist, and perennial psycho Bruce Dern, who are hell-bent on making sure there is no tomorrow for eighty thousand Super Bowl fans. The blimp-bombing finale is a little overinflated, but director John Frankenheimer made this terrifying trip from the alleys of Beirut to a hyped-up Miami an all-pro suspense chiller.

R / 1977 / Paramount

▲ BLAME IT ON RIO

Michael Caine may be one of the most charming and persuasive actors ever, but even his sure comic touch cannot save this sniggering sex farce, which uses statutory rape as its playful premise.

Caine and Joseph Bologna play business partners with bad marriages. Bologna is on the brink of divorce and Caine's wife, stridently acted by Valeria Harper, is fed up with her husband's neglect. That's when the boys decide to vacation in Rio with their respective teenage daughters. Model-turned-actress Michelle Johnson plays Bologna's 15-year-old, a zaftig free spirit who can't hide her yen for Caine even from his daughter, played by Demi Moore. Johnson, modest only in talent, displays her centerfold's body at every opportunity. (She and Moore strut onto the beach topless in front of their nonplussed daddies.) The climax, as it were, arrives when Johnson pulls off Caine's swim trunks. The ensuing explicit Caine-Johnson love scenes are a natural target for righteous indignation. Let's face it: Roman Polanski was arrested for doing what Caine does in this movie. It isn't surprising that Charlie Peters, whose tawdry work includes *Paternity* and *Kiss Me Goodbye,* wrote the screenplay. But what is incomprehensible is that such formidable talents as co-screenwriter Larry (*Tootsie*) Gelbart and director Stanley (*Singin' in the Rain*) Donen abet Peters ladling out this swill. Don't blame it on Rio, which, as photographed by Reynaldo Villolobos, has all the romantic innocence the film lacks.

R / 1984 / Vestron

▲ BLIND DATE

We all scoffed—heck, we even snickered—when Madonna, then late of the megabomb *Shanghai Surprise,* turned down this promising-sounding comedy. The desperately-seeking-a-hit pop star had blown her chance to work with class director Blake Edwards and *Moonlighting*'s red-hot Romeo, Bruce Willis, in his starring screen debut. Well, Madonna, you earned some apologies. You got the last laugh, which puts you way up on anyone who watches this witless exercise in frenzied farce. Our sympathies to Kim Basinger, who stepped into the title role. Despite her obvious beauty and talent, Basinger's credits read like a road map of movie disaster areas (*No Mercy, Mother Lode, 9½ Weeks, The Man Who Loved Women*). And she never struggled more futilely with a role. Playing a setup date for nerdy financial analyst Willis at an important client dinner, Basinger is meant to embody a rather nasty male chauvinist joke. Give this doll a sip of champagne

and she's a sexual cannibal. Give her another sip and she's a foul-mouthed harridan, able to wreck a restaurant as easily as her date's reputation. Dale Launer's mean-spirited script rarely gives Basinger a chance. When she's not drunk, she's dazed. Willis fares a bit better; you never doubt his innate appeal would survive this drivel. But director Edwards seems determined to bury his stars in an excess of sight gags, car wrecks, and brawls. He succeeds. Other fine actors, such as Emmy winners John Larroquette and William Daniels are also lost in the melee. Edwards's previous two films (*A Fine Mess, That's Life*) indicated that the dazzling stylist behind the *Pink Panther* films had lost his touch for mixing silliness and sentiment. Renting an Edwards classic (how about *Breakfast at Tiffany's?*) would provide the kick this movie does not. This *Blind Date* is a dog.

PG-13 / 1987 / N/A

▲ BLOOD BEACH

Once the only things to worry about at the beach were flip-top tabs, sand between the toes, or tripping over Frankie Avalon and Annette. But the Los Angeles strand that's the setting for this scare flick is also home to a creature that resembles a giant canister vacuum cleaner with a devouring attachment. It prowls under the sand, pulling victims down to a gritty fate. While it evinces the usual movie-monster taste for nubile bikini-clad starlets, it also gobbles up a fair cross section of the community. This is standard low-budget horror, bolstered by dry, what-the-hell performances from John Saxon and Burt Young as cops. What sticks in the craw are tossed-off smidgeons of sex, foolish gore, and a faded image, as if the film had been purposely overexposed. The plot is figuratively and literally a fright.

R / 1981 / Media

▲ BLOODBROTHERS

The De Cocos are a clan of Italian-American macho toughs, slugging it out and whoring around in the Bronx. But they're also loving, caring men who kiss and cry and say what they feel (often in vivid four-letter terms) and, mamma mia, they aren't even gangsters. Richard Gere plays a tenderly rebellious son and nephew to a couple of hard hats, Tony (*F.I.S.T.*) Lo Bianco and Paul (*Oh, God!*) Sorvino, and the long ghost story he tells the hospitalized children he works with steals the movie. With the exception of 1982's *An Officer and a Gentleman,* Gere hasn't been better (or even good) since. The women, alas, are pathetic stereotypes, and the anorexic kid brother strains credibility. But at least the warm-blooded De Cocos, drawn from Richard Price's bestseller, stand to redeem the famiglia from the Corleones.

R / 1978 / Warner

▲ BLOOD SIMPLE

A thriller that's fresh, frightening, and fiendishly funny, this film was independently made on a shoestring budget (about $1.5 million). It marked a remarkable debut for two brothers from Minneapolis—director Joel Coen and producer Ethan Coen. The pair collaborated on the script about a surly Texas bar owner (Dan Hedaya), his roving wife (Frances McDormand), the sexy bartender she slips out with (John Getz), and the fat detective (M. Emmet Walsh) whom the husband hires to kill the cheating couple. Things go haywire, just as in pulp fiction from James Cain to Dashiell Hammett, but the Coens and their brilliant cameraman, Barry Sonnenfeld, don't just shake up the lurid detective genre, they give it the roller coaster ride of its life. A footfall, a fan, a newspaper tossed against a window—all of them take on terrifying dimensions. The climax is a gruesome gag worthy of Hitchcock. The actors are fine, but Walsh, whose face is recognizable from *Straight Time* and *Reds,* is terrific. There hadn't been a creepier screen menace since Robert Mitchum's mad minister in *Night of the Hunter.* Walsh's last chilling laugh is the stuff of bad dreams.

R / 1985 / MCA

▲ BLOW OUT

Writer-director Brian De Palma seizes the audience's attention from the opening frame and holds it until the final goose bump. If the title recalls Antonioni's 1966 film, it's no accident. Instead of a photographer stumbling on the *Blow-Up* murder in a London park, De Palma's story focuses on sound effects technician John Travolta, who witnesses what may be a political killing on a deserted bridge near downtown Philadelphia. There are echoes of Chappaquiddick as Travolta rescues Nancy Allen from a rapidly submerging car. Then Travolta and Allen team up to unravel the mystery. The plot doesn't bear scrutiny; both Travolta and Allen take inexplicable chances. Character development is chucked in a movie like this too. But Travolta provides a disciplined performance as an innocent man caught in a conspiracy—a situation used so well by Hitchcock, whose influence permeates De Palma's films. Allen (then Mrs. De Palma) serves up a cut-rate version of her high-class hooker in *Dressed to Kill.* If De Palma stretches credibility and indulges in visual excess, he should be forgiven. He has as much panache and imagination as any filmmaker in America today.

R / 1981 / Warner

▲ BLUE CITY

Michelle Manning says she considered herself lucky in this, her directorial debut, because she was able to "fire guns, kill people, stage lovemaking sequences, destroy buildings, and blow up cars." Great. Now all she has to do is learn how to tell a story. The setting is a crooked Florida town, and Judd (*St. Elmo's Fire*) Nelson plays the son of the mayor. Nelson left home five years earlier when his dad married a voluptuous vamp, played by Anita (Broadway's *Nine*) Morris. Hoping for reconciliation, he returns home only to find that his father has been murdered. But what's supposed to be an emotional roller coaster is as flat as the Florida landscape. Nelson's career as a schoolboy basketball star, which fortunately for critics is discussed in the press material for the movie, is never mentioned onscreen. Thus, a potentially poignant scene in the beginning—when the boy leaves his basketball at his father's grave—is meaningless. When Nelson vows to find his father's killer, the most obvious suspect is his father's former partner, Scott (*The Right Stuff*) Wilson, who's now sleeping with Morris. In his crusade against Wilson, Nelson enlists a high school buddy, whose sister is Ally (*Short Circuit*) Sheedy. She just happens to work at the police station and can obtain files on the murder. There's a twist at the end that helps redeem the movie, but most of it is spent staring

up at Nelson's substantial proboscis as he issues threats like this one to Morris: "You're going to experience grief and woe of biblical proportion." Viewers may take that as fair warning.
R / 1986 / Paramount

▲ BLUE COLLAR

A film about three auto workers, this movie has trouble deciding whether it's *On the Waterfront* or a Socialist Workers party tract. Yet Richard Pryor, Yaphet Kotto, and Harvey Keitel have impressive moments—not only acting but interacting. Pryor is especially moving at times, restraining his penchant for playing all his characters as if they were black comics doing nonstop funky-jivy-honkie jokes. Director Paul Schrader (who had already written *Taxi Driver* and *Obsession*) lapses into unnecessary melodrama—the three men bog down in a contrived battle with their corrupt union—but he effectively uses the Checker auto plant in Kalamazoo as his main set. He also manages to capture some of the frustration and despair of people who feel as soulless and manipulated as fenders on an assembly line.
R / 1978 / MCA

▲ BLUE COUNTRY

Ah, the French. They sure know how to whip up a soufflé comedy. The trouble is, this one's so fluffy it just seems to float away. Brigitte Fossey plays a health-food nut who moves to the country and falls in love with a handsome young farmer but refuses to marry him. The farmer, played with offhand humor by Jacques Serres, agrees that their mutual independence is too good to spoil, so they settle in for a long romance. Director Jean-Charles Tacchella, who created the charming *Cousin, Cousine,* often skips the plot for some amusing but pointless digressions on life in the country. (In French with subtitles.)
Unrated / 1978 / RCA/Columbia

▲ BLUE THUNDER

For a silly, shallow, preposterously plotted film about a giant surveillance helicopter capable of wasting large cities, *Blue Thunder* is surprisingly absorbing entertainment, a real popcorn movie. Purportedly designed to keep L.A. safe from

terrorists at the 1984 Olympics (but really a tool of military madmen), the armor-plated police chopper can fly at 200 mph, provide instant computer readouts on targets, fire four thousand rounds of 20-mm shells in a single minute, and peek down a hooker's dress at one thousand feet. Nicknamed "Blue Thunder," this incredible hulk (adapted from a real helicopter, France's Aerospatiale Gazelle) can do everything but talk. That puts it at a distinct advantage over the actors, who must mouth the banal dialogue of writers Dan O'Bannon and Don Jakoby. Saddled with most of the lifeless lines is Roy Scheider, playing a dedicated L.A. cop who puts aside his problems involving lady friend Candy Clark, a near nervous breakdown, and recurrent nightmares of chopper duty in Vietnam to sleuth out the evils in *Blue Thunder*. After *Jaws* and *The French Connection,* Scheider could play this kind of part in his sleep—an understandable temptation given the futility of trying to steal scenes from a helicopter—but instead he gives his all. So do Warren Oates as his captain, Malcolm McDowell as a sniveling villain, and Daniel (*Diner*) Stern as Scheider's novice copilot. "You're supposed to be stupid," Scheider tells Stern. He's right. Bungling copilots are a movie convention, and *Blue Thunder* has a healthy respect for those. Director John (*Saturday Night Fever*) Badham even manages to make his flying machine look simultaneously like the mother ship in *Close Encounters* and the shark in *Jaws*. (He did, after all, work as an associate producer for Steven Spielberg.) But when it works, wow. John Alonzo's nighttime L.A. aerial photography is stunning, and tender hearts will be grateful that Badham wreaks tons of havoc but little gore. Aside from some nudity and four-letter words, *Blue Thunder* is as clean and one-dimensional as a computer display screen. It would have made a great video game.
R / 1983 / RCA/Columbia

▲ BLUE VELVET

David Lynch, the undisputed wizard of odd as writer-director of *Eraserhead, The Elephant Man,* and *Dune,* topped himself with this visionary classic. Funny and frightening, the film only occasionally makes sense. Even so, the feverish, erotically charged atmosphere is impossible to shake. Kyle MacLahlan, the stalwart hero of *Dune,* stars as a college student visiting his sick

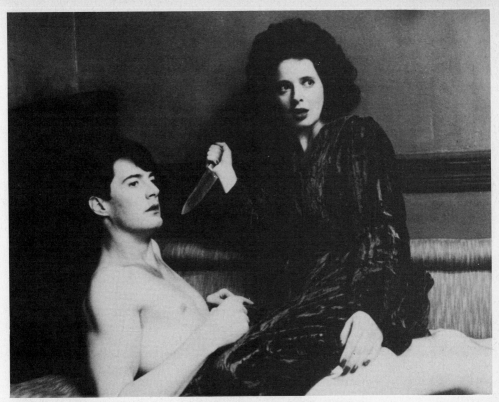

Blue Velvet: Kyle MacLahlan encounters one of the quirky moods of Isabella Rossellini in David Lynch's disturbing meditation on the pervasiveness of human instability.

dad in North Carolina. The setting is a small lumber town, the kind with a chirpy radio weatherman who, on a sunny day, advises listeners to "get out your chainsaws." Shortcutting through a field one afternoon, MacLahlan finds a freshly severed human ear. The police thank him for bringing in the appendage but offer no explanation. His curiosity aroused, MacLahlan coaxes a few clues out of a cop's smitten teenage daughter, a tremulous Laura (*Smooth Talk*) Dern. The clues lead to a voluptuous nightclub singer, played with torchy carnality by Isabella (*White Nights*) Rossellini. This is the point where the film and probably most video viewers come unglued. In a smoky bistro Rossellini sings endless off-key choruses of the old Bobby Vinton hit "Blue Velvet." Perhaps in revenge, a drug-pushing psycho, played by Dennis (*Easy Rider*) Hopper, bursts into Rossellini's apartment to force huge chunks of a blue velvet robe down her throat before sexually assaulting her. Hopper has kidnapped her husband and son to ensure her con-

tinued submission. Later, Rossellini at knifepoint forces amateur sleuth MacLahlan to strip and make love to her. He obliges, balks when she asks to be beaten to heighten her arousal, then obliges again. In short order the Eagle Scout is sucked into a vortex of violent crime and perversion. Despite absurd situations and the dippiest dialogue this side of *The Rocky Horror Picture Show,* the movie makes for vivid visual storytelling. Lynch, deservedly Oscar nominated as Best Director, is a genuine original. Whether you are attracted or repelled by Lynch's bizarre vision, one thing is for sure: You've never seen anything like it in your life.
R / 1986 / Karl-Lorimar

▲ BOBBY DEERFIELD

Forget the familiar climactic crescendo of emotion, the clutching couple disappearing into a tangerine sunset. The relationship here rambles on forever. Al Pacino plays a vapid but terribly sweet jet-set racing driver who denies his humble Newark, New Jersey, origins. Marthe Keller is a wealthy Italian going eccentric due to terminal illness. Their hot-cold meeting progresses into a hit-miss relationship. Once they do connect, they remain a most unlikely twosome—even though Pacino and Keller were a genuine number off-screen. Though the dialogue is drab and the plot aimless, Pacino's odd facial expressions are almost a diversion in themselves.

PG / 1977 / Warner

▲ BODY DOUBLE

A witty, suspenseful, dazzlingly erotic intrigue, this is a hellzapoppin' top thriller, and it restored director Brian De Palma as rightful heir to the Hitchcock throne despite audience indifference. *Body Double* is a variation on two Hitchcock masterpieces, *Vertigo* and *Rear Window*. The central character, played with shambling grace by Craig Wasson, is an L.A. actor getting by on TV work and cheap vampire movies. Just as Jimmy Stewart suffered from fear of heights in *Vertigo,* Wasson is claustrophobic. The villain uses that fear to make Wasson an accomplice to a gruesome murder. Wasson is housesitting at a high-tech aerie that commands a great view of the Hollywood Hills and the window of a rich housewife. Like Stewart in *Rear Window*, Wasson can't help watching. He becomes obsessed with this sleek brunette, played by the gorgeous Deborah Shelton. But his voyeuristic passion turns to fear when he spots an Indian on a nearby tower spying too. In a stunning and seductive De Palma set piece, without sound except for Pino Donaggio's evocative music, Wasson follows the woman from a shopping mall to a beachfront motel where he must confront his lust and his conscience. De Palma's all-seeing camera makes most other movies today look like the sloppy TV products they are. It would be a disservice to give away more of the plot, except to mention Melanie Griffith who gives a star-is-born performance as a porn star. Along with unraveling the mystery, De Palma also exposes the underlying issue of porn and violence. Feminists got on De Palma's case about a scene in which Shelton is assaulted by a man wielding a drill. De Palma films the incident (the man holds the drill between his legs) as if to incite such criticism, but the scene is done by

indirection and De Palma doesn't linger on it. Neither does he dehumanize his female characters: The women are so strong we want to know them better. The acting, including Guy Boyd's hard-nosed cop, is especially forceful. But the film belongs to De Palma, who brings to it all the richness of his craft as a master of mayhem without sparing intelligence. *Body Double* ranks with *Dressed to Kill* and *Carrie* as his best work.

R / 1984 / RCA/Columbia

▲ BODY HEAT

Here's a gorgeously lurid, great bash of a movie that restores the good name of celluloid eroticism. Screenwriter Lawrence (*Raiders of the Lost Ark*) Kasdan here proved himself a director with uncommon sureness of instinct. Even his familiar material—sexy wife tempts lover to kill husband—seems fresh, despite its similarity to *The Postman Always Rings Twice*. Heat is the film's motif—the steamy Florida setting raises everyone's passions to a fever pitch, especially small-time lawyer William (*Altered States*) Hurt's when he meets leggy, luscious (and married) Kathleen Turner. An alumna of the NBC soap "The Doctors," Turner made her screen debut with the impact of a Lauren Bacall. In one scene, Turner just stares smolderingly at Hurt through a window until he smashes the glass with a chair to get at her. *Body Heat* wallows in such excess (the sex scenes are as graphic as any since *Last Tango*), but Kasdan's incantatory style makes it work. So does Hurt, an actor with a core of humor and likable human weakness. Richard Crenna is wonderful as the husband, and a pre-"Cheers" Ted Danson is raunchy as Hurt's friend. But it's Turner you'll remember. With Kasdan's help she weaves a web of artifice that makes danger irresistible. The result is pulp transcended—a beautifully rhythmed film full of the pleasures of the unexpected.

R / 1981 / Warner

▲ BOLERO

For those aspiring actresses hoping to pick up some pointers from Bo Derek in this film: Yes, she does employ her revolutionary, all-purpose acting technique of nibbling on the tip of her fingernail. She employs it four or five times, in

Body Heat: Fairly oozing passion, William Hurt and Kathleen Turner embroil themselves in a plot full of murder, deceit, and disillusionment fueled by the sultry climate of a Southern town.

fact, to reflect determination, anxiety, shyness, pensiveness, and—although one can't be sure of this—even a subtle rebuke to her manicurist. Anyway, in *Bolero,* written and directed by her husband, John, Bo plays a rich young woman who graduates from college and sets out to lose her virginity. She first offers herself up to a desert sheik; after slopping honey all over Bo's naked body—with some nuts and whipped cream he could have made a ham sundae—he falls asleep. So is this a bad satire? No, it's a bad serious romance. For Bo tries to turn on a Spanish bull-fighter, played with extreme handsomeness by Andrea Occhipinti. Drama ensues when Occhipinti is gored by a bull, right in the unmentionables, but Bo is undaunted. To arouse Occhipinti's prurient interest, she even rides her horse around the bullring bareback—also barefront, baretop, and barebottom. When he still seems uninterested, she sighs, "You're a hard man to seduce." When they do get around to their love scenes, they perform soft-core-porn style: Occhipinti's bull-damaged area is not visible. Bo, however,

is right out there on display. Her facial expressions during lovemaking suggest not so much passion as, oh, seasickness or maybe a dislocated hip. John's camera grinds right along with her, proving for posterity that a woman can be impossibly beautiful and still seem not at all sexy. Trivia fans will note that, title notwithstanding, the Ravel composition that accompanied Bo's prettiness in *"10"* is not heard in this film; *Bolero's* music, written by Peter Bernstein and conducted by his father, Elmer, seems, especially during the film's lurid moments, more appropriate to Championship Wrestling.
Unrated / 1984 / USA

▲ THE BORDER

There is a movie struggling to get out of the jumble that director Tony (*Tom Jones*) Richardson has made of this tale of a Texas border patrol guard who, unlike his buddies, sees Mexican wetbacks as human. But the mix of modes—

social document, satire, shoot-'em-up—ultimately fights a losing battle with plausibility. Riding out the storm, however, is Jack Nicholson, who turns sad-sack guard Charlie Smith into one of his most compelling, compassionate roles. "I married a banana," he whines to wife Valerie Perrine (who plays her as such), but he grudgingly allows her to buy a water bed, furniture, and swimming pool, none of which they can afford. Perrine also sways him from signing on with the Park Service (he likes to feed the ducks, he explains) and into joining his border guard friend Harvey Keitel, who takes bribes for running illegal Mexican immigrants into the U.S. Keitel and Nicholson perform with fine, lunatic brio until the script takes a grim turn, revealing Keitel as a cold-blooded killer. Nicholson's interest in helping a Mexican woman (Elpidia Carrillo) and her child precipitates a violent climax. Director Richardson makes the mayhem repugnant and ghoulish, though Nicholson's performance goes far to redeem the film. "I want to feel good about something," he says, and his integrity makes the sentiment believable. The movie—with no sincerity or sureness of its own—is not.

R / 1982 / MCA

▲ BORN AGAIN

This is more a promo for the Billy Graham crusade than a feature movie. Based on Charles Colson's pious memoir, it tells of the former Nixon hatchet man's felicitous conversion to Christianity just before he went off to an Alabama prison. Dean Jones, born again himself in 1974, plays Colson with frightening zeal. As the long-suffering Mrs. Colson, Anne Francis is saddled with some of the dumbest lines since the White House tapes. Jay Robinson is so relentlessly unsympathetic as Colson's Jewish law partner that an anti-Semitic slant is suggested. With Harry Spillman's hilarious parody of Richard Nixon, the drama turns into limp comedy for a few moments—probably unwittingly. The distributor said Colson would donate any profits he earned from the film to charity; there weren't many. Discriminating audiences found ways to eliminate the middleman.

PG / 1978 / Embassy

▲ THE BOSTONIANS

Vanessa Redgrave picked up another Oscar nomination for playing, with radiant intensity, a 19th-century Boston woman dedicated to the suffrage movement. She meets a faith healer's daughter who has remarkable gifts as a public speaker and enlists her in the cause. Christopher Reeve, as an impoverished Mississippi lawyer, also has eyes for the young woman, played by Madeleine Potter. He tries to woo her away from Redgrave (the movie's sexual complexities are subtle and tantalizing) and thus sets up a romantic quandrangle—a man, two women, and a cause. Against the backdrop of proper Boston, the movie, from Henry James's novel, is often stuffy but rarely uninteresting. Reeve slips in and out of his drawl, but his performance remains his liveliest outside the *Superman* films. Linda Hunt adds interest as a woman doctor whose dialogue is used to explain the action. Nancy Marchand plays a scheming New York social matron, and the marvelous Jessica Tandy is all but wasted as the elder stateswoman of the suffrage movement, a kind of good-natured granny. The film has a rich, sumptuous look; the costumes are scenery in themselves; and the locations—Boston, New York, and Cape Cod—are shot with loving care by cinematographer Walter Lassally. James Ivory, who reached a peak with 1986's *Room with a View,* directed. Yet the movie is far too deliberate; watching it is like watching a stew simmer.

PG / 1984 / Vestron

▲ BOULEVARD NIGHTS

A stupidly brutal film about Mexican-American gangs in east L.A., this film prompted mayor Dianne Feinstein to call the movie "a threat to the safety of the citizens of San Francisco" and prevail on a theater owner to cancel it when four people were shot in a fight after a showing. Warner Brothers at one point was paying some movie houses for extra guards. It certainly wasn't worth risking your neck to see the "low-riders," those candy-colored '50s autos that bounce up and down on special hydraulic pumps. There's no thrill in the pretty girl (Marta Du Bois) or the thoughtful hood (Richard Yniguez) who is torn between the straight life and loyalty to his gang-doomed younger brother (Danny De La Paz). The

script, by Desmond Nakano, is a pointlessly faithful rendering of gutter language, with violent action and no insight into L.A.'s Chicano population. Executive producer Tony Bill (who previously made *The Sting* and *Taxi Driver*) should have been ashamed of himself.
R / 1979 / N/A

▲ BOUND FOR GLORY

Folksinger Woody Guthrie, touchingly played by David Carradine, travels the hobo route from Texas to California singing to and for the underdog. Glowing and reverently shot by Haskell Wexler (who won an Oscar for his efforts), this overlong (at 147 minutes) but underrated odyssey is the *Elvira Madigan* of the Depression. Also Oscar-nominated as Best Picture, it lost to *Rocky*.
PG / 1976 / MGM/UA

▲ THE BOUNTY

When Anthony Hopkins whips off his wig as he enters a court inquiry at the start of *The Bounty*, you know you're in for a revision as well as a remake of the old high-seas tale. It's clearly neither the classic 1935 Charles Laughton–Clark Gable original of *Mutiny on the Bounty* nor the clunky 1962 Trevor Howard–Marlin Brando version. This film sprouts all the state-of-the-art accessories of an '80s epic: stunning cinematography, a score by Vangelis, and a feisty cameo by Laurence Olivier as the admiral heading the investigation into the mutiny aboard her majesty's ship. Robert Bolt's screenplay also replaces pomp with psychologizing. It views Captain Bligh as both right and self-righteous, and there's even a suggestion of unrealized homoerotic love between Bligh (Hopkins) and his pal-turned-nemesis Fletcher Christian, played by Mel Gibson, who mobilized the mutiny. Despite these innovations, Australian director Roger Donaldson doesn't make the most of the adventure. Saddling himself with a flashback structure, he telescopes crucial sections, such as the Tahitian idyll during which Gibson falls in love with the native chief's daughter. The movie never arouses much feeling, even though it's a story about passion. When the elderly Tahitian chief breaks into sobs as his daughter chooses to leave their island, the scene is as disruptive as it is moving: It shows how emotionally frostbitten the rest of the movie is. Hopkins does a fine job as Bligh; he at least delivers hints of the emotional content that Donaldson neglects. But Gibson is treated like a decorative object; while he's photographed to advantage, he's never permitted any of the bravura intensity Gable exhibited. *The Bounty* ends up a curiosity: It's competent, yet as a remake it never justifies the retelling.
R / 1984 / Vestron

▲ THE BOYS FROM BRAZIL

The Ira Levin scenario, from his best-seller, is a potential winner. The tattered remains of Hitler's legions plot to create a Fourth Reich through genetic manipulation and a thirty-year master plan. Gregory Peck, obviously relishing every malicious second of his most villainous role since Captain Ahab in 1956's *Moby Dick,* is Joseph Mengele, the real German doctor whose life of atrocity ends up—in this fiction—with this perverted vision. Laurence Olivier, creating the character with his usual resourcefulness, is the Nazi hunter (loosely based on Simon Wiesenthal) who stumbles on the conspiracy. Unfortunately, director Franklin (*Patton*) Schaffner lets the story unravel in a series of grisly but strangely unsuspenseful murders (the best happens on a dam in Sweden), and what could have been a tense, shattering climax turns into a matter-of-fact The End. Olivier, Oscar-nominated as Best Actor (he lost to Jon Voight in *Coming Home*), is superb, and Uta Hagen, in a single scene as a former concentration camp guard, is memorable. The other actors, including James Mason, Rosemary Harris, and Denholm Elliott, are wasted, however, as is a chance for some effective Latin American color. (The Paraguay and Brazil scenes were shot in Portugal.) Unlike its subject, the film suffers from lack of ambition.
R / 1978 / CBS/Fox

▲ THE BOYS IN COMPANY "C"

There's no boogie-woogie bugle boy in this outfit, but there are all the other GI stereotypes: a streetwise black, a redneck, a hippie, a farmer, and, of course, an Italian from Brooklyn. Put the

Dodgers back in Ebbets Field and take away the paddies, and this slapped-together movie about Vietnam becomes another World War II flick in disguise—and not a very good one at that. The expletives fly like shrapnel and the cast full of then unknowns (Andrew Stevens and Craig Wasson, among them) substitutes shouting for acting. The climactic soccer match is curiously reminiscent of the football game in *M*A*S*H*.
R / 1978 / RCA/Columbia

▲ BRAINSTORM

Viewers may find themselves of two minds about *Brainstorm*. As a computer-age thriller, its vivid special effects help compensate for a standard and sometimes silly plot. However, as Natalie Wood's last movie, *Brainstorm* is something else again—a chance for her admirers to bid farewell. Natalie's death in a boat accident occurred just five days short of completing her role. Director Douglas (*Silent Running*) Trumbull finished the film without resorting to tricks, doubles, or jarring plot devices. It helped that Wood's character is peripheral to most of the action. The late actress is cast as the estranged wife of Christopher (*The Deer Hunter*) Walken, a scientist collaborating with workaholic Louise Fletcher on a "brainstorm" device enabling one person's thoughts, feelings, and even nightmares to be recorded on videotape and transferred intact to another person's brain. Cliff Robertson plays the corporate bigwig who sees the evil potential in the invention. In interviews Trumbull speculated that the advances in cybernetics, holography, and computer imagery may soon make "brainstorm" a reality. Fortunately, the movie is a good deal more fun than such poppycock suggests. Since video images can be made of everything from a coronary to an orgasm, the cinematic possibilities are endless, and Trumbull and his lab wizards make the most of them. He fails only when he tries to create an abstract visualization of death. The idea is an ambitious notion worthy of Stanley Kubrick but out of Trumbull's artistic grasp. Still, the actors perform way beyond the call of sci-fi duty, especially Fletcher, who does her juiciest work since winning the Oscar for *One Flew Over the Cuckoo's Nest*. And, of course, there's Wood, whose dark-eyed loveliness and keen intelligence shine through the flimsy material. She doesn't dominate *Brainstorm*, but she alone makes it luminous.
PG / 1983 / MGM/UA

▲ BRASS TARGET

Suppose Gen. George Patton died after World War II but not in a highway accident. Suppose he was murdered because he was about to discover who stole $250 million in German gold. That's the premise of this entertaining if hammy suspense drama. George Kennedy plays Old Blood-and-Guts and John Cassavetes an investigating officer. Sophia Loren, despite top billing, has only a bit part. The all-star international cast also includes Robert Vaughn, Max von Sydow, and Patrick McGoohan, who nearly steals the movie as a conniving American officer. Believers in conspiracy theories won't mind the holes in the script big enough to drive a panzer division through.
PG / 1979 / N/A

▲ BRAZIL

It took a war to get this beleaguered masterpiece to an audience. The combatants: director-writer Terry Gilliam, the old Monty Python animator, and Universal Pictures, his reluctant American distributor. In 1984, Universal president Sidney Sheinberg saw *Brazil* and pronounced it overlong, depressing, and less suitable to the screen than to a shelf. That's when producer Arnon Milchan cannily arranged a screening for the Los Angeles Film Critics Association, which promptly voted the film 1985's best. Thus a major studio was shamed into releasing a picture that reflected its maker's peculiar vision. Sure, it's Sheinberg's money (Universal put up $9 million of the $15 million budget). But he had to know that Gilliam's previous films, *Jabberwocky* and *Time Bandits,* showed him to lack even a nodding acquaintance with the conventional. Why hire a bizarre imagination if you intend to squash it? *Brazil,* Gilliam's most daring, demented, and demanding film, asks the same question. The resourceful hero, superbly played by stage actor Jonathan Pryce, is a bureaucrat who enjoys his dull job because it allows him time to fantasize about himself as the winged savior of a gorgeous blond, Kim (*C.H.U.D.*) Griest, held captive by

a giant samurai warrior. "Brazil" refers not to the country but to a romantic 1930s dance ditty; the film, set somewhere in England in the future, plays like *1984* as adapted by Jonathan Swift. (Gilliam wrote the wildly inventive script with Tom Stoppard and Charles McKeown.) Technology is still king, but everything is on the fritz. Computers that resemble primitive typewriters are capable of errors that kill. Investigating one such bungle, Pryce happens on the girl in his dreams. She is a tough-talking truck driver and has no interest in him. To get closer to her, he takes a promotion and enters a go-for-broke-and-blood world that doesn't allow for dreams. Gilliam paints this bleak universe with the most astonishing visuals since *Metropolis.* Terrorists swing across Art Deco towers like high-tech Tarzans; bombs reduce one part of an elegant restaurant to rubble while the unscathed diners merrily continue to munch. Gilliam also got remarkable performances from a large cast; Robert De Niro and Bob Hoskins as duct repairmen and Katherine Helmond as Pryce's plastic-surgery-mad mother are particular standouts. But the undeniable power of the film is the way its images keep digging into your memory. Gilliam can take pride in delivering on his promise to Sheinberg and the public: He gave both their money's worth.
R / 1985 / MCA

▲ BREAD AND CHOCOLATE

If there is no Italian word for "nebbish," one ought to be coined to describe Nino, the nonhero of this perspicacious, truly funny film. Nino, played with woebegone comic grace by veteran Italian actor Nino Manfredi, just wants to make an honest lira. But he is so frustrated he feels compelled to defend himself even to a family portrait of his in-laws. And though he manages to get a tryout as a waiter at a fancy restaurant in Switzerland, he loses that job, too, when he is accidentally photographed by tourists while urinating against a wall. Franco Brusati (he adapted *Romeo and Juliet* for the Zeffirelli version) directed this sensitive film which won a bundle of international honors—including the Italian critics' award and the Berlin Silver Bear. It deserved every one. (In Italian with subtitles.)
Unrated / 1978 / N/A

▲ BREAKER! BREAKER!

The frenetic energy that made American International's biker films such Grade-B fun is lacking in this unimaginative contribution to the CB genre. Although former karate champ Chuck Norris chops and kicks with gusto, the dearth of trucks on location keeps this low-budget saga about an evil California "speed trap" town from getting into gear. It didn't stop Chuck, though. The American Bruce Lee has been putting a dent in the box office ever since.
PG / 1977 / Embassy

▲ BREAKER MORANT

This Australian import is the movie *Heaven's Gate* should have been—a rich historical drama with convincing characters and well-laced action. The title comes from the nickname of the main character, a horse-breaker named Harry Morant, who fought for the British Army in its turn-of-the-century guerrilla war against the Boers in South Africa. Morant, beautifully underplayed by Edward Woodward (later TV's "Equalizer"), sees his best friend shot and horribly mutilated by the enemy. In rage, he orders the execution of some prisoners and an innocent German missionary and is court-martialed in a trial that rocks the British high command. Courtroom dramas can be stuffy, but this one, told mainly in flashbacks, has unflagging vitality, energized by Jack Thompson, a popular Australian actor, as Morant's impassioned defense counsel. The movie won ten awards in Australia and until 1986's *Crocodile Dundee* was that country's all-time highest grosser. Bruce Beresford, later to score in America with *Tender Mercies,* proves a director need not break the bank to make a grand movie.
PG / 1981 / RCA/Columbia

▲ BREAKIN'

Hollywood, with this film, jumped on the break-dancing bandwagon, feet churning frenetically if not with an impeccable sense of rhythm. Backed by Israeli producers Menahem Golan and Yoram Globus—their credits include *Revenge of the Ninja* and *The Wicked Lady*—this film takes the ghetto

dance scene that was so beautifully depicted in *Wild Style* and attempts to glitz it up, à la *Flashdance*. Set in Los Angeles, the story follows a jazz dancer, played by "Solid Gold" chorine Lucinda Dickey, who is trying to break into legitimate theater. She meets a pair of street performers, real-life breakers (or "lockers," in L.A. jargon) Adolfo "Shabba-Doo" Quinones and Michael "Boogaloo Shrimp" Chambers. Lucinda likes their style, and they like hers. The rest is predictable: They stick together and conquer a lecherous dance instructor as well as a snobby group of moguls. Yet the music—by such people as Al Jarreau and Rufus—is slick, and the dancing is vibrant, often spectacular. Dickey does all her own legwork and ingratiatingly combines an Elizabeth McGovern innocence with Sheena Easton sexiness. In more ways than one, she was among the freshest faces to hit the screen in quite some time—"fresh" is also street-dance lingo for "terrific." Quinones and Chambers are a funny, likable pair, although at times they come across as a couple of ghettoized Hardy Boys who don't ever get very far beyond calling each other "knucklehead." Overall, in fact, the film is, if anything, too restrained: It never quite manages to capture the real passion and energy of the streets. Even a love relationship between Dickey and Quinones is only hinted at, making it seem that Israeli director Joel Silberg and his three screenwriters shied away from anything as potentially controversial as an interracial romance. *Breakin'* is harmless entertainment—nice, but hardly "fresh."
PG / 1984 / MGM/UA

▲ BREAKIN' 2 ELECTRIC BOOGALOO

The heroes of *Breakin'* were all back: WASPy ballerina-turned-break-dancer Lucinda Dickey, neighborhood youth leader Adolpho "Shabba-Doo" Quinones, and his amiably mischievous sidekick Michael "Boogaloo Shrimp" Chambers. When last seen they had foiled some stuffed-shirt producers and break-danced into legitimate theater. Once more the villains are evil, three-piece-suited, establishment types who are out to turn the local community center into a shopping mall. This film takes time to get in gear, it provides little intelligent dialogue, and there's no reason to like the characters at first. But for those who slog through the opening 30 minutes or so,

the movie ultimately is fun. Quinones and Chambers are still likable, especially in a scene in which Shabba-Doo tries to teach Shrimp the fine art of approaching women. Director Sam Firstenberg nicely balances dancing and comedy, and in a fantasy sequence colorfully updates Fred Astaire's dance-on-the-walls scene from *Royal Wedding* for Chambers. (This was before Lionel Richie's *Dancin' on the Ceiling* video.) There's a good sound track by several artists, a happy ending, a simple message about brotherhood, and a glowing finale.
PG / 1985 / MGM/UA

▲ BREAKING AWAY

Very simple, very funny, and very well made, this comedy is about four high school chums—Dennis Christopher, Jackie Earle Haley, Dan Stern, and Dennis Quaid—growing up in Bloomington, Indiana. When they begin to feel life has passed them by because they didn't go to college—Indiana University is right in their backyard—inevitable skirmishes between town and gown follow. The climax is a two hundred-lap bicycle race the four friends enter to one-up the students. Of the four, Christopher is most affecting as a dead-end kind of kid pretending to be an Italian for macho effect. His befuddled parents, Barbara Barrie and Paul Dooley, are hilarious. Lovely Robyn Douglass is perfect as the sorority girl who falls for Christopher's tall tales. Though low-budget, the film was deftly directed, mostly on location in Bloomington, by Peter Yates and has a well-adjusted charm of a small Midwestern town. Steve Tesich's screenplay won an Oscar.
PG / 1979 / CBS/Fox

▲ BREAKING GLASS

At last, the fervid post-punk British rock scene had found a movie as sharp, sensuous, and gripping as the music itself. The hero, a nervy, hustling kid played by Phil Daniels, encounters singer Hazel O'Connor in an alley while she's slapping up handbills for her band and demands to hear a song. She hurls a few bars at him a cappella and then bristles, "Get the gist of it?" He does—in fact, he proceeds to manage her, operating on pure instinct. In a witty, beautifully edited series of vignettes, they audition a new band called Breaking Glass. Soon they land a big touring contract, and just as manager and client begin to click romantically, big-time producer Jon Finch takes over and everything starts to unravel. O'Connor, then 25, a fine singer from Coventry, wrote the thirteen songs on the sound track. She is a sexy, tender, sardonic, clowny fireball.

PG / 1981 / Paramount

▲ BREATHLESS

A Paris hood steals a car, shoots a cop, and runs off with an American girl, who finally turns him in. Standard film fodder. But back in 1960, in the hands of young screenwriter and debuting director Jean-Luc Godard, the film—*Breathless*—became an instant classic, inaugurated the New Wave in cinema, and made international stars of Jean-Paul Belmondo and Jean Seberg. In 1983, underground director Jim (*David Holzman's Diary*) McBride and his co-writer, L. M. Kit Carson, had the guts (some might say the gall) to remake and update it. They switched the locale to Los Angeles and the nationalities of the lovers, now played by Richard Gere and French newcomer Valerie Kaprisky, but kept the basic plot. And though Godard's striking original remains in every respect superior, McBride and friends put on quite a show. Godard was poeticizing American gangster films, especially Bogart's; McBride is waxing lyrical about American pop culture. The seedy neon glare of L.A. has never flared more luridly or luminously. The highly touted sex scenes also deliver. Kaprisky, then 19, lacks the late Seberg's elegant bitchiness but possesses a full-bodied sensuality and plays her nude scenes with Gere as if the cameraman had gone home. Though this is not one of Gere's lazy *American Gigolo* performances, he is less successful than his co-star. While he perfectly captures the jazzy, pretty-boy surface of his amoral character, he can't cut deeper. Belmondo had reserves of talent to draw the audience in; Gere is not as well endowed. Still, McBride covers most of the shortcomings with a flashy style that's just right for the material. Along with a fan's respect, he covers old Godard ground with an artist's eye and a rhythm all his own.

R / 1983 / Vestron

▲ BREWSTER'S MILLIONS

If there's one thing that Richard Pryor doesn't need in his comedies, it's a sidekick, particularly a comic one. Besides siphoning off the one-liners, a sidekick deprives Pryor of the posture that made him a movie star: the outraged outsider. One of the many mistakes that *Brewster's Millions* makes is providing Pryor with a best friend in the corpulent form of John Candy. Indeed, this spiteful comedy sabotages these two formidable comedians from its setup to its fade-out. When Pryor's rich uncle dies, the will stipulates that he may inherit $300 million only if he can spend $30 million in thirty days—and not have a penny to show for it at the end of the month. That premise has served as the basis for six previous movies. But this script by Herschel Weingrod and Timothy Harris, who wrote the equally money-mad *Trading Places,* ricochets from one lame situation to another as Brewster buys icebergs, rents the New York Yankees so he can pitch against them, and runs a joke candidacy for mayor of New York. Director Walter Hill never finds a workable pace or style. The only remotely provocative situation is a love triangle involving Pryor, Lonette McKee, who plays a paralegal, and Stephen Collins, who plays a lawyer. The interracial romance between the black McKee and the white Collins is not exploited or italicized; it's played strictly matter-of-fact. That's a welcome approach but inconsistent with the rest of this moralistic, old-fashioned movie. *Brewster's Millions* is such an incoherent, slapdash mess that even when the movie does something right, it looks like a mistake.

PG / 1985 / MCA

▲ THE BRIDE

Watching this rococo retelling of *The Bride of Frankenstein,* you begin to wonder if Gloria Steinem worked on the script. *The Bride* isn't really a remake; it's more a feminist revision of the legend. As directed by Franc Roddam, this pandering version forsakes Mary Shelley's plot for sexual politics that are anachronistic in the 1830s, the time in which the story is set. Indeed, without a rudimentary knowledge of the original plot, you may not be able to follow the movie. When Baron Charles Frankenstein (Sting) creates a female companion for his monster in the opening sequence, he announces, "I might make the New Woman—independent, free, as bold as a man." To make sure no one misses the point, Roddam cast Jennifer Beals, the video version of the New Woman, as Mrs. Monster-to-be. It sounds noble but it plays badly, particularly since Lloyd Fonvielle's screenplay doesn't practice the equality it preaches. After introducing the creature and her plight, the script ignores her. Instead it wanders off with her male monster counterpart (Clancy Brown), who has fled the castle and teamed up with a dwarf (David Rappaport). They join a Budapest circus and act out a Middle European variation on *Of Mice and Men*. Although it appropriates both *Frankenstein* and feminism, this schizophrenic movie is most interested in the character least associated with either subject: the dwarf, whom Rappaport endows with an ingratiating maliciousness. Rappaport and Brown sidetrack the story, but they make a more arresting couple than the monstress and her creator back at the castle. So does the late Geraldine Page who plays the housekeeper with all her scene-stealing brilliance intact. With no dialogue and no sexual chemistry between them, Beals and Sting traffic in the manufactured mooning seen on record album covers. In the end Beals gets what every idealized movie heroine of the '80s wants; her dignity, her identity, and her man—or, rather, her creature. The title is a misnomer: The film should have been called *An Unmarried Monster*.

PG-13 / 1985 / RCA/Columbia

▲ A BRIDGE TOO FAR

In this big, bloated World War II drama the Allies badly botch an attempt to capture a bridge in Holland from the Nazis. Like the real 1944 mission, Joe Levine's $26.5 million epic (from Cornelius Ryan's best-seller) takes off promisingly but soon bogs down in chaos and confusion—sabotaged by uncertain direction (Richard Attenborough) and a huge, top-heavy cast. Sean Connery glowers, Dirk Bogarde smirks, Michael Caine minces, James Caan looks stricken and Liv Ullmann soulful, as usual. Others, including Robert Redford (for $2 million), are lost in meaningless cameos. This was the real Star War. Oh, the money they lost on this one, with nary an Oscar nomination for their trouble.

PG / 1977 / CBS/Fox

▲ THE BRINK'S JOB

The title says it. This is not a heist, not a caper, but a job, occasionally based on the actual 1950 Boston crime. Where it might have been hilarious, it is merely amusing. Instead of gripping, it settles for interesting. William Friedkin, director of *The French Connection* and *The Exorcist*, apparently couldn't decide whether to make a caper flick or a quirky comedy, so we get a little of both and ultimately neither. The Brink's gang's bush-league break-in at a gumball factory is strictly slapstick, for instance, while the real Brink's robbery is played straight. Both work, but do they belong in the same movie? Dino De Laurentiis's $12.5 million budget bought a talented cast and some evocative set pieces of Boston. As the honcho, Peter Falk is at his genial best, and Warren Oates makes a fine World War II veteran going around the bend. But in the end, like the real-life Brink's gang, the perpetrators of this disappointing movie make too many mistakes and have to take the rap.

PG / 1979 / Warner

▲ BROADWAY DANNY ROSE

What does Woody Allen do when he doesn't have a classic like *Annie Hall* or *Radio Days* in mind? At times, he has made wrongheaded detours into serious drama (*Interiors*) and satire (*Stardust Memories*). But he settled for a pleasant minor key in *Broadway Danny Rose*. The movie, about a third-rate New York talent agent, is no more than a doodle, but it is always amiable and rises to moments of inspired lunacy. There's none of the cynical, smart-ass Woody this time. "My hand to God," Danny Rose promises his clients. And he means it, even when he's hustling a one-armed juggler, a bird act, or a fat '50s crooner, nicely played by Nick Apollo Forte. Danny's life changes when he falls for Forte's gum-chewing girlfriend, the kind of doxy who explains the demise of her first husband with a cryptic "Some guys shot him in the eyes." Mia Farrow plays this against-the-grain role with astonishing verve. Director Allen must hide her aristocratic eyes behind dark glasses to pull off the charade. No matter. She and Allen, real-life lovers, framed by Gordon Willis's black-and-white photography, make a playful, sometimes touching couple. If *Broadway Danny Rose* is not a Woody Allen

Broadway Danny Rose: Woody Allen as a second-rate manager of over-the-hill talent and Mia Farrow as a tough-talking doxie make an oddly funny and endearing couple—just as they do in real life.

banquet, it's no famine either. Like a good glass of seltzer, if goes down easily and lifts the spirits. **PG / 1984 / Vestron**

▲ BRONCO BILLY

Milder and mellower than usual, Clint Eastwood is still a man of few words and sometimes prone to violence, but essentially a likable guy. Clint calls himself Bronco Billy McCoy, a onetime New Jersey shoe salesman running a Wild West show. Billy is a huckster with a heart of gold who will do anything for his tattered troupe (including instigating a bungled attempt at a train robbery), and he always has a kind word for the "little pardners" in the audience. The character is much too good to be true; Eastwood knows it and plays Billy with a self-mocking, easygoing charm. Unfortunately, the same cannot be said for his protégée, Sondra Locke, who overacts annoyingly as a New York heiress who winds up in Clint's show. Eastwood's direction is slack

too; the film, which has a grainy washed-out look, just moseys along. It's amiable but aimless. **PG / 1980 / Warner**

▲ THE BROTHER FROM ANOTHER PLANET

Most modern movies are so impersonal and indifferently made that this low-budget comedy with a conscience catches you up immediately. Written, directed, and edited by John Sayles, *Brother* tells the tale of a mute black man from another planet, Joe Morton (formerly Dr. Abe Marsh on NBC-TV's "Another World"). After his spaceship crashes on Ellis Island, the alien makes his way to Harlem, where he is assaulted by a babel of sounds and a welter of smells and sensations. A social worker, nicely played by Tom Wright, gets him a job in a video arcade and a home with a white woman, her young son, and her black mother-in-law. Pursued by two outer-space bounty hunters, hilariously played by

David Strathairn and Sayles himself, Morton comes across a heroin-pushing Wall Streeter and takes up the job of cleaning the streets of drug traffic. As a Caucasian, Sayles may get hassled for creating (or even seeing the need for) a modern black hero, especially one he could find only in another world. But his nonpatronizing touch is, with few exceptions, unerring. While Sayles makes some points about the hardships of ghetto life, his gift is for individualizing characters, and here he gives it free play. His large, interracial cast could not be bettered. Leonard Jackson, Darryl Edwards, and Bill Cobbs turn street talk into an art as regulars at a Harlem bar, and standout cameos are delivered by Fisher Stevens as a subway hustler, Dee Dee Bridgewater as a jazz singer, and David Babcock as a preppy lost on 125th Street. Still, the star spot belongs to Morton. He wordlessly provides the film with its center and its remarkable poignancy. *Brother* lacks special effects, but it has real voltage, the kind that keeps you energized long after you've seen "The End."
PG / 1984 / Key

▲ BROTHERS

Bernie Casey, once a pass receiver for the Rams and 49ers, proves—mirabile dictu—that some ex-footballers can act. Unfortunately, he picked the wrong movie: a wanly disguised recap of the George Jackson (*Soledad Brother*) case and the arrest of Angela Davis (played by the flossy Vonetta McGee). Ironically, the real issue —whether Jackson was the victim of white prejudice—is buried by an unrelieved, black-is-infallible racism.
R / 1977 / N/A

▲ BRUBAKER

The story is based on a book by Thomas Murton, a penologist who tried to reform Arkansas's Cummins Prison Farm in 1967 and was fired by Gov. Winthrop Rockefeller. Only Murton is now called Brubaker, the locale is Ohio, and the obviously well-meant film seems preposterous. The script is full of farfetched happenings like Robert Redford as the warden playing polo with his inmates, and the characters are mostly one-dimensional. The state prison board is full of venal rednecks; the prisoners are depicted as just a bunch of good

guys being exploited. Redford is given too many lines like "I don't see playing politics with the truth." And director Stuart Rosenberg (he did *Cool Hand Luke* and *Amityville Horror*) is not entirely successful with his cast. Yaphet Kotto is, as usual, powerful as a trusty. Matt Clark, David Keith, and Richard Ward are effective as convicts. But Jane Alexander, as a governor's aide, is ludicrous. At times she drawls, at others she sounds suspiciously like Eleanor Roosevelt. Such distractions obscure the film's message, and prison reform is hard enough to sell. The classic *I Am a Fugitive from a Chain Gang* eloquently stated the case long ago. The mere existence of *Brubaker* indicates how much good it did.
R / 1980 / CBS/Fox

▲ BUCK ROGERS

What apparently was an attempt to turn Buck into a spaced-out James Bond is more like an especially bad episode of "Three's Company." The script is full of obvious double entendres. (Following Col. Wilma Deering [ex-English Leather model Erin Gray], Buck radios, "I'm right on your tail"—and that's one of the better jokes.) The evil Ardala (Pam Hansley) flounces seductively, but at five feet eight inches and done up in weird costumes and strange makeup, she often looks less like a space princess than a drag queen. As Buck, Gil Gerard is so overboard he makes one marvel again at Christopher Reeve's performance in *Superman*. Even Buster Crabbe's breathlessly naive rendering of Buck in the 1939 serial seems preferable. And those who have seen that relic will probably yawn at the by-now-standard *Star Wars–Galactica* special effects, longing for those saucepanlike devices villain Killer Kane used to put on the good guys' heads to turn them into zombies.
PG / 1979 / MCA

▲ BUDDY BUDDY

Cruddy cruddy! Billy Wilder directing everybody's favorite odd couple, Jack Lemmon and Walter Matthau, conjures up happy memories of *The Fortune Cookie* and *The Front Page*. For those who like it hot, though, this go-round is barely tepid. Matthau plays a gruff professional hitman, while Lemmon is a whining would-be

suicide who inadvertently interferes with a contract. The dreary sets have the look of a small-budget TV sitcom, the plot is predictable, and the script insistently resorts to profanity in a vain attempt to provoke laughter. In the movie's best moment, Matthau, disguised as a priest, reels off an unlikely string of Latin phrases (*e pluribus unum, nolo contendere*) when he is drafted by the police to administer last rites. As for the rest of this disappointing picture, may it *requiescat in pace*.
R / 1982 / MGM/UA

▲ THE BUDDY HOLLY STORY

An extraordinary performance by Oscar-nominated Gary Busey as the early rock 'n' roll star gives life to this above-par rock biography. Lanky, raw-boned, and all teeth, Busey (noted for ballooning and deflating his body with each film), recreates with uncanny skill the look and singing style of the composer of such '50s classics as "Peggy Sue," Oh Boy," and "That'll Be the Day." The story takes Holly from his Texas beginnings as a roller rink musician to his rise on the pop charts and, finally, his death at 22 in a plane crash that also killed the Big Bopper and Ritchie Valens. Don Stroud and Charlie Martin Smith are cast in Holly's backup band, the Crickets (which in real life briefly included Waylon Jennings), and Maria Richwine plays his pregnant young wife. They are all satisfactory, but the movie belongs to Busey and his driving, powerful portrayal.
PG / 1978 / N/A

▲ THE BUDDY SYSTEM

Richard Dreyfuss plays an unsuccessful writer-inventor, the creator of such useful devices as a talking scale that informs him, "You've gained seven pounds. If you want to put something in your mouth, try a gun." Susan Sarandon is a harried single mother who longs to become a court reporter. They meet, and the result is another one of those romantic comedies in which the principals gradually wear down their mutual resistance. This only rarely funny variation on the theme, directed by Glenn Jordan and written by Mary Agnes Donoghue, includes Nancy Allen, wonderfully ditsy as Dreyfuss's girlfriend,

and Edward Winter as Sarandon's soon-to-be former beau. Everyone struggles to hide behind very thin material, but at least one cliché has been avoided. Instead of succeeding at last as a writer, Dreyfuss takes the manuscripts of his novels and scatters them to the sea breezes. Maybe that's what should have been done with this script.
PG / 1984 / Key

▲ BURGLAR

Whoopi Goldberg and Bob Goldthwait between them have enough charisma to float a battleship, so they keep this comedy mystery bobbing along. Goldberg plays a San Francisco cat burglar who becomes an earwitness to a murder while hiding in the victim's closet. Goldthwait, as her best friend, a poodle groomer, tones his act down a little—to only a dull roar. Director Hugh Wilson, who did the first *Police Academy*, has always shown more talent for casting than anything else and this film is no exception. Lesley Ann Warren, as a style-conscious discount dentist, is sleazily funny; when she's arrested for the murder, her main concern is that she has to wear cotton underwear in jail. G. W. Bailey, another *Police Academy* alum, adds world-weary atmosphere as an ex-cop blackmailing Goldberg into stealing for him. Nobody gets much funny material. It's mostly on the level of Goldthwait reacting to a businessmen's bar: "I can't go in there; it's like *Yuppies from Hell*." Goldberg, alternately tough and sweet, is appealing, though, and Goldthwait's critical case of insecurity makes him sympathetic. Goldberg, of course, has to track down the real murderer to clear herself. This does not so much lead to a climax as get things over with so everybody can turn out the lights, but there is some distraction in the interim.
R / 1987 / N/A

▲ BUSTIN' LOOSE

Check out this mediocre patch job, if only to see how Richard Pryor transforms it into bracing entertainment. Pryor is cast as a parolee commandeered to drive eight kids on a rickety bus from a South Philly ghetto to Seattle. Their schoolmarm, Cicely Tyson (looking lovely in a spiffy wardrobe no teacher could afford), is determined to show these racially mixed misfits the good life. Since pyromania and prostitution are just a few of the naughty habits the tykes display, Pryor has his hands full. Veteran theatrical director Oz Scott lets things turn to sentimental goo near the end, but before that Pryor (who has to share the blame, since the story idea was his) has cajoled mirth out of everything from white guilt to the Ku Klux Klan. Considering that a near-fatal accident the year before almost prevented him from finishing retakes on the film, Pryor's *Bustin' Loose* is sweet triumph indeed.

R / 1981 / MCA

▲ BUTTERFLY

"Bad comes from bad," Stacy Keach tells Pia Zadora when she finds him at the shut-down Nevada silver mine he guards from scavengers. She has told him she is his long-lost teenage daughter, and Keach is talking about genes. In Hollywood, too, the rule applies, as this inane adaptation of James M. Cain's 1947 novel proves. Meshulam Riklis, Zadora's wealthy and generous husband, produced it to further her career. In the movie Zadora goes, as they say, from bed to worse. Keach is leaden though loaded with temptation for the seductive daughter who craves him. "Something you want?" he asks her. "How can I tell till I know what you got?" she snaps. With more thought, this could have been done as a campy satire—the *Airplane!* of incest, say, or a sort of Oedipus Reeks. Zadora, then touted as a new sex kitten, doesn't purr or slink—she squints, which can't be easy with her penciled eyebrows, lip gloss, and puffy cheeks. James Franciscus actually may be Zadora's daddy—and father of her baby. Then again he might not be. Only Orson Welles, the local judge who arbitrates it all, seems able to act his way clear of this disaster. Director Matt Cimber's one accomplishment is that by fitting the gargantuan Welles and the wispy Zadora into one frame, he unwittingly defined the upper and lower limits of Hollywood's physical and artistic stature.

R / 1981 / Vestron

C

▲ CABO BLANCO

A cynical American expatriate with a heart of gold runs a divey hotel-cabaret in a godforsaken tropical city, dominated by a Nazi and a corrupt police chief; then a beautiful girl with a European accent walks in. Are they playing it again, Sam? Not exactly, since the time is 1948, the locale is Peru, and this is not one of the most endearing films of all time. Even if Charles Bronson is no Bogart, he does contribute a resigned dignity as the American who offers sanctuary to Dominique Sanda. She's looking for a sunken ship full of German loot, and so is Jason Robards, who lowgears it nicely as the refugee Nazi villain. (He does have trouble with his German accent, though; vun minute ve haff it, the next we don't.) The plot is light on plausibility, and Bronson has to finesse some dreadful lines. When the corrupt cop, Fernando Rey, double-crosses him, Bronson declares, "There goes your soul, down the toilet." Still, director J. Lee (*The Guns of Navarone*) Thompson knows he isn't making a profound statement. As B movies go, this one is diverting and—nudity and violence aside—harmless enough.

R / 1981 / Media

▲ CALIFORNIA DREAMING

All the Californians in this pleasantly offbeat film want to go to Hawaii. Maybe that's the message. But the plot focuses on a naive Midwesterner (Dennis Christopher) out West for a crash course in volleyball and vixens from aging beach bum Seymour Cassel. Director John Hancock elicits engaging work from Cassel and enhances the scenery with Glynnis O'Connor and Tanya Roberts, in her pre-Angel days. A snappy sound track—the Mamas and the Papas' classic that provides the title is sung by America—complements fine surfing footage, even if the film sometimes lurches like a board out of control.

R / 1979 / N/A

▲ CALIFORNIA SUITE

Neil Simon plays—witty, mannered, and sophisticated—usually fail on film. But *Plaza Suite*'s West Coast cousin is an exception. Vignettes of five couples at war in the Beverly Hills Hotel are intercut smoothly and delightfully. Two of the pieces are erratic. Walter Matthau has a funny face and manner but not enough funny lines when his wife, Elaine May, finds a hooker in his room. Bill Cosby and Richard Pryor engage in what was obviously intended as a scherzo but which degenerates into sad slapstick. The *Suite*'s two andante movements, however, more than carry the movie. Tough New York writer Jane Fonda and laid-back California scenarist Alan Alda, a long-divorced pair, disagree painfully about their daughter's future. And Michael Caine plays a gay antique dealer married to over-the-hill actress Maggie Smith, who won a supporting Oscar. Affecting and funny, these two couples make the movie California Bittersweet.

PG / 1979 / RCA/Columbia

▲ CAMILA

In 1847, a young woman of the Buenos Aires upper class, Camila O'Gorman ran away with a handsome priest, Garther Ladislao Gutierrez. That real-life scandal is the story of *Camila,* directed by a 62-year-old Argentine grandmother who didn't start making films until she was in her forties. Argentine actress Susu Pecoraro plays the young woman with convincing passion. While dreaming of her one grand love, she is also developing a political consciousness in reaction to the patriarchal, dictatorial regime run by her family's friends. Spanish actor Imanol Arias, cast as Gutierrez, with intense emotional power plays a man who sheds his whole identity when he sheds his priestly vestments. At her first encounter with Arias, Pecoraro falls in love. He rebuffs her, inwardly battling the temptation she represents. But soon after that first meeting, they flee to the countryside posing as man and wife. The authorities pursue the lovers as criminals. While Pecoraro and Arias form the emotional core of *Camila*, the controlled direction of Maria Luisa Bemberg lends the film a charged verisimilitude. She vividly recreates the mannered society of 19th-century Buenos Aires and unflinchingly trains

her camera on such images as a rebel's head impaled on a pole by government assassins. There is a minor distraction: often ungrammatical, too literally translated English subtitles. This is still a remarkable film, exploring the connections between personal and political freedom in the most human terms. (Available both dubbed and subtitled.)

Unrated / 1985 / Embassy

▲ CANNERY ROW

The novels of John Steinbeck have inspired films that were good (*The Grapes of Wrath, Of Mice and Men, East of Eden*), bad (*Tortilla Flat*), and indifferent (*The Wayward Bus*), but none was so misbegotten as this meshing of two Steinbeck works—*Cannery Row* (1945) and *Sweet Thursday* (1954). Both books centered on a shut-down Monterey, California, sardine cannery and a community of hookers, bums, and dreamers in the 1940s. It's a world that first-time director David Ward, who also wrote the screenplay, takes pains to recreate. He is luckiest in his cast. Nick Nolte makes a forthright Doc, the baseball-pro-turned-biologist, who provides for his friends by selling marine animals to school labs. Debra Winger (replacing a sacked Raquel Welch, who sued and won a bundle for the insult) is potently sexy as the doxy who loves him. Winger's *Urban Cowboy* zip may be inappropriate for a period piece, but it's welcome since the film's pace is funereal. Every shot is lingered over as if the director were trying to squeeze art into it. John Huston's beery narration doesn't help. Worse is the set—a massive, jerry-built array of storefronts and connecting overpasses. Constructed on a huge MGM sound stage formerly used for Esther Williams epics, the set screams artificiality instead of atmosphere. In his Oscar-winning script for *The Sting,* Ward showed imagination to spare. Here, like the waters off Cannery Row, he's fished out.

PG / 1982 / MGM/UA

▲ THE CANNONBALL RUN

It didn't do much for the 55-mph speed limit and didn't win Burt Reynolds his Oscar, but this tire screecher is an affable time waster. It's based on a real road race—an illegal cross-country speed run. That allows director Hal Needham to muster an all-star cast including Farrah Fawcett, Roger Moore, Dom De Luise, Dean Martin, Adrienne Barbeau, Jamie Farr, and Sammy Davis, Jr., with bits by such off-screen types as Terry Bradshaw, Bianca Jagger, Mel Tillis, and Jimmy the Greek. It's reminiscent of *The Great Race,* a more ambitious and literate 1965 film. But Needham, who directed the first two *Smokey and the Bandits,* and screenwriter Brock Yates, creator of the actual Cannonball race and a driver himself, do much better by their hardware—the stunts are small masterpieces—than they do by their humans. They also settle for easy laughs—proctology jokes, leering at women drivers' "equipment," Tillis stuttering, and when all else fails, making cops look silly. It's a shame. Nice chemistry seems to be brewing between Reynolds and Fawcett, who charmingly plays an ecology freak. And something could have been made of a macho-macho confrontation between Reynolds and Moore, who never even exchange dialogue. But no matter. You'll likely watch the movie smiling, no small feat these days.

PG / 1981 / Vestron

▲ CANNONBALL RUN II

Burt Reynolds. Shirley MacLaine. Dom De Luise. Jamie Farr. Marilu Henner. Dean Martin. Frank Sinatra. Susan Anton. Catherine Bach. Joe Theismann. Ricardo Montalban. Sammy Davis, Jr. Tony Danza. Anyone who gets a thrill out of reading that list of names and who might find it amusing to watch them all move listlessly around a screen will find a fleeting moment of pleasure in this film. Just don't expect anyone to do or say anything amusing. The movie, a sequel to the 1981 cross-country auto race hit, was written by director Hal Needham, producer Albert Ruddy, and Harvey Miller. Any three boys chosen at random out of a junior high school locker room could have done a funnier screenplay. The humor relies on such ploys as placing a "155" over the "55" on a speed-limit sign, lines such as "I think those liars told the truth," and a variety of obscene gestures. De Luise has a nice moment or two, Henner manages a bemused charm, and Farr tries hard. But most of the cast walks—or drives—through the film. When Needham wheels out his trademark device of running outtakes

beneath the end credits, even they are boring. That makes them fit perfectly with the rest of the film.

PG / 1984 / Warner

▲ CAN SHE BAKE A CHERRIE PIE?

Can director Henry Jaglom make a coherent movie? Jaglom achieved cultish success with such films as *A Safe Place* and *Sitting Ducks.* Indeed, he deserves a gall award for using in this film a long clip featuring Orson Welles from *A Safe Place,* an ego trip within an ego trip. Unhappily, Patrice Townsend, the charmer who was Jaglom's star in *Sitting Ducks,* wasn't his star anymore (or his wife either) when he made this movie. Also unhappily, he had not lost Michael Emil, his brother and still his leading man. Emil takes up with Karen Black, a New York woman whose husband has just left her. Why she would be smitten by the bald, fast-talking, impossibly edgy Emil is unfathomable. His mere appearance on-screen is enough to make any normal person chew up a popcorn container out of nervousness. This aimless film may appeal to a few people on Manhattan's Upper West Side, where it was shot. Everyone else can safely miss it.

R / 1984 / Monterey

▲ CAN'T STOP THE MUSIC

Disco! Boogie! Get Down! Better yet, play cribbage. A $13.5 million disco musical, ostensibly about the rise of the group the Village People, this was many things: a waste of money, a gay propaganda piece, a promotion for the sound track LP, a mess. What it was not was a movie. The only thing louder than the even then passé music is the sound of reputations crashing. Veteran comic Nancy Walker directed (her first feature) like a blindfolded cop at a rush-hour intersection. Party-giver-turned-producer Allan Carr also co-wrote the script, including lines like "I didn't invent life, I'm just in it." Olympian Bruce Jenner perfects his wimp role. Valerie Perrine has the female lead, not an asset in a film where women are sexual bags, sexual barracudas, or both. Poor Tammy Grimes looks wretched as a head of a modeling agency. There are flashes of nudity (mostly male); kinky, flashy production

numbers with spiked heels cutting into biceps; and a funny cameo by Paul Sand that proves talent can exist in a vacuum. *Can't Stop the Music* also proves something else: there can be a movie musical worse than *Sgt. Pepper.*
PG / 1980 / Thorn/EMI

▲ CAPRICORN ONE

Like *Goldfinger,* this film is based on a ludicrous premise. And, like *Goldfinger,* it is witty, visually dazzling, and totally entertaining. An embattled chief of NASA (Hal Holbrook), unable to fund a planned mission to Mars, fakes it. He sends up a rocket but only after whisking astronauts James Brolin, Sam Waterston, and O. J. Simpson off to a Mars set in an isolated TV studio where he forces them to stage a "landing" by threatening their families. Director-writer Peter Hyams (his biggest previous credit was for writing and producing the undeservedly obscure *T. R. Baskin*) decorates the plot with marvelously paced and photographed set pieces. To cite three: a runaway car scene, shot from the perspective of driver Elliott Gould, a nosy reporter who becomes a target; a tense and funny soliloquy by the wisecracking Waterston, who tells himself jokes as he tries to scale a steep cliff; and a crop-duster flown by Telly Savalas. No one takes things too seriously; the result is the kind of movie they're not supposed to make anymore: pure fun.
PG / 1978 / CBS/Fox

▲ THE CAR

In this surreal version of the headless horseman, a beeping, skidding, roaring limo terrifies a sleepy desert town, mows down innocent bystanders, and exceeds the 55-mph limit—all without a driver. Steven Spielberg's 1971 TV movie, *Duel,* made art out of the same trash theme. (James (*Hotel*) Brolin plays the hapless sheriff who trails the bionic demonmobile, which has an indestructible chassis and tires that seem impervious to bullets, explosives, and miscellaneous road hazards. You may be less interested in seeing the movie than in finding out where you can buy the tires.
PG / 1977 / N/A

▲ CARAVANS

While filming in Iran, Jennifer O'Neill described this movie as "a mixture of *Cleopatra, Lawrence of Arabia,* and *Dick and Jane.*" Anyone fascinated by such an unlikely combination should give it a go. Otherwise, be warned that this film is a very poor man's epic. It is set somewhere in the Middle East, just after World War II. A U.S. Embassy underling (Michael Sarrazin) is dispatched into the arid wastes to find O'Neill, a U.S. senator's daughter who has married a native colonel and then disappeared. She turns out to be tenting up with nomad chieftain Anthony Quinn. Then things get really silly and boring. Sarrazin is ineffectual in a weak role, O'Neill looks smashing but out of place, and Quinn is his same old lovable, irascible, omni-national self. The Michener novel on which the film is based came out in 1963, and movie rights were tied up immediately. It took fifteen years for *this?*
PG / 1978 / N/A

▲ CAREFUL, HE MIGHT HEAR YOU

So artfully gruelling, so poignant is this study of a little boy's introduction to the hypocrisy, fears, and pain of the adult world that it won the 1983 best picture award of the Australian Film Institute. The movie is graced by a number of extraordinary performances, notably those of Wendy Hughes and Robyn Nevin. Hughes and Nevin create a palpable sense of tension as two sisters whose battle for custody of their nephew turns into a vicious contest in psychological manipulation. Nicholas Gledhill, who was 7 when the film was made, is remarkable as the boy whose mother has died and whose father has disappeared. A disarmingly subtle and appealing little actor, Gledhill earns sympathy and respect for his embattled character. He is so natural and unaffected that it's difficult to watch as his sense of the joy of life is gradually eroded by the grown-up cynicism he sees around him. The screenplay is based on a clearly autobiographical novel by Sumner Locke Elliott, the Sydney-born writer who eventually moved to New York, where he wrote for such programs as "Studio One" in the early days of television. Hungarian-born director Carl Schultz, most of whose credits were in Australian television, carefully manages to present things from a child's perspective—the boy often seems perplexed by the mere size of the adults he has to deal with. All this hardly makes for an enjoyable movie, but it is a profoundly touching one, full of sad truths about that most unhappy of our experiences—the loss of innocence.

PG / 1984 / CBS/Fox

▲ CARNY

Step right up, ladies and gents. See the World's Tallest Man, the Monkey Lady, and the Human Blockhead! And over here we have the Teen Queen (Jodie Foster), the weirdo (Gary Busey), and the Rock Star (Robbie Robertson)! Like the carnival midway itself, this movie is bright, brassy, edging on bizarre, and violent just beneath the surface. What makes it work are three perceptive performances. Foster provides a measured, mature portrayal of a small-town girl seduced by carnival life, among other things. Busey displays his versatility, and Robertson, who doubled as producer, exudes sensuality in his acting debut (he was in the Band's *The Last Waltz,* of course, but that was a concert film). The story itself careens uncertainly from comedy to romance to melodrama. Yet documentary filmmaker Robert Kaylor captures the curious demimonde of the carnies. His first feature pulls you in like a sideshow—it repels as it fascinates.

R / 1980 / CBS/Fox

▲ CASEY'S SHADOW

Your usual boy-meets-horse story, with some down-home corn and nasty villians thrown in, stars Walter Matthau as a crusty, eccentric father who stumbles across an astoundingly fast quarter horse. His youngest son, Casey, falls in love with the beast but nearly cripples it in a dumb dare with another kid. Will Shadow recover in time for the big race? Will the bad guys succeed in their diabolical plan to poison the whole stable? Well, the ending is predictably happy, with a thrilling climax and lots of yuks along the way. Martin Ritt directed.

PG / 1978 / RCA/Columbia

▲ CAT AND MOUSE

Another French police story, Claude Lelouch's romantic thriller drew favorable comparisons to the best of Hitchcock. That's extravagant, but the film is worth seeing. Veteran French actress Michele Morgan plays the wife of a millionaire who is shot to death in his country home. The flics suspect her, yet can't cinch their case— which is the essence of the story. The acting is formidable all around, especially that of Morgan and Serge Reggiani, who plays a detective not above committing a little larceny himself. And those eating scenes! You'll be starved by the time you figure out who did it if not before. (In French with subtitles.)

Unrated / 1978 / Columbia

▲ CAT PEOPLE

Back in 1942, *Cat People* crept from the B-movie basement to cult status because director Jacques Tourneur knew how to suggest the presence of evil without showing it. In updating the tale, Paul (*American Gigolo*) Schrader takes the opposite tack: Nothing is unseen, but the result is no less sinister. Plagued by erotic dreams of black leopards, a virginal Nastassja Kinski jets to New Orleans to see brother Malcolm McDowell. She learns they are descended from a race of cat people who can't mate with humans without reverting temporarily to their feline state and mauling the life out of their love objects. Nastassia is stunned. Brother Malcolm has already pawed a score of high-heeled hookers. Tired of being a ladykiller, he thinks his only hope is sex with Sis, but kittenish Kinski isn't buying it, having just fallen in love with handsome zoo curator John Heard. To tell what happens after Kinski and Heard pass the petting stage would be unfair except to warn the squeamish about the limb-tearing violence and kinky sex. Kinski and McDowell display enough skin to drive the R rating to its limits, and both find the fun in their roles without slighting their "terrible destiny." Schrader invests the story with an air of high-class decadence that is hypnotic and horrifying. Though screenwriter Alan (*My Bodyguard*) Ormsby can't cover all the plot holes, Albert Whitlock's visual effects, Tom Burman's makeup tricks, and Giorgio Moroder's driving

score (with theme lyrics by David Bowie) make logic irrelevant. Like the black cats themselves, the film is an object of beauty and terror.
R / 1982 / MCA

▲ CAT'S EYE

Creepshow and *Cujo* had their moments but after *Carrie,* no film based on Stephen King material until *Cat's Eye* had been so consistently witty and deliciously evil-spirited. It's a set of three King tales, two adapted from his 1978 book *Night Shift* and the third written for this movie. One involves a stop-smoking clinic run by gangsters, using mob tactics such as threatening the spouses of clients who backslide. Comedian Alan King adopts a marvelous all-business attitude as the clinic's boss, while James Woods gets to show his sense of humor as a would-be quitter. The second story pits Kenneth McMillan as a sadistic mob boss against Robert Hays, playing an aging tennis pro who has stolen McMillan's wife. McMillan offers to spare Hays if he can walk around a narrow ledge outside a high-rise penthouse, and that sets up a suspense story worthy of Poe, Hitchcock, or Serling. In the final segment Drew Barrymore is a little girl having bad dreams about a malicious creature who comes out of her bedroom wall. The creature, resembling what the offspring of Ernest Borgnine and one of the *Gremlins* might look like, wants to steal Barrymore's breath, but he has to fight his way past a stray cat. Director Lewis Teague and King, who did the screenplay, make every frame count; they can be forgiven for all the inside jokes, such as the frothing Saint Bernard a la *Cujo* that chases the cat during the opening credits. The movie isn't for children: The Barrymore sequence is nightmare fodder, for one thing. But for those who like to have their funny bones tickled and chilled at the same time, this film is perfect.
PG-13 / 1985 / Key

▲ CATTLE ANNIE AND LITTLE BRITCHES

You just know a Western with a cutesy title like that isn't going to be a sequel to *The Wild Bunch.* And sure enough, this is a West where there's plenty of shooting, but nobody ever seems to get hurt. It is populated by good-hearted outlaws, and gang leader Burt Lancaster is a prince of a bad guy. He is too good to be true, and Lancaster knows it, playing the role with just the right hint of self-mockery. The screenplay abandons credibility altogether when the outlaws hook up with two comely hoboes, *A Little Romance*'s Diane Lane and Christopher Plummer and Tammy Grimes's fiery daughter, Amanda. Director Lamont (*The Last American Hero*) Johnson has a confident eye, though sometimes he lets the story canter when it should gallop. Yet this modest movie is affecting and memorable as Plummer's film debut.
PG / 1981 / N/A

▲ CAVEMAN

It's bad enough that this fleshed-out Flintstones burlesque repeatedly stoops to flatulence, armpit odor, and worse for laughs. Nobody expected Shakespearean repartee, but even the film's potentially amusing caveman argot includes only fifteen words. The rest is grunting. Ringo Starr plays a moony misfit who aloondas (loves) the hostile tribe's local "10," lusciously embodied by his offscreen wife, Barbara Bach. He even fights off machas (dinosaurs) to get her ool (food), but it's all for nya (nothing). Barbara zug-gugs (mates) exclusively with her cave's fech (ugly, no good) leader, played with fech to spare by six-foot eight-inch, 280-pound Oakland Raider tackle John Matuszak. Ringo is helped by some perkily animated machas, especially a blissed-out Tyrannosaurus rex. They in fact supply the charm the film's bo-bos (humans) lack. Amid the belching and scatological jokes, first-time director Carl Gottlieb and co-writer Rudy (*Silent Movie*) De Luca provide the engaging Ringo with a few bright gags, notably the discovery of music over a campfire. But all told, *Caveman* is fech and hard to aloonda.
PG / 1981 / CBS/Fox

▲ CEASE FIRE

Relentlessly grim and pedantic, this film about veterans suffering from post-Vietnam stress syndrome probably would never had been released if its star, Don Johnson of "Miami Vice," had

not become such a hot ticket. He didn't have anything to be embarrassed about. The movie's faults—its inability to build up tension and its unrelieved, sledgehammer touch when there's a point to be made—are the faults of first-time director David Nutter and screenwriter George Fernandez, who adapted his own play, *Vietnam Trilogy.* Johnson himself is often affecting as an unemployed Miami man who keeps flashing back to his combat experiences; so is longtime character actor Robert Lyons, who usually plays a psychopathic gunman but here is a buddy of Johnson's going through the same anguishing delayed reaction to his war experience. Lisa Blount also suffers as Johnson's wife. Although the portrayal of a tragically persistent real problem is melodramatic in the extreme—Johnson seems to go berserk every ten minutes or so—nothing in it is implausible. But one can be truthful and sincere without being eloquent. And this movie, lacking verbal and visual eloquence, vividly demonstrates the difference between creating a work of art and making an announcement.
R / 1985 / Thorn/EMI

▲ THE CHALLENGE

There may be life in the B movie yet, judging from this pungent, no-flab update of a 13th-century samurai legend, set in present-day Japan. Scott Glenn, the mangy macho of *Urban Cowboy* and *Personal Best,* is an L.A. tough hired to return an ancient, magical sword to Kyoto, where its owner, Toshiro Mifune, the John Wayne of Japan, as a martial arts master, is waiting to take possession. Before Glenn can deliver the goods, he's nearly eliminated by Mifune's evil business tycoon brother, Atsuo Nakamura, who wants the blade too. Director John (*Birdman of Alcatraz, The Manchurian Candidate*) Frankenheimer has been handed more prestigious assignments but, to his credit, he doesn't appear to be slumming. He gives *The Challenge* his sock-bam best. The Japanese-American cast also adds authenticity. Mifune can exude dignity just standing still, while Glenn has the earnest squint of Clint Eastwood. There's a crafty screenplay by Richard Maxwell and John Sayles. As Sayles did in *The Howling* and *Alligator,* they poke fun at the genre's dialogue ("You're dead meat") and conventions (the climactic battle weapon is a stapler). Thanks

to the zest of its participants, *The Challenge* proves to be the thinking martial artist's film.
R / 1982 / CBS/Fox

▲ THE CHAMP

Despite the Hollywood actors' maxim "Never do a picture with kids or dogs," Wallace Beery won an Oscar for his role in the original 1931 *Champ,* even though 9-year-old Jackie Cooper was pitifully lovable. In this remake, Jon Voight's talents got KO'd by Ricky Schroder, then 8, who looks like a Campbell Soup kid, which he was. As the champ, Jon is a loser—a failed boxer, gambler, brawler, and drinker. His wife and the child's mother (Faye Dunaway, more of an ice queen than ever) has left them but reappears to see her son. Ricky upstages her too. Director Franco Zeffirelli uses Florida's beautiful Hialeah racetrack as the main location. The seamy side of the movie looks authentic too. But it is basically shameless, going for the tear ducts at every opportunity—and there are plenty. It is a must only for those who, for reasons of catharsis or masochism, like to end up surrounded by mounds of soggy tissues.
PG / 1979 / MGM/UA

▲ CHAMPIONS

Bob Champion's life story was tailor-made for a movie. In 1979, at the peak of his career as a jockey in England, he found out he had testicular cancer. Given only eight months to live, he underwent chemotherapy and, miraculously, recovered. Even more miraculous was what happened in 1981—Champion won the Grand National, Britain's steeplecase spectacular, aboard Aldaniti, a horse that had been destined to be destroyed after a serious leg injury. Despite the extraordinary drama of Champion's life, however, this movie just plods along. John Hurt portrays Champion, but like the rest of the film he just seems tired. While Jan Francis plays the woman who comes to love Champion despite his physical problems, the romantic subplot seems pasted on to the rest of the action. (Aldaniti plays himself convincingly.) The Grand National is stirring, but it is the only part of the movie that isn't conveyed in a kind of cinematic monotone.
PG / 1984 / Embassy

▲ CHANEL SOLITAIRE

Surprisingly affecting, this story of French fashion doyenne Coco Chanel unfolds around the time of World War I. Marie-France (*Cousin, Cousine*) Pisier ranges from feisty to ambitious to romantically vulnerable as Chanel. And, sacrilege, seems more ideally cast than Katharine Hepburn was in the Broadway musical *Coco*. The film maintains its dignity when it could easily degenerate into soap opera. It focuses on Chanel's turbulent romantic conflicts, relegating to subplot status her rise in couture—from seamstress to successful designer. Pisier goes after a dashing stud, an ex-cavalry officer played by Rutger Hauer, and then a cunning coal merchant, Timothy Dalton. Hauer and Dalton (the later James Bond) are superb. Once best friends, they confront each other in rivalry over Coco. Hauer (the loser) breaks down and weeps, asking his friend to embrace him. It's a moving moment.
R / 1981 / Media

▲ A CHANGE OF SEASONS

Bo Derek's post *"10"* was a "4" at best. Derek makes a splash only when she steps into a hot tub for an extracurricular (and explicit) whirl with Anthony Hopkins, her professor at a New England college. That's all during the first five minutes, though. The film almost had to be anticlimactic from there, and it is, thanks to the clichéd script. Shirley MacLaine plays Hopkins' wife, and after discovering that he is seeing Bo, she retaliates by bedding down with the first available man, the vaguely appealing Michael Brandon. Hopkins and MacLaine remain civilized about it all, even taking their lovers on a joint vacation. Only their 20-year-old daughter, played by an appropriately bratty Mary Beth Hurt, disapproves. By then, though, it's hard for a viewer to rouse more than a yawn.
R / 1981 / CBS/Fox

▲ THE CHANGELING

An old-fashioned haunted house story, pure but not so simple, this movie might tingle a few spines. Having just lost his wife and daughter in a tragic accident, a well-known composer (George C. Scott) rents an enormous Victorian mansion outside Seattle. It's hard to see why a grieving widower would want to live in such a huge establishment—but, anyway, Scott begins to hear strange noises, water faucets turn on by themselves, windows shatter for no reason. The usual stuff, yes, but in this case it is quite scary and there is a dandy unsolved murder at the bottom of it. Scott is very effective as a man obsessed with his house possessed, although he is forever walking down dark corridors and peeking behind closed doors long after normal people would have hit the road. Director Peter (*The Ruling Class*) Medak lets the plot unravel a little only at the film's climax; up to then he keeps the fine edge of suspense.
R / 1980 / Vestron

▲ CHAN IS MISSING

Clever people, these Chinese-Americans. Wayne Wang, a director from San Francisco, made this full-length movie for about the price of a family vacation in Hong Kong: $20,000. It is the first feature film made by and about Chinese-Americans. A mystery/comedy, it was filmed in black and white with an all-newcomer cast in San Francisco's Chinatown. Chan tells the story of two cab drivers, easygoing Wood Moy and his hip nephew Marc Hayashi. They chase around the Bay Area in search of Chan, a friend who has vanished with a wad of cash. As conflicting reports arise, the cab drivers become less interested in where Chan is than in who he is. A thief? A victim? A Communist? A Nationalist? In fact, the search for Chan seems intended to represent the Chinese-American community's search for its cultural identity. Sounds pretentious, but director Wang doesn't harangue about Yellow Liberation. In spite of technical crudities and a sometimes confusing story line, this is a minor triumph.
Unrated / 1982 / N/A

▲ THE CHANT OF JIMMIE BLACKSMITH

One of the best if bloodiest of Australian films. This movie is based on a true incident in 1900 when an aborigine went on a rampage, killing several farm families before he was caught. Raised by a missionary and his wife, Jimmie Blacksmith was led to believe he could be accepted by white

society. He was wrong. After a series of humiliations by white employers, he snaps, taking up weapons and avenging himself on the bigots. Actor Tommy Lewis, as Jimmie, adequately portrays the boiling anger that grows from disillusionment; Freddy Reynolds is superb as his half brother, a happy-go-lucky sort who unwittingly gets sucked into the violence. Roy Barrett nearly overpowers them both with a chilling portrayal of a sadistic white police officer. The photography is breathtaking, juxtaposing the brutality of a universal human struggle against sweeping backdrops. This was only the second feature from director Fred Schepisi, who later turned to American Westerns and such films as *Roxanne*.
Unrated / 1984 / N/A

▲ CHAPTER TWO

Neil Simon had lost his wife to cancer in 1974 and married Marsha (*Goodbye Girl*) Mason three months later. That story—with the touch of the Muse of One-liners—was a success on Broadway in 1977. The film version seems a bit cute and pat. James Caan, in the role Simon based on himself and which Judd Hirsch originated on Broadway, is convincing, as is Marsha Mason, in effect as Marsha Mason. So are the almost anorexically thin Valerie Harper as Marsha's meddling best friend and Joseph Bologna as Neil's meddling brother. This really isn't a *bad* movie. Just don't expect Simon's best.
PG / 1980 / RCA/Columbia

▲ CHARIOTS OF FIRE

The movie was casually conceived when producer David Puttnam moved into a rented house and found only a history of the Olympic Games to read. The result, a true account of two British runners who competed in the 1924 Paris Games, was a surprise smash, winning the Best Picture Oscar when the smart money was betting on *On Golden Pond* or Warren Beatty's *Reds*. The honor

Chariots of Fire: This 1981 Best Picture Oscar winner focused on members of the 1924 Olympic racing team, in particular on Scottish missionary Eric Liddell, stirringly played by Ian Charleson.

was deserved, despite carping from some critics about this British film's "Masterpiece Theater" reserve. Bah! It's a classy, absorbing gem. Ben Cross plays Harold Abrahams, the Cambridge-educated son of an immigrant Jewish financier. The young man's reaction to anti-Semitism was to prove himself better than the bigots as one of the top sprinters of the decade. Ian Charleson is Eric Liddell, an evangelical Christian born to Scottish missionary parents, who ran to glorify God (he dropped out of a race in Paris that was scheduled on a Sunday). The film tells both stories, and the contrasts are subtly striking. Sir John Gielgud and Ian Holm head up—but don't show up—director Hugh Hudson's excellent cast of mostly unknown British actors, among whom Nigel Havers and Alice Krige are standouts. The cinematography, too, is splendid. And, oh, that Oscar-winning Vangelis theme.
PG / 1981 / Warner

▲ CHARLIE CHAN AND THE CURSE OF THE DRAGON QUEEN

Oriental groups leveled charges of racism against this stereotyped comedy, but it is lovers of the old Charlie Chan movies who should have hollered. Peter Ustinov cuts a fine figure as the famed sleuth, so it's not his fault shrewd Charlie is reduced to a sitcom cop. Chan, based on a real Chinese detective, was created by novelist Earl Derr Biggers and first appeared in films in a 1926 silent serial, played by George Kuwa. There have been seven major Chans since: Kamiyama Sojin, E. L. Park, Warner Oland, Sidney Toler, Roland Winters, J. Carrol Naish, and Ross Martin. Director Clive (*What's New, Pussycat?*) Donner and writers Stan Burns and David Axlerod didn't provide enough wit or wisdom here to stuff a fortune cookie. The plot focuses on Chan's clumsy number-one grandson, who's half Chinese and half Jewish, played by WASPy Richard ("Battlestar Galactica") Hatch. Young Chan has his lox and eggs with soy sauce and wants to follow in grandpop's footsteps. Instead, Hatch and his fiancée (Michelle Pfeiffer) are kidnapped by villainess Angie Dickinson. At one point Chan advises: "When faced with the obvious, look elsewhere." Ah so.
PG / 1981 / Media

▲ THE CHEAP DETECTIVE

There are more stars than in the heavens (as MGM used to advertise) in this parody of—as well as homage to—the detective classics of the past. Louise Fletcher takes on the Ingrid Bergman role from *Casablanca*; Madeline Kahn is *The Maltese Falcon*'s Mary Astor, and Marsha Mason is Gladys George; Ann-Margret plays Lauren Bacall from *To Have and Have Not*. While these women hover around Peter Falk—a Lieutenant Columbo-cum-Sam Spade—Sid Caesar, Dom De Luise, Paul Williams, Phil Silvers, and others sneak in for vignettes. No matter who whistles it up, a spoof is just a spoof, but this one works better than the previous collaboration among Falk, producer Ray Stark, and scenarist Neil Simon, *Murder by Death*.
PG / 1978 / RCA/Columbia

▲ CHEECH & CHONG'S NICE DREAMS

Cheech Marin and Thomas Chong's *Up in Smoke* and *Cheech and Chong's Next Movie* grossed more than $160 million, not a small stash for a dopey comedy team. This follow-up is more of the same—predictable jokes about smoking dope, ribald sex (featuring gorgeous Evelyn Guerrero), and general zaniness. Cheech and Chong are selling marijuana by hiding it in ice-cream sticks, and their erratic drive through L.A. is hilarious for those who find reckless driving fun. Stacy Keach, who again plays a drug-crazed police sergeant, seems to turn into a giant lizard from smoking too much of the boys' weed. He ends up flicking his tongue at everything. Another model for youth, Dr. Timothy Leary, the 1960s guru of mind-bending drugs, appears as himself. For C&C fanatics only.
R / 1981 / RCA/Columbia

▲ CHEECH & CHONG'S STILL SMOKIN'

The Ferrante and Teicher of hip West Coast stoned-age humor go to Amsterdam. So much for the story line. Dialogue? Throw a "man" at the beginning and end of every speech, like "In the middle, man" and "You got it, man." Dope jokes? Read a menu offering "California salad"—marijuana leaves. Cracking up yet? Maybe grossness is where you're at. While a blonde is taking on both Cheech and Chong, there are intercuts of animal fornication (tortoises, deer, rhinos). Any successful gags are lost in the dumbness of it all. Artistically, if not chemically, Cheech and Chong are the most wasted talents in Hollywood.

R / 1983 / Paramount

▲ CHEECH & CHONG'S THE CORSICAN BROTHERS

It would seem that a venture into legitimate, drugless humor by Richard "Cheech" Marin and Thomas Chong should give the pair a chance to show off their true abilities, not more pandering to the seamier side of their devotees' taste. But this film crashes. It is a takeoff chronicling the lives of the two Alexandre Dumas characters, twins who wind up embroiled in the French Revolution. Half the gags are based on the Corsicans' supposed empathetic responses to each other (when one gets hurt, the other feels the pain), but this approach quickly wears thin. The rest of the humor takes a marked turn for the base, rambling endlessly around bodily functions, dumb blondes, and the sexual hang-ups of a Marquis de Sade-like character who is played with flaming abandon by Roy Dotrice. Perhaps the movie's most original bit, not to mention its most tasteless, involves one brother's accidental close contact with a horse's rear end. The comedy never rises above that level.

PG / 1984 / Lightning

▲ THE CHESS PLAYERS

Satyajit Ray, India's preeminent director, made this very funny film about, of all things, British colonialism. Set in 1856, it tells the story of two Indian friends, both idle noblemen, who do nothing but play chess all day. Their wives can't stand it: One throws out the chess pieces in a rage, while the other takes up with her husband's young cousin. Meanwhile, the British are making a few moves of their own, forcing the provincial ruler to abdicate, wiping out all vestiges of self-rule. The intricacy—and humor—of this political drama is mirrored in the friends' game, which comes to a near-violent climax as the troops are about to march on the royal palace. For those whose Urdu is rusty, there are English subtitles.

Unrated / 1978 / N/A

▲ CHILDREN OF A LESSER GOD

You're probably tempted to skip this movie. Admit it. When it sinks in that the title is familiar from the Tony-winning 1980 play about a teacher of the deaf, the dread is likely to mount. Hard experience shows that Hollywood's usual tendency is to hype and trivialize these inspirational dramas. Sure the critics rave. What else can they do without looking like a herd of uncaring ogres? If you see this movie, it may be only out of duty or guilt. And, boy, will you be surprised. *Children* turns out to be deeply romantic, a sensitive and sexy love story. William Hurt—fresh from his Oscar win for *Kiss of the Spider Woman*— plays the teacher, and he's never been more appealing. Arriving at a school for the deaf in Maine (the film was actually shot in Canada), Hurt uses jokes, profanity, and even the vibrations of rock music to move his students away from what he considers the crutch of sign language and into lipreading and speech. Then he slams right into a brick wall. Her name is Sarah. An incurably deaf former student, she is fluent at signing and regards speaking as an acceptance of inferiority in a hearer's world. She prefers cleaning the school toilets to the possibility of winning a better job through compromise. In a knockout screen debut that won her the Oscar for Best Actress, deaf theater actress Marlee Matlin, then 21, shows how Sarah's resentment won't let her relax. Even love doesn't leave her pliant; she's all ragged edges. Matlin's remarkably expressive face and body render Hurt's translations for her signings an unnecessary contrivance. Though student falls for teacher and moves in with him (onstage they got married), she won't agree to let him play miracle worker. Like most couples at odds, they also use sex—and anything else handy— to score points off each other. But the only victory is a grudging mutual understanding. Or so it was in the stage version. Onscreen, playwright Mark Medoff (who co-wrote the script with Hesper Anderson) has let his cold distrust of easy answers thaw into a sap-happy ending. And though first-time feature director Randa Haines (best known for the TV incest drama *Something About Amelia*) made that rare filmed play that looks like a movie, she shows an exasperating preference for making too many scenes postcard pretty. Haines and Nedoff are both to be credited, though, for allowing the student-teacher relationship to do the work of the play's deaf-rights preachiness. Hurt and

Matlin, who became real-life lovers during shooting, display a passionate urgency that is more profound than polemical. Exhausted from signing during one argument, they drop their hands and stare at each other with the wounded eyes of lovers who've run out of ways to express their need. The painful eloquence of their silence is unforgettable.
R / 1986 / Paramount

▲ THE CHILDREN OF THEATRE STREET

Princess Grace of Monaco lovingly narrated this feature-length documentary on the Kirov Ballet School in Leningrad. The film concentrates on three students, beginning with their stern audition—a cattle call where only those with the requisite "dancer's body" can even survive the first round. From there, it moves slowly through six long, painful, and confined years (training comparable to that of an NFL football camp) until the gangly underlings emerge in an explosive yet tremulous graduation performance. Explicit camera work catches the dancers' subtlest moves and reveals a humanistic Leningrad, contrary to the grim image of Russia. *Theatre Street* has a soft and informative touch that explains why, although America manufactures the best movies, hamburgers, and denim, Russia turns out the best ballet dancers.
Unrated / 1977 / Kultur

▲ CHILDREN OF THE CORN

Aw, shucks. This would-be chiller is based on a Stephen King story. (Yes, another one. Say, Steve, you haven't made any pacts with the devil that guarantee you a movie a week, have you?) It's set in Nebraska—though actually filmed in Sioux City, Iowa—where one day all the kids in town up and slaughter all the adults. The children are religious fanatics devoted to a being called He Who Walks Behind the Rows. This is not an usher but a something or other that burrows around underneath a cornfield, emitting a glow. For three years it lets the town's little darlings live happily ever after, or at least until they reach 19, at which point they are sacrificed. But then a young couple, Linda Hamilton and Peter Horton, happens by. Perhaps mistaking them for truant officers, the youths of the town get mur-

derous again. Little Robby Kiger and AnneMarie McEvoy, as the kids who manage to defy the rebellion's leaders, show some charm. But director Fritz Kiersch, in his first feature film, turned out something as satisfying as one of the unexploded kernels at the bottom of a popcorn bowl.
R / 1984 / Embassy

▲ THE CHINA SYNDROME

It begins as a routine assignment for a TV reporter (Jane Fonda) and her minicam photographer (Michael Douglas): an essay on a nuclear power facility. But as they tour the plant, a near disaster (for which the title is a code word) is barely contained by a mid-level engineer (Jack Lemmon). Corporate structures at both the power plant and the TV station scramble to cover up the incident. Then, as in the real-life case of Karen Silkwood and the Cimarron nuclear power facility in Oklahoma, which the movie loosely resembles, a courier with proof of dangerous abuses has a fatal car accident. (Mike Nichols' later *Silkwood* did that story better.) Like all the other protagonists in this film, Fonda is so relentlessly high-minded that the movie lacks passion. The only emotion, in fact, comes from Lemmon's performance as a man in conflict. As a thriller or a treatise about man versus technology, the movie works marvelously. It was also prophetic in view of the 1986 Soviet accident at Chernobyl. It is just painfully cold-blooded. While preaching about what's good for humanity in the abstract, the film lacks sensitivity to its flesh-and-blood characters.
PG / 1979 / RCA/Columbia

▲ THE CHOIRBOYS

In his fourth police novel, on which this movie is based, Joseph Wambaugh detailed the misadventures of a bunch of L.A. cops who gather in a park after work for what they cynically call "choir practice." It is an attempt to soften the ugly realities of their lives as cops. They handcuff one another to trees, take potshots at ducks, and drink themselves into oblivion. Although marvelously funny, Wambaugh's book was episodic, a hurdle that director Robert Aldrich is unable to clear. The black humor is there, but the justification for it isn't. Burt (*Rocky*) Young stands out in a large cast (Perry King and James Woods

63

were there too) that struggles gamely with thinly sketched characters. If you've read the book, this surprisingly tasteless movie is sure to disappoint you. If you haven't, it will merely confuse you.
R / 1977 / N/A

▲ CHOKE CANYON

It's not a glorious triumph of substance over style, but this old-fashioned adventure film offers a refreshing diversion from the big-budget blow-'em-ups. The hero is Stephen (*Brewster's Millions*) Collins, as a physicist with a ninety-nine-year lease on Choke Canyon, Utah, the one spot on earth where he can prove a theory that will bring safe energy to mankind. An unscrupulous corporate overlord, played by Nicholas (*The Falcon and the Snowman*) Pryor, wants to use the site to dump illegal nuclear waste. After destroying Collins's lab, he sends in veteran character actor Bo Svenson, suitably menacing as a hitman armed with portable rocket launchers, to finish the job. While the action, with its well-shot air chases through the canyon, is predictable, the script is layered with wit. Collins is such an engaging good guy that he can't kidnap Pryor's daughter (played by Karen Allen look-alike Janet Julian) without providing her with a few dozen take-out burgers and several buckets of fried chicken. "How could you put me in a pit?" she later complains. "It wasn't that bad," he says, "How would you like it?" "I like pits." Who could argue with logic like that?
PG / 1986 / Media

▲ CHOOSE ME

Genevieve Bujold plays a late-night talk-show host who counsels people on their sexual problems. Lesley Ann Warren is the owner of a seedy bar who calls Bujold on occasion to discuss the many men in her life. Keith Carradine, a former patient in a mental hospital, is given to outlandish lies. Rae Dawn Chong likes to pick up men at bars. The brief intersection of these lives is the basis of this movie, which is not the dark, moody film their backgrounds might suggest. Rather, it's a contemporary comedy about manners and morals in Los Angeles. The performances are especially strong. The action begins when Bujold, not knowing Warren is one of her frequent callers,

answers her ad for a roommate. The resulting couplings (and uncouplings) are wild, poignant, occasionally hilarious. It sometimes seems as if the movie started out as a drama but turned irresistibly funny in the filming, and director Alan Rudolph let it happen, with sardonically amusing results.
R / 1984 / Media

▲ A CHORUS LINE

The wave of dread starts early. You notice that, with rare exceptions, the dancers don't sweat. Director Richard Attenborough's *Chorus Line* is a sanitized, homogenized, conventionalized film version of the most successful musical in Broadway history. If you've never seen this milestone show onstage, where it belongs and blossoms, you may cadge some enjoyment out of watching an eager cast of newcomers strut onscreen. And the socko finish is a rouser. Still, this $24 million extravaganza is an empty shell, so cautious it lacks even the sleazy energy of a real desecration. A *Chorus Line*'s original director-choreographer, Michael Bennett, fashioned theatrical magic from a simple premise: seventeen dancers stand on an empty stage vying for eight spots in the chorus of a Broadway musical. What is it that drives talented kids to face rejection for a place on this anonymous line? Bennett dug his answers out of life, taping interviews with real gypsies (slang for chorus people); Marvin Hamlisch and Edward Kleban provided a score that celebrated every dancer who ever marched in step. Perhaps Attenborough and screenwriter Arnold Schulman thought this too New Yorky for a national audience. Their solution—beefing up the dutiful love story between the show's featured dancer, Alyson Reed, and the director, Michael Douglas—misses the point and muffles the emotion. So does turning a dancer's anthem to her craft, "What I Did for Love," into a ballad that Reed torch-sings to Douglas. With the monotony of a metronome, Attenborough trots out each member of his cast for a close-up show-and-tell. Under this hothouse staging, the performers visibly wilt. Choreographer Jeffrey Hornaday's halfhearted attempts to update the dancing for the '80s also misfire. "Surprise, Surprise," a new number performed by the talented Gregg Burge, plays like a Vegas disco routine or, worse, like something out of Travolta's *Staying Alive*. A sprinkling of vitality

does come through: a flashy opening no less effective for being cribbed from Bob Fosse's *All That Jazz,* the welcome sass from Vicki Frederick and Matt West, and a touching version of "At the Ballet," a song that links dance and childhood longing with agonizing simplicity. But *A Chorus Line,* a Broadway baby to the end, simply won't be torn from its theatrical stomping grounds.
PG-13 / 1985 / Embassy

▲ THE CHOSEN

Curses! This is still another horror movie that expropriates the New Testament Book of Revelation prophecy of an Antichrist who comes to destroy the world. Only this time the Apocalypse comes not as a little boy, as it did in *The Omen,* a gruesome monster, or even Pat Sajak. It is a normal-looking chap (Simon Ward) who wants to use a thermonuclear power plant being designed by his father (Kirk Douglas) as a doomsday device. Ward is effective in an easy role that mainly requires him to look sinister, but Douglas never seems able to muster much conviction for lines like "I'm not counting on God; I put my faith in nuclear energy." The plot—spotted with a little nudity and a lot of ugly violence (the top of one head is lopped off by a helicopter)—is so sluggish that the end of the world seems like a welcome prospect if it would get this kind of foolishness over with.
R / 1978 / CBS/Fox

▲ THE CHOSEN

When will Rod Steiger get another role he can sink his teeth into? This adaptation of Chaim Potok's best-selling novel offers him—and audiences—barely an hors d'oeuvre. It's the story of two Jewish boys growing up in Brooklyn during World War II. One, played by teen heartthrob Robby Benson, is the son of a rabbi. The other, Barry (*Fame*) Miller, is the son of a Zionist journalist. Their friendship is complicated by their respective fathers' opposing views on a Jewish homeland. The rabbi, played by Steiger, is against it; the journalist, Maximilian Schell, is for it. But the movie has no focus. One minute it's concerned with the friendship between the boys, which is so sweet as to have homosexual overtones. Next we see horrifying documentary footage of Nazi concentration camps. Then the movie lurches back to a spotty portrayal of the fathers. Steiger looks terrific in his white beard and earlocks, but the only time the movie comes to life is when he or Schell is on the screen, and that's not often enough. Benson is horribly miscast as the pious rabbi's son; his dewy-eyed sincerity is laughable. This movie's failure is especially shameful since, as the book proved, the subject is rich and fascinating.
PG / 1981 / CBS/Fox

▲ CHRISTINE

Hell has no fury like a Plymouth scorned, or so it would seem from director John Carpenter's adaptation of the scary Stephen King novel. This movie, about a car that runs amok, never gets into gear, though. The car, a version of the Plymouth model so popular for its sweeping fins, starts acting up on the assembly line, where it chomps an inspector's hand and then kills another auto-worker who dares flick an ash on its upholstery. Flash forward twenty years to California, where Christine (the car had been nicknamed by its mysteriously dead owner) sits in a weed-filled lot. A passing teenager, Keith Gordon, spies it and falls in love. He fixes up the car and himself: No longer the class nerd, he gets the most desirable girl in school, Katherine Ross look-alike Alexandra Paul. The class bullies trash Christine, which is a mistake, since she has a habit of cruising around at night, driverless and in a bad mood. Technically, the film is slick: At one point, Christine repairs herself before her owner's disbelieving eyes. Still, Carpenter has failed to make her as scary as, say, the truck in Steven Spielberg's 1971 movie *Duel.* (She does have it all over the villain of 1977's *The Car.*) The mood is often broken by insipid philosophizing; Gordon is stuck with an embarrassing speech about the heartbreak of being a twerp. *Christine* is not quite a lemon, but it's nobody's dream vehicle either.
R / 1984 / RCA/Columbia

▲ A CHRISTMAS STORY

Coy, cloying, and precious just for starters, this seasonal tale is about a 9-year-old boy who desperately wants a BB gun for Christmas. The movie is adapted from Jean Shepherd's novel *In*

God We Trust, All Others Pay Cash. Peter Billingsley, then 11, played the boy with grown-up sensitivity—he's efficient but not really a cuddlesome child performer. Darren McGavin, as the father, overacts no more than usual, and Melinda (*Close Encounters*) Dillon, as the boy's mother, lends some sweetness. So does Ian Petrella, who portrays Billingsley's whimpery little brother. There is some fun from a surly department store Santa, Jeff Gillen, and from Tedde Moore, who plays one of those maternal teachers in print dresses whom children of the '40s remember. It won't make anyone forget *Miracle on 34th Street* but shortcomings notwithstanding, this is workable fare as far as holiday films go nowadays.
PG / 1983 / MGM/UA

▲ CIRCLE OF IRON

For better or worse, the kung fu movie did not die with Bruce Lee. In this self-proclaimed "mystical martial arts adventure," the martial arts sequences are capably enough handled by lead players David Carradine and Jeff Cooper. In addition, Carradine has a pleasingly wry screen presence that keeps the picture from going comatose. Cooper plays a naive pilgrim who must undergo survival tests, most of which involve a lot of frenzied leaping and kicking, in his search for the *Book of Enlightenment.* It contains—no, not the latest advice from Joyce Brothers or Dr. Ruth—only "all the wisdom of the world." The pseudophilosophical screenplay is often so pretentious that it's funny. (In that respect, the film resembles *The Towering Inferno,* whose screenwriter, Stirling Silliphant, hacked out this script too.) The title, like so much else about this movie, sounds impressive but signifies nothing.
R / 1979 / Embassy

▲ CIRCLE OF TWO

The late Richard Burton carried a film or two in his day, and he tried to tote this one along. Burton, then 56, plays a Toronto artist whose muse and passion are revived by a liaison with Tatum O'Neal, 18, a schoolgirl who wants to be a writer. The premise is within reason, if barely. It's harder to accept the obnoxious supporting characters—her parents and friends, his art world associates—and the actors who play them quite

badly. Jules (*Never on Sunday*) Dassin's direction and Thomas Hedley's script are strained too. At one point O'Neal goes on a hunger strike when her parents won't let her see Burton. "That old gentleman happens to mean more to me than anything else," she wails. "The next time I eat, it will be with him." While she's a decent actress, O'Neal hardly seems attractive enough for the role, even though she records her first nude scene. Burton, meanwhile, gentlemanly underacts, yet his glances and monosyllables are so much more interesting than the rest of the movie they become a form of upstaging.
PG / 1981 / Vestron

▲ CITIZENS BAND

A minor American classic that gets better with each viewing. Written by Paul Brickman, who later scripted *Risky Business,* and directed by Jonathan (*Melvin and Howard*) Demme, this lyrical, generous-hearted comedy adopts the CB craze to examine what happens to citizens of a southwestern town who find a liberating release of expression as disembodied voices. Two *American Graffiti* grads, Paul Le Mat and Candy Clark, and a band of ratchet-jawing citizens use their rigs to preach, rescue shill, make love (of sorts), and even marry. Streetwalking is raunchily updated by Aliz Elias as a motorized lady-of-the-interstates. But the film is stolen by Ann Wedgeworth and Marcia Rodd as two housewives who find they're married—at the same time—to the same square-jawed trucker. In some areas the film is released under the title *Handle with Care.* Whatever name you find it under, you'll discover a hidden treasure.
PG / 1977 / N/A

▲ CITY HEAT

Having established in *Tightrope* that he can work up some serious dramatic acting, Clint Eastwood showed he can play for laughs too. Going palsy-walsy with Burt Reynolds as a cop and private eye in Kansas City in 1933, he winks, shrugs, and scowls menacingly through a send-up of old gangster movies. Directed by Richard Benjamin, this is an easygoing film. It's almost too good-natured, relying on fistfights and gun battles as if they were funny in themselves. But Eastwood

and Reynolds, trading wisecracks like Hope and Crosby, are relentlessly affable. A happy change of pace is seeing light performances by such usually serious actors as Rip Torn (who plays a sneering mobster), Jane Alexander (as the stereotypical private eye's secretary), and Tony Lo Bianco (as Torn's archenemy). Madeline Kahn does her typical superbimbo number to good effect, and Irene Cara gets to sing—her rendition of "Embraceable You" is touching. The plot, which has to do with a chase for some incriminating documents, is peripheral. It's the we're-all-here-to-have-a-good-time mood that counts, and few films offer such guilt-free enjoyment.
PG / 1985 / Warner

▲ CITY OF WOMEN

What if women took over the world? That's the premise of this hypnotically alluring Federico Fellini film. Marcello Mastroianni is travelling on a train. He spots a beautiful woman, tries to seduce her, then follows her to a land where women rule. Is this a dream or Fellini fantasy? Whichever—we learn at the end—the movie reconfirms Fellini's reputation as one of the most daring directors in cinematic history. This film, which he also wrote, resembles his earlier 8½, and Mastroianni again gives a superb performance. Stumbling through a feminist convention, hounded by cruising teenage girls, and finally taking refuge in the fortress of the last macho man, he is amused, mystified, and, finally, stripped of his protective male armor. Not that this movie is antifeminist—Fellini's wit skewers men as well as women. His story is, as usual, told in strikingly beautiful scenes and reinforces the idea that, at its best, pure cinema can be a kind of magic. (In Italian with subtitles.)
Unrated / 1981 / N/A

▲ THE CLAN OF THE CAVE BEAR

Daryl Hannah probably never had to worry about this movie doing for her career what *When Dinosaurs Ruled the Earth* did for Magda Konopka's. (If you're asking "Magda who?" you get the idea.) Based on the Jean Auel novel, this film makes no attempt to reflect the desperation of early man as the grim *Quest for Fire* did; nor is it one of those dinosaur-filled epics. It's more

like a prehistoric *Dallas,* with the Cave Bearites constantly squabbling over who's running the place, wondering who's going to mate with whom, and swapping family tales. They speak to one another in sign language and grunts, though the accompanying subtitles render their exchanges as Socratic dialogues conducted in Shakespearian English. Hannah plays an outsider whom the Clan regards as peculiar. It's easy to see why, since everyone else is heavily made up with jutting brows and pounds of hair, while Daryl is her blond, all-American self. She's supposed to be one of the Others, which makes sense only if the Others are a bunch of collegians who are running a mammoth-burger franchise nearby so they'll have some spending money at Malibu. Hannah is very inventive. She shows the Cave Bearites how to count and, by example, braid their hair cutely. She invents depression and then, while off moping in the woods, happens upon a cozy little hole in the mountain. She claims it for herself, thereby creating the concept of the vacation home. She is also obviously the first feminist, defying the male elders at every turn. Michael (*All the Right Moves*) Chapman directed, from a screenplay by John (*The Brother from Another Planet*) Sayles. They get the most out of their British Columbia locations. The film is never very involving, though, and the ending is rather abrupt. If you want Hannah to settle down into her cave, sweet cave at the end, you'll be disappointed.
R / 1986 / CBS/Fox

▲ CLASH OF THE TITANS

If you quiver at the prospect of two hours of elaborately staged, often hilarious Greek mythological kitsch, then *Clash* is for you. But if your taste also runs to gripping plot, fast-paced action, and characters perceptibly less mechanical than special-effects monsters, try Homer. As Zeus, Laurence Olivier is the sleepiest deity ever. As the young Perseus, handsome Harry Hamlin confronts savage foes with a sword and a shield that render him invincible, a helmet that renders him invisible, and a script that renders him inarticulate. Boy, did he find TV's "L.A. Law" just in time. The film does get help from beautiful Judi Bowker as Perseus's slinky heartthrob, Andromeda, but there isn't enough of her, not even when she emerges nude and glistening from

a Greek hot tub. Hamlin's then offscreen lady, Ursula Andress, is overdraped and underused as Aphrodite. And only incurable nostalgia freaks will go for director Ray Harryhausen's '50ish gimmicks: a Godzilla-like sea monster capable of unleashing a tidal wave by clearing its throat; a Pegasus that minces around backward and forward like those kitties in the TV cat food ads; and a mechanical owl cloned, it seems, from *Star Wars'* C-3PO. The movie's visual high points are a couple of well-designed effects involving three blind nags and a gruesome Medusa. "What more," Zeus wonders of young Perseus's strong build and dark good looks, "could any mortal desire or deserve?" Well, check local listings. This myth conception is easily avoided.
PG / 1981 / MGM/UA

▲ CLASS

Attention, boys and girls! Today's lesson is on the curious career of Jacqueline Bisset. In this alleged comedy, Miss Bisset plays a very rich, horny society wife who seduces a virginal preppie (Andrew McCarthy) in a glass elevator overlooking Chicago. The ensuing romance might be the crux of an interesting movie, but *Class* isn't really about sexual initiatives or mismatched lovers or anything pertaining to Bisset's character. Bisset's unlikely stud is also the roommate of her 18-year-old son (Rob Lowe). Director Lewis John Carlino is most interested in how the love affair affects that bosom-buddies relationship. In fact, Bisset effectively vanishes in the film's second half. We hear from her creepo husband, Cliff Robertson, that she has checked into a mental institution. In this occasionally amusing, frequently farfetched mishmash, the prep school shenanigans do have some charm. But because the movie is so coarse and misogynistic, the laughs are all sleazy. *Class* is a low-down comedy about highfalutin types. It's *Porky's* for people who wear Lacoste shirts. For homework, please compose an essay on why Bisset might have accepted such a role. *Class* dismissed.
R / 1983 / Vestron

▲ THE CLASS OF MISS MACMICHAEL

Play hooky. Unlike its spiritual predecessor, *To Sir with Love,* it lacks wit and warmth, even though it is the work of folks who know better.

Glenda Jackson is at her least appealing—severe and frumpy simultaneously. Oliver Reed has rarely given a good serious performance outside 1970's *Women in Love,* and his nasty headmaster here is no exception. And Michael Murphy, in another role as a whiny cast-off lover, is tiresome. Nothing works for director Silvio Narizzano—there is no story line, the lighting is dismal, and a grating punk rock tune even ruins the credits.
R / 1979 / CBS/Fox

▲ CLASS OF 1984

The prologue to this film cites new statistics about violence in our schools. But *Class of 1984,* a mix of *Blackboard Jungle, To Sir with Love,* and *The Warriors,* offers up a solution that is as old as Hammurabi: an eye for a bloody eye, a tooth for a knocked-out tooth, and a stiletto for a chain. Director Mark (*Roller Boogie*) Lester envisions high school as an armed camp, with metal detectors and surveillance cameras everywhere. At the student body's rotten core is Timothy (*The White Shadow*) Van Patten, the then 22-year-old half brother of Dick and Joyce. He gives a marvelous performance as the strutting, black-hearted psychotic who rules Abraham Lincoln H.S. with a gang of punks. Perry King plays his challenger, a naive new teacher who battles callous administrators as well as the thugs. (Ironically, King gave a much better performance as a leather delinquent in 1974's *The Lords of Flatbush.*) He remains committed to his profession until the gang brutally rapes his pregnant wife. That leads to a climax reminiscent of De Palma's *Carrie,* as the now feral King stalks his tormentors. His vigilante approach to education isn't very edifying; sweet Karen Valentine would have civilized the young misfits within three episodes of "Room 222." The subtheme about the need for changes in the juvenile justice system seems a rationalization for brutality. But the film has great verve and plays deftly on the emotions.
R / 1982 / Vestron

▲ CLOAK & DAGGER

In the caper comedies of not so long ago, the elusive object of desire was usually a fabled gem. Nowadays it's a computer program. Although officially an updated remake of *The Window,* a

1949 suspense movie starring Bobby Driscoll, *Cloak & Dagger* plays more like the bastard child of *WarGames* and a Hitchcock homage. Henry Thomas is a gadget-crazed kid who indulges in game playing, fantasy, and the companionship of an imaginary spy, Dabney Coleman. As a surrogate father figure, Coleman delivers the advice and affection Thomas doesn't get from his real dad, a preoccupied Air Force officer, also played by Coleman. When Thomas stumbles upon a real-life spy ring, he becomes the high-tech equivalent of the boy who cried wolf. Director Richard Franklin, who made 1983's *Psycho II*, seems more entranced by the scenery of San Antonio, where the film was shot, than the Hitchcock allusions of Tom Holland's script. *Cloak & Dagger* is the story of Thomas's rite of passage. When he becomes his own man, he casts off his imaginary pal and learns to appreciate his dad. But like a lot of adolescent comedies, this one sabotages its own theme. Since there isn't a brainy adult in the film, why would anyone want to grow up? Other movies can get away with pandering to kids through condescending portraits of adults, but not a movie that makes maturity its grand finale. Thomas's performance reflects a likable combination of intelligence and vulnerability. But Coleman just coasts on with his insensitive cad shtik, and most of the time *Cloak & Dagger* merely insinuates that growing up is the most egregious kind of child's play.
PG / 1984 / MCA

▲ CLOCKWISE

In this, his first screenplay, British playwright Michael (*Noises Off*) Frayn concocted a delightfully jaunty farce about one man's fight against time. John (*Monty Python*) Cleese, the headmaster of an exclusive prep school, must get to Norwich to make a historic speech before the all-England headmasters conference. He's a punctual and punctilious sort, but when he leaves for Norwich, Cleese begins debating with the ticket taker about the semantics of "right" and "left." Soon the train for Norwich has gone, the speech manuscript is on a train heading in the other direction, and Cleese is launched into a series of events that include stealing a car, vandalizing a phone booth, and kidnapping an old flame. All before teatime. Along for the chase is Sharon Maiden, one of Cleese's students. She just broke

up with the slow-witted music teacher who has trouble finishing his . . . that is, he can't end . . . well, it's that he has problems completing . . . Anyway, writer Frayn's oblique wit is equal to his eccentric characters. "It's not the despair," moans Cleese, realizing his chances of getting to Norwich on time are growing slim. "I can stand the despair. It's the hope!" Director Christopher (*The Jewel in the Crown*) Morahan makes wonderful sense of the whole thing. With Cleese in top form, *Clockwise* is 96 minutes and 4 seconds of fun.
PG / 1986 / HBO/Cannon

▲ CLOSE ENCOUNTERS OF THE THIRD KIND

Close Encounter of the First Kind: sighting of a UFO. Close Encounter of the Second Kind: physical evidence. Close Encounter of the Third Kind: contact! Richard Dreyfuss as a Muncie, Indiana, power company worker experiences all three when he has a brush with extraterrestrial visitors. Family and neighbors think he has simply short-circuited. Air Force brass and technocrats do all they can to discredit him. But Dreyfuss's obsession draws him onward—and upward. Director Steven Spielberg delivers a paranoid but nonetheless powerful message about ordinary people reacting to extraordinary circumstances. With twice the $9.5 million budget of *Star Wars, Close Encounters* is that much more intriguing. The only disappointment: We never actually climb aboard the glittering chandelier of a spaceship designed by *2001* special effects genius Douglas Trumbull. (That deficiency was rectified in 1980 when Spielberg issued a re-edited version of the film, *The Special Edition*.)
PG / 1977 / RCA/Columbia

▲ CLUB PARADISE

Like *Water,* another 1986 film it closely resembles, this comedy set in the Caribbean is frustrating. Not that it isn't funny. It is full of thoughtful, original humor that never relies on obscenity or cruelty and entertains its audience without pandering to it. The frustration comes from the feeling that an all-time great film, not just a good one, should come from a cast that includes Robin Williams, Peter O'Toole, Twiggy, reggae singer Jimmy Cliff, Steve ("Newhart") Kampmann, and the bulk of the SCTV alumni association—Rick Moranis, Andrea Martin, Eugene Levy, and Joe Flaherty among them. Williams, playing a retired Chicago fireman who moves to an island and uses his disability-settlement money to buy into a rundown resort run by Cliff, is subdued. He gets his laughs with dry delivery; when a racist visitor waxes nostalgic for the productivity of the days of slavery, Williams says, "Yeah, a good day's work for a good day's beating." Twiggy is captivating as Williams's lover, and O'Toole, as the British governor of the island, all but gives dissipation a good name. Among the others, Levy and Moranis sustain a funny subplot as inept women chasers (both named Barry), and the extraordinary Martin exploits her role as a yuppie wife looking for thrills. When a lost and hungry troupe of resort guests spots some sugarcane, Martin huffs, "I'm not about to eat real sugar." Levy answers, "All right, fine, we'll find you a Sweet 'n Low field." Director Harold (*National Lampoon's Vacation*) Ramis, who co-wrote the film with Brian Doyle-Murray, never stoops for an easy laugh. He seems capable, however, of making a movie with more momentum than this—one where the jokes build on one another instead of just sprouting up.

PG-13 / 1986 / Warner

▲ COAL MINER'S DAUGHTER

The title figure in this film bio was born into Appalachian poverty, got married at 13, and began birthin' babies, but became Loretta Lynn, one of country music's most enduring stars. The unpretentious, affectionate treatment was predictably popular with Loretta's fans, but it also garnered a much wider audience, thanks to strong performances from Tommy Lee Jones, Beverly D'Angelo, the Band's drummer Levon Helm, and especially Sissy Spacek, who took the gamble of singing Lynn's material herself and gambled her way into an Oscar. (D'Angelo sings the role of Lynn's idol-mentor, Patsy Cline.) Like its subject, the movie celebrates down-hominess, but city folk are likely to be won over too.

PG / 1980 / MCA

▲ COAST TO COAST

An aw-shucks truck driver (Robert Blake) escaping bill collectors meets up with a Beverly Hills woman (Dyan Cannon) who has just run away from a mental institution. They hop in a truck and head cross-country. Their misadventures include chases, women wrestling in a pigsty, making love in the snow, fisticuffs, and—as a finale—crashing a semi into a mansion. This trucking variation of an overworked plot (man meets woman in bizarre circumstances, with affection blossoming out of adversity) would make a fabulous half-hour TV episode, but it's a long haul strung out for 95 minutes. The movie bears more than coincidental resemblance to *Smoky and the Bandit*. Although Blake and Cannon are charming and attractive, director Joseph Sargent doesn't offer them much support.

PG / 1980 / Paramount

▲ COBRA

Even Sylvester Stallone's most devoted followers should have a hard time swallowing this neurotically stupid film. Stallone plays a ruthless Los Angeles cop who makes the Charles Bronson of *Death Wish* seem like a liberal member of the Supreme Court. Stallone is so full of paranoid self-righteousness that nearly everybody, including most of his fellow cops, is his enemy. The main bad guys are a cult of random murderers whose favorite pastime seems to be a ritual dance in which they click ax handles together. Most of the time the cultists are pursuing Stallone and the witness he is trying to protect, Brigitte Nielsen (Mrs. Stallone). The odds are usually around 135 to 1, but then, Sly never goes anywhere without as much weaponry as your average Marine division. Director George (*Rambo*) Comatos knows how to fill the screen. What he fills it with, however, is something else. Stallone's cop, supposedly an ace killer, seems like a cartoonish buffoon. At one point he stalks a shotgun-wielding maniac in a dimly lighted supermarket without ever taking his sunglasses off. In a strange way Stallone becomes sort of a reverse wimp, appearing frightened of responding to anyone except by choking them or blowing off their heads. Nielsen has little chance of making any impression. While the film argues that the judicial

system coddles criminals, its real message is that all anyone has to do to stop crime is swagger around like a 10-year-old bully, speaking loudly and carrying a couple of crates of hand grenades.
R / 1986 / Warner

▲ COCOON

Just a few minutes into this film from director Ron Howard and you begin to feel a revivifying, unmistakable charge. *Cocoon* is a tonic, a cousin to *E.T.* and *Close Encounters* but with a touching charm all its own. *Cocoon* also has something insightful to say about the way senior citizens have become the new aliens in our society, and there's sometimes a savagery of tone you don't expect in this type of mainstream moviemaking. That tone is welcome. So is the cast of veteran actors who match the best moments in Tom Benedek's script and compensate for its occasional vulgarity. Don Ameche, Hume Cronyn, and Wilford Brimley play three cantankerous codgers who live in a Florida retirement complex. A neighboring mansion is unrented, and the three gents like to sneak in and use the pool. One day the men notice strange-looking pods at the bottom of the pool. They belong to the mansion's new renters, Antareans (from another galaxy) on an expedition to pick up members of their crew left in the Gulf of Mexico on their last trip to earth. These crew members are protected inside the cocoonlike pods. Antareans, who have extended their longevity to thousands of years, don't resemble earthlings except when they put on their human skins. Then they look like Brian Dennehy, Tahnee Welch (Raquel's gorgeous daughter), and Tyrone Power, Jr. (you know who's gorgeous son). The Antareans rent Steve Guttenberg's fishing boat to round up their pals. But then Guttenberg peeps at Welch undressing, and she takes off everything, including her skin. Once Guttenberg is assured the aliens won't chew off his face, he relaxes. He even enjoys a bizarre love scene with Welch. But it's the old folks that concern Howard most. Swimming in the pool with the cocoons gives the men new life. They cavort like youngsters in scenes that allow three marvelous actors to deliver the performances of their lives. Cronyn's cancer goes into remission. He starts winking at his wife, played by his incandescent real-life mate, Jessica Tandy. Ameche (who won

a Best Supporting Actor Oscar) starts dancing up a storm with his sweetie, beautifully done by Gwen Verdon. And Brimley and wife Maureen Stapleton seriously ponder the Antarean offer to leave earth to live a productive life in a new galaxy. When pal Jack Gilford argues that he and his wife (Herta Ware) would prefer to face death on earth, *Cocoon* takes a plunge into serious waters: Society has made outcasts of our elderly. The Antareans are offering more than immortality; they're providing another chance at dignity. Mixing an unsparing social conscience with bracing, blissful entertainment, *Cocoon* came through as one of the '80s' best films.
PG-13 / 1985 / CBS/Fox

▲ CODE OF SILENCE

When Chuck Norris played a city detective in 1981's *An Eye for an Eye,* the result was abysmal. But *Code of Silence* is Norris's most satisfying, exciting film. Norris plays a Chicago cop embroiled in a drug vendetta between Italian and Colombian mobs. Director Andy David incorporates a variety of subplots; Norris's partner, Dennis Farina, for instance, keeps nagging him to retire so they can start a concession stand outside Wrigley Field. He also uses the Chicago environment effectively, employing such picturesque locations as Lincoln Park. *Code of Silence* also marked a number of firsts for a Norris film. Cast members don't deliver their lines as if they're just hearing them for the first time themselves. There is no mawkish love interest. Norris commits less manual mayhem than usual and actually loses one fight. (That defeat, however, is by a small army of steroid-stoked Colombians who hardly observe Marquis of Okinawa rules.) It's also refreshing to be able to describe one of Chuck's movies as gritty and not be referring to the film stock. Norris has always been bankable. In *Code of Silence,* mirabile dictu, he's good and still bankable.
R / 1985 / Thorn/EMI

▲ THE COLOR OF MONEY

Paul Newman makes everything he's learned in three decades of screen acting pay off in this forceful follow-up to his 1961 role as pool shark

71

Fast Eddie Felson in *The Hustler*. The film earned him his long overdue Oscar, but don't expect one of those ravaged, old pro performances. Newman, at 61, hadn't lost his looks, he had improved upon them. And his acting isn't lazy; it's eager, feral. He's in full maturity, and he's never been better. To the film's credit, Newman is not the whole show. Tom (*Top Gun*) Cruise, 24, is remarkably good as Newman's protégé-turned-nemesis; the teen dream is a real actor. For Newman's Fast Eddie, the sight of this naive, naturally talented kid at his game is "like watching home movies." Eddie, too, shot pool at first for the pure pleasure of playing. Learning to win or "dump" the game for money came later. Disillusion forced him to hang up his cue stick twenty-five years ago. Now a glib liquor salesman in Chicago, he stakes Cruise to a big bucks nine-ball tournament in Atlantic City, only to wind up taking on the kid himself. The pungent debut screenplay of novelist Richard (*The Wanderers*) Price hits a provocative high in showing how Newman wins back his innocence and passion for the game by corrupting Cruise. Director Martin (*Raging Bull*) Scorsese is peerless at mining the streaks of courage and excellence that might redeem such low-life sleaze. And Scorsese again proves himself a master with actors. Mary Elizabeth Mastrantonio (Al Pacino's sister in *Scarface*) deserved her Oscar nomination too, as Cruise's gold-digging girlfriend. "You're a hard broad," Newman tells her with undisguised admiration; she's also vividly smart, sexy, and a future star. Helen (*Desert Hearts*) Shaver shines as Newman's barkeep lady; their turning a discussion about omelets into a seduction is an erotic howl. Okay, you can carp. The later pool scenes lose their snap, and the ending seems more appropriate to *Rocky* than a no-bull drama. But the invigorating match of Newman and Cruise going at each other with full force makes *The Color of Money* a good movie bet.

R / 1986 / Warner

▲ THE COLOR PURPLE

Carrying to extremes the Mary Poppins dictum that "a spoonful of sugar makes the medicine go down," director Steven Spielberg has sprinkled the whole canister over his film version of Alice Walker's Pulitzer prizewinning novel. By pretti-fying or ignoring the poverty, racism, rape, incest, and lesbianism that course through Walker's stinging prose, Spielberg has made a movie your Aunt Fanny can see without blushing. Perhaps that was his intention. Despite the success of the book, films about the black experience in Georgia at the turn of the century don't exactly guarantee box office. So Spielberg made compromises, apparently to gain wider acceptance. There is much that entertains, entrances, and electrifies in the film. That's true at least if you can ignore Spielberg's cloying, calendar-art lyricism, outrageously overdrawn performances (Adolph Caesar, Dava Ivey) and Quincy Jones's poundingly obtrusive score. To his credit, however, he knows how to hook an audience. We meet Celie, the central character, at 14. And Spielberg gives the scenes of childhood (no one is better with young actors) a shattering poignance. Already Celie has had two children by a man she believes is her father, had her babies sold off to African missionaries, and been traded in marriage to a widower with four kids and a penchant for cruelty that includes separating her from her beloved sister. Newcomer Desreta Jackson plays the young Celie, and she is heartbreaking. The older Celie is played by comic actress Whoopi Goldberg in a justly celebrated screen debut (the National Board of Review named her 1985's best actress). Through her resplendent smile and wounded eyes, we see clearly a world that Menno Mayjes's screenplay barely hints at. Whoopi is a wow. It is too bad that Spielberg shies away from Celie's lesbian affair with her husband's lover, a beautiful blues singer deftly played by Margaret Avery. The relationship had less to do with sex than caring (men had only abused Celie), but the point—a major one—is lost onscreen. Spielberg's fabric-softener approach also hurts the work of the talented Danny (*Silverado*) Glover as Celie's husband. His last-minute transformation to goody-goody just won't wash. Talk show host Oprah Winfrey, another Oscar nominee, comes through as a vital, vigorous source of joy as Celie's liberated friend. Winfrey and Goldberg give the movie a sense of pride that is the film's final glory. When all the arguments end over whether Spielberg can make a serious movie or not (a silly debate really—*E.T.* was a serious and great movie)—that pride at least will make *The Color Purple* endure.

PG-13 / 1985 / Warner

▲ COMA

Coma did for hospitals what *Psycho* did for motels. Genevieve Bujold and Michael Douglas are surgeons at a respectable hospital in Boston (the city where Dr. Robin Cook, whose novel the film comes from, practiced ophthalmology). When a friend of Bujold's is admitted for routine surgery and suffers brain death, her suspicions are aroused. Through a labyrinth of computer files and cadaver-stocked labs, she pursues a mastermind who is guilty of both murder and a gruesome traffic in human organs. Authentic direction and screenplay by (Dr.) Michael Crichton and excellent performances are guaranteed to chill the blood.
PG / 1978 / MGM/UA

▲ COME BACK TO THE 5 AND DIME, JIMMY DEAN, JIMMY DEAN

Robert Altman, who after directing *M*A*S*H* and *Nashville* hardly earned a kind word for his movies, tried this as a Broadway play. When it closed—the reviews were widely hostile—he moved the production to a Manhattan movie studio and made this low-budget screen version on 16-mm film (blown up to 35 mm for theaters) in nineteen days. The trite story by Ed Graczyk still revolves around three lonely women in a small Texas town for the twentieth reunion of their teenage James Dean fan club. All have secrets, which are revealed as they carouse in the dime store that used to double as their clubhouse. The revelations, however, are alternately banal and unbelievable, and the frequent flashbacks from 1975 to 1955 are disconcerting. But Altman gets lively performances from a terrific cast. Hiding personal tragedy behind a facade of snappy patter, Cher is pure dynamite in the role that proved she really could act. And her comic byplay with sexy Karen Black and dowdy Sandy Dennis is a constant joy, especially when they indulge in an impromptu chorus of the McGuire Sisters hit, "Sincerely." A first-rate supporting cast, including Kathy Bates, Sudie Bond, and Marta Heflin, act as if they were performing in art instead of twaddle. And darn if they don't make us believe it, too, until the dime store melodramatics of the finale. Fault Altman if you must for his choice of material, but *Jimmy Dean* proves again that

he is without peer in bringing out the best in actors.
PG / 1982 / Embassy

▲ COMES A HORSEMAN

Somewhere deep inside the lavish, lumbering, modern-day Western (set in 1945) lurks a nice, simple movie trying to get out. Director Alan (*All the President's Men*) Pakula gussied it up with a lush Michael Small score, gorgeous Gordon Willis cinematography, and big bankable stars— Jane Fonda, James Caan, and Jason Robards. Fonda is fine as a stoic rancher battling change, and Caan is likably laconic as her business partner–lover, but Robards glowers his way through the role of the villain. The pace is agonizingly slow. The only reward for staying awake is the Oscar-nominated supporting performance of old-timer Richard Fransworth as the bunk-house philosopher. He's the diamond in a heap of dross.
PG / 1978 / CBS/Fox

▲ COMING HOME

Jane Fonda put this movie where her mouth was. Directed by Hal Ashby, *Coming Home* is a poignant love story with a political message wherein Fonda is married to the ever-neurotic Bruce Dern, this time playing a Marine captain whose fondest dream is to bring home a Commie machine gun from Vietnam. While he's away waging war, she's at home raising consciousness in a veterans' hospital. There she meets and falls in love with Jon Voight. The difficulties and confrontations that ensue when her husband returns from that war are predictable but powerful, the resolution less so. Voight, as a wheelchair-bound lifer, turns in a wonderfully touching performance. Fonda is Fonda: If you like her, you'll love her. Both Fonda and Voight won Oscars for their portrayals.
R / 1978 / CBS/Fox

▲ COMMANDO

Overheard in the crowd after a packed theater showing of this Arnold Schwarzenegger's expedition: "He makes Rambo look like Peter Pan."

"I think he's cute." "I think he looks like a tree trunk." "Didn't you love the scene where he dangled the guy over the cliff?" "No, I loved it when he jammed that hot steam pipe through the other guy's chest." "It wasn't as good as *The Terminator*. I don't like it when Arnold plays the good guy." "Good? Whaddaya talking about? He slaughters about three hundred people." "I know, but he's doing it to save his daughter." "Why did they make him talk? He can't talk." "It was funny when Arnold shot one guy and said, 'Don't bother him, he's dead tired.' " "That was funny? I bet you think Pee-wee Herman's a riot." "Terrific special effects, huh?" "Did you wear your glasses? The army that blew up in the end was cardboard." "What was it about?" "Don't be cute. It had a perfectly plausible plot: Arnold gets mad and wipes out the world. It's the same plot as *Conan the Barbarian*." "You saw *Conan*? I don't know why I go out with you." "Who was the girl in it?" "That was Rae Dawn Chong. Remember her in *Quest for Fire?*" "Yeah, I like her. She's talented. Great legs, too. Wonder who made her do this." "I told you we should have seen *Plenty*." "I want to see this again." "I hear the critics hated it." "Critics? With movies like this who cares about critics?" No argument.
R / 1985 / CBS/Fox

▲ THE COMPANY OF WOLVES

Some werewolf movies are a scream. Some are a howl. This one is a snore. The only aspect of the movie even remotely interesting lies in wondering what ever possessed Angela Lansbury to appear in it. She plays an old granny who lives in the middle of the woods—rocking, knitting, and muttering about how nasty men are. The beneficiary of Lansbury's advice is Sarah Patterson, who plays her granddaughter. She is a brooding sort, a neurotic Little Red Riding Hood, complete with red shawl, goody basket, and weird thoughts. Screenwriter Angela Carter and director–co-screenwriter Neil Jordan may have had some notion of making this horror film a metaphor about the relationship between men and women. But any sense they were trying to make is buried under all the Gothic sets, incessant scurrying about, and murky forests full of extraneous animals (you can't take a step without happening upon a rat, toad, snake, owl, rabbit, or weasel, not to mention the pack of wolves with glowing eyes). The film also has the most idiotic special effects this side of *Cat People,* with werewolves clawing their way out of their human forms. This process is neither scary nor interesting—it is just time-consuming and ineffably dull. That pretty well describes the whole movie.
R / 1985 / Vestron

▲ THE COMPETITION

Attempting a movie about a classical piano competition is akin to a box office death wish. (Editor's note: It was.) Still, *The Competition* mixes its music with a love story without compromising either. The film sets up Richard Dreyfuss, Amy Irving, and four other finalists in a race for a prize that can make a career. Dreyfuss, whose chances for success are running out at age 30, is desperate to win it. Irving, 21, is desperate to win him. Will she sacrifice her performance to get a man? The windup is predictable and a few of the subplots are numbingly so, yet writer-director Joel Oliansky successfully evokes the pressure-ridden world of the concert stage. Dreyfuss forsakes his usual cutesy mannerisms in his toughest work since *Duddy Kravitz,* and Irving complements him nicely. Also fine are Lee Remick as Irving's tart-tongued teacher and Sam Wanamaker as an egotistical conductor. But the movie's heart is its music.
PG / 1981 / RCA/Columbia

▲ COMPROMISING POSITIONS

The mystery-comedy was a staple of movies of the '30s and '40s. Think of *The Thin Man* or *The Falcon* series, or Van Heflin in *Grand Central Murder*. Then television, from "Mr. and Mrs. North" to "McMillan and Wife," pretty much exhausted the genre in much the same way it exhausted the Western. That's why it comes as such a pleasant surprise to see this breezy whodunit about the murder of a philandering Long Island dentist. Most of its charm comes from its cast, headed by Susan Sarandon as an ex-reporter-turned-housewife-turned-amateur-detective. Raul Julia appears as a homicide cop, Edward Herrmann as Sarandon's lawyer husband, and Judith Ivey as a wisecracking artist who thinks any woman not having an adulterous affair is peculiar. Susan

Isaacs' script, adapted from her 1978 novel, simultaneously manages to build suspense and stay playful. She allows a bantering attraction to develop between Sarandon and Julia. There's also an effectively biting scene between Sarandon and Herrmann, who wishes his wife would spend more time on her cooking and less on her sleuthing. Director Frank Perry too often lets the comedy overwhelm the mystery, going for broad caricatures and dwelling on lines that would have been a lot better off thrown away. Still, if you want something a little sexier and a lot better acted than anything you're likely to see on television in the next 90 minutes, here is a diverting escape.
R / 1985 / Paramount

▲ CONAN THE BARBARIAN

In that troublesome epoch after the successful quest for fire but before the invention of the Franklin stove, a young boy's parents in some unspecified but obviously evil-ridden land are slaughtered by marauders. The lad grows up to be a kind of comic book hero called Conan (Arnold Schwarzenegger). He's a sixty-watt bulb even in these Dark Ages; but boy, does he have muscles! He uses them to dice and slice his way ever nearer Thulsa Doom (James Earl Jones), who when not pillaging finds time to head up both a legion of flower children and a cult of snake worshippers. When not vacillating between unintentional humor and gory special effects, director John (*The Wind and the Lion*) Milius replicates scenes from such disparate predecessors as *Raiders of the Lost Ark, Demetrius and the Gladiators, Blazing Saddles,* and *The Seven Samurai.* When does homage become cribbing? Of the players, James Earl hams it up grandly, and the sinuous dancer Sandahl Bergman is smashing as Valeria, Conan's decidedly unbarbaric love. Schwarzenegger comes across like iron-deficient white bread. An epilogue announced there would be sequels. Sadly, the epilogue wasn't lying.
R / 1982 / MCA

▲ CONAN THE DESTROYER

Glistening, grunting, and groaning across the screen, Arnold Schwarzenegger stars in this sequel to *Conan the Barbarian.* This time he plays Conan with a sense of humor—he even manages to get drunk. Conan is enlisted by a wicked queen, Sarah Douglas, to accompany her virgin niece on a long, perilous journey to recover a precious magical horn. What Conan doesn't know is that both he and the niece, Olivia D'Abo, are going to get knocked off once they do the job. Schwarzenegger has a real cast of characters to help him out: Wilt Chamberlain, the former basketball great, makes his film debut as a towering (naturally—he's more than seven feet tall) bodyguard with bad intentions; disco singer Grace Jones, in her first film, is sleek and dangerous as a female warrior who is very handy with a pole; Mako, the friendly wizard in the first *Conan,* again plays a seer; and Tracey Walter is cast as the seemingly cowardly sidekick who always comes through in the pinch. The result is surprisingly funny—some of the gag lines could work for Johnny Carson if he pumped a little iron, and others are so dumb they're hilarious. Obviously director Richard Fleischer and screenwriter Stanley Mann are playing for laughs, and they fill the screen with wall-to-wall fun—the action is large-scale, the plot is suitably fantastic, and the climax, a fight to the death between Conan and a god brought back to life (the monster was designed by *E.T.* creator Carlo Rambalki), is slam-bang. Someday they're going to pit Conan against Rocky. Then we'll really see some biceps.
PG / 1984 / MCA

▲ THE CONCRETE JUNGLE

Sleazy, sickeningly exploitative, and made on the very cheap, this film uses one of America's most painful problems—its prison system—solely as an excuse to parade out scenes of sadism, degradation, and sex. It's all beneath contempt, of course, but what fun! Directed by Tom (*Prison Girls*) De Simone, it stars Jill St. John (R.J. Wagner's favorite lady) as a women's prison warden, Nita (*Bundle of Joy*) Talbot as her deputy and, as the inmates' "queen," Barbara (*The Devil at 4 O'Clock*) Luna, whose presence makes the joint look more like a home for aging starlets than a penal institution. Peter (TV's "Lawman") Brown appears as a drug smuggler who talks his young girlfriend, Tracy (*Happy Birthday to Me*) Bregman, into a smuggling attempt that lands her in prison. She is sentenced to one to three years and, apparently, to having her clothes ripped off by anyone who's in the mood, which, in this

place, is just about everyone. There are sexual assaults, razor fights, foul language, and even fouler writing, by Alan (*Parasite*) Adler. It lasts only 106 minutes, but trash haters may find it seems like a life sentence.
R / 1982 / RCA/Columbia

▲ CONFIDENTIALLY YOURS

No director took such obvious joy in making films as François Truffaut. This case in point, his last movie, is a black-and-white mystery that seems a homage to the French *film noirs* and the work of Truffaut's idol, Alfred Hitchcock. It is a loose-jointed, funny, quietly sexy romp. Jean-Louis Trintignant plays a real estate broker whose hunting companion and slutty wife are murdered within a few hours of each other. Since the hunting pal was the wife's lover, there is only one suspect. Trintignant's secretary, Fanny Ardant, has no doubt that he is guilty, but she loves him so she spends the rest of the movie trying to save him. More bodies turn up. A cop with an inferiority complex takes on the case. New suspects materialize, among them a priest, a pimp, and a movie-theater cashier. Plausibility is not the point; fugitive Trintignant, for instance, spends most of his time hiding in his own office, hardly the most plausible refuge. Truffaut and co-writers Suzanne Schiffman and Jean Aurel, though, let everyone in on their conceit: Events don't have to be true to life as long as they're true to the tone of the movie. Things whiz to a satisfying but unsurprising climax that includes one of many Hitchcockian touches, the police inspector discussing dinner with his wife (see *Dial M for Murder* or *Frenzy*). Francis Coppola, among others, might learn a lesson from this film: A director does not have to make a profound statement every time he rolls his camera. Sometimes it is sufficient just to have a good time. (In French with very bad subtitles: "Cannon" becomes "canon," "nice" becomes "niece," and the French word for sweat, transpiration, becomes "transpiration"—valid English but hardly idiomatic.)
PG / 1984 / Key

▲ CONTINENTAL DIVIDE

For a situation comedy with very little situation, this is quite a charming film. The premise is flimsy going on invisible: A muckraking Chicago reporter, John Belushi, is beaten up by corrupt cops, and his unusually sympathetic editor sends him on working R&R to Wyoming to do a story on a woman ornithologist, Blair (*Altered States*) Brown. Based in a lonely cabin in the Rockies, Brown is a tough bird herself, though inevitably she and Belushi get together. The screenplay is by the gifted Larry Kasdan (two years later he really hit paydirt with *The Big Chill*). He's a little on the sluggish side with his romantic comedy repartee, however—exchanges end with an "Oh, yeah?", a "Really!" or a cuss word just about as often as they do with a punch line. That leaves director Michael (*Coal Miner's Daughter*) Apted obliged to devote considerable attention to his majestic location (near Canon City, Colorado). He also does a lot of zooming in on footage of bald eagles soaring, swooping, and otherwise behaving like refugees from a dollar bill. Belushi was an adequate actor and a great physical comedian who could turn slamming his thumb with a hammer into a one-act play. Brown is winsome with her straight lines. Even if the ending drags on a little, the most hard-boiled of moviegoers are likely to shed a sentimental tear or two over the romance of it all.
PG / 1981 / MCA

▲ CONVOY

C. W. McCall's 1976 record smash was a lively trucker's anthem that helped galvanize the CB craze. But director Sam (*The Wild Bunch, Straw Dogs*) Peckinpah, with surprising lack of invention, turned it into a modern-day Western: Covered wagons were replaced by eighteen-wheelers, and the good-hearted outlaws evolved into truckers. Indeed, what's best about the movie is the trucks, huge and sinister beasts rumbling through glorious New Mexican landscapes. The action sequences are pure if relatively tame Peckinpah (no one is even killed), but the screenplay is a cliché-ridden imitation of Steven Spielberg's *Sugarland Express*. Kris Kristofferson's ponderous performance as the leader of what becomes a social protest movement is reminiscent of Jeffrey Hunter wondering how Christ should behave in *King of Kings*. And never has an actress chosen an emptier comeback vehicle than Ali MacGraw. This is one *Convoy* that went nowhere.
PG / 1978 / HBO/Cannon

▲ CORVETTE SUMMER

Vette enthusiasts should not get their hopes up, since this film bears the same relationship to sports cars that *Jaws* did to sharks—it's not for the serious student. The Corvette in question is saved from a junkyard and rebuilt—into better-than-mint condition—by a high school shop class, then stolen by a car-theft ring. That sends Mark Hamill, the class mechanic who has an almost abnormal passion for the car, in hot pursuit. The movie was shot before Hamill's *Star Wars* market value had risen enough to price him out of low-budget, drive-in fodder like this. So he can't really be blamed for the inane behavior he has to exhibit. Annie Potts, however, should have been boiled in artificial sweetener for her shudderingly bad try at playing a kookie but lovable, sexy but sweet would-be hooker who latches onto Hamill.
PG / 1978 / MGM/UA

▲ THE COTTON CLUB

Add this to the list of great movie opportunities missed. A speakeasy called the Cotton Club occupied a prime spot in Harlem from 1923 to 1936 (it's now a housing project). During these years the CC became a symbol for the Jazz Age. While the best black performers (Duke Ellington, Lena Horne, Cab Calloway) took the stage, the white proprietor, mobster Owney Madden, permitted only whites to sit at the club's cramped tables. The glitz-and-goons audience mixed the aristo-cracies of show-biz (Chaplin, Durante, Gloria Swanson) and crime (Dutch Schultz, "Mad Dog" Coll, "Lucky" Luciano). What a rich subject, especially for Francis Coppola, who had Mario (*The Godfather*) Puzo and Pulitzer Prize-winner William (*Ironwood*) Kennedy to collaborate with him on the story. A $47 million budget bought a star cast, headed by Richard Gere and Gregory Hines, and top technicians to get the look perfect. Well, the look is perfect. And the sound of that matchless pre-swing era music is mesmerizing. But what happened to plot, character, theme? Harlemites used to line up outside the club during the Depression to ogle the elite. Coppola, with all his budget, never shows any sense of the club's place within the black community. And the story is a mess—dozens of characters in a futile search for a connecting link. Gere is cast once again as a pretty boy, a cornet player going nowhere until he saves the life of Dutch Schultz. The mob boss hires him to escort his tough-cookie mistress, played flatly by Diane Lane, so Dutch's wife won't suspect he's playing around. Naturally Gere and Lane fall in love, but he's soon off to Hollywood where he becomes a star playing a gangster he models on Schultz. Gere's sex appeal might be an asset if he weren't so smug about it. Worse, his character has little to do with the Cotton Club. The movie is on more solid ground when it stays closer to the club. Hines is a marvel when he takes his taps to the floor with his brother Maurice and vet hoofer Charles "Honi" Coles, 72. The best acting is on the fringes. Bob Hoskins is smashingly effective as Madden, a gentle killer who loves horses, and Fred Gwynne makes something wonderfully touching out of Hoskins' henchman. But this gangster odd couple has the only involving rela-tionship in the film. And the movie's best direc-torial touch (an assassination intercut with a dance) is a near lift from the climax of *The Godfather*. Sadly, what could have redeemed Coppola only confirms his decline. *The Cotton Club* is a shell of a movie—dazzling on the surface but hollow at the core.
R / 1984 / Embassy

▲ COUNT DRACULA AND HIS VAMPIRE BRIDE

Christopher Lee, whose credits include *Dracula, Brides of Dracula, Dracula—Prince of Darkness, Dracula A.D. 1972, The Satanic Rites of Dracula,* and *Taste the Blood of Dracula,* was back to his old fly-by-night tricks. Peter Cushing, after going legit as the villain Grand Moff Tarkin in *Star Wars,* returns, too, as a new scion of the never-say-die Van Helsing family, which is to vampire extermination what the Heinzes are to catsup. Lee, having escalated his evildoing, plans bio-logical warfare, while Cushing, in addition to his standard kit of crucifixes, silver bullets, and wooden stakes, comes up with a new miracle ingredient: hawthorne bushes (potent since Jesus' crown of thorns derived from one). Not much else is changed, though, except that the violence is more graphic and the imperiled maidens are more nude. England's Hammer Films had long since drained the life out of this genre.
R / 1978 / N/A

▲ COUNTRY

As coproducer and star of *Country,* Jessica Lange shows a commitment to her subject—the plight of the contemporary American farm family—that infuses every frame. But don't fear a sincerity overdose. In fact, the film begins when Lange discovers a condom in her teenage son's room and tries to keep a straight face while confronting him. The kids in this Iowa family are as feisty as their crusty grandad, Wilford Brimley (who used a variation on the theme for TV's "Our House"). And though Lange shows deference to her husband, playwright-actor Sam Shepard, she's no doormat. Cooking breakfast with pink curlers in her hair, Lange is sassy and sexy. How refreshing to see a farm woman portrayed as something other than a taciturn drone. Real sparks fly between Lange and Shepard, and that's understandable considering their offscreen romantic relationship. While these early family scenes are wonderfully appealing, the film takes a serious turn when the federal government starts calling in loans it made to farmers. Shepard's frustrations lead him to drink and desertion. So Lange takes hold, rallying her children and the farm community. Red-faced from the cold, Lange delivers an eloquently powerful climactic explosion against injustice. But the film isn't always as surefooted. Reducing the government agency officials who force foreclosure to a collection of cardboard villains distorts a complex issue. The naiveté of farmers who buy more than they can afford is only suggested too. Perhaps *Country* was thrown off-kilter when screenwriter William Wittliff was replaced as director by Richard Pearce after Wittliff's differences with Lange and Shepard proved insurmountable. One fierce argument between Shepard and his son, beautifully played by Levi Knebel, has the disturbing primal edge often associated with the playwright's work. As an actor, Shepard is altogether remarkable in a difficult role. When he and Lange focus on the small details of farm life, they make *Country* come alive.

PG / 1984 / Touchstone

▲ COUP DE GRACE

There are two reasons to see this Franco-German movie. One is marginally historical—it portrays the long-forgotten skirmishes between Russian Bolsheviks and remnants of the German army in the Baltic states after World War I. The other is an effective performance by Margarethe von Trotta as a woman who turns Marxist after failing to seduce a German commander. (He seems to be a John Wayne sort, more interested in battles than blondes, though there are hints that he may be gay too.) Director Volker Schlondroff—von Trotta's husband, with credits like *A Free Woman* and *The Lost Honor of Katharina Blum*—has unclarified a lot of confusion. For one thing, why do the same characters speak French to each other one minute and German the next? *Magnifique? Nein.* With subtitles.

Unrated / 1976 / RCA/Columbia.

▲ CRACKERS

French director Louis Malle had at this point made four films in America. *Atlantic City* was oddly wonderful; *Pretty Baby* and *My Dinner with Andre* were oddly interesting. *Crackers* is just odd. The story: San Francisco layabouts Donald Sutherland, Sean Penn, Wallace Shawn, and Trinidad Silva decide to rip off pawnbroker pal Jack Warden. Meanwhile, when these Keystone Robbers aren't madly trying to crack safes, Shawn noshes on cat food, Penn plays the harmonica and dances at the same time, and Sutherland makes love with a meter maid on a horse's saddle. This is an intermittently amusing but puzzling film. Why did Malle bother?

PG / 1984 / MCA

▲ CREATOR

To call this movie harebrained would be an insult to rabbits everywhere. It is apparently supposed to be a subtly profound comedy about an old college biology professor, Peter O'Toole, who is trying to clone his long-dead wife. It comes across more as a silly combination of *Goodbye, Mr. Chips, Love Story,* and *Voodoo Man,* the 1944 horror howler in which Bela Lugosi keeps trying to revive his comatose Mrs. In this case, when the young girlfriend of the professor's student assistant has a stroke, it's clear that director Ivan Passer and screenwriter Jeremy Leven (a former neuropsychology fellow at Yale) can't decide whether they want a movie full of laughs

or one full of wisdom. What they end up with is one full of baloney, trashing such cast members as Vincent Spano as the student assistant, Mariel Hemingway as a ditzy girl in love with O'Toole, and David Ogden Stiers as the faculty bully. O'Toole, given frequent inane speeches about love and God, seems weary. His eyes are so often droopy, in fact, that the movie seems to be putting him to sleep. Why should he be any different from the rest of us?
R / 1985 / Thorn/EMI

▲ CREATURE

Not everything about this sci-fi space thriller seems stolen from 1979's *Alien*—some of it appears to have come from the two screen versions of *The Thing*. In the case of *Creature*, the crew of an American mission to one of Saturn's moons discovers the preserved bodies of beings that have been in hibernation for centuries, apparently building up their appetites for fresh meat. Sensing dinner time, one creature, who resembles *Alien*'s toothy monster down to the last drool, sets off to feast on the unknowing newcomers one by one. Luckily there's no character development to make us empathize with the crew, with includes a drippy corporate executive (Lyman Ward), a sexy doctor (Wendy Schall), and a security officer (Diane Salinger) who looks like Vampira. Co-writer/director William Malone's insipid script ignores futuristic technical lingo in favor of such lines as "Is anybody here?" "Where's Susan?" and "What's the matter with John?" Only Klaus Kinski brings any vitality to his role, zealously portraying a thoroughly frightened, slightly lecherous German scientist. Anyway, *Alien* fans should rightly resent their favorite monster being ripped off this way. It's a little like Macbeth showing up as a character on "The A-Team."
R / 1985 / Media

▲ CREEPSHOW

Directed by George (*Night of the Living Dead*) Romero and written by master of the macabre Stephen King, this anthology of five unrelated tales showcases the production design and special effects of Cletus Anderson and Tom Savini. The cast—which is twelve or thirteen cuts above what

this genre usually draws—includes Adrienne Barbeau, Hal Holbrook, Viveca Lindfors, E. G. Marshall, Leslie Nielson, Carrie Nye, and Fritz Weaver. The different segments are variations on a theme: about a murdered father returning from the grave to seek revenge, a sadistic husband who's out to punish his wife and her lover, a dumb farmer who discovers a dangerous meteorite, an old crate that holds a monster with a big appetite, and a rich man with a phobia about cockroaches. Marshall, as the buggy tycoon, provides the best performance, and author King, playing the farmer, is almost bad enough to be good. Romero's penchant for resuscitating corpses gets a little tedious. But *Creepshow*, given the genre, is all restraint, with no nudity, under-control gore, and a refreshing sense of understatement. Silence and uncertainty are, after all, much more terrifying than unrelenting hacking and chomping.
R / 1982 / Warner

▲ CREEPSHOW 2

With a little less sex and a lot less gore, the three segments in this mild chiller could have turned up on the syndicated TV series "Tales From the Darkside." No wonder, since that series's co-producer, George Romero wrote this screenplay. It is based on stories by Stephen King, but this collaboration has none of the inventive wit of the original King-Romero joint project *Creepshow*. (This one was directed by Romero protégé Michael Gornick.) In one segment Lois Chiles plays a woman who kills a hitchhiker in a hit-run accident. While there is a certain scary stubbornness to the victim's determination to haunt her, most of the goings-on in this film suggest routine movie-making. No film can be termed a shocker when its big surprise is the appearance of the sarong sweetie of the Crosby-Hope *Road* films, Dorothy Lamour. She and George Kennedy play owners of a small-town general store who are terrorized by three hoodlums until even their cigar store Indian statue—played by Dan Kamin in the most truly wooden performance of all time—seeks revenge. In the lame third segment, four college kids at a swimming hole encounter a carnivorous oil slick. King appears as a truck driver in one scene. But those who want to keep up with the King oeuvre may want to leave a light on so they can read one of his novels while watching this film. It's hardly worth devoting a whole attention span to.

R / 1987 / NA

▲ CRIA!

Prizewinning (Cannes and Berlin) Spanish filmmaker Carlos Saura gave his lady, Geraldine Chaplin, a most moving role as the fatally ill mother of 9-year-old Ana Torrent. The story unfolds in one sun-dappled summer of childhood, moving gracefully between tragedy and lyricism. (In Spanish with subtitles.)

PG / 1977 / N/A

▲ CRIMES OF PASSION

Within its 102 chaotic minutes, this film manages to arouse thoughts of Fellini, Bergman, Woody Allen, Hitchcock, *Deep Throat,* the Three Stooges, and your Uncle Ziggy's home movies. Occasionally it even arouses thoughts of what seems to be its point: preoccupation with sex. Directed by Ken Russell, the picture vacillates between giddy, nervous humor and bleak despair. Kathleen Turner plays a prim clothes designer who moonlights as an anything-goes hooker, not for the money but because she needs the attention. John Laughlin, a hunky young family man estranged from his wife, falls in love with Turner. Meanwhile, Anthony Perkins makes his *Psycho* character seem like the very model of well-adjusted humanity as he plays a would-be preacher whose prayers for Turner's lost soul are mixed with obscene remarks about her all-too-available body. Russell had to cut the film drastically to avoid an X rating, and he seems to have used a lawn mower on it. (Some sexually graphic scenes were restored for an expanded videotape version without clearing things up to any extent.) Characters and subplots disappear without explanation. Annie Potts as Laughlin's wife and Bruce Davison as his best friend are especially wasted. Russell seems to be trying to say something about society's hypocritical approach to sex. But like most Russell films, *Crimes of Passion* goes out of control; watching it is like trying to talk to someone in a fit of hysteria.

R / 1984 / New World

▲ CRIMES OF THE HEART

The last scene in this surprisingly arid film version of Beth Henley's 1980 Pulitzer prizewinning play shows Diane Keaton, Jessica Lange, and Sissy Spacek merrily grabbing at chunks of a birthday cake, gorging as if a prize awaited the one who gobbled the most. These powerhouse stars—playing sisters from Hazelhurst, Mississippi—go at the movie in the same way. In a year parched for all-out acting gusto, *Crimes* delivered a triple-threat display that fully deserves applause and awards. But the rest of the film is a mess. The seams in Henley's play (she did the adaptation) show up more glaringly when blown up to wide-screen size. Soap opera contrivances, crude flashbacks, and curled whimsy also blot the Southern Gothic landscape. But Henley's saving grace is her antic humor. Her McGrath sisters laugh to keep from toppling into an abyss of misfortune. Keaton, offering her strongest work in years, is the eldest sibling. She alone takes responsibility for her hospitalized granddaddy (Hurd Hatfield) and bemoans the "shrunken ovary" she thinks has shrunk her chances with a mail-order beau. Lange, never sexier, is the middle sister, a failed singer just returned from Hollywood and a psychiatric ward. Spacek, wonderfully funny and touching, is the baby who has just shot her politician husband in the stomach because she "didn't like his looks." (He didn't like her sneaking off with a 15-year-old black boy.) The girls' problems are complicated by the memory of a mother who hung herself and the family cat with a note explaining, "I had a bad day." Slack direction leaves the job of making us care for these oddballs to the actors, who do the job proud. We cheer when Keaton tells off her pushy cousin, played to a bitchy fare-thee-well by Tess Harper, and takes charge of her life. We're moved when Lange spends a night with her old boyfriend, acted with devilish charm by her real-life housemate Sam Shepard, and finds he doesn't want her back. And we're tickled when the guileless Spacek starts up a flirtation with her straight-arrow lawyer (David Carpenter), while facing a rap for adultery and attempted murder. As long as you don't expect miracles (it's a good, not great, movie from a good, not great, play), you'll find *Crimes of the Heart* a tangy movie treat.

PG-13 / 1986 / Karl-Lorimar

▲ CRITICAL CONDITION

The title is appropriate; this movie is ailing. It gets off to a healthy start, weakens midway, then limps to clichéd conclusion. Richard Pryor plays an eccentric entrepreneur who visits a loan shark to borrow $50,000, finds himself the center of a sting operation, and lands in prison. Faking insanity, he is transferred to the psychiatric ward of a New York City hospital just before a blackout sends the hospital into chaos. While Pryor is trying to escape, a fetching hospital administrator, played by Rachel Ticotin, mistakes him for a much-needed doctor and enlists his aid. Only Pryor could pull off the frenetic phony physician as he flimflams his way from ER to OR. He is befriended by hip orderly Ruben Blades, collides with head honcho Joe Mategna, and battles Bob Dishy, who will leave you in stitches as a doctor with malpractice phobia. As Pryor contemplates operating on a patient with a spinal injury, Dishy warns, "We can't expose the central nervous system to a lawsuit." Later, when a psychotic killer takes Ticotin hostage, the film becomes predictable and as funny as a fatal disease, with no real suspense to fill the gaps. The porous script, written by brothers Denis and John Hamill, newspaper writers whose collaborations include *Turk 182!,* leaves talented British director Michael Pated operating without an instrument.

R / 1987 / Paramount

▲ CROCODILE DUNDEE

Paul Hogan proved to be the biggest thing to come out of Australia since the winged keel. He had been best known in this country for the Australian tourism TV commercials. But in his own country Hogan was a media hero. It's easy to see why from this, his first feature movie: He gives one of the most likable performances of many a movie year. As the title character, Hogan plays a notorious croc poacher whose idea of civilization is a seedy pub in the middle of nowhere. A determined New York reporter, played by sexy stage actress Linda Kozlowski, seeks him out for an interview, and he takes her on a two-day trek through Australia's rugged back country. She talks him into going to New York, where the predictable pratfalls ensue (he is, for instance, propositioned by a man in drag). Most

of the movie is a showcase for his humor and her body. It's actually Hogan, though, who sustains the film by his considerable charm and swagger, disarming Kozlowski and everybody else. You can't help having a g'day at this one, mate.

PG-13 / 1986 / Paramount

▲ CROSS CREEK

Overly romantic and full of implicit announcements by director Martin (*Norma Rae*) Ritt that here is an independent-woman-before-it-was-fashionable movie, this is still an ultimately satisfying experience. It is based on the memoirs of novelist Marjorie Kinnan Rawlings. She was so determined to become an author that she retreated to an isolated Florida orange plantation in 1928 to write gothic novels. Her newsman husband accompanied her but soon left Rawlings to her new backwoods neighbors, who eventually inspired her most famous novel, *The Yearling*. Mary (*Melvin and Howard*) Steenburgen plays Rawlings, who died in 1953, with a remarkable combination of strength and vulnerability. Peter (*E.T.*) Coyote is warmly effective as the Cross Creek, Florida, hotel man Rawlings married. Two supporting performances were so good they won Oscar nominations: Alese Woodard as a servant and Rip Torn as the neighbor whose daughter became the model for Jody, the young hero of the *The Yearling*. Still, Ritt gets carried away with all this backwoods lyricism, crossing the line from idyllic to icky-poo. He comes off like a cinematic version of the French primitive painter Henri Rousseau, all agog at the purity of untamed nature.

PG / 1983 / Thorn/EMI

▲ CROSSED SWORDS

A run-of-the mill remake of Mark Twain's *The Prince and the Pauper,* this film seems to have been shot with leftover costumes, sets, and actors from the Richard Lester *Musketeer* movies. Apparently there wasn't any leftover humor. Twain's conceit is amusing enough, but Mark Lester's insipid performance in the film's dual central roles—as look-alikes at opposite echelons of the feudal system—cheats the script out of possible laughs. On the other hand, Oliver Reed is splendid as a lusty nobleman, Rachel Welch makes every effort to burst out of a dress several sizes too small, and George C. Scott does a nice turn as an outlaw chieftain.

PG / 1978 / N/A

▲ CROSS OF IRON

Gore fans will relish this classic of bunker madness expertly directed by Sam Peckinpah (*The Wild Bunch, Straw Dogs, The Getaway*). Machine-gun-ripped bodies and severed heads bounce to the tune of artillery fire as good Nazi James Coburn, leader of a retreating German platoon on the Russian front, bickers with bad Nazi Maximilian Schell, a lame aristocrat angling for an Iron Cross.

R / 1977 / Media

▲ CROSSOVER DREAMS

This pointed, perceptive comedy about a struggling Latin musician who signs a lucrative pop recording contract says a lot with little strokes of action and dialogue. Its protagonist, a talented "New Yorican" singer-songwriter, played by real-life salsa virtuoso Ruben Blades, has a manager, Frank Robles, who doubles as a furniture salesman. When Robles sends his client off to an audition with a sleazy record producer, Blades plans to take the subway, but his manager won't hear of it. "Today you ride a cab," he says grandly, then doles out four dollars. "If it's more than four dollars, get out of the cab." Leon Ichaso, a former advertising executive who directed the movie and wrote it with Manuel Arce, deftly shows that the big-time producer (Joel Diamond) who signs Blades is no more heartless and grasping than Blades himself. The difference is that when the singer's debut album flops and goes on sale for $1.99, the slick producer has other acts to exploit while Blades has nowhere to go but back to the old neighborhood to face the people he rejected. This, in the end, saves his soul. Moving as briskly and fluently as the salsa beat itself, the movie wears its Faustian mantle lightly. Among an exceptional cast, including Elizabeth Pena as the singer's long-suffering girl-

friend, Blades proves himself a natural in his screen debut. His innocence and charm are as well outlined as his callousness; he makes clear the cruel tug of war between ethnic identity and the hunger for outside validation.

Unrated / 1985 / Thorn/EMI

▲ CROSSROADS

You can tell what's wrong with *Crossroads* when you try to describe it to friends. Midway through a plot description, their eyes glaze over. That's a shame. *Crossroads* is such a well-intentioned film, you wish it were more substantial. At its best it's a musical drama that feasts upon the folklore of the blues, in this case pacts that musicians Robert Johnson and Willie Brown made with the devil at a Mississippi crossroads in the '30s. Fifty years later Joe Seneca, as Brown, and Ralph (*The Karate Kid*) Macchio, as his young white protégé, make an impromptu pilgrimage from New York City to that Mississippi site. As the title suggests, what matters more than the trip is the convenient metaphor: At this fabled intersection, rites of manhood are fulfilled. Macchio seeks the worldly experience that will let him master the blues, while Seneca seeks an absolution of his past. Debut screenwriter John Fusco and director Walter (*48 Hrs.*) Hill have made the material accessible but not involving, despite some strong blues compositions by Ry Cooder. Macchio undercuts his blind enthusiasm with a street-smart delivery. In Seneca, Hill found a picture-perfect actor. His whiskey voice, salt-and-pepper beard, and seasoned countenance lend authority to the film. If only *Crossroads* didn't lead him and its audience to a dead end.

R / 1986 / RCA/Columbia

▲ CRUISING

Appropriately framed by opening and closing shots of a garbage scow, *Cruising* is trash. Al Pacino seems as confused as any viewer will be in trying to make sense of his role as a rookie cop sent out to decoy a psychopathic killer of homosexuals. In Gerald Walker's novel, the Pacino character struggles with his own repressed homosexual tendencies until they explode in vio-

lence. But director William (*Exorcist*) Friedkin ignores any psychological motivation in favor of graphically exploitative scenes in the sadomasochistic nether world (e.g., embarrassing symbolic shots like a knife cutting into rare steak and two lit cigarettes burning on the ground). Had gay activists not stirred such a ruckus during the filming in New York, this distasteful portrayal of gay life-styles would have been justifiably ignored back in 1980. Best to keep it forgotten now.
R / 1980 / CBS/Fox

▲ CUBA

What starts as an intriguing story about love and politics in pre-Castro Cuba quickly bogs down in a tedious, cliché-ridden muddle. Sean Connery plays a soldier of fortune hired to help rid the island of Fidel's guerrillas. Brooke Adams, his onetime lover now married into the Cuban oligarchy, is unhappy because her husband, Chris Sarandon, is a philanderer. Sean soon distracts her from that problem. Then as the Batista regime crumbles he tries to get her out of Cuba. At this point the movie begins to resemble a James Bond thriller, with tank fights and other pyrotechnics. Director Richard Lester's customary sure touch lapses into moralizing. Castro's troops are portrayed as saints, while Batista's are all nincompoops and worse. The photography by David Watkin is superb—the movie was shot in Spain and it's lushly beautiful. And there are two fine supporting performances: Denholm Elliott plays a British gunrunner with a lovely mix of cynicism and swagger and Lonette McKee is convincingly sluttish as a factory worker. The rest of the movie would qualify it as the worst ever about Cuba if Omar Sharif's *Che!* hadn't been there first.
R / 1979 / Key

▲ CUJO

As films of unrelenting, throat-tightening terror go, this one makes *The Birds* seem like a mere gathering of friends of a feather. It makes *Jaws* seem like a movie about a mischievous fish. Taken from Stephen King's novel of the same title, *Cujo* is all the more remarkable because the menace involved is a Saint Bernard, one of those big, cuddly, lovable pooches who wouldn't hurt a flea and would walk a thousand miles through a blizzard to bring you a keglet of brandy. The catch is that rabies has turned this Saint Bernard into a fearsome monster. Most of the movie takes place in and around a disabled car inside which the dog has besieged Dee Wallace, best known as *E.T.*'s adopted mom, and Danny Pintauro, then 6, whose performance as Wallace's son is astonishingly mature. The car has broken down in a run-down, deserted mechanic's yard, and director Lewis Teague succeeds in building up a mood of claustrophobia and mounting panic as the heat and fear escalate inside the car. That Wallace has been having an affair with a local carpenter, played by her real-life husband Christopher Stone, adds some metaphysical overtones. Are she and her son being punished somehow for her guilt? The common, familiar nature of the setting, the people, the dog, the emotions make it easy to become involved in this grueling but engrossing kind of entertainment. The film was rated R, and despite its 6-year-old star, no one under 10 should be allowed to see it.
R / 1983 / Warner

▲ CUTTER'S WAY

Early in 1981, as *Cutter and Bone,* this cult film was generally panned and was yanked by United Artists before most of the country got to judge for themselves. Later that same year it was re-released with a supposedly less gruesome title (the old one did suggest a surgical training film). While the movie wasn't so worthless it deserved such short shrift in its first incarnation, it isn't a born-again classic, either. Ivan Passer, a Czech who previously directed five obscure features in this country, fails to make the story, which is about some quirky southern Californians caught up in a murder, either coherent or suspenseful. John Heard, however, delivers a performance that is at once witty and moving as Cutter, a crippled, half-blind, alcoholic Vietnam vet. Lisa Eichhorn, as Cutter's long-suffering wife, and Jeff Bridges, as a sometime gigolo named Bone, are both appealing too. But cutting through the murkiness may be more effort than it's worth for most viewers.
R / 1981 / MGM/UA

D

▲ DAMIEN—OMEN II

Unfortunately for all of us, though Gregory Peck tried to kill the little devil back in the original *Omen*—one of 1976's biggest movies—young Damien Thorn survived and now lives with his aunt (Lee Grant) and uncle (William Holden) in Chicago. Aided by a splendidly evil blackbird, Damien (Jonathan Scott-Taylor) dispatches almost every major character—sometimes ingeniously but always predictably.
R / 1978 / CBS/Fox

▲ DAMNATION ALLEY

Nuclear war is only marginally a more terrible threat than inane screenwriters who essay the subject. This time three Air Force men (Jan-Michael Vincent, Paul Winfield, and George Peppard, who affects a hilarious southern accent) set off across World War III-devastated America. They're heading, for unfathomable reasons, for Albany, New York. Along the way they pick up Dominique Sanda, a chanteuse stranded in Las Vegas, and fight off giant scorpions, killer cockroaches, and crazed desperadoes. There are some spectacular visual effects and an interesting "Land Master" vehicle, but mostly unintentional laughs.
PG / 1977 / Key

▲ DANCE WITH A STRANGER

In 1955 a woman named Ruth Ellis tracked down David Blakely, her race-car driver boyfriend, at a London pub. Outside in the fog she removed a gun from her purse and shot him dead. "Go and call the police" was all she said to the shocked witnesses. Ellis was convicted of murder and hanged in Holloway prison, the last woman to be executed in Great Britain. This film, directed by Mike Newell, examines the emotions behind the case, and not since *Room at the Top* has there been such a sizzlingly sexual bundle from Britain. Newell and his remarkable screenwriter, Shelagh Delaney, probe the class structure that doomed these two lovers. Ellis, as played by Miranda Richardson, is a working-class blonde itching to break into the Establishment. One night the wealthy young Blakely wanders into the nightclub where she's a hostess. He's taken with her smoky sensuality. She can't keep her hands off his body or her mind off what he represents. But the rigid social structure of the '50s makes a lasting union impossible. Blakely escapes into cars and drink. Rupert Everett, so good in *Another Country,* plays this weak character with ruthless honesty and an erotic languor. Richardson does startling things to help us see inside Ellis. In one scene, Blakely drives her to his family's estate and then loses his nerve about introducing her. Ellis catches only a glimpse of the gentrified life she wants so passionately. Richardson, without dialogue, renders her character's feelings faultlessly. She is smashing. So is the film.
R / 1985 / Vestron

▲ DANIEL

If good intentions were enough for a movie, *Daniel* would be an instant classic. Instead, Sidney (*The Verdict*) Lumet's adaptation of the 1971 E. L. Doctorow novel is a major disappointment. Part political drama, part history lesson, part crash course in parent-child psychology, this film is an unsatisfying hodgepodge. Doctorow's screenplay is a compare-and-contrast exercise between two generations of an American Jewish family. Mandy (*Ragtime*) Patinkin and Lindsay Crouse play fictionalized versions of Julius and Ethel Rosenberg, the American Communists executed in 1953 for conspiring to sell atomic secrets to the Russians. As Lumet presents them, the couple are dedicated, sincere activists; he coyly sidesteps the still-controversial question of their guilt. But twenty years after the couple's death, their children cannot withstand the burden of their notoriety. Their son, Timothy Hutton, has become a self-absorbed grad student, while daughter Amanda Plummer is a nerve-racked anti-Vietnam War protester obsessed with her parents' memory. Like Stanley Kramer, who lapsed into such preachy films as *On the Beach* and *Ship of Fools,* Lumet can be a causemonger. He dilutes

the drama of *Daniel* by embracing more issues than any film could possibly sustain. Among other things, Daniel tackles capital punishment, the right to privacy, ethnic-group assimilation, mental illness, and class warfare. And Lumet italicizes the issues' importance with a sanctimonious tone and a heavy-handed style: The film opens with an extreme close-up of Hutton lecturing the audience about forms of execution, a device returned to throughout the film. As the title character, Hutton is adrift in mannerisms; his performance lacks the intensity and resonance of his work in *Ordinary People* or *Taps*. There are overwrought supporting performances from Patinkin, Crouse, and particularly, from Plummer, who cannot overcome such deadening dialogue as "I forget what it is you're supposed to expect from being alive." Most of the time you feel like shouting: Off your soapbox, Sidney.
R / 1983 / Paramount

▲ DANTON

Andrzej Wajda, Poland's foremost director, fashioned this brilliant, hard-edged movie about the French Revolution. The time is 1793, the place is Paris, and the revolution, which started out with high hopes and the beheading of the king, is beginning to come apart. On one side is Robespierre, played by Polish actor Wojciech Pszoniak. He is first among equals, given to increasingly repressive measures as he sees the regime come under fire. His rival is Danton, a man of the people and the main threat to Robespierre's rule. They are on a collision course. As Danton, the loutish, swashbuckling popular hero, Gerard Dépardieu, is sensational. He plays the role broadly, recklessly. Beneath his goofy grin is the brain of a pure politician—and one who doesn't try to hide his lust for the good life, despite the professed ideals of the new egalitarian society. As Robespierre, Pszoniak is more than Dépardieu's match—his mannerisms, his movements all betray a man on the edge who, while coldly plotting the murders of his rivals, is also seemingly on the verge of a nervous breakdown. It's a bravura performance. The movie was shot in a kind of bold color that makes the action even more terrifying. There are, of course, unmistakable parallels to recent events in Poland. But this would not in any case be a cold, historical drama: It is like being face-to-face with the people who

have made history. It is intimate, exciting moviemaking. (In French with subtitles.)
PG / 1983 / RCA/Columbia

▲ DARBY O'GILL AND THE LITTLE PEOPLE

Faith and begorra, if it isn't Sean Connery, singin' the praises of Irish lassies in a brogue as thick as Irish stew. His own voice too! In this 1959 Disney film that later went into re-release, the pre-Bond Connery (who was 29 at the time) is an ingratiating romantic who can be outwitted by his ladylove (Janet Munro) and bloodied in a pub fight (he wins, but barely). Still, old Darby O'Gill (Albert Sharpe, the original Finian in Broadway's *Finian's Rainbow*) is the spark that makes the film burst with life—and imagination.
G / 1977 / Disney

▲ D.A.R.Y.L.

Combining suspense, science fiction, fantasy, and the formidable charms of a doe-eyed little boy, *D.A.R.Y.L.* stars Barret Oliver, then 11. Oliver (Wilford Brimley's grandson in *Cocoon*) is a skinny, strangely quiet kid who finds himself abandoned and with no recall of anything except his name, Daryl. At the start the boy narrowly escapes a high-speed chase on a treacherous mountain road. He is found in the forest and brought into a small town, where he is put in the care of a childless young couple, Michael McKean and Mary Beth Hurt. Surprisingly, Oliver adjusts effortlessly to his foster parents. In fact, there seems to be nothing he can't do. He dazzles his friends with his computer game wizardry, gives his math teacher a nervous tic because his answers are always correct, hits home runs in his first baseball game, and even makes his own bed. His foster mom begins to worry that "he doesn't seem to need anyone." In time, however, the once-distant Oliver becomes fiercely close to McKean and Hurt and to his mischievous best friend, played with wise-guy humor by Danny Corkill. Corkill shows Oliver the ropes, such as when he advises him to mess up sometimes. "Grown-ups like to feel they're making progress with you," he says. One day, though, Oliver is claimed by his "real" parents, actually a team of scientists working on a secret Pentagon project.

The boy learns his name is an acronym for Data Analyzing Robot Youth Lifeform. He is human, but his brain is microcomputer. His life turns into a high-tech nightmare as he is poked at and observed in his eerie, antiseptic room. When the scientists conclude that the boy has developed such emotions as anxiety and fear, the Pentagon brass decide to terminate him. One general says, "That's all right for America but hardly what we need at the Department of Defense." *D.A.R.Y.L.*'s script can be a little too cute—the malevolent military figures are hardly more than cardboard cutouts. Nonetheless, Australian director Simon Wincer, who has an easy technological fluency and a penchant for sneaky plot twists, pulls out the stops in building the suspense as Oliver attempts to escape. Though *D.A.R.Y.L.* stretches the limits of credibility, it is saved by Wincer's direction and by the warm, simple performances of McKean, Hurt, and especially Corkill and Oliver, two camera naturals, performing instinctively with poise and disarming humor. For moviegoers with sky-high imaginations and mushy hearts, *D.A.R.Y.L.* satisfies like a summertime chocolate-chip ice cream cone.
PG / 1985 / Paramount

▲ **DAS BOOT**

A German U-boat crew as the good guys? It's been decades since World War II, and this film was made in Germany. So the Jerries do come off as real people in this close-up look at life under the sea. Based on a novel by German submarine veteran Lothar-Gunther Buchheim, the film is relentlessly realistic. After setting out in 1941 and sinking an Allied tanker, the sub is ordered to make a suicidal run through the Strait of Gibraltar, then crawling with British patrol boats. Depth charges and tension follow. When American producers were thinking of making this movie, there was talk of either Paul Newman or Robert Redford in the lead role, played by Jurgen Prochnow. But even with the unknown German cast the film's claustrophobic atmosphere and mounting excitement proved a potent box-office lure, winning a much-coveted Oscar nomination for director Wolfgang Petersen. (In German with subtitles.)
Unrated 1982 / RCA/Columbia

▲ **DAWN OF THE DEAD**

More is definitely less when it comes to rending live bodies and cannibalism. That is the lesson of this sequel to *Night of the Living Dead*. Director George A. Romero unwittingly made a stomach-churning cult film back in 1968 but took a while to follow in the Hollywood tradition of "If at first you do succeed . . ." Like *Night, Dawn* was shot in and around Pittsburgh, this time largely at the $50 million Monroeville Mall shopping center. Romero was still using casts of unknowns, too, but in the black-and-white original, suspense and revulsion were nicely balanced. Here, the cascades of Technicolor gore become more numbing than disgusting.
Unrated / 1978 / Thore/EMI

▲ **DAY OF THE ANIMALS**

The script says all those bears, cougars, wolves, rattlesnakes, and eagles start attacking people because of radiation pouring through the depleted ozone layer. It seems more likely that they were outraged to be in a film so humiliating to animals that the ASPCA ought to use it at benefits. At that, the animals outperform the human cast of Lynda Day George and husband Christopher, Leslie Nielson, and Michael Ansara, who seems less concerned with fighting the beasts than with keeping his hair in place.
PG / 1977 / Media

▲ **DAYS OF HEAVEN**

No film has ever captured the beauty of the American plains better. Writer-director Terrence Malick, an ex-MIT philosophy lecturer whose only previous work was the acclaimed *Badlands,* set up one gorgeous scene after another: a train crossing a scaffold bridge silhouetted against the sky, threshers chomping through a gold-colored wheat field, an old farmer sitting wearily in front of a barn. They're portraits, gorgeously shot by Oscar winner Nestor Alemandros, and worthy of Fellini, Kubrick, or John Ford. But they're also incessant. Malick has trouble with his plot too. It's about a World War I–era ne'er-do-well (a miscast, method-acting Richard Gere) who flees Chicago from the Texas Panhandle, then talks

girlfriend Brooke Adams into marrying a terminally ill farm owner. Malick resorts to close-ups of Gere and the lovely Adams looking vacant, and he splashes on violence like hot sauce. While there are remarkable performances by Linda Manz, as Gere's tough-talking sister, and playwright Sam Shepard in his film acting debut as the farm owner, they only accentuate that, for all its prettiness, the film can't compete emotionally with the not dissimilar *Grapes of Wrath.*
PG / 1978 / Paramount

▲ D. C. CAB

No fare. Written and directed by Joel Schumacher, who wrote *Car Wash* and directed *The Incredible Shrinking Woman,* this film about a ramshackle taxi company in Washington was apparently supposed to be one of those jolly working-class rebel comedies. It's mostly a working-class mob scene, with jokes along the lines of "Albert doesn't have no political convictions; he's an American." The cast includes Mr. T, Max Gail, Adam Baldwin, Gary Busey, Marsha Warfield, and a few dozen more people, all of whom seem to be constantly standing around in small rooms. The plot eventually leads to the kidnapping of two children of a diplomat, hardly a surefire comic concept. The closest thing to humor is when Mr. T gives one of his stern-faced lectures on right living, and the camera slowly zooms back to reveal that he's standing on the steps of the Lincoln Memorial. Even that may not be hilarious, folks, but it's all there is.
R / 1984 / MCA

▲ DEADLY BLESSING

Count your curses; there are a lot worse demonic epics around. Director Wes Craven, also responsible for 1973's *Last House on the Left,* uses a deft scare-relax-scare-relax-REALLY-SCARE rhythm. He employs it here to shower hellfire and brimstone on a young Los Angeles woman, Maren ("Battlestar Galactica") Jensen, who marries a member of an ultraconservative religious sect and then compounds her mistake by homesteading next door to her spooky in-laws. Something satanic is afoot. Not to mention the sect's menacing

patriarch. He's played, of course, by Ernest Borgnine. (If he does many more of these murderous chillers, someone is bound to give him dialogue like: "Who do you want to do in tonight, Marty?" "I don't know, who do you want to do in?") Veteran actress Lois Nettleton also appears, enjoyably, as a drawling waitress with a strange daughter. Susan Buckner, a former beauty queen, is appealing as a city friend of Jensen's. Jensen herself effectively conveys both stark terror and an unreasonable if admirable pluck. Craven's ending is packed with fast surprises—one too many, in fact. The climax steals devices from both *Hamlet* and *Faust,* which this film does not otherwise resemble.
R / 1981 / Embassy

▲ DEAD OF WINTER

Though this film doesn't quite live up to the cleverness of its title, director Arthur Penn manages a stylish thriller. He even subscribes to the atypical notion that a woman can take care of herself. Indeed, the men in this movie are wimps or crippled. Mary Steenburgen is a struggling New York actress auditioning to replace the female star who has walked off the set of a movie. The casting agent, unctuously acted by Roddy McDowall, is stunned by Steenburgen's likeness in looks and voice to the original. He brings her to an old, isolated house in upstate New York where a psychiatrist-turned-producer, Jan Rubes, gives her a screen, or rather, scream test. Steenburgen unwittingly becomes a central character in murder and blackmail. She has to give the performance of—and for—her life. But Penn overdoes things by throwing in every suspense-raising gimmick in the genre: squeaky doors, a raging blizzard, cut telephone lines, a two-way mirror, drugged tea, and more. They're so obvious (and peripheral), though, they actually help highlight the plot's inventiveness, concocted by first-time feature writers Marc Shmuger and Mark Malone, college friends of Penn's son. This is Penn's second suspense film in a row—*Target* wasn't exactly a bull's-eye—and its not the sort of thing he does best. (Such character studies as *Bonnie and Clyde* and *Little Big Man* are more like it.) Nevertheless, *Dead of Winter* won't leave you out in the cold.
R / 1986 / Drn

▲ THE DEAD ZONE

Warning to horror fans: This is not the kind of blood-and-guts movie you might expect from a Stephen King story. It's enjoyable nonetheless. In a knockout performance, Christopher Walken plays a small-town school teacher who's banged up in a car accident and comes out of a coma with the ability to foretell the future. He tells his nurse that her young child will be caught in a fire; he helps the local cops solve a series of grisly rape-murders; he predicts a student will die in an ice-skating accident. So far, so good. Then Walken latches on to another vision: He sees that a hard-driving candidate for the U.S. Congress, Martin Sheen, will someday plunge the wold into a nuclear war. Should he intervene? The movie gets a little wobbly here, and the plot turns seem trite. Up to then, though, it's a first-class thriller with a sharp cast. Brooke (*Cuba*) Adams plays Walken's girlfriend. Tom (*Alien*) Skerritt is the local sheriff. Colleen Dewhurst is the rapist-murderer's mother, and Herbert Lom, known to *Pink Panther* fans as Inspector Clouseau's hapless boss, is marvelous in a serious role as a sympathetic doctor. Director David Cronenberg's sense of pace is acute; the editing by Ronald Sanders is seamless and suspenseful. And the movie establishes that chills can be generated without explicit gore and violence. (Cronenberg later forgot the lesson with his remake of *The Fly*.)
R / 1983 / Paramount

▲ DEAL OF THE CENTURY

Imagine Chevy Chase walking up to you on the street. He has Sigourney Weaver and Gregory Hines with him. He begins to talk about the ominous international trade in weapons. A smile starts to form on your lips as you wait for the punch lines. An hour later, you're still waiting. It dawns on you: We're talking pedantic lecture here, not humor. Anyone who doesn't merely want to imagine that experience and feels like being bored stiff for a couple of hours should see this film. While it was billed as a "black comedy," there are few attempts at humor. Chase shoots himself in the foot (twice). He moans at one point: "I think I'm going to vomit on the floor." An excessive amount of footage is devoted to the phallic symbolism of rockets being launched or keeling over on the pad. To give the

benefit of the doubt to screenwriter Paul (*Risky Business*) Brickman, the film seems well intentioned; and certainly the arms business is fair game for both criticism and lampooning. But directory William (*Crusing*) Friedkin has no flair for comedy. And he fatally misuses the cast: Chase is wrong as a weapons dealer, Hines is a washed-out pilot who turns to a born-again faith—that's only one of the many aimless plot turns—and Weaver portrays a woman with gorgeous legs who's only around for scenic value. They all seem at times to have wandered into a documentary. Chase, especially, seems mesmerized, and audiences are likely to feel a snooze coming on too. Title notwithstanding, this movie is no bargain.
PG / 1983 / Warner

▲ DEAR DETECTIVE

The lady is a cop! And a good one at that in Philippe De Broca's comedy. Annie Girardot—less leggy but more endearing than that old Yank policewoman Angie Dickinson—plays a beautiful police inspector hot on the trail of a dangerous killer. She drives like a maniac, packs a big black gun, and fights the usual sniggering sexism at the office. Along the way she falls in love with a bumbling college professor (Philippe Noiret) who has some rather old-fashioned ideas about working women. The ending is a little too cutesy, but *Dear Detective* is still an enjoyable spoof on all those detective movies that traffic in blood and guts. It was remade in the U.S. with Brenda Vaccaro in 1979. (In French with subtitles.)
PG / 1978 / N/A

▲ DEATH ON THE NILE

One of Agatha Christie's most popular mystery novels was turned into this sumptuous whodunit with a dazzling cast of character actors obviously relishing the chance to drop and pick up clues. Peter Ustinov plays the mustachioed detective Hercule Poirot, taking over from Albert Finney, who did the role in 1974's hit, *Murder on the Orient Express*. Poirot turns up in Egypt shortly after the murder of a beautiful young heiress (Lois Chiles). There's no shortage of suspects: a love rival (a marvelous Mia Farrow), a rich dowager (a cunningly crusty Bette Davis), a Swiss doctor

(Jack Warden), and a vengeful beauty (Olivia Hussey). Angela Lansbury almost steals the show as a sex-starved novelist, and Maggie Smith, as Davis's tough secretary, is priceless. David Niven plays Poirot's sidekick so subtly he often upstages Ustinov by downstaging himself. The action is slow at first, but gorgeous scenery whiles away the time. Then once everyone is gathered in the drawing room of a Neil cruise ship, suspicions begin to fly. Like *Orient Express,* this is sharp, diverting fun.
PG / 1978 / HBO/Cannon

▲ DEATHRAGE

An Italian production, this low-budget film doesn't pretend to be anything more than a good, solid shoot-'em-upper. Yul Brynner, in one of his few screen roles, is effective as a jaded Mafia hitman out to avenge the mob's savage slaying of his younger brother. His vendetta takes him to Naples, where he chases the bad guys all over town and encounters bountiful Barbara Bouchet. She spends most of the movie taking off her clothes. Director Anthony Dawson wisely kept the dialogue to a minimum and emphasized the bang-bang. The result, while not the *Son of French Connection,* succeeds in a slam-bang sort of way.
R / 1977 / N/A

▲ DEATH SHIP

Talk about incredible hulks. This one is a World War II Nazi prison ship that's been sailing for thirty-five years—with no crew—looking for people to molest. Then who should show up but Richard Crenna, Sally Ann Howes, Kate Reid, and a few lesser lights. They're cast adrift when George Kennedy's ocean liner is rammed by the Nazi juggernaut. Then, while everyone is floating around, the death ship sneaks up on them, and what else can they do but climb aboard? They learn the ship can steer itself, open and shut doors, show Hitler movies, and make people run in slow motion. It can also talk to Kennedy in German and convince him to take over its captain's chair. (One thing the ship can't do is provide subtitles, so non-German speakers never know what it's saying.) The violence is tedious and ugly. The only highlight is the debut of a 50-year-old Canadian coast guard ice-breaker, the

N. B. McLean. In the title role, it stirs more emotion with one turn of its crankshaft than the *Love Boat* ever managed in a whole season.
R / 1980 / N/A

▲ DEATHSPORT

Even serious fanciers of movie violence are likely to find that this one contains a coup de grace or two too many. Set in the year 3000 (when the death penalty has been abolished but some criminals are condemned to mortal combat in arenas), the film is full of blood, fire, nudity, and hacking with swords. That's the thoughtful part. David Carradine as the hero more or less, was setting a new standard for sublime-to-ridiculous transition, having gone from Ingmar Bergman's *The Serpent's Egg* to this product of Roger Corman's B-movie assembly line. Neither Carradine's presence nor Claudia Jennings' skill at taking off her clothes should prevent viewers from feeling insulted.
R / 1978 / Warner

▲ DEATHTRAP

Faithfulness to the original is both the charm and the curse of this film version of Broadway's longest-running comedy thriller. Ira Levin's 1978 play was adapted by screenwriter Jay Presson Allen and director Sidney (*Murder on the Orient Express*) Lumet with special care to keep all the chicanery and dastardly plot twists intact. He did not succeed, however, in opening up the story for the camera. Michael Caine's the playwright so anxious to have a hit show he'd kill for it, even if the victim might be his wife (Dyan Cannon) or protégé-lover (Christopher Reeve). To say any more would be unfair to those who do not know the ingenious story line. Beyond the surprises are Lumet's strenuous efforts to conceal *Deathtrap*'s one-set stage origins. He hangs his camera from every corner of Caine's East Hampton home, but the tricks only heighten the claustophobia. *Sleuth,* the 1972 stage-to-screen mystery co-starring Caine and Laurence Olivier, suffered from the same problem but benefited from a lighter touch. Lumet has directed his actors to such a high pitch they often seem to be playing a second balcony. Cannon and Irene Worth, as a medium who lives next door, are overbearing.

Reeve does the desired damage to his Superman image by kissing Caine full on the mouth. But no matter how gamely played, his part is ill-focused. Caine, at least, allows the humor to seep through the cracks in his character. Still, the film's artifice dulls what seemed most diverting onstage.

R / 1982 / Warner

▲ DEATH WISH II

There is something to be said for this film: It provides the same vicarious relief for those seeking revenge against urban crime that pornography provides for those in need of sex. Whether this is meritorious or simply vile is another question. As in the original 1974 *Death Wish,* Charles Bronson plays Paul Kersey, an architect whose family falls victim to thugs. In this one, his housekeeper and his daughter (who was raped and driven insane in the first film) are raped and murdered. The plot is his one-man vigilante hunt for the gang responsible. Carnage and implausibility are rampant; competent writing and acting are not. Even the estimable Vincent Gardenia, as the same New York cop who tracked Bronson in the original movie, doesn't have a convincing word to say. Bronson's off-camera wife Jill Ireland, who plays his steady here, rejects him in the end. Otherwise he escapes retribution to visit more violence on criminals in the fulfillment of future *Death Wishe*s.

R / 1982 / Warner

▲ DEATH WISH III

For an actor, the guaranteed quickest exit from a film is playing Charles Bronson's friend in the *Death Wish* vigilante series. The closer you are, the faster you go. In this clumsy, botched second sequel, directed by Michael Winner (who directed I and II), Bronson's dearest buddy, played by Francis Drake, is dispatched just as the credits are rolling. And as soon as a virtuous lawyer, played by Deborah Raffin, beds down old Charlie, she, too, gets bumped off. All this provocation is supposed to pave the way for Bronson's inevitable cathartic vengeance. But *DW III* has none of the jazzy pace of the original film, in which Bronson turned the streets of Manhattan

into a shooting gallery. Instead, this time architect Bronson gets the unlikely approval of New York police chief Ed Lauter to protect, in his free time, the poor, decent folk of a Brooklyn tenement from brutal punks. The film sluggishly makes its way to a series of wildly violent confrontations. The stage directions for the last few minutes must have been easy: "He shoots, shoots, shoots, and shoots again."

R / 1985 / MGM/UA

▲ THE DEEP

Can Nick Nolte hold his breath long enough to get the gold before Robert Shaw dynamites the sunken Spanish galleon and Jackie Bisset's wet suit dries? Such are the deep, if not profound, questions posed in this waterlogged saga of scubaing for treasure in Bermuda, from Peter (*Jaws*) Benchley's best-selling paperback. There are diversions—a scene of sharks feasting, a bloody voodoo ritual, a moray eel attack, and Nolte and Bisset buddy-breathing—before we come up for air. But the supposedly revolutionary underwater photography is unexciting, the acting is drippy, the plot inane, and . . . oh, see it anyway. Sad truth: Jackie's wet T-shirt photo will be remembered longer.

PG / 1977 / RCA/Columbia

▲ THE DEER HUNTER

Robert De Niro is explosive in this stunning Vietnam movie, one of the best early cinematic attempts to deal with the war. True, there are some problems: Director Michael Cimino takes too long getting De Niro and his two buddies (Christopher Walken and John Savage) from a steel town in Pennsylvania to the rice paddies of Indochina, but once they arrive the film is gripping, suspenseful, and at times unbearably tense. De Niro plays the monomaniacal hero who saves his friends from seemingly certain death. In one scene they are all forced to play Russian roulette with their Viet Cong captors. Walken and Savage are both impressive as tough guys who slowly come apart under the pressure, and Meryl Streep as the girl left behind, is perfect. This was the real beginning of her esteemed career. More than just another war movie, this is a story of how

some people learn to survive and others don't. The memory of this triumph must have kept Cimino going through his subsequent series of mega-flops.
R / 1978 / MCA

▲ DEFIANCE

Jan-Michael Vincent stars as an out-of-work merchant seaman who walks tall on New York's rough-and-tumble Lower East Side. His ship didn't come in with this role, but he does lend a certain laconic strength as he is reluctantly drawn into a showdown with the Souls, a gang led by the splendidly sinister Rudy Ramos. Unlike gang films where hoods just whack one another, the Souls prefer terrorizing helpless citizens, raiding church bingo games, and beating up Art Carney, slumming in a supporting role. Director John Flynn lacks any light touch, the dialogue seems awkward, the love scenes are dreadful, and the climatic battle is shot confusingly in half light.
PG / 1980 / Vestron

▲ THE DELTA FORCE

This B-grade production is actually two films in one; both are witless and artless. The title refers to a crack American antiterrorist squad. Unfortunately for action lovers, these commandos, led by a long-in-the-tooth Lee Marvin, are pretty much leashed up until the movie has nearly ended. The bulk of *The Delta Force* is spent detailing events similar to 1985's hijacking of a TWA jet to Beirut. Director Menahem Golan's attempt at realism is severely hampered by implausible details and a dim-wattage cast that might have been left over from an Irwin Allen extravaganza: Joey Bishop, Robert Vaughn, George Kennedy, and Shelley Winters. There's a docu-pretension in the first reel, but that is dropped for the sake of a blazing-ballistics finale in which the Arab hijackers prove to be craven weaklings. No one will be more disappointed by *The Delta Force* than the fans of Chuck Norris, who plays Marvin's second in command. The scant moments he spend snuffing Arabs are about as exciting as it would be to watch him toss a salad.
R / 1986 / Media

▲ DEMON SEED

Scientist Fritz Weaver creates an all-knowing, all-doing computer that runs even further amok than *2001*'s HAL. Not only does *Proteus IV* lust after Weaver's wife, Julie Christie—which is reasonable enough—but it succeeds in impregnating her. Although sci-fi plot holes and tedious light-show effects (again à la *2001*) detract, Christie is controlled and affecting, especially considering that her leading man is a huge tetrahedron with electronic eyes, a steel hand, and a heart of FORTRAN.
R / 1977 / MGM/UA

▲ DERSU UZALA

Such landscapes! Such cinematography! Such a dreadfully slow movie! The 1975 Oscar winner for best foreign film—a Japanese-Russian production released in the U.S. for the first time in 1978—tells of the odd friendship between a Russian surveyor and his elderly guide, a hunter who still grieves for his dead wife and children. When the old man, Dersu Uzala, goes blind, he moves to the city to live with his young friend, but the life does not suit him. Unhappy, he returns to the forest, and the outcome is shockingly violent. Director Akiro Kurosawa said he was trying to warn against despoiling nature, but his long, beautifully constructed scenes may tax even the sort of ardent conservationist who likes to watch redwoods grow. (In Japanese with subtitles.)
G / 1975 / Embassy

▲ DESERT HEARTS

You've seen her before. She's a free spirit and an untamed force. She can spark passion in the most passive, uptight, downtrodden square around. She can teach a person about life, love, and sex— usually not in that order. From such classics as *Cabaret* to such clinkers as *The Girl from Petrovka,* the movies have enshrined this lady: the libertine liberator. In *Desert Hearts* she rides again, but there's a twist: Her consort is another woman. Despite the addition of sexual switcheroo (and a relatively explicit love-making scene), there's nothing really new or novel taking place in this film. As soon as you see those dainty white gloves on English professor Helen Shaver, who has come to Reno in 1959 to get a divorce, you know she's going to get her proper little life dirty very soon. Her emancipator proves to be a spunky casino change-maker, Patricia Charbonneau, who had a small role in *Without a Trace*. She resides on the ranch where Shaver mopes while she awaits her divorce decree. Adapted from the 1964 cult novel *Desert of the Heart,* by Jane Rule, this romance falls for all the clichés of the genre: As usual the working-class woman awakens the intellectual to life's erotic and exotic possibilities but, as usual, the class differences prohibit a lasting romance. "We've been saying good-bye from the beginning," Shaver tells her lover at their teary farewell. Making her feature debut, filmmaker Donna Deitch treats her heroines' sexuality as a matter of fact, but her direction is nevertheless defensive. She directs every scene with the emotions italicized, as if she's got to convince the audience that these events warrant our attention. Her good ole girls talk too loud, laugh too hard, and cry too often. In the process of pleading for sexual tolerance, *Desert Hearts* does some discriminating of its own: The movie seems to be decreeing that rural folks just feel a lot more than city slickers. It's guilty of country chauvinism.

R / 1986 / Vestron

▲ DESPAIR

German director Rainer Werner Fassbinder succeeded in his first work in English in making a schizophrenic movie about schizophrenia. Dirk Bograde, in a bravura performance, plays a Russian emigré running a chocolate factory in pre-Hitler's Germany. He discovers his wife's affair with her cousin, and he has a sneaking suspicion that he's going mad. But right around the time he arranges to have the man killed, the movie tries to enter his head—and loses its own. Only when the cops come after him do we get back on track and appreciate what the director has been trying to show us—a crack-up from the inside and out. British playwright Tom Stoppard adapted the screenplay from Vladimir Nabokov's novel of the same name. The result is a marvel of literate, elegant dialogue and, if nothing else, Fassbinder deserved credit for not being afraid to take chances.

Unrated / 1979 / Warner

▲ DESPERATELY SEEKING SUSAN

In this class-clash comedy Rosanna Arquette, a frustrated Fort Lee, New Jersey, housewife whose husband runs a hot tub business, drives an expensive car with the plates TUB N SPA. You can judge a comedy by the cleverness of its license plates, and by that standard, as well as most others, *Desperately Seeking Susan* has a fresh and funky perspective. It doesn't hurt that rock diva Madonna, making her movie debut, was the co-star, and *Susan* is indeed a material girl of a movie. It can't get enough crazy props, odd gadgets, and bright pink doodads. For that matter, Leora Barish's script is overdressed to kill an audience. Incorporating amnesia, mistaken identity, stolen artifacts, stalking hit men, and suburban social lives (all in the first reel), the movie nearly asphyxiates on its plot twists. When Arquette becomes involved with a hipster, played by Madonna, she inadvertently assumes Madonna's identity. Arquette takes up with a likable guy in the East Village, while Madonna bamboozles her way into Arquette's suburban sanctuary. Director Susan Seidelman takes much too long to get the peculiar rhythms of her movie percolating. And for a castigation of the status quo, *Susan* at times comes off like the first punk sitcom. But Seidelman, whose first movie was the $80,000 *Smithereens,* graduated to the big leagues with grace. She didn't cash in her counterculture temperament. She made that rare creation—a comedy that possesses the moral ambiguity of an arresting drama. *Susan* has a screwy sensibility fueled by an appreciation of atmosphere and a kookie code of honor. Seidelman isn't hipper-than-thou, either: Madonna, the coolest character, is the most dishonest. She fabricates murder accusations without batting an eyelash. Fortunately, Arquette has a goofy grace that makes her role's implausibilities palatable. Madonna appears completely at ease, perhaps because the part form-fit her persona. In fact, Seidelman cast wisely right down to the walk-ons. It's hard to resist a movie that contains such diverse talents as deadpan comedian Steven Wright and Lina Wertmuller's favorite jail matron, Shirley Stoler. Watching *Desperately Seeking Susan* is like attending a terrific loft party. It's different, it's infectious, and you never know whom you'll run into next.

PG-13 / 1985 / Thorn/EMI

▲ THE DEVIL AND MAX DEVLIN

Think of this as the flip side of *Heaven Can Wait*. Like Warren Beatty, Elliott Gould gets snuffed in the prime of life. But instead of going Upstairs, Gould goes straight to the Bad Place because he was a nasty Los Angeles landlord as a mere mortal. Like Beatty, however, Gould works out a deal so he can return to the land of the living. He becomes a fire-and-brimstone recruiter, and his targets are an ambitious young rock singer (played by screen newcomer Julie Budd), a klutzy motorcyclist (David Knell), and an adorable kid who desperately wants a daddy (Adam Rich). Since this is a Disney film, these characters are all impossibly clean-cut. Steven Hilliard Stern, who directed *Running,* seems to have adopted a devil-may-care approach to his lead players. The most memorable aspect of Gould's performance is his apparent inability to shave properly, and Bill Cosby is strangely restrained as one of Lucifer's lieutenants. If there's a Purgatory for movies, this one belongs there.
PG / 1981 / Disney

▲ A DIFFERENT STORY

"Different" is only half the story. The first 45 minutes of this low-budget romantic comedy are offbeat and amusing. A homosexual (played by Perry King) shares his L.A. digs with a lesbian (Meg Foster). They form the oddest of couples, and the role-reversing permutations are handled deftly. She works; he doesn't. She's a mess; he's tidy. But when their relationship of convenience turns heterosexual (surprise! surprise!), the production lapses into predictability and tedium, though King and Foster are both effective.
R / 1978 / CBS/Fox

▲ DINER

Peering back at the youth of two decades ago has become something of a cinematic pastime from *American Graffiti* to *Porky's.* It has also become achingly repetitive. No wonder MGM was skeptical about releasing *Diner,* a low-budget, all-non-star (but not anymore) look at a handful of buddies who hang out at a Baltimore eatery, circa 1959. Astonishingly, the movie turned out to be the best and boldest of the genre—and a pierc-ingly intelligent comedy. Writer Barry (*And Justice for All*) Levinson, debuting as a director, shows an eye for detail as astute as his ear for dialogue. Among the guys in *Diner,* the top compliment is "She's death," the hot debate is whether Sinatra or Johnny Mathis provides the best make-out music, and the ultimate fantasy is sex. The reality is mostly sexual panic. Daniel Stern is married but can't abide talking to his wife, vividly played by Ellen Barken. Steve Guttenberg is scheduled to walk the aisle but won't unless his fiancée first passes a "monster football quiz." Most moving is the self-destructive Kevin Bacon, who'll "do anything for a smile," even sell his date for $5. At the center is Mickey Rourke, the one ladykiller in the bunch, a beautician trying law school at night. All the performances are remarkable. But the ultimate triumph is Levinson's. He captures both the surface and the soul of an era with candor and precision. Other films have promised as much. *Diner* delivers.
R / 1982 / MGM/UA

▲ THE DISAPPEARANCE

Winter in Montreal. One cold gray day follows another. A professional hitman, played by Donald Sutherland, returns home to his wife (Francine Racette), for whom he has lost enthusiasm. When she disappears, however, he suddenly finds himself obsessed with tracking her down. This film is so relentlessly bleak and Sutherland so detached that it is impossible to care about his mission. More's the pity, because British director Stuart (*Test of Violence*) Cooper has assembled an excellent supporting cast. Racette, who later became Mrs. Sutherland, is just right as the sultry cipher who vanishes. Christopher Plummer and John Hurt show up all too briefly. Unfortunately, Cooper's studied direction telegraphs what few plot twists there are. The success of *Body Heat* may have signaled the return of the film noir, but there was never much of a call for a film gris.
R / 1981 / Vestron

▲ DIVA

It's tempting to call this just another French cops-and-robbers film. But it's a tour de force that put its director, Jean-Jacques Beineix, in the front

ranks of French moviemakers with his first feature. The plot is intriguing, if sometimes confusing: An 18-year-old Paris mailman, played with perfect self-effacement by Frederic Andrei, loves opera. His fascination is an American diva who won't record her voice for fear of diluting her art. One night the young mailman secretly tapes her performance, and when two Taiwanese record pirates find out, the chase is on. That's only the beginning. Another tape accidentally dropped in his mail pouch implicates a high-ranking police inspector in a drug-and-prostitution ring. When the crooked cop finds out that this tape exists, he, too, sets out after the mailman. Director Beineix and his cameraman, Philippe Rousselot, show an uncommon touch. The scenes are like paintings: a dangerous chase through the subways of Paris, an abandoned lighthouse at dawn. As the diva, Wilhelmenia Wiggins Fernandez is dazzling, a portrait of arrogance and beauty. But this is a director's movie, and Beineix is superb. (In French with subtitles.)
R / 1982 / MGM/UA

▲ DIVINE MADNESS

Bette Midler is a natural high, but this filmed concert, taped in three days at the Pasadena Civic Auditorium, is really no more than a big-screen TV special without the bleeps. (Miss M's vulgarity, abetted by her trashy trio, the Harlettes, comes through unsanitized.) This is less a movie than a chance to cash in on a tour without the extra effort that distinguished the Dylan-Baez documentary *Don't Look Back* or the Band's *The Last Waltz*. Except for an opening gambit in which harried head usher Irving Sudrow prepares his charges to cope with Bette aficionados, director Michael Ritchie's light touch is rarely perceptible. This is all Midler—nineteen songs—and she's not always at peak form. Two numbers, "Paradise" and "Street Shuffle," are inexcusably ragged, and her comedy set pieces (lounge singer and bag lady) are, to be generous, overlong. She delivers a medley from her debut film, *The Rose*, a stirring version of Dylan's "I Shall be Released," and a mesmerizing Tom Waits chant, "Shiver Me Timbers." Surprisingly, however, her quietly definitive interpretation of James Taylor's "Millworker," which she did on tour in those days, is missing; somewhere between stage and screen, ballad gave way to belt. It's a

shame. As she proved with her bravura performance in *The Rose,* there is more to Bette than just her upper registers.
R / 1980 / Warner

▲ THE DOCTOR AND THE DEVILS

If pedigree alone could produce a good movie, *The Doctor and the Devils* would glide to glory. In the '40s Dylan Thomas wrote the original script that playwright Ronald Harwood has adapted for this gothic drama. At some point this true story of an ethics-versus-science standoff may have accommodated the melancholy poetry and pungent morality that mark the Welsh poet's work, but as directed by Freddie Francis, it looks like *Frankenstein* played out on the set of *Oliver!* In late 19th-century England, a notorious scientist is paying grave robbers to supply fresh cadavers for his classes. The not-yet-Bonded Timothy Dalton, who plays the mad doc, acts as though this were a role the young Laurence Olivier overlooked. The difference is that Olivier would have played the part; Dalton merely poses for it. Eventually his backdoor bribes prompt one nasty pair to create new corpses for quick money. Can science answer for the consequences? Can blood money spark a sluggish economy? Can bad doctors really give good dinner parties? Like its hero, the movie never answers any of the ethical dilemmas it parades. Indeed, Francis proves to be the movie's most inept grave robber. He exhumes Thomas's screenplay to no apparent purpose. His movie pretends to address serious issues while it makes its own point with close-ups of severed feet bottled in formaldehyde.
R / 1985 / Key

▲ DOCTOR DETROIT

Here are some of the people to blame for this insulting, childish, unprofessional comedy film: actors Dan Aykroyd, Howard (*Head of the Class*) Hesseman, and Donna (the real-life Mrs. Akyroyd) Dixon; director Michael (*Some Kind of Hero*) Pressman; screenwriters Bruce Jay (*Stir Crazy*) Friedman, Carl (*Jaws*) Gottlieb, and Robert Boris, who wrote the novel *Blood Feud* and the TV miniseries derived from it. The film stars Aykroyd as a Milquetoasty Chicago college professor who gets involved with a pimp (Hesseman) and

his stable of hookers (one of whom is Dixon). To make a very long 90-minute story short, in a battle for turf with a mob leader Aykroyd assumes the identity of an eccentric gangster from Michigan. And then nothing funny happens. It's a tip-off to everyone's desperation that so much footage is devoted to scenes of people walking, running, or driving. These aren't even chase scenes, just tedious travelogues of Chicago streets. Obscenities are liberally sprinkled through the script, as if they are by themselves funny or as if the audience is stupid enough to think so. Aykroyd seems out of shape both physically and comedically; the only time he ever hints at using his talent is a party scene in which he does one of those funky mechanical-man dances. The movie does accomplish one thing: It makes Jerry Lewis's *The Nutty Professor,* which had a similar theme, seem like the masterpiece some Lewis partisans have long claimed it to be.
R / 1983 / MCA

▲ THE DOGS OF WAR

Based on Frederick Forsyth's novel, this thriller is long on plot and short on character. The action spans four continents, following a modern-day mercenary, Christopher Walken, who is hired by one of those sinister, faceless conglomerates that crop up in so many movies these days. Director John Irvin, a veteran of British television and documentaries, mounts suspense nicely during the fast-paced first half, but the script weakens as Walken and his troops prepare to overthrow a dictator in a West African country in order to install the puppet of the evil multinational moguls. Walken matches his intense performance in *The Deer Hunter,* but his character seems one-dimensional. There's a violently colorful finale, though, and assuming one doesn't look for much else, this is a satisfying adventure.
R / 1981 / CBS/Fox

▲ THE DOMINO PRINCIPLE

Gene Hackman's talent is the real victim in a plot to kill the unnamed resident of a San Clemente-type compound. As Hackman's bubble-headed wife, Candice Bergen relies on a verge-of-tears mien that isn't meant to be funny but is. Neither the title nor the movie has anything to do with

Southeast Asia, foreign policy, or anything else of interest.
R / 1977 / CBS/FOX

▲ DONA FLOR AND HER TWO HUSBANDS

One of Brazil's all-time top films, this is such an erotic delight it was later remade as *Kiss Me Goodbye,* with Sally Field, James Caan, and Jeff Bridges. Directed by 23-year-old Bruno Barreto and shot in Bahia, Brazil's answer to San Francisco, the original tells the story of a young woman who can't seem to forget her dead husband. Never mind that he was a drunk, a philanderer, and a compulsive gambler—he was also a terrific lover, something her second spouse clearly is not. Sonia Braga is bewitchingly beautiful as the young widow, and Jose Wilker sparkles as the roguish husband who returns to haunt her dreams. Lots of laughs, with some very steamy love scenes that confirm they do more in Brazil than drink coffee and malign soccer referees. (In Portuguese with subtitles.)
Unrated / 1978 / Warner

▲ DOWN AND OUT IN BEVERLY HILLS

Although you can't tell from this one-joke comedy, director Paul Mazursky is perhaps the most savvy cultural commentator in American movies. *An Unmarried Woman* and *Moscow on the Hudson* bear witness to that. But Mazursky mixes those original efforts with Americanized versions of European film classics. This time he grafts Jean Renoir's 1932 masterwork *Boudu Saved from Drowning* onto a modern Beverly Hills setting. Richard Dreyfuss and Bette Midler are the nouveau gauche couple who take in hobo Nick Nolte after he attempts suicide in their pool. It's a terrific idea, but as with such past Mazursky hybrids as *Alex in Wonderland* (his Fellini tribute) and *Willie and Phil* (à la Truffaut), you wonder why Mazursky insists on playing cultural ambassador. Overly faithful to *Boudu* at times, he's stuck with a schematic tale of salvation—Nolte systematically brings happiness to each family member. Even when Mazursky cuts loose on today's fads—dog psychiatrists, fire walking, a teenage son who talks to his parents only via videotape—the comedy plays like déjà vu. A telling comment on the picture is that the character viewers tend to remember most is Mike the Dog, the hottest mongrel act in movies since Lassie. The unholy trinity in the leads, Dreyfuss, Midler and, to a lesser degree, Nolte, give italicized, condescending performances. It's the kind of acting in which the stars wink at an audience to say, "We're not really like these icky people." The audience is told only that these folks are superficial and silly—the outlook of those Rodeo Drive jokes that populate Johnny Carson's monologues. It's surprising Mazursky suffers from such a poverty of perspective.

R / 1986 / Touchstone

▲ DOWN BY LAW

It's always a bad sign when you start rooting for the poisonous snakes. Those viewers who are still awake midway into this movie may well find themselves doing just that, however. Tom Waits, John Lurie, and Roberto Benigni play New Orleans jail escapees lost in a swamp, and when Waits begins to worry about how many serpents there are in the area, it looks as if something might actually happen. No such luck. Not even a frog shows up. Director Jim Jarmusch, trying to follow up his 1984 cult success *Stranger Than Paradise,* mostly has his characters sit around and insult one another. There seems to be a lot of improvising of dialogue. Let's hope, anyway, that nobody bothered to write down such lines as "Holy Toledo! Can you believe this?" Waits, the growly blues singer, has a dark, simian kind of presence, and Benigni, an Italian comedian, provides scraps of amusement by quoting American poets, including one he calls Bob Frost, in Italian. Lurie seems to undergo a personality transplant offscreen, changing inexplicably from a surly pimp into an aw-shucks kind of guy. While he has a strong visual sense, filling the screen (in black and white) with Felliniesque images of seedy New Orlean neighborhoods and scummy swamps, he seems to prefer tedium to plot. This is at best a self-parody of overintellectualized, underproduced films. You could create more impact by throwing feathers at a marshmallow.

R / 1986 / Key

▲ DRAGONSLAYER

Mickey Mouse may have thought he had it rough as a sorcerer's apprentice when he had to cope with all of those ill-tempered brooms in *Fantasia.* But in this Disney production, would-be wizard Peter (*Sophie's Choice*) MacNicol faces a more fearsome foe: an 800-year-old dragon who has a taste for medieval virgins and is given to arsonous rampages when his advances are unrequited. MacNicol inherits the magical mantle when his master, Sir Ralph Richardson, croaks. Then he challenges the dragon, Vermithrax Pejorative, who steals nearly every scene he's (she's?) in. The dragon was easily the best creation of mechanical malevolence Hollywood had come up with since Jaws. (Effects are by Brian Johnson, progenitor of *Alien*'s creature.) Romance also blossoms between the young hero and Caitlin Clarke, a beauty he tries especially hard to keep from becoming dragon fodder. An innocent adventure that's technically slick and lacking in pretense, this film should provide a nice scare for kids, and maybe a few for the grown-ups too.

PG / 1981 / Paramount

▲ THE DRAUGHTSMAN'S CONTRACT

What is the movie about? Only director Peter Greenaway, a veteran of British television, knows for sure, and he's not telling anybody, certainly not the audience. The curious thing is that it's so deftly acted it's still almost fun to watch, no matter how confusing—or simply absent—the plot is. A wealthy 17th-century woman, Janet (*Nicholas and Alexandra*) Sulzman, hires a young, handsome, and very arrogant draftsman, Anthony Higgins, to draw twelve pictures of her house and grounds while her husband, an offensive lout if ever there was one, is away. Part of the deal—it is written into the contract—is that the draftsman will sleep with the mistress of the estate, which he does with great gusto. (The scenes of them coupling are hilarious—in one moment of passion he undoes her dress with a pair of scissors.) Then her daughter gets into the act—she wants the draftsman the same way, and gets him. But there's something else afoot here. About two-thirds of the way into the movie, the draftsman appears to be involved in a plot to murder the master of the mansion. At least it seems that's what's going on. There are so many loose ends and crazy cul-de-sacs it's impossible to tell exactly what's happening. For instance, periodically a naked man appears in the background. Why? If this was meant to be an elaborate mystery, it certainly fails. Greenaway is, obviously, the guiltiest party around, since he made this too-eccentric film.

R / 1983 / N/A

▲ DREAMER

The subject is bowling. Sure, the sport is engaged in by more than 50 million Americans, but so is washing dishes, and the dramatic possibilities are roughly comparable. To make matters worse, the screenplay was compiled from dusty sports movie clichés. Take a struggling young competitor (Tim Matheson), give him a former champ (Jack Warden) for a mentor, and throw in a beautiful girl (Susan Blakely) to say things like "I think you love that crummy old baseball bat/golf club/bowling ball more than me." Suffer the consequences. Considering the material, the cast struggles gamely. Matheson gets by on his *Animal House* charm and throws a pretty mean hook besides. But director Noel Nosseck rolled the cinematic equivalent of a gutter ball.

PG / 1979 / CBS/Fox

▲ A DREAM OF PASSION

When Melina Mercouri, as a Greek movie star, returns home to do *Medea* on the stage, she becomes obsessed with an American woman (Ellen Burstyn) who, like a modern-day Medea, has murdered her children to punish her husband for infidelity. Jules Dassin—the producer, director, and writer (as well at Mercouri's husband)—creates a fascinating, often frightening, *Persona*-like study of transference between the two women. Indeed, Dassin includes a lengthy clip from the Bergman classic. Mercouri delivers a powerful, multidimensional performance that, she once said, "I love more than anything I've ever done." Burstyn combines foul-mouthed rage and child-like innocence in the demanding role of the murderess. Some scenes from *Medea* itself run overly long, but even then they help to build the impact of this forceful film.

R / 1978 / CBS/Fox

▲ DREAMSCAPE

Anyone who has ever wished it were possible to videotape dreams and keep them to view at leisure would appreciate this compact, imaginative fantasy thriller. Dennis Quaid plays a psychic who makes his living betting on horses. Then he gets shanghaied into a research project that involves sending people who are awake into dreams of those who are asleep—via telepathy. Max von Sydow is the relatively benevolent scientist heading the project, but Christopher Plummer, as the head of a supersecret government agency, sees the research as a possible weapon. All of this could have done nothing more than remind people of the 1940s song popularized by Artie Shaw and Hot Lips Page, "Take Your Shoes Off Baby (and Start Running Through My Mind)." But the effects and hysterics are kept so well under control by director Joseph Ruben, and the film is so well acted, that it is easy to muster 98 minutes' worth of suspended disbelief. Quaid is especially engaging. He works up some nice romantic by-play with Kate Capshaw; their love scenes are old-fashioned, which is to say clothed, yet sexy nonetheless. Plummer adds sublime villainy as the spymaster with the smile and heart of a crocodile. The attempts to portray what a dream would look like from the outside are intriguing too. This is not sheep-jumping-over-fences stuff but Daliesque nightmares full of eerie light, smoke, endless caverns, and strange creatures. Somebody connected with creating this film obviously has spent a few troubled nights. It may be going too far to have the climactic battle fought inside the nightmare of U.S. President Eddie Albert, who is being haunted by specters of a nuclear holocaust. In the old days the basic idea of this movie would have been condensed into a half-hour "Twilight Zone." But this is a rare, modern science fiction film: It neither insults the intelligence nor upsets the stomach.

PG-13 / 1984 / Thorn/EMI

▲ DRESSED TO KILL

Imagine *Psycho* as it might be conceived by the editor of a skin magazine, and you'll have some idea of what to expect from this gory whodunit about sexual hijinks and homicide in Manhattan. What raises it above the usual sub-Hitchcock riff

is writer-director Brian De Palma, whose visual audacity and wicked wit rarely fail him. He is, of course, a Hitchcock disciple, and the film is both reverent spoof and sexual tease. Looking indecently gorgeous, Angie Dickinson plays a frustrated wife given to propositioning her shrink (Michael Caine) as well as the occasional passing stranger. A long sequence, in which Angie picks up Ken Baker at the Metropolitan Museum and the two tear at each other in a cab en route to his apartment, can stand with the screen's most erotic moments. Nancy Allen (Mrs. De Palma at the time) also registers a strong contribution as a wholesome hooker with an eye for art and for Angie's teenage son, nicely underplayed by Keith Gordon. No excuses can be made for De Palma's perverse fascination with slashed throats and arteries, but except for the bloodbaths, this is a dazzling, high-gloss chiller.
R / 1980 / Warner

▲ THE DRESSER

This Ronald Harwood adaptation of his 1980 play about a fading Shakespearean actor and his valet won a passel of Oscar nominations including Best Picture. Albert Finney plays the actor who is on the verge of a breakdown. Tom (*King Rat*) Courtenay is the valet trying to coax his master into just one more performance of *King Lear*. They have powerful scenes together, each patronizing the other. Finney, though, overdoes the madman notion a little, and Courtenay overdoes the mincing, simpering, flouncing ninny role a lot—it doesn't take a gay rights activist to be offended by the portrayal. (Both of them, in any case, were nominated for Oscars.) Edward (*Edward and Mrs. Simpson*) Fox is part of a corps of sturdy British stage veterans who play Finney's ramshackle World War II troupe of aged, infirm and, as he puts it, "nancy-boy" armed forces rejects. Director Peter Yates, who has done such quintessentially American films as *Bullitt, The Friends of Eddie Coyle,* and *Breaking Away,* is, in fact, English. He effectively conveys the camaraderie of wartime England in general and of the small theatrical company in particular. Students of acting and things theatrical cannot fail to be moved.
PG / 1983 / RCA/Columbia

▲ THE DRIVER

You know you're in trouble when the characters don't have names and the actors never bother to change clothes. But it's really time to worry when you learn director Walter (*Hard Times*) Hill set out to make "more than just another chase picture." What we get, of course, is much, much less. The screenplay gropes unsuccessfully for the pseudoexistential appeal of that other automobile vehicle, *Vanishing Point*. Ryan O'Neal is a professional wheelman of few words and high rates who locks bumpers with Isabelle (*The Story of Adele H.*) Adjani and fanatical cop Bruce Dern. Suddenly there's more than money at stake. Oo-ow, heavy. O'Neal drives like a wild man but acts like a zombie. Lovely Isabelle handles her bad lines badly, while Dern simply added another page to his already bulging book of crazies. Granted, there are several well-choreographed chases and crashes, but movie fans cannot live by bent metal alone.
R / 1978 / CBS/Fox

▲ DUEL

When this film first appeared as an ABC-TV "Movie of the Week" in November 1971, its director was an unknown. In the intervening years *Jaws, Close Encounters of the Third Kind, Raiders of the Lost Ark,* and *E.T.* were unreeled, and whatever else you want to call Steven Spielberg, "unknown" is out of the question. "Money in the bank" might be more like it, and this slightly altered version of the '71 film that appeared in 1983 can only have been designed with that in mind. Not that the movie is negligible, especially for a TV film, and most especially for a first-time director. Written by Richard (*The Incredible Shrinking Man*) Matheson, it is a man-against-machine fable, with Dennis Weaver as a motorist who becomes involved in a life-and-death chase with a menacing diesel truck on a lonely highway. Weaver is terrific as the harried victim, and Spielberg, at age 23, was able to maintain the tension, despite the original TV commercials, and didn't let the improbability of the tale weigh him down. On your next stop at the video store, there will be worse choices than this.
PG / 1983 / MCA

▲ THE DUELLISTS

Back in the days of the Napoleonic wars, Keith Carradine is an intellectual young Hussar who is forced to fight a duel with fellow officer Harvey Keitel, for reasons that are never clear to them or anyone else. In between slash-and-hack sword-fests, both age unconvincingly while Carradine loses his mistress (then real-life roommate Cristina Raines) and his reputation. Then he risks losing his life for a notion of *honneur* that, while perhaps authentic, seems gallant in the extreme. At least this rendering of Joseph Conrad's *The Duel*, director Ridley Scott's first feature, pleasures the eye—if pretty scenery and a lot of blood are one's predilections.
PG / 1977 / Paramount

▲ DUET FOR ONE

Ever since Julie Andrews won an Oscar for her 1964 film debut in *Mary Poppins,* she has been battling her sugarplum image. She was tough, terrific and, yes, sexy in her second film, *The Americanization of Emily* (still her best performance), but the public wanted her G-rated. Andrews worked very little for a decade after the expensive debacles of *Star!* and *Darling Lili.* But in 1979 her writer-director husband, Blake Edwards, launched her comeback in *"10"* as the older woman trying to win Dudley Moore from Bo Derek. Two more hits with Edwards followed; *S.O.B.* and her male drag role in *Victor/Victoria.* In 1985 she had the only memorable scene in Edwards's *That's Life,* telling off a whining Jack Lemmon. First-rate performances, but all in comedies directed by her husband. At 51, Andrews was determined to test her mettle in a heavy (and we mean heavy) drama. She found her challenge in *Duet for One,* directed by Russia's Andrei Konchalovsky, playing a famed concert violinist stricken with multiple sclerosis. Konchalovsky mucks it up royally with portentous dream sequences, close-ups of rolling wheelchairs, and ham acting from the usually reliable Max von Sydow, Alan Bates, and Rupert Everett. He uses Andrews mostly for shock value: See Julie spout the f word. See Julie sprawling nude to seduce a junkman. See Julie hit the sack with her lesbian maid. See Julie swallow sleeping pills when she can't cope with her creeping paralysis. Andrews fights to maintain her grace (and her character) under the pressure of Konchalovsky's huffing and puffing. But the movie is claptrap. Her talent is something Julie Andrews need not labor to prove. By George, she's got it.
R / 1986 / HBO/Cannon

▲ DUNE

This ambitious, $42 million film version of Frank Herbert's perennial sci-fi best-seller (first published in 1965) must have been something of a shock to previewers who labeled it a disaster. For a long (137 minutes), occasionally dull, and often incomprehensible movie, *Dune* was a box-office success. The success was deserved. Despite its flaws (shared with the book), *Dune* was the most visually stunning movie fantasy in a long time. Writer-director David Lynch (warming up for *Blue Velvet*) realized Herbert's vision of life on four planets, circa 10191, with a palpable accuracy. The heroes are stalwart, the villains hissable, the monsters creepy, the atmosphere decadent and decayed. Don't expect a *Star Wars* joyride. *Dune* is a determinedly dark vision, hardly appropriate for the kiddie matinee crowd. What Lynch does not achieve, sadly, is cohesiveness. The story, weighed down by symbolic references to the Bible, Jung, the Holocaust, and the kitchen sink, requires a scorecard for strangers to the book. But Lynch was fortunate with his actors. Kyle MacLachlan does wonders with the impossibly difficult role of Paul Atreides, the young messiah who must wrest the planet Dune from the evil Harkonnen family and stop the production of a hallucinogenic spice that allows its users to glimpse the future. While MacLachlan wrestles with the mystical mumbo jumbo, the villains have fun. Kenneth McMillan, his face festooned with boils, has a field day as the sadistic Baron Harkonnen. And rock star Sting, as the baron's bad-boy nephew, has a scene-stealing sexual arrogance that is mesmerizing. The film is rich in cameos, from Linda Hunt's housekeeper to Jose Ferrer's emperor of the universe. These performaces and Lynch's superb camera eye make *Dune* an outrageous and original entertainment.
PG-13 / 1985 / MCA

E

▲ THE EAGLE HAS LANDED

Although it has all the right ingredients—a more or less plausible plot (Nazi paratroopers attempt to kidnap Churchill), crackerjack actors (Michael Caine, Donald Sutherland, Robert Duvall), and spiffy lenswork—this ends up another big-budget film with a low return. It's a could-have-been thriller that isn't, from a director, John (*The Great Escape*) Sturges, who once knew how.
PG / 1977 / CBS/Fox

▲ EASY MONEY

An R-rated movie with nothing but sight gags, dirty jokes, and Rodney Dangerfield doing his bulging-eyeball number. This was the unrespected comedian's first starring vehicle. He plays a children's photographer who likes to eat, drink, and gamble with his buddies. He's a slob. Then one day his very rich mother-in-law, Geraldine Fitzgerald, decides it's time to reform him. If he stops drinking, smoking, and gambling, and loses a lot of weight, the family department store is his. The movie's subplot has far more potential for humor and interest—Dangerfield's daughter, played by Jennifer Jason Leigh, gets engaged to a Latino, and this provides more laughs than Rodney's incessant no-respect shtik. When things go wrong on the wedding night, Leigh runs home to Daddy. Her lovesick husband, Taylor Negron, and his best buddy do a lot of what appears to be rejected Cheech and Chong material trying to win her back—which comes almost as a relief from the tedium of the rest of the movie. Dangerfield just seems locked into a one-joke routine. After a while he wears down the audience.
R / 1983 / Vestron

▲ EATING RAOUL

Despite its title, *Eating Raoul* is neither a porn flick nor a strange gourmet guide but a rare high-camp comedy that proved palatable to more than art house audiences. Paul Bartel and Mary Woronov play Paul and Mary Bland, a middle-class couple who dream of opening a country restaurant (Chez Bland) outside of Los Angeles. Meanwhile, they're debt-ridden and plagued by sexual swingers who infest their apartment building. When one of the swingers tries to rape Mary, Paul fatally conks him with a skillet, stuffs his body into a garbage bag, and deposits the remains in the building's trash compactor. They keep the $300 in his wallet, however, and thereby discover a new source of financing for Chez Bland. They advertise kinky sex ("We do anything") in a local paper and soon are entertaining all manner of weirdos, each of whom is dispatched with the skillet and relieved of cash. Then Raoul (Richard Beltran), a thief posing as a locksmith, discovers their scam and demands a cut of the action. The plot really does thicken rather than sicken because Paul and Mary are the most wimpy, deadpan murderers imaginable. Bartel, who also directed, co-wrote the script as a vehicle for himself and Woronov, a longtime friend. Since no Hollywood studio was interested in financing the offbeat project, Bartel enlisted actor friends, scrounged film stock, and shot ten minutes here and ten there until the movie was finished on less than a $1 million budget.
R / 1982 / CBS/Fox

▲ EDITH AND MARCEL

For sheer joy in movies, it's hard to beat French director Claude Lelouch—his 1965 *A Man and a Woman* is one of the romantic classics. This story of the tragic real-life love affair between chanteuse Edith Piaf and boxer Marcel Cerdan is just as good. Cerdan, who briefly held the middleweight title, died in a 1949 plane crash—the starting point of the movie, which flashes back to the Piaf-Cerdan meeting and follows the course of a parallel love story between two ordinary French citizens who had a special love for both the boxer and the singer. Evelyne Bouix, a newcomer and just about a dead ringer for *A Man and a Woman*'s Anouk Aimée, plays both Piaf

and the ordinary Frenchwoman, and her performances in the two roles brilliantly blend the saucy and the sublime. (Piaf's music is rendered via recordings, though three new songs, written by Francis Lai and Charles Aznavour, are sung by the French rock singer Mama Bea.) Marcel Cerdan, Jr., takes on the task of playing his own father. His gap-toothed look and gentle manner make him a heart stealer. The atmospherics are convincing too. The film roams from war-torn Europe to the grimy fight scene in New York, where Cerdan loses the middleweight title in a bout with Jake La Motta. This is a grand kind of moviemaking that is every bit as heroic as the improbably melodramatic real events on which it's based. (In French with subtitles.)
Unrated / 1984 / Cinémathèque

▲ EDUCATING RITA

In this quietly memorable film, Michael Caine plays a rumpled, burned-out English professor who couldn't care less about his students and prefers Johnny Walker to William Shakespeare. Enter Julie Walters, a saucy working girl dressed in a tight miniskirt and a clinging sweater. Her hair is peroxide blond with little pink wings, but her mind is sharp: She comes to Caine's class as part of a remedial program. What ensues is a romantic comedy with lots borrowed from *Pygmalion*. But the Oscar-nominated performances by Caine and Walters make the film distinctive. Walters is a vivid presence from her first tottering entrance on high heels to the final scene, where she and Caine bid farewell at an airport. (He leaves for an enforced sabbatical in Australia after one too many drunken revels.) The director is Lewis Gilbert, who did three James Bond films. He also did *Alfie,* which featured Caine's best performance until *Rita.* Caine deftly underplays his role, combining humor and vulnerability. The supporting cast is also superlative. Michael Williams, as a fellow professor having a secret affair with Caine's live-in girlfriend, is hilarious (he always pretends he's just stopped by to use the phone). The movie isn't really about academic life—it's about how a young woman reawakens a tired older man's appetite for life—but let's give everyone an A anyway.
PG / 1983 / RCA/Columbia

▲ 8 MILLION WAYS TO DIE

Jeff Bridges's performance as an alcoholic cop is the only reason to get involved in this adaptation of a Lawrence Block novel directed by Hal (*Coming Home*) Ashby. The plot, set in Los Angeles, is a mix of *The Lost Weekend* and *Klute.* After he's been sneaking some sips on the job, Bridges kills a drug suspect and is forced into a leave of absence. Six sober months later he meets a kookie call girl, Alexandra (*American Flyers*) Paul, who wants to change professions but is too afraid of her pimp, TV actor Randy Brooks. When she is murdered, Bridges goes on a two-day binge. (He's so convincing you can almost feel the pain of his hangover.) Then he starts investigating Brook's role in Paul's death, which leads him to another hooker, Rosanna Arquette (much less sparkly than usual). There's another suspect as well: a drug boss played with real lunatic brio by Andy (*The Untouchables*) Garcia. By this time everyone is talking in such impenetrable drug world jargon that it's hard to tell who might have done what to whom. It's also hard to care. The picture has some of the grim mood of the '40s films noirs it resembles, without having any of the twists and turns peculiar to those movies. Good as he is, Bridges can't compensate for the scarcity of ideas.
R / 1986 / CBS/Fox

▲ 84 CHARING CROSS ROAD

The premise of this film—a twenty-year epistolary liaison between a New York writer and the manager of a London antique bookstore—doesn't sound all that inviting. But don't be scared away; *84 Charing Cross Road* is as beguiling as a letter from a long lost friend. To be sure, this film doesn't leap off the screen at you (most of the movie is comprised by recitations by Anne Bancroft and Anthony Hopkins), but anyone who has a love for words will adore it. The movie is based on a memoir by TV writer Helene Hanff about her correspondence with Frank Doel during the '50s and '60s. Bancroft is in love "with the England of English literature," but can never find the exact editions of classics in New York. So she responds to an advertisement in the back of a literary magazine from Marks and Company, a London bookstore that specializes in out-of-print

books. They fill her request and then some, and she sends them long, bright letters and boxes of food in postwar rationed London. She longs to visit England (even though she knows Hopkins is married) but keeps postponing the trip because her money either goes to doctor bills or the costs of her meager life. Director David Jones's film is punctuated with silly soliloquies, as Bancroft talks straight to the audience, à la *Equus* or more lamentably, *Ferris Bueller's Day Off*. At times Bancroft is cloying and excessively emotional (the film was produced by her husband, Mel Brooks, who bought the rights to the story as a twenty-first anniversary present for her). But she contrasts well with the wonderfully understated Hopkins. It is a delight to hear and watch him as he writes her about the latest book he's found for her or to thank her for the packages. Most of all the film is rich in period detail, especially in the bookstore, where leather-bound volumes of the likes of Thomas Hardy and John Donne cover the walls. The opening for "Masterpiece Theatre" could have been filmed here. No need for Alistair Cooke to spell things out, though: Bancroft's and Hopkins's mutual passion for the English language is palpable.
PG / 1987 / N/A

▲ ELECTRIC DREAMS

A fantasy about a computer that takes over the life—and love life—of a novice hacker, this is an easy-to-like movie. Lenny Von Dohlen is straight-faced as a klutzy, lovable San Francisco yuppie who buys a personal computer he calls Edgar. Everything runs smoothly until he and Edgar begin to vie for the affections of Virginia Madsen, a concert cellist who becomes enamored of the PC's musical compositions, thinking they're Von Dohlen's. It's a high-tech triangle: boy, girl, and oversexed machine. True love triumphs, but is it a match made in heaven or Silicon Valley? While Von Dohlen and Madsen make a charming screen couple, Bud Cort steals the film as the voice of Edgar, a villain with a printed circuit where his heart should be. Whether scheming to ruin Von Dohlen's credit rating or calling Dr. Ruth Westheimer for advice on love, Cort displays the same sly charm and caustic wit that made him so endearing in the 1971 cult classic *Harold and Maude*. Director Steve Barron, responsible for Michael Jackson's "Billie Jean"

video, resists the temptation to make this a 96-minute MTV special, taking time to develop the strange triangular relationship. Barron does dip into his video repertoire, though, synchronizing explosive visual effects with an equally slick sound track that includes songs by Giorgio Moroder, Culture Club, Heaven 17, and Electric Light Orchestra's Jeff Lynne. It all comes together as an escapist package that is exactly what it should be: viewer-friendly fun.
PG / 1984 / MGM/UA

▲ THE ELECTRIC HORSEMAN

It was Robert Redford's first big part since *All the President's Men* and, like a fine Burgundy, he had improved with the years. The role of a TV cowboy fed up with the tawdry business of pitching himself was obviously one Redford felt empathy for. Jane Fonda is a TV journalist, largely restricted to trotting gamely after Redford, as the "Ranch Breakfast Cowboy" takes off for greener pastures. He has all the lines and most of the charm. Country-music star Willie Nelson made an interesting movie debut as Redford's manager and sings most of the sound track as well. More of the footage that was devoted to the purple mountains' majesty should have gone to Willie and Valerie Perrine, who plays Redford's wife. Still, the movie highlights most of what is great about Westerns: a wonderful chase, folksy wisdom, love, humor, scenery, and an electric cast.
PG / 1979 / MCA

▲ ELENI

Few films come with more commanding credentials: In 1983 former *New York Times* reporter Nicholas Gage wrote a deservedly praised book about his mother, Eleni Galzoyiannis. She was a Greek peasant who was imprisoned, tortured, and executed before a firing squad in 1948 (during the three-year civil war in Greece) for trying to save her five children from being forced into Communist indoctrination camps. Nicholas, Eleni's only son, was 9 when (along with his sisters) he was sent to Massachusetts to join his father, who had lived there since 1939. Later, as a *Times* foreign correspondent in Athens in 1977, Gage used his position to investigate his mother's death.

His book, the result of six years of interviews, is both a vivid rendering of Eleni's world and a scrupulous account of Gage's probe. The movie is neither—miscast, melodramatized, its truths misshapen by Hollywood histrionics. Kate Nelligan, the Canadian-born British-trained performer widely regarded for her work onstage (*Plenty*) and in film (*Eye of the Needle*), is woefully wrong as Eleni. Her grand manner, actressy technique, and florid intonations are more appropriate to classic Greek tragedy than to this simple tale of human dignity. The priceless Linda Hunt is more like it as Eleni's neighbor, but Hunt disappears in a blink. John Malkovich as Gage is also a letdown, nearly turning the passionately committed son into a spoiled neurotic. Screenwriter Steve Tesich and director Peter Yates, who collaborated on the lyrical *Breaking Away*, had seemingly lost their touch. The film is awash with close-ups, yet there's little real intimacy. Eleni's story had such dignity, it didn't have to be hyped. The exaggeration is especially surprising when you consider that Gage himself is listed as the film's coproducer. The book's only eyewitness to Eleni's execution describes her as the woman who "screamed and fell to the ground in the instant before the guns opened fire." On-screen, Nelligan, though previously tortured by having her feet beaten, stands ramrod straight, her arms raised exultantly. In the book, Gage takes a gun to his interview with the judge responsible for his mother's death but conceals it, deciding instead to reveal the culprit's identity to the press. In the movie Malkovich brandishes the gun like a modern-day Bogart. Of course such compromises are common practice in an industry where integrity often takes second place to box office. Eleni Gatzoyiannis deserved better.
R / 1985 / Embassy

▲ THE ELEPHANT MAN

There are two things this vivid, mesmerizing film is not. Although Mel Brooks's company is the producer, it is not a comedy. It is also not taken from the award-winning Broadway play, which was primarily fiction. The movie claims to be the true, if dramatized, account (from several historical sources) of John Merrick, hideously deformed at birth and resigned to life as a circus freak until rescued by a London surgeon. As Merrick, John Hurt is disguised with latex. At first, the effect is horrific. But before long Hurt exposes the tortured man beneath. It is an unforgettable performance in a film full of marvelous actors: Anthony Hopkins as the surgeon, Wendy Hiller as a sympathetic nurse, John Gielgud as a hospital official, and Freddie Jones as Merrick's creepy sideshow keeper. Only Anne Bancroft is subpar in the underwritten part of an actress who introduces Merrick to Victorian society. Director David Lynch, whose only previous credit was the cult film *Eraserhead,* overdoes the horror. But aided by Freddie Francis's evocative black-and-white photography, Lynch captures the dark underside of a society that exploits its freaks. Despite the excess, this is a uniquely memorable film.
PG / 1980 / Paramount

▲ EL NORTE

As this superb Mexican import begins, a Guatemalan villager has been gunned down by government troops who suspect that he is a revolutionary. His son and daughter, in their late teens, flee to Mexico, knowing their lives are also in danger. But their real goal is "el norte"—the U.S. Their tortuous journey leads them to an abandoned sewer, through which they crawl into California. Once settled in a rundown section of Los Angeles, the young man, played by David Villalpando, finds a job as a busboy, and his sister, Zaide Silvia Gutierrez, becomes a domestic. They find that the American dream, so promising from a distance, can disintegrate. Villalpando is eventually betrayed to the immigration authorities, and Gutierrez comes down with a deadly disease, the result of rat bites in the tunnel. Despite its sobering theme, the film provides some nice flecks of humor. Gutierrez, working for a wealthy Beverly Hills matron, can't figure out an automatic washing machine and ends up doing the laundry by hand, letting it dry on the grass by the pool. Director Gregory Nava, a Mexican-Basque graduate of U.C.L.A.'s film school, co-wrote the script with his wife, Anna Thomas, a cookbook author (*The Vegetarian Epicure*). Their documentary tone creates a convincing contrast between the lush hills of poverty-ridden Mexico and the squalor of rich Los Angeles. The result is a disturbing movie about hope and disappointment. (In Spanish with subtitles.)
R / 1984 / CBS/Fox

▲ THE EMERALD FOREST

Director John Boorman started with a naturally dramatic story: An American engineer working in Brazil is picnicking with his family when his young son is kidnapped by Indians. The father spends ten years searching the jungle for the boy (the plot is based on a real incident). While that premise ought to be enough for a movie, Boorman mostly uses it to excoriate modern society. He makes a sloppy case of it. For one thing, the Indians are often ruthless, sometimes cannibalistic, given to sadistic initiation ceremonies and hallucinogenic drugs. For another, it is dishonest for Boorman to use the skills and technology of an industrialized country to make a movie belittling industrialization. He also resorts to idiotic mumbo jumbo. The boy can turn into an eagle and fly around, inciting frogs to start big storms by croaking. While Boorman's son Charley as the kidnapped boy, Powers Boothe as the father, and Rui Polonah as an Indian chief lend the film dignity, its real star is the rain forest. Photographed by Philippe Rousselot, the jungle is full of rich beauty, yet man's creations also can be full of nobility and beauty. By biasing his argument so cheaply, Boorman loses the sympathy he's trying to arouse.
R / 1985 / Embassy

▲ EMPIRE OF THE ANTS

A Florida real estate junket (including a pre-"Dynasty" Joan Collins) arrives at a remote swamp just when some huge mutant ants tire of eating sugar and decide to add protein to their diet. After half the group has been shredded, one woman consoles the terrorized survivors by saying, "We're all on edge." The dialogue goes down the anthill from there. In 1954's *Them!* even the ants were better actors.
PG / 1977 / Embassy

▲ THE EMPIRE STRIKES BACK

Remember *Casablanca II? Son of the Wizard of Oz? The Revenge of Ben Hur?* Of course not, because long, long ago in a movie capital far, far away, people dared not tarnish the memory of classics by exhuming them for sequels. This movie, of course, was *Star Wars II,* and while it's hardly the worst sequel ever made—*Exorcist II* retired that trophy—it's not up to the original either. The spacecraft-laser-battle gimmicks are familiar now, so even though these are the most special of the special effects, they are no longer so fascinating. Worse, the more one sees the main characters, the less appealing they become. Luke Skywalker is a whiner, Han Solo a sarcastic clod, Princess Leia a nag, and C-3PO just a drone. Nor will the acting of the performers who play them—Mark Hamill, Harrison Ford, and Carrie Fisher—stand much scrutiny, especially in comparison with Alec Guinness, in a cameo as Ben Kenobi, and James Earl Jones, again masterful as the evil voice of Darth Vader. There is a delightfully conceived and executed elfin guru named Yoda. Also charming is George Lucas's continuing homage to his favorite things. *Hamlet, Tarzan, The War of the Worlds,* Jack London's story *To Build a Fire,* and even "Star Trek" seem to be saluted. (Lucas gets executive producer credit this time, while Irvin Kershner, who had sequel experience on *The Return of a Man Called Horse,* directed, and sci-fi veteran Leigh Brackett and Lawrence Kasdan wrote the sometimes sluggish screenplay.) There are a couple of surprising plot twists as Luke confronts the not quite so goody-goody side of his nature. The ending is emotionally unsatisfying, though, and that's no accident. Lucas said this was to be only the first of eight sequels, though the batteries in Luke's light sword seemed to wear out after *Return of the Jedi.*
PG / 1980 / CBS/Fox

▲ THE END

A comedy about dying may not be everyone's cup of hemlock. Still, Burt Reynolds at least took a chance in his second directorial venture. (The first was *Gator.*) *The End* is a series of cameos in what's left of the life of a sleazy real estate dealer who has a fatal blood disease. With Sally Field (Burt's then real-life lady) playing his hippie honey, Joanne Woodward his divorced wife, Myrna Loy and Pat O'Brien his parents, Kristy McNichol his daughter, Carl Reiner his doctor, and Dom De Luise his nutso abettor in a suicide project, Reynolds has little time for character development. But since semi-fun is had by all, *The End* pretty much justifies the means.
R / 1978 / CBS/Fox

▲ ENDLESS LOVE

"Do you think I'm too small on top?" asks Brooke Shields of her 17-year-old lover (Martin Hewitt) as they lie naked in her bedroom in her parents' house. Such trite *Blue Lagoon*ish dialogue trivialized this film adaptation of Scott Spencer's first-rate 1979 novel of obsession. Banished from Brooke's life by her parents, Hewitt sets fire to their house thinking he can stage a fake rescue. Instead, he is almost too late. Arrested, he is sent to a mental institution for two years and, even when released, is kept apart from his love. His compulsive attempts to get her back made for a voluptuous poisoned flower of a book. Onscreen, bathed in director Franco (*Romeo and Juliet*) Zeffirelli's misty-glow photography, the story has lost its venom. Hewitt's ardent obsession is rendered merely as thwarted love interest, pumped by the Diana Ross–Lionel Ritchie theme song. There are compensations, though, in this too slick production—like the way Shirley Knight turns Brooke's on-the-edge-of-a-cliché mother into a mercurial, delicate, passionate woman. The director has also done well by Hewitt, more than a promising newcomer. As for Brooke, then 16, she was too awkward and squeaky-voiced to be considered a persuasive actress. As everyone connected with the movie went to great lengths to point out, a double replaces Shields in the nude scenes. But more than anything else in this empty movie, her beauty makes us see what Spencer saw of the joy in love and the ache in its loss.
R / 1981 / MCA

▲ THE END OF THE WORLD IN OUR USUAL BED IN A NIGHT FULL OF RAIN

Except for its all-time title length, Italian director Lina Wertmuller's first English-language film was disappointing. Candice Bergen plays an American photographer married to Giancarlo Giannini, an Italian journalist with Communist sympathies. The story serves up Wertmuller's typically lavish portions of sex and politics, while portraying a long night in the crumbling marriage of this odd couple. The music is terrific, the cinematography breathtaking, and Wertmuller's energy is everywhere evident. But, aside from Giannini, the acting is strangely uneven, and in Bergen's case just plain awful. The rumors of conflict on the set between the director and her beautiful star were supported by the final product.
R / 1978 / N/A

▲ ENIGMA

This spy saga seems relatively as weighty and substantial as a Nancy Drew mystery. Martin Sheen stars as an American working for a radio propaganda operation in Paris. Because he had once lived in East Germany, he is recruited by American intelligence to return there and steal a Soviet encoding device. His success naturally sets off a flurry of concern in East German intelligence circles, driving Derek (*I, Claudius*) Jacobi, in particular, to heights of hateful villainy. Jacobi is second-guessed by the KGB, led by New Zealand actor Sam (*My Brilliant Career*) Neill, who seems strangely likable. Meanwhile Sheen teams up with a former lover, played by Brigitte Fossey. She worms her way into the KGB chief's heart and bed en route to his trade secrets. Sheen is efficient in an undemanding role, Fossey seems sincere enough, and director Jeannot (*Jaws II*) Szwarc gives the film a swift pace and glossy coating. But there are too many implausible elements in the script by John (*Gandhi*) Briley. What self-respecting KGB officer, for instance, would not know he was being seduced by the ex-girlfriend of a suspicious American? The showy plot twists and superficial complexity do lead to an enigma, but it is not a very intriguing one: What was all the fuss about?
PG / 1983 / Embassy

▲ ENORMOUS CHANGES AT THE LAST MINUTE

Based on short stories by Grace Paley, adapted for the screen by John Sayles, and co-directed by three independent filmmakers, this loosely connected trilogy weaves an affecting portrait of three New York women. They're all struggling to achieve self-sufficiency amid the pressures of failing romances and the vagaries of family life. Their stories combine in a spare, intimate film with the look of a home movie. In the first and most assured segment, directed by Ellen Hovde and Muffie Meyer, Ellen Barkin portrays a 26-year-old trying to keep her three children fed and happy after her husband abandons the family.

She spends days hassling with rude welfare clerks and nights staring aimlessly out her window, until she finds unexpected comfort when an old high school flame, now balding, overweight, and married, reenters her life. Barkin's performance is disarmingly simple and direct as she progresses from a frightened, deserted wife to a tough single parent. The second segment, directed by Hovde and Mirra Bank, is about one of Barkin's neighbors, Lynn Milgrim. She lends a brittle intensity to her role as a bitter divorcee cowed by her responsibilities to her two sons, to her neglectful lover, and to her parents, who are growing dotty in a retirement home. This strangely flat episode revolves around a macabre hysterical visit that Milgrim makes to her parents. The final and funniest segment, directed by Bank, concerns a kindhearted social worker, Maria Tucci. Long-divorced and childless, she counsels teenage drug addicts and unwed mothers. She worries constantly about her father, a critical old man obsessed with his own mortality. When she attracts a cabbie 15 years her junior—played with warmth and wit by Kevin Bacon—she has an impulsive affair with him and becomes pregnant. Soon Tucci's teenage clients are offering advice to her. Tucci's natural grace and subtlety add to the tale's charm; her pained, ironic smile at once obscures and reveals her fear and loneliness. *Enormous Changes at the Last Minute* is a fitting title for this unique film: It has much to say about the hardships, surprises, and rewards women encounter in the search for love and autonomy.
Unrated / 1985 / N/A

▲ ENTER THE NINJA

With the blood and guts kept out of sight and some James Bondesque humor filling the gaps, this film manages to leap over many of the martial arts film's clichés. Franco Nero plays the Ninja, an American import to Japan. (A Ninja, we learn, is one well versed in the medieval Japanese pastime of Ninjutsu, or "art of assassination.") Equipped with every hand-to-hand combat move imaginable, he travels to Manila, where he visits an old war buddy, Alex Courtney, and the buddy's rifle-wielding wife, sexy Susan George. Also in town are a resident bully known as "The Hook," played for fun by the roly-poly Zachi Noy, and an evil corporate genius (Christopher George). He seems intent on ruling the world but

will settle for the Philippines. Enter our Nero with the usual aplomb-filled dropkicks, and everything is tidy again. Writer Dick Desmond's script is often campy, and George is amusingly villainous. Director Menahem Golan avoids the genre's "violence is golden" rule, for which he deserves a pat on the back but nothing more strenuous.
R / 1981 / MGM/UA

▲ THE ENTITY

The demon in this very farfetched scare flick is invisible but persistent and extremely noisy. It sounds, in fact, much like a disco rhythm track paced for, say, a Donna Summer sizzler. When the title phenomenon visits Barbara Hershey, playing a single mother of three, it has its effect, variously making her gyrate, slam herself against walls, press down on her gas pedal, and otherwise act up. Mostly, though, it seems to have sex on its mind. Hershey seeks help from a shrink, played amusingly by Ron Silver (in supporting roles, he was the best thing about both *Best Friends* and *Lovesick*). Then she tries some local parapsychologists. The most likely explanation for her problem seems to be some undue affection she recalls her father's lavishing on her when she was a girl. But this is not a movie about Freud; it's a movie about "subcarnate reality," says one parapsychologist. He has the last word, and in an unconsciously hilarious finale in which Hershey seems to be trying to seduce a hose filled with liquid helium, he tries to send the menace back whence it came. Supposedly based on a "true" incident in California, *The Entity* was part of a sub-fad of horror films—those about young women being ravaged by oversexed spirits (see, or don't see, 1982's *The Incubus* and *Demon Rage*, for example). That this one is directed by the respectable Sidney Furie (*The Ipcress File, Lady Sings the Blues*) doesn't make it any less ridiculous.
R / 1983 / CBS/Fox

▲ ENTRE NOUS

Diane Kurys is a first-class scavenger. For her warm and perceptive character studies, the French director-screenwriter usually ransacks her own history and experience. *Entre Nous* was her third

such enterprise, and Kurys turned her observant eye on her parents. In the city of Lyons in 1952 Isabelle Huppert thrives as the pretty bourgeois wife of a garage owner (Guy Marchand) and the mother of two young daughters. At the school recital of one daughter, she meets Miou-Miou, a sophisticated sculptor who lost her first husband in World War II and has misguidedly married a fledgling actor with big career plans and little else. As these two women share a succession of everyday dramas and domestic obligations, they seal a friendship that spoils their marriages. Miou-Miou forsakes her husband and son, while Huppert awakens to both the sexual and career possibilities that await women of her caliber. Like her compatriot François Truffaut, Kurys has a gift for clear-eyed compassion; she colors even the blackest event or character with shades of gray. Although *Entre Nous* is a celebration of the emotional and sexual bonds between women, Kurys doesn't indiscriminately indict her male characters. She acknowledges the crimes of the heart that are committed in the name of emotional emancipation. As the heroines, Huppert and Miou-Miou exhibit vibrancy and range that neither previously displayed. But as exceptional as the actors are, this film is primarily Kury's triumph. She is masterly at turning an accumulation of small details into a haunting tableau. (In French with subtitles.)
PG / 1984 / MGM/UA

▲ EQUUS

On Broadway, British playwright Peter Schaffer's story of a doubt-ridden psychiatrist trying to find out why a young boy has blinded six horses was thoroughbred drama. This slow-moving, self-conscious film version finishes out of the money. Directed by Sidney Lumet, *Equus* (Latin for "horse") stars Richard Burton as the shrink (a part he played memorably, if briefly, on the stage) and elastic-faced Peter Firth, who created the role of the sexually disturbed boy on Broadway. Joan Plowright is superb as Firth's Bible-quoting, confused mum, and Burton's frequent soliloquies—directed straight at the camera—are suitably tortured. But all the tension and stark symbolism of the stage production are dissipated as the movie plods like an old wheel horse to its inevitable conclusion.
R / 1977 / MGM/UA

▲ ERASERHEAD

Charlotte Stewart of "Little House on the Prairie" plays Mary X, who with her factory-worker lover Henry (film newcomer John Nance) produces a horrible premature "baby," far more grotesque than Rosemary's. Besides the blood-spitting, gut-oozing horror, there's a little sci-fi, a little low comedy, some flying fetuses, and a rolling severed head (later molded into an eraser), making this one of the most repugnant, yet fascinating, movies ever shown. Writer-director-producer David Lynch's aspiration to high art (filming in near darkness, droning white background sound, a grant from the American Film Institute) either keep it from being blatantly ridiculous or make it more so, depending on the audience's tolerance. Still, the picture has been selling popcorn with the midnight crawler cult on both coasts for years (as did the similar *Night of the Living Dead*). And Lynch, who followed up this one with *The Elephant Man, Dune,* and *Blue Velvet,* kept making movies that stir up controversy and change the way we look at the world. He's a genuine original.
Unrated / 1978 / RCA/Columbia

▲ THE ESCAPE ARTIST

Griffin O'Neal, Ryan's much-publicized and troubled son and Tatum's brother, is superbly freckled and nonchalant as a small-town kid hooked on the legend of his dead father, "the greatest escape artist who ever lived, after Houdini." The kid is driven to emulate his dad's tricks (helped by his wacky aunt and uncle, Joan Hackett and Gabriel Dell, who have a struggling magic show). Along the way Griffin becomes a smooth picker of locks and pockets, and lifts a wallet crammed with $100 bills from Raul Julia, the son of the town's mayor. The mayor is played by Desi Arnaz the elder, in his first film in twenty-six years. The heist sets in motion an effortlessly eccentric, absorbing series of plot turns. Julia persuades the boy to pull off some jobs for him, including cracking his own father's safe. Kids will take particular delight in the affable O'Neal as he hot-wires a Caddy and locks himself inside a mailbox to flee a knife-wielding Julia. The film, scripted by Stephen Zito and Melissa (*E.T.*) Mathison from David Wagoner's novel, is deftly directed by Caleb Deschanel. Arnaz is wonderful

as the corrupt mayor; Julia is just right as his nutty, good-for-nada son. And the debut of O'Neal, at seventeen, gives this little gem of a film a special magic.
PG / 1982 / Vestron

▲ ESCAPE FROM ALCATRAZ

In 1962, three men escaped from the island fortress that was this country's most notorious maximum security prison—thought, after fourteen previous attempts had failed, to be escape-proof. This movie details the intricate planning for the break, masterminded by bank robber Frank Morris. (None of the three fugitives were ever found.) Directed by frequent collaborator Don Siegel, Clint Eastwood does his silent stuff to perfection. As the seedy Morris, his mind moves behind his eyes, and there are enough prison dustups to give him a chance to flex his more physical talents. The cast of unknowns is excellent, notably Frank Fonzio, as a con with a pet mouse, and a white-hating librarian, Paul Benjamin. Patrick McGoohan, without his British accent, is the vindictive warden. But it is the escape plan that makes this a picture of old-fashioned, dark, tense excitement.
PG / 1979 / Paramount

▲ ESCAPE FROM NEW YORK

The year is 1997. The U.S. has apparently survived a war with Russia. Manhattan has been turned into a maximum security prison with a thirty-three-foot-high wall around it. "To enter," the movie ad boasted, "is insane, to escape is impossible." Maybe the first part is true but not the second. With the profits he made from low-budget horror fodder like *Halloween* and *The Fog*, John Carpenter finally got to direct and co-write a film he conceived back in 1974, when he was still John Who. The President (Donald Pleasence) is kidnapped and held captive on the island; police chief Lee Van Cleef gives inmate Kurt Russell the assignment to free the Prez. Gratuitous savagery and implausibility ensue. With the exception of the stark sets and Carpenter's dramatic synthesizer compositions, played loud enough to give a scalp massage, the film is predictable and clichéd. Russell, who starred in Carpenter's TV movie *Elvis*, has a patch over

one eye, but for all his grunts and dumb sneering, he'd be better if it were over his mouth. Mrs. Carpenter, Adrienne Barbeau, provides little more than a world-class jiggle as the companion of mad scientist Harry Dean Stanton. Soul star Isaac Hayes is the evil Main Man, cruising in a limo through the rotten Big Apple (actually, most scenes were shot in St. Louis). This film is really about escaping in L.A.—to the kind of maximum security and freedom a director wins through bankability.
R / 1981 / Embassy

▲ E.T.

What do you say now about the biggest money-maker in motion picture history? Let's start with how good it is. In *E.T.* (it stands for Extra-Terrestrial), director Steven Spielberg combined the gimmick-a-minute intensity he brought to *Jaws* and *Raiders of the Lost Ark* with the emotional intimacy he started to develop in *Close Encounters of the Third Kind*. The result was his most personal film and his best. *E.T.* packs the classic fairy-tale wallop of *The Wizard of Oz* and *Peter Pan*, from which it openly borrows. The story concerns an alien creature trapped alone in a California suburb after his fellow E.T.s beat a hasty retreat in their spaceship. A young boy, beautifully played by Henry Thomas (a young Texan discovered in *Raggedy Man*), comes to his aid. With the help of older brother Robert MacNaughton and kid sister Drew Barrymore (John Sr.'s granddaughter), Henry hides the E.T. in his bedroom away from his mother, Dee Wallace. Melissa Mathison's screenplay is a perfect blend of intelligent humor and sentiment. E.T., designed by effects wizard Carlo Rambaldi (who also worked on *Alien* and *Close Encounters*), is the scene stealer. Whether he's stalking the house in a bathrobe, learning English from a child's computer game, or accidentally getting soused on beer, the E.T. is sure to steal hearts, seize imaginations. When the creature's life is in danger, and Spielberg turns loose his arsenal of dazzling yet controlled effects, the movie yanks a viewer into the fray. The ending is unforgettable, as is the entire film. But more than that, E.T. remains one of the greatest Hollywood films ever made. It seems inconceivable now that *Gandhi* won the Best Picture Oscar in the Year of *E.T.* But the Academy has always preferred stodgy, pseudo-art to the thrill of being richly entertained. Spielberg need not feel slighted. Years after other Oscar-winning films have been forgotten, *E.T.* will endure to fill future audiences with a sense of wonder. By any definition, this one is a classic. **PG / 1982 / Still not available in video at presstime.**

▲ EVERY WHICH WAY BUT LOOSE

Every which way puts it mildly, since this so-called comedy rambles along willy-nilly—and back to willy again. With Clint Eastwood at the wheel, the trip is not totally disagreeable. He follows his fists east from California in pursuit of aspiring country-western singer Sondra Locke. Sondra's pipes are passable, but the best tunes come from Charlie Rich and Mel Tillis (in the flesh) and Eddie Rabbit, who sings the surefire title track. However, not even superfine pluckin' and singing' can totally compensate for two ludicrous subplots concerning a motorcycle gang and an off-duty cop obsessed with Eastwood's capture. Some laughs are provided, though, by Clint's sidekicks, Geoffrey Lewis and an engaging orangutan named Clyde. (Ruth Gordon's crazy-old-lady shtik seems just tiresome.) Though hardly up to hard-edge *Dirty Harry* standards, this Eastwood effort will placate his fans and treat them to some terrific twanging in the bargain. **PG / 1978 / Warner**

▲ THE EVIL DEAD

If there are any ancient Sumerians around, they ought to sue for defamation of character, since they are blamed for the curse that leads to all the havoc in this imbecilic horror movie. Set in a lonely cabin in Tennessee, it is directed by a young Detroit filmmaker, Sam Raimi, with no sense of style. His technique: Turn people into ghoulish fiends and follow that up with a lot of bleeding and gut-spilling. As soon as the vines and trees start attacking—they manage to rape a young woman in one particularly ugly scene—it is clear that only a huge dose of weed killer could have saved this film. To what perverse strains of human nature do movies like this appeal? **R / 1983 / Thorn/EMI**

▲ THE EVIL THAT MEN DO

Charles Bronson films operate on the principle that the more malevolent the villain inciting Charlie's wrath, the more liberal his license to gain revenge. In this case he raises the stakes of graphic violence above even that of *Death Wish* movies. Bronson plays a professional killer lured out of serene retirement by Jose Ferrer, a kindly professor. Apparently easily swayed by humanitarian causes, Bronson agrees to track down a sadistic doctor who has been advising Latin American countries on the finer points of torture. Theresa Saldana appears as Bronson's partner in vengeance; this was a bizarre film for her comeback after a near-fatal assault by an apparent psychopath in Los Angeles in 1982. Bronson disposes of the doc's henchmen one by one, like someone peeling the leaves off an artichoke, and J. Lee Thompson, directing his fifth Bronson film, missed few chances to boost the body count. The settings in and around Guadalajara, Mexico, are lovely—when they can be seen between the blood spatters. **R / 1984 / RCA/Columbia**

▲ EVIL UNDER THE SUN

Murder on the Orient Express was more surprising, and *Death on the Nile* was more sumptuous. But *Evil Under the Sun*—the third of Agatha Christie's Hercule Poirot stories to reach the screen in recent years—is the most fun. Monsieur Poirot, the Belgian master detective, here in the portly person of Peter Ustinov, is at a plush Adriatic resort in the summer of 1938 when what else but foul play turns up. The murder victim is a showgirl (played with great verve by Diana Rigg) whose gold-digging ways have led her to walk out on a hit play and its producers (James Mason and Sylvia Miles) and marry a millionaire (Denis Quilley). All gather at the resort hotel, whose owner (the incomparable Maggie Smith) hates Rigg almost as much as Mason and Miles do. Other potential suspects include Rigg's stepdaughter (Emily Hone), a Hollywood gossip (Roddy McDowall), a discarded lover (Colin Blakely), and a wronged third party (Jane Birkin), whose gigolo husband (Nicholas Clay) has been dallying with Rigg. It's up to Poirot, of course, to sleuth out the culprit. Whether he is taking his morning swim by standing ankle-deep in water

and pantomiming a breaststroke or railing against mispronunciation of his name, Ustinov's Poirot is a delight. The whole cast, under Guy Hamilton's direction, is first-class, but Rigg and Smith steal the show with some expert bitchery, especially in a hilarious duet of *You're the Top* that turns into an upstaging contest. Another pleasure that underscores the action is the array of Cole Porter tunes, superbly arranged by John Lanchbery. As one of them has it, *Evil Under the Sun* is "delightful, delicious, and de-lovely."
PG / 1982 / Thorn/EMI

▲ EXCALIBUR

Picture Camelot with its songs replaced by slice'em and dice 'em bloodletting worthy of today's horror films, plus just a bit of Monty Python madness. That will give you some idea of the visually stunning, verbally overwrought retelling of the Arthurian legend by John (*Deliverance*) Boorman. The director said he pictured an evocation of "man's lost oneness with nature" (one of his preoccupations), and the superb location photography in Ireland vividly makes us long for primeval times. But the script, which Boorman co-wrote, carries a deadweight of decadence. While switching the legend's focus from Arthur to Merlin is an intriguing concept, Nicol Williamson's low-comic anachronistic playing of the magician doesn't mesh with the stiff-upper-lip heroics of Nigel Terry's Arthur or Nicholas Clay's Lancelot. Helen (*Caligula*) Mirren fares little better as Arthur's incestuous sister, who is fond of hanging knights from trees and watching birds peck their eyes out in close-up. There are hacked limbs aplenty, and the sex is kinky enough to stir envy even in Ken Russell. Many naked women couple with knights in full, spiky armor. That the director uses his own daughter, Katrine, for one such encounter is hardly chivalrous. Neither is the movie, which, despite moments of high style and wit, too often substitutes mayhem for magic.
R / 1981 / Warner

▲ EXORCIST II: THE HERETIC

This reincarnation of the 1973 smash (in the all-time top 20 box-office ratings) suffers from distressingly silly dialogue and a badly contrived plot. The late Richard Burton, looking constantly tortured (perhaps by embarrassment at being seen in such drivel), is the priest trying to literally beat the devil out of poor Linda Blair, who went on to spend the rest of her career on the B-picture circuit. Oscar winner Louise Fletcher is wasted in another cuckoo's nest role. This horror show has its only moments in the final scene, where the last Welsh actor tries to save Linda—and us—from facing an *Exorcist III*. So far he's succeeded.
R / 1977 / Warner

▲ EXPLORERS

Steven Spielberg's name appears nowhere on this teen space-adventure flick. Perhaps he was too busy turning out *Back to the Future* and *The Goonies*. Still, the spirit of Hollywood's Mr. Magic hovers. *Explorers* director Joe Dante, who worked with Spielberg on 1984's *Gremlins*, knows a hit formula when he borrows one. Take kids, computer effects, creatures cuddly or blood-curdling, then mix and serve to a teen audience. Dante's *Gremlins, The Howling*, and the kiddie terror segment of *Twilight Zone—The Movie* displayed a devilishly original humor that cut through the goo; however, Dante is working along more traditional lines here. Three California teens build a spaceship and set off to unlock the secrets of the unknown. It helps that *Explorers* is a state-of-the-art space toy. The kids construct their craft out of junk shop parts, making a welcome, homey contrast to the film's wow visual effects by George Lucas's Industrial Light and Magic outfit. It helps also that the boys—sensitive Ethan Hawke, nerdy River Phoenix, and brash Jason Presson—are natural and appealing. Their space trip may be familiar, but they make it fun. Strangely, things go awry at just the point the real jolts should start: when the boys make alien contact. Dante and screenwriter Eric Luke develop a surprising conceit. Expecting to meet creatures with the wisdom and grace of those in *Close Encounters*, the trio finds instead Robert Picardo and Leslie Rickert, two bubble-brained alien fanatics for '50s TV. The joke is funny, but the effect is a downer for the boys and, for that matter, the kid in all of us. By exchanging the wonder-of-space myth for the earthbound message that TV isn't good for kids, *Explorers* proves too clever for its own good.
PG / 1985 / Paramount

▲ EXPOSED

The casting is promising: Nastassja Kinski, an international movie star despite her limited acting abilities, plays opposite Rudolf Nureyev, once king of the ballet, seemingly on course in his second career as a movie star. Sadly, the expected sparks never fly. It's not the actors' fault. James (*Fingers*) Toback, the director-writer-producer, flails about like a mad-hatter. The film, a disjointed, almost farcical international thriller, is devoid of sensible plot, character, and dialogue, which doesn't leave much. Kinski, showing more range as an actress than in any of her previous films, is a bored college student who drops out for the big-time world of New York modeling. She soon gets caught up in a bizarre plot to catch an international terrorist, played by Harvey Keitel—a good actor once again stuck in a mediocre role. Nureyev is a concert violinist in pursuit of Keitel, although it is never clear why. Nureyev's plot to use Kinski as bait could have produced an exciting twist, but in Toback's hands the development makes no sense. All that takes place is a lot of dashing back and forth between New York and Paris. The characters don't get anywhere, and it's not much of a trip for the viewer, either.
R / 1983 / MGM/UA

▲ EXTREME PREJUDICE

If you're in the mood for a cartoonish shoot-'em-up, with touches of "Mission Impossible" and *The Wild Bunch,* you could do worse than this film. It's a variation on those '30s films with James Cagney and Pat O'Brien as boyhood friends now on opposite sides of the law. Nick Nolte, a Texas Ranger in a border town, has grown up so pure-hearted he wears his white hat even when sitting behind his desk. Powers Boothe, a drug dealer operating out of Mexico, is so mean he crushes scorpions in his bare hand for fun. A third side in this triangle of violence is provided by a high-tech government commando unit. They're going after Boothe by robbing a bank in Nolte's town where the drug money is laundered. When director Walter Hill sticks with gunplay, he keeps the momentum going. The dialogue is another matter. The ramrod-straight Nolte has to say such things as "He's polluting this town with drugs and turning it into a sewer." Maria Con-chita Alonso, as a cantina singer in love with both Nolte and Boothe, actually mutters "crazy gringo" at Nolte. Boothe acts his way out of a lot of lost lines. He even generates a smile when, just before the big gun battle, he says to Nolte, "Let's get this over with. It's almost 4 o'clock." Hill draws blood only in the literal sense of gory violence. There is no issue here. But for a movie that isn't really about anything, *Extreme Prejudice* keeps the screen occupied reasonably well.
R / 1987 / NA

▲ THE EXTERMINATOR

Don't get your hopes up, pest-control fans. The villains in this poor man's version of *Death Wish* are human. Make that poor producer's version, since every expense was spared. The cast's big name is Christopher George, whose career was most visible on 2 A.M. TV reruns of *Rat Patrol.* He plays an honest cop halfheartedly chasing a vigilante who vows to rid New York City of crime after a Vietnam buddy is mauled by a street gang. To his credit, Robert Ginty works at playing the vigilante with some subtlety, though when he looks queasy after stuffing a mobster into a meat grinder, it's hard to tell if the character or the actor can't quite believe what he's doing. Also noteworthy is special effects man Stevie Kirschoff, clearly expert at making junky old cars blow up in spectacular fashion. Writer-director James Blickenhaus crams in excessive sadism, violence, and obscenity in a movie that indicts the Establishment as well as overt criminals. There seems to be little difference between corrupt officials being foiled and homosexual procurers being sauteed.
R / 1980 / Embassy

▲ EXTREMITIES

As a victim of attempted rape in this film version of the William Matrosimone play that died off-Broadway in 1983, Farrah Fawcett is riveting. She needed to be. Despite some effective TV emoting (*Murder in Texas, The Burning Bed*), Fawcett saw her screen career fizzle in the four movies (*Somebody Killed Her Husband, Sunburn, Saturn 3, Cannonball Run*) she made after fleeing the high floss of "Charlie's Angels." With a basically bland personality, Fawcett requires material that snaps an audience to attention. *Extremities,* for all its weaknesses, is no slouch at snap. Fawcett plays a woman stalked by a rapist (James Russo) who cons himself into her house, taunts her, then paws and beats her. Russo, who created the role onstage, gives an award-caliber performance. But director Robert (*Short Eyes*) Young's leering camera too often substitutes sensationalism for characterization: Watch Fawcett's nipple being bitten in close-up, her body paraded in spike heels and black negligee for a pervert's delectation. Before Russo can proceed with the rape, Fawcett blinds him with bug spray and cages him in a fireplace. That was hard to believe onstage, harder in the movie. Spewing hatred, Fawcett is planning to bury the creep alive in the garden when her roommates walk in—Diana (*Silkwood*) Scarwid and Alfre (*Cross Creek*) Woodard. They aren't real characters, merely mouthpieces used by Mastrosimone to debate pat moral questions about rape and vengeance. The endless argument that ensues is hogwash. So is the movie, despite strong, stinging work by Fawcett and Russo.

R / 1986 / Paramount

▲ AN EYE FOR AN EYE

The nimble Chuck Norris still gets his kicks from karate. But the Great White Box-Office Hope of martial arts cinema needs a script. His lines here can put you out faster than a savage kick to the attention span. Director Steve Carver is a Roger Corman disciple whose credits include Angie Dickinson's biggest embarrassment, *Big Bad Mama.* He cast Norris as a San Francisco cop who quit the force to avenge the murder of his partner during a drug investigation. The murder trail leads back to—surprise!—a secret society. Norris's nemesis is the titanically blubbery (four creases in the back of his neck) ''Professor'' Toru Tanaka, a 290-pound pro wrestler, whose emoting is limited to stomps and grunts. Christopher Lee, fiendish even without his Dracula fangs, is dapper as a villainous TV executive. While Norris succeeds in saving the free world from the Asian poppy crop, he can't rescue his fans from the even more insidious Hollywood poppycock.

R / 1981 / Embassy

▲ EYE OF THE NEEDLE

A stripped-down version of Ken Follett's 1978 best-seller, this thriller may disappoint fans of the novel, if not fans of film. Set in Britain during World War II, it's the story of a German spy who discovers plans for the Allied invasion of Normandy, then desperately tries to get the information to Hitler. Donald Sutherland's performance as the spy is icily impeccable as he murders his London landlady when she catches him transmitting information, then flees across England to a rendezvous with a German sub. While waiting for his U-boat to come in, Sutherland seduces Kate Nelligan, the gorgeous wife of a cripple. Nelligan's performance as a sex-starved wife is erotic and engrossing; her agonizing over whether to kill the man she loves gives the film a slambang ending. The problem is that the novel's richness lies in the conflicts of the spy's smudged psychological makeup, and none of that carries over into the movie. (Stanley Mann did the screenplay.) Sutherland just comes across as a bad guy we'd be happy to see bumped off, and that cheats the audience.

R / 1981 / CBS/Fox

▲ EYES OF LAURA MARS

The ayes have it for this slick murder mystery. Faye Dunaway, looking very pale, plays a high-fashion photographer fond of shooting fake murder scenes for her magazine ads. Then she starts having eerie visions: She claims she can see real murders as they're taking place. The cops think she's cuckoo, of course, but when the killer comes after her the suspense is harrowing, if carefully manufactured. Tommy Lee Jones is perfect as the sympathetic detective who falls in love with Faye, Rene Auberjonois oozes jealousy as her gay assistant, and Brad Dourif is spooky as the chauffeur with a suspicious past. The ending is a surprise, though not a very convincing one. But the fun is watching Dunaway and her kinky models doing their own version of the world of Helmut Newton. Jon Peters produced and his then lady, Barbra Streisand, sang the theme song, *Prisoner.* Whatever happened to them?

R / 1978 / RCA/Columbia

▲ EYEWITNESS

Director Peter Yates and screenwriter Steve Tesich, who teamed up on *Breaking Away,* scored again here with a classy mystery. William Hurt plays an office building janitor who finds a tenant murdered and then, in order to meet a TV newswoman he's long admired from afar, pretends to know more than he does. (The plot is based on Tiesch's own struggling days as a janitor, when he used to fantasize about CBS's Lesley Stahl.) Hurt is terrific, creating a memorable movie character in the bright, witty but unambitious janitor. Sigourney Weaver, as the newswoman, is appealing too: Together she and Hurt strike sparks reminiscent of Jane Fonda and Donald Sutherland in *Klute.* The supporting cast also provides peripheral fascination. Christopher Plummer, as Weaver's lover, a world-weary leader of an underground group that helps Jews escape the Iron Curtain, manages to be wary and ruthless at once. James Woods, as Hurt's old Marine buddy and a prime suspect, puts a scary edge on a nervous character. Kenneth McMillan, as Hurt's bitter paraplegic father, packs years of pain into a couple of minutes onscreen. And Pamela Reed, as Hurt's girlfriend, is beautifully frumpy; in one marvelous scene they joyfully tell each other "I don't love you" once they realize the nonfeeling is mutual. Yates does toss off a potentially harrowing scene where Hurt seems to be trapped in a trash compactor. And the ending, which packs in far too many coincidences and implausibilities, is deflating. But this film has rare energy and style.

R / 1981 / CBS/Fox

F

▲ FADE TO BLACK

Here is a film that asks the question: What was Rick's last name in *Casablanca?* It never gives the answer (Blaine). That is not the only way in which it fails to deliver. The movie preys on other movies—with allusions to *Psycho, Dracula, Hopalong Cassidy,* and *White Heat* and characters with names like Stella and Professor Moriarty. Played for laughs, that might have worked. But as written—and directed—by Vernon Zimmerman, the film is lugubrious and the characters unpleasant. Dennis Christopher gives a humorless performance as a movie freak who masquerades as various screen characters to do away with people he dislikes. Linda Kerridge is the only likable character, startlingly sexy and effective as a Marilyn Monroe look-alike. Zimmerman's camera does create some memorable images, often held for several seconds before the screen fades—you guessed it—to black.

R / 1980 / Media

▲ THE FALCON AND THE SNOWMAN

Christopher Boyce and Andrew Daulton Lee grew up together in southern California, were altar boys together, went to the same schools. Then in 1975, when they were in their early twenties and Boyce was working for a high-tech company that was processing supersecret information from CIA spy satellites, they sold some secrets to the Soviet Union. Both were sent up for long stretches in prison on espionage convictions. This movie is based on their story, first dramatized in Robert Lindsey's 1979 book of the same title. Director John Schlesinger has taken big chunks of that book and added a few twists to make an absorbing, fast-paced movie. Timothy Hutton (remarkably unaffected) plays Boyce, the falcon-loving loner, and Sean Penn (shamelessly aping Robert DeNiro) is Lee, a coke dealer constantly on the run between California and Mexico. Why Boyce decided to sell the information to the Soviets is never really clear. Perhaps his difficulties with his authoritarian father, played by Pat Hingle, made him recklessly rebellious. Perhaps his faith in government had been shaken by the Vietnam war and Watergate, making him seek a sort of revenge against his own country. The movie only hints at these motivations. Nor is it clear how Boyce persuaded Lee to be his courier, running information to the Soviet embassy in Mexico City. The Soviets are portrayed as loutish comic-book characters who slurp their soup. But the scenes between Hutton and Penn, as things begin to unravel, brim with tension. This film ends before Boyce escaped from a Lompos, California, federal prison in 1980. He was recaptured nineteen months later, and that tale could someday make for an exciting sequel.

R / 1985 / Vestron

▲ FALLING IN LOVE

It's not often that a movie suffers because the actors are too good. This is one of those rare occasions. This film co-stars Robert De Niro as a nice suburban New York guy, a construction engineer who is devoted to his family and is about as exciting as a lawn mower. Opposite him is Meryl Streep as a nice suburban New York woman, a commercial artist who is as sexy as a jar of applesauce. As they're written—by playwright Michael Cristofer—the characters are pleasant, bland, unimaginative people. Banality defined, De Niro and Streep act the heck out of their parts; anyone who has ever doubted that either is a great actor need only see this film. They indeed seem like real people. It is not, however, terrifically entertaining to watch a man and woman being mundane for two hours as they commute on the train a lot and drift into an affair. The supporting cast is eccentric. De Niro's real-life pal Harvey Keitel lends his usual weaselly intensity to his role as the engineer's philandering friend. Jane Kaczmarek manages to make an impact as De Niro's wife, despite being saddled with some ludicrous wounded-spouse lines. But Dianne Wiest, as Streep's loose-living buddy, seems uninterested and looks as if she is always smelling something putrid. And David Clennon, as Streep's doctor-husband, acts perpetually terrified of nothing in particular. The film was directed by Ulu Grosbard, who should be given credit for trying to make a movie about average people living average lives. He accomplishes one thing: He demonstrates why most of us don't find

large audiences gathering to watch us make toast or read the paper.

PG-13 / 1984 / Paramount

▲ FAME

What was the state of the American dream, circa 1980? English director Alan Parker offered one entertaining answer in this ambitious, exuberant film. He follows eight fictionalized students at Manhattan's High School of Performing Arts from enrollment auditions to graduation day. A stereotypical sample—four boys, four girls, two blacks, one Puerto Rican, one gay—the kids are performers first and students second. They think nothing of tumbling out into the streets and staging an impromptu dance atop passing cars. As in Milos Foreman's *Hair,* the plot adeptly tightropes the line between realism and fantasy. Michael Gore (Lesley's brother) composed a lively score, highlighted by a funky, frenzied number called "Hot Lunch Jam" and the Oscar-winning "I Want to Live Forever." The standouts of the talented, mostly unknown cast were Irene Cara and Gene Ray, a dazzling dancer. Comedienne Anne Meara contributes a thoughtful performance as an empathetic English teacher. Although there are hints of pretentiousness and an obvious debt to *A Chorus Line,* this movie is a sparkling celebration of music and life.

R / 1980 / MGM/UA

▲ THE FAN

Detailing a fan's homicidal designs on a star, this ghoulish thriller may be accused of exploiting John Lennon's murder. Hollywood is certainly not above such things, but *The Fan* is based on Bob Randall's 1977 novel and thus antedates Lennon's death. If that lets the film off one hook, there are plenty more to hang it on. While the gap between fan and fanatic is a worthy subject for examination, this attempt sheds more blood than light. Though Lauren Bacall lends her striking presence, she has little opportunity to be more than a sitting duck. Playing a 50ish film star about to make her Broadway musical debut, Bacall is plagued by a handsome young psychotic, sharply etched by Michael Biehn. Her secretary, Maureen Stapleton, warns her about his perverse, obscene letters, but Bacall shrugs it off until a series of

Fame: Irene Cara and company sing and dance to the Oscar-winning title tune from this high-spirited film (later a TV series) about students at Manhattan's High School for the Performing Arts.

brutally graphic slayings of those near and dear to her sends her into panic. In the intervals, there's a tossed-in romance with ex-husband James Garner and a Marvin Hamlisch musical number (''Hearts Not Diamonds'') so lethargically staged you'd never guess what a delight Bacall can be in the theater. Only the splendid Stapleton emerges as a rounded character. Director Edward Bianchi, who gives the film the glitz of a TV commercial (his regular job), lacks the perception a Brian De Palma could have brought to the story. A moralizing last scene, reportedly tacked on by producer Robert Stigwood, is much too little and too late.

R / 1981 / Paramount

▲ FANDANGO

Screenwriter-director Kevin Reynolds, a Steven Spielberg protégé, made his feature debut with this intermittently funny movie about five Texas frat brats who finish college in 1971 and decide it's time for an inebriated pilgrimage across the desert. What follows is a sodden celebration of wild-oats sowing, car stealing, treasure hunting, and bond sharing among serious drinking buddies. Kevin Costner, not too long before he became Eliot Ness, is the group's leader—a con man who can no longer avoid a draft notice. Costner does seem as if he could talk a riled-up rattler out of his fangs—he has an easy charm and for a southern California native, a not-too-affected Texas twang. Sam Robards (son of Jason, and Lauren Bacall) sensitively portrays the group's other draftee, who breaks up disastrously with his fiancée—''She was at her shower, so I told her dad.'' Judd Nelson is the group's car owner and odd man out, a hysterical ROTC ''weenie.'' Nelson overdoes his fits of pique—his growling and nostril flaring are grating. Chuck Bush (whom Reynolds discovered in a 7-Eleven) is a 365-pound Belushi-type slob. Bush delivers an antic performance in a role consisting of grunts, feats of brute strength, and boorishness (he slobbers beer while perusing Gibran's *The Prophet*). Brian Cesak is the fifth frat brother. On the road Reynolds shows some spark, as in the scene in which the boys attempt to hook Nelson's inoperable Caddy to a passing freight train. Too often, though, Reynolds's direction is unfunny and redundant. The boys compulsively moon passersby, for instance. Things get downright sappy too: Costner dreams about a young blonde romping in a field of purple wild flowers. *Fandango's* real problem is that it doesn't know what to be—a love story? an anti-war statement? a socially conscious *Animal House II?* Stranded in the desert, Costner drawls, ''Going nowhere is the privilege of youth.'' It is not, however, a privilege afforded to movie directors.

PG / 1985 / Warner

▲ FANNY AND ALEXANDER

Ingmar (*Cries and Whispers*) Bergman claimed that this 194-minute historical epic would be his last film. The great Swedish director couldn't have asked for a more extraordinary coda to an incomparable career. Despite the equal billing of the title, the emphasis is on 10-year-old Alexander (Bertil Guve), who observes and absorbs the strange behavior of his large and wealthy family, which operates a theater in a provincial Swedish town at the turn of the century. When Alexander's father dies, his mother comes under the spell of the evil local bishop, who weds her and wars with the kids. Before Alexander and younger sister Fanny can escape to the home and bosom of their wise, worldly grandmother, they must endure a string of hardships and peculiar supporting characters. That threatens to turn the movie into a semiautobiographical Bergmen version of *David Copperfield.* In fact, in its texture, temperament, and narrative sprawl, *Fanny and Alexander* more closely resembles a satisfying 19th-century English novel than the stark, sad psychodramas that Bergmen is renowned for. The director's concerns are, as usual, social hypocrisy, the inevitability of death, the claustrophobia of relationships. But this time Bergmen's perspective is remarkably sweet-tempered, and his story is accessible and engrossing. *Fanny and*

Fanny & Alexander: Pernilla Allwin and Bertil Guve star as the children through which writer-director Ingmar Bergman rapturously relives his own early life in this lovely and, Bergman says, last film.

Alexander is both a highlight and an anomaly of his distinguished life's work. (In Swedish with subtitles.)

R / 1983 / Embassy

▲ FAST BREAK

Although this basketball movie is as predictable as an easy slam dunk, it's also as much fun. Its appeal does not come from Gabriel Kaplan and his self-conscious "Kotter"-like performance as a New York hoop freak hired to coach at an obscure Nevada university. The movie's strength comes rather from the ringers who play for him. Instead of having actors make fools of themselves trying to play basketball, casting director Lynn Stalmaster recruited real-life players and prayed they could act. It works. Ex-UCLA captain Mike Warren teams up with pro star Bernard King and Mavis Washington (who formerly played for a women's championship AAU team) to form a nucleus both off court and on. (Warren was so good he later became a regular on TV's "Hill Street Blues.") The screenplay has enough laughs and plenty of good basketball, if no surprises. The climactic game goes down to the final second, just as you knew it would. Still, all things considered, it's a lot more exciting than your average midseason game in the National Basketball Association.

PG / 1979 / RCA/Columbia

▲ FAST TIMES AT RIDGEMONT HIGH

This very funny film revolves around a group of California teenagers much more devoted to laughs and sex than to education. There's the carefree surfer, Spicoli, who a classmate says "has been stoned since the third grade." As played by Sean Penn, Spicoli is a masterful comic creation. Whether he's ordering pizza delivered to his history class or dreaming of finding the perfect wave, Penn is a howl. Today's viewers, who know only the sullen, photographer-punching actor, will find this performance a revelation. It's almost enough to forgive him for the *Shanghai Surprise* fiasco he did with his wife, Madonna. And Penn's not the whole show. There is the naive, studious couple—Jennifer Jason-Leigh, the late Vic Morrow's daughter, paired up with Brian Backer. There's the con man (Robert Romanus) and the school's "woman of the world" (model Phoebe Cates), who carries off the snooty character with a bit of bubble-bursting vulnerability. Judge Reinhold is the school's straight arrow, whose greatest claim to fame is his "head fryer" job at All-American Burger. If they're all Hollywood stereotypes, anyone who has attended high school in the U.S. will recognize them. Rock journalist Cameron Crowe went undercover at a California high school to research the book that spawned the movie. His screenplay is as amiable as his book, and this movie, directed by first-timer Amy Heckerling, resembles every summer's fun song—no more profound, no less enjoyable.

R / 1982 / MCA

▲ FEAR CITY

It's easy to see why everybody's scared. The municipality in question seems to be populated by only four kinds of people: topless dancers, gangsters, cops, and psychopathic killers. Who's going to clean the blood off the streets? Who's going to sharpen the knives? Who's going to make coffee? Not only that, but you'd be scared too if you had to read lines like "Let's get out of this cesspool" and (this from a cop talking about a sleazy mob character) "What really burns me up about him is, he's arrogant." The only surprising thing about this inanity is that director Abel Ferrara could entice credible actors into it. Melanie Griffith plays one of the dancers with considerably more subtlety (and sexiness) than anyone else displays. Tom Berenger is a dancers' agent with criminal connections; he mainly flashes back to when he was a boxer and killed someone in the ring. Billy Dee Williams, as a homicide detective, has to be hamming it up on purpose; no actor so accomplished could be this bad accidentally. Rossano Brazzi, as a mob capo, spends all his time sitting at a tiny table in an Italian cafe looking forlorn, as if he's wondering which wrong turn he took on the way from *South Pacific*. At the end there's a battle between Berenger and the killer, a martial arts expert. The fight produces enough raw, mangled flesh for a dozen hamburgers.

R / 1985 / Thorn/EMI

▲ FEDORA

The tragedy of this movie is not that it's so bad but that it came from veteran director Billy Wilder (*Some Like It Hot, The Apartment, Front Page*). Marthe Keller struggles through the role of a Garbo-like actress in seclusion on a Greek island while William Holden, as a down-and-out producer, tries to lure her out of retirement. When he turns up at her villa, he discovers strange goings-on and suspects Keller is being held captive by a mysterious Hungarian countess (Hildegard Knef) and a boozy doctor (Jose Ferrer). The lines are trite, the acting barely adequate (even Henry Fonda's cameo as himself is an embarrassment), and the plot almost nonexistent. Halfway through, the characters begin explaining the story to one another—a sure admission of defeat in moviemaking. Wilder, who co-wrote the script, drops old Hollywood names, irrelevantly, rather than advance the story. This is not the sort of thing Wilder will be remembered by.
PG / 1979 / MGM/UA

▲ FELLINI'S CASANOVA

A bizarrely made-up Donald Sutherland as the all-time rake comes off a chilly fop pawing through a cast of thousands in the misty regions of the director's imagination. Two and a half hours of sensory overload.
R / 1976 / N/A

▲ FERRIS BUELLER'S DAY OFF

After the credits roll at the end of John Hughes's comedy, Matthew Broderick appears in his bathrobe to address the audience. "You're still here?" he says with surprise. "Go on—go home." It's an original moment, yet symptomatic of what's wrong with the latest teen feature from adolescent-obsessed writer-director Hughes. He's so determined to amuse an audience, he won't even let people exit in peace. The plot pivots on an archetypal kid's fantasy: getting away with playing hooky. As etched by the talented Broderick, the title character is a suburban Tom Sawyer. Looking for action and company on this impromptu holiday, he bamboozles his best pal, Alan Ruck, who makes a fascinatingly neurotic Huck Finn. Broderick also enlists his girlfriend,

Mia Sara, cast as a bland Becky Thatcher. But on a day that Broderick describes as a watershed, Hughes merely takes him on a routine tour of Chicago landmarks. In fact, Broderick is upstaged by his director. In search of a solid laugh, Hughes detours the plot, chucks characters arbitrarily, and even includes a gratuitous rendition of "Twist and Shout" performed by everyday citizens of Chicago. Watching *Ferris Bueller* is like going to a party given by a pushy, overzealous host. You can't really have a very good time when the party giver is constantly insisting that you enjoy yourself.
PG-13 / 1986 / Paramount

▲ FFOLKES

Ffunnily enough, the most intriguing thing about this ffilm is its title. Once that's explained—it's the surname of the hero rendered, as per an Olde English practice, with a capital "F" as "ff"—there isn't a lot to keep people amused. Oh, Roger Moore gets his jollies playing ffolkes, who, according to the ads, "loved cats, ignored women, and is about to save the world." There's a bit of hyperbole in that claim, since all he really saves are a couple of North Sea drilling platforms and the 25 million pounds that hijacker Anthony Perkins demands for ransom from the British government. Perkins' quirky performance gets a little tiresome, but James Mason maintains a properly stiff upper lip as a crusty admiral. Director Andrew McLaglen handles the action sequences adequately yet fails to stir much electricity. The verdict: what else but ffair?
PG / 1980 / MCA

▲ THE FIENDISH PLOT OF
DR. FU MANCHU

When it comes to outrageous accents, laughable disguises, and wacky humor, film comedy was a sellers' market—Peter Sellers, that is. This, his last movie, is a rather tepid story, though. It features an English cottage that doubles as a hot-air balloon and contains about four good laughs. When not-so-nasty old Fu Manchu (Sellers) turns 168, he is suddenly deprived of his precious youth elixir. Scouring the earth for the rare ingredients, Fu locks mustaches with a retired Scotland Yard superintendent (Sellers again) who has a strange

attachment to his lawn mower. Directed by Scotsman Piers Haggard, the film has a dour look. Sellers keeps his tongue in check, establishing his non-sequitur interpretation of Fu with lines like "Call me Fred, that's what they called me at Eton." While the superintendent works out as a delightfully dotty character overall, Sellers' performance may be too muted for those expecting something approaching Inspector Clouseau. The brilliant actor's farewell isn't the film people might have wanted him to use as an exit.
PG / 1980 / Warner

▲ THE FIFTH MUSKETEER

No wonder Columbia hesitated to release this film, which is no relation to the Richard Lester *Musketeer* series but a remake of 1939's *The Man in the Iron Mask*. That classic, starring Louis Hayward and directed by James Whale (he did the first *Frankenstein*), was a stylish swashbuckler based on the Dumas tale about twin pretenders to the French throne. This version features the unlikely if likable Beau Bridges doubling as both twins. The loyal musketeers are his dad, Lloyd, Cornel Wilde, Jose Ferrer, and Alan Hale, Jr., whose father was in the '39 version. Ursula Andress, the most diverting part of the film, plays a wearer of low-cut dresses. But nobody has enough to do. The movie was edited from what would have probably been X-rated, and what's left fails as both adventure and parody.
PG / 1979 / RCA/Columbia

▲ 52 PICK-UP

Only an extremely easy grader would call this a B movie, though that's what it should have been—and a good one too. Adapted from an Elmore Leonard novel by Leonard himself and John Frankenheimer, it stars Roy Scheider and Ann-Margret. Scheider plays a married Los Angeles businessman who is being blackmailed because he had an affair with a young hooker; Ann-Margret is Scheider's wife and a political candidate. John Glover, an Emmy nominee in NBC's *An Early Frost*, plays the glib psychopath behind the blackmail scheme that turns into murder. Scheider's solution to the problem starts out as

wildly improbable, and he loses credibility every frame. That would have been all right if the pacing, dialogue, and music had some flash. Instead, Scheider paces around saying, "Who would believe that these people could just come in and take over your life?" A potentially fearsome confrontation between him and Ann-Margret is dissipated; they may as well be arguing about who forgot to take out the garbage. Only the villains have any energy, and that's because Glover and the old "Mod Squad" hero Clarence Williams III get to act totally crazy. Frankenheimer knows how to make engrossing films, as *Manchurian Candidate* and *Black Sunday* proved. He would seem the ideal director to do an updated '40s B film, where within an unlikely crime plot amusing characters reel off snappy lines. This movie, however, never generates enough cinematic life to allow a willing suspension of disbelief to get started.
R / 1986 / Media

▲ FIGHTING BACK

"Enough is enough" is the credo of the hero of this nerve-wracking film, which could have been called a cousin of *Death Wish*. Tom (*Alien*) Skerritt plays a south Philadelphia Italian grocer who is driven to establish a vigilante group (and thence moved into politics) by a tidal wave of crime in his neighborhood. The man is provoked early, often, and gruesomely, so that the film can get on with the joyous and cleansing motif of a righteously indignant man exacting revenge on "punks and dudes." Patti Lu Pone, Broadway's original Evita, is wasted as the grocer's wife. She abhors his vindictive confrontations until, in an infuriatingly gratuitous scene, she discovers their house ransacked and the family dog hanged in the shower. That tears it for her. Now everybody is into wanton violence. But the damage has been done, especially to any intelligent viewer's sensibilities. Yaphet Kotto is an implausible black community leader, and Michael Sarrazin is ludicrous as a sympathetic policeman. The director, Lewis Teague, who did the good-natured horror film *Alligator,* has made of this movie an endless muddle. Long before Skerritt's character has reached his boiling point, viewers are more likely to send this one back to the video rental store.
R / 1982 / Paramount

▲ FINAL CHAPTER—WALKING TALL

The legend of corruption (and head) busting of southern sheriff Buford Pusser was picked pretty clean by *Walking Tall,* parts I and II. The lack of material is painfully evident in this third and final installment (Pusser died in a car accident in 1974). After some nasty but predictable work with his famous hickory stick, Pusser (nicely played by a hulking Bo Svenson) loses his job as sheriff. Then, in a curious bit of déjà vu, we relive the filming of the original movie and, in one odd scene, Svenson actually watches Joe Don Baker (the first Pusser) perform onscreen. Silly, silly, silly.

R / 1977 / Lightning

▲ THE FINAL CONFLICT

This is the third and, as the title reassuringly indicates, the last chapter of the *Omen* trilogy, which started back in 1976. You may remember that young Damien Thorn is the Antichrist, an altogether nasty sort potent enough to do away with both Gregory Peck and William Holden. Now, it seems, he has grown up to be a titan of industry, U.S. ambassador to England, and a likely candidate for president. Things look bleak indeed for the human race. As in earlier installments, Damien systematically eliminates anyone who looks at him sideways—often dispatching them in ingenious fashion. Directed by Graham Baker, darkly handsome Sam (*My Brilliant Career*) Neill gives the devil his due in the central role, yet his diabolical soliloquies seem more silly than sinister. The loyal opposition is provided by a band of Italian monks and a talk-show hostess played by Lisa (*All Things Bright and Beautiful*) Harrow. A slight improvement on *Omen II,* this is the most predictable of the Damien series, and movie fans may say a hearty amen to the revelation that they have been delivered from this particular cinematic evil.

R / 1981 / CBS/Fox

▲ THE FINAL COUNTDOWN

There is something demeaning about a movie starring a boat. Here the U.S.S. *Nimitz* (the world's largest nuclear-powered aircraft carrier, playing itself) hardly deserves the affection lav-ished on it by director Don Taylor. Planes zoom off into the blue yonder only to return minutes later in a joyless celebration of technology. Time warp is the theme. Although the subject was handled better in 1979's *Time After Time,* the scenario has possibilities: A bizarre storm off Hawaii sweeps the *Nimitz* back to December 6, 1941. The captain (Kirk Douglas) has the foreknowledge and firepower to change history—but does he dare? Other pressing questions are: What is a fine actor like Martin Sheen doing in this movie? What strange bond exists between Katharine Ross and her collie? Was it paternal duty or poor judgment that led Kirk to star in son Peter's first effort as a producer? As a Navy recruiting film, this might have floated; as a feature, it's dead in the water.

PG / 1980 / Vestron

▲ THE FINAL TERROR

While they probably never bragged about it, both Daryl Hannah and Rachel Ward have featured roles in this 1982 film. It is of the boys-and-girls-vs.-the-monsters-in-the-woods genre, and it feels like a class project from the USC film school—one that got a D plus. It's never clear exactly who this group of young people is or what the monster is up to. Adrian Zmed is in the cast, too, and while he, Hannah and Ward avoid embarrassing themselves, this is still gibberish. (In one scene, Ward saves Hannah from bleeding to death after her throat has been cut by the monster; Ward sews up the foot-long wound right there in the forest, using needles from a first-aid kit.) To call the release of this film cynical is to understate the case by several quanta; if it weren't for the exploitable success of Hannah and Ward, the movie would no doubt have been left moldering in whatever crypt holds all those lousy ideas that never make the screen.

R / 1984 / Vestron

▲ FINGERS

Strange and disturbing, this film features Harvey Keitel as an aspiring concert pianist (get the title?) who becomes inextricably involved in shady gangland dealings. He delineates his deeply disturbed character with lots of nervous energy and very little substance. The gritty Manhattan loca-

tions and Tisa Farrow, Mia's younger sister, are the only redeeming aspects of this otherwise pointless and nasty movie, directed by the idiosyncratic James Toback.
R / 1978 / N/A

▲ FIRE AND ICE

That sex and violence are the focus of this animated sword-and-sorcery movie shouldn't come as any surprise. Director Ralph Bakshi's other animated features, *Fritz the Cat, Heavy Traffic,* and *American Pop,* all had a vulgar, macho edge. The bad guys in this case hang out on a large glacier that is moving inexorably south to swallow up all humanity. The evil genius behind this icy invasion is a white-haired mama's boy named Nekron, who sits on an ice-carved throne that is shaped like a human skull. The good guys are the folks who inhabit the warmer regions and are ruled by the good King Jarol. One night Nekron's drooling, subhuman henchmen show up and kidnap the voluptuous daughter of Jarol, Princess Teegra, who sometimes acts like a centerfold model. The hero, Larn, turns out to be a blond-haired, blue-eyed WASP sort. (Skin color in this film consistently denotes good and evil, which seems racist.) There are too many chase scenes and too many *Star Wars* pyrotechnics. Those who find titillation in this kind of thing can probably manage to hang on for the ride; anyone else is likely to be offended, and, worse, bored.
PG / 1984 / RCA/Columbia

▲ FIREFOX

Clint Eastwood produced, directed, and stars in this spy-fi thriller about the Soviet-American race for firepower supremacy. The title is the nickname for a Russian-built MIG-31 equipped with a system that destroys oncoming targets by translating pilot brain waves into laser-beam devastation. Eastwood plays a burned-out, ex-POW, a Vietnam-era fighter pilot who is considered the only man alive capable of stealing Firefox from the Russians. Forget the obvious implausibility of his very recruitment, since he suffers from physically crippling flashbacks. The script (by Alex Lasker and Wendell Wellman) is full of hilarious "Russian"-accented English and seems adapted more from a Berlitz manual for screen-

writers than from Craig Thomas's speedy 1977 novel. The plot makes the Russian military brain trust out to be impossibly bumbling fools who don't seem bright enough to have discovered thirty-watt bulbs for their war room. The climactic dogfight recalls *Star Wars* (effects maestro John Dykstra worked on both films). But it's only Luke Skywalker trapped inside Dirty Harry's soul as Eastwood mutters such macho gems as "Let's see what this baby can do" and "I'm coming home." Some things never change, especially Clint's dialogue.
PG / 1982 / Warner

▲ FIREPOWER

What does the U.S. Government do in the movies when it can't track down the bad guys? Right, it hires an ex-villain or two to do the job. This time the protagonist is James Coburn, characteristically sparing of dialogue though prolific in the action department, blasting his way to Antigua in search of an archcriminal. While he is delayed momentarily by Sophia Loren—the widow of one of his early blastees but not the sort to hold a grudge—Coburn and partner O.J. Simpson devote most of the film to mayhem. That is just as well, since nothing else of interest is going on. This is an old-fashioned B movie—just a little sexier and more violent. It can be seen or disregarded with impunity, except perhaps by Victor Mature fans, who have a chance to catch their old favorite in a cameo.
R / 1979 / CBS/Fox

▲ FIRESTARTER

Despite the fact that every other minute some villain bursts into flame, this film never quite catches fire. Based on the Stephen King novel about a little girl who can make anything burn just by willing it, the movie is oddly lacking in suspense. It does boast an extraordinary cast. Drew Barrymore, at 9, played the heroine, mixing a touching little-girl vulnerability with the more fiery aspects of her personality. George S. Scott acts the devil out of his part as a ruthless hitman who works for a government agency that wants to kidnap Drew and turn her into a superweapon. David Keith mixes hysteria and paternal concern as Barrymore's father, who is, not incidentally, telepathic. Art Carney adds a little gem of a performance as a kindly, tough-minded farmer. The cast also includes Louise Fletcher, Martin Sheen, Moses Gunn, and Freddie Jones, and none of them are clinkers either, at least until Barrymore commences charbroiling them. Such a splendid cast makes it easy to overlook idiotic plot turns and some sloppy editing. The movie, though, lacks momentum. What should be a powerful climax, when Barrymore finally confronts Scott, is tossed off. Maybe it would be wrong to expect subtlety from director Mark Lester, whose previous films include *Truck Stop Women*. Or maybe we were all Stephen Kinged out when this film appeared. He himself has become a monster— The Horror Author Who Consumed the Pop Culture.

R / 1984 / MCA

▲ FIREWALKER

Sometimes you are just in the mood for one of those generic, frozen chicken potpies—easy, comfortable, just the right amount of sustenance. Sometimes you are just in the mood for a movie like this pointless, artless, and mostly witless adventure spoof. What saves it are three casually winning performances by Chuck Norris, Lou Gossett, Jr., and Melody Anderson. Norris, the martial arts movie hero, does not make much of a leading man. He looks and sounds a lot like Sonny Bono, for one thing. He is also so small that Gossett towers over him in physical stature as well as acting ability. Norris seems so amiable and unpretentious, though, that it's easy to like him. He and Gossett play a couple of hapless treasure seekers who end up in a Central American jungle with Anderson and her map showing the location of a cache of Aztec gold. Gossett is always a substantial presence and never tosses off even the lamest of lines (and he had plenty of chances), so the banter between him and Norris seems quite engaging. Anderson, whose TV credits include "Manimal" and "Police Woman Centerfold," puts so much spirit into her role of a not-so-dumb blonde that she makes an entertaining something out of nothing too. First-time screenwriter Robert Gosnell's script is full of lifeless lines like "If we keep sticking our necks out, somebody is going to chop off our heads." The whole production, directed by J. Lee (*Murphy's Law*) Thompson, has a very low-tech look that extends down to what seems a light bulb shortage; the screen is dim most of the time. Even Anderson, Gossett, and Norris can't strike up enough interest to make things more than mildly diverting. Considering the material, however, that is quite an accomplishment.

PG / 1986 / HBO/Cannon

▲ FIRST BLOOD

Call it *Rambo 1*. Based on David Morrell's brutal 1972 novel, *First Blood* is a kind of *Deliverance Meets the Deer Hunter*. Sylvester Stallone plays a former Green Beret Congressional Medal of Honor winner trying to track down an old Army buddy in a small town in the Northwest. He finds that his friend had died of cancer he blamed on Vietnam. When police chief Brian Dennehy arrests the bedraggled Stallone for vagrancy, a fingerprinting session triggers Stallone's nightmare flashbacks of VC torture. He goes berserk, tramples a dozen cops, and escapes to the mountains where he becomes the object of a massive manhunt. As the bodies pile up, the law brings in Richard Crenna, the colonel who first trained Stallone as a killing machine. "We can't have you out here wasting friendly civilians," scolds Crenna, who is nonetheless proud of his guerrilla pupil's prowess. Stallone cunningly uses camouflage, kills animals for food and, in a gruesome film first, actually stitches his own arm wound. The script by Michael Kozoll, William Sackheim, and Stallone makes a few hackneyed stabs at social comment, but they are dropped in, not dramatized. (Will Hollywood ever tire of insulting Vietnam vets by portraying them all as victims?) *First Blood,* directed by Ted Kotcheff, is an adolescent male fantasy pure and simple. To its credit, though, it looks like Chekhov compared to the cartoon follow-up in *Rambo*.

R / 1982 / Thorn/EM

▲ FIRSTBORN

A lot of early '80s films featured the kind of kid who was an archangel of adolescence destined to bring insensitive grown-ups to their senses. In that era of pandering to teenage audiences, this characterization may be the most odious yet: It reduces all adults to idiots. In *Firstborn*, which aspires to Judy Blume meets John Updike,

Christopher Collet is essentially St. Teen of the Suburbs. His recently divorced mother, Teri Garr, gets involved with an intimidating loser, Peter Weller, who moves in with Garr and her two sons. The creep has grand dreams and lousy schemes, including a cocaine deal that Garr finances after she comes under his influence (and that of his cache in the closet). Screenwriter Ron Koslow writes some TV-snappy exchanges, but this drama is afflicted with recycled-movie mentality and self-righteous morality. Essentially the villain serves the same purpose as the beast-in-the-basement monster of horror films: He exists primarily to threaten the household back into family togetherness. Director Michael Apted, who proved himself an ace on atmosphere with *Agatha* and *Coal Miner's Daughter,* goes astray in the suburbs. The details are either implausible or distorted. Collet's high school fields what looks like the world's largest lacrosse team, for instance. And we never learn what Garr does for a living—if anything. She's defined entirely in terms of her outdoor activities—she does more gardening than a royal grounds keeper. As always, Garr is a great asset. Her wounded-puppy face evokes instant empathy. She adds some shades of gray to this black-and-white, heroes-and-villains script. But there's no electricity between her and Weller. He confuses preening with acting. Though Collet is likable, his performance mainly consists of more pained looks per minute than you get in an aspirin commercial. *Firstborn* has the synthetic pathos of a bad sympathy card.
PG / 1984 / Paramount

▲ THE FIRST DEADLY SIN

Early in the second stage of his movie career, Frank Sinatra delivered memorable dramatic performances in *From Here to Eternity* and *The Man with the Golden Arm.* After that, however, his acting, musicals excepted, was characterized mostly by insouciance in a series of monotonous tough-guy, wise-guy roles. This, his first feature film in ten years, offered tantalizing glimpses of how effective an actor he could have been. Playing a weary, ready-to-retire New York City cop trying to catch a psychotic murderer, he displays real flashes of warmth, wit, and vulnerability. Director Brian Hutton, however, whose top credit was *Where Eagles Dare,* at times lets Sinatra get away with offhand readings, at others cuts him

off in mid-emotion. A preposterous script from Lawrence Sanders's hit novel doesn't help. Only the supporting cast provides some interest, albeit of an eccentric kind. Faye Dunaway establishes a record of sorts by playing her whole part as Sinatra's wife dosing in a hospital bed. Martin Gabel, as a museum curator assisting on the case, is phenomenally hammy. James Whitmore employs all his upstaging tricks as a medical examiner. And David Dukes does a twitchy, road show De Niro as the killer. The result may not be a sin, but it is a transgression.
R / 1980 / Warner

▲ FIRST FAMILY

With an actor living at 1600 Pennsylvania Avenue it was only a matter of time until a White House spoof. "Remember when comedy was King?" declared the ads. "Now he's President." The idea of Bob Newhart as Chief Executive is funny; spending 104 minutes watching him act presidential is only moderately so. True, Gilda Radner is delightful as the sex-starved First Daughter, and it's amusing when Cabinet members dress up as pumpkins, rabbits, and turkeys at a party. But where does one go from there? Buck Henry directed his own screenplay, which disintegrates about halfway through the firm. That's surprising, since Henry wrote the scripts for *Catch-22* and *The Graduate.* Maybe *Bonzo* wasn't so bad after all.
R / 1981 / Warner

▲ FIRST LOVE

So this is college. For William Katt, later TV's "Greatest American Hero," the golden days of autumn are filled with soccer games, scholarship jobs, and Dante lectures. His nights are filled with beautiful Susan Dey. Although the film—like their love—falls short in the end, director Joan Darling elicited surprising performances. Katt is strong and sensitive, while Dey melts the screen as the soft, seductive girl of his dreams. So what if the movie is sappy, simplistic, and cliché-ridden? Weren't we all in our campus days?
R / 1977 / Paramount

▲ FIRST MONDAY IN OCTOBER

Dumb luck's not just for lotteries. It can also work for movies. This film version of the 1978 Broadway hit starring Henry Fonda and Jane Alexander (in roles filled onscreen by Walter Matthau and Jill Clayburgh) is a plodding attempt to wring a few laughs out of a woman's being appointed to the U.S. Supreme Court. In another time it would have thumped its way to TV and then oblivion. But with Judge Sandra Day O'Connor's appointment to the highest court, the film profited from the coincidence. If only that superb timing could have been transferred to the actors, writers, and director. Jerome Lawrence and Robert E. Lee's bargain-basement drama is threadbare, and Ronald (*Poseidon Adventure*) Neame's direction is congested. Each line is stated as if the actors had been electrically prodded. "A woman can ovulate and think at the same time," declaims Clayburgh, whose smirky performance as an Orange County conservative carries little of Alexander's stage conviction. On Broadway, the redoubtable Fonda was emotional yet not ludicrous in the role modeled after liberal William O. Douglas. Matthau all but slobbers. Though the plot throws in an obscenity case and a corporate cover-up, the politics stay at sitcom level. "She makes the bench smell better," observes one justice of the comely Jill. Verdict? Guilty on all counts—of triteness and trivialization.
R / 1981 / Paramount

▲ THE FIRST NUDIE MUSICAL

No, Cindy Williams doesn't reveal any more skin here than she did on "Laverne and Shirley." That settled, there's plenty of other undressing—including an all-nude tap-dancing chorus line—in this low-budget, irreverent parody of both porn flicks and the 1940s Andy Hardy let's-make-a-musical movies ("Hey, my dad's got a barn!"). All the numbers smack of college-boy humor, such as a tango called "Perversions," but the energy and high spirits are irresistible. Co-director Bruce Kimmel turns in an uneven but protean performance as screenwriter, lyricist, and actor. On screen, he almost steals the show as a naive director.
R / 1977 / Media

▲ THE FIRST TIME

Claude Berri directed this clever little French comedy about a teenage boy's sexual coming of age. The boy, played winningly by Alain Cohen, has lust in his heart and dirty books under the mattress. Along with three school chums, he tries to seduce every female within his grope—and usually fails. Finally he meets the girl of his peach-fuzz dreams. But she lives in Canada, and once again his love goes unrequited. The film is part of Berri's transparently autobiographical trilogy (*Marry Me! Marry Me!* and *Le Sex Shop* were about the same character as a young man) and is fluffy stuff. But anyone who has suffered through the heartbreak of puberty should enjoy a few embarrassed laughs. Good acting all around, especially Charles Denner as the father who thinks his son should be studying instead of leering. (In French with subtitles.)
Unrated / 1978 / N/A

▲ F.I.S.T.

Sylvester Stallone has more dramatic punch than might be expected as the star of this saga of the labor movement. It begins in the '30s, with Stallone as a muscleman who unloads trucks but has no clout with the bosses or sweetheart Melinda Dillon; by the '40s he's a dedicated local leader of the Federation of Interstate Truckers (hence the title) and married; by the '50s he's a national leader and in big trouble with a U.S. senator (Rod Steiger) investigating labor's mob connections—all à la Hoffa. The story, while *Rocky*-esque, requires more range from Stallone and, under director Norman Jewison, he delivers as a bigger-than-life leader. Excessive length (2½ hours) and an inconclusive ending mar the picture but don't destroy it—thanks to superb location shooting of Depression-era factories and solid acting.
PG / 1978 / CBS/Fox

▲ FITZCARRALDO

The subject of this intense, hypnotic, erratic movie is obsession—that of the main characters and perhaps more interestingly that of West German director Werner Herzog himself. Klaus Kinski, Nastassja's dad, plays a half-mad Irishman living

in a young town along the Amazon earlier in this century. It is his half-baked dream to bring grand opera to the mud shacks that line the river. To do it he must first make a lot of money, so he concocts a scheme to harvest rubber from an inaccessible section of the Amazon. His solution: Drag an old steamer from a nearby river up over an Andean mountain so it can carry the rubber part of the way. The image of the steamer being slowly winched over a mountain is the central metaphor of the film, which is based on a true story. It could also summarize Herzog's struggle to get the movie made on location. In addition to finding himself in the middle of a brawl between two factions of the resident Indian tribe, Herzog also lost the services of his two original stars, Jason Robards and Mick Jagger. Robards came down with a case of galloping dysentery, and when production stopped, Jagger, who had done three months' shooting, had to leave for other commitments, including a concert tour. Then there was Herzog's disputes with his longtime star, Kinski, who had appeared in *Aguirre, the Wrath of God* and *Wozzeck,* among other Herzog films. Their collaboration is, as always, fascinating. Kinski brings a berserk quality to almost anything he does. In this movie he is all dyed blond hair and filthy white suits as he impersonates the deranged opera buff. This film is similar to *Aguirre,* which was a metaphoric portrayal of Germany under Hitler disguised as a Spanish conquistador adventure. The ending on this one is strangely out of sync, happy where it should have been tragic. (In German with subtitles.)
PG / 1982 / Warner

▲ FIVE DAYS ONE SUMMER

To make this film, set high in the Swiss Alps near St. Moritz, director Fred (*A Man for All Seasons*) Zinnemann shot in caves and crevasses, during avalanches, on glaciers and sheer rock walls, in numbing temperatures at breathtaking altitudes, and from pitching helicopters. Too bad Zinnemann didn't have a better script to go with all the filmmaking heroics. Then 75, he said he wanted for more than thirty years to make a movie from Kay Boyle's story, *Maiden, Maiden.* This movie, the realization of that long-deferred ambition, concerns middle-aged doctor Sean Connery, his mountain-climbing guide, played by newcomer Lambert Wilson, and a young woman who loves both men, played by another new discovery, Betsy Brantley. Very little happens; two men climb a mountain, but only one comes down. And while the scenery alone should make this movie special, it is shot with a postcard sensibility that often makes the mountains seem familiar rather than forbidding. There is some entertainment, mostly provided by the charm of the two young actors. And Sean Connery plays Sean Connery just fine.
PG / 1982 / Warner

▲ THE FLAMINGO KID

Although this comedy was director Garry Marshall's second theatrical film after a long TV sitcom career, it has the heartfelt emotion of a first novel. Like those writers who mine their own passages to manhood for material, Marshall has turned to the place and approximate time of his own adolescence, the '60s, for a frequently delightful movie. Marshall's remembrance of things past is like a Philip Roth story as Sid Caesar might have rewritten it. Set in Brooklyn in 1963, it chronicles the summer in which unsophisticated Matt Dillon gets an adult education as a cabana boy at the ritzy El Flamingo, a Queens beach club. There he encounters a world of glamorous types, including the club's ace card player, Richard Crenna, who becomes Dillon's mentor and surrogate father. Using '60s songs and cha-cha lessons, among other things, Marshall has shrewdly streaked the movie with period details that anchor the plot and illuminate the characters—an idiosyncratic bunch who are as interesting to us as they are to his naive hero. As Crenna's bored wife, Jessica Walter alchemizes a small part into a fascinating personality. Dillon does a clever comical riff on his usual brooding outsider, playing down his standard defiance and playing up his vulnerability. Marshall sustains the sweetness of his movie, if not its surprises. The script he coauthored with Neal Marshall (no relation) advertises its plot developments before they occur, and the resolution skids into "Laverne and Shirley" pseudo-sentiment. But the movie is ingratiating even when it's clunky. Watching *The Flamingo Kid* is like looking at a nostalgic home movie with an oldies album on the stereo.
PG-13 / 1985 / Vestron

▲ FLASHDANCE

True, it is something like a *Saturday Night Fe-verette*. But this spirited rock musical about a young factory worker–go-go dancer in Pittsburgh who aspires to be a ballerina is the best kind of adolescent fantasy: colorful, involving, and full of leaping, prancing energy. Jennifer Beals, the Chicago-born actress who was then a Yale drama freshman, stars and is wonderful; she has one of those magical faces that seem innocent one moment, darkly knowing the next. She's onscreen and dancing most of the time or seems to be. Actually, her double Marine Jahan did most of Beals' fancy footwork. Anyway, both ladies deserve credit for distracting viewers from the dopey plot. How does it happen, for instance, that a 17-year-old girl, even one anxious to build a nest egg so she can study dancing, manages to get a job as a welder? Why would she fall in love with her dippy plant foreman—especially as he is played by "Search for Tomorrow" alumnus Michael Nouri, who looks so much like Chico Marx you keep expecting him to pull out his seltzer bottle? What happened to her family? The screenplay, by *Rolling Stone* writer Joe Eszterhas and Tom Hedley, takes some mawkish turns too: Beals' mentor dies just before Beals gets her big chance—"Dance one for the Gipper" seems to be the unspoken line. The music, though, including original tunes by Giorgio Moroder and records by such rockers as Irene Cara and Joan Jett, is slick and urgent. Director Adrian (*Foxes*) Lyne and cinematographer Don Peterman also set up an appealing if ostentatious sideshow of lighting effects. Lyne obviously profits from Beals' presence, but he never condescends to the youthful audience he's aiming for. While Lyne himself was 42 at the time of filming, he seems to remember and respect how splendid it is to be young, ambitious, in love, and able to laugh about it all.

R / 1983 / Paramount

▲ FLASH GORDON

In the 1930s movie serial based on cartoonist Alex Raymond's intergalactic hero, the buxom female leads flounced around in what appeared to be nightgowns, and the spaceships looked like flying soup cans with sparklers attached. But what made that series the epitome of camp was the unselfconscious earnestness with which Buster Crabbe played Flash. Memories aside, this remake is disarmingly likable, striking a nice compromise between nostalgia and now. Sam J. Jones, discovered on *The Dating Game,* plays a vulnerable and contemporary Flash. The sets and effects are more polished (the film minimizes laser battles and such gimmickry), and the score by the rock group Queen is electronic. Many of the clothes and gadgets, however, invoke the '30s originals. So does Melody Anderson who, like Crabbe's heroine, Jean Rogers, radiates wide-eyed innocence. Max von Sydow portrays Ming the Merciless, the planet Mongo's emperor, with wicked elan and some of the same nervous gestures of Charles Middleton, the original Ming. (When asked why he's attacking the earth, he responds, "Why not?") Ornella Muti is cast as his daughter, Princess Aura. As for those contemporary ingredients, sex and violence, director Mike Hodges made them only slightly more overt than in the '30s version (which is still in TV reruns). One complaint: The serial's most endearing creatures were omitted this time. They were, of course, those idols whose arms, legs, hands, heads, and torsos, as well as feet, were made of . . . yes, the Clay People.

PG / 1981 / MCA

▲ A FLASH OF GREEN

Few films so thoroughly eschew commerciality or challenge audiences to such an unflinching exploration of the human psyche. Ed Harris stars as a newspaper reporter in a small Florida town in 1961. Harris's professional life is a string of stultifying committee meetings and horrible highway accidents. He is dull-eyed, mechanical, the truly detached observer. Harris's personal life is lonely and painful. His wife is incapacitated in a hospital. He harbors an unrequited passion for his widowed friend, played affectingly by Blair Brown. Harris presents an easy target for Richard Jordan, the manipulative county commissioner who wants to rig an environmentally disastrous real estate deal. Jordan bribes Harris to spy on the conservation group organized by Brown. Floating in amoral inertia, Harris capitulates with little hesitation. His journalism skills give him a knack for prying into people's lives. But when his betrayals touch off rampant blackmail, nervous breakdowns and, inevitably, violence, he

faces a more penetrating challenge of conscience. Combining reticence with expressive physicality, Harris infuses his character with palpable tension. Jordan delivers as a small-time politician obsessed by his own delusions. Director-screenwriter Victor Nunez shows a commanding hand in his casting and evocative cinematography—he captures a fleeting tropical light that induces a deceptive ennui. Nunez's film never sinks into the B-movie melodrama of the similar *The Mean Season,* though it sputters at the end. Even so, *A Flash of Green* is a visceral, gritty tale of one man's fall from grace.
Unrated / 1985 / Media

▲ FLETCH

Throughout his erratic movie career Chevy Chase had honored at least one principle in his comedy: He had never relied previously on costume changes for laughs. As investigative reporter I.M. Fletcher, the hero of a popular mystery novel series by Gregory McDonald, Chase is tracking down a California drug scam. In the process he impersonates, among others, a quack doctor, a bumbling mechanic, a beach bum, and a toastmaster at a dinner for the American Legion. But it's the sight of Chase as a Los Angeles Laker in an Afro wig that is the real tip-off to the movie's troubles. The Laker getup is entirely gratuitous—it's a dream sequence that appears to exist solely to let Chase look ridiculous. Although it possesses the smart-mouth sensibility of a hipster comedy, *Fletch* is really a comic strip with a "Dynasty" twist. The only hook is what outlandish outfit will the hero wear next? Like Eddie Murphy in *Beverly Hills Cop,* Chase plays a chameleon con man in pursuit of justice. But Murphy required only a swish of the wrist or an indignant expression to assume his disguises. Ironically, while Chase's manic, prop-cluttered performance evokes the worst of Jerry Lewis, the character is better suited to Chase's persona than any of his other movie roles. A pathological jokester, Fletch courts trouble with his cutting up. When burly cops manhandle him, he taunts, "Why don't you two go down to the gym and pump each other?" Like Chase in his best "Saturday Night Live" skits, this guy mocks the conventional so that he can be what he most wants to be—an outsider. But the lazy screenplay by Andrew Bergman doesn't even bother with the fundamentals of character

or motivation. Surprisingly, director Michael Ritchie doesn't bolster the script's string of vignettes with any of the quirky background action that once distinguished his work. In his best movies, such as *Smile,* Ritchie showed himself to be an astute student of behavior. Here he performs more like a traffic cop at a costume fitting.
PG / 1985 / MCA

▲ THE FLIGHT OF THE EAGLE

This film is too long, but it was a deserved Oscar nominee for 1982's Best Foreign Film. It is based on a true adventure—the doomed 1897 expedition of three explorers who tried to fly from Sweden to the North Pole in a hydrogen gas balloon, then crash-landed thousands of miles from civilization. Max von Sydow plays the expedition leader, S.A. Andrée—a cold, willful man fanatically dedicated to becoming the first man to fly to the North Pole. The colors in the film are astonishing, further confirmation that director Jan (*The Emigrants*) Troell, who also served as cinematographer, has a masterful eye. There is one particularly poignant touch: The original explorers were found dead thirty-three years after they became lost— and actual photographs, found in their cameras, have been intercut with the rest of the film. But the shift of the movie's focus to a psychological drama of survival is badly handled. At times the boredom of being marooned at the North Pole is conveyed all too realistically. (In Swedish with subtitles.)
Unrated / 1982 / Active

▲ FM

Station manager Michael Brandon presides over purist hip Los Angeles radio station QSKY, whose staff includes disc jockeys Martin Mull, Eileen Brennan, Cleavon Little, Cassie Yates, and Alex Karras. Everything is laid-back, cool, and groovy until the station's money boys attempt to dilute its "integrity" with some slick Army recruiting spots. It's not much of a plot, but what the movie lacks there it makes up for in fast pacing and wall-to-wall sound track. There's nothing original—just favorites by folks like Neil Young, the Eagles, Red Foley, and live concert appearances by Jimmy Buffett and Linda Ronstadt. As a "creative-radio" deejay who expresses his neu-

roses on the air, Mull is nearly as funny as he was on his short-lived TV series, "America 2 Night."
PG / 1978 / N/A

▲ THE FOG

All the ingredients of a classic horror movie are here—ghosts, corpses that return to life, and, best of all, an eerie, supernatural fog that envelops a seaside hamlet in California. Even as the credits unreel, clocks stop, car windows shatter, TV sets turn themselves on and off. That opening may be a little too reminiscent of *Close Encounters*, but this is still a doozy of a chiller—an intricate tale of intrigue and terror stirred by a century-old shipwreck. Director John Carpenter doesn't miss a grisly trick in his infinitely more polished follow-up to his 1978 fear-jerker, *Halloween*. His real-life wife, Adrienne Barbeau, heads a strong cast as a sultry-voiced disc jockey of a radio station situated on a Big Sur–like cliff. Janet Leigh co-stars, while John Houseman and Hal Holbrook pop up briefly but effectively. The denouement is overwrought with not-so-special effects, but for a project that, in contrast to some sci-fi flops, creeps in on little cat feet. *The Fog* left some mightly big paw prints on the genre.
R / 1980 / CBS/Fox

▲ FOOL FOR LOVE

It's not hard to get cranked up for a film of such formidable firsts: *Fool for Love* is the first of Pulitzer prizewinner Sam Shepard's some forty plays to be adapted to the screen. It also represents the first major appearance by Shepard as an actor in one of his own works. Shepard is an original (there's never been a serious dramatist who was also a Hollywood dreamboat); he's a maverick who adopts violent actions, absurdist humor, and poetic speeches to take theater into uncharted realms. For this film Shepard found a kindred spirit in director Robert Altman, whose experiments with filmed drama (*Come Back to the 5 and Dime, Jimmy Dean, Jimmy Dean; Streamers; Secret Honor*) broke new ground. Their collaboration bashes its way into your head and heart. Like most of Shepard, though, *Fool* is also ornery, exasperating, and often stifled by symbols. The scene is a seedy New Mexico motel on the edge of the Mojave Desert. A cowboy, Shepard, drives up in a tin trailer crowded with the horses he uses at rodeos. But he is after a different prize now: Kim Basinger, a short-order cook who is also the cowboy's half sister. Their father, played by a ghostly Harry Dean Stanton, occasionally comments on the action. Altman's fluid camera work helps lighten the symbolic load and heighten the kiss-kiss-bang-bang relationship of Shepard and Basinger. The gorgeous (and, as a result, often underrated) Basinger turned the waitress into a tortured child who wants to kill her obsession with Shepard by killing him. "Right in the moment when you're sure you've got me buffaloed," she tells him, "that's when you'll die." And Shepard subtly reveals the fears that haunt his macho cowboy. He insults Basinger's klutz of a boyfriend, tersely done by Randy Quaid, and lassos objects (a jukebox, a bedpost) that replace the truths he can't get a fix on. Shepard and Basinger ignite a sexual bonfire whose embers are haunting. Like it or not, understand it fully or not, this movie is going to shake you.
R / 1985 / MGM/UA

▲ FOOTLOOSE

"Let's dance," shouts Kevin Bacon near the end of the picture. If only he'd said something earlier. While the similar *Flashdance*'s story was just a thread to connect musical numbers, *Footloose* favors talk over action. No sooner does director Herbert Ross start things off with a bouncy credit sequence than we are bogged down in exposition. Bacon, a Chicago street kid deserted by his father, lives with his mother in a regressive midwestern town that outlaws dancing. The fictional town is run by a sobersided minister, John Lithgow. But his high school daughter, Lori Singer, gets her kicks by standing in front of moving trains. Clearly this girl needs an outlet. She finds it in Bacon's drive to reopen the town to rock 'n' roll. Bacon, so brilliant in *Diner,* and Singer, the sexy, long-legged veteran of TV's "Fame," make an attractive screen couple. Choreographer Lynne Taylor-Corbett, however, gives them only a snippet of a dance together. (Bacon's gymnastic dance feats are done by double Peter Tramm.) *Footloose* uses music primarily as background, which is too bad since the nine tunes screenwriter Dean Pitchford wrote with various collaborators have definite get-up-and-go, especially "Let's Hear It for the Boy." There is fun to be had in *Footloose,* but the movie never stays on its feet long enough to sustain the enjoyment.

PG / 1984 / Paramount

▲ FORCED VENGEANCE

In the chop! kick! clunk! splat! school of movies, karate expert Chuck Norris's films are relatively clean. The gore—by today's standards—is minimal. The martial arts action, though, does give this supposed thriller a modest amount of excitement. Good thing, too, because the plot is rickety with age. A crime syndicate wants to move in on a small, honest gambling house in Hong Kong, where Norris is in charge of security. Naturally the owner won't sell, and he and his son are dispatched by the Mob. Norris quickly moves to save the one surviving member of the family, jet-setting daughter Camila Griggs. With her in tow, Norris and his girlfriend, played by Mary Louise Weller, set off on a wild trip. Eventually the hoodlums catch up. That sets off a final round of whacking and stomping as Chuck attempts to get to Mister Big, who in a nice reversal turns out to be Mister Little. Michael Cavanaugh, as a harpoon-wielding villain, shows some signs of life, and veteran David Opatoshu, as the casino owner, provides much of the acting in evidence. Norris has developed either a mastery of the cool, laid-back approach or a sincere sense of boredom about these things, which wouldn't be unreasonable.

R / 1982 / MGM/UA

▲ FORCE 10 FROM NAVARONE

"If we don't blow that bridge, those Yugoslavs will be dog meat." Can a movie with a line like that be all bad? You bet. Although it opens with footage from *The Guns of Navarone,* this fatuous follow-up has nothing in common with the 1961 classic. Robert Shaw and Edward Fox (in the original Gregory Peck and David Niven roles) are sent to Yugoslavia during World War II to eliminate a German agent. They hook up with Force 10, an American mission headed by Harrison Ford that is out to destroy a strategic bridge. As a recent graduate of the *Star Wars* school of one-dimensional acting, Ford seemed like a weaker

actor than he is. The story is predictable, and the dialogue is riddled with clichés that went out with the Hula Hoop. Sadly, Shaw died soon after the film was finished and, though he tackles his part with typical dignity and humor, this is not the way a fine actor should be remembered.

PG / 1979 / Warner, Vestron

▲ FOREVER, LULU

Let's all just pretend this film never happened, in deference to the distinguished career of its star, German actress Hanna (*The Marriage of Maria Braun*) Schygulla. She plays a struggling novelist on New York's lower East Side who happens upon a small fortune in drug money when she accidentally holds up a dealer. This may not sound like much of a comdy, but it sounds a lot better than it plays. Director Amos Kollek wrote the lame dialogue, then set up some dull scenes and cast them with compulsive overactors. That excludes rock singer Deborah Harry. While she is in the movie (and gets second billing), she has only about two lines, spending most of the time hanging around the periphery of various street scenes looking frowsy. Schygulla floats through the production with a regal serenity, though even an actress of her commanding presence could no more carry this film than she could tote a piano across the Sahara. While she appeared in the TV miniseries "Peter the Great," this was her first American feature, and when she says (in only barely accented English), "Take a hike, babe. You're history." it's hard to avoid cringing. In structure, location and plot, this film bears some resemblance to *Desperately Seeking Susan,* but most of the resemblance is in the desperation department.

R / 1987 / N-A

▲ THE FORMULA

Just before World War II ended, the Nazis were rumored to have developed a formula for producing synthetic fuel efficiently. This movie, an adaptation of Steve Shagan's best-seller, begins with that premise and conjures up an international conspiracy to suppress the formula in order to preserve the high price of oil. When George C. Scott, as an L.A. cop, investigates the murder of a friend and stumbles onto the conspiracy, he

ends up chasing all over the world—and into the arms of beautiful Marthe Keller. But the fun of this flick is in Scott's encounters with Marlon Brando, who plays the eccentric head of an oil cartel by recycling some *Godfather* quirks. When these two actors get together, it's like watching two elephants waltz—both are fat and funny. Otherwise director John (*Rocky*) Avilden has come up with a mostly, er, formula adventure.
R / 1981 / MGM/UA

▲ FORT APACHE, THE BRONX

Puerto Rican leaders in the south Bronx protested this cops-and-killers film set in a New York precinct nicknamed after an embattled outpost in a 1948 John Wayne Western. Indeed, in the attempt to capture the sense of the place, the script tends to be melodramatic, exploitative, and despairing. Paul Newman plays an idealistic veteran of the force, while Ed Asner, a tough captain assigned to shape up the precinct, acts mostly by folding his beefy arms and glowering. Both also occasionally forget to use their dese-and-dem Bronx accents. Director Dan Petrie doesn't follow through on the cop killing that sets the film in motion but focuses instead on an affair between Newman and a darkly seductive nurse with a heroin problem, Rachel Ticotin. The result is a mess as drama but a marvel for Newman's all-stops-out performance.
R / 1981 / Vestron

▲ 48 HRS.

"$#@%it, you @<11>«<12>&#ing watermelon, let's **%# @<S1>«<14> go and %$$ @@<S1>«<14>ing <S1>«<14> it!" That is not code, although it might as well be. It is the essence of the dialogue and plot of this movie, which will be remembered for the impressive feature debut of Eddie Murphy. He proved that he can be as ferociously funny a screen presence as any in movies. For the record, the film is about a foul-mouthed cop, Nick Nolte, using a foul-mouthed inmate, Murphy, to catch some foul-mouthed cop killers. But it's the byplay between Murphy and Nolte and Water Hill's vigorous direction that made this such a box-office winner. Murphy's scene in a redneck bar, rousting the patrons with borrowed police credentials, is by

now a screen classic. "I'm your worst nightmare," he tells the crowd, "a nigger with a badge." Alternately profane and provocative, *48 Hrs.* is the perfect video laugh ticket for grown-ups after the kids go to bed.
R / 1983 / Paramount

▲ FOR YOUR EYES ONLY

First-time director John Glen packed this, the twelfth 007 thriller and Roger Moore's fifth, with all the familiar Bond tricks. There's devilish gadgetry, a double-helix plot about salvaging a supersecret British computer, villains with a flair for spectacular mountain ski chalets and underwater hideaways, and a very high per capita rate of nearly nude females. In one electrifying chase, a stuntman speeds along the solid ice curl of a bobsled run—on skis—at what feels like one hundred fifty miles an hour. The dazzlingly dapper star is, of course, Moore, wryly wrinkled eyebrow and all. "My nightie is slipping," one conquest murmurs huskily. "So is your accent, Countess," Oh-Oh Seven replies, seeing through the slinky spy's cover as easily as her lingerie. There are fine roles for bubbly ice skater Lynn Holly Johnson, as a sexy Olympic hopeful, and Topol, as a pistachio-popping Bond ally. Carole Bouquet, who deserved the role for her legs only, is an otherwise flat—well, almost—heroine next to predecessors like Barbara Bach, Britt Ekland, and Ursula Andress. And the traditional foreplay finale, despite the shot of two facing pairs of bare feet (Moore's and Bouquet's), is less provocative than dumb. Still, it's comforting to have 007 stylishly triumphant and making movies safe for entertainment.
PG / 1981 / CBS/Fox

▲ FOUR FRIENDS

Steven Tesich saluted the American dream in the estimable *Breaking Away*. Two years later he was back to bury that same dream—and the result is truly depressing. The story, Tesich says, is based partly on his own life. A Yugoslav immigrant boy, played by Craig Wasson, grows up in Tesich's hometown, East Chicago, Indiana. He meets three friends, and they become fellow travelers through '50s sock hops, the civil rights movement, the drug culture, and other periods of Americana, all

the while vying for the same woman, an annoyingly mannered Jodi Thelen. Director Arthur (*Bonnie and Clyde*) Penn has made it all look stylish, and he gets some real heat into the big, emotional scenes, especially a wedding that erupts in violence. His eclectic cast (which includes James Leo Herlihy, the author of *Midnight Cowboy*) is mostly admirable. Among the young unknowns who star, Reed Bimey, as Wasson's MS-stricken college roommate, is best. But the story is full of callow clichés. That these oversimplifications are precisely the ones an immigrant might arrive at does not make them any easier to stomach or to understand. Despite its faults, the film remains haunting, a noble failure from Penn, whose misses are more intriguing than the hits of his less adventurous colleagues.
R / 1981 / Warner

▲ THE FOUR SEASONS

"Face it," shouts Carol Burnett to Alan Alda, "you married a middle-aged woman with a good sense of humor and dry skin." Alda and Burnett are one of three couples whose communal vacations (one a season) form the basis of this funny, rueful look at the crimes committed in the name of friendship. As writer, director, and actor, Alda lacks the killer instinct to cut past the comfortable first layer of social satire. He can get awfully gooey at times, but his wry way with lines makes for pleasing entertainment, especially for the over-40 set who've long been waiting for an inning on screen. Burnett is quite good; so is Alda's supporting cast, including Len Cariou and Sandy Dennis. Their divorce shakes the group, notably when he takes up with a young sprite, nicely played by Bess Armstrong. And when Jack Weston rages at Rita Moreno, "Your thoughts drop from your brain to your tongue like a gumball machine," the remark combines bite and affection. So, at its best, does the movie.
PG / 1981 / MCA

▲ FOXES

The camera pans slowly across the cluttered room. Four teenage girls lie sleeping, alluring yet innocent. Shot in extremely soft focus, this dreamlike opening image is visually entrancing. The trouble is that the photography is not the only

fuzzy aspect in this ambitious but aimless movie about growing up circa 1980. It creates a frighteningly realistic universe of broken homes, booze, drugs, and sex. Unfortunately the story has about as much direction as its characters, skipping nervously from rock concerts to bad trips to loss of virginity. First-time director Adrian Lyne—pre-*Flashdance*—might have made the California version of *Breaking Away*, but his film is marred by soap-opera situations. Sally Kellerman plays a bitchy mom and sweet Scott Baio skateboards in and out of the screenplay, but the real star is Jodie Foster. At 17 she was no longer the wisecracking kid from *Taxi Driver*, but an intelligent, bordering-on-beautiful actress.
R / 1980 / Key

▲ FRANCES

With a superb lead performance from Jessica Lange, this is a horror story based on life, not nightmare. Willful, beautiful, fiercely talented, Frances Farmer was a 1930s star of film (*Come and Get It*) and stage (*Golden Boy*). She was also an atheist, a leftist, a druggie, and an alcoholic and ended up in a series of mental institutions. There she was subjected to brutal experiments in electroshock and perhaps even a lobotomy and to countless assaults by men who paid hospital orderlies for a chance to rape her movie star's body, institutionalized for five years (many insist she was never insane). Farmer was 36 when released in her mother's custody in 1950 and 56 when she succumbed to cancer in 1970. She ended her life hosting a B-movie afternoon TV show in Indianapolis, the seemingly complacent pawn of hucksters who exploited her past fame. Farmer's persecution, perhaps because it suggests a collusion of family, psychiatry, and government to repress dissent, inspired two books (one her own), two off-Broadway shows, an independent film, *Committed*, and a CBS-TV movie with Susan Blakely. *Frances* has special impact because of the uncanny way Lange, who had grown astonishingly in range since 1976's *King Kong*, gets under Farmer's skin. Her scenes with Farmer's jealously neurotic mother, brilliantly played by Kim Stanley, make up for the bewildering shortcomings of the screenplay, which skimps on Farmer's political activism, talent (we never see her act), and even her husbands (only one of three is mentioned). Instead, the usually reliable

Sam Shepard, Lange's real-life fella, is brought on to play a ludicrous fictional lover in Farmer's life; he keeps coming back into her life like a boomerang, and a dumb boomerang at that. He also provides stilted, pointless narration. How distressing that Farmer, who always despised the falseness in her Hollywood movies, should have her own life similarly mis-served. Still, Lange and Stanley, both winning well-earned Oscar nominations, go a long way in cutting through the gloss laid on with galumphing heaviness by debuting director Graeme Clifford (he edited such films as *The Postman Always Rings Twice*). The two women pay tribute to Farmer's memory by tugging at the conscience as well as the heart.
R / 1982 / Thorn/EMI

▲ FRATERNITY ROW

Employing a batch of yeasty young stars and USC students, Charles Gary Allison produced (and scripted) this low-budget gem as part of his Ph.D. dissertation. With documentary accuracy, the 1950s rites of the Greek system pass from schmaltzy serenades and pinnings to cruel black-balls and hazings. The climax is in a horrifying spring semester "hell week." The villainous "Chuck Cherry," Gamma Nu Pi's pledge-monger supreme, is played by stuntman Scott Newman, Paul Newman's son, whose untimely death ended a most promising career.
PG / 1977 / N/A

▲ THE FRENCH LIEUTENANT'S WOMAN

Already all but canonized on the basis of five performances in films that merely hinted at her possibilities, Meryl Streep finally took on her first picture-carrying role. As the title character in John Fowles's fluid 1969 novel, a 20th-century look at Victoriana shot through with Freud and feminism, Streep unleashes everything she's got. Intuitive, rapt, real—she is dizzyingly sensual in a role that brought her another Oscar nomination. (She won her first for 1979's *Kramer vs. Kramer*.) But director Karel *(The Loves of Isadora)* Reisz and screenwriter Harold Pinter guide her down a bumpy road. Trying to find a cinematic equivalent for a Fowles device (he sometimes offers various ways of looking at the same scene), Pinter created an awkward movie-within-a-movie format. Streep is a governess seduced by her French lieutenant and cast out by society. But the audience is not permitted simply to watch her steal the affections of an above-her-station gentleman, the superb young Jeremy Irons, from his intended, Lynsey Baxter, and then make him suffer as she has. The absorbing tale is constantly interrupted with a contemporary love story between Streep and Irons, playing two modern actors making a film. The only result is confusion, and even Streep seems self-conscious in these scenes. Most everything else is exactly right. Reisz shot the film in Lyme Regis, England (where Fowles now lives) using many of the book's actual locations. Freddie Francis's impassioned camera work, especially Streep on the storm-swept seawall, is a grand sight. It's tempting to dismiss this difficult, demanding film for its faltering step. Better to salute it for its daring.
R / 1981 / CBS/Fox

▲ FRIDAY THE 13TH

Apart from bloodthirsty mosquitoes, execreble cuisine, and short-sheeted beds, working at a summer camp has never been considered particularly perilous. But after seeing this gory mess, future counselors are sure to demand hazardous duty pay. A sylvan New Jersey setting turns macabre when, one by one, the newly arrived staff of Camp Crystal Lake is dispatched in increasingly gruesome fashion. With one murder every 9.1 minutes, director Sean S. Cunningham tries to keep the murderer's identity unknown with the clichéd technique of using hand-held cameras to stalk the victims from a killer's eye view. The mayhem concludes with an annoying series of false endings, one of which is shamelessly lifted from *Deliverance*. It's still a guaranteed jolt, though, as is Betsy Palmer's go-for-it performance as a camper's mom. The rest of the largely unknown cast, headed by Andrienne King and Harry Crosby (Bing's son) head a cast of unknowns who perform adequately until their services are mercifully terminated.
R / 1980 / Paramount

▲ FRIDAY THE 13TH—A NEW BEGINNING

Let's face it. Nobody interested in this kind of movie wants to know how intelligent the dialogue is or how carefully the director blocks out his

The French Lieutenant's Woman: Meryl Streep is the infamous lady and Jeremy Irons the Victorian gent who falls under her spell in this fascinating though flawed film version of John Fowles's novel.

scenes or how well the actors are able to articulate their emotions. What you want to know is, do lots of people get chopped up? The answer is yes—lots and lots of people get chopped up. They also get stabbed, skewered, impaled, and slit. This is not a movie for fans of blunt instruments. Those who remember the end of *Friday the 13th—The Final Chapter* in which Jason, the hockey-masked killer, got himself cleavered right in the noggin, may well wonder how the series could plausibly be continued. In the Hollywood slash-and-cash genre, though, where there's a till there's a way, and the *Friday* series had turned out to be money in the bank. Danny Steinman directed this sequel with occasional flashes of humor. John Shepard plays the grown-up version

of the boy who put Jason away in *The Final Chapter,* and Richard Young portrays the therapist who is treating Shepard, perhaps for the trauma associated with having done away with such a popular monster. They're all incidental to the gallons of artificial blood that flow all over the place, of course.
R / 1985 / Paramount

▲ FRIDAY THE 13TH—PART II

Question: How can there even be a sequel to a movie in which all the characters have died? Answer: In Hollywood, anything is possible when the original grosses $35 million. One thing can be said for producer-director Steve Miner: He sticks slavishly close to the spirit of the first film. Again, the story concerns a group of camp counselors more intent on foreplay than oar-play. The scares are there when the inevitable psychopath strikes, but shock becomes more like tedium with each successive murder until the only suspense is, who else is doomed? The former jock in the wheelchair or the cooing couple in the bedroom or the spunky blonde in the Volkswagen? Yes, yes, and hard to say. Most everybody meets a grisly demise.

R / 1981 / Paramount

▲ FRIDAY THE 13TH—PART III

Jason, the grotesque hatchet murderer of 1980's original and 1981's Part 2, is back with still more axes to grind—not to mention planting them in the heads and abdomens of anyone who strays onscreen. (It's a quibble, of course, but by this time, with three dozen or so grizzly murders to account for, the police of Crystal Lake, where the *Friday* films are set, might show a little more diligence about catching the rascal responsible.) This time the dirty work is done in 3-D (unavailable on video) which doesn't make much difference except that now instead of just your credibility being strained, your eyes are too. Director Steve (*Friday 2*) Miner actually uses the technique to show just how an eye would look popping out of the head of a handsome hero whose skull is being squished by a maniac. As a personal favor to the witless, talentless screenwriters and cast involved, none of their names will be mentioned here except for Richard Brooker, the ever-hulking Jason III. He plays his role wearing a hockey mask, anyway, and therefore doesn't have to worry about any one he knows recognizing him. He doesn't have any lines, either, but, as pop musicians might say, he's got real good chops.

R / 1982 / Paramount

▲ FRIDAY THE 13TH—THE FINAL CHAPTER

When last seen Jason, the hockey-masked fiend, had an ax embedded in his skull. He never was the easily discouraged type, though, and he was back again for the fourth film of this interminable horror series. He had indeed become a pretty sympathetic character. It can't be an easy life trudging around for two hours doing away with one lousy teenage actor or actress after another. Anyway, it's clear that this was a low-budget movie. The biggest name in the cast is Lauren-Marie Taylor—seventeen letters. The film is cheaply set in a couple of old houses in the woods. The biggest budget item must have been the gallons of phony blood that swamp the screen. Joe Zito directed, showing no sense of pace, humor, or anything else except the ability to yell to his actors, "Stab him in the back" and "Cut her throat with a saw." Nobody under 13 should be allowed to see this movie. Nobody over 13 should want to.

R / 1984 / Paramount

▲ FRIGHT NIGHT

Chris Sarandon makes a nice modern vampire— a fellow who wears turtlenecks, likes to dance, and has a gentle demeanor making him resemble Mister Rogers with a severe overbite. William Ragsdale and Amanda Bearse make an appealing enough teenage couple in jeopardy. Roddy McDowall, as a TV horror-show host pressed into service to perform some real-life vampiricide, has some funny moments. But basically this movie was made a lot better by Roman Polanski back in 1967 as *The Fearless Vampire Killers*. This is a harmless film (if far too gory for young children). But it does inspire a campaign to drape films about garlic and wolfsbane around screenwriters' typewriters.

R / 1985 / RCA/Columbia

▲ FROM THE LIFE OF THE MARIONETTES

Ingmar Bergman's meditation on modern marriage is also one of his bleakest films, which is saying a lot. Using a cast drawn from the Munich stage, he tells a tale of a business executive who confesses to a psychiatrist friend that he's had dreams of killing his wife. The shrink—who has designs on the wife—reassures him. Then the husband murders a whore who has the same first name as his wife. Much of the story is told in flashback, with the murder coming early on, so there's no suspense. Usually Bergman's explanations are more interesting than the events; here they are just banal. The acting is excellent, and

Walter Schmidinger, who plays a homosexual acquaintance of the couple, is exceptional. But where Bergman's other movies about domestic upheaval have had a compassionate side, *Marionettes* is coldhearted. (In German with subtitles.)
R / 1981 / USA

▲ FULL METAL JACKET

You are staring down the barrel of a Viet Cong sniper's AK-47, its sight trained on an American Marine. You can almost feel, as well as hear, the satisfying click of the trigger and the gentle explosion as the round is fired. You see the bullet hit, the blood spurt. It's only later you realize that against loyalty and intellect, against all your senses, you have been seduced into empathy with the sniper—not with the politics of the person behind the weapon, or with the character, but empathy with the act of killing. The allure killing has for a lot of people—most of us, maybe, in varying ways—has been powerfully evoked in a stunning, upsetting, indelible film. Director Stanley Kubrick has long been a master of probing the dark corners of the human mind. Think of *A Clockwork Orange, Dr. Strangelove, Paths of Glory*. The setting for most of this film is Vietnam, 1968, but this is certainly not a "Vietnam movie" in the way *Platoon* was. This film uses the war; it doesn't attempt to explain it. As a Marine patrol moves through the wreckage of Hue during the 1968 Tet offensive, fires rage everywhere—somebody obviously remembered the Vietnam vet saying, "When I die, I know I'm going to heaven, because I've served my time in hell." An officer asks a sergeant, Matthew (*Birdy*) Modine, why he has both a peace symbol pinned to his flak jacket and the words "Born to kill" scrawled on his helmet. "I think," Modine says after reflecting, "I was trying to suggest something about the duality of man." It is through Modine, indeed, that Kubrick seems to explore that duality. The first third of the movie, set in Marine boot camp at Parris Island, seems to be about the therapeutic value of violence. (Lee Ermey, who was a real-life DI, gives a drill-instructor performance to rival Lou Gossett's in *An Officer and a Gentleman* or Jack Webb's in 1957's *The DI*.) Modine remains above the skirmishing most of the time, a literate, humane young man whose attitude toward the Marines seems dilettantish. Yet when he gets to

Vietnam, he becomes swept up in the rush of war; he seems to hate the dying, yet love the killing. Don't expect to be lectured; Kubrick engages the intellect much more subtly. There is succinct, economical writing—by Kubrick, Michael Herr (a Vietnam correspondent and author of the acclaimed *Dispatches*), and Marine vet Gustav Hasford. There is an almost unbroken succession of arresting images. And there is an impeccable cast, headed by Modine, who makes his blood lust seem all the more hateful because he obviously knows better. Adam (*Ordinary People*) Baldwin, as a grunt who has forgotten everything but how to fight, and newcomer Vincent D'Onofrio, as a struggling recruit who is both borderline retarded and overweight, are both powerful too. Behind it all is Kubrick, whose genius—and perhaps burden—is to see the insanity in us all and to make it seem so terrifyingly normal.
R / 1987 N/A

▲ THE FUNHOUSE

The plot is surefire horror movie fodder. Two young couples decide to hide overnight in a carnival fun house, not knowing there's another tenant—a monstrous killer. While the director, Tobe (*Texas Chainsaw Massacre*) Hooper, ought to have moved on to better things, he is a master of this gore-and-sadism genre. His heroine, Elizabeth Berridge, was straight out of the Jamie Lee Curtis School of Comely Innocent Victim, and Cooper Huckabee has a klutzy, Harrison Fordish-like charm as her date. The film features an excruciatingly tense final confrontation too. It's a satisfying scare to those whose wits aren't already dulled by the chiller glut.
R / 1981 / MCA

▲ FUN WITH DICK AND JANE

Ironically enough, the only impact social critic Jane Fonda makes in this thudding satire on American capitalism is by looking gorgeous. No wonder her *Workout* video income dwarfs the proceeds from her films. If you're not devoted to her or co-star George Segal, playing a suburban couple turning to crime to meet the mortgage payments, a pointlessly vulgar toilet scene is reason enough to skip this.
PG / 1977 / RCA/Columbia

▲ THE FURY

This was the *Star Wars* of ESP believers—a classy, funny melodrama of the netherworld. It concerns the kidnapping of a teenage boy with eerie mental powers (Andrews Stevens) by a government agency. Kirk Douglas, who plays his father, has never gritted his teeth to greater advantage. Carrie Snodgress (who was making a career comeback after devoting seven years to singer Neil Young) is appealingly wide-eyed as Kirk's woman friend. Amy Irving (in her first major role) is admirably understated as another psychic teen, and John Cassavetes, the agent behind all the trouble, is blithely sinister. Co-starring is blood; spurting, oozing, gushing, dripping, and even coagulating. In fact, director Brian De Palma, whose dad was a surgeon, seemed to be working out a fixation on the stuff. The ESP stunts may also strike some as excessive, yet the film is so carefully directed—with a dazzling opening, masterful lighting, changes of pace, and sophisticated special effects—that it's easy to become absorbed. Mind over lack of matter, as it were.
R / 1978 / CBS/Fox

▲ F/X

F/X has a nifty premise: It tries to marry the tone of a Hitchcock thriller to the effects of a Spielberg opus. Like the heroes of first-class Hitchcock films, Bryan (*The Thorn Birds*) Brown anchors the action as an average Joe who gets enmeshed in unsavory circumstances when he momentarily gives in to his greed. He plays a top-notch special effects man whose credits include *Vermin From Venus* and *Rock-a-Die Baby*. New York Justice Department officials ask him to stage a fake assassination of a mobster-turned-squealer, who will then disappear into the witness relocation program. Or so Brown thinks. The plot complication escalates. Brown becomes the hunted instead of a hunter, and the movie totters. In addition to unreliable government types, he has on his trail an honest but nonconformist New York cop who doesn't think the mobster is dead. Although well-played by the reliable Brian (*Cocoon*) Dennehy, that character robs *F/X* of its tension and the no-exit paranoia that these thrillers must pivot on. He also robs Brown of his role. Didn't the filmmakers have any confidence in their hero? Surprisingly, *F/X*, which is industry lingo for "special effects," proves stingy with its own gimmicks. You might expect Brown to resort to a cavalcade of tricks. Instead, director Robert Mandel saves most of his tricks for the climax. Mandel, who made a respected first feature in 1983's *Independence Day*, doesn't deliver the technical virtuosity the material dictates, and he can't camouflage the script's contrivances. *F/X* could have been a freewheeling warning about the consequences of fantasy life. Instead it leaves an audience stranded in a no-man's-land of make believe.
R / 1986 / HBO/Cannon

G

▲ GABRIELA

The combination of Brazilian sex goddess Sonia Braga and Italian superstar Marcello Mastroianni ought to light up the screen. This, alas, is a dim bulb of a movie. The expected fireworks between Braga and Mastroianni, who usually can say more with a wink than most actors can say with a whole script, never happen. Braga plays a peasant woman in a small Brazilian town who is hired by the local tavern owner, Mastroianni, to be his cook. She soon winds up in his bed, and Marcello even marries her—mainly to discourage the lascivious glances that other men cast at her every time she walks by. The plot seems tailor-made for Mastroianni, but its comic potential is dissipated in a strange, boring portrait of the town. (The film was shot in Parati, a Brazilian coastal village.) Brazilian director Bruno Barreto, who also directed Braga in *Dona Flor*, seems at times to be emulating Federico Fellini, who always populates his films with bizarre characters. Barreto's weird faces just seem weird, however, not fascinating. Braga seems stuck in one attitude—the naughty girl who delights in her naughtiness. Even Mastroianni, who knows how to milk a script, comes up dry. (In Portuguese with subtitles.)

R / 1984 / MGM/UA

▲ GALAXINA

Lovable as they might be, the *Star Wars* films offer themselves up for a tour de force parody, with their inept acting, bratty characters, excess gimmickry, nitwit philosophizing, and teaser endings. Mel Brooks finally took advantage of the opportunity with *Spaceballs*. This movie tries to profit from that vulnerability and fails by light years. Avery Schreiber, best known to those who remember the TV series "My Mother the Car," is mildly funny as the captain of a space police cruiser who keeps wanting a pizza. And there's a nice sendup of the space tavern in *Star Wars*— a place with a sign saying "human restaurant" that turns out to have people on the menu, not reading it. The laughs are scarce, though, and the acting lacks flair. The hero, Stephen (*Loose Change*) Macht, is a cipher. Former *Playboy* model Dorothy R. Stratten, who was murdered by her estranged husband in August 1981 in Los Angeles, plays the title character, an affectionate robot. Her beauty and natural charm remain the film's only claim on the memory.

R / 1981 / MCA

▲ GALLIPOLI

Peter Weir, the Australian director whose *Picnic at Hanging Rock* helped give Down Under films a leg up in America, turned his perceptive eye on his country's involvement in World War I in this film. The locus is the battle at Gallipoli in Turkey, where thousands of Australian troops were massacred while trying to establish a beachhead in 1915. But this is not a conventional war movie. The battle occupies only the last few minutes. It is about two young, idealistic members of the Australian Light Horse regiment who meet as track competitors, enlist as "mates," and travel some seven thousand miles to uphold their

country's honor. Weir makes every scene an event. The cast, led by American-born Mel Gibson and newcomer Mark Lee, is extraordinarily skilled, the photography is superb, and the story moves. The film's two Australian expatriate producers, newspaper mongul Rupert Murdoch and Robert (*Grease*) Stigwood, honored their native country with this superlative work.

PG / 1981 / Paramount

▲ GANDHI

Director Richard Attenborough spent $22 million and twenty-two weeks slogging across the Indian subcontinent. He enlisted hundreds of thousands of extras to pull together this 3-hour-and-30-minute biography of India's spiritual-political leader and prophet of peaceful resistance. The project, as he repeatedly told the press, was his life's ambition. How could the Academy not reward Attenborough's perseverance with a crowd of Oscars, including Best Picture? They couldn't. *Gandhi* won eight Oscars. With hindsight, most of us probably realized at least two other 1982 nominees, *E.T.* and *Tootsie,* are superior films. But Gandhi has epic size, prestige, a saintly hero. So Academy voters overlooked the picture's stodgy, reverential approach to its subject. You should, too, if you're planning on a video rental. So let's concentrate on the good parts. Gandhi is an historically sweeping film that succeeds in capturing the humanity of its magnetic central figure. Half-Indian British stage actor Ben Kingsley, hitherto unknown in America, plays the Mahatma. And he manages to fill the role with humor, passion, and conviction in a series of tableaux spanning fifty-five years, from Gandhi's arrival as a young London-educated lawyer in South Africa, where he's rapidly transformed from popinjay to politico by anti-Indian prejudice, to his 1948 assassination by a Hindu fanatic in New Delhi at age 79. Brutal and beautiful images convey the efforts of the man whose otherworldly guise belied his political genius for rousing Indian masses to civil disobedience against British rule. John Gielgud and South African playwright Athol Fugard have brief but strong moments as two of Gandhi's colonial opponents. Less memorably, Martin Sheen finds himself stuck in the cardboard part of a *New York Times* correspondent; Candice Bergen comes across as still and self-conscious in the role of *Life* photographer

Margaret Bourke-White; and Ian (*Chariots of Fire*) Charleson turns his eyes heavenward again as an insipidly pious priest who doesn't have any function other than to counterbalance all the British villains on the landscape. The real counterbalancing compensation comes in Kingsley's Oscar-winning performance, which captures both Gandhi's divine light and his irresistible simplicity.

PG / 1982 / RCA/Columbia

▲ GARBO TALKS

Though Sidney Lumet has directed some fine film dramas (*Network, The Verdict, Serpico*), he is justifiably not celebrated for the lightness of his touch. Broadway confections such as *The Wiz* and *Deathtrap* sank like potato latkes when Lumet tried to float them onscreen. But of all Lumet's latkes, this comedy is surely the most unappetizing. The usually lovely Anne Bancroft feverishly overacts the role of a Jewish mother in Manhattan who learns that a brain tumor has given her only six more weeks to drive the world crazy. She has just one wish—to meet her idol Greta Garbo. Her nebbishy accountant son, played by Ron Silver, is determined to find the elusive Swede and serve her up to Momma in the hospital like so much smorgasbord. Silver hires a detective to stake out the star and poses as a delivery boy to get into her apartment. He even follows her to Fire Island, but there he meets only a homosexual, played by Broadway wonder Harvey (*Torch Song Trilogy*) Fierstein, who provides one of the film's few touching moments when he confesses his loneliness to Silver. The rest is frenzy. Silver risks his life, his marriage (the wife is shrilly caricatured by Carrie Fisher), and his job. Evidently Lumet finds all this endearing and hilarious. In truth it is tiresome and flat. You can feel the actors straining for laughs, though Hermione Gingold's voice on an answering machine is a genuine howl, and Didi D'Errco does something special with a small role as an Actors' Equity receptionist. Near the end, Silver develops an appealing relationship with a struggling actress, attractively played by Catherine Hicks, and together they finally catch up with Garbo. It's really Betty Comden in slouch hat and slacks, but even the aura of Garbo can still evoke magic. There's a real charge when GG sweeps into Bancroft's hospital room. But Bancroft's final monologue (she talks, Garbo listens) is artificially extended and embarrassingly maudlin, just like the movie. Lumet simply doesn't know how to put a cork in it.

PG-13 / 1984 / CBS/Fox

▲ GARDENS OF STONE

'Ten-*shun!* Since *Platoon* grossed more than $100 million and was decorated in Oscar glory, it was only a matter of time before a new army of Vietnam films began box-office and publicity maneuvers. This one concerns Sergeant Clell Hazard, a combat vet of World War II, Korea, and Vietnam. As Hazard, James Caan delivers an impressive comeback performance (he spent five years concentrating on raising his son). Given the minefield of clichés he must circumvent, Caan's achievement is even more admirable. The sarge aches to train recruits to survive jungle fighting. Instead he is detailed to "toy soldier" duties with the Old Guard burial unit at Arlington National Cemetery. The graves, growing at the rate of fifteen per day in 1968, are the stone gardens of the title. Based on a novel by Nicholas Proffitt, a former *Newsweek* bureau chief in Saigon (and a member of the Old Guard), the film means to salute the Vietnam dead by telling the story of one of them. Played by newcomer D. B. Sweeney, he is an idealistic enlisted man hankering to leave his Old Guard berth and leap into battle. Naturally Caan feels paternalistic, as does his profane buddy, acted with bluster to spare by James Earl Jones. The premise is suffocated, however, by director Francis Coppola's polemics. Ronald Bass, a Harvard lawyer-turned-screenwriter, sets up the film like a legal brief. These "toy soldiers" are the salt of the earth and you *will* believe it. No hostile witnesses admitted, excepting stereotypes. The bad guys are the hazy bureaucrats and the press who helped turn public respect for soldiering into contempt. When the propaganda stops the audience is treated to a *From Here to Eternity* rehash about love and war that inhibits a first-rate cast, including Dean Stockwell, Mary Stuart Masterson, and a wonderfully sexy Anjelica Huston as a peacenik reporter who falls for Caan. Moreover, by using Sweeney's funeral to begin and end the film (a ploy the book resisted), Coppola washes *Gardens of Stone* in sentiment. For a director whose finest work (*The Godfathers, The Conversation, Apocalypse Now*) shows a clear-eyed scrutiny, the reliance on melodrama is inappropriate even if it is understandable. During filming, Coppola's son Gian Carlo died at 23 in a boating accident. Cast members spoke of how that loss permeated the production. When Caan eulogizes Sweeney as a boy known only to an honored few ("I knew him. I won't forget"), the honest emotion shows up everything that's missing in the rest of the film.

R / 1987 / N/A

▲ THE GATE

The ads for this movie made it seem a lot scarier than it really is, but it's still a passable addition to the teen scream scene. A series of strange events leads to the uncovering of a mysterious hole in a house's backyard. The parents get out of the house just in time for a vacation, while teens Stephen Dorff and Christa Denton, along with neighborhood friend Louis Tripp, are left to do battle with their worst nightmares: a multi-limbed monster under the bed, a zombie who bursts through walls, and a giant *Aliens*-like creature who engulfs almost the entire house. (Parents can be scared, too, if they liken this last guy to an adjustable-rate mortgage that just ballooned out of control.) In a wry touch, Tripp discovers from one of his heavy-metal LPs that they've unlocked the gate to hell. Playing the album backwards—à la those "Abbey Road" myths—tells them how to close it. Canadian Tibor Takacs directed his first American feature with aplomb, but the real stars of this film are the special effects team of Randy Cook and Craig Reardon. True, a movie that exists solely for special effects purposes is on the empty side. But to paraphrase Woody Allen, as empty experiences go, this is a pretty good one.

PG-13 / 1987 / N/A

▲ THE GAUNTLET

Another Clint Eastwood cop flick, this is a mindless excuse for violence. This time Dirty Harry stars as a washed-up flatfoot assigned to escort a mob witness to Phoenix. Along the way, Clint discovers (a) that he's been double-crossed by his boss, and (b) that his prisoner is a sexy, hard-boiled hooker he, naturally, falls in love with. Sondra Locke, just beginning her association with

Eastwood, is adequate as the bare-chested sidekick, and Pat Hingle makes a real try at acting the good cop. Everyone still winds up looking ridiculous. Even the final scene, with an armorplated bus slowly making its way through a hail of police bullets, can't save this one.

R / 1977 / Warner

▲ GET OUT YOUR HANDKERCHIEFS

French director Bertrand Blier's sense of humor is curious if not downright incomprehensible. (The same is true of the National Society of Film Critics, which voted this the best film of 1978.) Gerard Dépardieu plays a frustrated young husband who can't make his wife laugh. As a solution, he gives her to another man (Patrick Dewaere), who's even less successful. Finally, in a jump in the story line that will leave audiences with a severe case of whiplash, the wife (Carole Alure) takes up with a precocious 13-year-old boy she meets at a summer camp, and they seem to live happily ever after. (She, of course, gets pregnant.) There are a few funny moments: The sight of two grown men being given an intelligence test by a teenager is one. But overall, the comedy is so airy it floats right off the screen. (In French with subtitles.)

Unrated / 1978 / Warner

▲ GHOSTBUSTERS

Forget the bad taste, bathroom humor, and tacky sight gags: *Ghostbusters* is irresistible nonsense. Dan Aykroyd and Bill Murray (the "Saturday Night Live" alumni appearing on the big screen together for the first time) play off each other with such prankish assurance that all is redeemed. Along with pal Harold Ramis, the boys portray university parapsychologists tossed out of academia for their unorthodox ways. Going into business to serve the public's "supernatural elimination" needs, the team, sporting proton packs and neutrana wand, tools around Manhattan in an Ectomobile (it's not supposed to make sense). Gorgeous Sigourney Weaver is one of their first customers: the fridge in her apartment is a gateway to hell. Psychic phenomena run amok. The ghosts are an untidy lot—they cram leftovers, belch, and spew goo on everything in sight. But it's the Akyroyd-Murray high jinks that provide

139

Ghostbusters: **As the spirit breakers in question—very much in question—Harold Ramis, Dan Aykroyd, Bill Murray, and Ernie Hudson confront an especially fearsome apparition.**

inspired lunacy. Facing a spirit with a firm "Freeze, potato face," Aykroyd is a hoot. And whether it's a come-on ("I make it a rule never to sleep with possessed people") or a complaint ("It slimed me, it slimed me"), Murray's delivery is a fail-safe mechanism for laughter. Director Ivan Reitman keeps the Aykroyd-Ramis screenplay zipping right along, creating something like *Abbott & Costello Meet the Exorcist.* Aykroyd and Murray make the perfect tonic for raising spirits.
PG / 1984 / RCA/Columbia

▲ GHOST STORY

All too soon this film gives up the ghost that is its main attraction and lets you know who is haunting four apparently likable codgers—Fred Astaire, Douglas Fairbanks, Jr., John Houseman, and Melvyn Douglas—and why. After that, the best thing to do is admire those wonderful old troupers, though you expect Houseman to finish every speech with a sales pitch for a brokerage house or a car. The young South African actress who plays the mean-spirited spirit, Alice Krige,

is undeniably intriguing. She ranges from a zaftig voluptuary, who makes apparitions in something less than a sheet, to a skin-and-bones specter. But director John (*The Dogs of War*) Irvin doesn't wring much tension from Peter Straub's best-seller, and the ending is less scary than sickening.
R / 1982 / MCA

▲ THE GIFT

A kind of celluloid soufflé, this French sex farce isn't perfect but it never flattens. Written and directed by Michel Lang, a Parisian with a big following in France, it stars Pierre Mondy as the cuckolded husband (twenty years' worth) of Claudia Cardinale. He is a bank functionary with two bratty kids and a back that goes out at the worst times. When he retires, his cronies pony up $1,000 for his retirement gift—the services of a jet-setting hooker, played by a deliciously sensuous Clio Goldsmith, who accompanies him by train on a business trip to Venice. She keeps her assignment a secret, so he imagines he's gotten lucky, and she finds the old dog not a bad trick

himself. Mondy is delightfully kinetic in his bumbling role. And Goldsmith, the gift, is spectacular, wrapped or unwrapped. The plot accelerates to a finale in Venice, where Jacques François, as Mondy's boss, makes his move on the jilted girlfriend of Mondy's son. She rejects him. He apologizes for "brushing" her. "Your hands don't brush," she snaps. "They scrub." The humor ranges from bitter Gallic to galling. Would a director from any other culture try to squeeze a half hour of raucous film comedy from a train compartment? Lang tries, too hard sometimes. With a coup like Goldsmith, why bother with slapstick? (In French with subtitles.)
R / 1982 / Thorn/EMI

▲ GILDA LIVE

This film version of Gilda Radner's successful trip on Broadway is first-class entertainment by America's funny valentine. Directed by Mike Nichols (Lorne Michaels did the Broadway show), Radner hits the marks with her ragtag gang of endearing "Saturday Night Live" characters: Judy Miller, Emily Litella, Roseanne Roseannadanna, and Lisa Loopner. But the showstopper is Radner as herself singing Michael O'Donoghue's naughty "Let's Talk Dirty to the Animals," doing an audition in which she tap dances out of step, and singing her own lyrics about the lost innocence of high school. A couple of the bits come off heavy-handed. Was it necessary, for example, for Radner to powder her leotard around the bust and groin in a parody of Olympic gymnast Nadia Comaneci? But the film adds backstage glimpses of the fierce energy that went into the show and exhibits Radner's ability to slip in and out of character in seconds. Her supporting cast is excellent: Don Novello as Father Guido Sarducci, the Vatican gossip columnist, would have stolen the show if Radner hadn't been in such good form.
R / 1980 / Warner

▲ GINGER AND FRED

Clashes between gentle sentiment and crass reality have, of course, cropped up once or twice before in Federico Fellini's films. But neither he nor anyone else has ever depicted that conflict in such a bittersweet swirl of cynicism and emotion as Fellini succeeds in doing with this picture. His wife, Giulietta Masina, and Marcello Mastroianni play a couple who once had a moderately successful (if obviously second-rate) dance act modeled on Fred Astaire and Ginger Rogers's movie relationship. They are reunited, after thirty years, for an appearance on an Italian TV show that seems to be a cross between "That's Incredible!" and "Entertainment Tonight." Not only do they have to deal with their reactions to each other—they were lovers as well as partners—but they also find themselves at first puzzled, then furious at being programmed with a polyglot group that includes punk rockers and a monk who thinks he can fly. Masina has never made a Hollywood film and is relatively unknown to American audiences, but she is a magnificent actress. She infuses this role with a touching mixture of pride, regret, and a wry kind of humor born of the resignation of middle age. Mastroianni is equally affecting as a used-up man who knows that he is a has-been—and that he wasn't ever much in the first place. Fellini's delight is almost palpable as he sets up his climax: the couple's actual appearance on the show. They're racked with doubt over whether they can even dance at all, let alone recapture the mediocre splendor of their youth, and Fellini milks the scene mercilessly. It is corny, melodramatic, and altogether irresistible. Like all Fellini films, this one is filled with extravagance, asides, and in-jokes probably only his butcher would understand. But even the overstuffing is fascinating in this case, perhaps because it is juxtaposed with such an intimate, personal story. (In Italian with subtitles.)
PG / 1968 / MGM/UA

▲ GIRLFRIENDS

This was director Claudia Weill's first feature film, and it almost works. Melanie Mayron (the hitchhiker in *Harry and Tonto*) plays a young woman coming of age in the jungle that is professional photography in New York. But she soon discovers that fixation on a career has its price. After an unhappy affair with a married rabbi (Eli Wallach), she is left devastated and alone. The problem is that the movie is shot like a documentary, full of quick scenes without much emotional depth. That is possibly due to Weill's previous experience—she directed twenty *Sesame Street* episodes and codirected Shirley MacLaine's

1975 journal about China, which won an Oscar nomination. Still, Weill showed promise until a big studio flop, 1980's *It's My Turn,* stalemated a once promising career.
PG / 1978 / Warner

▲ GIVE MY REGARDS TO BROAD STREET

Paul McCartney said he thought up the idea for this movie in the back seat of a taxi. It looks it. He plays a rich rock musician who discovers that the master tape of his latest album is missing. The suspect is a low-level record-company worker with a criminal record. So far so good, but the story is quickly abandoned for a lot of music, and it's of mixed quality. McCartney sings a medley of old Beatles favorites near the beginning, giving the film an especially sad and nostalgic tint. The plot seems almost incidental, as if the movie were created just as a vehicle for Paul's singing. Some of the numbers are dazzling. A rendition of "Eleanor Rigby" involves an elaborate flashback in which McCartney plays a 19th-century gentleman on an outing in the country. And there are some good new tunes like "Not Such a Bad Boy" and "No Values," which features Paul in leather jacket and ducktail, hearkening back to the early days of the Beatles. But the dialogue is weak, the movie is occasionally downright incoherent, and too many scenes and characters seem to have no meaning. Ringo Starr appears, naturally enough, as the drummer. His real-life wife, Barbara Bach, plays a reporter-groupie. Mrs. McCartney, Linda, is everywhere evident, and singer Tracey Ullman plays the suspect's girlfriend (as opposed to his wife). McCartney might have made quite a fascinating movie out of the life of a middle-aged superstar. Or he might have made a good old-fashioned concert film with none of the fictional frills. But he took the middle road, and it turns into mush.
PG / 1984 / CBS/Fox

▲ GLORIA

Tart, tangy, and as butt-chewing rough as Bogart in his heyday, Gena Rowlands emerges as a remarkably believable gun moll in this comedy-drama, written, directed, and produced by her husband, John Cassavetes. She plays a gangster's lady on the far side of 40 trying to retire quietly

from the mob in a rundown Bronx apartment. When some hoods massacre her Puerto Rican girlfriend (Julie Carmen, in a quick but vividly sexy appearance) and her Anglo husband (Buck Henry), Rowlands takes reluctant custody of their 7-year-old son (Juan Adames). The two go on the lam, but the audience should not expect the sitcom sentimentality of *Lucy Meets the Godfather.* The bond between the child-baiting Rowlands and her street-smart charge is complex and convincing. Though overlong, the film is free of the director's usual self-indulgent camera angles and repetitive dialogue. Cassavetes, who has worked with his wife five times previously, most notably in *A Woman Under the Influence,* has never devised so strong a showcase for her talents. Whether tossing the absurdly amorous kid out of bed ("I outweigh you sixty pounds") or brandishing her .44 Magnum at some gangsters ("Okay, you bananas, up against the wall"), Rowlands (a deserved Oscar nominee) delivers.
PG / 1980 / RCA/Columbia

▲ THE GODFATHER, PARTS I AND II

Law enforcement officials justifiably argue that Francis Coppola's two *Godfathers* glamorize the sordid, dishonorable, and destructive netherworld of organized crime. Everyone else can wallow shamelessly in this 6-hour-plus double-dip treat with Al Pacino, Robert Duvall, Diane Keaton, Robert De Niro, James Caan, John Cazale, and Marlon Brando, as Don Corleone. In 1977, Coppola combined the two films (for TV and video), straightening out the chronology and adding scenes cut from the originals. Any way you look at it, the *Godfather* saga, combined winner of nine Oscars (including two Best Picture prizes) stands as the greatest American gangster picture ever made. Don't kid yourselves about *The Untouchables.*
R / 1972/74 / Paramount

▲ GODZILLA 1985

When *Godzilla, King of Monsters* was released in 1956 it had a subliminal theme: the memory of the Hiroshima and Nagasaki tragedies, which remained fresh in the minds of Japanese and American audiences alike. The film's prehistoric creature, risen from the radioactive dust of the atomic age, was a horrifying product of man's world. Of course most people still perceived it as a charmingly dumb monster movie, and during the '60s and '70s a string of Japanese haute shlock ripoffs featured such monsters as a giant moth and a flying turtle. This, the first real sequel (never mind *Godzilla vs. the Smog Monster*) brings back Raymond Burr in the newspaperman role that was spliced into the Japanese original for American moviegoers. It also updates the antinuclear statement implicit in the original film. An explosion on a small Pacific Island revives the silver screen's most toothsome ham from a thirty-year beauty rest that clearly didn't work. He munches on a nuclear power plant, sweeps his tail into Tokyo skyscrapers, and causes general havoc. The Japanese, Soviet, and American governments, respectively portrayed as dignified, trigger-happy, and irresponsible, try to find a non–nuclear solution to the giant menace. There are too many fast cuts, the dubbing of the Japanese actors' voices is bothersome, and the actors play second fiddle to the monster and the other special effects. It's not easy to stretch three basic destruction scenes over 91 minutes of screen time, either. Still, *Godzilla 1985* has a nostalgic appeal, and the old beast is certainly more watchable than some of his cinematic relatives.

PG / 1985 / New World

▲ GOIN' COCONUTS

In this alleged comedy-mystery Donny and Marie Osmond play themselves, which couldn't have been that easy. Pursued by underworld types after Marie inadvertently accepts a necklace holding a clue to hidden treasure, they encounter a Strangeloveish nasty played with typical (though not unfunny) heavy-handedness by Kenneth Mars. There are also a lot of Nelson Riddle tunes for the smiling siblings to sing between chases, so even a non-Osmond devotee may find something to enjoy. But basically, little happens. Under no circumstances confuse this with the Marx Brothers' glorious old classic *The Coconuts*.

PG / 1978 / N/A

▲ GOING BERSERK

John Candy, Joe Flaherty, and Eugene Levy, all alums of the ''SCTV'' comedy series, are masters of satire. They proved it again in this movie when they sent up kung fu movies and the old ''Father Knows Best'' show. The film was directed and co-written, however, by David Steinberg, whose comedy style is that of a stand-up, joke-pause-joke-pause-kicker comedian. That approach doesn't fit the more complex SCTV kind of humor, and the result is a movie that goes not berserk but slowly. It's good-natured and relatively tasteful for a modern comedy (that means the drug and penis jokes aren't too gross). Candy plays the lead as a maladroit, one-car limousine-service owner who's engaged to a congressman's daughter and pursued by a crooked religious cult; he is always at least on the verge of being funny, even when he's just standing around. But the film is listless, and the supporting cast is feeble. (An exception is Richard Libertini as the sleazy leader of the cult.) The drab, slightly sour TV actress Alley Mills is a particularly bad choice as Candy's fiancée. It had also become increasingly evident that the SCTV troupe, even more than the original ''Saturday Night'' not-ready players, were ensemble performers. When Candy, Flaherty, or Levy is alone onscreen the pace falters even more than usual. There are plenty of idle moments during which to long for an episode of Monster Chiller Horror Theater, one of those drop-in visits by that perennially obnoxious talk-show guest Bobby Bittman, or any of the other SCTV routines that were so consistently funny.

R / 1983 / MCA

▲ GOING IN STYLE

Growing old can be a dreary business. Sitting on park benches, feeding pigeons, and waiting for Social Security checks do not make for snappy conversation. Nor do they provide the foundation for a particularly entertaining movie—not even when venerable actors like George Burns, Art Carney, and Lee Strasberg are cast as the pigeon feeders. The film flashes only briefly to life when the three old codgers pull a bank job to relieve their boredom, in unspoken homage to another old hand, they sport Groucho Marx glasses during the heist. The casting is perfect: Burns, Carney, and Strasberg look old, act old, and at 84, 61, and 78, weren't exactly a youth corps. Yet considering the mother lode of acting talent and experience assembled here, director Martin Brest's first commerical effort fell flat. It is mildly diverting without being funny. When the end comes,

it is not unwelcome, for protagonists and audience alike.
PG / 1980 / Warner

▲ GOIN' SOUTH

It was billed as a comedy-Western, but there was nothing terribly funny about this film, which Jack Nicholson stars in and also directs. Mary Steenburgen (then a charming newcomer he had discovered) saves Nicholson, an outlaw, from hanging by marrying him—but only because she needs a man to help her dig for gold. He has only one use for a woman, and though she denies him that, he has to stick with her to avoid the noose. John Belushi made his film debut in an outlaw role that landed mostly on the cutting-room floor. They should have restored Belushi and cut some of the dialogue. The level of sensibility is low ("Woman loves an outlaw like a boy loves a stray dog," says one wise man) and plummets ever lower when Nicholson's wife finally comes to love him only after he rapes her. The story is thin and uninspired. Nicholson's direction is slack. Head north.
PG / 1978 / Paramount

▲ THE GOLDEN CHILD

There's no one better than Eddie Murphy when he plays the right guy in the wrong place (or vice versa). This movie, however, is so wrong there's no guy right enough to fix it. It would have been reasonable to expect more from Murphy under a director like Michael Ritchie. With a few good lines, Murphy could have held even *Heaven's Gate* together, yet Dennis Feldman's script makes even Eddie grind to a halt. The Golden Child, destined to save the world, is kidnapped by Charles Dance, an agent of the Devil. The child is to be rescued, it is written, by the Chosen One. Murphy, as a finder of missing children, inherits the job. (It might have been funnier had he been, say, a shoe salesman.) Murphy must go to Tibet with the exotic Charlotte Lewis to bring back a dagger that Dance says he'll trade for the child. As the viewer, your job is to find the film amid the smokescreen of special effects and lousy lines. Good luck.
PG-13 / 1986 / Paramount

▲ GOLDEN GIRL

For blond bombshell Susan Anton, this could have been her Big Break in feature films. It wasn't, though she may be the least to blame. Anton plays a runner trying for an impossible three gold medals at the Olympics. But as she demolishes one foe after another at the trials, she discovers an awful fact: She's been biologically engineered by her mad-scientist father (Curt Jurgens). How she reacts is supposed to be the core of the movie, although any drama is lost in the poor plotting and astonishingly sloppy editing. There's also some lame-to-competent acting by James Coburn, a slick agent who sees commercial possibilities in Anton; Leslie Caron, frail but beautiful as a psychiatrist; and Robert Culp, in a nasty performance as a Cosell-like TV reporter. The real problem, though, is director Joseph Sargent; he couldn't make up his mind whether he was making *The Bionic Woman II* or *Gidget Goes to Moscow*.
PG / 1979 / CBS/Fox

▲ THE GOODBYE GIRL

Thanks to an original screenplay by Neil Simon, this film boasts a delicious dose of saucy and mind-tickling dialogue. Marsha Mason, then Mrs. Simon, is an over-the-hill chorus-liner whose Manhattan apartment serves as a revolving door for struggling actors on the way up—and out. Until, that is, a failed Richard III, eloquently portrayed by Richard Dreyfuss, enters the scene. His verbal jabs coupled with a pleasantly rumpled demeanor produces an enchanting, cuddly leading man. His performance won an Oscar. Quinn Cummings also steals hearts as Mason's 9-year-old daughter, cynically commenting on her stage-struck old lady.
PG / 1977 / MGM/UA

▲ GOODBYE, NEW YORK

In this likable comedy, a ditzy New Yorker, Julie Hagerty, quits her boring insurance job and, while she's at it, leaves her coked-up, philandering husband as well. She hops on a plane to Paris, a place she has always wanted to visit. Popping a few Valiums to relax, Hagerty passes out and

The Goodbye Girl: The cream of Neil Simon's film comedies stars Marsha Mason as a suspicious divorcee and Oscar winner Richard Dreyfuss as the struggling actor who wears down her resistance.

misses her stop. When she awakens she is in an Israeli airport with no money, no luggage, and no idea what to do. How Hagerty clumsily finds her way among tough kibbutz farmers and the urban Israelis of Tel Aviv and Jerusalem lies at the heart of this genial movie, written and directed by Amos Kollek, the son of longtime Jerusalem Mayor Teddy Kollek. On the kibbutz Hagerty mucks around in cow pens in high-heeled pumps. She wants to prove herself so badly that she accepts a challenge to devour sixty green bananas in a sitting. The sight of the dainty Hagerty determinedly stuffing fruit in her mouth as fast as she can is almost painfully funny. Kollek also co-stars as a horny but softhearted soldier who helps Hagerty out in the hope that she'll assuage his loneliness. While Hagerty gets most of *Goodbye, New York*'s pratfalls, Kollek, who possesses the same self-deprecating aplomb as Judd Hirsch, gets the comedy's best lines. When Kollek is on patrol with his military buddies, he complains about the lack of women. "I like a little sex with my violence," he says.

Kollek's script and direction are plain silly, but the warmth and relaxed humor of *Goodbye, New York* coupled with Hagerty's wide-eyed charm make this movie diverting armchair travel.
Unrated / 1985 / Vestron

▲ GORKY PARK

Two men and a woman are found savagely murdered in Gorky Park. They have been shot and their faces have been sliced off. Obviously, this is a case for "the best policeman in Moscow," a sallow fellow played by William Hurt. In the course of solving the vicious crime, Hurt rounds up the Russian equivalent of the usual Cold War suspects: some KGB officers; a visiting New York cop whose idealistic brother was one of the victims; a suave, devious American businessman (portrayed to smarmy perfection by Lee Marvin); and a pouty, dissident ex-student (Polish actress Joanna Pacula), who, for better or worse, seems to have pilfered Nastassja Kinski's mannerisms.

Martin Curz Smith's best-selling *Gorky Park* was a crackling police procedural-cum-travelogue; the grim details of life behind the Iron Curtain were as convincing as they were eye-opening. This movie, in which Helsinki co-stars as Moscow, isn't so persuasive. Director Michael (*Coal Miner's Daughter*) Apted seems to have confused aridity with atmosphere. Apted's apparent point is that life in contemporary Russia can be almost as routine as life in America, but he force-feeds that view through a parade of sterile scenes. Then he concentrates on some mumbo jumbo about the Soviet monopoly on sable furs, diluting what is essentially a story about the tragic fate of a good cop. Hurt doesn't salvage much either. Playing the detective with a distractingly heavy accent, he recedes into the wallpaper, as if he is afraid to project anything. (Sometimes, less is less.) This may have been a robust novel, but it's an anemic movie.
R / 1983 / Vestron

▲ GOTCHA!

Bold, spiny, and flushed with a screw-you-buster sexuality that evokes Debra Winger and Barbara Stanwyck without mimicking those ladies. Linda Fiorentino has a mesmerizing, original presence. She dominated her debut, *Vision Quest,* but with *Gotcha!* she has encountered the same second-film jinx Rebecca De Mornay met with in *The Slugger's Wife.* Equally influenced by the Hardy Boys, Alfred Hitchcock, and *Risky Business, Gotcha!* poses as a spy adventure. Its focus is college kid Anthony Edwards, whose campus espionage games are only an audition for the real thing when he takes a summer trip to Europe. There he meets Fiorentino, a Mata Hari with the severe look of a young Geneviève Bujold. After giving Edwards his sexual initiation, Fiorentino continues with a course in secret agentry, using the man-child as her unwitting courier in East Germany. Edwards, going through a kind of gullible's travels, gets to endure an emotional rite of passage into manhood. Wonderfully wry as the libidinous best friend in *The Sure Thing,* Edwards is ingratiating, yet not idiosyncratic enough to flesh out this TV-slick script. Director Jeff Kanew displays his single imaginative flourish in a sight gag in which speeded-up film makes a cab ride through Paris look like a slalom race. This material might have worked if, say, the late

German director Rainer Werner Fassbinder had reshaped it into a perverse comedy. As it is, Fiorentino, with the stark look and implacable demeanor of a Fassbinder heroine, languishes.
PG-13 / 1985 / MCA

▲ GO TELL THE SPARTANS

Relatively inconspicuous in the Vietnam war film derby, this was the best early entry (and still is despite all the later thunder over *The Deer Hunter, Coming Home,* and *Platoon*). High among this small, tough little film's virtues is the commanding presence of Burt Lancaster. He plays a crusty Army major in the early days of U.S. involvment who sees nothing but disaster at the end of the tunnel and can't do anything about it. His immediate problem is rescuing a bunch of raw recruits from an outpost about to be overrun by the Viet Cong (played by Vietnamese refugees). There are the usual military stereotypes: the burned-out sergeant (Jonathan Goldsmith) whom the youngsters look to for leadership, the play-it-by-the-book lieutenant (Joe Unger), and the naive draftee (Craig Wasson) who learns the true meaning of heroism under fire. The script wobbles a little when it goes in for cheap antiwar rhetoric, but director Ted (*Magnum Force*) Post gave an authentic feeling to the film, a feeling of pain. Here is a movie that did not deserve to be forgotten.
R / 1978 / Vestron

▲ GRACE QUIGLEY

In 1973, Katharine Hepburn read a script treatment by A. Martin Zweiback. It was a black comedy about an eccentric elderly lady and a contract killer who team up to mercifully "give the rub" to senior citizens who are tired of life. Hepburn loved the idea and touted the script at various studios, all of which balked at underwriting such a peculiar venture. Undaunted, Hepburn partly financed the movie and brought *Grace Quigley* to the screen. If only it were the triumph that determination deserves. This movie is, however, a muddle of confusing plot turns, lousy timing, and contrived joviality. *Quigley* begins when Hepburn witnesses hitman Nick Nolte offing her unctuous landlord. The wily Hepburn corners Nolte, blackmailing him down to a bargain-basement contract murder. When Hepburn

tells him she is to be the victim, the guilt-ridden assassin scurries to his psychologist with psychosomatic pains and a nosebleed. Hepburn, meanwhile, inexplicably has a change of heart, deciding to stay alive and dedicate herself to providing the "ultimate solution," with Nolte's help, for old, lonely people. Soon Hepburn is managing a booming business and the orphaned Nolte is calling her "Mom." They provide a painless demise for a frail oldster, played by the sweetly deadpan William Duell, who wants to be a tenant of the hereafter before he has to pay another month's rent. They also do a carbon monoxide poisoning (at a group discount) for some friends who exit singing *When Irish Eyes Are Smiling*. Then Hepburn orders Nolte to do in a rat of a cab driver just because he has stolen her shoe. *Quigley* has its genuinely funny moments, but in the last third of the movie, Zweiback and director Anthony Harvey lose control. They skitter wildly away from their offbeat, socially conscious comedy and end up with a clunky farce, complete with a high-speed hearse chase. Not even Hepburn and Nolte can keep the film from toppling off the edge.
PG / 1985 / MGM/UA

▲ GRAND THEFT AUTO

The real crime is the movie itself. Long before he made his *Splash,* Ron Howard wrote, directed, and starred in this film, in which he elopes to Las Vegas with his rich girlfriend, nicely played by perky Nancy Morgan (Mrs. John Ritter). Sadly, she remains chaste while chased by a typical assortment of California fruits and nuts—including a lisping twit played by someone named Collins Hedgeworth. When the action flags there is always another spectacular spinout or car crash—so many of them there apparently wasn't any money left for a script doctor. Save your money and visit your local demolition derby.
PG / 1977 / Warner

▲ GRANDVIEW, U.S.A.

Jamie Lee Curtis had become such a smart, witty, and sexy actress by this point in her career that she makes this otherwise stupid, shoddy movie intermittently tolerable. She plays a 27-year-old divorcee who runs a near-bankrupt demolition derby in a small town (the film was made in Pontiac, Illinois). She has a ridiculous fling with a high school twerp, C. Thomas Howell, though she really loves Patrick Swayze, an unhappily married construction worker. Nothing that happens approaches life. The director was Randal Kleiser, who seems to be auditioning for MTV—badly, in one dream sequence where Howell imagines himself to be a rock star. The production values are atrocious; the photography is washed out; the sound muddy; the editing slipshod. What is a nice actress like Curtis doing in a movie like this?
R / 1984 / Key

▲ GRAY LADY DOWN

A submarine movie, this one should never have left port. Subs, perforce, tend to be confining, and after 111 minutes of nonaction, one begins gasping for air. The "Gray Lady" of the title is a nuclear sub that has been rammed by mistake and plummets 1,450 feet to a precarious resting place on the continental shelf. What follows is basically a promo for newfangled Navy vessels, notably something called a DSRV, which—although we're never told—stands for Deep Submergence Rescue Vessel. Nothing, however, not even a pleasantly wry performance from David Carradine, can rescue this sinker.
PG / 1978 / MCA

▲ GREASE

Critics nitpicked like crazy back in 1978 when Robert Stigwood produced the film version of the Broadway musical smash. John Travolta was bad-mouthed for once again playing the hood-with-a-heart he had already mined from TV's "Welcome Back, Kotter" to film's *Saturday Night Fever*. In her starring film debut, pop singer Olivia Newton-John was (at 29) considered too advanced in years to play a '50s teen. The age argument was used even more negatively against Stockard Channing, then 34. But, heck, none of that mattered to the public who made the filmed *Grease* one of the biggest box-office hits in screen history. The public was right. Watching the picture today, you see a Travolta who was rarely more charming, a wonderfully appealing Newton-John, a peppy and peppery Channing, and an old story about '50s proms, perms, and hot rods given new life by an energetic cast and high-stepping choreography from Patricia Birch. And we're still hearing those allegedly "forgettable" songs, "Hopelessly Devoted to You," "Greased Lightning," "You're the One That I Want." Sure, it isn't art or even realism. Who ever said it should be? All *Grease* offers is a good time. It still delivers.

PG / 1978 / Paramount

▲ GREASED LIGHTNING

Richard Pryor as Wendell Scott, the first black to bend fenders with the good ol' southern boys who invented stock car racing, keeps this vehicle on track all the way to the checkered flag. The obligatory lard-bellied whites who threaten the hero are played mostly for laughs, and racial epithets fly like watermelon seeds, but then this true story is designed to be a heartwarming tale—not social history. Beau Bridges as a white racer who befriends Pryor, Cleavon Little as Pryor's racing partner, singer Richie Havens as his mechanic, and Pam Grier as his wife stand out in a fine supporting cast. Look for black politicians Julian Bond and Maynard Jackson in bit parts.

PG / 1977 / Warner

▲ THE GREATEST

The Champ, regrettably, was a punchless actor, even playing himself, but what keeps this tendentious biography off the ropes are film clips carefully culled from Muhammad Ali's best fights. (Who remembers Henry Cooper, Zora Folley, and Cleveland Williams?) Ernest Borgnine is Angelo Dundee and James Earl Jones appears briefly as Malcolm X. Ali himself apes Rocky, earnestly jogging to a swelling theme song. But the joke was on him. Though the film flopped, Whitney Houston turned his theme into her personal anthem and a 1986 Top 10 smash.

PG / 1977 / RCA/Columbia

▲ THE GREAT SANTINI

Robert Duvall is a gung-ho Marine fighter pilot approaching middle age. Returning home from a typically rowdy overseas assignment, he discovers his family has grown up—and turned rebellious. Duvall's conflict with his unmacho 18-year-old son, a high schooler who doesn't want to follow in the old man's footsteps, is the

focus. Though there is some ugly violence, their confrontations are always gripping and sometimes oddly delightful. Michael O'Keefe is the son, and he's marvelous; Blythe Danner plays Duvall's long-suffering wife, and Lisa Jane Persky steals a scene or two as an ugly-duckling daughter with a smart mouth. Writer-director Lewis John Carlino, whose only previous directing credit was *The Sailor Who Fell from Grace with the Sea,* is guilty of a few lapses in an otherwise fine film: The subplot involving a racial murder is awkward. But whatever the movie's shortcomings (including a misleading title), they are more than made up for by a white-hot performance from Duvall, himself a military brat whose rear admiral father always wanted him to go to Annapolis.

PG / 1980 / Warner

▲ THE GREAT TRAIN ROBBERY

It takes a little while to build up a head of steam, but once under way, *Train* is a great ride. Sean Connery is debonair (as always) as the mastermind of a plot to lift a gold shipment (a similar event actually occurred in 1855). His cronies are an actress (Lesley-Anne Down) and a locksmith (Donald Sutherland), and the gang's meticulous preparation—making impressions of four separate safe keys—is as much fun as the heist. The actors are charming (though 007 in a top hat may give momentary pause), and the clichés are all there, from Victorian vamp to jumping from car to car on top of the train. Streamlined and pleasantly predictable, the movie is just like the book, which is a high compliment. They should be similar. Michael Crichton, who wrote the 1975 best-seller, adapted it for the screen, and also directed.

PG / 1979 / CBS/Fox

▲ THE GREEK TYCOON

Only the names and a few facts have been changed for this simple-minded cinema à clef. The story—a President's widow who marries a Greek multimillionaire—is so familiar that Theo Tomasis (Anthony Quinn) and Liz Cassidy (Jacqueline Bisset) hardly need an introduction. Furthermore, Quinn and Bisset manage to look so reminiscent of the originals that acting is barely necessary. They walk through a lush Mediterranean setting,

The Great Santini: In one of his most powerful and moving performances, Robert Duvall plays a rowdy Marine air ace who treats his teenaged son, played by Michael O'Keefe, like a rebel soldier.

with props like a 250-foot yacht, helicopters, Halston and St. Laurent fashions, and worry beads.
R / 1978 / MCA

▲ GREMLINS

Despite the horror-flick title, *Gremlins* is a movie of wicked wit and startling invention, and it has a heart that's at least a match for the special effects. Executive producer Steven Spielberg bought the script from New York University film student Chris Columbus, hired B-movie master Joe Dante to direct, and came up with an $11 million movie that puts most bigger budget bombs to shame. *Gremlins* opens like a Frank Capra movie in a small, picture-perfect, middle-American town called Kingston Falls. Zach Galligan plays a shy bank clerk with a nice girlfriend, Phoebe Cates, nice parents (country singer Hoyt Axton and Frances Lee McCain), and a new pet, called a mogwai. (Dad picked up the cute, four-toed fuzzball as a gift during a visit to Chinatown.) The creature, which the hero christens Gizmo, has the charm of E.T. and the wisdom of Yoda. But mogwais tend to multiply, and there are special rules for their care and feeding. When the rules are broken, mogwais become gremlins who like to play tricks that aren't always funny. The film changes course dramatically in the second half. And the sudden turn to violence is jarring (parents take note). To say more would be dirty pool. But Spielberg, Dante, Columbus, and company prove to be expert at raising laughter, tears, and goose-flesh—all in a good-humored, fascinating way. Galligan and Cates are an exceptionally appealing couple, and Polly Holliday as the town's richest and meanest citizen, has a high old time taking off on Margaret Hamilton in *The Wizard of Oz.* It's Gizmo who will win you over, though, and the gremlins who will jangle your nerves. They may represent the dark side of Disneyite fantasy, but as sure as the Seven Dwarfs, they're on the march into screen legend.
PG / 1984 / Warner

Gremlins: What begins as a cute story of lovable furry creatures turns into a peculiar sort of nightmare filled with such evil-eyed, evil-doing characters as these guys.

▲ GREYSTOKE

No movie based on Edgar Rice Burroughs's Tarzan stories has ever been so elegantly photographed. None has been so superbly acted. No previous Tarzan film has been so serious in intent. And none has been so stodgy and lacking in charm and fun. Half the film, directed by Hugh Hudson, is devoted to Tarzan's infancy, childhood, and adolescence after his parents—Lord and Lady Greystoke—are shipwrecked and die on an African coast. He is raised by a tribe of chimpanzees who teach him what every young ape should know about finding grubs, swinging from vines, and showing affection by patting and scratching. Tarzan's foster family, played by humans in ape outfits, is impressively simian; zoologist and chimp expert Dr. Roger Fouts was the film's technical adviser. Star Christopher Lambert mimics primate behavior convincingly. The footage John Alcott shot on location in Cameroon is gorgeous. But then Tarz encounters a Belgian explorer, played preachily by Iam Hom. He teaches the ape-man to talk (both English and French, no less) and convinces him to go back to Scotland. There the ape-man meets his grandfather, portrayed with wonderful dignity and sparkle by Sir Ralph Richardson in his last film performance. He also meets Jane, played by model Andie MacDowell (with a voice dubbed by Glenn Close), and spends a lot of time confronting civilization's hypocrisies. By now this is no adventure film, and it's hard to avoid longing for one of those menaces Johnny Weissmuller's Tarzan battled: a rubber crocodile he could wrestle into submission, say, or one of those lost jungle kingdoms ruled by Maria Ouspenskaya. Lambert sure can do intensity and bewilderment. He isn't the most physically imposing Tarzan, though. And he spends too much time cradling dying creatures, from his chimp mom and dad to Richardson. Is he a lord of the jungle or an undertaker? Even the film's ending is abrupt and emotionally flat. But then it seems an insurmountable mistake to take a beloved fantasy adventure character such as Tarzan, dissect him, and use him as a vehicle in a message movie. It's like making a psychological drama about Santa Claus. **PG / 1984 / Warner**

▲ GUNG HO

Randolph Scott fans may be disappointed that this is not a remake of his 1943 combat epic. But director Ron (*Cocoon*) Howard does seem to be refighting World War II in this movie about a Japanese auto company that opens a plant in an economically troubled Pennsylvania town. Dwelling bitterly on racism, ignorance, sexism, unemployment, and despair, this ostensible comedy isn't funny. In one key scene, Michael (*Johnny*

Dangerously) Keaton, who plays the leader of the American workers at the plant, sneers at Gedde (*Volunteers*) Watanabe, the manager, because Japan lost the war. Keaton seems to be the only one who knows the movie is even supposed to be funny. As much as he mugs and twitches, he is trapped in a series of loud arguments about Japanese management techniques. At times Howard and his *Splash* writers, Lowell Ganz and Babaloo Mandel, seem to be flag-waving, burdening Keaton with a long union-hall speech about how U.S. workers are "getting our butts kicked"—no laughs

intended, none generated. Only Watanabe's performance adds much human feeling. Howard himself is guilty of a strange kind of hypocrisy: He crows about American values, though he spent three weeks shooting in Argentina because he found a factory location there. In *Cocoon* he deftly blended comedy and social commentary. In *Gung Ho*—the title is not even Japanese but Chinese for "work together"—he made a film that is not much of anything except two hours long.
PG-13 / 1986 / Paramount

H

▲ HAIR

Okay, so the Age of Aquarius seems like the Dark Ages by this time, and "Let the Sun Shine In" got more air play than it deserved even back in 1969. Still, the stage play makes for a fresh, fun movie. The songs (cleverer than most Broadway numbers) and Twyla Tharp's wonderful choreography have been smoothly integrated into visually striking scenes. The story is also better developed. John Savage is a draftee from Oklahoma looking for a good time in New York before induction. He runs into a crowd of freaks, falls in love with a high-class chick (Beverly D'Angelo), and, of course, gets turned on. He goes off to the Army, anyway, and when Treat Williams, Don Dacus of the rock group Chicago, Annie Golden (of punk's The Shirts), and Dorsey Wright show up as his boot camp to shake him loose from combat duty, the trip turns into a bummer. A decade's perspective helps Czech-born director Milo Forman deromaticize the flower children a little, but the overall effect is still a high. This was the dawning of the age of '60s nostalgia.
PG / 1979 / CBS/Fox

▲ HALF MOON STREET

Sigourney Weaver traveled zillions of miles to get from *Aliens* to this loony British thriller. Better she should have gone to Tipperary. The

film's main appeal will be to people who long to see Ms. Weaver take her shirt off. Nothing much else of interest happens. Weaver plays an American economist working—and getting bored—in England. So naturally she becomes a high-priced call girl. One of her clients is Michael Caine, a renowned diplomat whom some Arab types want to kill to keep him from mediating a dispute. Weaver and Caine fall fitfully in love, which might account for her mindless behavior, such as naively failing to notice that the Arabs are setting her up to get at Caine. She seems otherwise rational, though, and director Bob (*La Balance*) Swaim trots the plot along such obvious lines that her foolishness leads nowhere. The film just sputters to a conclusion.
R / 1986 / Embassy

▲ HALLOWEEN

No one suspected at the time that this efficient, low-budget horror flick would spawn two sequels, dozens of ripoffs, and Jamie Lee Curtis's reputation as Queen of the Horrors. Director and cowriter John Carpenter merely set out to give "trick or treat" a new meaning, which he indeed did. A 6-year-old boy knifes his sister to death on Halloween. Fifteen years later the killer escapes from a mental hospital and returns to his hometown for more mayhem—again on October 31. Although there isn't even a ghost of an explanation for his choice of night or victims, there are scares aplenty. The cast was mostly unknowns except for an evil-looking Donald Pleasence and Curtis, then 20, who looks convincingly terrified as the plucky teenage babysitter who tangles with the killer. As to why audiences didn't ask Curtis's reasons for not turning on the lights when she enters a dark room or for hiding herself in a closet instead of running away, the answer is elementary: They're too scared to ask questions, that's why. A classic creepshow.

R / 1978 / Media

▲ HALLOWEEN II

If *Halloween* was the treat horror movie of 1978, this sequel is certainly the trick. The original, directed by John Carpenter, told its sordid tale with skill and economy: A child murders his promiscuous sister and 15 years later escapes from a mental institution on Halloween night to wreak havoc on a trio of nubile baby-sitters in the old neighborhood. Carpenter relied more on suspense than graphic slashings, making fear a palpable presence. With Debra Hill, Carpenter co-wrote and coproduced this film too, but he left the directing chores to newcomer Rick Rosenthal. The result is a wildly silly, gut-spilling film that demeans the original and will disappoint any audience that expects more than gore. The film picks up exactly where its namesake left off. Surviving baby-sitter Jamie Lee Curtis is rushed to the hospital, while the madman remains on the loose. The nurses jiggle around in peekaboo bras, and staffers perform acrobatic sex acts in the therapy room whirlpools. Since the camera never reveals a single patient except the comatose Curtis, no one seems to mind the orgasmic commotion except the killer, who enjoys plunging hypodermic needles directly into his victim's eyeballs. Donald Pleasence is once again in hot pursuit as the doctor, but the main thing here is the body count.

R / 1981 / MCA

▲ HAMMETT

No, this isn't a biography of (Samuel) Dashiell Hammett, one of the founding fathers of the hard-boiled detective novel. This film, set in San Francisco in 1928, is rather along the lines of

Michael Apted's *Agatha,* which starred Dustin Hoffman and Vanessa Redgrave in a tale extrapolated from the life of Agatha Christie. Frederic (*The Rose*) Forrest, fedora atilt and cigarette dangling insouciantly from his lips, plays Hammett. At the request of an old Pinkerton colleague (Hammett actually worked for the detective agency for a few months), Forrest goes off in search of a young woman, prowling the claustrophobic, cacophonous streets of Chinatown, looking world-weary and talking in machine-gun bursts. En route, he and pal Marilu (''Taxi'') Henner encounter Peter Boyle, Lydia (*Doctor Detroit*) Lei, and even Elisha Cook, Jr.—Wilmer the ''gunsel'' in the movie version of the real Hammett's *Maltese Falcon.* Francis Ford Coppola was the film's executive producer; its director was German New Waver Wim (*Paris, Texas*) Wenders, who, with the help of production designer Dean Tavoularis, provides the film with a wealth of atmosphere. The surprises and quadruple-crosses are snappily handled, and the acting is appropriately stylized. Hammett himself, who eventually all but forsook writing to serve as Lillian Hellman's mentor, probably had little in common with the character created by Forrest—though his stories certainly did.

PG / 1983 / Warner

▲ THE HAND

Disarming in more ways than one, this chiller is about a comic-strip artist, Michael Caine, who loses his drawing hand in a car wreck and finds it coming back to haunt him murderously. No big deal; Alan Alda's dad, Robert, got mixed up in a similar accident in the sturdy 1946 film *The Beast with Five Fingers.* In the grasp of Caine and director Oliver Stone, however, this minor notion is executed so well it becomes a major pleasure. Caine plays it straight, going edgy and sweaty as he begins to lose his wife, chilly Andrea Marcovicci, to a consciousness-raising movement and another man. Stone, who won an Oscar for writing *Midnight Express* but had previously directed only the obscure *Seizure,* adroitly milks the plot. Because even the most mean-spirited of hands is not all that menacing, Stone heightens the mood by ominous shifts to black-and-white, glaring flashes, and lots of storms. He uses his cast well, especially fascinating newcomer Annie McEnroe, as a sweet but foul-mouthed coed Caine falls for. Stone also leaves some questions open, even after a climactic mano-a-mano confrontation between Caine and his ex-appendage. Are the attacks we keep seeing real or imagined? Is the vagabond hand real or a creation of Caine's unconscious? If it's real, how does it manage to get from Vermont to California—thumbing rides, spending money hand over fist, or letting its fingers do the walking? No matter; in this case one is happy the devil finds work for idle filmmakers. As for Stone, he found a more serious outlet for his talents in 1986's acclaimed *Platoon.*

R / 1981 / Warner

▲ **HANKY PANKY**

Remember the classic bystander-embroiled-in-espionage movies, such as Alfred Hitchcock's *The Thirty-Nine Steps* and *North by Northwest,* the Bob Hope vehicle *My Favorite Blonde,* and *Arabesque,* with Gregory Peck and Sophia Loren? The director of this film, Sidney Poitier, and his writers, Henry Rosenbaum and David Taylor, obviously do. The problem is, they don't remember those classics well enough to emulate their verve, tension, and wit. Gene Wilder, as a Chicago architect, is linked with a murdered agent and a lost computer tape that holds the key to a weapons project. Gilda Radner plays the Madeleine Carroll/Eva Marie Saint/Sophia Loren role. The Grand Canyon has been thrown in instead of Mount Rushmore. The stars resort to yelling and constant double takes to get laughs. Wilder and Radner, husband and wife offscreen, are as endearingly vulnerable as ever. But the film looks as fake as their mutual affection looks real.

PG / 1982 / RCA/Columbia

▲ **HANNAH AND HER SISTERS**

What do you say when you happen on a movie this elating, this full to the brim with humor, heartbreak, and ravishing romance? The usual fever of adjectives—terrific, titanic, transcendent—sounds puny. A plot synopsis—three sisters search for the right man in New York—sounds trite. Even the fact that Woody Allen wrote and directed it and plays a leading role is not much help. This is Allen's most ardent, ambitious, and brilliant film, uncharacteristically crowded with character and incident. The spilling-over effect, letting emotions run amok, releases a generosity in the filmmaker that rushes to the rescue when his comic darts draw blood. The result yields some of Allen's most personal observations yet on the feelings for parents, siblings, children, bedmates, and buddies we categorize as love. Allen, a hypochondriac TV producer, is the ex-husband of Hannah, played by a radiant Mia Farrow. She, with a propensity to gain children in ways that range from the usual to adoption and artificial insemination, is an actress now married to a financial adviser expertly done by Michael Caine. Caine has found himself in lust with Farrow's sister Lee, played by the meltingly lovely Barbara Hershey. Hershey is living with a neurotic artist, lampooned by that master of Bergmanesque angst, Max Von Sydow. In the neurosis department, though, Von Sydow is a piker compared to Farrow's other sister, Holly, played by Dianne Wiest in a bonfire of a performance. Wiest, perpetually wincing from the rejection she suffers as actress, singer, writer, and lover, lets her sisters have it in a restaurant scene that cuts to the nerve as well as the funny bone. Watching Wiest and Allen, two maladjusted urbanites nursing each other's ego bruises, proves hilarious and surprisingly poignant. Their emotions are no less real for being susceptible to time. (Allen's screenplay, as well as Caine's and Wiest's supporting performances, won Oscars.) The melancholy attached to love's impermanence suffuses the film. At a climactic Thanksgiving family dinner, Hannah's parents—beautifully acted by Maureen O'Sullivan (Mia's real-life mom) and the late Lloyd Nolan—gather around the piano to sing Rodgers and Hart songs about love found and lost. Allen's camera roams the room picking up the same stories, hauntingly etched on the faces of his characters. In the music world an enduring ballad like those sung here is called a standard. You watch *Hannah and Her Sisters* with the intoxicating impression that you've been in on the birth of the film equivalent.

PG-13 / 1986 / HBO/Cannon

▲ **HANNA K**

Even Costa-Garvas had to make a clinker sometime, and this is it. The Greek-born director, who was nominated for an Oscar for *Missing,* turned to some new political biases in this film. But this

153

time he wields them in an artless frenzy. His argument is that the Israelis, through paranoia, are turning their country into a police state. Jill Clayburgh plays an American-born Jewish lawyer trying a difficult case in a Jerusalem courtroom. Her client is a tall, blue-eyed Arab accused of sneaking into Israel as part of a terrorist gang. Clayburgh, saddled with a truly moronic part, is about as believable as she would be playing Clarence Darrow. Consider her plight: In addition to showing herself incompetent in court, she's got two men on the hook and a third is nibbling. She is pregnant by her courtroom adversary, the smooth-talking district attorney—Gabriel Byrne, an Irish actor—who is convinced that the Arab (played by Mohamed Bakri, an Israeli) is a terrorist. Clayburgh phones her husband, from whom she is not yet divorced. He flies from Paris to counsel her and plead for her to return to him. Flash forward a year, Jill is still in Israel, she has had her baby, she and the district attorney are barely on speaking terms, and her Arab client is on a hunger strike in prison. This is only the beginning. In keeping with Clayburgh's naive character, she gets Bakri paroled into her custody—and he moves into her basement. Do they become lovers? Is he really innocent? Can she ever resolve her problems with men? Why didn't they call this *An Unmarried Woman Goes to Israel?*
R / 1983 / MCA

▲ THE HANOI HILTON

A kind of psychological *Rambo,* this film seems devoted to the proposition that we won the Vietnam war because many of our POWs survived. In fact this is a sad exploitation of those POWs, many of whom are credited as advisers to the film, appropriating fictionalized versions of their experience for a political purpose. There have been many powerful POW films in the past: *The Bridge on the River Kwai, Stalag 17, King Rat, The Rack.* They succeeded because a POW camp is an obvious arena in which to study the character of men—both captives and captors. When this film, directed and written by Lionel Chetwynd, sticks to the story of the individual Americans in the camp, it is engrossing. The actors playing those prisoners, including Michael Moriarity, Jeffrey Jones, Stephen Davies, Lawrence Press-

man, and Paul Le Mat, are consistently moving. Chetwynd compromises their performances, however, by preaching at every opportunity. Even Jane Fonda's hardest critics would cringe at the doltish behavior of the actress character (played by Gloria Carlin) who visits the Hanoi prison camp to sweet-talk the POWs into confessing guilt. The camp commander (Filipino-American actor Aki Aleong) is a one-dimensional brute, as is a Cuban officer (Michael Russo), who drops in to flaunt his sadistic impulses. Chetwynd undercuts himself too. The liberation of the prisoners, potentially a most moving scene, is just another excuse for flag-waving. Most offensive is the fact that he misuses the real POWs his film is about. These surely are men who have been misused enough for one lifetime.
R / 1987 / N/A

▲ HANOVER STREET

A super sweet love story, this period piece is set in London in 1943. Harrison Ford is an American flyer with a scar on his chin, said to be dashing; Christopher Plummer is a British officer with a scar on his lip, said to be boring. Lesley-Anne Down is married to the latter and in love with the former. As long as she is around, acting gracious or pained, the movie is pedestrian, despite shots of flying coyly intercut with the lovemaking. When the two men meet on a mission behind German lines, the action picks up, thanks to some sensational chase scenes. Once back in London, however, director Peter Hyams resorts to such pedestrian lines as "In a minute I'm going to turn and walk away" and the sort of schmaltz no one has seen since World War II flag wavers like *Mrs. Miniver.*
PG / 1979 / RCA/Columbia

▲ HAPPY BIRTHDAY, GEMINI

There's no cause for celebration. Based on the Broadway play *Gemini,* the movie is hopelessly stagebound, in spite of its grandiose claim to have been shot entirely on location in south Philadelphia. The seven main characters—each progressively more disagreeable—have roughly equal screen time, although the focus is on Alan Rosenberg, as a Harvard student about to turn 21

and going through a sexual identity crisis because he swings both ways. Robert Viharo turns in the film's best performance as Rosenberg's confused, good-natured father. With "hair like hepatitis" and nonstop mugging, Madeleine Kahn gets a few laughs as the loopy neighbor, but her portrayal is one-dimensional. Incredibly, this humorless exercise was written and directed by Richard Benner, who dealt with sexual hang-ups so masterfully in 1977's *Outrageous!* Blow out the candles, please.
R / 1980 / N/A

▲ HAPPY BIRTHDAY TO ME

Moldering on the compost heap of horror quickies is this rich-kids-on-campus blood gusher. Melissa Sue Anderson, the lovable blind daughter of that paragon of family entertainment "Little House on the Prairie," inexplicably chose to make her movie debut as a brain-damaged student who may or may not be cutting up her schoolmates to punish them for being rude at her birthday party. It's a credit to Anderson that she fashions a performance of pluck and poignancy out of a convoluted plot and anything-for-a-jolt direction by J. Lee (*The Guns of Navarone*) Thompson. The rest of the cast, including Glenn Ford as a sympathetic shrink, is mostly body count. The true horror is reserved for unsuspecting TV followers of Melissa Sue.
R / 1981 / RCA/Columbia

▲ HARDCORE

George C. Scott, as a devoutly religious businessman whose young daughter suddenly disappears into the sleazy L.A. porno scene, is good as always. Even better is Season Hubley, who plays the hooker Scott pays to help find the missing girl. She delivers a smashing, sexy performance. The others aren't bad either: Peter Boyle slavers effectively as a leering L.A. detective who likes to make it with the runaway girls he's supposed to catch, and Dick Sargent is appropriately uptight as Scott's Bible-quoting brother-in-law. But writer-director Paul Schrader, who wrote such powerful screenplays as *Taxi Driver* and *Blue Collar,* seems almost prissy in dealing with such an explosive topic as kiddie

porn. He can't seem to decide between moralizing and titillating. The result is an uneven, mostly depressing movie.
R / 1979 / RCA/Columbia

▲ HARDLY WORKING

In the '50s and '60s you could take a Jerry Lewis movie to the bank, which Paramount and other studios delightedly did. Critically, Lewis was regarded by some people—most of them French—as a comedian on a par with Chaplin and Keaton. His previous comedy, however, *Which Way to the Front,* had been released in 1970. (His cherished serious film about a World War II concentration camp, *The Day the Clown Cried,* was shot in 1972 but never finished due to legal disputes.) The comic himself directed this independently financed comeback try about a clown who goes through a succession of odd jobs after his circus folds. Lewis is so willing to play for old laughs that the opening sequence is a montage of clips from his hits. Many children will enjoy this film. Lewis still has quick, deftly clumsy hands made for slapstick, and nobody is better at knocking over a pitcher of water on a stuffed shirt. But to adults this poky movie may seem a bit sad. Lewis's once-manic energy is barely suggested in a few labored outbursts, and his lovable bewilderment is now more like bitterness. What was endearing in an innocent youth is plain wretchedness in a man of 55. Is there a more sophisticated, Pink Pantheresque comedy in Jerry Lewis the actor? It is a question, alas, that can't be answered by Jerry Lewis the director. His talents as a dramatic actor, however, were amply displayed under the direction of Martin Scorsese in 1983's *King of Comedy.*
PG / 1981 / N/A

▲ HARD TO HOLD

Fast women, fast cars, living on the razor's edge—such are the hardships of a Hollywood rock star's life. For those who haven't had enough of such travail, director Larry Peerce created this 93-minute cliché to hammer the point home once again. Soap opera and recording star Rick Springfield, in his movie debut, played a poor little super-rocker. Really just looking for true love,

155

he's trapped in his prison of glitz. Try to hold back the tears, everyone. Springfield, trying to bounce from his musical success into Hollywood the way he careened off "General Hospital" into musical stardom, is laughable. But then screenwriter Tom Hedley packs the script with such howlers as "It's tough being a star. People think it's all tits and champagne." Springfield's bubble-dumb rock voice chirps annoyingly throughout most of the sound track—he wrote seven of its songs, too—and yet he performs onscreen for only six minutes. Janet Ellber, who becomes the object of Springfield's romantic obsession, is right out of central casting, the "Girlfriend, Pop Star's Snooty" section: She's an intellectual who's never even heard of Rick and resists his five-dozen-roses advances until she is convinced he is more or less human. Will Ellber leave on the proverbial jet plane? Will Springfield rush straight from a concert to the scene of her departure? Will they hug and kiss ecstatically? Hard to take is more like it.

PG / 1984 / MCA

▲ HARPER VALLEY PTA

The early box-office success of this film is mystifying since it was based on a silly ten-year-old hit song, includes no real names, and relies on a clunk-on-the-head sort of subtlety. Barbara Eden (TV's old "Jeannie") plays the miniskirted mom who confronts the stuffy PTA and in the process exposes the vices—gambling, drunkenness, and promiscuity, for starters—of Harper Valley (effectively evoked by Lebanon, Ohio). The markedly professional supporting cast includes Nanette Fabray, Pat Paulsen, Louis Nye, Ronny Cox, and as Eden's daughter, Susan (Audrey Rose) Swift. But the main point is plain old institution-baiting.

PG / 1978 / Vestron

▲ HARRY & SON

There have been a lot of young actors for whom Paul Newman might have qualified as a father figure: Tom Cruise, Sean Penn, and Timothy Hutton, among others. They're Newman's professional offspring in their poise and avoidance of artifice. (The Cruise-Newman affinity was

later exploited in The Color of Money in 1986.) But if there is one actor with no family resemblance to Newman, it's Robby Benson, who plays the aspiring writer-son in this blue-collar ballad. Unlike Newman, Benson always makes the audience aware that acting is going on: His every sentence is an exercise in melodrama. In a drama about a stunted father-son relationship, such miscasting flirts with catastrophe, and Harry & Son cannot afford the flirtation. As coproducer, coauthor, co-star, and director of this enterprise, Newman hasn't put his usual ironic spin on the material either. Instead, he embraces the genre's clichés. An unemployed construction worker learns to express love for his boy after suffering through more physical and emotional trials than Job. Whatever motivated him, Newman doesn't let his passion surface. Indeed, Harry & Son is everything a typical Newman performance is not: sentimental, unfocused, unconvincing. Only in its final moment does the movie display any power. When a tough-minded friend, Joanne Woodward, mourns Harry's fate, her expression and economy, by comparison, magnify the faults of the film.

PG / 1984 / Vestron

▲ HARRY AND THE HENDERSONS

It waits until the lights are out. It stalks you relentlessly and strikes just when you think you're going to have a good time. It's . . . it's . . . it's another limp ripoff of E.T.! When John Lithgow and Melinda (Close Encounters of the Third Kind) Dillon are driving home from a camping trip with their two kids and crash into Bigfoot not once but twice, it's a sign of things to come. When they get him home, his cloying cuteness more than compensates for the bad smell that daughter Margaret (My American Cousin) Langrick constantly complains about. Harry, played by 7'2" Kevin Peter Hall (who also played the monster in Predator), even cries when Lithgow tries to take him back home. Harry manages to escape, and after numerous sightings in the Seattle area everyone flocks to Lithgow's sporting-goods store for guns. His father, played by M. Emmet (Blood Simple) Walsh, decides to make the store "B.H.Q." (Bigfoot headquarters) but is disappointed when Lithgow makes a life-size drawing of the alleged beast. "I wanted King Kong and you brought me a giant gerbil,'' Walsh tells Lithgow in the film's funniest line. The rest of the film is a race by Lithgow, characteristically engaging despite the inept material, and anthropologist Don Ameche to save Harry from French trapper David Suchet. Director and co-writer William Dear came up with few jokes and repeats them again and again, perhaps a reflection of his background in TV commercials. Even children, for whom this film was obviously intended, are likely to lose their patience. In the end when Suchet says, ''It's over,'' Ameche responds, ''Over? It's just beginning.'' That there could be more out there like this is a scary thought indeed. PG / 1987 / N/A

▲ HARRY'S WAR

For anyone who's been audited by the IRS, this film is sheer joy—or at least vicarious revenge. Karen Grassle, the wife of mailman Edward Herrmann, wants a divorce because he's not aggressive enough. Then, suddenly rejuvenated, he responds to a plea for help from an old friend, Geraldine Page, the delightfully daft owner of a dilapidated antique-cum-war-surplus shop. She's been audited and dunned for $190,000 in back taxes because she has been taking charitable deductions for what she doles out to assorted oddball friends. In tax court, she offers no defense, and finally collapses and dies, leaving Herrmann her estate. When he finds his inheritance plastered with ''U.S. Government Property'' placards and his bank account attached for back taxes, he appeals to a wonderfully pompous IRS district director, David Ogden Stiers. Retorts Stiers: ''I am the United States Treasury. What are you?'' Herrmann declares war and, in one scene that audiences cheered aloud, drives a World War II armored car into a TV studio where Stiers is expounding on the joy of paying taxes. When the feds besiege his property with enough tear gas, guns, and ammunition to overrun a couple of battalions of tax rebels, the press arrives and Herrmann gives a speech via TV minicam, declaring, ''Hitler would have loved the IRS.'' Those to whom the multiform horrors of April 15 are always fresh in the mind can only sympathize. PG / 1981 / N/A

▲ HAUNTED HONEYMOON

Connoisseurs of haunted-house comedies aren't likely to rank this among prime examples of the genre, such as Abbott and Costello's Hold That Ghost or Bob Hope's Ghost Breakers. Director Gene Wilder and his co-writer, former art director Terence Marsh, left too many lame lines in this film about a couple who returns to the man's hoary family estate to get married. ''His memory's going,'' Wilder says of a forgetful butler. ''I wish we were,'' replies Gilda Radner. Wilder also wasted too many opportunities, frittering away any number of scenes that seem to have been chopped off just as they were starting to get funny. A lot of them involve Radner. Mrs. Wilder in real life, she plays his fiancée in the film and seems almost painfully subdued. She's not a bad straight woman; it just seems an underuse of her talent. There's a cathartic tone to the scene in which she does a raucous rendition of ''Ballin' the Jack'' with Dom De Luise, who deftly plays Wilder's grandmother (as a prim sort of dowager with a five o'clock shadow). It's reminiscent of the ''Puttin' on the Ritz'' number Wilder did with Peter Boyle in Mel Brooks's Young Frankenstein. Indeed, Wilder seems doomed to invidious comparisons with Brooks, who directed The Producers, in which Wilder made his movie-acting breakthrough. As writer-director of such films as The Adventure of Sherlock Holmes's Smarter Brother, The World's Greatest Lover, and The Woman in Red, Wilder has turned out pleasant, sporadically funny comedies. None of those films, however, approached the wild yet carefully crafted humor Brooks generates when he gets a film rolling. Wilder almost seems too gentle, too lacking in Brooks's willingness to display an edge of nastiness. While Haunted Honeymoon has its entertaining moments, it makes Wilder seem almost complacent, like a ballplayer who's content to get one hit a game. PG / 1986 / HBO/Cannon

▲ HEAD OFFICE

Eventually it is pounded into submission by its own cartoonish heavyhandedness, but this anti-big-business satire scores some points. That's partly due to its sheer savagery. ''Are you executive material?'' one character asks another. ''Do you mean, can I play hard ball?'' ''No, I mean, can you kiss ass?'' There are also some winning performances. In an age of smirky, self-congratulating comic actors, Judge (*Beverly Hills Cop*) Reinhold lays way back as a shiftless son of a U.S. senator who goes to work for a multinational conglomerate. While Reinhold demonstrates a Jimmy Stewart-like good-hearted naiveté, Jane (TV's *The Sun Also Rises*) Seymour does a nicely smarmy turn as a woman executive who's sleeping her way to the top as fast as she can get her clothes off and on. There are nice bits by Danny De Vito, Rick Moranis, and Don Novello as a chauffeur who tries to lure women into his limo by offering to play them a Julio Iglesias tape. Newcomer Lori-Nan Engler provides an appealing fresh young face for Reinhold to fall in love with. Writer-director Ken (*Airplane II*) Finkleman, a Canadian, takes his whacks at such bits of business as closing plants in a one-company town and high-stakes lobbying in Washington. While he has made his point long before the slapdash ending and gets a little preachy, he's funny enough to redden faces in boardrooms all over the country.

PG-13 / 1986 / HBO/Cannon

▲ HEARTBEAT

Though only dedicated aficionados of Beat Generation lore will fully appreciate this slice of the on-the-road myth surrounding '50s literary avant-gardists Jack Kerouac and Neal Cassady, the film is more than cultish indulgence. While erratically paced and maddening in its omissions (Kerouac's bisexuality is ignored), the script is otherwise faithful to its inspiration: the unsentimental saga of the two men written by fellow traveler Carolyn Cassady. Sissy Spacek shows her remarkable range as the sophisticated Carolyn, traversing an emotional minefield between John Heard's sensitive, gentlemanly Jack and Nick Nolte's primal, self-centered Neal. Laszlo Kovac's inspired cinematography raises just another picaresque epic of gettin' high and gettin' by into real artistry. The film even makes self-destructive impulses seem more poignant than puerile.

R / 1980 / Warner

▲ HEARTBREAKERS

Directed and written by little-known Bobby Roth and acted by a cast devoid of big names, this film could easily escape notice. Don't let it. Few movies have done such an honest, unapologetic job of exploring the frustrations of middle-aged Americans. Peter Coyote plays a painter who has a lot of integrity but no money. His best friend, Nick Mancuso, is a businessman with a lot of money and little peace of mind. Coyote lives, unhappily, with Kathryn Harrold. Both he and Mancuso also end up lusting after Carole Laure and Carol Wayne, the crazy-as-a-fox bimbo on the ''Tonight Show.'' Coyote and Mancuso adroitly underplay the pulsing mix of affection and envy between them; each shows a lot more ability to deal with his friend's failures than with his successes. Laure is icily detached, and Harrold is tired of struggling. Wayne is altogether charming as a model who, in seducing the two men at the same time, does a striptease that is at once innocently clumsy and feverishly sexy. Roth seems to be in something of a rush to wrap up the loose ends at the finish, swirling through a series of plot resolutions that makes the film tidier than it needed to be. But he doesn't fall into the trap of overplaying his story or resorting to clichés. He seems satisfied to create recognizable characters whose lives are intimately involving.

R / 1985 / Vestron

▲ HEARTBREAK RIDGE

For all his excesses, John Wayne never really let himself become a caricature. Clint Eastwood, by most measures the inheritor of Wayne's mantle as national Hero Laureate, is not so fortunate. Then again, he has only himself to blame since he directed this film. It's about a battle-weary Marine sergeant who can't hear someone clear his throat without being so offended he is moved to utter eighty or ninety obscenities and bust heads and elbows, none of them his own. The movie is disappointing in other ways too. For one thing, the gruesome battle referred to in the title, a major confrontation of the Korean War, is not in this film, except as a historical inspiration to the modern Marines it focuses on. Screenwriter Jim Carabotsos is a Vietnam vet. Yet he seems to have no idea of how men fight, get along, or

talk. A man, about to do a favor for another man but apparently fearful the action will be misinterpreted as an act of affection, snarls, "This doesn't mean I want to trade warm spit with you." Grim noncom Eastwood and the undisciplined squad of young Marines he inherits, as well as their officers, are all stereotypes. And the battle they eventually fight in is the 1983 invasion of Grenada. While it was no doubt more than enough war for the men who fought in it, Grenada is hardly the stuff of which glory is made. The only moments in the film that have the texture of reality are Eastwood's encounters with Marsha Mason, the ex-wife who is still jealous of the corps. Whether it's Eastwood's natural gallantry coming into play or some honest-to-goodness acting, he defers to Mason in such a vulnerable way that he seems more like a man, less like a cardboard figure. It is the only thing he does in the film that seems to mean anything.
R / 1986 / Warner

▲ HEARTBURN

Shirt-chasing Jewish prince leaves self-mocking Jewish wife for shiksa goddess. Nora Ephron made something freshly funny of that plot line in her 1983 best-seller by lifting many of the details from the breakup of her own marriage to Watergate journalist Carl Bernstein. (The split was precipitated by Bernstein's affair with Margaret Jay, wife of a former British ambassador, while Nora was pregnant with their second child.) That there would be a movie version was inevitable. The decidedly non-kosher casting of Meryl Streep and Jack Nicholson was not. The two WASPy leads make no sense as the real Ephron and Bernstein. The book's ethnic flavor is lost, along with its roman-à-clef allure. Eventually, though, you realize that director Mike Nichols and screenwriter Ephron (who also wrote Nichols' *Silkwood*) wanted it that way. They are after something deeper here than the tale of one wronged wife who uses her rapier wit to bloody her rat husband. The emphasis now is on how hard it is to sustain a modern marriage when you toss in the grenades of career, friends, children, and temptations to infidelity. When Streep, as a tart-tongued magazine food writer, meets Nicholson, a womanizing Washington, D.C., columnist, neither is blind to the other's failings as a potential mate. Streep's fa-

ther, beautifully played by Steven (*Yentl*) Hill, has to cajole her to the altar. But the pair's attraction is never in doubt. Both Streep and Nicholson seem palpably turned on by the other's wit and energy. Then marriage and parenthood slowly work changes. She enjoys the everyday details of householding, he does not (watching Nicholson struggling to read Beatrix Potter to his tot is a howl). When he begins slipping out with an undersecretary's wife (the stunning Karen Akers), Streep (again pregnant) takes the baby to her father's apartment in New York. After a reconciliation attempt flounders because of Nicholson's continued cheating, she bashes his face with a key-lime pie. Nichols's knack for finding the sting in every joke remains unparalleled. And Streep and Nicholson share an unforgettable moment: In the hospital for the birth of her second baby, she and the husband who no longer figures in her future recall the more promising day when their first child was born. With heartpiercing candor, the measure is taken of what gets lost in a marriage. Forget the critics who dumped on this project because it wasn't what they expected and try this hilarious, heartbreaking film next time you're at the video store. You might be surprised.
R / 1986 / Paramount

▲ HEART LIKE A WHEEL

A car races up and down a back road somewhere in upstate New York. The driver giggles happily as he hoists his young daughter up onto his lap and lets her take the wheel. That's the enticing beginning of an unfairly neglected film. The little girl is portraying Shirley Muldowney, who in real life went on to become a three-time winner of the National Hot Rod Association Championship. She's the only driver, male or female, to win the title more than once. That she had to triumph not only against other drivers but against the onus of being one of the few women in drag racing is the dramatic core of this movie. Muldowney is played by Bonnie Bedelia, an actress who hadn't made a feature movie since 1978's *The Big Fix* but is known for such TV films as *Salem's Lot*. Married young to a local boy who works in a gas station, Muldowney quickly establishes herself as the fastest thing on four wheels, turns a weekend hobby into a profession—and loses her husband

along the way. On the drag-racing circuit, Muldowney takes up with another racer, Connie Kalitta—played by Beau Bridges—who becomes her chief mechanic and lover, although his philandering eventually drives them apart. Director Jonathan Kaplan, whose previous effort was *Over the Edge* (he also directed *White Line Fever* in 1975), wisely kept this movie from being pitbound. The racetrack scene is energetically depicted, but he's really after the story of how a woman—or anyone, for that matter—manages to overcome huge odds to achieve what she wants. In that sense, this is certainly an all-American success story. Bedelia's performance is a deftly shaded one: She is soft when she should be (especially in the domestic scenes with her young son, John) and steely when she finds she is going to have to go it alone. Leo Rossi as her husband is sympathetic, and Bridges provides a reminder that brother Jeff is not the only member of the family who can act. This is a rare auto-racing film that has a human heart at its center, not just a carburetor.
PG / 1983 / CBS/Fox

▲ HEAT

To accentuate the positive, this is the perfect entertainment for people who would enjoy watching Burt Reynolds, Peter MacNicol, and Diana Scarwid mill around Las Vegas for an hour and a half, waiting for a movie to happen. Other than that it is a remarkably pointless, lame waste of time, written by William Goldman from his own novel. The director is listed as "R. M. Richards," though the film was actually directed by a consortium that included Dick Richards, who quit after he and Burt got into a brawl. To call the plot moronic would be to give it the benefit of the doubt. Reynolds is a Vietnam veteran who has become a professional bodyguard in Vegas because he is such an efficient fighter. While he has obviously seen a Bruce Lee movie or two—he can fight in slow motion—his specialty is edged weapons. (Reynolds indeed seems to have taken a paper shredder to the script.) MacNicol, a rich, chattery nerd, wants Burt to teach him bravery. Karen Young, a hooker who has been sadistically assaulted by a mobster's son, wants revenge. Young is among a number of characters who wander idly in and out of the story. The events before, during, and after the inevitable

fight-out are not remotely plausible. Nor are they stylish or interesting. At one point Reynolds and MacNicol are talking in an alley and MacNicol says, "Why don't we go back to the city lights and find some of that glitter and glitz?" So they go stand on a building and talk some more, then continue the chat in a hotel room. At one point, Scarwid, a casino blackjack dealer, breaks into tears when Reynolds blows $100,000 in one hand at her table. It couldn't have been too hard for her to get motivated to cry; all she had to do was think about what a shlocky movie she would be associated with for the rest of her career.
R / 1987 / N/A

▲ HEAT AND DUST

Set in the India of past and present, *Heat and Dust* has plenty of both eras, though it's a bit short on narrative drive. But then atmosphere has always been the key element in the films of director James Ivory, producer Ismail Merchant, and screenwriter Ruth Prawer Jhabvala. The trio's collaborations, including *The Householder* and *The Europeans,* all would have a lot of catching up to do to achieve a snail's pace. (Not until 1986, with the lyrical *A Room With a View,* did they finally find the right balance). Still, the lulling sensuality of *Heat and Dust* may cast a spell on patient viewers not weaned on Spielberg. Julie Christie plays a modern Englishwoman obsessed by the scandalous past of her great-aunt (Greta Scacchi). The aunt had come to India in the 1920s as the bride of a stuffy British civil servant (Christopher Cazenove) and had run off with an Indian prince (Shashi Kapoor). Determined to understand what got into Auntie, Christie travels to India to research the facts and gets hooked on a married Indian guide (Zakir Hussain). The film flashes back and forth between both stories as the mystery unravels over a very slow 130 minutes. Christie, who could command attention clad in sackcloth and ashes (her wardrobe's not much better here), helps the time pass. And newcomer Scacchi makes the aunt a figure of true beauty and dignity. But it's India's reigning superstar, Shashi Kapoor (he's done at least 210 films), who is called upon to represent the seductiveness and the hypnotic pull of his country. He's just not up to the task—at least by Western standards. Pudgy, perhaps from too many trips to the tandoor, Kapoor sports an inane grin,

a charmless manner, and a voice like Yoda. Why he's considered such a hunk in his own country is the film's abiding mystery.
R / 1983 / MCA

▲ HEAT WAVE

My Brilliant Career's Australian star Judy Davis has a marvelously responsive face, which can register defiance and fear at the same time, seem at once hostile and sensual, appear both beautiful and shattered. And she gets plenty of chances to demonstrate her range—too many chances, in fact. This is an overwrought story about a group of poor Sydney people opposing a new apartment project that will force them to leave their homes. Davis plays the anarchist leader of the group; newcomer Richard Moir is the leftist-turned-Establishment architect who designed the project. Director Phillip Noyce uses color and light to create an all-but-tangible mood of heat and oppression, but the film disintegrates into a morass of symbolism (the project is named "Eden," and viewers are beaten over the head with the biblical implications of man's unworthiness). The movie will be forgotten. Davis won't.
R / 1983 / Thorn/EMI

▲ HEAVEN

Look in vain here for the humor and heart Diane Keaton brought to her role in *Annie Hall*. In her dilettantish debut as a director, Keaton is hell-bent on getting the poop on paradise from a randomly chosen group of Los Angeles citizens. She started her hundred or so video chat sessions in 1984, asking such questions as: "Are you afraid to die?" "What is heaven?" and "Is there sex in heaven?" Though many of the interviewees address her by name on camera, Keaton is never seen or heard. Her contribution was to splice these interviews with campy old movie and TV clips and music that sounds like a hereafter hit parade ("My Blue Heaven," "Over the Rainbow," etc.). For all the dazzle, the film emerges as pure prattle, alternately exploitative or patronizing. The wacko comments run the gamut. One person defines heaven as a place where there will be "wonderful bodies." Another compares reaching the pearly gates to winning an Oscar. A recent poll by *USA Weekend* reported 67 percent

of Americans believe in hell. If they sit through this maddening film, the other 33 percent are bound to come around.
PG-13 / 1987 / N/A

▲ HEAVEN CAN WAIT

The "enough with reality, already" syndrome has taken over Hollywood in recent years. And the scripts that don't blast off into the future blast back into the past. First there was a play, *Heaven Can Wait,* adapted for film in 1941 as *Here Comes Mr. Jordan* with Claude Rains. Then Warren Beatty resurrected the notion, indulging his Warren-of-all-trades conceit by co-writing, co-directing (with Buck Henry), producing, and starring as a Rams quarterback who's prematurely snuffed by an overzealous bureaucrat in heaven. Returned to earth in the body of an industrialist whose murder is being plotted by his wife (a deliciously dotty Dyan Cannon) and male secretary (Charles Grodin), Beatty's sole concern is getting his new body in shape to play football—until he meets schoolteacher Julie Christie. Along the way there is fun, football, romance, and thoroughly satisfying unreality. Movies are supposed to be like this. Oscar certainly got excited at the time, doling out nine nominations with Beatty tying the Orson Welles record as writer-director-producer-star. Poor Warren didn't actually win a thing, though. Perhaps that's the price of doing a movie purely for the fun of it. Back in 1978, the heavy dramatics of *The Deer Hunter* struck the Academy as more like it as Best Picture.
PG / 1978 / Paramount

▲ HEAVEN HELP US

"Bless me, Father, for I have sinned. This is my first confession."

"What are your sins, my son?"

"I'm not a son, Father. I'm a comedy. . . . Well, actually, I cannot decide if I'm an antic comedy or a melancholy drama. That's one of my sins, which are multitudinous."

"What else?"

"I have taken an excellent and ripe premise—growing up Catholic at an all-boys high school in the mid '60s—and abused it."

"How many times?"

"The usual: twenty-four frames per second. I reduce complicated and comic relationships between priest and students to a series of sado-masochistic encounters. I think running mastur-bation gags are real funny. I treat—"

"Slow down. Speed-rapping has no place in the confessional."

"But, Father, I have so much to confess. I could have been somebody."

"Do you have any merely venial sins?"

"Sure. Donald Sutherland plays the school principal as if he's doing Dame Edith Evans's impersonation of a priest."

"Are any of your sins original?"

"No, that is my biggest transgression. I've abandoned a bunch of young actors, and I'm afraid of burning in hell, Father."

"What's your idea of hell?"

"Debbie Reynolds as the Singing Nun."

"Anything to say in your defense?"

"At least I don't try to pass off Julie Andrews as an 18-year-old novice."

"All right, for your penance, say three hundred Our Fathers and watch *Going My Way* ten times. And ask St. Jude, the patron saint of hopeless causes, to intercede for you. Are you familiar with the miracles of St. Jude?"

"Sure, he's my agent."

"Now, make a sincere act of contrition."

"Thanks, Father, and let's have lunch."

PG / 1985 / Thorn/EMI

▲ HEAVEN'S GATE

Now a synonym (along with *Ishtar*) for movie turkey, this bloated 225-minute exercise in direc-torial self-indulgence remains an endurance test even when watched on a home VCR with the speed forward button close at hand. Fresh from his Oscar-winning *The Deer Hunter,* director Mi-chael Cimino saw his reputation drown in the waves of his own incompetence. Cimino attempts to inflate a Wyoming range war of the 1890s into an epic, complete with sweeping panoramas, ex-pensive set pieces, an ear-splitting sound track, and a cast of thousands, including Kris Kristof-ferson, Christopher Walken, and Isabelle Hup-pert. It won't work. Somewhere in this huge, heartless $36 million movie lurks an arresting little Western, but Cimino was clearly not ready to settle for anything small.

R / 1980 / MGM/UA

▲ HELL NIGHT

As part of a joint sorority-fraternity hazing, two college coeds and two male friends spend a night in a candlelit, supposedly haunted manor near campus. Their nasty pals rig up a few early scares, but of course these sharp collegians refuse to admit there are real ghosts about and of course there are. The menace turns out to be an agile hulking half-man, half-linebacker type, whose specialty is twisting heads around 180 degrees. Linda Blair knows where her head is at, but she's so bored (hey, after doing *The Exorcist* at 14, we understand), she sighs, "What are we doing here anyway?" It's a line sure to elicit viewer sym-pathy. You won't have any trouble sleeping after *Hell Night,* or through it, for that matter.

R / 1981 / Media

▲ A HERO AIN'T NOTHIN' BUT A SANDWICH

Hokey but not insubstantial, this film brought Cicely Tyson and Paul Winfield together for the first time since their hit *Sounder.* Surprisingly, the two Oscar nominees are overshadowed by Larry Scott, who plays a bright, troubled student at a Los Angeles junior high. Puzzled and hurt by the disappearance of his father, the boy turns to heroin, steals from his own family, and ends up in a drug rehabilitation center. Scott turns in a warm, believable performance as an adolescent struggling for instant maturity. Although the screenplay sags periodically, he is always there to stretch it taut again.

R / 1978 / N/A

▲ HERO AT LARGE

Slower than a spent bullet! Barely able to leap park benches in a single bound! Even when he's decked out in blue tights, red cape, and yellow boots, John Ritter makes an unlikely superhero, yet the big "A" on his chest stands for "Captain Avenger." He was just another out-of-work actor until he foiled a holdup in Greenwich Village and became an overnight hero. Silly as all this may sound, it's amusing, thanks in large part to the engaging performance director Martin (*The Lords of Flatbush*) Davidson coaxed from Ritter, mer-cifully devoid of his "Three's Company" double

takes. Anne (*Paradise Alley*) Archer is witty and alluring as the girl next door. The film falters when it takes its comic-book morality too seriously.
PG / 1980 / MGM/UA

▲ HEROES

Henry Winkler never did quite make the quantum leap to the big screen from his hit TV series, "Happy Days." In *Heroes* he plays a Vietnam vet trying to blot out a nightmare and reconstruct his life. But he comes off more like a zany punk. His quirky girlfriend (Sally Field), whom he meets in a bus station, is the best thing not only in his life but in this movie. The two of them are mostly on the run, en route to some illusory place where Winkler hopes to set up a worm farm with former Army buddies. When the dream collapses, Field assures Winkler that he still has a future—with her.
PG / 1977 / N/A

▲ THE HIDDEN FORTRESS

George Lucas claimed this 1958 Japanese film was the inspiration for *Star Wars,* and it's not hard to see why. Set against the backdrop of Japan's 16th-century civil wars, the movie focuses on two bumbling farmers who happen upon some gold pieces hidden in the wood they are using to build a fire. Before the two can make off with the booty they are intercepted by Toshiro Mifune, who plays a fearsome-looking but likable general; he tells them that if they join him to help a beautiful princess escape, he'll let them keep the gold. The princess has been deposed by a rival dynasty. If you imagine her as Princess Leia and the general as Han Solo, you begin to get the idea. And if you stretch it a little, the farmers, who constantly squabble but can't seem to live without each other, could be R2D2 and C-3PO. The movie was directed by Akira Kurosawa, who is a favorite of Lucas's. This film was made in black and white, and although it's a bit tedious (the endless climbing uphill and down to get to the secret fortress is awful), the battle scenes are spectacular, the byplay between the farmers witty, and the wide shots of the battle and the Japanese countryside breathtaking. (In Japanese with subtitles.)
Unrated / 1984 / Media

▲ HIDE IN PLAIN SIGHT

This film was getting bad reviews even before it opened. Worse yet, they were emanating from its director, James Caan, who was miffed at MGM over its shooting instructions and the editing of the movie. The release was postponed eight months. It wasn't worth the wait. This is a "dramatization of a true story" about the Witness Relocation Program, first implemented in 1967 when a small-time Buffalo hoodlum turned state's evidence against a pair of crime bosses and was given a new identity. Spencer Eastman's screenplay concentrates on factory worker Thomas Hacklin, whose ex-wife runs off with the informer, taking Hacklin's two kids. Caan is affecting as a man of limited education battling against a stone-wall bureaucracy. Jill Eikenberry is appealing as his new girl and Robert Viharo is perfectly cast as the hood. Caan shot the film in Buffalo—often in the same places where real events unfolded thirteen years before. But his directorial debut is marred because the film lacks both the immediacy of a documentary and the inventiveness of fiction.
PG / 1980 / MGM/UA

▲ HIGH ANXIETY

Director-star Mel Brooks is a psychiatrist who takes over an institution for the "very, very nervous." Soon some very strange things start happening there, mostly sent-up scenes from Hitchcock movies and Hollywood in-jokes. Cloris Leachman and Harvey Korman are heavy into S&M, not to mention murder and mayhem. Madeline Kahn is the kind of girl who has everything—and it all matches. To win her, the shrink has to fight off high anxiety, a Brooksian version of *Vertigo*—or is it *Frenzy?* Whichever, the audience suffers through a takeoff that, despite a few funny traumas (notably Brooks's nightclub rendition of the title song), doesn't quite take off.
PG / 1977 / CBS/Fox

▲ HIGH-BALLIN'

The charmingly irresponsible and handsomely grubby eighteen-wheel jockeys in this time-killer are Peter Fonda and country singer Jerry Reed, seen and heard in *Smokey and the Bandit.* They meet predictable obstacles: highjackers, a ruthless

163

trucking baron, and blizzards that seem to strike every time they get behind a wheel. There's also a woman driver, of course, Canadian Helen Shaver (who later reaped the rewards of starting the hard way with a juicy role opposite Paul Newman in the 1986 hit, *The Color of Money*). It's all pretext to shoot big semis crashing into things. There's little pretension here, only the sort of honest action movie that went out with Randolph Scott Westerns.
PG / 1978 / Vestron

▲ HIGHLANDER

This picture is a mesmerizing triumph of style over substance. Director Russell Mulcahy, a music video director, turned what might have been just another wacky fantasy adventure into a moody combination of *Blade Runner, The Terminator,* and your last really good nightmare. The plot centers on Christopher (*Greystoke*) Lambert, who plays a Scottish warrior destined to fight a battle that will determine the fate of the earth. He's 468 years old, one of a band of immortal knights who have been waiting for the Gathering, which seems to be the Super Bowl of knightdom. The origin of their strength isn't clear. Even Sean Connery as Lambert's mentor (played so earnestly he's like Yoda with a good hairpiece) doesn't know. When Lambert asks Connery, he replies, "Why does the sun come up? Or are the stars merely pinholes in the curtain of night?" Right, uh, well, thanks, Sean; let's keep in touch. Mulcahy uses all manner of light effects as he cuts back and forth between 16th-century Scotland and modern Manhattan. All the backlighting, silhouetting, ominous shadows, and stark rays of light become entities of their own. Roxanne (*The Verdict*) Hart, as a police forensics expert, is a comely enough foil, though she's one of the worst screamers ever. Most women shriek more at the checkout counter when they find out their paper towel coupon is out of date than Hart does when she's dangling by one hand stories above the ground. Lambert is no Schwarzenegger in physique, and his accent isn't as muscular either. But he does have those Brando-like feral eyes. Anyway, the climactic battle has less to do with him and archenemy Clancy (*The Bride*) Brown than it does with the special effects.
R / 1986 / HBO/Cannon

▲ HIGH ROAD TO CHINA

Maybe he should have taken a slow boat. Maybe he should have tried the Shanghai Express. Maybe he should have just stayed in Hawaii. In any case, this proved to be an unfortunate pathway to feature films for Tom Selleck, the brawny star of TV's "Magnum, P.I." Seleck's character has a John Wayne appeal—laconic, swaggering, but sensitive, given only to the wholesome macho vices—smoking, drinking, and swearing. As a former World War I ace hired to fly debutante Bess (*The Four Seasons*) Armstrong to Afghanistan to find her lost father, he is a hero men can admire and women can lust after. But after a stylish first scene involving a Milquetoasty clerk being stalked by a gunman, this movie musters little energy. Armstrong, who brings to mind Julie Andrews with a case of the blahs, is bratty where she's supposed to be spunky. Director Brian Hutton, whose previous credits were not exactly a list of all-time greats—*Kelly's Heroes, X Y & Zee, Night Watch,* to name three—lets scenes drone on and strikes up little in the way of responses among his performers. Writers S. Lee Pogostin and Sandra Weintraub Roland are also culprits, since the film cried out for some snappy interchanges between Selleck and Armstrong and they mostly snipe at each other. There's only a slogging trip through Afghanistan, Nepal, and China—they all look alike, which isn't surprising since most of the film was shot in Yugoslavia. Only splendid aerial footage of old biplanes keeps things from getting soporific. In its promotions, the film raised comparisons with *Raiders of the Lost Ark,* but the best comparison it can hope for is merely invidious.
PG / 1983 / Warner

▲ HISTORY OF THE WORLD—PART I

Mel Brooks's film suffers from his typical overload of juvenile plays on words and ram-it-down-their-throats vulgarity. With some hilarious scenes degenerating into disgusting ones, this is a real carrot-and-shtik job. *History* shows Brooks in five vignettes (the Dawn of Man through the French Revolution). They lack the manic brillance of his classic "2,000-Year-Old Man" LPs with Carl Reiner. Still, there are moments of inspired lu-

nacy. When Moses drops the one of his three stone tablets bearing commandments eleven through fifteen, it shatters, and he says, "Make that ten commandments." A Spanish Inquisition production number recalls the classic "Springtime for Hitler" scene from *The Producers*. But not even Sid Caesar, Dom De Luise, Cloris Leachman, Madeline Kahn, Gregory Hines, Shecky Greene, Harvey Korman, and the stunning Mary-Margaret Humes can save the rest of the film. The last frames promise a Part II featuring "Hitler on Ice" and "Jews in Space." It hardly helps. As Louis XVI, Brooks turns to the camera three times and mumbles, in New Yorkese, "It's good ta be da King." In Hollywood it's even better ta be da writer, producer, and director of your own self-indulgent trash.
R / 1981 / CBS/Fox

▲ THE HITCHER

C. Thomas (*Soul Man*) Howell, driving alone through the desert, dozes off but awakens just in time to avoid an eighteen-wheeler. He might just as well have stayed asleep rather than go through the ordeal that ensues. Howell picks up the title character, Rutger (*Blade Runner*) Hauer, and soon Hauer has a knife near Howell's eye and is asking such trivia questions as, "Do you have any idea how much blood jumps out of a guy's throat when you cut his neck?" With his intense eyes and rugged physique, Hauer is convincing as the roadside psychotic who has a thing for dismembering motorists. But he isn't interested in killing Howell; as a matter of fact he wants Howell to stop him. "Why?" Howell asks. "You'll figure it out," Hauer tells him. But he never really does. Nor does the audience. Perhaps it's all just to showcase John (*Witness*) Seale's striking desert photography, which is as gorgeous as the story is gruesome. Or maybe it's to set up such spectacular state-of-the-art stunts as the two police cars that do simultaneous pirouettes through the air and then somersault down the highway. *The Hitcher* is a respectable double debut for writer Eric Red and director Robert Harmon. But the story is repetitive. And when Hauer uses the sexy Jennifer Jason Leigh as a trailer hitch, things are stretched a little too far.
R / 1986 / Thorn/EMI

▲ HOME OF THE BRAVE

True, this is a musical film. But don't expect *The Sound of Music, Shall We Dance?* or *Grease*. Don't expect a concert film either, though it's closer to that than anything else, except perhaps the visualization of a dream. The movie was written and directed by, and stars, multimedia performer Laurie Anderson, and whatever else it is, it's fascinating. Shot over ten days at a Union City, New Jersey, theater in 1985, the film focuses on Anderson's singing, dancing, and recitations. But all kinds of things are going on. People walk around onstage wearing robotlike masks that make them resemble C-3PO. A rear-stage screen shows a succession of images ranging from a grocery list to a giant radar antenna. Cadaverous Beat novelist William Burroughs comes out and does a macabre jitterbug with Anderson. Anderson telephones her keyboard player, Joy Askew, who is standing just across the stage, to discuss the next bit. What's surprising is how cohesive all these elements seem; they're related in mood and attitude if not in substance. What's more, Anderson and her choreography consultant, Wendy Perron, appear to have planned every movement with relentless precision. The stylized percussionist David Van Tieghem, for instance, is as much a kinetic presence as a musical one, and even Burroughs' doddering seems precisely calculated. Anderson herself is an entrancing dancer, seductive and oddly menacing; at times she has the demeanor of a stalking tiger, smiling as she waits for her next meal. Her composing and singing are sly and satirical, if rarely direct: "Hey look! Over there!/It's Frank Sinatra/Sitting in a chair./And he's blowing/Perfect smoke rings/Up into the air. And he's singing:/Smoke makes a staircase for you/To descend. So rare." The film bogs down in the middle, due mostly to Korean musician Sang Won Park, whose performance seems alien even in this anarchic context. And Anderson would have a hard time making a case that the film successfully uses technology to criticize itself (as she said it does). Her argument is so impressionistic—the thesis is never really stated—it could easily slip by unnoticed. That hardly matters, though. The sounds and shapes with which she fills this movie make it a primarily sensual experience. Thinking about it just gets in the way of the enjoyment.
Unrated / 1986 / Republic

▲ HONEYSUCKLE ROSE

This is essentially a showcase for the considerable talents of country-western star Willie Nelson. Willie is thinly disguised as a singer named Buck Bonham whose winning smile and sing-songy voice permeate the movie, and he also wrote four new songs for it. Although it is basically a concert film (noncountry fans, be warned), there is a lot going on backstage. Dyan Cannon is radiant as Nelson's understanding yet independent wife, and Amy Irving exudes a smoldering sensuality as the girl who leads Willie astray. This is perhaps Cannon's most affecting performance, and both she and Irving display unexpected skill as singers. There are few surprises in the direction by Jerry Schatzberg, but his camera adroitly captures everything from a Texas-size family reunion to the near hysteria of a live concert. (The title has nothing to do with Fats Waller's great song, by the way; it's the name of Buck's ranch.) Though the movie is about twenty minutes too long, it seems almost un-American to complain about that kind of excess when it's filled with down home boys playing down home music.
PG / 1980 / Warner

▲ HONKY TONK FREEWAY

At the end of this movie, there is a colossal car crash that pretty much sums up the preceding 100 minutes: noisy, messy, and not nearly as funny as it was meant to be. British director John Schlesinger, who made a wow film about Americans called *Midnight Cowboy,* tackles the subject again, using that most American of art forms—the "road" picture. Structured in vignettes like *Nashville,* the screenplay follows an unconnected cast of characters as they converge on the tiny town of Ticlaw, Florida. The citizens of Ticlaw are ticked off because they didn't get an exit off the new interstate, and they go to great lengths—like painting the town pink and offering free gas—to lure the tourist trade. Schlesinger's eye is sharp, but he is as subtle as a jackhammer. Though it's meant to be a comedy, the film is so aggressively strident that it's not much fun. In a huge cast, Beverly (*Coal Miner's Daughter*) D'Angelo stands out as a man-crazy waitress, who feels that "the International House of Pancakes is the one consistent thing in my life." So does Daniel Stern, who played Cyril in *Breaking*

Away, as a spaced-out hitchhiker. And the late Geraldine Page as a hilariously nasty nun shows a bit of what we missed when Anne Bancroft was cast on film in the stage role Page created so memorably in *Agnes of God.*
PG / 1981 / Thorn/EMI

▲ HONKYTONK MAN

Clint Eastwood traded in his six-shooter for a six-string Gibson guitar to portray a tubercular, down-and-out country songwriter driving out of Dust Bowl Depression toward the dream of a Grand Ole Opry audition in Nashville in the 1930s. Along for the ride is his wide-eyed nephew, played with familiar Eastwood impassivity by his real-life son, Kyle, then 14. The story is about the trip to Music City, and along the way Uncle Clint shows the awestruck kid how to drink, visit whores, bribe troopers, and duck a shotgun marriage. The kid reciprocates—helping Unc steal some chickens, flee a jail, and elude a bull. Because Eastwood is so predictably tough and taciturn, he loses something after two hours. And while cinematographer Bruce Surtees has created some gorgeous images, director Eastwood didn't mine the picaresque potential of the plot. There is little action, and when Eastwood croons, it's in a style as authentically down-home as Merv Griffin's.
PG / 1983 / Warner

▲ HOOPER

Fast, good-natured, and light, this movie deserved its success at the turnstiles. Burt Reynolds, as the king of Hollywood stuntmen, faces the inevitable challenge from the kid (Jan-Michael Vincent). So much for the plot, but it all cruises along pleasantly enough largely because of Reynolds's easygoing charisma. As in life, at the time, Sally Field plays Burt's honey. (She was wasted, but why feel sorry for her now after she's won two Oscars?) Comedian Robert Klein is cast wonderfully as an unpopular director. Hal Needham (an accomplished stuntman himself) actually directs the nonstop wrecks, leaps, and fistfights, and the stunning earthquake finale of a bizarre movie within a movie. Reynolds pulls off some of his own stunts; several doubles perform the rest. Except for a smugly self-indulgent final

freeze, *Hooper* is another enjoyable example of the good-ole-boy comedy that good ole Burt does better (or used to) than anyone else.
PG / 1978 / Warner

▲ HOOSIERS

Even in his *French Connection* heyday, Gene Hackman was something of a sham as a movie star. Hackman doesn't have the charisma to carry a movie on his own personality, which isn't meant as a slam. Like Robert Duvall, he's a character actor occasionally miscast in star roles. In his most successful outings, Hackman doesn't go around posturing like a star—he serves the vehicle instead of vice versa, which is the case in this immensely likable period drama about that tortured love affair between the state of Indiana and the sport of basketball. Out of the overused underdog scenario, *Hoosiers* fashions a recognizable, wrenching, and most satisfying story. As with the best sport films, it's more interested in the players than the playing. As a once-disgraced basketball coach, Hackman moves to a small town in 1951 to pilot a misfit team of high school students to a championship season. With a less gifted filmmaker, the movie could have been an inappropriately fevered movie about sports enthusiasts. But director David Anspaugh, a veteran of "St. Elsewhere," tempered his drama with an impressive introspection. He doesn't force-feed an audience ersatz Americana. His memorable tableaux possess the ambivalence of Edward Hopper instead of the unalloyed optimism of Norman Rockwell. As written by Angelo Pizzo, a Bloomington, Indiana, native who displays real affection for the citizens of the title, *Hoosiers* observes instead of preaching. Pizzo writes about real folks without being folksy too. Besides Hackman, *Hoosiers* is graced with a superb cast, including Barbara Hershey, who elevates what could have been a throwaway role as an unlikely love interest. There's a reason the teammates look and act their roles so convincingly: Among the nine members of the squad are seven Indiana natives who are making their movie debuts. Ironically, the point man in this movie—Dennis Hopper, who brilliantly complements his performance in *Blue Velvet*—isn't actually on the team. As the town's Dickensian drunk, Hopper, who earned an Oscar nomination, mimes the benign side of the parochial mentality. As one from the heart and the heartland, *Hoosiers* is a contender in any season.
PG / 1986 / NA

▲ HOPSCOTCH

The travel budget for this comedy thriller must have been seven figures, what with location work in Austria, Germany, England, and the U.S. Thanks to a crafty performance by Walter Matthau, however, the finished product is more than just travelogue. With his gigantic jowls, basset-hound eyes, and shambling walk, Matthau makes an unlikely CIA agent; yet he carries it off. (Early in his career, he successfully played a straight CIA role in *Charade*.) Relegated to a desk job, a disgruntled Matthau retaliates by sending his unpublished memoirs to the Russians and the Chinese. The CIA, of course, is soon on his track, but blustery Ned Beatty, as the CIA director, is always one step behind. As in *House Calls*, Matthau teams up with Glenda Jackson, and the curious match-up works again. Director Ronald Neame wisely leaves Matthau to his own devices and changes the venue often enough to stimulate action. As spy flicks go, the suspense is strictly routine, but Matthau makes it an agreeable experience.
R / 1980 / Embassy

▲ HOT DOG THE MOVIE

This is, indeed, a worst. While there have been plenty of undergraduate jiggle-giggle films, this one is unrelievedly vulgar, exploitive, insulting to its audience, and much less than it might have been; it is in a lack of class by itself. The opening credits run over a dazzling ski sequence featuring stunt skiers Lan Parrish and Rob Huntoon. From then on, the movie is all downhill, literally and figuratively. Directed by Peter Markle, it concerns a freestyle ski competition at Squaw Valley, California. The usually likable David Naughton plays a mildly alcoholic veteran of the slopes. John Patrick Reger plays an insult-snarling German champion. Patrick Houser is the aw-shucks newcomer to the ski tour. Tracy N. Smith makes her debut as the neo-flower child Houser picks up on his way to Squaw Valley. Also featured are the breasts of former *Playboy* model Shannon Tweed; the rest of her body has a supporting role.

Plentiful are scenes involving nudity (women only, of course), off-color and off-the-mark jokes, and stupid anti-German prejudice. The film is so relentlessly juvenile that nothing about it seems enjoyable. It couldn't meet the eligibility requirements even to be considered sophomoric.
R / 1984 / Key

▲ HOT PURSUIT

If you've already seen every movie around and have nothing more enjoyable to do—getting a tooth pulled, say—then watch this movie. Star John (*The Sure Thing*) Cusack at least is likable enough even if this movie's a treadmill on which he goes nowhere fast. Done correctly, as for example Laurel and Hardy showed, this kind of frustration film can be a howl. Co-writer–director Steven (*Tron*) Lisberger's movie, however, is just plain irritating. Cusack plays a prep student who has to make up a chemistry test, forcing him to forego a trip to the Caribbean with newcomer Wendy Gazelle and her family. When he does get to leave, Cusack just misses a car, then a plane, a bus, and a boat Gazelle is on. The jokes miss with the same regularity. But the film goes from neutral to reverse when the yacht Gazelle and her family are on becomes the target of murderous hijackers led by comedian Jerry Stiller. One hopes Robert (*The Jagged Edge*) Loggia, "Dallas's" Monte Markham, and Shelley (*Brian's Song*) Fabares enjoyed the paid vacation they got in Mexico, where the movie was shot. While the postcardlike photography and the pleasing sound track might be fine for a family slide show, they don't quite add up to a feature film.
PG-13 / 1987 / N/A

▲ THE HOTEL NEW HAMPSHIRE

Given Hollywood's woeful track record with adapting novels, it's natural to expect little in this film version of John Irving's book. In fact, admirers of Irving's fiercely comic prose can justifiably carp that in this case writer-director Tony Richardson has only skimmed the book's surface. At least he was more faithful than director George Roy Hill was with Irving's *The World According to Garp*. Richardson's graphic style—remember his *Tom Jones*—is a closer match to Irving's

literary extravagance and, at its best, approaches a Marx Brothers madness. The plot concerns an eccentric New England family: Father Berry (Beau Bridges) buys hotels across two continents while Mother (Lisa Banes) keeps following along. Older son Frank (Paul McCrane) is gay; daughter Franny (Jodie Foster) loves the boy who led a gang rape of her; brother John (Rob Lowe) leches after sister Franny; sister Lilly (Jennie Dundas) is a dwarf; brother Egg (Seth Green) is deaf. Thanks to a first-rate cast—especially Foster and Lowe—the family feeling is beautifully caught. The movie goes off-course when the scene switches to Vienna. Wallace Shawn as Freud, Amanda Plummer as a radical, and Nastassja Kinski as a woman so scared of life she hides in a bear costume are literary conceits that don't translate to the screen. But when the family is battling life's adversities, the film makes for an entertaining three-ring circus.
R / 1984 / Vestron

▲ HOT LEAD AND COLD FEET

Lukewarm entertainment. Jim Dale, the British actor who won a Tony as Broadway's Barnum, is the biggest plus in this comedy Western. He is also its only plus, playing three roles: a crotchety old land grabber and his twin sons, a black hat and a white hat who compete for dad's legacy. Don Knotts, whose eye-popping shtick had long since gotten old, is the deputy sheriff, Darren McGavin the crooked mayor, and Karen Valentine the schoolmarm. The film is full of contrived scenes, like the "process" action shot where Dale is obviously flailing around in a studio, safe as a pillow, while rapids are projected on a screen behind him. The usually reliable Disney organization should have been embarrassed, especially in 1978, the 50th birthday of Mickey Mouse.
G / 1978 / Disney

▲ THE HOUSE BY THE LAKE

If your idea of a happy ending is one villain having his throat cut, another being burned alive, a third sinking in a bog, and a fourth getting run over, this movie is for you. Not that the bad guys don't deserve it, having spent 89 minutes raping, murdering, pillaging, and—worse—overacting.

But the violence lacks focus, unlike that in Sam Peckinpah's *Straw Dogs,* whose revenge-against-hoodlums theme was similar. Here, however, a woman—a superliberated model played with edgy conviction by Brenda Vaccaro—rises up to smite the evildoers and, presumably, warm the hearts of feminist vigilantes everywhere.
R / 1977 / N/A

▲ HOUSE CALLS

Walter Matthau, a widowed doctor, does make house calls. That's because he's a would-be Lothario, let loose on a world of scrumptious women, to his friend Richard Benjamin's despair. One of Walter's patients is Glenda Jackson, a spunky divorcee with more than a touch of sass, who makes it quite clear that she's not interested in a philanderer. Nor does she approve of the good doctor's hospital politicking. (A senile chief surgeon, Art Carney, is killing patients accidentally, but heir apparent Matthau won't toss him out.) Glenda and Walter give their relationship a two-week trial run anyway, in what seems to be a golden-ager's *Goodbye Girl.* They make a very odd but intermittently entertaining couple.
PG / 1978 / MCA

▲ HOWARD THE DUCK

If you want to know why many grown-ups don't watch movies anymore, try suffering through this ludicrous curiosity. It's based on the cult Marvel Comics character, a wiseass duck who lives on another planet that mirrors ours. But if Howard has movie-star potential, this movie buries it. Instead of honoring the spirit of Steve Gerber's fowl creation, which dishes out droll social commentary, *Howard* keeps splitting its personality. First it's a culture-clash-across-the-cosmos comedy. Transported from his planet to earth, Howard lands in Cleveland, where he befriends punk singer Lea (*Back to the Future*) Thompson. Then the script turns into a high-tech edition of *The Exorcist* as scientist Jeffrey (*Amadeus*) Jones, who was going to send Howard home, metamorphoses into a tyrannical monster. From there the film careens from car chase to fistfight to quack-up (indiscriminately indulging in duck puns along the way). Howard gets upstaged by the villain, and his idiosyncratic personality gets reduced to smart aleck. He's like David Letterman in a Halloween outfit. Watching an actor waddle around in the unimpressive costume (eight players are credited with the part), you don't know if you're seeing a movie or a shopping mall opening. Besides its enormous expense (reportedly costing between $22 million and $50 million), *Howard the Duck* comes with prodigious pedigrees. George Lucas, who originated the project, served as executive producer; his company provided the special effects. Director Willard Huyck and producer Gloria Katz, the husband-and-wife team who co-wrote the script, authored the smashing screenplay for *American Graffiti.* It's particularly depressing that filmmakers of such distinction would only want to overpower audiences with sights and sounds. This pointless creature-feature seems like only an indignity.
PG / 1986 / MCA

▲ THE HOWLING

The hero of this bracing horror is Rob Bottin, then 21, who created special effects to rival those in *Altered States.* We're in traditional werewolf territory, but Bottin's makeup wizardry is absolutely unique. Actors become drooling, snout-nosed beasts without trick photography in scenes that won audience gasps—deservedly. There are unexpected laughs as well, thanks to the screenplay by John (*Return of the Secaucus Seven*) Sayles and newcomer Terence Winkless. Their satirical shots hit everything from self-help groups to Wolfman Jack. The protagonist, Dee Wallace (the mom in *E.T.*), is a TV anchorwoman who uses herself as bait to land a sex maniac (Robert Picardo) and bigger ratings. Then Patrick (*The Avengers*) Macnee, a smoothie TV shrink, invites Wallace to unwind in his isolated northern California health spa, inhabited by the suspicious likes of John Carradine, Slim Pickens, and lupine nympho Elisabeth Brooks, who brings fresh meaning to the cliché "animal magnetism." Before long werewolves are making it hairy for everyone. Director Joe (*Piranha*) Dante keeps the brew bubbling with B-movie references and clips from the 1941 classic *The Wolf Man,* complete with anti-werewolf tips from Maria Ouspenskaya. Between the gooseflesh and the giggles, it will keep you howling, too, full moon or not.
R / 1981 / Embassy

▲ HOW TO BEAT THE HIGH COST OF LIVING

Can there be a funny film about inflation? Yes, and this is the zany proof. Jane Curtin plays an abandoned housewife with plenty of bills and no bucks. Her pal Susan Saint James needs money for an abortion, and another friend, Jessica Lange, is also broke. What to do? Why, hit a shopping center, of course. The girls—sort of "Charlie's Angles" with more brains and less sanctimony—plot to steal a big ball full of money that's used as a promotion gimmick by store owners. It's a made-for-television caper idea, perhaps, but brought off with flair. Robert Kaufman's script is hilarious, poking fun at everything from pantyhose to politics. Richard Benjamin, as Lange's oversexed veterinarian husband, almost dominates the movie, and Eddie Albert adds a wonderful cameo as Saint James's ex-Marine father, whose wife has gone gay. Saint James is funny, and Lange made something of a breakthrough after her nondescript roles in *King Kong* and *All That Jazz*. Curtin, in her first major movie role, proved to be a virtuoso comedienne on the big screen too. Jane Fonda's and George Segal's *Fun with Dick and Jane* took a similar approach to a similar problem, yet ended up sour and ponderous. This is light, bright, and appropriately detached from reality.
PG / 1980 / Vestron

▲ HUMANOIDS FROM THE DEEP

Most monsters are put into movies to defend their territorial imperative, find some electricity to eat, or go to work for a mad scientist. Of course, they have to get the leading lady in their clutches first. The characters in this epic look like cousins of the *Creature from the Black Lagoon* and make no secret of their intentions, which are all dishonorable. They're out to mate with human women in a Pacific Northwest fishing village, and their idea of foreplay is knocking a wall to smithereens en route to the damsel of their dreams. Otherwise, this is standard horror from prolific producer Roger Corman. The cast is professional—Doug McClure, Vic Morrow, and the picturesque Ann Turkel. There's a message: Genetic manipulation is a menace. The malefactor is a cannery trying to manufacture chunkier seafood. There are also some mild jokes and good fake scares on the way to real ones. The ending is grotesque, but it's hard to dislike a movie where the hero's ultimate weapon—pouring gasoline on the water and lighting it—produces about a dozen pathetic square feet of flame, yet kills the monsters anyway. (While this film is not to be taken seriously, many people will be offended, since what the humanoids are up to is rape, however phantasmagoric.)
R / 1980 / Warner

▲ THE HUNGER

In this modern tale of the supernatural, David Bowie has a problem: He's 200 years old and in love with Catherine Deneuve, who's about four thousand years his senior. That they both look great has nothing to do with sessions at the skin stretcher's—they're vampires. Bowie and Deneuve haunt Manhattan's punk discos scaring up potential blood donors to keep up their life-style, which puts Dracula's to shame. They live in a gorgeous town house, teach classical music to teenagers, and keep a crematorium on the premises to dispose of their emptied vessels. Presumably, Deneuve keeps a hairstylist hidden as well, since she's always immaculately coiffed. The trouble comes when Bowie starts aging rapidly. It's an occupational hazard with Deneuve's lovers—their looks go after a few hundred years, after which they get moldier but never die. Bowie's aging is accomplished by makeup artist Dick Smith, who did the same thing for Dustin Hoffman in *Little Big Man*. Hoffman was an Indian and Bowie isn't, but they come out looking the same; perhaps Smith has only one old man in his repertoire. Anyway, at this point the film becomes a softcore lesbian vampire movie as Deneuve takes a new lover, a perky doctor played by Susan Sarandon. Their much-touted love scenes are visually dazzling and sensationally silly. Bowie and Sarandon do wonders with little and Deveuve, at 40, is ravishing. But it's no surprise that director Tony (*Top Gun*) Scott comes from British TV commercials or that he's the brother of director Ridley (*Alien, Blade Runner*) Scott. The Scotts are known for wasting little time on character, and *The Hunger* isn't so much film-directed as interior-decorated. The result, especially for a vampire film, is curiously bloodless.
R / 1983 / MGM/UA

▲ THE HUNTER

Having become a star on TV's "Wanted—Dead or Alive," Steve McQueen was a natural choice to play Ralph "Papa" Thorson, a real modern-day bounty hunter who tracked down some five thousand bail jumpers. Thorson's life sounds like ready-made movie material, but it doesn't quite work out. McQueen delivers a pleasant, unadventurous performance as a man of few words who loves his girl (Kathryn Harrold), collects old toys, and can't drive worth a damn. Like Thorson wrestling a stick shift, the screenplay moves in fits and starts while the direction of TV veteran Buzz Kulik veers from the offbeat humor to straight action. There are several chases, the best of which features a car and a huge thresher in a Nebraska cornfield. Yet the film lacks momentum. The only element of suspense—when will the demented ex-con try to kill Thornson?—is ignored for so long the showdown, which could have been a heartstopper, seems out of place. (In 1986, Rutger Hauer played a modern-day descendant of McQueen's old TV character in a feature titled *Wanted: Dead or Alive*.)

PG / 1980 / Paramount

▲ HURRICANE

His disappointing 1976 *King Kong* apparently taught Dino De Laurentiis nothing about remakes. Though he spent $22 million and four months in Bora Bora to redo a 1937 Dorothy Lamour–Jon Hall picture for this project, he might just as well have established a museum for Gauguin paintings. Such a gesture would have translated the life and color of Polynesia more accurately and created a tax deduction. But no, he dragged Ingmar Bergman's gifted cinematographer, Sven Nykvist, to the island, then did not permit him to shoot the scenery, preferring to dwell on the signs and moans of a couple of tiresome lovers— a head chief, Hawaiian Dayton Ka'Ne, and the U.S. governor's daughter, Mia Farrow. (Small wonder Nykvist fell for Farrow off-camera; she looks gorgeous, even as an 18-year-old. This was in Mia's pre-Woody Allen days, though.) The script inspires howls at moments of theoretically high drama. When, after an interminable wait, the Great Storm comes, the great disappointment is that it doesn't sweep all previous footage out to sea.

PG / 1979 / Paramount

I

▲ ICE CASTLES

She's a small-town girl from the Midwest and a natural-born ice skater. He's the hockey player left behind when she goes after fame and fortune. Then, just on the brink of a try at the Olympics, she's injured. He saves her from despair. Lynn-Holly Johnson, who does all her own very impressive figures, and Robby Benson are innocent and appealing. Tom Skerritt, as the possessive pop, and Colleen Dewhurst, as coach, are also fine. All the beautiful winter scenery and warm-blooded sentimentality are pretty standard, but it's guaranteed to make people cry, and little girls who see it will immediately want to become skaters.

PG / 1979 / RCA/Columbia

▲ ICEMAN

In the frozen Arctic, a mining company worker uncovers the body of a man entombed in the ice. Rushed to a nearby research outpost, this human popsicle is discovered to be both prehistoric (40,000 years old) and alive. Those who remember *The Thing* (Howard Hawks's 1951 version or John Carpenter's 1982 remake) might expect the monster to come to life and start ripping off heads in true horror-film fashion. Forget it. Australian director Fred Schepisi is after something more ambitious. As scientists study the iceman in a sealed artificial environment, Schepisi tellingly observes modern man confronting his past. It's a great movie subject, intelligently conceived and gorgeously photographed, but the dialogue by

Chip Prosner and John Drimmer is deadening. Most of the talk involves an obvious debate between Timothy Hutton, as an anthropologist who sees the monster as a man, and David Strathairn, as a surgeon who sees all men as specimens. Mediating is Lindsay Crouse, as the station's research director. Strathairn and Hutton are strong actors, but Crouse is disappointing. Her idea of how to play a woman of science is to act as if she possessed no trace of humor. Happily, whenever the iceman gets to his feet, so does the picture. Hong Kong-born actor John Lone gives the Neanderthal large doses of welcome wit, especially when he joins Hutton in a guttural duet on "Heart of Gold." Lone's performance and Schepisi's often poetic imagery make the preposterous seem possible. They turn this potentially trivial film into something haunting and beautiful.

PG / 1984 / MCA

▲ THE IDOLMAKER

As *Willie and Phil* proved, Ray Sharkey has the talent, drive, and vitality to carry an entire film on his shoulders. But Atlas himself might stumble under the burden of Edward De Lorenzo's script for *The Idolmaker*. Based loosely on the life of Bob Marcucci, the hard-nosed South Philly promoter who discovered '50s faves like Frankie Avalon and Fabian, the movie attempts to dramatize the behind-the-scenes Sturm und Drang that turned underaged (and often undertalented) pretty boys into moneymaking music machines. Though Marcucci served as technical adviser and Peter Gallagher and Paul Land acquitted themselves nobly as the pomaded idols, the dialogue is trite. Further, Jeff Barry's original songs have been arranged in too contemporary a style; instead of sounding like nostalgically bad old songs, they sound like bad new ones. The film's few good moments are owed largely to director Taylor Hackford's eye for zippy "American Bandstand" theatrics and to Sharkey's live-wire performance. Whether he's hustling little old ladies (in Italian yet) or standing in the wings pathetically aping the gyrations of his onstage creations, he's mesmerizing. The rest of the movie is as vibrant as two hours of Fabian's greatest hits.

PG / 1980 / MGM/UA

▲ IF EVER I SEE YOU AGAIN

In 1977, Joe Brooks was the perpetrator of *You Light Up My Life,* both song and movie. In his follow-up indulgence, he writes, produces, directs, composes the music for, and stars. Brooks plays a TV jingle writer in the lovably silly role that used to go to Irene Dunne. Revlon model and former Charlie's Angel Shelly Hack has the chic Cary Grant part. They have an affair in college, and he falls down in the snow. She tells him to get lost. They meet again twelve years later. An artist by then, she is painting big blobs that look like Robert Motherwell rip-offs. Every scene is interminable. One shudders at the kind of ego trip that would have followed if this turkey had been a box-office hit. But viewers wisely decided to look elsewhere for someone to light up their lives.

PG / 1978 / RCA/Columbia

▲ IF YOU COULD SEE WHAT I HEAR

Too cute and insufficiently touching, this story of a young blind man could be dismissed as ludicrously implausible were it not for the fact that it is based on the real experiences of Boston-born folk singer Tom Sullivan. Even so, as cinema we're not talking triumph. Sullivan, overplayed by Marc Singer with a jerking, goony, uningratiating fierceness, refuses to accept his blindness, which was caused just after his birth by too much oxygen in a faulty incubator. His compensations are phenomenal: He jogs, putts like Nicklaus, wrestles on his Providence College team, sings in clubs, studies psychology, expertly tosses darts in Irish pubs, skydives, and drives a friend's sports car. He scores so effortlessly with women that his sidekick, R. H. Thomson, ponders cruising with a white cane to improve his sex life. Sullivan eventually falls in love with a black student keyboardist, Shari Belafonte Harper, who is much more exciting to look at than to listen to. This may be Sullivan's saga, but director Eric Till has portrayed him as if he were making *Pollyanna as Told to the Preppy Handbook.* There are so many cheap sight gags and oh-my-gosh faux pas that, though the heartwarming climax proves love is blind, it also shows this film is lame.

PG / 1982 / Vestron

▲ I'M DANCING AS FAST AS I CAN

Movies have shown the perils of the hard stuff—from booze to drugs. So it was only a matter of time until Valium, America's most widely prescribed tranquilizer, got big-screen treatment. Based on the best-selling 1979 autobiography of CBS documentary producer Barbara Gordon, the film depicts Gordon's addiction to the drug. Played by Jill Clayburgh, Gordon is a workaholic with disabling anxieties who can't function without massive daily doses of Valium. She pins pills inside her clothes, stashes them in tissue boxes and, in emergencies, cadges them from friends who always seem amply supplied. The turning point comes when Gordon is berated for her habit by the subject of one of her documentaries, a dying cancer patient done to an acid-tongue turn by the late and great Geraldine Page. With the not-too-helpful support of her brutal lover, Nicol Williamson, who has problems of his own, Clayburgh quits her shrink of ten years and goes cold turkey. That leads to convulsions, hallucinations, and commitment to a mental institution, where she eventually recovers with the help of a therapist, sharply etched by then newcomer Dianne (*Hannah and Her Sisters*) Wiest. All this is harrowing; stage and TV soap director Jack Hofsiss, in his film debut (he was later paralyzed in a swimming pool accident), and screenwriter David Rabe (Clayburgh's husband) fill the screen with raw emotional fireworks. Before you flush your own Valium, though, remember not all medical experts agree that Gordon's experience is relevant to most patients. As a crusade, the film is far from conclusive.
R / 1982 / Paramount

▲ INCHON

Those IRS and congressional investigators who were worried about the wealth of Korean evangelist Rev. Sun Myung Moon should have encouraged him to make more movies. The Reverend Moon and his Unification Church enterprises were the primary financiers of this $48 million bomb, and their investment blew higher than the Korean War epic's special effects. Named for the site of Gen. Douglas MacArthur's 1950 amphibious landing that outflanked the invading North Koreans, *Inchon* is vapid and disjointed. There are some convincing battles, and director Terence (*Thunderball*) Young's crowd scenes utilize enough extras to make Cecil B. De Mille look like a hermit. But Sir Lawrence Olivier as MacArthur appears physically gaunt and poorly made up. There is a silly attempt, too, à la *Doctor Zhivago*, to portray the upheavals of history through the smaller fortunes of lovers, a remarkably chic refugee, Jacqueline Bisset, and a manfully squinting Marine, Ben Gazzara. One wonders only when the hand of Reverend Moon, who is credited as "special adviser," will appear. It does, in a mawkish final shot based on a real incident, when MacArthur gazes toward heaven and recites to an assembled multitude the Lord's Prayer.
PG / 1982 / N/A

▲ INCORRIGIBLE

Nobody every played an amoral, unscrupulous, but lovable rogue like Jean-Paul Belmondo. Nobody could ever look quite as sweet, innocent, or disillusioned as Geneviève Bujold. Yet both were strained to the breaking point in this French film, and they crack a little from time to time. Belmondo is cast as a con man who has just been released from prison and into the care of probation officer Bujold. He bounds from scam to scam and bed to bed, all the while falling into her uncalculating clutches. The plot is frenzied, not to say breathless, and J-P, at 47, was a little old for this sort of thing in 1975 when the movie was shot. It was released in 1980 in the U.S., presumably to profit from the growing popularity of its director, Philippe de Broca, who had made *King of Hearts* and *Dear Detective*. The film does indeed have a certain outre charm, something like those adorable, dotty films saved so often by Cary Grant. (In French with subtitles.)
Unrated / 1980 / N/A

▲ THE INCREDIBLE MELTING MAN

Yecch! When it comes to melting, the Wicked Witch of the West had it all over this disgusting fellow who leaves gobs of goo everywhere and chomps on his victims à la *Night of the Living Dead*. After dining out on several citizens of a California town, the title character (played by the not legendary Alex Rebar) does a nice onscreen impression of a toasted cheese sandwich. Too bad he doesn't do it 86 minutes earlier.

R / 1978 / N/A

▲ THE INCREDIBLE SHRINKING WOMAN

Lily Tomlin showed her big-screen potential in a farce that reduces her to the size of a figure on a portable TV set. As a suburban housewife shrunken by overusing products like a feminine hygiene spray that also kills cockroaches, the thumb-sized Tomlin soon becomes a media event and a nervous wreck. "To my family I'm a doll, to my dog a chewstick," she groans. Her hubby, tersely underplayed by Charles Grodin, starts reading "Marriage Without Sex" manuals, and her kids hawk tickets to gawk at Mom. Enter the bad guys—Ned Beatty, Henry Gibson, John Glover—with plans to kidnap Lily and shrink the world. Enter, too, a laboratory gorilla named Sidney, a worthy rival for Yoda in the cuddly creature department. The effects are dazzling, as Lily is tossed down a garbage disposal, carted off in a grocery bag, and nearly drowned by a doll that wets. Smaller moments are nicely realized too. Clad in a pink negligee, Lily tries to embrace her sleeping husband, only to be whooshed away by air escaping his pillow. Satire is seldom as pointed or poignantly funny. Credit Jane Wagner's lively script and director Joel Schumacher's unerring pace. For the film's heart, thank Tomlin—a giant, unshrinkable talent.

PG / 1981 / MCA

▲ THE INCUBUS

According to demonology, an incubus is an evil spirit that ravishes women in their sleep. Sleeping victims, of course, cannot heighten suspense, so the incubees in this somnolent suspense thriller are all awake, screaming and kicking. John Cassavetes meets his mortgage payments by portraying a doctor, a new arrival to a New England village that is beset by a rash of rapes and murders. Erin (*The Class of 1984*) Flannery is the doctor's daughter. She's in love with a boy, played as if on bad PCP by Duncan McIntosh, whose recurring nightmare seems to key the horrific attacks. As far as terror is concerned, British director John (*Dirty Mary, Crazy Larry*) Hough has filled *The Incubus* with enough red herrings

to feed the Norwegian navy. The scariest element of the film, however, is how much old-timer John Ireland, as the town's police chief, resembles Alexander Haig. Kerrie Keane makes her film debut as a reporter who is actually . . . well, to avoid spoiling the suspense, let's put it this way: She's not a candidate for an Oscar.

R / 1982 / Vestron

▲ INDEPENDENCE DAY

The title refers to the day on which Kathleen Quinlan, a spunky aspiring photographer, must decide if she will leave the stifling small fictional town of Mercury, New Mexico. Can she desert her dying mother, her father, and her boyfriend, David Keith, to pursue an art school scholarship in L.A.? Keith (seen as Richard Gere's lovesick crony in *An Officer and a Gentleman*) wants her to stay. He's dropped out of college, pumps gas, and is going for his fourth straight July 4 local drag race trophy. "I've been out of Mercury," he pleads, "and there's nothing out there." Along the way to the Big Decision, writer Alice Hoffman and director Robert Mandel show us that Middle American life in Mercury can be about as bizarre as life in the big city. The marvelous Dianne (*Hannah and Her Sisters*) Wiest, as Keith's emotionally brittle sister, and Cliff De Young, as her abusive husband, provide a sinister background that heightens Quinlan's quest for psychic and geographic emancipation. Quinlan acts with a piercing, quirky intelligence; Keith, with his earnestly creasing brow, again proves he is underappreciated. There are few fireworks and little to celebrate except the acting in this somber drama, but it is absorbing.

R / 1983 / Warner

▲ INDIANA JONES AND THE TEMPLE OF DOOM

For its first hour this film, directed by Steven Spielberg from a story by George Lucas, was a worthy sequel to 1981's megasmash, *Raiders of the Lost Ark*. It opens with Kate Capshaw singing "Anything Goes," mostly in Chinese, at a Shanghai nightclub in 1935. Harrison Ford—returning as the superintrepid archaeologist Indiana Jones—is among the listeners. Soon a wild, colorful brawl ensues. Capshaw, Ford, and their

henchboy—played charmingly by Ke Huy Quan, the son of Vietnamese refugees—flee via roadster, trimotor plane, life raft, and elephant. But this time they're in a drought-stricken Indian valley, embroiled in a search for a sacred stone. All the verve, wit, and happily cartoonish imagination that made *Raiders* such a triumph seem to be back. But what then follows may be the most unconscionable 45 minutes in movie history, a relentless, tedious stream of graphic brutality. Children are whipped and kicked. One sacrifice victim's heart is torn out of his chest and then—somehow still alive—he is slowly deep-fried in a pit of molten something-or-other. People are chained, shot, ground up, crushed, stabbed, poisoned, thrown to crocodiles, clubbed, attacked using voodoo dolls, bounced off rocks, and drowned. This is all depicted in the most detailed, sadistic way. It was an astonishing violation of the trust people have in Spielberg's and Lucas's essentially good-natured approach to movies intended primarily for kids. If they had set out to prove that they could get away with anything—insult the intelligence of viewers and literally make them sick—they couldn't have done it more effectively. Ford is his usual laconic self. When he drinks a trance-inducing drug, it's all but impossible to tell if it's working, since there's often so much trance in his basic acting style. While Capshaw is attractive, her character is almost all helpless-dumb-blonde; she isn't allowed to develop any of the sexy spunk Karen Allen showed in *Raiders*. Weak acting and underdeveloped characters are the least of this film's problems, though. The ads that said "This film may be too intense for younger children," were fraudulent. No parent should allow a young child to see this traumatizing movie; it would be a cinematic form of child abuse. Even Ford is required to slap Quan and abuse Capshaw. But then there were no heroes connected with this film, only two villains; their names are Spielberg and Lucas.
PG / 1984 / Paramount

▲ I NEVER PROMISED YOU A ROSE GARDEN

Kathleen Quinlan moved from *American Graffiti* and *Lifeguard* to this career role, a compelling portrayal of a young girl on the harrowing road back from mental illness. The screenplay of Joanne Greenberg's best-seller is often trite, but some scenes are striking—especially those showing the fantasies of the girl and the maddening ennui of a women's mental ward. Bibi Andersson is sympathetic as the shrink, Susan Tyrell fine as a rowdy inmate, and Sylvia Sidney insanely funny in a cameo.
R / 1977 / Warner

▲ IN GOD WE TRUST

But not always in Marty Feldman, who directed and starred in this film preaching against the worldly greed of some modern fundamentalist sects. Feldman had forgotten the commandment, Thou Shalt Not Bore Thy Flock. Like his *The Last Remake of Beau Geste,* this one lapses into tedium. Feldman was a natural second banana, not, as he seemed to think, a Chaplin, Keaton, or Woody Allen. He plays a monk who is sent to Los Angeles to raise money for his monastery's mortgage payment and ends up jousting with big-and-small-time charlatans. Feldman's halting script martyrs some delightful actors. Louise Lasser plays a hooker with dry, matter-of-fact charm. Peter Boyle, an itinerant religious novelties salesman, underplays as best he can. And Andy Kaufman, as a pompadoured TV evangelist, has scant verbal material to work with. Anyway, it isn't *Elmer Gantry*.
PG / 1980 / N/A

▲ THE IN-LAWS

The ingredients are familiar, but the collaboration of the stars, Alan Arkin and Peter Falk, has the strange, discordant charm of, say, a mixed grill. A demented secret agent (Falk) meets an uptight, law-abiding New York dentist (Arkin) just before their children's wedding. It takes three wacko chase scenes, but Falk lures Arkin away from his root-canal work to a banana republic to help unload a satchel of stolen Treasury engravings. Chaotic encounters with two Chinese pilots and a mad dictator (Richard Libertini) who talks baby talk to himself come later. The film is a showcase for the underappreciated comedic talents of Arkin, and Falk, even if he never could quite hang up his Columbo persona along with the raincoat, is likable. The film is ideal for resting the intellect.
PG / 1979 / Warner

▲ THE INNOCENT

Director Luchino Visconti, a giant of modern Italian cinema, died in 1976, just before this film was completed. Too bad: The final U.S. version clearly lacks the master's touch. Giancarlo Giannini plays a philandering husband who is shocked to learn that his wife is pregnant by another man. Unable to talk her into an abortion, he pretends to be the child's father—and then decides to kill it. Lovely Laura Antonelli, a specialist in taking off her clothes, plays the wife, and Jennifer O'Neill is surprisingly good as the mistress. But the story is disconnected and often dull. Giannini, perhaps sensing disaster, fought hard to have twenty minutes of the original footage put back in before the movie's U.S. release. It didn't help much. (In Italian with subtitles.)
Unrated / 1979 / Vestron

▲ IN PRAISE OF OLDER WOMEN

The Canadian film industry was probably set back a year or two by this awful exploitation of May-December romances. Tom Berenger plays a sex-starved young boy who becomes a sex-starved young man whose erotic odyssey takes him from Budapest during the 1956 Hungarian uprising to Montreal. Along the way he hooks up with a variety of cradle-robbing older women; among them: Karen Black, as an unhappy professor's wife; Susan Strasberg, a violinist with a political conscience; and Canadian actress Helen Shaver, who finally gives young Berenger his comeuppance. Adapted from Stephen Vizinczey's novel of the same name, this shameful movie was softcore porn masquerading as an R-rated feature.
R / 1979 / CBS/Fox

▲ INSIDE MOVES

In the opening scene, John Savage is seen falling eerily from a tenth floor window. Savage survives his unexplained suicide attempt but is badly crippled. Then he happens upon a tavern inhabited by a motley crew of invalids; even the bartender, played by David Morse, has a bum leg. Savage finds Morse the money for an operation, and soon he is a hotshot pro basketball star. (Despite the title, there are few basketball scenes.) The question: will he remember his handicapped "family"? The answer: a sermon on friendship that's as heavy-handed as a bad TV show for teens. Still, this is a remarkably human film, especially for director Richard Donner, whose important previous credits were *Superman* and *The Omen*. If the plot sometimes rings false, the touching characterizations more than compensate. Amy Wright, as Morse's hooker girlfriend, and Diana Scarwid, as the waitress Savage falls for, are outstanding. The eclectic cast also includes wheelchair-bound jazz musician Bill Henderson and Harold Russell, the handless businessman and Oscar winner for *The Best Years of Our Lives* who also gained fame as head of the President's Committee on Employment of the Handicapped. Together the actors achieve an ensemble effect that's rare on film.
PG / 1980 / CBS/Fox

▲ INTERIORS

Movieland's foremost funnyman, Woody Allen, made this the most grueling, unfunny movie since Bergman's *Scenes from a Marriage*. Grim meditations about the meaning of death, art, and relationships bubble to the serene, visually striking surface of the film, only to evaporate in so much metaphysical fizz. The late Geraldine Page delivers a remarkable performance (she earned an Oscar nomination) as a woman caught in a late-in-life divorce (from E. G. Marshall). His new wife, brilliantly acted by Maureen Stapleton (another Oscar nomination), is a vulgarian meant to represent the life force lacking in Page's family. Page has raised her three daughters (Diane Keaton, Marybeth Hurt, and Kristin Griffith) in an atmosphere of cold, WASPish elegance, wherein problems are frozen or intellectualized. Trapped in their mother's perfectly decorated compartments, all three are struggling to get free, and where Allen's carefully crafted film falls short is in not resolving this conflict. Maybe he doesn't know how it comes out. But in, say, *Annie Hall,* an audience can at least laugh at essentially insoluble problems. This picture offers no such relief.
PG / 1978 / MGM/UA

▲ IN THE REALM OF THE SENSES

Seized by U.S. Customs after a screening before the New York Film Festival in 1976, Japanese director Nagisa Oshima's controversial depiction of the sexual obsession of a geisha and her lover had to be sprung by the courts. Though customs officials were first, they weren't the last to be shocked by the graphic sex and a bloody mutilation scene. Still, *Senses* is a powerful and uncompromising study of the erotic passions that destroy. (In Japanese with subtitles.)
Unrated, but definitely for adults only / 1977 / N/A

▲ INTO THE NIGHT

Here's the setup: Jeff Goldblum plays an aerospace engineer who suffers from insomnia and a cheating wife. One sleepless night, he gets out of bed and drives aimlessly around Los Angeles—all to the evocative sound-track accompaniment of blues pioneer B. B. King's guitar and vocals. Parked at the L.A. airport, he ponders escape to a more exciting world. But this woebegone Walter Mitty can't even dream up another world. So director John Landis and screenwriter Ron Koslow do it for him. Presto, a gorgeous blonde, Michelle Pfeiffer, chased by a band of thugs, jumps into his car, and the two drive off into an L.A. night world of dames, decadence, and danger. Some setup. The plot, involving Pfeiffer's knowledge of stolen emeralds, is, to say the least contrived. But as a wish-fulfillment fantasy for the tired businessman, *Into the Night* is a pip. Pfeiffer is a knockout of the first order who here displayed a flair for comedy. She even manages to hold her own with the scenery, which is no mean feat. Landis and his skilled cameraman, Robert Paynter (they collaborated on Michael Jackson's *Thriller* video), give the L.A. midnight hour an irresistibly tacky sheen—especially when playing peekaboo around Rodeo Drive and Frederick's of Hollywood. The film's best bits, such as those involving Bruce McGill as an Elvis impersonator, Irene Papas as a dragon lady of real estate, David Bowie as a British hitman, and country music's Carl Perkins as a playboy's bodyguard, combine the snap of slapstick with the menace of *Maltese Falcon* melodrama. But Landis's penchant for graphic violence often curdles the comedy. On the surface, *Into the Night* was flashy, forgettable fun. Something else may have been bubbling beneath that surface, however; when the film was released, Landis was facing his trial on charges of involuntary manslaughter in the deaths of three actors during the filming of his *Twilight Zone—The Movie* in 1982. It seemed clear from *Into the Night* that many of Landis's colleagues wanted to offer him moral support. A number of directors, including Landis (as a member of the Iranian secret police), make cameo appearances in the film. Among them are Paul (*Moscow on the Hudson*) Mazursky, Roger (*Barbarella*) Vadim, Lawrence (*The Big Chill*) Kasdan, Jonathan (*Swing Shift*) Demme, David (*The Fly*) Cronenberg, and Muppet master Jim Henson. Their presence means little to the plot or to the uninitiated members of the audience. But that demonstration of directorial camaraderie adds to this high-gloss piece of Hollywood professionalism something resembling a heart. (Landis was acquitted of the charges in 1987.)
R / 1985 / MCA

▲ INVADERS FROM MARS

The original 1953 film was a naively effective salute to childhood paranoia. Jimmy Hunt first could not convince anyone that he had seen a spaceship land near his backyard; then everybody, including his parents and the police, started turning into Martians. This remake by director Tobe (*Poltergeist*) Hooper does not seem seriously intent on scaring anyone. Neither is it enough of a send-up to be funny. Karen Black plays a school nurse, the only person who believes Hunter Carson, then 10 (Black's son in real life), when he says his mother and father, Laraine Newman and Timothy Bottoms, have turned into Martians. Louise Fletcher plays a mean-tempered teacher at Carson's school, which is named after William Cameron Menzies, the director of the 1953 *Invaders*. (In another inside joke, Jimmy Hunt came out of retirement—he was a sales manager for a tool supply company—to play the police chief in this version.) James Karen is a Marine general who is finally persuaded to take on the Martians in their non-earthly form in which they resemble ham hocks with teeth. Fletcher and Black are especially corny, broadly overacting as if to make sure everyone

knows that they'd really rather be doing *Macbeth.* Hooper himself inserts a clip from his 1985 film *Lifeforce,* which could not even save itself let alone another film. Maybe when the real Martians finally come, they at least will get something out of this movie: a thrill, a chuckle, a light snack, whatever.
PG / 1986 / Media

▲ INVASION OF THE BODY SNATCHERS

There have been two classic versions of Jack Finney's classic sci-fi story. While the 1956 original was spare, in black and white, and nightmarish, this one is extravagant, in color, and nightmarish. The plot is the same—seed pods from outer space turn people into emotionless vegetables—with a couple of exceptions. One is to transplant the nasty weeds' attack from a small town to San Francisco, and it was a mistake; the siege atmosphere and the aliens' takeover seemed more plausible in a limited area. But the new script is wittier, the effects bloodier (and more interesting), and Denny Zeitlin's score a goosebump breeder. The enthusiastic, ironically inclined cast includes, most notably, Donald Sutherland, Brooke Adams, Jeff Goldblum, and Leonard Nimoy. (The 1956 film's star and director, Kevin McCarthy and Don Siegel, do cameos.) Remakes of grand old films are to be discouraged, but director Philip Kaufman (he later did *The Right Stuff*) gets away with this one on style and verve.
PG / 1979 / MGM/UA

▲ INVASION U.S.A.

In a role that is ultraviolent even by his standards, Chuck Norris plays a former intelligence officer who is America's only apparent defense against an invading horde of mostly Communist terrorists. Landing on a Florida beach, the Red menace fans out for slaughterous attacks on shopping malls, amusement parks, and churches. The only pattern to their targets is that a feisty photojournalist, feebly played by Melissa Prophet, happens to be there all the time. "They're turning people against each other, and even worse, against authority," moans an FBI man, in case anyone has missed the film's Cold War-era reactionary overtones. The subversion of the American way indeed seems all too easy, but the terrorist leader, a Soviet officer portrayed with the requisite psychotic bloodlust by Richard Lynch, makes a fatal error. Lynch has recurring nightmares about his former nemesis, Norris. So taking time out from their busy havoc-wreaking schedule, Lynch and cohorts travel to the Everglades to rub out Norris. From that point to the silly toy-soldier climax in Atlanta, Chuck puts some serious crimps in the Reds' well-laid plans. For the first time in his long career, Norris's character operates without a code of honor, as well as without the balletic karate moves for which he is known. Director Joseph Zito has in fact made both good and bad guys equally one dimensional and unlikable. All viewers can root for is more mayhem. There's plenty of that, anyway.
R / 1985 / MGM/UA

▲ I OUGHT TO BE IN PICTURES

Like good wine, Neil Simon doesn't always travel well. On Broadway, *I Ought to Be in Pictures,* though second-rate Simon, was at least amiable fun. Somewhere on its way to the screen, the play lost most of its bounce. The plot centers on Dina Manoff, repeating her stage role as a budding Barbra Streisand of 19 who leaves Brooklyn for Hollywood to look up her screenwriter father (Walter Matthau). He's the rat who deserted her, Mom, and little brother sixteen years before to make his mark in Tinseltown. Daughter hopes Dad will help get her into pictures. Actually, Matthau is barely scraping by himself, the brightest spot in his drab life being an affair with studio hairdresser Ann-Margaret, a divorcee with two kids. A-M, by virtue of some lovely underplaying in an atypical part (she is hardly your standard drudge), is herself the brightest spot in the movie. She seems to be living her role, not projecting it. Matthau indulges in less mugging than usual, but his basset hound face has already crossed over into permanent caricature. Manoff, the daughter of Lee Grant and a ringer for Mom, displays the same dynamism that won her a Tony on Broadway, but director Herbert (*Pennies from Heaven*) Ross either didn't encourage or didn't permit her to modulate. The wisecracks and whimsy that worked onstage seem forced at close camera range. A climactic telephone scene in which a reluctant Matthau calls his ex-wife while Manoff and Ann-Margret listen in is both funny and touching. It's the right combination, one Simon clearly has been striving for, but when it comes it's too little and way too late.

PG / 1982 / CBS/Fox

▲ IPHIGENIA

This beautifully mounted film has all the passion and grandeur so often missing from Greek tragedy on the stage. Directed by Michael (*Zorba the Greek*) Cacoyannis, it tells the story of King Agamemnon, who was forced to sacrifice his daughter in exchange for the safe passage of the fleet sent to rescue Helen of Troy. Tatiana Papmoskou, then 14, whom the director discovered on a plane from London to Athens, plays the doomed daughter; Irene Papas is stunning as Iphigenia's anguished mother, and Costa Kazakos superb as the father who must make the horrible choice. (In Greek with subtitles.)

Unrated / 1977 / Columbia

▲ IRON EAGLE

One of the reported reasons for President Reagan's hesitation to take military action against Libya was a fear that an American pilot would be shot down and held captive. That is what happens in this Rambo-goes-to-the-Middle-East. After his plane is hit by an antiaircraft missile, Tim (*Volunteers*) Thomerson is tried as a spy by an Arab country and sentenced to death. When the U.S. Government decides there is nothing it can do diplomatically or militarily, the downed pilot's 18-year-old son, Jason (*The Heavenly Kid*) Gedrick, and retired colonel Lou (*An Officer and a Gentleman*) Gossett, Jr., commandeer a couple of F-16s to rescue him. The rescue attempt is hardly believable, but the aerial scenes (shot over Israel using Israeli Air Force planes) have to be some of the flashiest ever filmed. And it's a treat to hear Gossett reel off such teeth-clenched lines as "There's somethin' about maniacs messing with good men that always pisses me off." David Suchet, as a Middle East despot who talks like Bela Lugosi, plays the villainy to the hilt. When director Sidney (*The Entity*) Furie yelled "action" on this one, he meant it. This is a fast-moving, chauvinist's delight, corny enough in its macho posturing to be a real crowd pleaser.

PG-13 / 1986 / CBS/Fox

▲ IRRECONCILABLE DIFFERENCES

In its own lackluster way, this comedy about a youngster who wants a divorce from her warring parents represents a disturbing genre, the sit-con. Although the situation has potential, the execution is little more than a scam. After Drew Barrymore drags her parents into the courtroom, the testimony triggers lengthy flashbacks that occupy the bulk of the film. But the flashbacks don't focus on the girl's problems; instead they tell the cocktail-chatter history of her parents, a professor-turned-director and his writer wife. Played with a sly, wink-of-the-eye affection by Ryan O'Neal and Shelley Long, who is endearing if not always inventive, the couple find themselves seduced and abandoned by the high life. But what director Charles Shyer really wants to lambaste is show business. In fact, the few original jokes in the screenplay, which Shyer coauthored with Nancy Meyers (his collaborator on Goldie Hawn's *Private Benjamin*), are clever commentaries on the state of the artless in southern California. O'Neal and TV model Sharon Stone, who plays his discovery, make a musical *Gone with the Wind*. When Stone belts a brassy Streisand-like number amid the corpses after the burning of Atlanta, the comedy shows a fresh sensibility. The bittersweet reconciliation at the end plays more like patchwork than resolution. What little interest the film generates is about the real-life inspirations for its characters. Is this partly the story of the marriage of Peter Bogdanovich (pre-Cybill Shepherd) and production designer Polly Platt? *Irreconcilable Differences* is a Beverly Hills cinema à clef party game masquerading as a movie.

PG / 1984 / Vestron

▲ ISHTAR

Those who were rooting for this long-delayed, overhyped, outrageously priced comedy—$50 million or so—to fall on its fat one financially were not disappointed. But leave the accountants to lament the indulgence of paying starring superegos Warren Beatty and Dustin Hoffman some $11.5 million in salaries (about triple the entire cost of, say, *A Room With a View*). It's the movie that counts, and in this case it doesn't count for much. Far from being the *Heaven's Gate* of comedy, as advance poop had it, *Ishtar* is merely a muddle. Writer-director Elaine May may have intended a send-up of the Bob Hope–Bing Crosby *Road* pictures. But the tackiness of those movies (shot on studio back lots) was part of their charm. Here elephantine production values, including location filming in North Africa with real camels on a real desert, bury the nuggets of barbed wit in the script. May's subtle humor (best appreciated in *A New Leaf* and *The Heartbreak Kid*) doesn't play in Spielberg country. The film's early scenes, set in Manhattan, work best. Beatty, 50, and Hoffman, 49, are 30ish singer-songwriters. An agent, sharply done by Jack Weston, offers sound discouragement: "You're old, you're white, you've got no shtick." But the boys persevere. For a while it's fun listening to the frog-throated duo croak out purposely bad songs, many composed by Paul Williams. The sassiest is "Love in My Will," in which Hoffman serenades a couple celebrating their 55th anniversary with morbid lyrics about the "big sleep." These tunes, a daunting twenty-six of them, move quickly from cute to not-so-cute to cloying. The plot involves a club date the boys do in Morocco, where a search for the secret map of the mythical kingdom of Ishtar embroils them in international intrigue. Reliable Charles Grodin gets a few laughs as a slimy CIA operative, but Beatty's ravishing real-life lady of the moment, Isabelle Adjani, is wasted playing a terrorist. The two stars show the strain of carrying the picture. Beatty goes along with the casting joke of playing the nerd sidekick to Hoffman's slick loverboy. But zany antics aren't his forte. Hoffman's impishness serves the film better until the sheer weight of the production grinds him down. Near the end, lying exhausted after a sandstorm, Beatty and Hoffman find themselves perused by two hungry vultures. "We're not dead, we're just resting," the boys wail. Maybe. Viewers, enduring the torpor of *Ishtar,* are likely to side with the vultures.

PG-13 / 1987 / RCA/Columbia

▲ THE ISLAND

The burning question raised by this movie is how much can Michael Caine see without his glasses? Sometimes he wears them, sometimes he doesn't, yet he never seems affected either way. Of course, one is supposed to be concentrating on the six hundred boats that have disappeared in the Caribbean over a three-year period. Caine plays

a journalist who promises his son a weekend trip to Disney World but ends up bobbing about the Bermuda Triangle. To be fair, the first 20 minutes are suspenseful in the best Peter Benchley tradition. Barely glimpsed interlopers menace pleasure craft in lovely tropical surroundings. But the moment the assailants' identity is revealed—they are a band of buccaneers who have survived on an uncharted isle for three hundred years—the film falls apart. Director Michael Ritchie contributes much mayhem (accompanied by a strange, swashbuckling score) but little of the humor that salvaged his *Semi-Tough* and *Smile.* Caine is plucky in the central role; still, he would have had a better time at Disney World. So would you.

R / 1980 / MCA

▲ THE ISLAND OF DR. MOREAU

As H. G. Wells's mad scientist, Burt Lancaster more or less succeeds in turning tigers, bears, and hyenas into men, but he can't turn this dog of a script into a movie. Search out the more convincing, less pretentious 1933 version, *Island of Lost Souls,* with its primitive camera work and appropriately tortured performances by Charles Laughton and Bela Lugosi. This new version offers intriguing acting by Michael York, the gorgeous but basically talentless Barbara Carrera, and the lush scenery of Saint Croix.

PG / 1977 / Warner

▲ ISLANDS IN THE STREAM

Maudlin malarkey, postcard photography, and calypso Muzak make this version of Hemingway's last book hard to take. But George C. Scott—who magnificently conceals his professed dislike of acting—deftly portrays a restive, Pop-like sculptor languishing in the Bahamas.

PG / 1977 / Paramount

▲ I, THE JURY

Private eye Mike Hammer was created by Mickey Spillane in his 1947 blood-and-guts potboiler *I, the Jury.* The book was denounced for its blunt sex and violence and, natch, went on to sell 6.5 million copies. Spillane's eleven subsequent

Hammer books spawned five movies, a syndicaterd comic strip, and a 1958 TV series with Darren McGavin. Here Armand (*Private Benjamin*) Assante kicks around the broads and the bad guys as Hammer. This updated version, written by Larry (*It's Alive*) Cohen, is gorier, kinkier, and sillier than anything Spillane ever imagined. Assante's Hammer is out to revenge the death of a one-armed cop friend who had saved his life in Vietnam. Police Captain Paul Sorvino keeps begging him, "Please try not to kill more than two or three people a day." Assante's search leads him to the Mafia, the CIA, and a sex clinic run by curvaceous Barbara Carrera. Richard T. Heffron directed swiftly and efficiently, but the violence is unrelievedly sadistic. Assante's climactic escape in a car fueled by rum and lighter fluid is analogous to the entire film: a series of fits and starts.

R / 1982 / CBS/Fox

▲ IT LIVES AGAIN

Why would anyone do a sequel to 1977's boring and artless *It's Alive?* Try a gross of more than $6 million. This movie was not just another cheapie money-maker, however; it was probably the most repugnant film since 1932's *Freaks,* with none of that movie's social comment. The monsters are babies who literally zoom off the delivery table looking for jugulars to rip. They were only glimpses in the original; this time master monster-maker Rick Baker, who created King Kong the Younger and *Star Wars'* flaky barflies, has worked up ugly little beasts. The talented Frederic Forrest and Kathleen Lloyd meanwhile seem sullen, as if they wished, sensibly, they were somewhere else. There may be eight or nine people in the world who would enjoy this film; none of them are pregnant women or children awaiting a new sibling.

R / 1978 / N/A

▲ IT'S ALIVE

If there were an Oscar for Best Performance by an Actor in a Film That Makes *The Alligator People* Seem Profound, John Ryan would have nailed it. Ryan (previously consigned to minor gangster film roles) plays the father of an infant mutant who bounds out of the womb and starts biting and clawing people to shreds. Ryan acts with such persuasive intensity you suspect someone forgot to tell him actors are supposed to walk through this kind of part. Maybe he knew, as many of us did not, that director Larry Cohen—assisted by the eerie score from Hitchcock's music man Bernard Herrmann—had spawned a cult horror classic.

R / 1974 / Warner

▲ IT'S MY TURN

Director Claudia Weill put together this impressive film. Jill Clayburgh is a slightly neurotic, klutzy, brainy professor who does complex mathematical formulas in bed and cuts herself unwrapping a Cuisinart. She lives with Charles Grodin, a property developer, who would rather make jokes than talk. When Clayburgh goes to her father's wedding in New York, she meets Michael Douglas, the son of her dad's new bride. Douglas is a brash and breezy ex-baseball player, best known for robbing Reggie Jackson of a crucial home run in Detroit with a spectacular catch. In their mutual attraction lies the plot, a modern twist on boy meets girl because he's married (shakily) and she cohabits. Intertwined are some truthful, humorous comments on families and 1980-style relationships. Weill manages to sustain the credibility of her characters throughout. They could be part of anyone's family, which makes them more identifiable and endearing and the film a romantic, witty, intelligent love story.

R / 1980 / RCA/Columbia

▲ I WANNA HOLD YOUR HAND

It's February 1964, and four mop-topped lads from Liverpool are greeted on their first trip to New York City by crazed hordes of admirers. Among them are four high school birds who would do almost anything—this is in the pre-groupie era—to see the Beatles. The girls' slapstick shenanigans work best when director Robert Zemeckis (a protégé of executive producer Steven Spielberg) permits them high camp—when, for instance, Nancy Allen (who went on to bigger things) fondles Paul McCartney's guitar and almost passes out. Eddie Deezen, a Jerry Lewis

clone, also shines as a Beatleabilia entrepreneur. The inevitable focal points, though, are the Fab Four themselves, in newsreel and ''Ed Sullivan Show'' footage, cleverly intercut with orgasmic concert scenes. This is not a music movie— Beatles records are on the sound track only as a background. But despite some downright silliness and some actors overaged for their youthful roles, the unknown cast and then unproven director Zemeckis (who later did *Romancing the Stone*) turned out a respectable bit of whimsey.
PG / 1978 / N/A

J

▲ JABBERWOCKY

Perennially befuddled Monty Pythonite Michael Palin wanders into the realm of King Bruno the Questionable. There he hopes to make a fortune so that he can marry Griselda Fishfinger, who looks like a distant relative of Petunia Pig, but he ends up stuck with Bruno's beautiful blond daughter. Unfortunately, the film doesn't live up to its premise, and director Terry Gilliam (Python's animator) relies excessively on splattering blood and strewing corpses to get laughs.
PG / 1977 / RCA/Columbia

▲ JACOB THE LIAR

From East Germany, of all places, this affecting and sometimes comic story is set in a Jewish ghetto in Poland during World War II. Jacob Heym (Czech actor Vlastimil Brodsky) inadvertently overhears a Gestapo radio broadcast saying the Russians are approaching—and, in spreading the word, boasts that he owns a forbidden radio. Badgered for news, Heym invents lies that bring cruel hopes until the inevitable shipment to the concentration camps. This Oscar-nominated film is affectingly acted by Brodsky and Manuela Simon as his niece. (In German with subtitles.)
Unrated / 1977 / N/A

▲ JAGGED EDGE

In this unintentionally funny murder melodrama (a surprise box-office hit), Glenn Close plays a corporate lawyer forced into a criminal case involving her stuffy firm's wealthiest client. As played by Jeff Bridges, the client is one of those charmers who have everything: old money, material goods, a great job (he runs a San Francisco newspaper), and a beautiful wife. Well, he had a beautiful wife. At the start of the film, the wife—an heiress who provided the money, goods, and job—is being brutally murdered, ritually cut by a knife with a jagged tip. The D.A., snakily played by Peter Coyote, accuses Bridges. Money is not the only motive. Bridges's paper has been smearing the D.A.'s tactics in editorials that might cost the D.A. a future Senate seat. Aha! Then there's the tennis pro (Marshall Colt) who's into S&M, the dead wife's girlfriend (tartly done by Leigh Taylor-Young), who lusts after Bridges, and everyone but the butler. Screenwriter Joe Eszterhas ham-handedly rounds up the usual suspects as if he thought the old Perry Mason TV series was the last word in sophisticated jurisprudence. Life can still be breathed into courtroom drama as long as it has surprise (*Witness for the Prosecution*), atmosphere (*Anatomy of a Murder*), or a riveting performance (Paul Newman in *The Verdict*). *Jagged Edge* misses in all departments. Close tries, but her role is criminally misconceived. We're supposed to see her as an intelligent career woman and divorced mother, but it's difficult to admire the ethics or logic of a lawyer who goes to bed with her client and then reacts like a child when she thinks he's lying. The scene that gets the most laughs, next to the use-every-cheap-horror-trick-in-the-book ending, comes in the courtroom. Close doesn't merely sit shocked when a surprise witness undercuts the man she loves. Director Richard Marquand, who did *Return of the Jedi* and is perhaps more accustomed to evoking human emotion in foam rubber characters like Yoda, has Close cup her hand over her mouth and pop her eyes wildly in a double take worthy of *Abbott and Costello Meet Frankenstein.*

R / 1985 / RCA/Columbia

▲ JAWS 2

The moral still is: If you're swimming and hear ominous cello music, you are about to be eaten by a giant shark. About everything else is the same, too, though the classy flourishes added to the 1975 original by Robert Shaw (already gobbled up), Richard Dreyfuss (other fish to fry), and director Steven Spielberg (not interested) are gone. The same dopey mayor is worrying about the tourist trade, another great white shark has heard about a good feeding ground off Amity, Long Island, and Roy Scheider, fulfilling a commitment to Universal, appears again as the police chief. He is to be commended for not just walking through, though his character is hopelessly addicted to staring at the ocean. The problem is that the best gimmicks were used the first time around, and despite a couple of tense who'll-be-main-course-and-who'll-be-dessert sequences, the $25 million sequel turns out to be only ordinary.

PG / 1978 / MGA/UA

▲ JAWS 3

Some fishermen think all they have to do is toss a hook overboard to land a big one. The producers of this sequel once-removed obviously figured they just had to toss their fish into the water to come up with a huge catch at the box office. Sorry, fellas; it won't float. Well, actually, it floats all right, but the giant shark in this case—it's a thirty-five-footer—doesn't swim especially well. Maybe the mechanical monster that played the shark in *Jaws* sequels was getting old (the fins are always the first to go). Or perhaps it decided to try for a more meaningful interpretation of the role. But this great white shark doesn't even motor fast enough to catch up with a bikini-wearing cutie on water skies. It just trolls leisurely along until it has a victim cornered, then gulps him down. Not much else happens. Dennis (*The Right Stuff*) Quaid and Bess (*High Road to China*) Armstrong think they have the shark penned up in Sea World (the Florida marine center, playing itself), but the shark seems to feel it has

dropped into a fast-food establishment and nibbles on a few peopleburgers. It takes them without cheese, but given the caliber of acting in this film, it can't help but get a few bites of ham. Quaid, as chief engineer of the park, is more nondescript than heroic, while Armstrong is on the gushy side. She's a marine biologist so conscientious that moments after the shark has swallowed two of her colleagues, her only concern is that her dolphins have survived. Lou Gossett, playing the park owner, affects a terrible ghetto accent, perhaps hoping he won't be recognized. Director Joe Alves, the original *Jaws* production designer, is so bland his work is hardly noticeable. *Jaws 2* was a sorry enough sequel; this one (shown in 3-D in theaters) really wears out the idea's welcome. The fearsome shark now seems more like the fish who came to dinner.

PG / 1983 / MCA

▲ JENNIFER

Like *Carrie,* already the grandma of telekinesis movies, *Jennifer* has a let's-get-even theme, only this time it's vengeance with vipers. Lisa Pelikan (the young Vanessa Redgrave in *Julia*) plays a poor girl attending a snooty private school for rich kids, some of whom tease her mercilessly and finally kill her pet cat. That's a mistake, since as a child of the Bible Belt she handled deadly snakes during frenzied revival meetings. Pelikan acts with as much reserve as the scenario allows, but the end is predictably gruesome, with huge rattlers and boas slithering around fanging and constricting folks on command. What's the reptilian equivalent of "turkey"?

PG / 1978 / Vestron

▲ THE JEWEL OF THE NILE

Twentieth Century-Fox had to sue Kathleen Turner for $25 million to get her to honor her contract to appear in this sequel to *Romancing the Stone.* From the looks of it, maybe she would have been better off just coughing up the money and sparing everyone a lot of tedium. Turner is so creative and communicative an actress that she could turn ninety minutes of making toast into an exciting event. But making toast is a profound experience in comparison with the plot of this movie. While

Jewel of the Nile: Michael Douglas and Kathleen Turner huddle through a dismal sequel in which the biggest menace they face is the ever-present danger of being upstaged by Danny De Vito.

Turner is reunited with Michael Douglas, their screen relationship seems to be wearing thin. In *Stone,* her romance novelist falling in love with his adventurer was one of the all-time cute meets. This time the couple is sailing around the world with the passion oozing away, when an East African potentate lures Turner away to write a history of his revolution. The potentate is played by Greek actor Spiros Focas as if he is competing in an Omar Sharif imitation contest and coming in third. At least semivillain Danny De Vito, who was saddled with idiotic slapstick routines in the first film, gets some lines this time. When he is introduced to the holy man who is called "Jewel of the Nile," De Vito snarls, "Yeah, and I'm the Kumquat of Queens." But most of the time everyone seems to be going through the motions of an adventure comedy—top of the train fight, torture scene, desert chase—with little verve. Director Lewis (*Cujo*) Teague got everybody to show up and say their lines and stay in focus. He didn't however, get anybody to entertain.
PG / 1985 / CBS/Fox

▲ **JINXED**

Talk about bad luck titles. Bette Midler's comedy follow-up to her Oscar-nominated dramatics in *The Rose* got crucified by critics and died on the box-office vine. The premise is certainly limp. Midler is a would-be Vegas lounge singer shacked up with gambler Rip Torn, who slaps her around when he's not putting a jinx on blackjack dealer Ken Wahl that seems to compel Wahl to deal winning hands. If that sounds like strange comedy on paper, rest assured it doesn't play any clearer on screen. What does play, and gloriously, is Bette. But she is stymied at every turn by Bert Blessing's and David Newman's banal script, Don (*Dirty Harry*) Siegel's deadpan direction, and Vilmos Zsigmond's often unflattering photography. Bette's reported unhappiness with making the movie (and Wahl's and Siegel's mutual problems with her) shows on screen. It took four years for Midler to regain her stride with *Ruthless People, Down and Out in Beverly Hills,* and *Outrageous Fortune.* Jinxed, indeed, but not forever. It clearly takes more than one bad movie to keep Bette Midler down.

R / 1982 / MGM/UA

▲ JOHNNY DANGEROUSLY

Director Amy Heckerling had obviously seen her share of those gangster films of the '30s and '40s. She clearly knew how little they resembled the scummy life of real criminals. She also knew how entertaining those movies were, as this good-natured, relaxed parody of the ganster film genre shows. (The title, by the way, is not as unlikely as it may seem. There have been serious films called *Johnny Allegro, Johnny Angel, Johnny Apollo, Johnny Cool, Johnny Eager, Johnny Hamlet, Johnny Holiday, Johnny Nobody, Johnny O'Clock, Johnny Rocco, Johnny Trouble,* and *Johnny Stool Pigeon,* a 1949 film starring Howard Duff.) Michael Keaton plays the title character, a newsboy who becomes the protégé of gang boss Peter Boyle. All the clichéd characters are present: Joe Piscopo is the trigger-happy mobster out to replace Keaton; Marilu Henner, the golden-hearted moll; Maureen Stapleton, the ever-ironing mom. Griffin Dunne is Johnny's ultra-straight, would-be lawyer brother, and Glynnis O'Connor is Dunne's sweetie pie girlfriend. Ray Walston adds a deft series of blackout bits as a newsstand operator constantly being bombarded with flying bundles of papers. The humor ranges from outrageous slapstick to quiet throwaways—a bumper sticker on one mob car reads "I brake for gangsters"—and there's never a mean-spirited moment. Keaton, who has

the personality of soggy Frosted Flakes, is much too bland to parody actors like Cagney or Bogart. That allows Piscopo, who never succeeds in committing much else in the way of crime, to steal the picture from its nominal star. The film moves so briskly that its deficiencies can be overlooked. It makes you want to say, "All right, you dirty filmmakers, you've got us. We're coming out laughing."

PG-13 / 1985 / CBS/Fox

▲ JO JO DANCER, YOUR LIFE IS CALLING

As vanity projects go, Richard Pryor's comedy-tragedy—mea culpa ranks somewhere between *All That Jazz* and Fellini's *Amarcord.* The picture is not as self-indulgent as you might expect, but it never transforms autobiography into art either. As star, director, producer, and coauthor, Pryor follows the "Entertainment Tonight" school of filmmaking—he mistakes his career history for the stuff of parables. Without Pryor's notorious 1980 free-basing accident, which provides both the opening and the climax, there would be no movie (and no audience for it). Even at its most memorable, this film is still a celebrity's fan dance, tantalizing the audience with did-this-really-happen foreplay. While Jo Jo Dancer lies near death in a hospital, his alter ego takes the renegade comic on a tour of his life. All the well-known Pryor landmarks are visited: the Midwest whorehouse where his mother worked while Pryor was growing up, the small-town dives where he honed his craft, the Hollywood Hills where he executed his emotional tailspin. As a first-time director, Pryor displays a fine sense of comic counterpoint; he shrewdly follows most of the pathos with punch lines. But Pryor sidesteps the improvisatory, dangerous comedy that first made him popular. Unlike Pryor the performer, this movie proves most successful when it's least angry—in the early club scenes in which Jo Jo gets an adult education from Damon Runyon-esque types and a stripper named Satin Doll, wonderfully portrayed by Paula Kelly. Pryor even homogenizes his happy ending. When Jo Jo recovers his will to live, the cure isn't the balm of comedy or the soul-saving power of performing. He simply recovers because most movies last only about 97 minutes. When *Jo Jo Dancer* works, it's a surprisingly sweet memoir of a past that never was; when it misfires, you feel as though you're watching a remake of *It's a Wonderful Life* performed by graduates of the Betty Ford Center.

R / 1986 / RCA/Columbia

▲ JOSEPH ANDREWS

Tony Richardson, who directed *Tom Jones,* obviously hoped to filch from Fielding another bawdy 18th-century success. But despite plenty of ruddy cheeks and English countryside, *Joseph Andrews* doesn't always work. Ann-Margret is lovely as a voluptuary trying to seduce her sensitive footman, Peter (*Equus*) Firth. In fact, every woman the young lad meets tries to bed him, with the obligatory rude slapstick ensuing. An eating scene cribbed from *Tom Jones* doesn't seem nearly so provocative the second time around.

R / 1977 / Paramount

▲ THE JOURNEY OF NATTY GANN

In the beginning of this endearing film, we find out how well the 15-year-old girl who is the title character can take care of herself. At a Depression-era union meeting, the girl's father, Rick (*Swamp Thing*) Wise, is giving a speech that William Jennings Bryan would have been proud of. Meanwhile, the girl, inspiringly played by newcomer Meredith Salenger, is smoking her first butt in a men's room stall with two boys. When one makes a disparaging remark about her dad, Salenger gives the kid the ol' one-two. Written by Jeanne (*The Black Stallion*) Rosenberg, this girl-and-wolf movie was distributed by the Disney Studios, but it was part of the nouveau-Disney mentality. It is as charming as anything done when Uncle Walt was alive, yet it has enough grit to be interesting for adults. Salenger begins her journey in Chicago, after her unemployed dad reluctantly accepts the last seat on a company bus headed for the state of Washington. He doesn't have time to find his motherless daughter and leaves her a note saying that he'll send for her. When Salenger's landlady wants to turn her over to the orphanage, the girl decides to head to Washington on her own. She soon meets up with hobo John (*The Sure Thing*) Cusack, who teaches Salenger the tricks of the trains. She also picks up a half-dog, half-wolf canine companion, and soon they are sharing food, caves, and railroad cars. When the girl is caught stealing a bull with a band of young transients and is put in a juvenile detention center that's run like a concentration camp, the plot is stretched a little thin. This is especially true when Salenger escapes and climbs into the trunk of a car that just happens to be going right to the place where her pooch is being kept. It also seems unlikely that Cusack and Salenger would kiss at the end of their journey. Nevertheless, this is good family fare, with an appealing cast and some picturesque locations in the Northwest.

PG / 1986 / Disney

▲ JOYRIDE

In this low-budget, oddly endearing film, a trio of innocent-faced, foul-mouthed kids take off from California's San Fernando Valley for Alaska in a converted Pontiac hearse. What salvages the flick, produced by Bruce Cohn Curtis, great-nephew of Columbia mogul Harry Cohn, are finely tuned performances by four second-generation actors: Desi Arnaz, Jr., Robert Carradine, Melanie Griffith (Tippi Hedren's daughter), and Anne Lockhart, daughter of June. Griffith fans may want to ferret this one out.

R / 1977 / N/A

▲ JULIA

A haunting story about two women who renew their fondly remembered girlhood friendship, this film is set against the ominous backdrop of prewar Nazi Germany. Based on Lillian Hellman's autobiographical memoir *Pentimento* and lovingly directed by Fred Zinnemann, the narrative takes Lillian (Jane Fonda) on a dangerous trip to Berlin to meet Julia (Vanessa Redgrave), who has forsaken her medical studies for anti-Fascist political activity. The performances are glowing, if remote. (Jason Robards plays Hellman's lifelong lover, Dashiell Hammett, and Meryl Streep makes her film debut.) This was a breakthrough film, pitting two strong women against each other in the leads. Redgrave won an Oscar, as did Robards in his supporting role.

PG / 1977 / CBS/Fox

▲ JUMPIN' JACK FLASH

Whoopi Goldberg has massive amounts of personality, every ounce of which she has to call upon to make this picture what it is: a pleasantly diverting, affable adventure comedy. Eyes rolling, body flouncing, dander rising, she is on-screen almost continuously, playing a bank computer operator who inadvertently gets involved in a spy case. (A British agent trapped in Eastern Europe patches into her international line and asks for help.) As people like Bob Hope and Woody Allen previously showed, comedy and international politics are perfectly compatible; as people like Chevy Chase and Dan Aykroyd previously showed, that compatibility is not always easy to demonstrate. Goldberg has to overcome some handicaps. The film's four writers couldn't, for instance, think of anything else for her to do but scream a lot of the time. She also can hardly get through a line of dialogue without tossing in a pointless obscenity, which can hardly amuse anyone with any sense and is likely to alienate many people. Director Penny Marshall, who directed a number of "Laverne and Shirley" episodes but had never done a feature before, acted a little like all those Chicago Bears coaches who for years didn't do much of anything except make sure the ball got into Walter Payton's hands. They might not have won any championships that way, but they did make things fairly entertaining. While there's a considerable amount of talent in the supporting cast—Carol Kane, John Wood, Stephen Collins, Annie Potts—they have hardly anything to do. It's almost wholly up to Goldberg, and even for those long stretches when she is just sitting at her terminal trading messages with the spy, she keeps a ferocious hold on the audience's attention, and their affection.
R / 1986 / Warner

▲ JUNGLE WARRIORS

People who like movies with great acting have it easy. They can watch, say, *Richard III* with Olivier, Gielgud, and Richardson, or *The Godfather* with Brando, Pacino, Duvall, and Keaton. But never before *Jungle Warriors* did one movie's cast contain so many names synonymous with bad acting: Van Pallandt, Gortner, Danning, Vernon, Cord, and Smith. No matter how wretched a line is, these actors can make it sound even more wretched. Set in an unnamed Latin American country (it was shot in Mexico), the movie has a script that suggests a cross between the label of a tomato soup can and a pornographic novel with the sex taken out. John Vernon, Alex Cord, Sybil Danning, and Paul Smith are gangsters involved in a drug-smuggling war. Marjoe Gortner is a director and Nina Van Pallandt a photographer; their plane full of gorgeous models, headed for an advertising "shoot" in the jungle, crashes into the crooks' hideaway. Director Ernst Von Theumer has something to disappoint every one: The action is confused, the violence tedious, the dialogue of the "What the hell's going on here?" school. The gorgeous models even keep their shirts on. Anything would be more fun than seeing this movie, including sitting in a traffic jam or getting a paper cut.
R / 1984 / N/A

▲ JUST A GIGOLO

This drama of post-World War I Germany capitalizes on the presence of rocker-turned-actor David Bowie. As he showed in 1976's *The Man Who Fell to Earth,* Bowie can spark the dimmest of movies—and things are pretty murky here. Bowie is cast as an idealistic Prussian soldier who sees his values crumble amid the rise of Nazism. In love with vivacious Sydne Rome, a Sally Bowles–type club singer, he wants marriage and kids. She wants sex and success. Director David Hemmings seems never to have heard of *Cabaret.* He presents the obvious with a sense of real discovery. Worse, Joshua Sinclair's screenplay brims with such blather as: "There comes a time in every man's life when he stops making the same mistakes as Napoleon." Huh? But Bowie, who turns from martinet to paid escort, is a stylish sight onscreen. He's a hoot with aging widow Kim Novak, but it's not until a veiled, almost immobile Marlene Dietrich appears that the film shows any fire. Then 76, she is heartbreaking as she torches the title song to a defeated Bowie. The film marked her last screen appearance outside of Maximilian Schell's award-winning documentary, *Marlene,* where only her voice is heard. But her presence, however brief, is deeply felt. Dietrich and Bowie are cut from the same star cloth. Even in this zircon of a movie, they gleam like diamonds.
R / 1978 / N/A

▲ JUST BETWEEN FRIENDS

When a movie makes an impact and speaks eloquently, you expect it to move well and look good too. When it doesn't, the movie is usually dismissed as too much like television. That's the unfortunate fate of *Just Between Friends*. Writer-director Allan Burns, a founding force of "The Mary Tyler Moore Show," filmed his own script with an unimaginative, often inert camera. He clearly writes better than he directs. He has created a most intriguing, ingratiating quartet of grown-up characters. It's as if he has placed a seismograph in suburbia, registering the tremors of sorrow that run down these clean streets. The script pivots on some contrivances. Mary Tyler Moore plays a Pasadena housewife who makes a new best friend, TV reporter Christine Lahti, at an exercise class. Moore doesn't know that Lahti is sleeping with her husband, Ted ("Cheers") Danson—to the dismay of Danson's best friend, Sam (*The Killing Fields*) Waterston. With compassion and piercing dialogue, Burns transcends what could have been a routine sitcom setup. Although she has the most sympathetic role, Moore heightens the rigidity that makes her borderline unsympathetic. It's a brave move, and it works. Similarly, Danson rescues his cad from complete villainy. Waterston is funnier and slyer than he's ever been. And Lahti, who stole *Swing Shift* from Goldie Hawn, proves a most adroit klepto here too. "I keep having to make these decisions between my career, which I'm good at, and my life, which I'm not," laments Lahti. No other actress around better depicts the contradictions in contemporary career women. Even her tall, angular body seems at odds with itself—one minute graceful, the next gawky. She won an Oscar nomination for playing a 1940s variation on this character in *Swing Shift*, and she's a major reason *Just Between Friends,* despite being a clunky piece of moviemaking, is undeniably affecting.
PG-13 / 1986 / HBO/Cannon

▲ JUST TELL ME WHAT YOU WANT

Picture aging (then 41) ingenue Ali MacGraw slugging comedian Alan King with her purse in New York's elegant Bergdorf Goodman's. It's an unlikely scene, much less duo, but in this case the casting is perfect. King plays a power-mad Jewish magnate, MacGraw his ambitious gentile mistress, and together they are a delightfully funny team. Considerable credit must—obviously—go to director Sidney Lumet for making King a touch endearing and MacGraw more than a bit convincing. The two wage a romantic battle royal with a cast of admirable supporting performers, notably Myrna Loy as the businessman's faithful secretary and Dina Merrill as his faithless wife. All proceeds according to the magnate's plan until MacGraw falls in love with a young off-Broadway playwright (Peter Weller). Weller is appealing in his first major movie role, hanging in there in a tug-of-war over Ali. Who wins? Never mind, but in real life she ended up with Weller.
R / 1980 / Warner

▲ JUST THE WAY YOU ARE

For a movie that campaigns for the social acceptance of a woman with a brace on her leg, *Just the Way You Are* has a nasty habit: It cuts to more close-ups of feet than a Busby Berkeley dance musical. Starring Kristy McNichol, this romance chronicles the humiliations and hardships of a handicapped American musician who finds her self-respect and self-reliance during a ski vacation in the French Alps. As executed by screenwriter Allan Burns, who wrote for "The Mary Tyler Moore Show," and *La Cage aux Folles* director Edouard Molinaro, who was making his English-language debut, there's an underlying hypocrisy to the tale. By constantly calling attention to its heroines' afflictions, it's guilty of the same offense for which it condemns some characters. Despite the smattering of sex and nudity, this could just as easily have hit the screens in 1955. As with the throwaway romances of that period, it's all scenery and pious moralizing. True to the European adventures typical of that day, it also features the usual "the continent can cure you" philosophy and a disposable male lead, Michael Ontkean, whose dimples go deeper than his characterization. What leavens this exercise, to some extent anyway, is McNichol's performance. As an actress, she's promiscuous with her good humor and goodwill: She flirts with everybody in the film and the camera as well. Like Debra Winger or Sissy Spacek, she is unimpeachably forthright with the camera. But McNichol's directness only serves to italicize the embarrassing artifice of the script. *Just the Way You Are* isn't really moviemaking. It's pamphleteering.

PG / 1984 / MGM/UA

K

▲ KANGAROO

This screen version of D. H. Lawrence's semiautobiographical novel about his self-imposed exile to Australia in 1922 is a showcase for some strong performances by Colin Friels as Lawrence and July Davis as his German-born wife. Down Under Friels encounters a country with ''no history. Nothing has been paid for in blood.'' But he soon finds himself caught between a blue-collar socialist faction and a revolutionary group of World War I vets led by the title character, a misguided fascist ably played by Hugh Keays-Byrne. In this truly foreign land—and in their sometimes strained, sometimes passionate relationship—Davis is the willful catalyst, Friels the introspective observer. She is taken aback by the male-dominated society; he takes detailed notes on its colorful speech. Friels is a versatile, subtle actor. He won Australia's 1986 Best Actor award for his performance as the slow-witted title character in the comedy *Malcolm*. Davis, who won Australia's 1986 Best Actress award for this role, is frail yet inwardly stalwart. Spouses in real life, they made a captivating pair. Add Tim Burstall's solid direction and some beautiful photography, and *Kangaroo* is a solid pleasure.

R / 1987 / N/A

▲ THE KARATE KID

Ralph Macchio plays the New Jersey kid who moves to California with his mother. Naturally he's made unwelcome among the kids at school, especially by William Zabka, a blond karate nut, and his gang of thugs. They get really mad when Zabka's ex-girlfriend, Elsabeth Shue, takes a shine to the new boy. Then Macchio, whose winning smile makes up for his exaggerated swaggering, hooks up with an old Japanese handyman, and his life changes. The handyman, played with disarming calm by Noriyuki ''Pat'' Morita, teaches the youngster to be a martial arts wizard, but one with a heart. It all leads, of course, to a big climax at a karate tournament where Ralph faces down the bully. It's predictable and strained, but who cares? Director John Avildsen won an Oscar for *Rocky* in 1976; that movie, despite its embarrassingly clunky style, was a rousing hooray-for-the-good-guys flick. So is this. The wonderful parts of this film are those involving the kid and the old guy; there is something magical about the old man's balanced, compassionate view of life. Morita also proves that economy is effective when it comes to acting. The movie sags badly when it lapses into the obligatory teen-romance story. Shue has no real role except to cheer for her new boyfriend. The film is so deftly calculated to arouse audience sympathy, though, that it's hard in the end to avoid joining her.

PG / 1984 / RCA/Columbia

▲ KARATE KID, PART II

The Karate Kid was one of 1984's smashes, grossing more than $100 million. That tale of the underdog overcoming tremendous odds was based on the relationship between the teenage Daniel (Ralph Macchio) and his personal martial arts mentor Mr. Miyagi (Noriyuki ''Pat'' Morita). With enough action to satisfy the popcorn gobblers, it was a complete summer movie. Part II was born with an obvious predicament for director John Avildsen: how to reestablish yet broaden Macchio's and Morita's story without rehashing the original. It was a losing battle. In this sequel, Morita humbles his nemesis from the original movie (Martin Kove), and six months later Macchio

The Karate Kid: En route to becoming a reluctant but nonetheless adroit practitioner of the martial arts, Ralph Macchio gets in a few practice licks with his mentor, Pat Morita, Jr.

announces that his mother is moving and his girlfriend has left him. So when Morita receives a letter telling of his father's illness, he heads for his native Okinawa, with Macchio in tow. They find that all is not as Morita left it forty-five years before. For starters, his village is now part of a U.S. air base. Morita also has trouble with the local landlord (veteran character actor Danny Kamekona). Long ago, the landlord lost his honor when Morita stole his wife-to-be (Nobu McCarthy). "In Okinawa, honor has no time limit," says Morita, explaining why his former friend still holds the grudge and intends to fight him to the death over it. Despite the inevitable confrontations—one of them matches Macchio against Kamekona's nephew (Yuji Okumoto)—the fighting is again not at the film's heart. Honor, custom, and tradition are its focus, and the decidedly slow

pace and beautiful village scenes, shot in Hawaii, lend some integrity to the plot. Morita also returns to his first love (McCarthy), while Macchio finds a new one (Tamlyn Momita). Morita brings the same charm to the role that won him a 1984 Oscar nomination, and Macchio and the rest of the cast are workmanlike. But the film is ultimately too predictable, even somewhat tiresome, and *Karate Kid, Part II* goes down kicking.
PG / 1986 / RCA/Columbia

▲ THE KEEP

It's 1941, and somewhere deep in the mountains of Romania, the Nazis have set up housekeeping in the local castle. Strange things start happening. First, all the crosses on the tombs in the castle glow eerily; then the German soldiers start dying in horrible ways, their heads blasted open, their bodies burned. That is the spooky premise for this movie, which was directed by Michael Mann, who did the intriguing *Thief* with James Caan and later produced TV's "Miami Vice" and "Crime Story." This film has a spectacular look— the forbidding castle and townspeople appear like something out of the Grimm's fairy tales. The mood, thanks to a sound track by Tangerine Dream (who also scored *Thief*), is aptly eerie. But the plot is muddled. A monster trapped in the castle wants to get out. Enter Scott Glenn. An ageless semi-demon himself, he has come to fight it out with the evil force, anti-Nazi or otherwise. Then there's Ian McKellen, a Jewish history professor headed for a concentration camp until the Nazis bring him in to help solve the mystery. The movie collapses when the monster appears. It is a cross between Darth Vader and the Incredible Hulk. Its eyes and mouth glow red. It roars. It provides guffaws. The only saving grace of *The Keep* is Alberta Watson, a Canadian actress who plays McKellen's daughter. She at least occasionally relieves the runaway nightmare that this movie becomes.

R / 1984 / Paramount

▲ THE KENTUCKY FRIED MOVIE

Though a few of the spoofs in this cult comedy success fall flat, most are good for a giggle, especially the takeoffs on disaster movies, aspirin commercials, and happy-talk news shows. Most of the performers were (and remained) unknown, with a few surprise cameos—including Richard A. Baker, who played Dino De Laurentiis' *King Kong,* appearing as an ape named Dino. The film's director, however, was John (*Twilight Zone—The Movie*) Landis, and its idea came from Jim Abrahams and David and Jerry Zucker, who later created *Airplane!*

R / 1977 / N/A

▲ KEY EXCHANGE

If nothing else, this film represented a breakthrough in the Ban the Yuppies movement. It probes the subtleties of that eternal question: How committed do you have to be before exchanging apartment keys with your chic, cool, cynical Manhattan mate? Broadway actor Ben Masters plays a suave mystery writer. He's afraid to meet the father of his semi-steady girlfriend, Brooke Adams, assistant producer of a TV talk show hosted by Tony Roberts. Subplot-wise, Masters' bicycle-racing friend, Daniel Stern, and his new wife, Nancy Mette, are breaking up just a few days after they got married. Boys meet girls, boys lose girls, boys and girls behave like utter jerks. The only scene that sustains any comedy is one in which Masters wanders accidentally onto Roberts' TV panel during a discussion of infertility among couples and ad-libs a speech on the poignant problems of being a "sterile single." First-time feature director Barnett Kellman was nominated for an Emmy for "Another World"; maybe he should have paid a trifle more attention to television. Just about any episode of "The Mary Tyler Moore Show" had ten times as much humor and humanity as this movie.

R / 1985 / Key

▲ THE KIDNAPPING OF THE PRESIDENT

A Canadian production that has the slickly packaged look of a medium-budget, made-for-TV movie, this predictable political thriller is about a terrorist who tries to ransom a U.S. President for $100 million in diamonds. Until the President is actually nabbed, tension mounts nicely, recalling the far superior *Day of the Jackal*. But once the Chief Executive is shackled inside a security truck in Toronto's Civic Square, the story—like the Prez—has nowhere to go. William Shatner plays the Secret Service director with a pop-eyed anxiety unbecoming to his Captain Kirk calm. Old-timers Van Johnson and Ava Gardner are simply embarrassing as the jittery Vice-President and his ambitious wife. Only Hal Holbrook rises above the mundane with his wry portrayal of the President. Director George Mendeluk handles the action capably but without demonstrable flair.

R / 1984 / Continental

▲ THE KIDS ARE ALRIGHT: THE WHO

It's all there—the swooping, guitar-smashing violence of Peter Townshend, the maniacal drumming of Keith Moon, the Buddha-like presence of John Entwistle, and the tight-jeaned charisma of Roger Daltrey. The film has some funny moments: the group tearing off one another's clothes during a TV interview, Moon mock-trashing a motel room on a tube special, and Townshend's hilarious nonanswers to dumb questions by journalists. And one doesn't have to be a Who fan to be electrified by such songs as "Who Are You," "Tommy," and "Won't Get Fooled Again." But the rock documentary is at best limited: concert scenes, interviews, and more concert scenes. After a while the sequences can get boring, and there's something sad about tracking The Who from 1967 to 1978. Partially it's the knowledge of Moon's death later in 1978, but a film like this is also too-graphic proof of the aging process—for audiences as well as performers.

PG / 1979 / Thorn/EMI

▲ THE KILLING FIELDS

If you're rationing your video rentals to only extraordinary films, here's one to pick. Based on an article by *New York Times* correspondent Sydney Schanberg, *The Killing Fields* is the story of Schanberg's relationship with his Cambodian interpreter, Dith Pran, during the war between the revolutionary Khmer Rouge and the U.S.-supported Lon Nol government. Schanberg won a Pulitzer Prize for his reporting. Pran, who also risked his life in Schanberg's service, had to flee into Cambodia's death-ridden countryside with millions of other refugees after Khmer Rouge troops occupied the capital, Phnom Penh, in April 1975. From then until October 3, 1979, when Pran crossed the border to Thailand, Schanberg, who had returned to the U.S., tried to locate him. Pran's story—four years of lonely horror—is the heart of this almost unbearably moving film. First-time feature director Roland Joffe and screenwriter Bruce Robinson made the details of Pran's life a paradigm for the fall of Cambodia— a lush, cultured country used as battle fodder by world powers. Their film rings with a justifiable sense of rage but avoids Hollywood hyperbole. The superb documentary cinematographer Chris Menges brings the stamp of unflinching reality to every frame (he won an Oscar for his efforts).

The Killing Fields: Sam Waterson *(white shirt)* portrays an earnest *New York Times* correspondent who becomes horribly entwined in the vicious civil war in Cambodia.

From the faces of 10-year-old orphans in uniform to muffled explosions that result in bloody death, Menges's camera sees war as it is. The acting is equally authentic. Sam Waterson plays Schanberg with a piercing intelligence that allows for human flaws. And John Malkovich, portraying a photographer who uses drink, drugs, and humor as a support system for living in hell, adds to his reputation as an actor's actor. But the film, haunting and haunted, belongs to Dr. Haing S. Ngor as Dith Pran. A Cambodian physician, Ngor was tortured when the Khmer Rouge began persecuting the educated class (he pretended to be a taxi driver for four years, finally escaping to Thailand). Ngor had never acted before (Joffe saw his face in a friend's wedding photos). He won a Best Supporting Oscar but perhaps what he does isn't so much acting as presenting an agonizing human reflection of war.
R / 1984 / Warner

▲ KILLPOINT

The ads said Richard Roundtree gave his "toughest and roughest performance since Shaft." The audience is never really sure, though, as he only appears in about a quarter of the film. The rest of Killpoint offers the blood, bullets, and bad acting prevalent in low-budget cops-versus-kingpins flicks. Brutal crimes are being committed in southern California with the use of automatic weapons stolen from a National Guard armory. A federal agent in charge of the case, Roundtree calls on Leo Fong (also the film's associate producer and fight choreographer) an aging martial arts expert/cop bent on revenge since his wife was murdered by thugs (haven't we heard that one before?). Cameron Mitchell is sleazy as a crime boss, and Stack Pierce is menacing as his right-hand man. But the film goes nowhere. The scenes are confusing, the acting wooden, the violence gratuitous. And none of it seems the same without that Isaac Hayes Shaft sound track.
R / 1984 / Vestron

▲ KING DAVID

At least nobody can blame the writers for this one. When it comes to providing all the ingredients for a terrific movie—action, political intrigue, sex, war, art—you just can't beat the boys who pounded out the Old Testament. In translating the rocks-to-riches story of the Jews' King David to the screen, however, director Bruce Beresford took an astoundingly literal-minded, credulous approach. The film has none of the scope of mythology. Yet none of the characters seem like real people either. Nobody ever says anything normal like, "Wow, that Goliath is a big son of a gun" or "Another bowl of manna, please." Instead, average people go around proclaiming to no one in particular, "The God of Israel, He is the Lord of Hosts," as if they all hope they'll end up being quoted in the Bible. Richard Gere plays David as a mumbly lech who seems to have left his charisma in the shepherd's hut. When he gazes at himself in a mirror, the notion of retitling the movie Israelite Gigolo seems awfully hard to resist. And when David celebrates the arrival of the Ark of the Covenant in his city, Jerusalem—the Bible describes him as "dancing and making merry" (1 Chronicles 15:29)—Gere seems more to be auditioning for the "Solid Gold" chorus than paying his respects to his Deity. Beresford rouses some life only in the many scenes of battle and miscellaneous violence. There his motto seems to be: Two heads are better than one, especially if you can lop them both off and let them bounce on the ground. Edward Woodward has his moments as the paranoid Saul, David's predecessor, and Cherie Lunghi, as David's first wife, Michal, denounces him in the movie's only really passionate scene. But the pace drags. Anyone facing the temptation to watch King David is advised to remember that old video renter's commandment: Thou shalt not squander thy time on biblical epics.
PG-13 / 1985 / Paramount

▲ KING KONG LIVES

King Kong has been a lot of things. Never, however, was he such a big bore. The story picks up where the 1976 remake ended. Kong has survived that nasty fall off the World Trade Center in New York, though he needs an artificial heart implant. The surgeon is Linda Hamilton, who knows from big apes, having co-starred with Arnold Schwarzenegger in The Terminator. She installs what looks like a monster food processor in Kong's chest, and it is soon going pitter-patter

over Lady Kong, a giant female gorilla discovered in Borneo by Brian Kerwin. While Hamilton and Kerwin get to know each other, the Kongs stomp around the countryside on a honeymoon that includes snapping people in half. Special-effects master Carlo Rambaldi had two forty-five-foot Kong models on hand, but a lot of the footage was shot using live actors in gorilla suits. The actors costumed as the Kongs are so ungorilla-like that the merely hokey becomes cartoonish. Sequel purposes are served, however. A son of Kong is born, and he too seems likely to lead a life of reluctant destruction unless someone can get him a scholarship to Ohio State—or teach him to type so he can review movies.
PG-13 / 1986 / Karl-Lorimar

▲ KING OF COMEDY

As a TV talk show host kidnapped at gunpoint, Jerry Lewis invests King of Comedy with a performance of astonishing restraint. Gone is the spasmodic, physical Jerry of yore. Instead, he paints a wickedly accurate portrait of a celebrity exhausted and straitjacketed by success. This is a major character but, sadly, Lewis's role proves peripheral to the matters at hand. What director Martin (Raging Bull) Scorsese and critic-turned-screenwriter Paul D. Zimmerman are offering is a caustic but curiously labored treatise on celebrity obsession. Robert De Niro plays a struggling comic who, in his daydreams, sees Lewis as his mentor. In fact, Lewis and his assistant (well played by ex-Angel Shelley Hack) continually give him the brush. When De Niro involves his innocent girlfriend, Diahnne Abbot (Mrs. De Niro in real life), in his obsessions, the line between fantasy and reality blurs dangerously. De Niro abducts Lewis with the help of Sandra Bernhard, a rich young neurotic who holds Lewis captive in her candlelit Manhattan apartment while De Niro demands a spot on Lewis's show as ransom. The kidnappers are sick, suffering characters deserving of compassion, but they get precious little from Scorsese, who views them always from a safe, superior distance. De Niro's last-minute rise to fame is the film's ultimate sick joke. Perhaps burning over the criticism he received for Taxi Driver—a film that co-starred De Niro and Jodie Foster and allegedly influenced John Hinckley—Scorsese used King of Comedy as an act of

exoneration, not contrition. He implies that the press should bear the brunt for glamorizing and even inciting criminal behavior. On the evidence here, such reasoning seems spurious. The acting excellence of Lewis, De Niro, and especially Bernhard, a stand-up comic new to the screen, may make King of Comedy glitter. But Scorsese, refusing to share responsibility for the society he mirrors, wears a hollow crown.
PG / 1983 / RCA/Columbia

▲ KING OF THE GYPSIES

Another big hype from that prince of promo, Dino De Laurentiis, this movie is at least adorned by stunning photography from Ingmar Bergman's cinematographer Sven Nykist. There's also an often engrossing glimpse of the Romany lifestyle from best-selling author Peter Maas, exquisite background music from jazz violinist Stephane Grappelli, and an exciting performance by then-newcomer Eric Roberts. Roberts portrays a '70s New York gypsy both attracted to and repelled by his grandfather (Sterling Hayden), the king of the gypsies. As Hayden grows older, he passes over his alcoholic son (a thankless role Judd Hirsch deserved a crown for attempting) and named Roberts his successor. The grandson would prefer not to be king, precipitating a gypsy-style Godfather crisis. Susan Sarandon and Brooke Shields (reprising their mother-daughter act in Pretty Baby) brighten the background, but even they can't steal the horse from under Roberts.
R / 1979 / Paramount

▲ KING SOLOMON'S MINES

Why would anyone offer the lead in this woeful comedy adventure to Richard Chamberlain? More puzzling still, why would Chamberlain, with a substantial career going for him at 50, accept such a dumb role? This project bears no resemblance to the 1950 version of the H. Rider Haggard story about adventurers searching for Solomon's mythical riches. That film reeked with dignity, from the lead performers, Stewart Granger and Deborah Kerr, to the Masai (who staged a memorable dance sequence), to the plains animals (filmed by Robert Surtees in a spectacular stampede). In this movie everything is camped up, far past even the playful tone of Romancing

the Stone. Sharon Stone, who plays Chamberlain's love interest, is a student of the Bo Derek school of acting, and a dropout at that. Her reading of the line, "Where's my father, you cheap-suited camel jockey?" is a film milestone. Director J. Lee Thompson, whose light touch was exhibited in *The Guns of Navarone,* offers a glimmer of hope when some cannibals dump Chamberlain, Stone, and a batch of vegetables into a huge pot set over a fire. Just our luck, though. They escape, leaving only the audience to stew.
PG-13 / 1985 / MGM/UA

▲ KISS ME GOODBYE

Only a magician could levitate Charlie (*Paternity*) Peters' script for this comedy. And director Robert (*Same Time, Next Year*) Mulligan just loaded on more ballast. Casting wildly against type, he has given Sally Field the central role of a widowed New York socialite haunted by the ghost of her first husband as she prepares to remarry. James Caan is equally miscast as the ghost of a Broadway choreographer. If Jeff Bridges fares better in the hapless role of the Egyptologist fiancé, that may be simply because it's hard to imagine anyone who could make more of his insipid material. The movie is an unfortunate remake of 1978's Brazilian *Dona Flor and Her Two Husbands.*
PG / 1983 / CBS/Fox

▲ KISS OF THE SPIDER WOMAN

Tense, charged with intellectual energy, and witty with the dark humor of despair, this film by Brazilian director Hector Babenco is mesmerizing. A major source of its power is the acting by William Hurt and Raul Julia. Anyone who sees this film will have a hard time forgetting the characters. In a plot taken from a novel by the Argentine-born writer Manuel Puig, Hurt and Julia are cell mates in a prison in Brazil. Hurt is a brazen homosexual, imprisoned for child molestation; Julia is a political prisoner, being tortured because he won't betray his comrades. Most of the film takes place in their cramped cell, but so wide-ranging are the ideas and so expansive is the acting, the movie never seems confined. Hurt richly deserved the Oscar he won for the film, providing what surely must be the best gay performance ever by a major actor, looking and acting like the queen he says he is, but never resorting to cliché or camp. Julia amazingly manages to avoid being upstaged even though his is a quieter performance as a man so tortured by the need to feel dedication that he refuses to admit to any human weakness. Hurt's way of passing the time, conjuring up in minute detail the plots of dreadfully romantic movies, sets up the contrast: He seems totally irresponsible, concerned only with trivial pleasures, while Julia insists on his idealism. The two men's relationship evolves in such a natural way that when Julia finally lets Hurt seduce him, more in gratitude for Hurt's kindness than out of lust, the scene is just a love scene—its homosexuality seems irrelevant. There's also an effective subplot involving the prison officials' attempt to suborn Hurt, promising him freedom if he can extract the information they want from Julia. And Sonia Braga, who appears as the always overdrawn heroine of Hurt's movie plots, provides the right touches of surrealism. This is a prison movie to the same extent that *Hamlet* is a ghost story. What it is really about is the capacity of the human spirit to surprise, in beautiful ways as well as ugly ones.
R / 1985 / Charter

▲ KNIGHTRIDERS

It is impossible to sit through this movie with a straight face. But it's not a comedy, just awesome in its absurdity. On the surface, *Knightriders* is a simple tale about a modern-day Renaissance fair featuring knights who joust on motorcycles. There's a king and a queen, a good knight and a bad knight, and they live by ancient chivalric code. Harmless enough stuff. Yet, as the film drones on (and on and on for 150 minutes), writer-director George Romero seems intent on a message, not too cleverly couched in lots of silly existential talk about the evils of today's society. The pretensions get pretty funny. Viewers will howl at what is surely the most unintentionally hilarious, hyper-maudlin funeral ever filmed. In a cast of unknowns, most of whom were destined to stay that way, only Ed Harris is memorable, not for his performance, which is lousy, but for surviving this turkey to go on to a distinguished acting career. Romero, best known for his effectively gruesome *Night of the Living Dead,* strayed too far from his strength. Symbols keep popping up the way Groucho Marx's duck used to on *You Bet Your Life.* One that recurs is a forbidding black bird, looking constantly on the verge of saying "Nevermore." Or maybe it's "Never mind."

R / 1981 / Media

▲ KOYAANISQATSI

The title (pronounced Co-yon-uh-SCOT-si) is Hopi for "life out of balance." And this extraordinary 87-minute visual tone poem on nature, man, and technological self-destruction is a remarkable argument that a catastrophic lack of balance is pervasive in modern America. The film is less a documentary than a series of impressionistic images—from clouds and dunes to Los Angeles freeways and Manhattan streets. The concept and overall vision belong to director Godfrey Reggio, the hypnotic score to avant-garde composer Philip Glass, and the exquisite photography to cinematographer Ron Fricke. Reggio, then 43, was based in Santa Fe, New Mexico, and sometimes his vistas are spread across mountain ranges, while at other moments they're condensed in the experiences written on a single face in close-up. There are scenes of laundromats and video-game parlors in Chicago, Las Vegas, and San Francisco. There is man-made destruction—nuclear tests, for instance—juxtaposed with nature sequences. The film is, in visual impact, more akin to Lucas and Spielberg than to documentaries. "The idea was to look at ordinary daily life from an extraordinary point of view," Reggio said. "I want people to escape to reality, rather than from reality, as they do with other films. My film is a little like a cat that barks." His work is, indeed, an uncanny kind of cinematic beast, original and fascinating.

Unrated / 1983 / Pacific Arts

▲ KRAMER VS. KRAMER

There is so seldom even one great performance in a movie that three is too much to expect. For that reason alone, this story of a couple battling for custody of their young son is a remarkable achievement. Dustin Hoffman gives the dramatic performance of his career as the ambitious advertising exec who discovers there's more to life than success. Meryl Streep achieves the near-impossible, remaining sympathetic while committing the un-American horror of deserting her child. And, amazingly, Justin Henry, at 7, overcomes his cherubic looks and preciousness in his acting debut. Much of the credit must go to scriptwriter-director Robert (*The Late Show*) Benton. He never permits the camera to linger on scenes that are set up to be heart-tuggers, but crisply moves through a string of opalescent vignettes. The film, Benton, Hoffman, and Streep (as Best Supporting Actress) won Oscars. The film's only failing is its unlikely resolution (taken from the novel by Avery Corman, upon which the movie is based)—not that audiences will notice through their tears.

PG / 1979 / RCA/Columbia

▲ KRULL

It rhymes with dull. Any reasonably bright 10-year-old practitioner of Dungeons & Dragons fantasy games could have come up with as intriguing a plot as this, the pallid heart of yet another epic about swords, sorcery, and damsels. Set on the planet Krull, which bears a remarkable resemblance to medieval England, its hero is a prince, Ken (TV's Marco Polo) Marshall. He acquires a lot of magical powers, though his most amazing feat consists of looking like Kurt Russell. The heroine is a princess, Lysette Anthony, who is captured by a villain known as the Beast. It's easy to see how he got his name, since he has a bulbous head and is nineteen or twenty stories tall; it is less easy to see what he thinks he and the princess have in common. He wants to make her Mrs. Beast, nevertheless. Helping Marshall are a bush-league wizard (who accidentally turns himself into a basset hound), a cyclops, a young boy, a gang of bandits, and an old princely adviser. There's a lot of horseback riding, sword and laser battles, and foolhardy attacks. The film isn't too violent, gory, or sexy. It's not too entertaining either.

PG / 1983 / RCA/Columbia

L

▲ LA CAGE AUX FOLLES

Michel Serrault won the Cesar, France's Oscar, in this comedy, portraying an aging female impersonator in a St. Tropez nightclub. His lover, masterfully played by Italian actor Ugo Tognazzi, manages the club whose name (which roughly translates "The Madwomen's Cage") provides the movie's title. When Tognazzi's son gets engaged the fun begins. It centers on the son's attempts to hide his father's life-style from his prospective in-laws, climaxing at a prenuptial dinner that more than makes up for earlier lapses. Italian director Edouard Molinaro mostly avoids the cheap laughs so often resorted to in movies about gay life. The film inspired a couple of lackluster sequels and a hit Broadway musical. (In French with subtitles.)
R / 1979 / CBS/Fox

▲ LA CAGE AUX FOLLES II

The original *Cage aux Folles* was a vaguely risqué, charming confection about a pair of middle-aged homosexuals in the south of France. It achieved instant cult status and has grossed more than $40 million in the U.S. This sequel lacks the sense of discovery. What made the first *Cage* special was that it caught us off guard; now we know the situation, and the laughs seem forced. Still, Ugo Tognazzi, the long-suffering straight man, and Michel Serrault, the outrageous vamp, continue to play their roles with gusto. Edouard Molinaro directs with the same sardonic eye. No moviegoer will be able to resist the marvelous scene when chronic transvestite Serrault, dressed in overalls, pretends to be a macho window washer. An absurd spy-counterspy plot intrudes on the bittersweet humor, but fans of the original who seek out this follow-up shouldn't be more than mildly disappointed. (In French with subtitles.)
R / 1981 / CBS/Fox

▲ THE LACEMAKER

Swiss director Claude Goretta fashioned a delicate drama about a shy young girl's first love affair—and its surprisingly tragic consequences. Isabelle Huppert glows as a beauty parlor apprentice who meets—and moves in with—a lanky, kindhearted university student, played to perfection by Yves Beneyton. The young lovers soon find that differences of class and ambition—she aspires to be a hairstylist, he a university professor—are irreconcilable, and their idyllic relationship slowly unravels before the sympathetic eye of the camera. (In French with subtitles.)
Unrated / 1977 / N/A

▲ LADYHAWKE

Once upon a time there was a $21 million movie that wanted to make medieval romance compelling for a contemporary audience. It had castles and jousts and evil curses and lots of talk about meeting one's destiny. It had great-looking sets and Italian scenery (you know a movie's in trouble when people tell you how great the scenery and sets are). It even had a fantastical plot about the tortured love between a beautiful maiden, Michelle Pfeiffer, and her noble soldier-lover, Rutger Hauer. Because a hypocritical bishop loves the lady, he puts a curse on her and the soldier, which keeps the pair "always together, eternally apart." During the daylight hours Pfeiffer is transformed into a hawk who must accompany her lover on his shoulder. After the sun sets she returns to human form, but Hauer takes on the shape of a wolf. Despite the pomp and pageantry of *Ladyhawke,* the concept is inadvertently kinky instead of cosmic, since it's not exactly romantic to watch a moon-eyed fellow nuzzle a hawk. The plot also muzzles the actors, who must do most of the emoting with animals; they don't have anything to react to except howls and chirps. While Matthew Broderick had top billing, the script treats him like a peripheral character, a young thief who serves as a messenger for the lovers. Director Richard Donner and co-screenwriter Tom Mankiewicz brought an engaging note of skepticism to their previous pop-legend collaboration, *Superman,* but their touch here is humorless. *Ladyhawke* is a damsel in distress only a sorcerer could salvage.

PG-13 / 1985 / Warner

▲ LADY JANE

American audiences can hardly be fascinated with a movie about a minor crisis of the English monarchy in the 16th century, especially one that also dwells on intellectual discussions of the Christian sacraments. What justified releasing this film here were the smashing performances of two young British actors, Helena Bonham (*Room with a View*) Carter and Cary Elwes. Carter, then 19, plays Jane Grey, the young cousin of queens Mary I and Elizabeth I who was installed as queen in a political coup on the death of King Edward VI. Elwes, then 23, plays Jane's husband, Guildford Dudley, whose father engineered the coup. Queen Jane's reign—which turned into a sort of adolescent Camelot—lasted nine days before the rightful heir Mary ousted her and eventually had her beheaded. The intensity of Carter and Elwes makes not only their romance but the palace intrigue seem tolerable. But this often seems like a bad "Masterpiece Theatre" pilot that got lost on the way to PBS. Trevor Nunn, a legitimate theater director (*Cats, Nicholas Nickleby, Les Misérables*), gave his first film a lot of pomp, hardly any circumstance.

PG-13 / 1986 / Paramount

▲ LA GRANDE BOURGEOISIE

You don't have to understand the finer points of Italian proletarian politics to become involved in this fin de siècle story of a socialist lawyer who tries to save his sister from her malevolent nobleman husband by killing him. Lina Wertmuller's protégé, Giancarlo Giannini, a deglamorized Catherine Deneuve, and Fernando Rey are thoughtful and movingly baffled as they slowly lose control of their lives. (In Italian with subtitles.)

Unrated / 1977 / Vestron

▲ LA PASSANTE

Romy Schneider's last film may not have been her best, but it certainly offers a fond look at one of Europe's most elegant and talented movie stars. Schneider, who was born in Austria, died in 1982 after a lengthy illness. She had also been despondent over the accidental death of her son, David, in July 1981. This, her sixtieth film, was a project she developed herself—the title means "The Passerby." The movie begins with Schneider greeting her businessman-husband (Michel Piccoli) on his return to France from a trip overseas. As chairman of an international amnesty group, he spends much of his time trying to persuade repressive governments to treat political prisoners more humanely. While in Paris he discovers that an old Nazi nemesis is also there, masquerading as a Paraguayan embassy official. Overcome with rage, Piccoli kills him—and the film then becomes a series of scenes from his trial intercut with flashbacks of what made him do it. The flashbacks show Piccoli as a boy in Berlin in 1933, just as Hitler was coming to power. Piccoli's father is murdered by the Nazis in a horrifying street scene, and the boy's legs are broken in the attack. Later his foster parents are also hounded and finally killed by Hitler's dreaded storm troopers. Schneider plays two parts, one as Piccoli's wife who faithfully attends his trial, and the other as the foster mother. Her dual role is disconcerting at first, and the storytelling is a bit clunky—the murder of the ex-Nazi comes almost too soon in the story. But once the movie settles down, it gathers emotional intensity and becomes a moving testament to those still scarred by Hitler's nightmare, as well as a moving farewell from Romy Schneider. (In French with subtitles.)

Unrated / 1983 / Pacific Arts

▲ LASERBLAST

A nice hicktown kid is getting pushed around a lot—until he finds power and revenge with a laser gun and a magic pendant he stumbles upon in the desert. Trouble is, the gun and pendant turn young Kim Milford into a monster with green skin, fangs, and silver eyes. Two giant lizards from another planet have him locked in their computerized sights all through the movie without ever explaining why. A CIA type who tries to figure it out gets no further than we do. Some

mild sci-fi sex is thrown in, but this is the very definition of a low-budget aimless horror film.
PG / 1978 / Media

▲ LASSITER

Maybe they can still make good B movies after all. While it has no pretensions to art or social commentary, this caper film is a stylish, witty, escapist's delight. It helps if the escapist is also a Tom Selleck fan. Selleck displays an offhand charm in the title role—he's a cat burglar in pre–World War II London enlisted by British authorities to steal some gems from the German embassy. Selleck playing a cat burglar is like Woody Allen playing a tight end. But no matter. There is a spirited supporting cast, including Jane Seymour, Lauren Hutton, Bob Hoskins, Ed Lauter, and Joe Regalbuto. Ken Thorne's Dixielandish period music is delightful. David Taylor's script is compact and wry. At one point a Gestapo agent asks Selleck if he is an admirer of German culture. "Where I come from, we like things a bit lighter," Selleck says. "Oh," the Nazi sneers. "You mean like Mickey Mouse." Director Roger Young, whose TV credits include "Lou Grant" and Selleck's "Magnum, P.I.," frames some attractive London scenes and sets a snappy, sexy pace. As for Selleck, he and his mustache are in fine form. He is not afraid to look silly (at one point he ends up wearing Hutton's dressing gown), and he exploits that charming vulnerability. If he didn't make anyone forget Laurence Olivier or Cary Grant, he at least pushed Burt Reynolds into the back of people's minds for a while.
R / 1984 / Warner

▲ LAST EMBRACE

It's what movie people call a "cute meet," right out of The Goodbye Girl—Janet Margolin is subletting Roy Scheider's apartment, and they both refuse to quit the premises. He's an agent of some kind recovering from a nervous breakdown. She seems to be a nice girl who can help him. Then they get caught up in an attempted murder: his. The plot (based on The Thirteenth Man by Murray Teigh Bloom) is absolutely baffling. Whose side is John Glover on? What is Chris Walken up to? But director Jonathan Demme makes something undeniably disturbing and erotic

out of this mystery. Margolin's bathtub scene steamed up theaters and men's glasses everywhere. And the Niagara Falls climax is a pip. Here is just the type of underrated and undiscovered pleasure video was invented for.
R / 1979 / MGM/UA

▲ THE LAST MARRIED COUPLE IN AMERICA

"Endangered species," reads the lettering on the sweat shirt built for two that George Segal and Natalie Wood wear in this movie's ad campaign. The sweat shirt is referring to the beleaguered institution of marriage. The premise is simple: All of Segal and Wood's "happily married" friends get divorced. Predictably, they separate too. What little spark the film has is generated by its lead players, convincing in their mid-marriage crisis. Dom De Luise gets some laughs as a plumber turned porno actor, as does Valerie Harper as a liberated divorcee. Not much can be said for director Gilbert Cates.
R / 1980 / MCA

▲ THE LAST METRO

One of director François Truffaut's last and best films, this one is set in France during the Nazi Occupation. It focuses on a small Paris theater run by Catherine Deneuve in the absence of her husband (Heinz Bennent), who as a Jew must hide from persecution in a cellar. Enter Gerard Départieu as an actor who uses his rakish reputation to mask his role in the French Resistance. This is the ménage à trois situation of Truffaut's Jules and Jim, just as the director's affection for the actor's life also suggests Day for Night. But here both themes seem richer, more mature. In a time when free speech is forbidden, the work of the artist becomes a true commitment. The barrel-chested Départieu is raffishly funny claiming to crave women like warm croissants. But the film belongs to Deneuve, who has never looked more heart-stoppingly beautiful. Nor had she ever acted with such luminous strength as she does here, playing a woman torn between loyalty to her husband and passion for the actor. There is no nudity, but one love scene under a table becomes an erotic cinema landmark revealing no more than Deneuve's long legs and black patent pumps.

With so much sly wit, intelligence and heart—all under the sure hand of Truffaut—*The Last Metro* glides effortlessly into greatness.
Unrated / 1980 / Key

▲ THE LAST OF THE BLUE DEVILS

A remarkable documentary, this loving look at Kansas City jazz by a lawyer who never before shot a frame of movie film is a delight for jazz fans. Bruce Ricker, a white New Yorker practicing law in K.C. in 1974, hung out in the black musicians' old union hall, where he heard some survivors from the city's golden age of jazz. He hired a cameraman and, for $12,000, staged a reunion. It brought Joe Turner and Jesse Price from L.A. and Count Basie and his band from a gig fortuitously nearby. They joined other alumni of the 1920s' Oklahoma City Blue Devils, which begat the '30s bands of Basie and Jay McShann. Ricker intercut new film of them with black-and-white clips, including an old TV kinescope of Charlie "Bird" Parker and Dizzy Gillespie. Five decades intershuffle as Big Joe Turner pours out a spine-prickling 1944 "Piney Brown Blues"; the Blue Devils rip through Basie's "Squabblin' " in 1929; Jesse Price and McShann, forceful as ever, sing the blues in 1974; Bird unleashes a multidimensional "Hot House" in 1952; Lester Young lives again in a 1957 tenor solo; the 1974–75 Basie and 1932 Bennie Moten bands both perform "Moten Swing"; and Turner belts "Shake, Rattle and Roll" in concert and on film from 1956. "We were doing rock 'n' roll," says the big man, "before anybody ever heard of it."
PG / 1980 / N/A

▲ THE LAST REMAKE OF BEAU GESTE

The late Marty Feldman, a graduate of the Mel Brooks school of comedy, made his directing debut in this parody of the three film versions of the P.C. Wren Foreign Legion novel. It amounts to an 84-minute Hollywood joke (pages flipping off calendars to indicate passage of time, and so forth). Slapsticking along with Feldman are Michael York (as Beau), a voluptuous Ann-Margret (an often unappreciated comedienne), and Peter Ustinov as a sadistic Legionnaire. Feldman even gets stoned with Gary Cooper, irreverently cross-cut from the classic 1939 version.
PG / 1977 / N/A

▲ LAST RESORT

There aren't many movies that are actually painful to watch. This is an excruciating exception. The credits list a director and two writers. That's hard to believe. It seems as if everyone is just winging it. The result is obnoxious mayhem, not outrageous mirth. Perhaps you can forgive the no-name actors, but Charles Grodin should have known better. In a plot plainly similar to *Club Paradise,* Grodin plays a big-city salesman who leaves his job behind by taking his family to a tropical resort. There they are served TV dinners to go along with the egregious stage show put on by the sex-crazed counselors. Grodin pleads with his family to give the place, with its paper-thin walls and mud-spouting showers, a chance. Grodin's wife, played by Robin (TV's "The White Shadow") Person Rose, loosens up only after she starts getting high. Armed guards are everywhere because guerrillas lurking in the hills want to overthrow the club. Whatever for is anybody's guess. Never has a movie had a more appropriate title.
R / 1986 / N/A

▲ THE LAST STARFIGHTER

Anyone who's had fantasies about the ultimate video game will appreciate this film. Lance Guest plays a recent high school grad who lives in a trailer park. When not doing chores for his mother, he plays a video game called Starfighter. One night, with his girlfriend, Catherine Mary Stewart, and little brother looking on, he scores a record number of points. Soon Guest is visited by a strange man in a space-age car and then kidnapped to another galaxy, where his skills behind the video stick are enlisted in the cause of an intergalactic war. It's a bit of *Star Wars,* some *E.T.,* and a lot of "Star Trek." It all fits, thanks to the tongue-in-cheek script by first-time writer Jonathan Betuel and the mostly light touch of director Nick Castle. Guest plays two roles, the starfighter and a robot double sent to keep his girlfriend company while he's off saving planets. The film's funniest scene comes when the robot tries to romance Stewart, imitating the saccharine endearments of another couple nearby. Chris Hebert, as the kid brother, is hilarious, doing a great take when he sees the robot screw his head off to clean his ear. And Stewart, as the girl-

friend, adds freshness, not to mention beauty. Dan O'Herlihy plays a Wookie-like sidekick, and a lot of the other starfighters look like rejects from the *Star Wars* bar scene. The climactic fight between Guest and the bad guys is zippy, all of it done with computer graphics, not models. The movie is warmhearted too. What other teenager comes by to pick up his girlfriend in his own spaceship?
PG / 1984 / MCA

▲ THE LAST SURVIVOR

Give an Air Sickness Bag Award to this grisly, gruesome, Italian film. Supposedly based on a true story, it tells of a research team stranded on a jungle-covered island inhabited solely by Stone Age primitives. For 83 minutes you can watch the natives chomp on crocodiles, bats, and occasionally, each other. At one particularly stomach-churning moment a subtitle reads "scenes of cannibalism photographed from real life." As if the dietary aspects are not unsettling enough, the dubbing is sure to put anyone off his feed.
R / 1978 / N/A

▲ THE LAST WALTZ

Martin Scorsese originally earned his shot at directing as editor of *Woodstock,* the prototypical rock concert movie. Here he portrays another watershed, the last concert (Thanksgiving, 1976) of The Band, the formative country rockers of the '60s and sometime backup group for Ronny Hawkins and Bob Dylan. Their performance is intercut with amusing interviews revealing the wit and intelligence of The Band members, particularly guitarist Robbie Robertson, who produced this film. Robertson later turned actor, in such films as *Carny,* while drummer Levon Helm showed up in *Coal Miner's Daughter* and *The Right Stuff.* But the music is the thing, and the guests—including Eric Clapton, Emmylou Harris, The Staples, Muddy Waters, and particularly Van Morrison and Dr. John—all add excitement and perform to beat The Band. But they hardly upstage the headliners. Shooting was well choreographed, and the sound is four-track Dolby.
Unrated / 1978 / CBS/Fox

▲ THE LAST WAVE

Richard Chamberlain, in his post-Kildare years, ranged from *Hamlet* to *Centennial* to *The Thorn Birds.* He is, however, all but swamped by this farfetched Australian voodoo saga directed by Peter Weir, about a corporate tax lawyer who becomes obsessed with a murder case involving urbanized aboriginal tribesmen. The heavy-handedness and clichéd dialogue make the film seem rather like a made-for-TV throwaway. Olivia Hammett, a product of Aussie TV, gives a fine performance as the attorney's patient wife, and Chamberlain has his sturdy moments—as when he discovers he's literally some sort of shaman of doomsday. Recommended only for those movie fans who are deeply into aboriginal culture or the occult.
PG / 1979 / Warner

▲ THE LATE GREAT PLANET EARTH

So this is the way the world ends. Not in fire or ice, not even with a bang or a whimper, but by making us sit through a god-awful movie. Based on Hal Lindsey's 1970 best-seller, this pseudo-documentary hails from the *In Search of Noah's Ark* school of filmmaking. Lindsey tries to document the impending apocalypse with biblical prophecies (primarily from Revelation, which provided similar speculative fodder for *The Omen*). Stock footage of natural disasters, famine, killer bees, and nuclear blasts is supplemented by dreary interviews with scholarly types and Lindsey himself. The film is alternately ridiculous and offensive, the bad taste peaking in conjecture about which current world leader may in reality be the Antichrist. Orson Welles, narrating in his most portentous baritone, asks, "Is there some significance to all this? Some deeper meaning?" He never asked a sillier question.
PG / 1979 / N/A

▲ THE LATE SHOW

One of the most joyous and underrated films of the '70s came from *Kramer vs. Kramer* writer-director Robert Benton. A paunchy, old-school private eye, Art Carney, teams with an L.A. loonie, Lily Tomlin, to solve one last grimy case. A quirky chemistry develops between the hard-boiled and the flipped-out. That Oscar ignored the sheer perfection of this screen teaming remains a blot on the Academy.

PG / 1977 / Warner

▲ LA TRAVIATA

Opera buffs may enjoy it the most, but this big-screen version of Verdi's classic should be fun for anyone. It is lavishly mounted and beautifully sung, with New York Metropolitan Opera stars Placido Domingo and Teresa Stratas appearing in the lead roles. For those who may not be familiar with the Camille-like story: Stratas plays a beautiful woman with a shady past who finds herself pursued by a love-struck young merchant's son, played by Domingo. They proceed to embark on a passionate affair that is interrupted by a visit from the young man's father, who has found out that Stratas once was a courtesan. He decides he cannot agree to give his daughter away in marriage so long as the family honor is tainted by the scandal of his son's affair. Stratas, gorgeous and at times looking almost like a dreamy Barbra Streisand, eventually gives in to the father's pleas to stop the affair, but then later she changes her mind. After a considerable amount of hemming and hawing—all of it immensely entertaining—the lovers seem to have found happiness, but wait . . . In any case, it's not really the story that is the point here. The music, of course, is sensational, and James Levine, leading the Met orchestra, and Stratas and Domingo are in peak form. This is not simply a filmed version of an opera that is usually performed onstage, though. The setting, Paris around 1850, is recreated in dazzling fashion, and the lighting and direction by Franco Zeffirelli—who is best known for his 1968 movie rendering of *Romeo and Juliet*—contribute to the movie's enormous visual appeal. Seeing *La Traviata* is something like going to one of those spectacular all-day wedding celebrations that you wish would never end. (In Italian with subtitles.)

G / 1983 / N/A

▲ LEGAL EAGLES

Robert Redford was nearing 50 at the time, and in this eager-to-please comedy-thriller, his twenty-fifth film in twenty-five years as a screen actor, you can tell he wants to party. It was about time. The super-hero stiffs he had been playing the past decade have made us forget the glory days of *Butch Cassidy and the Sundance Kid, The Way We Were,* and *The Sting.* Aging (not badly but visibly), anxious about increasingly vicious critical raps and a diminishing hold on the box office, Redford had obviously decided to try to lighten up. In *Legal Eagles* he plays a nervous, insomnia-racked assistant D.A., the first mere mortal he had portrayed since 1967's *Barefoot in the Park.* He tap dances in the bathroom, croons an off-key chorus of *Singin' in the Rain,* makes a mess as a single father cooking breakfast for his teenage daughter (Jennie Dundas), romances a feisty colleague (Debra Winger), jumps in the sack with Winger's leggy client (Daryl Hannah), gets dumped in the East River (yes, those golden locks do get mussed), and risks death trying to solve a complicated case of art fraud and murder. The part was originally intended for Bill Murray, but Ivan Reitman, who directed Murray in *Stripes, Meatballs,* and *Ghostbusters,* reworked the role for Redford. The teaming of schlock director and class-act star sounds better than it plays. Redford looks uncomfortable when the slapstick turns too broad, and all those ga-ga close-ups work against humanizing his character. The script by Jim Cash and Jack Epps, Jr., whose first effort—*Top Gun*—proved a box-office skyrocket, presents another kind of problem. Trying for the kind of sophisticated comedy-romance Tracy and Hepburn did so splendidly, most notably as sparring lawyers in 1949's *Adam's Rib,* Cash and Epps get the surface right, yet muff the feeling. The film, set in the Manhattan art scene, has a luster the dialogue can't match. Winger, a take-charge actress who seems incapable of making a false move on camera, gets more sparks out of Redford than any of his co-stars since Streisand. Their appealingly unhurried relationship serves to remind us of what we've been missing since teenage-sex comedies drove witty adult romance off the screen. But too often Redford and Winger are obscured by Reitman's pyrotechnics (this film has more fire scenes than *The Towering Inferno*). *Legal Eagles* should have uncorked as a champagne comedy. Instead, it all too quickly runs out of fizz.

PG / 1986 / MCA

▲ THE LEGEND OF BILLIE JEAN

Into the crowded idiom of teen movies, *The Legend of Billie Jean* introduced a new archetype: the Mall Outlaw. It's the sort of story that used to be merely the basis of a Bobbie Gentry single. But this featherweight folktale is endowed with the hallmarks of an adolescent's poem: persecuted heroine, melodramatic narcissism, and the fantasy of a youth underground. When some rowdies wreck the scooter of Billie Jean's younger brother, she demands justice. Instead she gets a sexual assault from one of the rowdies' fathers. As happens in all such ballads, a gun goes off by accident, and Billie Jean goes on the lam from the Corpus Christi trailer park where she lives. As played by Helen Slater, Billie Jean is Rambo, the Pied Piper, and Pat Benatar all rolled into one Botticelli blonde. She catches Jean Seberg's *Saint Joan* on the late show and impulsively cuts her hair short. She then videotapes a message of vindication that makes the local news and makes her Joan of Arc of the trailer park. When Billie Jean's crusade is usurped by her peers—teens throughout Texas adopt her close-cropped look—the movie is onto something: the convenience and disposability of clone culture. But to sustain this media-mad hallucination, *Billie Jean* needed a more whacked-out director than Matthew Robbins, who co-wrote *The Sugarland Express,* which this movie often echoes. Intoxicated by its own improbabilities and buoyed by a strong performances, *Billie Jean* is a nutty, trashy, good bad movie.

PG-13 / 1985 / Key

▲ THE LEGEND OF THE LONE RANGER

For connoisseurs of clinkers only. The story of John Reid, the masked man who avenged the murders of his parents and his Texas Ranger brother with the help of his Indian buddy, Tonto, has fascinated generations since 1933 when it debuted as a radio serial originally written by Fran Striker. In 1938 it began a thirty-three-year run as a cartoon strip and in 1949 became a TV series with Clayton Moore and Jay Silverheels (they also played in two spin-off feature films). The new Kimo Sabe is Klinton Spilsbury, an actor whose inexperience necessitated dubbing his voice by James Keach. Trouble? You betcha.

Spilsbury, who grew up in Chihuahua, Mexico, is more pinup than actor. Only his faithful steed Silver is prettier—and he even does his own whinnies. Tonto, played by another hunk of beefcake, Michael Horse, was saddled with speeches that sound like warmed-over Brando rallies ("One day all nations will be brothers"). But let's be kind. There is something here to quicken the pulse: the sound of the *William Tell* Overture and a hearty "Hi-yo, Silver."

PG / 1981 / CBS/Fox

▲ LETHAL WEAPON

Thanks to a peculiar chemistry and a terrific script, Mel Gibson and Danny Glover lift this movie above mere TV-cop fodder. Gibson is usually cast as the strong, silent type, so it's a nice surprise to see him play a loud, brash Los Angeles police detective. He's suicidal because his wife of eleven years was just killed in a car accident. When he's transferred from narcotics to homicide to give him a break, the effect is a little like taking a drive during rush hour to calm your nerves. His new partner, however, is older family man Glover, who's very much interested in staying alive. Glover's coolheadedness creates an engaging contrast with Gibson's wild-eyed intensity. They have one thing in common: Both served in Vietnam. Now one of Glover's war buddies, Tom Atkins, is mixed up in a huge, ruthless heroin operation. Atkins wants to give away the company secrets, and an enforcer makes sure he takes a rather drastic form of early retirement. Ringleaders Mitchell Ryan and Gary Busey (who seem underused) torture Glover and Gibson to find out how much the cops know, setting up the predictable revenge when Gibson finally Rambos his way free. Although *Lethal Weapon* applies to Mel Gibson's martial arts abilities (and perhaps his state of mind), it could also apply to 24-year-old writer Shane Black's pen. It's wickedly witty. Asks Glover of Gibson: "Did you ever meet anybody you didn't kill?" Things eventually get out of hand, especially for those who don't like a lot of phallic gun caressing and scantily clad, tied-up women. The movie eventually degenerates into one big shootout. But then subtlety obviously wasn't what director Richard (*Superman*) Donner had in mind, and in this case there's

something to be said for all-out guns-blazing action.
R / 1987 / N/A

▲ LET'S SPEND THE NIGHT TOGETHER

The searing rock energy of the Rolling Stones's 1981 U.S. tour was captured on vinyl by their *Still Life* LP. Here is the major motion picture. Director Hal Ashby captured Jagger, Richards, and the others, in some wonderfully intimate glimpses from outdoor (sunny Arizona) and indoor (New Jersey) venues. Jagger, for instance, belts one tune so close to the camera you see his upper molar fillings and popping carotids. As for guitarist Keith Richards, well, phone home, spaceman, and keep those power chords hot. Unfortunately, the film plods along and offers too little. Aside from some bizarre spliced-in newsreel-type scenes of a starving man, an immolation, and a few fleeting backstage teases, it's almost all performing footage. Fans already know the Stones onstage. Why not give their worshipers something priceless, something even scalpers couldn't extort—the humanizing chit-chat, the wearying travel scenes, the girlfriends? Ashby does accomplish one grand coup—a hilariously accelerated time-lapse sequence of the construction of a stage site. Much more could have been made of this project, even without the grim realism of their 1970 tour film, *Gimme Shelter*. There is just too much vain self-celebration going on.
PG / 1983 / Embassy

▲ LETTER TO BREZHNEV

Adapted by Frank Clarke from his 1981 London play, this film is another gem from the bristling new British cinema. Clarke, like director Chris Bernard and stars Alexandra Pigg and Margi Clarke (Frank's sister), is a member of Liverpool's Everyman Theatre, and all were making impressive screen debuts. Pigg and Clarke play two scrappy Liverpudlians, one on welfare, the other yanking out chicken gizzards for a living. Tottering on high heels, uttering dialects as thick as their makeup, these punk princesses pick up two Russian sailors at a club. Clarke simply beds her sailor (Alfred Molina), but Pigg sees her man,

sensitively played by Peter (*Equus*) Firth, as the focus for all her romantic longings. When he returns to the Soviet Union, she writes a letter to Brezhnev asking permission to live there with the man she loves. Raunchy in the extreme, *Letter to Brezhnev* is also hilarious and heartbreaking. Pigg (who once wrestled pythons onstage) and Clarke (a punk comic on British TV) are both smashing.
R / 1986 / Karl-Lorimar

▲ LIANNA

Director John Sayles tackles a tough subject, lesbianism, and makes it into a worthwhile movie by adopting a low-key (also low-budget) approach that seems more direct and honest than that of, say, *Personal Best*. Set in an unnamed college town in New Jersey, the film begins as a story of marital infidelity. Lianna, played by Canadian actress Linda Griffiths, finds out that her husband, Jon De Vries, a disgruntled English professor, is fooling around with some of his students. She even spots him one night rolling around with a coed in a children's sandbox during one of those dreary faculty parties. Lianna then signs up for a course in child psychology, and before too long she too is having an affair—with the instructor, played by Jane Hallaren. The movie has a hard, flat look that gives it a realistic tone; an explicit love scene between the women doesn't really shock, simply because it is presented so unpretentiously. All the performances are fine, and Robyn Reeves is wickedly funny telling Lianna the ins-and-outs of the employment scene in a college town. Another humorous scene is when Lianna, newly liberated from her husband and living alone in an apartment, bumps into another tenant in the basement laundry room. "I'm gay," she announces proudly. The other woman, who couldn't care less, says, "I'm Sheila." Sayles, who also wrote the movie (as he did his previous film, *Return of the Secaucus Seven*), has a cameo role: He's a film instructor on the make for Lianna until he discovers she's having a lesbian affair. His awkward response is quietly hilarious. The whole movie works, in fact, because it is so understated—Hollywood would never do it this way. Sayles made this $300,000 movie in his hometown, Hoboken, New Jersey.
R / 1983 / Vestron

▲ LIFEFORCE

Anyone noting that this film was directed by Tobe Hooper, whose credits include *The Texas Chainsaw Massacre* and *Poltergeist,* will not expect *Lifeforce* to be *Little Women.* Hooper has, though, developed a reputation for doing things with style—however brutal and frenetic—and that's one thing lacking in this film about invaders from space trying to siphon off humanity's vitality. Some of its special effects, by John Dykstra, are flashy, but the lightshow excesses become reminiscent of *Ghostbusters.* The plot, in which an Earth space mission brings back hostile creatures to England, will remind horror buffs of *The Creeping Unknown,* a dreary 1956 movie starring Brian Donlevy. The acting, by Steve Railsback as a returned astronaut and Peter Firth as a British security officer, will remind bank tellers of people milling around in line waiting to cash their paychecks. The life-draining proclivities of the aliens lead to a vampirish subplot, which would have opened the way for clever jokes if Dan O'Bannon and Don Jacoby's script had even a drop of wit. Hooper tries to get mileage out of parading Mathilda May around nude. But May, like the cadaverous extras, gets tiresome. It would have been better to have more transfusions of energy offscreen and fewer on.
R / 1985 / Vestron

▲ LILI MARLENE

At 35, the German director Rainer Werner Fassbinder had already made forty movies, an astonishing output. This one, with a story line involving a young woman caught in the maelstrom of Nazi Germany, is a weak imitation of his own *The Marriage of Maria Braun.* Hanna Schygulla again stars, portraying a cabaret singer whose song (the movie's title) catches on with the German troops. But before the war Schygulla had an affair with a Swiss Jew, and when he turns up in Berlin, trouble begins. Schygulla is coolly elegant, and Fassbinder's beer hall scenes are hypnotically atmospheric. But as her lovesick paramour, Giancarlo Giannini, the hero of such Lina Wertmuller films as *Seven Beauties,* is subdued, almost a cipher. Fassbinder himself seems unable to settle on one story, choosing instead to tell bits and pieces of various lives. Fassbinder

at half speed is still good, but this film is a disappointment. (In German with subtitles.)
R / 1981 / N/A

▲ LILY IN LOVE

Prince Charles, talk to your mother at once. It's time Maggie Smith—that consummate actress who lends her grace, beauty, and delicious wit to this effervescent romantic comedy—was dubbed a Dame. What more does Smith have to prove to join the likes of Peggy Ashcroft and Wendy Hiller in the loftier ranks of the Order of the British Empire? Onstage she's played the classics from Shakespeare to Ibsen. She's won two Academy Awards (*The Prime of Miss Jean Brodie, California Suite*). She's collected the British Oscar for *A Private Function.* She's won the British Tony for *The Way of the World.* Charles, is your mum paying attention? Have her take a break from the pomp and circumstance to catch *Lily in Love.* Smith is cast as a playwright whose actor husband, devilishly well played by Christopher Plummer, is an aging ham of the John Barrymore school. Smith doesn't want him in her new movie (the part calls for a young, handsome European), so Plummer dons a wig, fakes an accent, and transforms himself into an Italian aristocrat. Only the couple's manager, snappily done by Broadway lyricist Adolph Green, is in on the secret. That's the plot, loosley based on Ferenc Molnar's play *The Guardsman,* which the Lunts filmed in 1931. The fun comes in watching Plummer try to seduce his wife into an affair with another man (himself as the Italian rake) and then hate her for succumbing. Plummer's shameless overacting is a delight, but Smith is the film's glory. Her Lily is a woman who aches for romance. How long can she be fooled by her husband's disguise? Onstage such illusions are easier to sustain. In this film, clumsily directed by Hungarian Karoly Makk, the harsh close-ups of Plummer's makeup quickly pull the wool from the audience's eyes, if not Lily's. But technical mishaps and crude plotting can't daunt Maggie Smith. She brings heart and conscience to her role, turning a film soufflé into something more substantial. There's a touch of magic about this kind of acting. Dame Maggie Smith. Sounds right, doesn't it?
PG-13 / 1985 / Vestron

▲ LION OF THE DESERT

One of the things all those petrodollars put the Arabs in position to buy was a new image. This film, about Italy's occupation of Libya from 1912 to 1943, is mostly a brazen propaganda paean to the courage, dignity, and all-around nobility of the Bedouin. Its director, Moustapha Akkad— the Syrian-born American who was responsible for the dreadful 1977 film *Mohammed, Messenger of God*—here belabors for 160 minutes the point that the Fascists under Mussolini were not only evil but also incompetent. In the process Omar Mukhtar, a real-life guerrilla leader, is all but deified. Mukhtar is played by Anthony Quinn, who spent so much time in desert movies (he also played Mohammed's uncle) he probably never got the sand out from between his toes. He is very majestic yet very passionless. Oliver Reed, cast as the ruthless general sent by Mussolini to make the caravans run on time, does his Mr. Mean number. Yes, he slaps his riding crop into his hand in frustration. There is nonstop action, alternating between scenes of Italian atrocities and relatively clean-cut, if bloody, Arab revenge. It is a one-sided polemic of a historical situation that hardly needed one. And, ironically, it was filmed in Libya and received the logistical support of that country's government, which had become as foolishly predatory and adventurist as was Mussolini's Italy.
PG / 1981 / USA

▲ LITTLE DARLINGS

Two of America's most popular juvenile actresses, hardly sweet 16, were put in revealing outfits and a plot that hinges on which will lose her virginity first. Tatum O'Neal, who plays the rich girl at summer camp, and Kristy McNichol, the tough street kid, deserved far better. O'Neal looks mature and poised enough to be running the camp and far too old to be a camper. But because she is a deft professional, she avoids embarrassment. McNichol, who at 17 was actually a year older than Tatum, fits in more comfortably and, despite the succession of hopelessly dumb scenes, is able to arouse some feeling. Young Matt Dillon appears, too—he also survived. The one disaster in the cast is Armand Assante as the counselor O'Neal tries to seduce.

Both screenwriters were women, but the film is smutty and sexist, exploiting young girls' interest in physical matters rather than empathizing with it. The title could have been *Little Floozies*.
R / 1980 / Paramount

▲ THE LITTLE DRUMMER GIRL

Diane Keaton will be a long time living down this film version of John Le Carré's provocative best-seller about the morally bankrupt world of international espionage. Forget that the movie doesn't live up to the book. How can we forgive Keaton for a comically intense performance that distorts what may be Le Carré's most complex work? Director George Roy Hill, who mismanaged the screen translation of Kurt Vonnegut's *Slaughterhouse Five* and John Irving's *The World According to Garp,* must also shoulder some blame—along with screenwriter Loring Mandel —for hammering Le Carré's finely calibrated prose into pulp. The book introduced Charlie, a struggling British actress with pro-Palestinian leanings who fell for an Israeli intelligence operative and became a double agent. Her mission was to help the Israelis trap the elusive Khalil, a Palestinian terrorist. Le Carré was illustrating the seductiveness of terrorism and reflecting his own disenchantment with the irreconcilable claims of both sides. Onscreen Charlie, the plain-faced Brit, is transformed into the cute American Keaton. Joseph, the Israeli agent whose sexual magnetism is supposed to be strong enough to compel Charlie to switch allegiances, is played by Yorgo Vayagis, a charmless actor notable only for his paunch. How will these two ever convey the "seductiveness of terror" for those unfamiliar with the novel? Sami Frey is better and sexier as the legendary Khalil. And Klaus Kinski, as an Israeli intelligence chief who coolly orders an assassination and then phones his wife for a bit of family gossip, steals what there is of the picture. Kinski is pure Le Carré. Keaton is pure Hollywood. Her scenes in training at a PLO camp should send shivers down the spine; instead Keaton can't stop trying to endear herself to the audience. Near the climax, Hill splatters the screen with gore to make his point. The effect is shocking but too late. Keaton's star turn has transformed a good, perhaps great, book into an indefensibly bad movie.
R / 1984 / Warner

▲ THE LITTLE GIRL WHO LIVES DOWN THE LANE

In a kind of *Lolita Meets Psycho*, precocious Jodie (*Taxi Driver*) Foster singlehandedly pulls of an arsenic-and-blue-denim chiller. Alternately nymphet and tomboy, she cleverly conceals the death of her parents and leases a New England house from a shrill snob (piercingly portrayed by Alexis Smith) and her pervert son (Martin Sheen). To keep questions unasked, the 13-year-old neatly wastes the curious with poison. Shirley Temple and Margaret O'Brien were never like this.
PG / 1976 / Vestron

▲ LITTLE MISS MARKER

Walter Matthau kept saying *Little Miss Marker*, the Damon Runyon story that helped make a champ of Shirley Temple in 1934, had never been done right before this version. This was very puzzling, since little seems changed from the 1934 screenplay, though torch singer Bangles Carden turned into a lady named Amanda, for Julie Andrews's sake. Sure, it's fun to watch Matthau; he's a very tough Broadway inhabitant indeed, who goes soft for this beautiful little doll left to him as collateral on a bet by her daddy. But is he more right than Adolphe Menjou was in 1934? Menjou, who was an elegant gent, made a perfect betting-parlor slob as Sorrowful Jones, and he talked Runyon like a native. Matthau, one of the movies' born slobs, is good, but he doesn't upset the form charts. (He's in a dead heat with Bob Hope, who was in a 1949 version with Lucille Ball.) A lot of the Runyon flavor—names like Bonnie the Gouge, Sore Toe, Dizzy Memphis—is missing, too. That leaves Little Miss Marker. To make it work, she has to be the cutest kid you've ever seen. Does Sara Stimson fill the bill? Absolutely, for the younger citizens. But for anyone who's ever seen that Temple filly run, the entries were closed long ago. Shirley will always be the class of the little-doll field.
PG / 1980 / MCA

▲ A LITTLE NIGHT MUSIC

Oh, dear, Elizabeth Taylor never could sing, and she wasn't exactly at her playing weight in this era. But that's not the major problem with this embarrassing movie adaptation of the Tony-winning Broadway musical, which was itself based on Ingmar Bergman's *Smiles of a Summer Night*. The fault certainly lies not in other stars: Len Cariou, Laurence Guitard, Diana Rigg, Lesley-Anne Down, and Hermione Gingold. Producer Eliot Kastner reportedly had to go begging, though, to find a distributor, New World Pictures. That's probably because of the cliché-ridden screenplay and Harold Prince's inept directing. Even Stephen Sondheim's splendid music comes out badly mangled. When he wrote "Send in the Clowns," Sondheim didn't mean for them to be a producer and a director.
PG / 1978 / Embassy

▲ A LITTLE ROMANCE

About the only good moment in this perfectly awful film occurs when director George Roy Hill screens some clips from his celebrated *Butch Cassidy and the Sundance Kid*. That's at the beginning, and it's all downhill from there. Diane Lane plays an American teenager living in Paris with her rich stepfather (Arthur Hill) and on-the-make mother (Sally Kellerman). When she meets and falls in love with a young French boy (Theonious Bernard), Mom throws a fit—and the story lurches off into absurdity. The problem is that director Hill saddles two pubescent children with grown-up emotions that make them seem as if they are playacting more than they really are. Poor Laurence Olivier's role as a kindly old diplomat borders embarrassingly on camp.
PG / 1979 / Warner

▲ A LITTLE SEX

In fact, you get hardly any sex in this dismal comedy set in self-consciously hip Manhattan. Screenwriter Robert DeLaurentis and director Bruce (TV's "The White Shadow") Paltrow cast Tim (*Animal House*) Matheson as an ad director who wants to marry his girlfriend to prove he can give up skirt-chasing. After all, as he whines to his brother, Edward Herrmann, "Why can't I have a cup of coffee with a woman without winding up in bed?" He spends too many mornings in "other people's showers," he complains. Life's tough. Reform through marriage to Kate Capshaw, a grade school teacher, proves even worse. Matheson walks around gawking at women; his head swivels more on Madison Avenue than Linda Blair's did in *The Exorcist*. To save the marriage, he rationalizes a few harmless cheats. The rest is pure adulterated nonsense. Matheson is almost too pretty for the role and without depth; Capshaw, playing a character devoid of motivation or sense, at least makes a visually smashing debut, looking like a younger, frizzed Julie Christie.

R / 1982 / MCA

▲ LITTLE SHOP OF HORRORS

Just when you thought Hollywood had lost the knack for making musicals, along came this raucous rib-tickler to put a song and scare in your heart. Based on the off-Broadway musical hit, *Little Shop* is packed with irresistible silliness. Rick Moranis plays Seymour, a shnook who tends plants in a tacky flower shop. Three singing street urchins named Ronette, Crystal, and Chiffon (delightfully sh'bopped by Michelle Weeks, Tichina Arnold, and Tisha Campbell) act as a chorus for the drama ahead. Seymour pines for Audrey (Ellen Greene), a ditzy blond flower arranger with a penchant for push-up bras and abusive men. One day Seymour happens on a tiny fly trap plant. When the bud starts burgeoning to bozo size, Seymour sees his chance at winning fame, money, and his woman. There's a catch: The plant, winningly designed by Lyle Conway, thrives on blood. "Feed me, Seymour," sings the "mean green mother from outer space" in the potent voice of Levi Stubbs of the Four Tops. Seymour finds plant food in the person of Audrey's sadistic boyfriend (Steve Martin), a biker dentist who enjoys torturing his patients. In black Elvis wig and leather jacket, Martin is savagely funny. Greene, in the part she originated onstage, does a star-making turn. Singing of her dream life as a housewife who "cooks like Betty Crocker and looks like Donna Reed," she never patronizes her role. Screenwriter-lyricist Howard Ashman and composer Alan Menken, whose score is sly and sassy, give her two movie-stopping ballads ("Somewhere That's Green" and "Suddenly, Seymour"). There are tasty bits by John Candy, Christopher Guest, James Belushi, and especially Bill Murray as Martin's most masochistic patient. If director Frank Oz misplaces the show's pocket-size charm in mounting a big-screen climax, he more than compensates by showing that musicals can still be magic.

PG-13 / 1986 / Warner

▲ LITTLE TREASURE

Any movie that has Margot Kidder, Burt Lancaster, and Ted Danson in its cast starts off with such an advantage, you'd think it couldn't help but be at least moderately involving. Oops. Kidder demonstrates that enchanting combination of vulnerability and armor-hided stubbornness at which she is so adept. Danson is so relaxed and easygoing it's impossible not to identify with him. Lancaster is lovably grizzled and blustery. But they have almost no movie to use all that acting in. Writer-director Alan Sharp, who had written such shoot-'em-up films as *Ulzana's Raid* but had never directed before, seems to have no sense of the way people really talk and/or no ability to embellish the way they talk in a literate way. His plot is not convincing for a second. Lancaster is an ex-bank robber who has spent most of his life in Mexico, where he invites his estranged daughter, Kidder, for a visit. Danson, an ex-seminarian, has run off to Mexico for reasons never really made clear. The treasure of the title is some buried loot Lancaster stashed in New Mexico; the search for that cache becomes the movie's focal point. The three principals and such deft supporting actors as John Pearce and James Hall pull the film along for a while, but they might as well have been dragging a set of refrigerators across the Mexican desert that was the main location. It's interesting to watch for a little while but all too obviously pointless.

R / 1985 / RCA/Columbia

▲ LOCAL HERO

Bill Forsyth wrote and directed this enchanting story of a young oil conglomerate hotshot, played by Peter (*Animal House*) Riegert, who is dispatched from Houston to sweet-talk residents of a Scottish coastal village into selling drilling rights to their land. With the same offbeat, idiosyncratic humor that made his *Gregory's Girl* a winner, Forsyth immerses Riegert's computer whiz

in the hypnotic rhythm of life in a remote corner of the world. The village life is so beautifully textured it has the same seductive effect on audiences as Riegert experiences in the film. Some scenes—when actors are silhouetted against the deep blue twilight horizon, shimmering clear water and distant mountains—verge on the mystical. (The sound track, by Dire Straits' Mark Knopfler, flows hauntingly, too.) Indeed, after Riegert phones home to talk about the northern lights with child-like wonder, his boss, Burt Lancaster, choppers in to see Paradise Found for himself—providing the setup for an utterly transporting climatic twist.
PG / 1983 / N/A

▲ THE LONELY GUY

According to this sometimes satisfying, frequently stalled comedy, being without a lover in New York City is more dangerous than riding the subways at four in the morning. Adapted (by *Taxi* vets Ed Weinberger and Stan Daniels) from Bruce Jay Friedman's *The Lonely Guy's Book of Life,* the plot chronicles the misfortunes of a lovelorn greeting-card writer whose girlfriend forsakes him for a ballet dancer. In the title role Steve Martin expertly sustains the cartoonish character through what is essentially a series of single-again skits: getting a dog, prowling the bars, and meeting the perfect woman (Judith Ivey), who then rejects him "because you're so right for me." Despite Martin's facility, pairing him with director Arthur Hiller was one of Hollywood's worst shotgun marriages. Martin's wit and delivery mock traditional comedy, while Hiller, who, after all, directed *Love Story,* is a slave to convention. In those moments that combine social commentary and surrealistic humor, Martin rises above the directorial mismatch. When Martin's pathetic pal (Charles Grodin) throws a party peopled only by cardboard cutouts of famous folks or when Martin goes up on his roof to call the name of his beloved and finds a dozen other guys doing the same thing, the comedy is both inventive and incisive. But more often it undercuts its star's unorthodox talents. Providing able assistance are Grodin, a frumpy misfit on the social circuit, and Dr. Joyce Brothers, whose sexual habits serve as the punch lines for some funny sight gags.
R / 1984 / MCA

▲ LONELY HEARTS

The Australian cultural invasion reached the point where films as slight as this one—which is a sort of *Marty Goes to Melbourne*—were thrown into the import bin. Like the '50s TV play and movie in which Rod Steiger and then Ernest Borgnine portrayed aging men in desperate searches for romance, this is a quiet story about a shy couple trying to overcome years of social isolation. Norman Kaye, a stage actor making his movie debut, plays a piano tuner who, at 50, finds himself alone after years of caring for his mother. Wendy (*My Brilliant Career*) Hughes is the sexually insecure spinster he meets through a dating service. They are both involving actors, though Hughes seems a touch too terrified by her parents and everything else, while Kaye seems a little too much in control. *Lonely Hearts* won Australia's 1982 Best Film award, and Paul Cox was nominated for Best Director. Americans, though, may find it on the oversubdued side and not sufficiently expressive to compensate for the lack of action.
R / 1982 / Embassy

▲ LONELY LADY

Garbage in, garbage out, as the computer folks say. This movie is based on the 1977 Harold Robbins novel and directed by Peter Sasdy, whose credits include *Welcome to Blood City.* The film stars Pia Zadora. Anyone who watches such a movie expecting intellectual edification deserves what he or she gets. Zadora plays a young woman who is still in high school when she not only manages to marry a top-level screenwriter three times her age but immediately begins to rewrite his scripts. She soon leaves him and starts cutting a sexual swath through Hollywood, like a buzz saw through cardboard. She becomes a success, but at what cost? Let's see, that was $11.95 for the shoes, $20.50 for the dress, $115.73 for the eye makeup. Zadora is appealing in her forlorn way but laughably unconvincing as a writer of serious screenplays. Fan letters to John Travolta, maybe; screenplays, never. The rest of the cast is similarly incredible. Pia's screenwriter husband is played by Lloyd ("Dynasty") Bochner, whose basic acting style is to tuck his chin into his chest and speak in very deep, meaningful tones. He overacts wildly, though even Olivier couldn't do much with a line like "That's life: hurting and being hurt." Director Sasdy elicits universally hammy performances from everyone in his cast, which also includes Jared ("Dallas") Martin. It's so hard to take anything about the film seriously that even a rape scene involving a garden hose is not offensive, only silly. None of which, of course, is likely to do anything to daunt Zadora's husband and favorite financier, Meshulam Riklis, who bankrolled this travesty. What the heck. Why not give Lady Macbeth a whirl, Pia?

R / 1983 / MCA

▲ LONE WOLF MCQUADE

To call this the best film martial artist-actor Chuck Norris has made should not mean that he had any 1983 Oscars sewed up. Let's not forget his standards were set by such movies as *The Octogon* and *Goon Guys Wear Black*. But this one is far more elaborately plotted, by writer B. J. Nelson, and well directed, by Steve Carver. The title character is a maverick Texas Ranger who is so gung ho about kung fu that his superior takes him off the Big Case: going after David Carradine, who is similarly kung-gung but deals arms to "terrorists and stuff." Thrown in are a subplot about Norris's kidnapped daughter; a dwarf in a wheelchair (Daniel Frishman); the stunning Barbara Carrera, who gets her kicks from both kung fu men; an amusing Tex-Mex Ranger pal (Robert Beltran); some crisp combat scenes; and a slow-motion love scene finishing in a puddle with Norris caressing Carrera and Carrera caressing a garden hose. You may not leave the theater humming "Chuckie's in Love," but it's nice for once to see Norris end up with something other than a mangled body to keep him company. Best scene is the one in which Norris, buried alive in his hyper-souped Land-Rover, drives right out of his shallow grave. It's straight from *Night of the Living Dead*.

PG / 1983 / Vestron

▲ THE LONG RIDERS

Jesse James rides again—sort of. With inescapable logic but questionable results, director Walter Hill hit upon the notion of casting the real-life

brothers Keach (Stacy and James) as the historical brothers James (Frank and Jesse). Then he contracted the Carradine clan (David, Keith, and Robert) to play Cole, Jim, and Bob Younger, and hired Randy and Dennis Quaid and Nicholas and Christopher Guest also to portray onscreen siblings. Hill's visual approach is arresting as it was in *The Warriors*, and his penchant for shooting gunfights in slow motion with plenty of ketchup flying about recalls Peckinpah at his peak. Once the all-in-the-family novelty wears off, though, so does the raison d'etre of this otherwise straightforward retelling of an oft-told Western tale.

R / 1980 / MGM/UA

▲ LOOKER

What this film reminds you of is the vapid kind of girl to whom the title alludes—a beautiful package with nothing between the ears. The premise is promising: writer-director Michael (*The Andromeda Strain*) Crichton envisions a time in the not-so-distant future when our actions could be regulated by hypnotic suggestions from TV screens. A slow-witted plastic surgeon (Albert Finney), whose patients keep dying, stumbles on a dastardly plot involving manipulation of the masses by computer-created images. He befriends lovely Susan Dey (she later hit it luckier with TV's "L.A. Law") in a battle against megalomaniac James Coburn. The performances are uniformly wooden. Crichton has some passing fun with TV commercials, but the screenplay is futuristic folderol . . . folderol . . . folderol. You are falling deeply asleep. You will do as we say. You will not waste your money on renting this movie.

PG / 1981 / Warner

▲ LOOKING FOR MR. GOODBAR

Director Richard Brooks turned a stunning book into this unpleasant movie. In the central role of a woman who is a dedicated schoolteacher by day and a sex-starved prowler of singles bars by night, Diane Keaton dominates the film with a frightening hot/cold, kind/cruel portrayal of schizophrenia. It's an enduring, powerful performance, Keaton's best in some ways. But with

the exception of then-newcomer Richard Gere's searing portrayal of a switchblade-wielding stud, the secondary characters are reduced to simple stereotypes by the noisome direction, wasting the talents of such people as Tuesday Weld, Tom Berenger, LeVar Burton, and William Atherton. While Brooks does stage a stunning climax, the rest of the film is like the sex it depicts—cold, impersonal, and ultimately disappointing.
R / 1977 / Paramount

▲ LOOKIN' TO GET OUT

It's not much of a plot: Jon Voight and Burt Young are two New York gamblers on the run from loan sharks. They fly off to Vegas and with the help of a waiter with a system try to hit the jackpot in a no-limit blackjack game. Complications ensue in Vegas when Voight meets old flame Ann-Margret, an ex-hooker now living with wealthy hotel owner Richard Bradford and a young daughter, who turns out to be Voight's child. The climax, smacking uncomfortably of *The Sting,* offers little surprise. As star, coproducer, and writer (with Al Schwartz), Voight is obviously after something deeper than the TV movie surface implies. His bravery extends beyond casting his ex-wife (Marcheline Bertrand), daughter (Angelina), and girlfriend (Stacey Pickren) in the same film. There is dedication and skill here, and Voight's energy gives the film backbone. But *Lookin' to Get Out* never makes it as caper, comedy, or character study. Flexed for spontaneity, the result is mostly strain. Despite cogent supporting work by Young and a remarkably subdued, poignant Ann-Margret, plus sympathetic direction by Hal (*Coming Home*) Ashby, the script dribbles away its potential with repetition and hokum.
R / 1982 / CBS/Fox

▲ LORD OF THE RINGS

Animator Ralph (*Fritz the Cat*) Bakshi had the courage at least to take on J. R. R. Tolkien's cult classic. No matter how expert his adaptation, however, many of the trilogy's most devout worshipers were bound to be disappointed. As it turns out, unfortunately, almost all of them were. For those non-hobbitual Tolkien readers, this saga

of a place called Middle-earth is not only dull but impossibly confusing. The technological cartoon display is lacking in, of all things, animation; drama has been sacrificed for panorama. While it's awash with color and sophisticated drawing, the film picks up only when one minor but perfectly rendered character, the pathetic Gollum, comes sniveling onto the screen. The rest of the interminable 2 hours and 11 minutes is one listless, endless battle scene. The final insult is that this is just the first half of the story, with the end left unresolved until some distant "Rings II." Frodo preserve us.
PG / 1978 / Thorn/EMI

▲ THE LORDS OF DISCIPLINE

No, this is not a sequel, not *Another Officer and a Gentleman,* even though David Keith (Richard Gere's heartsick pal in *AO&aG*) stars. He plays a morally upright, politically liberalized cadet at a southern military academy who is entrusted with safeguarding the campus's first black student. (The film, set in the mid '60s, is based on Pat Conroy's novel of the same name.) Keith soon learns of a menacing secret society of cadets who get off on terrorizing the black, apparently with the acquiescence of the academy's power structure. It's not a bad premise, but problems crop up: the endless ranting and hazing, cute in *Private Benjamin,* unsettling in *An Officer and a Gentleman,* here is just plain excessive. It seems time to declare a movie moratorium on demeaning tactics intended to instill discipline and honor. Another question: Why are no girls in the plot? The audience needs them in a grim flick like this almost as much as the cadets do on weekends. As for the black cadet, played with laughable stoicism by a Golden Gloves fighter from New York named Mike Breland, if he is really a test case in early '60s civil rights in a lily-white southern military institute, where's the NAACP? The courts? The media? How could the masked thugs carve their logo in the kid's back without at least making Walter Cronkite's news? A film like this demands some hint at least of reality to make the melodrama seem plausible. Keith handles his role well, but he was still waiting to be discharged into a film that could stretch his considerable talents.
R / 1983 / Paramount

▲ LOSIN' IT

Directed by Curtis (*The Little Dragons*) Hanson and starring Tom (*Top Gun*) Cruise, Jackie Earle (*The Bad News Bears*) Haley, and Shelley Long late of TV's "Cheers," this latest example of the horny-high-schooler movie is an asinine waste of time. Sleep. Cut the grass. Play mah-jongg. Eat a doughnut. Do anything, but don't reward the greedy condescension of the producers by paying to rent or buy it on video. Okay, you adore Shelley, dote on Cruise. Believe us, you will like them longer if you never see how far the mighty once fell into the movie quicksand.

R / 1983 / Embassy

▲ LOST IN AMERICA

A Los Angeles couple give up their high-paying jobs, drop out of society, and head across the country in a motor home. They're determined, says director/co-writer/star Albert Brooks, to find themselves and "touch Indians." What ensues, however, is not a comedic journey but a 91-minute ego trip for Brooks. He is onscreen almost the whole time, and he has not only given himself the best lines but also nearly all the lines. Though he's often funny in his backhanded, skewed, bitter way, this comedy has no focus. It's not clear whether the materialistic world that he has left behind or the dull wilderness he's entered is being lampooned by his preachy monologues. The only clear theme has to do with nostalgia for the Peter Fonda–Jack Nicholson–Dennis Hopper film *Easy Rider,* which is mentioned so often that its plot becomes clearer than *Lost in America*'s. Julie Hagerty plays Brooks's wife to no great effect, though in her defense it must be said that Lady Diana could have shown up in this role and nobody would have noticed, so overbearing is Brooks. Among the supporting cast, only producer-director Garry Marshall, in a rare acting gig, has any impact; he is cast as a Las Vegas casino manager whom Brooks tries to con into refunding money Hagerty has lost. Most of the film seems as lightly conceived as if the script were written on a napkin at lunch. At one point Brooks is stopped for speeding by an Arizona cop; when the cop learns of Brooks's passion for *Easy Rider,* he lets him go. The scene is typical, one long straight line waiting for a punch that never comes. It's as if Brooks is saying, "A funny thing happened to me on the way to this movie, but I'm not going to tell you what it was."

R / 1985 / Warner

▲ LOVE AND MONEY

Producer-writer-director James Toback, a Harvard grad who refused to quit after his first film, *Fingers,* bombed in 1978, mentioned in his official bio that he "never studied filmmaking." Don't think it doesn't show. His farfetched plot concerns a mild-mannered Los Angeles banker whose sudden love for the wife of a Howard Hughes-like mogul draws him into an assassination plot in a banana republic. The hero, Ray (*Willie and Phil*) Sharkey, finds himself forced to deliver such lines as these (to Italian starlet Ornella Muti): "I'm your father. You're my mother. I'm your husband. You're my wife. I'm your chauffeur. You're my car." Sharkey is as good as can be expected but, like Hollywood veteran King Vidor (who this time acts instead of directs), Klaus Kinski, and Armand Assante, he is totally wasted.

R / 1982 / N/A

▲ LOVE AT FIRST BITE

When Drac came back this time, it was to a disco beat. The transmogrified Transylvanian fetches up in the Big Apple in the 1970s with a sweet tooth for fashion model Susan Saint James. The tone is one of camp (high) and comedy (low). George Hamilton is a delightful Count—charming and handsome, drolly sighing, "Just once I'd like to go out and eat . . . potato chips." Saint James, though, is all wrong and, as a psychiatrist who is out for the Count, Richard Benjamin is, well, out for the count. Although the film is occasionally hilarious, many jokes thud, and the "bat" who doubles for Hamilton could set special effects back ten years. In his first feature, TV commercials director Stan Dragoti (then Cheryl Tiegs's hubby) concocted a sporadically trenchant spoof but seems to have bitten off a little more than he could chew. The film did set off a wave of horror send-ups, if that can count as a saving grace.

PG / 1979 / Warner

▲ LOVE CHILD

The producer of this film, Paul Maslansky, came upon his plot during a 1979 "60 Minutes" broadcast. *Love Child* is based on the experiences of Terry Jean Moore, a young Florida woman who was sentenced to fifteen years of imprisonment and probation for a $5 robbery. She subsequently became pregnant by a guard in a maximum security institution and successfully fought to bear and keep her child. Director Larry (*Goodbye, Columbus*) Peerce created a movie that undergoes a metamorphosis nearly as remarkable as the process of becoming a mother. What starts out as a disturbingly gritty look at an unfeeling, Draconian penal system ends up as an almost heartwarming hymn to love and hope. Screen newcomer Amy Madigan gives an astonishingly mature and convincing performance as Moore, a tough-talking but fragile woman cast down into a Stygian prison population of what she calls "crazies, sneaks, and dykes." Beau (*Norma Rae*) Bridges offers one of his best efforts as the seemingly tender guard who leaves town in a hurry with his wife and kids after learning that he has impregnated Madigan. Mackenzie Phillips is also fine in an unexpected, bizarre turn as a butchy, tattooed lesbian who turns out to be just about as full of human kindness as Bridges is empty. *Love Child* is a gripping, well-acted film, and if you can't handle the grueling beginning, stick with it; it'll change.
R / 1982 / Warner

▲ A LOVE IN GERMANY

Only once has an actress in a non-English-speaking role won an Academy Award. That was when Sophia Loren got an Oscar for the Italian-made *Two Women*. If quality was any barometer in such contests, though, Polish-born Hanna Schygulla—known principally for the eighteen films she made with German director Rainer Werner Fassbinder—would have been a shoo-in for an Academy Award. (Sally Field got it in real life for *Places in the Heart*.) The range and subtlety she brings to this film transcend language barriers and subtitles. The luminous Schygulla, at the peak of her powers, plays a hausfrau in a small German town during World War II. She falls in love with a young handyman, Piotr Lysak, while her husband serves in the army, but this is no common tale of adultery. Polish director Andrzej Wajda is concerned with exposing the infectious spread of Nazism into the fiber of German life. Schygulla's lover is a Polish prisoner of war, and the law expressly forbids, under penalty of death, sexual relations between Germans and "inferior" foreigners. The law, of course, cannot be enforced without local informants. Most movies about this period put the onus of evil on the Nazi hierarchy. Wajda uses this film to indict those allegedly "good" Germans, exemplified by Marie-Christine Barrault as a scheming neighbor and Bernhard Wicki as a cowardly doctor, who allowed human rights to be trampled for their own venal ends. In this context, Schygulla's progressively heedless and hopeless love affair with the Pole—who refuses to deny his heritage in order to save himself—takes on heroic proportions. Schygulla charts her character's course from eroticism to political passion with dazzling virtuosity. Her final scene of disgrace is shattering.
R / 1984 / RCA/Columbia

▲ LOVE ON THE RUN

Few artists so relentlessly attempted to rewrite their lives in their work as French director François Truffaut. This is another in the series starring Truffaut's alter ego, actor Jean-Pierre Leaud, that began in 1958 with *The 400 Blows*. Here Leaud is a writer obsessed with fiction that is faintly disguised autobiography and mostly about his calculating relationships with women. Flashback clips from *The 400 Blows* provide a tragic perspective (also reminders of how spectacular Leaud, then thirteen, was in that film). But this is basically a comedy, filled with the beautiful women Truffaut likes to think of himself surrounded by—Marie-France Pisier, Dani, and Dorothée in this case. It is typically fluid, self-deprecating, and in a cynical French way, delightful. (In French with subtitles.)
Unrated / 1978 / Warner

▲ LOVESICK

They could have called this film "14," since it is another case of Dudley Moore playing a middle-aged man consumed by lust for a young

woman, and the object of his fixation in this case, Elizabeth McGovern, is at least the equivalent of Bo Derek, adjusted for inflation. Or they could have called it *Play It Again, Marshall,* since it resembles *Play It Again, Sam,* which was written by *Lovesick* writer-director Marshall Brickman's old buddy Woody Allen. Or they could have decided not to bother with it at all, which would have been best for all concerned. Moore, as a New York psychoanalyst, is likable enough, but most of the movie's jokes are visual, and he spends much of the film reacting. Eventually he just seems reacted out. McGovern, as a new-in-town playwright from Illinois, looks like the thinking man's Brooke Shields; she's so infectiously charming a couple of unflattering close-ups that accentuate her face's chubbiness don't hurt her. What does hurt is that she doesn't have any funny lines either. And the *Play It Again, Sam* gimmick, which involves an apparition of Sigmund Freud instead of Bogart, is disastrous. Alec Guinness plays Freud as if he were Obi-Wan Kenobi with an Austrian accent, and the byplay between him and Moore is embarrassing; there is even a Freudian slip joke. The stalwart supporting cast includes John Huston, Alan King, David Strathairn, Ron Silver (whose Al Pacino-like portrayal of an overbearing actor is the film's highlight), and artist Larry Rivers, out of his element as an actor. That there is no real point to the proceedings is forgivable. Light comedy has its place. This film, though, is so fluffy it floats right off the screen.
PG / 1983 / Warner

▲ LOVE STREAMS

Hollywood's maverick director John Cassavetes fashioned this dark, exciting, and ultimately entrancing movie about the lives of a brother and sister, played by Cassavetes and his wife, Gena Rowlands. Cassavetes directed and co-wrote the screenplay; he also wrote some of the music. The character he portrays is an alcoholic novelist addicted to women. The opening scenes in a dim club, where he falls in love with Diahnne Abbott, a second-rate chanteuse, are breathtakingly beautiful. Rowlands is on the verge of a nervous breakdown—or maybe she already had it. In the midst of a divorce from her husband, Seymour Cassel, and a bitter custody battle over their daughter, Risa Martha Blewitt, she decides to move in with her brother until the storm has passed—a literal storm as well as a figurative one. The movie weaves Cassavetes's and Rowlands's lives together over a few days of madness in Los Angeles as they fight, try to comfort each other, and keep from slipping into total emotional disintegration. At one point Rowlands brings some horses, chickens, and goats home in order to give her brother something to love. The movie title is her definition of love: It never ceases, only flows forever in a stream. Cassavetes over the years has acted in big commercial movies (*The Dirty Dozen, Rosemary's Baby, The Fury*) to finance his own smaller, more personal films. With some exceptions, like 1980's *Gloria,* they have been strangely inaccessible. This one is different. Although at times it is harsh and violent, *Love Streams* is the director's most straightforward and involving movie.
PG-13 / 1984 / MGM/UA

▲ LOVING COUPLES

Surprise: Marriage, not infidelity or divorce, wins this one. The victory comes, of course, only after some fooling around that is so innocently portrayed that the R rating seems indefensible. James Coburn is a workaholic doctor; his wife, Shirley MacLaine, also a doctor, is bored and neglected. After she leaves him for a patient, Stephen Collins, Coburn moves in with Collins's ex-girlfriend, Susan Sarandon, a TV weather girl. The movie can't decide whether it is farce or a morality play, but there are funny scenes. Coburn plays his role broadly, sometimes substituting wide-screen, toothy grins for wit, and Collins seems almost too pretty as a Beverly Hills real estate salesman whom women instinctively want to bed. But MacLaine, then 46, looked wonderful, and the delight of the movie is Sarandon, whose quirks are endearing. A subplot involving Collins and Sally Kellerman as a home buyer who wants to see only the bedrooms is amusing, if heavy-handed. After a diverting 110 minutes, sex object Collins gets his, which should please almost everyone.
R / 1980 / Vestron

▲ LUCAS

Despite, or perhaps because of, the fact that this movie about teenagers has no big name Brat Packers to showcase, it is engrossing. From the looks of it, writer-director David Seltzer might have gone to the John Hughes school of film-making: He treats teenagers as intelligent human beings with a wide range of emotions, not just as beer-guzzling sexual automatons. Corey (*Murphy's Romance*) Haim gives a captivating performance as a 14-year-old free-thinking nerd who's an accelerated student at a local high school. He befriends and then falls in love with a slightly older, exceptionally cute girl, Kerri (*The Goonies*) Green, who has just moved to town. There's a great chemistry between them as they spend an idyllic summer together that translates beautifully on film. She sees him as unique as she shares his passion for insects and classical music. But when school starts, Green starts going out with the star football player, Charlie (*Platoon*) Sheen. Wildly jealous, the pint-sized Haim cons the football coach into letting him play in the opening-day game, risking injury and ridicule. This isn't just another *Rocky–Karate Kid* film, though. In his directorial debut Seltzer manages to avoid the stereotypical conclusions that so often dominate teen flicks. Instead he seriously explores the emotions of adolescents caught between friendship and love at an age when it's especially easy to confuse the two.

PG-13 / 1986 / CBS/Fox

▲ LUST IN THE DUST

It's hard to resist a movie most critics hate so much. "Witless," sniffed a reviewer for *The New York Times*. "Awful," echoed Rex Reed, who added that in his opinion the film "produces the kind of green reaction you get from eating a rancid burrito." Well, what did they expect from a whacked-out Western parody starring has-been '50s hunk Tab Hunter and three hundred-pound female impersonator Divine—*High Noon*? What *Lust in the Dust* delivers instead is tacky, hit-and-miss hilarity. Just the sight of Divine gussied up in full dance-hall-girl drag riding a donkey that weighs less than she/he offers more laughs than a barrel full of teenage sex comedies. And Hunter, wearing the de rigueur serape, apes Clint Eastwood's clenched teeth to perfection. Lainie Kazan also makes a spirited contribution as Divine's brothel-owning sister. Separate halves of a treasure map have been tattooed on the siblings' ample derrieres. (Their cheek-to-cheek union is a consummation devoutly to be missed.) But these are ladies who know how to give an audience a chops-smacking good time; so do Cesar Romero as a crooked padre, Geoffrey Lewis as a bandit leader, and especially Nedra Volz as a diminutive hooker known as Big Ed. It's a long way from Noel Coward or even Mel (*Blazing Saddles*) Brooks, and director Paul Bartel could have goosed up the pace a bit, but those in search of a smattering of cheap laughs will find *Lust in the Dust* the perfect oasis.

R / 1985 / New World

M

▲ MACARONI

Few films have had a starting point as charming as this Italian production directed by Ettore Scola. An American, Jack Lemmon, is in Naples on business when he is accosted by an Italian, Marcello Mastroianni. While a serviceman in Italy after World War II, Lemmon had had a romance with an Italian woman, then jilted her.

Mastroianni is the woman's brother. To protect his sister's feelings, he had started writing letters to her in English under Lemmon's name and was never able to stop. The sister has long since married, but she is still enthralled with Lemmon. And why not? Mastroianni's letters have made him seem to be a combination of James Bond, Superman, and Albert Schweitzer. It's a wonderful idea, especially as Lemmon comes to identify with his mythical self in the letters. It's also gratifying to see these two distinguished actors playing against each other, Lemmon all American intensity and nervousness, Mastroianni resigned, with an eternity of patience. But this film is far more casual, far more loosely structured than most Italian movies. Lemmon often lapses into those exaggerated cringes of exasperation he's famous for as if to fill what he perceived, correctly, to be dreadful lulls in the proceedings. The humor in the situation is largely unexploited. The one scene where it's pursued, in which Mastroianni's family insists that Lemmon demonstrate the piano-playing prowess he has often written about, seems only a setup to let Lemmon demonstrate that he is in real life an accomplished pianist. The film's ending is also so horribly sentimental you feel like kicking the screen.

PG / 1985 / Paramount

▲ MACARTHUR

Gregory Peck looks and acts uncannily like the old general in this predictable and flat reenactment of the road from Corregidor to Korea. The big moments are all there: "I shall return," he says. He wades ashore for the photographers. He rehabilitates Japan, overruns Korea, denounces war, and tells Congress that "old soldiers never die." The filmmakers tried for the ambivalence that worked so well in Patton, but Peck has no telling scenes to play. His MacArthur is at once a Great Historical Figure and an old, vain bore. The battle scenes are bloody and loud. MacArthur's aides hand him earplugs. You'll have to supply your own.

PG / 1977 / MCA

▲ MACARTHUR'S CHILDREN

After World War II, Japan's culture, as well as its territory, was occupied by American troops commanded by Gen. Douglas MacArthur. The emotion and turmoil of that experience provide the background to this sometimes stunning, sometimes puzzling film directed by Masahiro (The Demon Pond) Shinoda. It focuses on three children in early adolescence. All are students of a teacher whose husband returns from the war having lost a leg. Shinoda has an eye for screen landscapes worthy of Fellini; most of his scenes

are beautifully framed. The motivations behind the action are often bizarre, at least to a Westerner, and sometimes the characters' reactions seem unaccountable. Perhaps no subtitle can explicate cultural differences. There is also a too predictable showdown baseball game between the children's school and a contingent of U.S. soldiers. But the film does have its penetrating moments, partly because of the expressive performances by the youngsters, Takaya Yamauchi, Yoshiyuki Omori, and Shiori Sakura, and by the actress playing the teacher, Masako Natsume. Shinoda succeeds to some extent just by raising the question of how the Japanese absorbed the profound shock of the MacArthur period. One day they were fighting a vicious war against the U.S., the next day they were in effect America's protégés. Where, indeed, did all of the animosity go? (In Japanese with subtitles.)

PG / 1985 / N/A

▲ MADAME ROSA

In a just world, Simone Signoret might have won her second Oscar for her performance in this Gallic film as a former streetwalker who runs a boardinghouse for the children of young Pigalle hookers. (She had won in 1959 for Room at the Top, and this movie itself did take the Best Foreign Film Oscar.) Tough and blustery one moment and heartbreakingly feeble the next, Mme. Rosa is an ideal showcase for the versatility of Signoret. Samy Ben Youb is also affecting as a young Arab who was raised by Rosa, a Jew, and becomes her protector. Director Moshe Mizrahi settles for a distasteful and disappointing ending that is also unhappily reminiscent of Psycho. Yet he largely succeeds in maintaining the humor and dignity of a film that could easily have been crude and maudlin. (In French with subtitles.)

Unrated / 1978 / Vestron

▲ MAD MAX

Viewing this film is a lot like opening up one of those "Secret Origins" comic books that tell how Superman or Spider Man got his start in the superhero business. Such efforts, though not as well crafted as their descendants, offer insights into the character's past. The "prequel" to the surprise 1982 hit The Road Warrior, this 1979 Australian film had a limited run in the States. But thanks to Mel Gibson's triumph in *The Year of Living Dangerously*, Max got another chance at building a box office. Today, it's a video staple. Gibson, in the title role, plays a leather-clad highway patrolman in a futuristic Australian out-back. He is driven to a frenzy of vengeance by a gang of bikers who attack his wife, son, and best friend. As in *The Road Warrior*, his weapon is a souped-up auto, which sets up chase scenes that make "The Dukes of Hazzard" seem like a hayride—a feat director George Miller engineered with a meager $1 million budget. Dramatically, however, the film is inconsistent. And it has been dubbed, turning the Australian dialect into a form of southwestern American, which means Mad Max has little of the flavor of *The Road Warrior*. But it does have action to spare, and in Gibson one of the few authentic action stars of the 1980s. **R / 1979 / Vestron**

▲ MAD MAX BEYOND THUNDERDOME

There is something to get excited about in this third chapter of the Mad Max series: the power-house presence of Tina Turner. Even the usually unflappable Mel Gibson lifts a libidinous eyebrow when Tina swoops in for her Big Entrance. Play-ing a villainous character called Aunty Entity, Turner sports spike heels, an endless supply of eyeliner, and costumes cut to reveal more cleav-

Mad Max Beyond Thunderdome: No matter that this third *Max* chapter lags be-hind its predecessors, tantalizing Tina Turner is the perfect new ingredient to spark Mel Gibson's action heroics.

age than Stallone did in *Rambo*. Don't ask where she does her shopping. The film is set in the bleak near future, post-apocalypse. Never mind that everyone else runs around in rags, blistered from the fallout: Tina looks terrific. What's realism got to do with it? Turner eyes Gibson like a piece of prime beef. "One day cock of the walk," she sasses, with a pelvic thrust that's cut many a man down to size, "next day a feather duster." Turner isn't all the film has in it, but she is its sole source of fun. The rest is the usual head-bashing business of getting Max in and out of scrapes. This would be tired stuff if it weren't for two things: Gibson's strength and sexuality in the title role and Australian filmmaker George Miller's brilliant visual style. Miller is a master with the camera, as he proved in *Mad Max* in 1979 and its first sequel, *The Road Warrior,* in 1982. Co-directing (with George Ogilvie) this time, he hasn't lost his knack for casting oddballs to people his grim landscape. The niftiest is the two-headed Master Blaster, consisting of a dwarf (Angelo Rossitto) who sits on the head of a muscleman (Paul Larrson). When Max takes on this deadly combo of brain and brawn, the film is at least the equal of its predecessors. Where No. 3 falters is in the introduction of a group of stranded children, survivors of the atomic holocaust but too young to remember more than fragments of their past life. Miller allows Max, who won over the action junkies as a nihilistic hero, to go sappy at the sight of these tykes. Miller even shamelessly rips off parts—the worst parts—of *Indiana Jones* and *Dune* to refashion Max as a messiah. Save the sentiment for Spielberg, George. It won't wash with the madness in Max.

PG-13 / 1985 / Warner

▲ MAGIC

The title conjures up images of rabbits coming out of hats, but this picture is not kid stuff. The only transformation that takes place is when Anthony Hopkins, a ventriloquist and magician on the verge of the big time, suffers a personality split and, per horror film convention, insinuates his darker side into his dummy. Simultaneously he and childhood sweetheart Ann-Margret are falling in love, a project doomed not only by the deterioration of his mind but also by the fact that she is married. Actor-turned-director Richard Attenborough (*Gandhi* and Oscar were still a few years away) contrasts murder and madness with beautifully serene Catskill scenery to cast a tense spell. But his work can't compare with the 1945 British chiller, *Dead of Night,* with Michael Redgrave as the ventriloquist. Rent this one at the video store only if *Dead of Night* is out. What's worth your time and attention in *Magic* is the acting. Burgess Meredith, as Hopkins' manager, and Ed Lauter, as the husband, are excellent. And so is the underappreciated Ann-Margret. But Hopkins, who learned card tricks and ventriloquism for his demanding role, provides most of the razzle-dazzle: His performance is true onscreen magic.

R / 1978 / Embassy

▲ THE MAIN EVENT

In a weight class far lighter than any of the *Rocky*s, this movie has comedy potential. A woman perfume mogul is embezzled into bankruptcy and left with only the contract of a boxer who won't fight. There are good moments, such as the ring scene in which the exec, Barbra Streisand, dumps ice into the trunks of her reluctant stallion, Ryan O'Neal. Or when she seduces him while both are wearing long johns. But most of the time the film is out of the control of director Howard Zieff. Though O'Neal handles himself nicely in the ring, he has no sense of comedic timing outside it; his gestures are too late and too wild, his smiles look dumb when they should be knowing and vice versa. Streisand runs slightly amok, alternating between her frenetic, coarse, speed-talking mode and her vulnerable-after-all dreamy smile. Back when they were less pretentious, O'Neal and Streisand made a delightful pair in Peter Bogdanovich's *What's Up, Doc?* But *Main Event,* which could have been a contender, isn't.

PG / 1979 / Warner

▲ MAKING LOVE

A lot of good intentions went into this tale of an eight-year marriage that breaks up when the doctor husband (Michael Ontkean) tells his TV executive wife (Kate Jackson), "I find I'm attracted to men." For once, a commercial American movie avoids the extremes of the gay world and places its subject squarely in the middle of an average home. That it does so with obvious sympathy for its characters is commendable. That its screenplay, by Barry (*Gable and Lombard*) Sandler, leaves no cliché unturned is calamitous. "If it feels good, do it," says Ontkean's first male lover, a writer played by Harry Hamlin. Counters Ontkean: "I'm not gay, just curious." Author Sandler confessed that he got himself through a similar sexual identity crisis in part by writing this script. But the movie—with its false reassurances and sentimentality—remains cloudy throughout. As directed by Arthur Hiller in the same tear-jerking style he imparted to *Love Story,* the characters ring trite, not true. The actors are not to blame. Ontkean and Hamlin play their controversial love scenes with discreet and believable passion. Kate Jackson, free of her TV Angel confines, uses her frightened-colt's eyes and quiet integrity to speak with an eloquence the script never hints at. Lucky in its timing and performances, *Making Love* remains a major theme still seeking the right interpreter.

R / 1982 / CBS/Fox

▲ MAKING MR. RIGHT

Hmmmmmm. Maybe it was Madonna who made *Desperately Seeking Susan* what it was after all. Certainly this follow-up by *Susan* director Susan Seidelman showed an astonishing absence of charm and style. Ostensibly a comedy about a Florida woman, performance artist Ann Magnuson, who falls in love with an android, the movie is a brainless, heartless, gutless travesty. The humor is insipid, establishing only that penis jokes can be as tedious and puerile as breast jokes. The romance—this is a woman who gets passionate about a machine, remember—is pathetic. And while there is obviously rich opportunity for satire in a role-reversal film that makes fun of male sexism, Seidelman and her screenwriters, Floyd Byars and Laurie Frank, take only the cheap shots. They cower whenever a tough issue appears. This is the movie equivalent of kids dumping a pile of garbage on someone's front porch in the middle of the night and then running like mad. Seidelman and company don't even follow up on their own ideas. When, for instance, the android, John Malkovich, gets loose in human society for the first time, he encounters a child, which should provide all kinds of comic potential. The opportunity is totally ignored. Malkovich portrays the android as a toddling, wide-eyed scamp, as if he had gotten his ideas by watching *Bedtime for Bonzo* and episodes of "Leave It to Beaver." Magnuson, who plays a public relations whiz breaking up with her Congressman boyfriend, employs a tone of embittered resignation that this sour film hardly needs. But then she may have been feeling glum at being saddled with the movie's main burden: making a case that women would be better off rid of men. Now there may be some merit in this. It would save us from having to deal with another Attila the Hun, G. Gordon Liddy, or Sylvester Stallone. The point would have to be argued with considerably more intelligence and wit than it is here, though. When the reverse idea—using androids to replace women—was suggested in *The Stepford Wives* in 1975, the film was widely decried as a stupid, sexist waste of everyone's time. Ditto.

PG-13 / 1987 / N/A

▲ MALCOLM

The title character of this disarming Australian comedy, deftly played by Colin Friels, is a slow-witted Melbourne tram builder. He also happens to be a mechanical genius. He's fired for using spare parts to make a personal trolley car, so he's forced to take in a boarder. Enter John (*Careful He Might Hear You*) Hargreaves, as a gruff, bumbling ex-con, and stage actress Lindy Davies, as Hargreaves' girlfriend. When Hargreaves discovers the devious possibilities of Friels' innocent inventiveness, the three go from unlikely roommates to even less likely partners-in-crime. Davies' earthiness is a perfect complement of the high-strung Hargreaves and the naive Friels, as she is alternately lover, teacher, and mother hen. Hargreaves is sweetly smarmy, and Friels is wonderful, barely concealing a knowing grin behind his childlike demeanor. His gadgetry, which runs from a car that splits in half to bank-robbing robot ashtrays, is clever, yet never steals the film. Written by David Parker and directed by his wife, Nadia Tass—the couple mortaged their home to help raise production money—*Malcolm* is a charming tale replete with pointed humor.

PG-13 / 1986 / N/A

▲ MALONE

"Ex-cop. Ex-CIA. Ex-plosive," read the ads for this movie. They forgot ex-cessive, ex-cruciating, and ex-ceptionally boring. Burt Reynolds plays the title character. He is a company hit man who is tired of his job—suffering from assassination overkill, as it were—and decides to retire and drive around Oregon. Naturally he happens upon a rich, right-wing megalomaniac who is building a nationwide paramilitary organization. Reynolds does a good job of getting into the world-weariness of his character, barely mustering the enthusiasm to say his lines. Of course the lines *are* mostly blather. This may be due to the fact that screenwriter Christopher Frank usually writes in French. Reynolds, Cliff Robertson, as the right-winger, and the rest of the cast do seem to hesitate a lot, as if they can't bring themselves to utter such dialogue. Scott Wilson, as the Vietnam vet who befriends Reynolds, and Cynthia Gibb, as Wilson's teenage daughter, maintain some dignity. Director Harley Cokliss seems to have given up, though. The final shoot-out is especially listless. The model for films about strangers besieged in hostile towns, *Bad Day at Black Rock,* with Spencer Tracy (John Sturges directed), has more tension in any randomly chosen minute than there is in this whole film. If only Reynolds chose his movie properties as carefully as he does his hairpieces.

R / 1987 / N/A

▲ THE MAN FROM SNOWY RIVER

In the first few seconds of *The Man from Snowy River,* based on the 1898 poem by A. B. Paterson, silhouetted horses run wild across a shimmering sunset. Australian director George (*The Road Warrior*) Miller and screenwriter John Dixon are telling us this is going to be a film of unabashed romanticism. Surprisingly, they get away with it. Newcomer Tom Burlinson plays a mountain lad who must seek work in the valley after his father dies. Dad's old buddy, Kirk Douglas, a peg-legged free spirit, bids him farewell. Then Burlinson is hired as a ranch hand by a well-heeled cattle breeder, also played by Douglas. The two are, of course, long-estranged brothers, feuding for twenty years since a dispute over the woman they both loved. She married the cattle breeder, and their daughter is the spirited Sigrid Thornton.

Before Burlinson can win her away from her father, however, he must capture a prize colt that has run away with the wild horses who stampede across the countryside. Burlinson effectively combines a Harrison Ford bravado with the bumbling innocence of Michael York in *The Three Musketeers.* Douglas is excellent in the dual roles; Thornton, Lorraine Bayly as her aunt, and Aussie star Jack Thompson offer strong support. Thanks to the actors' conviction and the innocence of spirit maintained by Miller, a story that could have lapsed into schmaltz stays credible.

PG / 1983 / CBS/Fox

▲ MANHATTAN

Woody Allen took another chance with this film, almost as daring in its way as *Interiors.* The risk is giving his basic comedy character—the sex-obsessed, angst-ridden schlemiel—a hard edge. Playing a 40ish TV writer who thinks about writing short stories like *Castrating Zionist,* Allen has the usual problems with woman: He's twice divorced, and his nasty second wife (Meryl Streep) left him for another woman—and then wrote a book about it. This time, though, he gets mad once in a while—at Streep and, when he first meets her, at a testy journalist, Diane Keaton. More important, he displays genuine tenderness (only toyed with in *Play It Again, Sam* and *Annie Hall*) in his relationship with a precocious 17-year-old, charmingly played by Mariel Hemingway. The film has some annoyances: too many New York jokes, another overagonized performance by Michael Murphy, and perhaps excessive churlishness in Keaton's characterization. But as a slightly ironic comedy-romance (it's shot, beautifully, in black and white by cinematographer Gordon Willis and the background music is all Gershwin), the film is a success of classic proportions.

R / 1979 / MGM/UA

▲ THE MANHATTAN PROJECT

As Woody Allen's collaborator on such classic screenplays as *Annie Hall* and *Manhattan,* Marshall Brickman teethed on cutting-edge comedy. As director of his own loopy screenplays *Simon* and *Lovesick,* Brickman had trouble achieving the

same success—on the screen or at the box office. For his third feature Brickman initiated a back-handed career change: He's challenged himself to make a conventional, routine movie. The bad news is that he mastered the task. This script, which Brickman coauthored with Thomas Baum, concerns a suburban high school student (Chris Collett) who manufactures an atomic device. When news of it leaks out, he becomes the focus of a boyhunt by the usual military madmen and a scientist (John Lithgow) who is dating Collett's mom (Jill Eikenberry). Collett's girlfriend (Cynthia Nixon), who plays a kind of *Silkwood* of Sigma Chi, gives the movie its only real spark. Out of this material Brickman could have concocted an adolescent *Dr. Strangelove,* but instead he settles for a public service announcement: It's a lousy idea for anyone to play with nuclear weapons. In the past Brickman's comedies were criticized as snobbish, uptown exercises. But in pursuing a commercial crossover he's gone too far in the other direction. While an advocacy adventure such as *The Manhattan Project* depends upon plausibility, Brickman peppered the script with contrivances. Here the race-against-time finale goes off without a bang because the movie has proceeded without any heart. Like its hero, this movie is frighteningly ordinary.
PG-13 / 1986 / HBO/Cannon

▲ THE MANITOU

A manitou, in Indian legend, is a supernatural force that pervades the natural world. Unfortunately, a supernatural idiocy pervades this picture, which is nothing more than a Red Man's (and poor man's) *Exorcist.* Tony Curtis's ex-girlfriend, played by Susan Strasberg, develops a tumor that turns out to be the fetus of a 400-year-old medicine man. "It" exits Susan's body—sort of crawling out through her back—and begins hurling fireballs, causing earthquakes, and turning an entire hospital floor into a deep freeze. Tony and old Cochise himself, Michael Ansara—nicely playing a modern medicine man—team up to try to stop the devilments. Though they persevere through some very scary moments and startling special effects, they are ultimately done in by that deadliest peril, the silly plot. Give it back to the, uh, producers.
PG / 1978 / CBS/Fox

▲ MANNEQUIN

Here's the plot: Boy meets girl mannequin, who comes to life at night. Boy loses mannequin. Boy gets mannequin. No kidding, that's all there is to it. Andrew McCarthy and Kim Cattrall play these stick figures with none of the embarrassment that this amateur enterprise warrants. Newcomer Michael Gottlieb directs as if he's never even seen a sitcom. To label this movie "entertainment" is to perpetrate consumer fraud.
PG / 1987 / N/A

▲ MAN ON THE ROOF

A Swedish-style whodunit, scripted and directed by Bo (*Elvira Madigan*) Widerberg, with Carl-Gustaf Lindstedt as a perspicacious officer stalking a cop killer. The blast-the-sniper-out finish is beautifully botched by the Stockholm police, with the tension relieved by such unlikely touches as sauna and sugar cake breaks.
Unrated / 1977 / N/A

▲ THE MAN WHO LOVED WOMEN

François Truffaut directed this story of one man's obsession with women of all kinds—models, widows, deaf-mutes, pretty young nurses, et al. In the end his skirt-chasing quite literally leads to his demise, but the scenes of seduction and pursuit in between are funny and affecting in typical Truffaut fashion. Watch for lovely Leslie Caron's comeback appearance as a long-ago lover and a quick Hitchcockean cameo by the director himself. The film was remade with less success in 1983 by Blake Edwards, with Burt Reynolds as the title character and Julie Andrews as his shrink. (In French with subtitles.)
Unrated / 1977 / RCA/Columbia

▲ THE MAN WITH BOGART'S FACE

Humphrey Bogart's memory was honorably served with Jean-Luc Godard's *Breathless* and Woody Allen's *Play It Again, Sam.* Still, an amusing movie might have been made about a film buff who has plastic surgery so he'll look like Bogart, buys a '39 Plymouth, and hangs out a sign, "Sam Marlowe, Private Investigator." This one, though,

is bad—very bad. Robert Sacchi looks and talks like Bogart. The plot, a cross between *The Maltese Falcon* and *The Big Sleep,* is serviceable. The problems are straight lines that don't lead anywhere and confusion about whether this is a parody. Only Misty Rowe of "Hee Haw" as the dumbest and blondest of dumb blondes, exaggerates enough to show she's kidding. Among the background players, Michelle Phillips, Olivia Hussey, and Sybil Danning are at least attractive, and Franco Hero, Herbert Lom, and Victor Buono are notably shrewd; two Bogart contemporaries, George Raft and Mike Mazurki, do cameos. Otherwise the film doesn't amount to a hill of beans.
PG / 1980 / Key

▲ THE MAN WITH ONE RED SHOE

Director Stan Dragoti must have thought he had it made. Borrow a hit idea—the old standby of the innocent man mistaken for a spy—from the French comedy *The Tall Blond Man with One Black Shoe.* Cast Tom Hanks, doing his basic befuddlement routine. Then put in the middle the CIA, the modern cinematic equivalent of the Keystone Kops. Add slapstick. Presto, surely you have a terrifically funny film, right, Stan? But wait . . . the plot is played so broadly it seems aimed at eight-year-olds. Hanks, acting like a second string Bill Murray, seems hapless more often than he seems mistreated by fate. And the CIA types, who include Lori Singer, Charles Durning, Dabney Coleman, and Ed Herrmann, are total oafs. (Jim Belushi and Carrie Fisher, who have small roles as friends of Hanks, are the only contributors who seem fresh.) The French indeed have a word for this kind of thing: ennuyant. That means borrrrrrring.
PG / 1985 / CBS/Fox

▲ THE MAN WITH TWO BRAINS

This semi-sci-fi comedy is, at its best, another good matchup for star Steve Martin and director Carl Reiner, who first teamed in 1979 with *The Jerk.* Martin plays an egotistical surgeon whose revolutionary invention is a screw-top skull that facilitates brain surgery. While the notion seems workable—especially when Martin tries to perform two operations at the same time—the film quickly gets entangled in a cumbersome plot. But

a lighthearted spirit saves the day. Kathleen (*Body Heat*) Turner plays a professional black widow who systematically nags her hubbies to death while seducing every other man in sight. Turner proves a game comedienne, throwing herself into silliness with appealing abandon. One of the film's most hilarious scenes comes when Martin throws the slut out crying, "Into the mud, scum queen." David (*Time Bandits*) Warner is also fun as a mad scientist who keeps the entire innards of a Victorian castle in his condominium. Okay, the jokes are hit and miss, but Martin and Turner prove to be a surprisingly solid and memorable team.
R / 1983 / Warner

▲ MAN, WOMAN AND CHILD

This followed the trend of such tear-jerking kid movies as *Six Weeks, Six Pack,* and *Table for Five,* but it may have been the worst of a bad lot. The fault lies not with the excellent cast headed by Martin Sheen and Blythe Danner but with Erich Segal and David Z. Goodman, who co-adapted the screenplay from Segal's four-hankie 1980 bestseller. The waterworks in Segal's *Love Story* were nothing compared to what transpires here. Sheen plays an L.A. humanities professor—a happy hubby to Danner and a devoted dad to two youngsters, Arlene McIntyre and Missy Francis. Almost instantly disaster strikes. A call from France reveals that a woman he had bedded a decade earlier has died in a car accident, leaving a son born from the affair whom she never told Sheen about, not wanting to break up his marriage. The boy—Sebastion Dungan, an exceptionally appealing child actor—arrives in L.A. and the ugly secret gets out. Sheen weeps because he doesn't want to send the boy back to France; Danner weeps because she does, and also sneaks in a revenge flirt with a writer (an alarmingly pudgy David Hemmings); the daughters weep because they can't believe old dad had an affair; and poor Sebastion weeps, presumably because everyone else is doing it. Given this assignment, the best thing director Dick (*Farewell, My Lovely*) Richards could have done was pass around tissues on the set. There is some comic relief from Maureen Anderman and Craig T. Nelson as family friends, but this soggy plot could sink any actor—at least any except Danner. Here is a passionate, intelligent, criminally misused stage

actress giving her best to trash—it's the only true cause for weeping in the film.
PG / 1983 / Paramount

▲ MARCH OR DIE

Gene Hackman grumbles expertly as a combat weary Foreign Legion major ordered to lead his men into the Sahara on an archeological treasure hunt after World War I. Joining the ragtag squad is Terence Hill, who portrays a cocky cat burglar out to seduce Catherine Deneuve, an archeologist's daughter. Her porcelain perfection cuts like a Chanel ad through the dusty haze. Except for the melange of accents, the heroic and romantic mesh nicely in an agreeable latter-day B-movie.
PG / 1977 / N/A

▲ MARIE

Sally Field had her *Norma Rae,* Meryl Streep her *Silkwood,* and Vanessa Redgrave her *Julia,* so it was only fitting that Sissy Spacek should have a real-life crusader to play. These roles practically guarantee Oscar nominations. Why then is this movie so curiously hollow and unconvincing? Marie Ragghianti, the woman Spacek portrays, would seem a surefire subject, as she was in Peter Maas's 1983 book *Marie: A True Story.* A divorced mother of three, Ragghianti, a former beauty contestant, won a job in 1974 as Tennessee's extradition officer through the auspices of T. Edward Sisk. He was a college pal then serving as legal counsel to Tennessee Gov. Ray Blanton. Sisk, played with oily charm by Jeff Daniels, saw Ragghianti as an easily manipulated cream puff. He was wrong. Rising to the chairmanship of the state's Board of Pardons and Paroles, Ragghianti discovered that the governor's aides were selling clemencies. She blew the whistle, got sacked, and sued for reinstatement in a well-publicized 1977 trial that helped put Blanton and his aides in jail. Spacek brings her considerable skill to the role, but she can't lick the script, by John Briley, which ignores the woman in favor of the saint. Spacek's Marie is one-dimensionally noble. Director Roger Donaldson maintains a furious pace in the vain hope of distracting attention from the gaping holes in the script. Only in the climactic trial scenes (in which Watergate attorney and Ragghianti's real lawyer Fred Thompson plays himself) does *Marie* rise to the subject. Thompson's witty, cut-the-bull directness reminds us of what the rest of the film lacks: the ring of truth.
PG-13 / 1985 / MGM/UA

▲ MARLENE

Don't try to categorize this hypnotic hodgepodge as documentary, detective story, or celebrity biography. Just settle back and enjoy a mesmerizing film. Actor-director Maximilian Schell took on the formidable task of telling us about the enduring sex siren and Teutonic terror named Marlene Dietrich. Dietrich, in declining health, was a recluse in Paris. In 1982 she allowed Schell to audiotape interviews with her at home but refused to face a camera. "I've been photographed enough," the star of forty-eight movies chided the man with whom she acted in 1961's *Judgment at Nuremberg.* Schell almost dropped the project. Instead, he devised a form that allows the audience to share in solving the mystery of Dietrich. We watch as Schell and his crew reconstruct Dietrich's apartment in a studio and study photos and newsreels of her life. Through it all we hear that husky Dietrich voice, by turns cranky, caressing, and contentious. Throw out the glamour stuff, she tells Schell, while we see a film clip of temptress Marlene singing her trademark "Falling in Love Again" from *The Blue Angel* in 1930. "Nein, nein, I wasn't erotic," she says. "I was snotty." In that same year's *Morocco* with Gary Cooper, she shocks as a nightclub singer garbed in a man's suit and kissing a female patron full on the lips. How apt that Dietrich's last film, 1978's *Just a Gigolo,* co-starred her with that other specialist in androgyny, David Bowie. "Rubbish! Kitsch!" she shouts as Schell confronts her with her work on film and in concert. She's lying, of course. You can hear the pride in her voice when she describes working with Josef von Sternberg, Orson Welles, Spencer Tracy, Hitchcock. If her memory of her Berlin childhood has lapses (she describes herself as an only child, conveniently forgetting her older sister, Elisabeth), her hatred of what Hitler did to her homeland rings fierce. Through Schell's expert wheedling, the husk of cynicism that Dietrich uses to guard her feelings is eventually cracked. For those too young to know Dietrich, this remarkable film stands as a primer on an extraor-

dinary woman and the epoch on which she made a mark. For those who lived through some of those times with her, if only on screen, *Marlene* is a case of falling in love again.
Unrated / 1986 / Embassy

▲ MASK

We see him first through a window, his back to the camera. He is a trim, long-haired youth, about 15, with a collection of baseball cards and Springsteen posters on his wall. When he turns front, there is a temptation to laugh. The boy seems to be wearing a grotesque mask that elongates and enlarges his face. But this mask doesn't come off. Rocky Dennis was born with this disfiguring condition (the medical term for it is craniodiaphyseal dysplasia), which doctors had predicted would kill him years before he reached his teens. This movie, directed by Peter Bogdanovich, is based on a true story. What makes *Mask* so involving, besides Rocky's astonishing story, are two splendid star performances. After her Oscar-nominated portrayal in *Silkwood,* Cher no longer had to prove to the world that she could act. But even her admirers might have been astonished by the heat and bite she brings to the role of Rusty, a single mother whose dependence on drugs and too many wrong men never diminishes her fierce drive to get her son the medical attention, education, social acceptance, and love he deserves. As Rocky, Eric Stoltz is near miraculous. With only his eyes visible under Mike Westmore's layers of foam-rubber makeup, Stoltz shows us a boy, normal in every way except for the calcium deposits that have disfigured his face, struggling to prove that there is deep emotional power behind the cliché: What matters is what's inside. Bogdanovich handles the anguishing mother-son relationship with disarming directness. A small scene in which Rocky shows his mother his face in a fun-house mirror (the distortion has served to regularize his features) is shattering. And Rocky's love for a blind summer camp counselor, beautifully played by Laura Dern, deftly avoids the icky-poo sentimentality it could have lapsed into. Sadly, other parts of the film sink into exactly that kind of maudlin trap. And Bogdanovich isn't as conscientious with some of the story's minor characters. The way stalwart Sam Elliot and the rest of the leathery, leering gang who befriend Rocky are portrayed seems more than a little contrived. Their idea of outlaw antics is racing their Harleys without helmets. These bikers also offer Rocky so much teary support they threaten to dry up audience emotions. Still, the impact of Rocky's story disarms nit-picking. The smashing talents of Cher and Stoltz makes *Mask* both an affecting tribute to Rocky and a movie to touch the heart and the conscience. Have handkerchiefs ready.
PG-13 / 1985 / MCA

▲ MASS APPEAL

Jack Lemmon is a priest with a real cushy life. His parishoners love him, and he drives a Mercedes and tells funny stories from the pulpit. Then Zeljko Ivanek, a seminarian, challenges Lemmon. Irritated but intrigued, Lemon befriends the young man. Charles Durning plays the tyrannical rector of Ivanek's seminary who wants to bounce Ivanek because of the kid's uppity attitude. This begins what ought to have been an absorbing drama of an older man's reexamining the ideals that got him into the priesthood and a young man's dealing with his own passionate commitment. Sadly, the movie—adapted by Bill C. Davis from his successful Broadway production—is notable for its lack of dramatic buildup. A lot of the film smacks of low-grade sitcom. But Ivanek and Lemmon have some affecting moments together, especially in one scene when Lemmon comforts a woman whose mother has just died, while Ivanek finds himself incapable of doing the same for the granddaughter. And the climax, where Lemmon addresses the congregation and pleads Ivanek's case, is oddly unmoving.
PG / 1985 / MCA

▲ MAX DUGAN RETURNS

Marsha Mason shows up in unflattering blond curls that look like Barbra Streisand wig rejects from *A Star Is Born.* The movie doesn't suit her either, which is even more surprising. *Max Dugan Returns* marked Mason's fifth and last film collaboration with her then husband, Neil Simon, and three of them (*The Goodbye Girl, Chapter Two,* and *Only When I Laugh*) brought her deserved Oscar nominations. Not this time, Marsha. Simon wasn't scraping bottom as he did in 1982's awful *I Ought to Be in Pictures,* but despite a

cute moment here and there, Max Dugan is lamentably lame comedy. Mason plays a wise-cracking widow fighting an uphill battle to raise her teenage son, Matthew Broderick, on her skimpy teacher's salary. Just when her life gets a romantic lift from an L.A.P.D. detective, Donald Sutherland, up pops her ex-con father, Max Dugan (Jason Robards), who left home twenty-six years before. To make amends, the terminally ill Max starts spending his misbegotten gains on his family, dropping everything from video equipment to a Mercedes at their doorstep. The gift-giving has an engaging fairy-tale quality thanks to Robards's roguish charm, and there's an exceptionally appealing debut performance from Broderick, then 20, the son of actor James ("Family") Broderick. Unlike the frenetic Mason and the miscast Sutherland, Robards and Broderick frequently manage to break out of the Simon mold of snappy one-liners to find rhythms that are natural and recognizably human. The scene in which Robards hires real-life Chicago White Sox batting coach Charley Lau to improve his grandson's game is a hoot. For the rest, Simon and director Herbert (*California Suite*) Ross rarely rise above the sitcom level. This is second-rate Simon—pure formula and purely forgettable.
PG / 1983 / CBS/Fox

▲ MAXIE

In her final film appearance, Ruth Gordon has a lovely moment. Surrounded by photos of her youth (they're real), she dances haltingly and movingly to a 1920s tune—her eyes flashing with a yearning, youthful vigor that years failed to dim. Gordon's role is a small one and superfluous, really, to the plot, but then paying last respects to a beloved actress and screenwriter is the only reason for seeing this film. *Maxie* is a disaster—a brew of curdled whimsy chockablock with cutesy dialogue and career-crushing performances. Glenn Close, an intelligent actress who should know better, takes on a disastrous dual role. As Jan, she's a dull wife to librarian Mandy Patinkin and a dutiful secretary to San Francisco Bishop Barnard Hughes. As Maxie, the spirit of a dead flapper who inhabits Jan's body when the mood strikes her, she's a hard-drinking, over-sexed echo of the Roaring Twenties. The Patricia Resnick script, clumsily sculpted from Jack Finney's 1973 novel *Marion's Wall,* hinges on

supposedly sidesplitting identity mix-ups. At a stuffy cocktail party for Patinkin's boss (Valerie Curtin), Close does her Sybil multipersonality number. As Maxie, she gets drunk and disorderly, sings an impromptu version of "Bye Bye Blackbird," and takes hubby home for a hot night in the sack. Jan gets the next day's hangover. Harshly lit and directed by Paul Aaron, Close is embarrassingly unsuited to the broad shenanigans that Barbra Streisand pulled off with such aplomb in the similarly themed *On a Clear Day You Can See Forever.* And Patinkin allows his wimp role to swallow his skills. Both these actors might understandably have wished for the film to vanish quickly and quietly into the ozone, as Maxie herself does at the climax.
PG / 1985 / Thorn/EMI

▲ MAXIMUM OVERDRIVE

Stephen King the ubiquitous called this, his directorial debut, a "moron movie." He wasn't just being modest. There's not much right with this splatter-thriller based on a King short story. It focuses on a North Carolina truck stop where, in the aftermath of earth's passing through the tail of a comet, things go haywire. Electric knives attack their handlers, lawn mowers maul their masters, and eighteen-wheelers form a wagon train and start crunching anyone in their path. The down-home folks besieged by mechanical foes are led by Emilio (*St. Elmo's Fire*) Estevez, as a short-order cook, and Pat (*Brewster's Millions*) Hingle, as his slimy good-ole-boy boss. There are too-obvious allusions to Hitchcock's classic *The Birds.* King's direction is lacking—direction itself, for one thing. What comic edge he tries to add is lost in overdone southerner parodies, resulting in, at best, minimal entertainment.
R / 1986 / Karl-Lorimar

▲ THE MEANING OF LIFE

This Monty Python film opens with a "short feature": A cadaverous group of insurance clerks mutiny against their bosses, convert their office building into a pirate ship, and sail off to pillage Wall Street, firing file cabinet drawers like cannonballs. It's an example of the inventiveness that characterized the BBC comedy team in its

TV series and movies. The rest of the film rarely matches its beginning. But there are a few moments when bad taste is raised to high comic art. Best is an early sketch in which working-class Catholic papa Michael Palin comes home to his pregnant wife and brood of perhaps a hundred children to lead them in an anti-birth-control hymn, "Every Sperm Is Sacred." Some of the sketches drag on interminably or harp repetitively on the British stiff-upper-lip theme. For instance, a group of soldiers in a trench celebrate their commanding officer's birthday as bombs explode around them. Two are bound to repulse the uninitiated and delight the Python pack: One involves a forced liver transplant from a live, screaming "donor," and the other features an eight-hundred-pound human monstrosity who for ten minutes spurts streams of vomit all over the clientele of a fancy French restaurant. As ever the inspired turns from Palin, John Cleese, Eric Idle, and Graham Chapman are cause for celebration.
R / 1983 / MCA

▲ THE MEAN SEASON

As its tough-guy title suggests, *The Mean Season* speaks in the vernacular of '50s movie melodramas: Ominous clouds race across the skyscape, terrified damsels in distress cringe in close-ups, saxophones insinuate on the sound track, and cynical newspaper editors snarl challenges like "This is the one you've been waiting for." Guess again, guy. When burned-out newspaper reporter Kurt Russell gets phone calls from a serial murderer who is a major fascination in Miami, he becomes part of the story he's covering. Like *Deadline U.S.A.* and *Sweet Smell of Success,* this big-city melodrama mediates on the way the media and the damned use, abuse, and upstage each other. Adapted from John Katzenbach's 1982 novel, *In the Heat of the Summer,* this face-off is essentially *Frankenstein* on the front page. Katzenbach's ironic twist was that the reporter and the killer constantly alternate in the roles of monster-creator and creation. Russell gives the creep more fame, while the killer bestows on Russell more prestige with his calls. "It's becoming a collaboration," protests the reporter's live-in girlfriend. Played by Mariel Hemingway, she's a screaming ninny with integrity. She wants her fellow to run a small-town paper in Colorado.

It's a shock to see the sexy-sturdy Hemingway with her shortstop shoulders standing around petrified, but that's just one of the movie's many incongruities. Director Phillip Borson telegraphs his plot developments. While Borson overdosed on atmospheric touches in his first feature, *The Grey Fox,* this movie is almost devoid of atmosphere. Any episode of "Miami Vice" would provide a better feel for the peculiar social climate of the city. There's a terrific concept for melodrama here, but instead of propelling the action along, Leon Piedmont's condescending, pedantic script keeps stopping to announce themes. "You're the story," the villain tells Russell in their climactic confrontation. "You stole it away from me. You became the star." What do the filmmakers think these pronouncements are supposed to be—subtitles for the slow learning people in Middle America? *The Mean Season* sounds as if it were written by the town crier.
R / 1985 / Thorn/EMI

▲ THE MEDUSA TOUCH

Brian De Palma's *Carrie* and *The Fury* had teenagers wreaking death and destruction through telekinesis—that is, the power of mind. Well, this shows that older folks, specifically the *Exorcist II* himself, Richard Burton, are fully as capable of nasty deeds as young folks. He plays a deranged writer who kills his parents, knocks a jumbo jet from the sky, and wants to wipe out the queen of England. Lee Remick is the psychiatrist who tries to destroy her mad patient. That leaves a friendly cop (Lino Ventura) to try to avert disaster. Fans of this sort of nonsense will be entertained. But what to think of Burton's dabbling in horror movies? At least he never got around to *The Attack of the Creature with Perfect Diction.*
PG / 1978 / CBS/Fox

▲ MELVIN AND HOWARD

That's Howard as in Hughes—the billionaire, pioneer of commercial aviation, lover of beautiful movie stars, and ailing recluse who died in a plane whisking him from Mexico to Houston for surgery. Among the strange footnotes to the Hughes legend was the claim by a Nevada gas station

attendant, Melvin Dummar, that he was an heir of Hughes. Hughes intended to reward him, Dummar insisted, for rescuing him on the road to Las Vegas one night. Director Johnathan Demme dramatized Dummar's tale with limited success. When Dummar, played effectively by Paul Le Mat (the hot-rodder in *American Graffiti*), and Hughes are onscreen together, the movie soars. Jason Robards as Hughes is splendid. But most of the film dissects Dummar's usually boring life. The women *are* fun: Mary Steenburgen proves a consummate comedienne as Dummar's on-again, off-again wife, and Pamela Reed as his second spouse sounds the right note of stridency. Overall, the movie is as outlandishly unconvincing as, say, Dummar's claim to the Hughes fortune.
R / 1980 / MCA

▲ MENAGE

This surprisingly powerful French sex farce starts with the outrageous and builds from there. A couple, played by the pouty Miou-Miou and the balding Michel Blanc, argue loudly in a restaurant. Enter a big, barrel-chested stranger, Gerard Départieu, who stops the fight by tossing a handful of francs at the woman and flirtatious glances at her Milquetoast husband. Traditional sex roles hold no interest for writer-director Bertrand (*Going Places*) Blier, who revels in playing against audience expectations. A thief, Départieu teaches the couple to break into the houses of the rich; he also charges their lives with a fierce eroticism. He beds the wife but saves his heart and the tenderness of seduction for the husband, a romantic whose male resistance is eventually worn down. "I'll make you a princess," Départieu tells Blanc. He nearly does. Before this galvanically funny film winds to a disturbing conclusion, Départieu and Blanc, in drag, have joined Miou-Miou in her new profession as street hooker. All three now fantasize about lives of utter conventionality. The canny Blier has drawn potent performances from his cast. Miou-Miou proves a deadpan delight as she watches the men in her life desert her for each other. Blanc, who shared the 1986 Best Actor award at Cannes with Bob (*Mona Lisa*) Hoskins, makes something moving out of a role that could be a caricature. And Départieu remains the glory of the French cinema—a sex symbol without a trace of vanity, an actor who will try anything. With those spicy ingredients, *Menage* serves up the tastiest French dish in ages. (In French with subtitles.)
Unrated / 1986 / CBS/Fox

▲ THE MEN'S CLUB

There are bad, boring movies no reasonable person would expect to be otherwise. Then there are bad, boring movies like this one, frustrating because they could have been so much better. The plot, about a group of middle-aged men trying to achieve some kind of emotional connection, offers all kinds of opportunities. The cast includes such actors as Roy Scheider, Frank Langella, Harvey Keitel, David Dukes, Treat Williams, Craig Wasson, and Richard Jordan. Among the women who appear are Stockard Channing, Gwen Welles, Ann Wedgeworth, Marilyn Jones, Jennifer Jason Leigh, and Penny Baker. It's a big ensemble cast with nary a weak link. The weak links got to the film earlier: Leonard Michaels, in adapting his own novel, and director Peter (*The Ruling Class*) Medak, in allowing the film to drift. There is no focus, no momentum, no pace. There's a long knife-throwing sequence, for instance, that degenerates into a surreal nightmare. Then the men end up in a high-class brothel where they pair off for snippets of scenes that lead to a dotty happy ending. Flashes appear of what might have been—Dukes castigating Scheider for his philandering, Leigh seducing Langella—but nothing lasts long enough to make any impact, and the characters don't ring true. (One example: Scheider plays a former major league baseball star with a .320 lifetime batting average, yet he shows no signs of the financial rewards that accrue to even mediocre ball players these days.) A better writer might have finessed all these lives into one movie. Michaels, however, seems neither cutting, perceptive, nor witty enough. Where are Pinter, Shepard, and Stoppard when we need them?
R / 1986 / N/A

▲ MEPHISTO

Klaus Maria Brandauer, playing an obscure German actor in the 1920s, goes to visit his girlfriend. After some bizarre dancing, they wrestle violently, then make love. The sense of menace—it seems he might kill her—never leaves the

movie, as Hungarian director Istvan Szabo probably intended. *Mephisto* won the 1982 Oscar for Best Foreign Film. Brandauer, the Austrian who later appeared in *Out of Africa,* is sensational; his caterwauling, manic, success-obsessed actor is a dazzling achievement. As he claws his way from a regional stage in Hamburg to directorship of the Nazi-run state theater in Hitler's Berlin, Brandauer adapts to his environment like a chameleon. But slowly he realizes he has sold his soul to the Devil. And Brandauer's actor is best known for playing Mephisto—the Devil himself. Karin Boyd is the girlfriend whose sexuality gives way to a sensitivity that makes her a sane guidepost in the actor's life. Instead of a straight-line story, Szabo jumps from time to time, giving impressions, sometimes in half scenes. It's like flipping through old photographs from an era too terrifying to understand. (In German with subtitles.)
Unrated / 1982 / N/A

▲ MERRY CHRISTMAS, MR. LAWRENCE

David Bowie had appeared previously in three films, all of them on the bizarre side: *The Man Who Fell to Earth, Just a Gigolo,* and *The Hunger.* This peculiar movie did nothing to spoil his record. It's a joint Japanese-British production in which he plays an English officer captured on Java during World War II by the Japanese. He is brought to a prisoner-of-war camp at the edge of the sea, where he displays his defiance and distaste for his captors by eating flowers and pouting. In one scene he marches up to the head of the camp, Ryuichi Sakamoto (in real life a famous Japanese singer-composer), and kisses him on the cheek. There is, in fact, a heavy homosexual accent to this film. The director, Nagisa Oshima, one of the most controversial in the Japanese cinema, made the highly erotic *In the Realm of the Senses* several years ago. But his sensual approach gives this movie an almost lurid quality. What could have been an arresting drama becomes instead a strange dance between captives and captors, done with all the elegance—and stiffness—of a Japanese tea ceremony. The most remarkable performance is by Broadway veteran Tom Conti, who plays with considerable subtlety the Mr. Lawrence of the title, a fellow British prisoner. Sakamoto, too, is effective, displaying a combination of tenderness and maniacal rigidity. But the best moment belongs to Takeshi,

who plays the dumb sergeant given to cruel outbursts (a few scenes are very bloody). At the end of the story, when he is about to be executed as a war criminal, he is visited by Conti. The scene is heartbreaking, chilling, and the best reason to see the movie, aside from the wonderful soundtrack, which was written by Sakamoto. Too bad the rest of the film is a *Bridge Over the River Kwai* with shaky superstructure.
R / 1983 / MCA

▲ MICKY AND MAUDE

Farce is becoming a lost art in movies, with the flat contrivances of *Porky's* and *Police Academy* palmed off on a new generation as the genuine article. Happily, a master practitioner of farce, Blake Edwards, offered this refresher course. Watch closely, children, and learn: Take a silly plot about a TV journalist, Dudley Moore, whose lawyer wife, Ann Reinking, says she is too busy to conceive the baby he craves. Then mix in complications: Moore has an affair with a beautiful cellist, Amy Irving, who announces she's pregnant at the same time his wife does. Edwards builds his movie on sand, and the strong wind of logic does some structural damage, especially at the end. What's astonishing is how his wit and intelligence flesh out cardboard situations. Moore helps by squeezing every laugh out of his juiciest role since *Arthur*. Irving is wonderfully endearing, and Reinking—variously funny, touching, and sexy—exploits her role adroitly.
PG-13 / 1985 / RCA/Columbia

▲ MIDDLE AGE CRAZY

Movies about men's midlife crises had been done before—Burt Lancaster in *The Swimmer* and Jack Lemmon in *Save the Tiger* are two interesting examples, with outstanding performances. But those predecessors do not explain why this film is unsatisfying. Nor does blame lie with the present protagonist or cast. Bruce Dern, as a Houston contractor who turns 40 and anxious at the same time, is a model of sanity in comparison with psychos he has often played, and Ann-Margaret, as his wife, plays another bimbo-ish role expertly. The problem is a naive script by TV writer Carl Kleinschmitt, his first for a motion picture. Totally cynical for 93 minutes, he turns totally romantic for two. His dialogue is all clichés: "Couldn't we go somewhere, just the two of us?"; "Dad, you never listen"; "I never realized how much I love you." Dern keeps lapsing into dreary fantasies about a younger woman and/or a $40,000 sports car. A-M's character is schizophrenic, all simpering devotion one moment and cold calculation the next. In one scene Dern sits alone, while crying, watching a videotape of birthday tributes from his family. It shows how powerful he could have made this role if bad writing hadn't foiled him.

R / 1980 / N/A

▲ MIDNIGHT EXPRESS

Not a pretty picture, this is a true-life story of an American who got busted in Turkey for trying to bootleg out two kilos of hashish. Brad Davis, a newcomer, is cast as Billy Hayes, on whose book the film is based. Despite repeated efforts to free him from prison, Hayes was subjected to almost five years of brutal horror: beatings, homosexual rapes, and harassment by sadistic guards and other prisoners. Randy (*The Last Detail*) Quaid plays the hotheaded prison pal who plans their eventual escape, and John (*The Elephant Man*) Hurt is marvelous as an Englishman gone mad. Though Oliver (*Platoon*) Stone won an Oscar for his script, the dialogue often lapses into banality. Director Alan ("Fame") Parker has the good sense to emphasize the action, vividly helped along by Giorgio Moroder's propulsive score (another Oscar winner). Since the Turkish characters come off like thugs or worse, unsurprisingly the film was shot in Malta.

R / 1978 / RCA/Columbia

▲ A MIDSUMMER NIGHT'S SEX COMEDY

In another attempt to prove he's more than a laugh machine, Woody Allen filtered his urban neurotic sensibility through Ingmar Bergman's 1955 pastoral comedy, *Smiles of a Summer Night*. No harm in that. The result is sumptuously shot, stylishly acted, and fitfully charming. It's just not Woody Allen. Taking flight from the life-sized contemporary world of *Annie Hall* that his critics and fans think he does best, writer-director Allen once again cribbed from the old masters—in this case Shakespeare as well as Bergman. While hardly the solemn mess of *Interiors* or the bilious if mordantly funny *Stardust Memories, Sex Comedy* is still Woody out of water and floundering. Much of the ditsy dialogue seems out of sync in what appears to be Old World surroundings. As in Bergman's film, the period is turn-of-the-century mixing three couples during a weekend in the country. Woody, a crackpot inventor, and wife Mary Steenburgen have opened their home for the wedding of philosopher Jose Ferrer to free-thinking Mia Farrow. Along for the festivities are medical Casanova Tony Roberts and his free-loving nurse, *Airplane!*'s Julie Hagerty, who gives the film's most beguiling performance. The game is change partners, a sexual roundelay laced with tragedy that Bergman pulled off with finesse. Woody's okay with the laughs, getting off a few good jokes (he won't have sex with Steenburgen on the kitchen table because "that's where we eat oatmeal"), sight gags (he invents a machine that puts bones into fish), and fortune cookie bons mots ("Sex alleviates tension, love causes it"). Woefully inept, however, are Woody's attempts at tragic resonance. Roberts is too lightweight an actor to wring pathos out of a suicide attempt. And even Ferrer, though in fine form, cannot raise a lyrical spirit from dull material. The film remains memorable for marking Woody's first professional collaboration with his offscreen lady, Mia Farrow, a fine but neglected actress he later helped bring to full potential.

PG / 1982 / Warner

▲ MIKE'S MURDER

Debra Winger is a bank teller with an out-of-tune piano, a mother who phones frequently, and a future. Mark Keyloun is a pretty-boy tennis instructor with a sideline in cocaine. Their lives are welded by sexual attraction. When Keyloun is murdered, Winger ignores everyone's advice to stay out of it and searches for explanations. There are no Philip Marlowe voiceovers in this rigorously unromantic movie about the seedy side of Los Angeles. Nor is there any question about who done it. Director-screenwriter James Bridges instead builds an atmosphere of menace around the random motions of his rootless characters, who bounce about like pinballs in their hunt for love and money. In a finely modulated performance, Winger is convincing as the middle-class girl who wanders into an outlaw world. As

Keyloun's hopped-up confederate, Darrell Larson is frightening and pathetic, and Paul Winfield contributes a fine supporting performance as a wealthy, gay sybarite. But Winger's real co-star in this beautifully textured film is the city itself. With its sun-saturated pastels and rustling palms, L.A. has never looked more sinister or more seductive.

R / 1984 / Warner

▲ THE MIRROR CRACK'D

Here's an Agatha Christie whodunit that has improved with age thanks to the bracing bitchery of Elizabeth Taylor and Kim Novak as two 1950s movie queens fighting it out in the ego sweepstakes. La Liz plays an aging actress who suddenly finds herself the center of a murder plot. But the mystery is less intriguing than the catty dialogue. "Bags, bags, go away," says Taylor staring into a mirror at her dark circles, "come right back on Doris Day." Tony Curtis plays Novak's slimy producer husband in a caricature of old Hollywood. Geraldine Chaplin, as Taylor's prim secretary, has perhaps the best motive for doing her in. But Angela Lansbury as Christie's dowdy detective Miss Marple is reduced to observing the action from afar while her very English nephew, Edward Fox, ferrets out the killer. Lansbury ends up playing a more fully realized version of this character with great success on TV's "Murder, She Wrote." But the most unexpectedly touching moments come in watching Taylor with her *Giant* co-star Rock Hudson, cast here as her anxious director husband. In the light of Hudson's later AIDS-related death, their scenes together take on a special poignance. Give this one a second look.

PG / 1981 / Thorn/EMI

▲ MISCHIEF

Is anyone in Hollywood not making a movie about adolescence these days? If there is, would he please continue to refrain? This film about the perils of puberty in Nelsonville, Ohio, in the 1950s was directed by Mel Damski, with no sense of originality. You have your virginal nerd, Doug McKeon. You have your outcast greaser with Richard Gere looks and a heart of gold, newcomer Chris Nash. ("You may not be the greatest stud in the world," he tells McKeon, "but at least you've got a family.") You have your high school princess, Kelly Preston, and her slightly-less-glamorous-but-sweeter friend, Catherine Mary Stewart. You have your preppy bully, D.W. Brown. Toss in some jokes about condoms and making out in Studebakers, some blustering parents, lots of ludicrous fights, some hot rods, and a few mentions of James Dean, and you have a movie, or at least what Damski would like to palm off as a movie. His characters are so self-obsessed and faithless, they're not even likable. (McKeon doesn't help matters with his whiny performance.) In fact, Damski and screenwriter Noel Black are so witless and unimaginative they achieved something nearly impossible in this kind of movie: They make the adults seem far more sympathetic than the kids.

R / 1985 / CBS/Fox

▲ MISSING

You have a son who is living in a South American country shaken by revolution. He is thrown into jail by the new government, and no one seems to know where he is. That's Jack Lemmon's plight in this story based on the disappearance of American writer Charles Horman during the 1973 Chilean military coup. With Costa-Gavras directing his first American feature, there can be little doubt that his real target is U.S. complicity in the toppling of the Marxist Allende regime. Lemmon, playing a New York businessman, arrives in the Latin-American nation to find that his distraught daughter-in-law, Sissy Spacek, has all but lost hope. The heavies are played heavily, from the Chilean troops roaming the streets shooting at random to the stony American military and civilian officials who, in Costa-Gavras's mind, always put economic interests ahead of people's lives. Costa-Gavras drills that notion home with monotonous regularity. Played against this background, the human drama has less poignancy than it should. Lemmon and Spacek try mightily and won well deserved Oscar nominations for their efforts, but they are often done in by a script that substitutes rhetoric for dialogue.

PG / 1982 / MCA

▲ MISSING IN ACTION

Chuck Norris films were once known for murky cinematography, disjointed plot, nebulous character development, thudding dialogue, and bad acting. *Missing in Action* is no *Citizen Kane,* but it was a professional effort and, for grind-'em-up fans, Norris's best vehicle. As a retired Army colonel, Norris is consumed by his nightmares of the Vietnam war and the eight years he spent as a POW. When he returns to Ho Chi Minh City with a Senate committee investigating the issue of MIAs, he soon waxes indignant at the behavior of the Vietnamese representatives. Soon old Chuckles is decimating battalions of rotten Commies, and he has never been more menacing. Director Joseph Zito, incorporating frequent flashbacks, keeps combat in your face throughout. The supporting cast is erratic. M. Emmet Walsh, as the booze hound Norris recruits to help him, plays a stereotype, not a real person. Ernie Ortega looks much more like a delinquent from east L.A.'s barrio than he does a Vietnamese commandant. The film's ending seems anticlimactic too. Whatever else it's lacking, however, one thing this film is definitely not missing is action.
R / 1984 / MGM/UA

▲ MISSING IN ACTION 2— THE BEGINNING

In terms of cinematic professionalism, *Missing in Action* was a step forward for Chuck Norris. This hurried prequel, however, amounts to at least two steps backward. Sodden and uninvolving, *MIA2* is related to the original only in that it uses the same central character, Norris, as an American Army officer captured in Vietnam. In *The Beginning,* Norris has been engaged in a ten-year battle of wills with the commandant of a POW camp, Soon-Teck Oh. To pressure Norris into signing a confession of war crimes, the commandant heaps such diabolical indignities on the Americans as choking one GI's pet chicken and fibbing to Norris, "I didn't want to tell you this. Your wife is planning to remarry." The film lacks the hand-to-hand action on which Norris built his reputation. Making his directorial debut, Lance Hool (he produced a number of Charles

Bronson films) displayed paltry amounts of creative, natural, and technical resources.
R / 1985 / MGM/UA

▲ THE MISSION

Winner of the Golden Palm for Best Picture at the 1986 Cannes Film Festival, this Oscar-nominated $18 million epic stars Robert De Niro and Jeremy Irons as two 18th-century Jesuit priests converting the Guarani Indians in the remote mountains of Paraguay. Already we're not talking *Crocodile Dundee;* this is serious stuff. Or at least—as directed by Roland (*The Killing Fields*) Joffe—it pretends to be. For all its earnest intentions, *The Mission* is a ponderous mess, approaching a fascinating period of history with a misplaced reverence for the Hollywood cliché. Chris (*The Killing Fields*) Menges's breathtaking photography—shot in Argentina and Colombia—serves to prettify and soften the film's indictment of church and state for political expediency. The Guarani, arranged against the stunning backdrop of Argentina's Iguacu Falls, are seen as giggling innocents who are as quick to learn a Christian hymn as to dump a priest off the falls when their paradise is threatened. A vivid and varied culture never gets more than lip service. The Guarani are seen as mere pawns for slave traders and a Vatican willing to sacrifice the Indians to avoid pressure on the Church in Europe. *The Mission* wants to point an accusing finger, but the targets are papier-mâché. The politicians are caricatured bad guys, the Jesuit do-gooders merely setups for martyrdom. As a slave trader-turned-priest, De Niro simmers through most of the movie; he's programmed to explode. Irons, the preacher of nonviolence, is his opposite. Both renounce their vows in order to stay with the Indians, but one fights, the other doesn't. The largely silent De Niro fares better than Irons, who is saddled with most of the platitudes in Robert (*A Man for All Seasons*) Bolt's script, such as, "If might is right, then love has no place in the world." Ray McAnally, of Ireland's Abbey Theatre, has it worse. As the compromising cardinal who rationalizes his actions against the Guarani, he is the film's narrator and nagging conscience. In the last scene he stares out at us accusingly; if he is to blame for turning his back, so are we all. Since the film has fudged and oversimplified the issues

on every side, the gesture, like the movie, comes off as empty and infuriatingly smug.
PG / 1986 / Warner

▲ THE MISSIONARY

And now for something completely different from coproducer, scriptwriter, and star Michael Palin, a charter member of the Monty Python gang. Sure his film is a comedy, set principally in Edwardian England and with lavish heyday-of-the-Empire details. But it is so sparing of slapstick that it rises mercifully above being *Monty Python Visits Masterpiece Theatre.* Palin plays a Church of England missionary who, upon returning from Africa to his long-faithful fiancée, Phoebe (*Brideshead Revisited*) Nicholls, is called to found a mission for fallen women by the London docks. He's waylaid first by a lady patron, the marvelous Maggie Smith, who's desperate to shed her profoundly rich and boorish lord, Trevor Howard, and then by all twenty-eight ladies of the street, to whom Palin ministers not wisely but too well. Love, honor, and duty eventually prevail, but not before some timeworn hypocrisies among the rich and the clergy are ridiculed yet again. The performances are superb, in line with Palin's original hope for "a cast of excellent actors with a sense of comedy rather than comedians with a sense of acting." Is this a dig at his fellow Pythons? Though one funny sequence sends up *Chariots of Fire,* director Richard Loncraine and Palin can't resist lingering lovingly over landscapes and period finery. Who would have expected Palin to turn into a totally serious filmmaker?
R / 1982 / Thorn/EMI

▲ MISUNDERSTOOD

Bad schmaltz is a crime against the audience, but when a schmaltzy film exploits kids, the offense is an unforgivable felony. A shamelessly manipulative tearjerker, *Misunderstood* depends on two young boys and one Prince Valiant haircut for its effects. The boys are the sons-cum-victims of a distant dad, who has just become a widower. In the course of the longest 90 minutes this side of *Staying Alive,* the father learns to love his black-sheep son, scold the little darling son, adjust to the loss of his wife, and dodge falling objects. As the stone-hearted dad, Gene Hackman has

none of the immediacy and economy he usually displays. Henry Thomas fares better as the maligned older son, but Huckleberry Fox, so touching as Debra Winger's younger son in *Terms of Endearment,* does most of his acting with his bangs. Thanks to a script that considers youngsters nothing more than screenwriter's pawns, *Misunderstood* is the cinematic equivalent of parental neglect.
PG / 1984 / MGM/UA

▲ MODERN ROMANCE

To comedian Albert Brooks, love is like a jar of molasses—sweet, sticky, and difficult to get out of. As writer/director/star of this mordantly funny movie, Brooks plays a hip Hollywood film editor with an on-again, off-again romance with bank officer Kathryn (*The Hunter*) Harrold. When they break up, Brooks sets out to prove—with amusingly mixed results—that "one is not the loneliest number." As Brooks showed in his shorts for "Saturday Night Live" and his feature *Real Life,* his sense of humor is an acquired taste; it is at its offbeat best here as he pokes fun at everything from *Heaven's Gate* to jogging. Brooks may not have the zany genius of Woody Allen, but his humor is sneaky, subtle, and often bang on target.
R / 1981 / RCA/Columbia

▲ MOHAMMAD, MESSENGER OF GOD

The religious tract that so upset the D.C. Muslims when it was released suggests that Mohammad bored all those converts into submission, assisted by a drowsy Irene Papas and a stupefied Anthony Quinn. The film hardly does justice to an important and fascinating story but was clearly intended to be reverent, not blasphemous. Released in some areas as *The Message.*
PG / 1977 / USA

▲ MOMENT BY MOMENT

After one frame of John Travolta in bathing briefs with a sweet look on his face, fans will figure they've died and gone to Malibu heaven. But Travolta's grinny appeal and Lily Tomlin's skill as a character actress are both short-sheeted in this bedtime gale. It's a post-teen *Summer of '42*

with a tough (but innocent) kid and an older, richer woman falling for each other, on the beach, naturally. John and Lily look disturbingly like brother and sister and seem awkward in the sack—which is unfortunate since they spend a lot of time there. While the premise is affecting, so little happens in the plot, scripted and directed by Tomlin's producer pal Jane Wagner, that their romantic reversals become tiresome, and the movie is a major disappointment.
R / 1979 / N/A

▲ MOMMIE DEAREST

Whether or not you believe that the late screen legend Joan Crawford was guilty of the monstrous child abuse her adopted daughter Christina alleged in her 1978 best-seller, you'll have to admire Faye Dunaway's wickedly zestful portrayal. Dressed to perfection by Irene Sharaff, Dunaway looks every inch the part, with padded shoulders, ankle-strap shoes, thick eyebrows, and red scar of a mouth. But her achievement goes deeper than makeup. Dunaway often plays Crawford as Caligula—thrashing her daughter with wire hangers, pummeling her with a cleanser can, and chopping off her golden locks in a punishing rage. Astonishingly, Dunaway also provides insights into Crawford's fear of aging, poverty, and obscurity that are barely hinted at in Christina's book. Still, don't expect an objective biography. *Mommie Dearest* reduces Crawford's marriages, affairs, films, and even adopted son Christopher to shadowy presences. This is a duel of wills between mother and daughter. Director Frank (*Diary of a Mad Housewife*) Perry aims each shot for the jugular—and rarely misses. Mara Hobel and Diana Scarwid are wonderful playing Christina the child and the adult, respectively, but it's Dunaway, greedily attacking her role, who proves most riveting. In this glossy, gaudy Hollywood kind of movie, she makes her very own kind of truth.
PG / 1981 / Paramount

▲ MONA LISA

Balding, bug-eyed and built like a bull terrier, Bob Hoskins may be the most unlikely movie star material since the young Jimmy Cagney. But this London stage sensation (*True West, Guys and Dolls*) makes his own rules. His film send-off as a mobster in 1980's British import *The Long Good Friday* earned him cult status, and then he began stealing Yank flicks (*Cotton Club, Sweet Liberty*) in second-fiddle parts. But like the man said, you ain't seen nothin' yet. In *Mona Lisa,* a stinging drama for which he won the Best Actor prize at Cannes and an Oscar nominaction, Hoskins roars like a house afire through a once-in-a-lifetime role. He plays an ex-con, a petty thief who took the rap for his gangland boss (a sleazy Michael Caine) and now expects some reward. Instead, he gets abuse. His wife won't let him near their home, and Caine palms off a demeaning job on him: driving a high-priced black prostitute (Cathy Tyson) on her rounds. At first Tyson is appalled by this unsightly bantam cock with a loud mouth and a wardrobe to match. So she sets about transforming him with elegant clothing, lessons in etiquette and, later, her trust. The striking Tyson makes a dazzling debut, finding both the shrewd promoter and scared child in this haughty hooker. Naturally, Hoskins falls hard. She is his Mona Lisa, the mysterious beauty of the Nat King Cole song he constantly plays. The song (an Oscar-winning 1950 standard) is a key to his character—he's a bruised romantic who wants to believe in happy endings. There aren't any, of course. Though he carts Tyson around like a prom date, he can't shut his eyes forever to what she does upstairs while he waits in the car. In helping Tyson find the object of her own romantic obsession, Hoskins finds the truth about himself in a violent confrontation that doesn't allow for illusions. Director and co-writer Neil (*The Company of Wolves*) Jordan has an unerring eye for random glints of humanity even in these squalid surroundings. And Hoskins, unexpectedly moving as he builds a new life out of his shattered fantasies, created one of the great characterizations of recent times. Prepare to be wowed.
R / 1986 / HBO/Cannon

▲ THE MONEY PIT

Step right up, folks, fork over the price of a video rental, and watch the pit swallow your money before you can cry foul over this labored farce. There's a good comedy movie in the subject of an urban couple trying to build a country house that drains their patience and bank account. That movie was 1948's *Mr. Blandings Builds His*

Dream House, starring Cary Grant and Myrna Loy. This sledgehammer update seems perversely geared to bring out the worst in all the top talents involved. The biggest mystery is why executive producer Steven Spielberg chose to provide this film with the inflated jokiness of his jumbo fiasco, *1941.* Director Richard Benjamin, known for his success with period films (*My Favorite Year, Racing with the Moon, City Heat*), here goes thuddingly contemporary. And the actors visibly strain for laughs; you can see them sweating. Tom Hanks, who proved himself an adroit charmer in *Splash,* calls instead on the shrill antics that crushed his follow-up roles in *The Man with One Red Shoe* and *Bachelor Party.* Shelley Long, who can be a sweetheart on TV's "Cheers," can also be cloyingly cute when a script leaves her stranded as David (*The Black Bird*) Giler's *Pit* script frequently does. Even such expert Broadway actors as Maureen Stapleton, Joe Mantegna, and Philip Bosco lapse into caricature. True, Alexander Godunov (who made a strong acting debut in *Witness*) isn't bad as Long's sex-crazed ex-husband. But a comedy in which a ballet dancer still struggling with English gets the most laughs is its own worst enemy. Like the white-elephant house from which it takes its title, *The Money Pit* should have stayed closed for renovations.
PG / 1986 / MCA

▲ MONSIGNOR

The ads for Christopher (*Superman*) Reeve's 1982 film began: "Forgive me, Father, for I have sinned." And how! It's as if a stray piece of kryptonite had drained Reeve of the charm and talent he delivered as the Man of Steel. For a change of pace, he plays a fighting, fornicating Irish-Catholic priest who rises out of the Chicago slums to serve as a WWII Army chaplain. Reassigned to the Vatican when the souls he slays outnumber the ones he saves, Reeve uses his financial savvy to bolster the Church's budget by tying up with the black market and Mafia don Jason Miller. The Church, in the person of Fernando Rey's Cardinal Santoni, looks the other way. The script, by Abraham Polonsky and Wendell Mayes, comes down heavily on the Vatican but lightly on evidence or logic. The love story is even worse. Hiding his identity behind an Army uniform, Reeve seduces a nun played by Geneviève Bujold who, at 40, is cruelly miscast.

"I'm living with a need to tell you something," says Reeve in his best Barbara Cartland manner, but he doesn't. Bujold learns the truth when she spots Monsignor Reeve in church with the Pope and stares him down in front of the congregation. Not since Patty Duke damned the deity in *Valley of the Dolls* has a film provoked such steady and unintended laughter. Things don't get better as the film spans three decades, and Reeve is made to age through makeup that looks like a light flour dusting. Director Frank Perry, apparently still high from his *Mommie Dearest* campfest, went over the edge with this film. Perhaps Perry thought Reeve's popularity was enough to make audiences swallow 2 hours of staggering ineptitude. Not a prayer.
R / 1982 / CBS/Fox

▲ MONSTER IN THE CLOSET

The minutes stretch out in front of you like eons. You begin to count backward from 25,000, desperate for ways to pass the time. You worry that you will fall asleep and leave the TV on all night. Such are the dreadful possibilities that await those who watch this film. It is not, as the title suggests, a parody about a gay werewolf. This is a routine monster movie with no wit, no imagination, no nothing. MTV veteran Bob Dahlin misdirected a cast that includes Howard Duff, Donald Moffat, and Stella Stevens, as well as attractive newcomers Donald Grant and Denise DuBarry. They all embarrassed themselves just by being associated with this movie. Let's not make it worse for them by watching it.
PG / 1987 / N/A

▲ MONTY PYTHON LIVE AT THE HOLLYWOOD BOWL

This offering reprises some of the English TV comedy troupe's best known sketches. Captured at a four-day appearance at the Hollywood Bowl in 1980, and featuring the compleat Python (Graham Chapman, John Cleese, Terry Gilliam, Eric Idle, Terry Jones, and Michael Palin), *Live at the Hollywood Bowl* revisits such classic settings as the Ministry of Silly Walks and the Whizzo Chocolate Company—makers of that toothsome confection, crunchy frog. Here, too, is a Pope taking Michelangelo to task for his rendering of the *Last Supper,* which includes twenty-eight disciples, a kangaroo, and three Christs. The exasperated painter responds, "You want a bloody photographer is what you want." Screens set up on either side of the stage showed Gilliam's malevolent animated sequences as well as some funny filmed gags—for instance, a soccer game between the big names in Greek and German philosophy. This is really a film for those new to Python material or for those diehards who can never get enough, even of something not completely different.

R / 1982 / Thorn/EMI

▲ MOON IN THE GUTTER

Jean-Jacques Beineix won France's Cesar Award for the Best New Film of 1982 with *Diva,* and no prize could have been more deserved or suggested more promise. That film electrified audiences worldwide with its jarringly garish and erotic set design and cinematography, combined with a whiplash plot line and New Wave hipness that never let up. *Moon in the Gutter* is, astonishingly, everything *Diva* was not. *Moon* is unrelentingly sleazy, morose, self-indulgently tedious, and pretentiously "dark." Gerard Dépardieu plays a hulking but sensitive stevedore in an unnamed but vaguely Third Worldish port city, haunted by the throat-slashing suicide of his virginal sister after she is raped (off-camera, in the film's opening sequence). Beineix, who co-wrote the screenplay with Olivier Mergault from David Goodis's 1953 novel, gets plenty of help from set designer Hilton McConnico in evoking scenes of dockside squalor that give the film its funky gloom. In fact, the props get more care than the script. Dépardieu never really goes after his suspicions but pursues the sister (Nastassja Kinski) of the man who is one of the rape suspects, a rich vagrant who lives "uptown" and drinks himself into oblivion every night at a local dive. Kinski drives a red sports car and gets off on slumming, while Dépardieu dreams of "a clean city"—and his sister's redemption. We can't spoil the ending because there isn't any—the story is never resolved. Kinski can pout in four languages, though nothing of substance flows from those supernaturally sensual lips and eyes. In the end, Beineix sacrificed good storytelling, character depth, and dramatic tension for the sheer narcissistic rush of

artsy image making for its own sake. What a regrettable waste of talent.

R / 1983 / RCA/Columbia

▲ MOONLIGHTING

Who'd have guessed the isolation felt by Poles living abroad would be the theme of a great movie. Director Jerzy (*The Shout*) Skolimowski, a Polish expatriate, and onetime collaborator of Roman Polanski's, wrote the screenplay. It's about four Warsaw construction workers who come to London to renovate the town house of their wealthy boss, then find themselves completely cut off from their native country when martial law is declared at home. Only one of the workers—the foreman—speaks English, and so he becomes the others' sole link to the outside world. Their story combines suspense and psychological revelation with healthy doses of comedy (slapstick, at that) in a tight, coherent mix. The acting is also superb: In a casting coup for a low-budget film, Jeremy Irons agreed to play the foreman, reportedly to show that he could go beyond the elegant types he played in *Brideshead Revisited* and *The French Lieutenant's Woman.* He succeeds completely. Still, most of the credit for this film goes to Skolimowski, who was writing it when martial law was declared in 1981. That event made an already striking film even more timely and powerful.

PG / 1982 / MCA

▲ MOONRAKER

No James Bond film has ever won a major Oscar. (*Thunderball* and *Goldfinger* were honored for effects.) But producer Albert Broccoli, who turned out most of the Connery-Moore 007s, deserves one for maintaining such a high level of entertainment in the face of predictability. This one is a little long. Richard ("Jaws") Kiel, surviving villain from *The Spy Who Loved Me,* is onscreen too much. The women don't quite live up to the aesthetic standards set by such earlier Bond beauties as Ursula Andress, Britt Ekland, and Barbara Bach. (The main heroine is Lois Chiles, playing a CIA agent.) But the series' spectacular photography, gimmickry, verve, and wry wit are still abundant. The opening sky-diving sequence is magnificent, both visually and dramatically.

Michael Lonsdale is perfectly droll as the latest nasty trying to conquer Earth. There's a brilliantly choreographed laser battle between two space-walking armies. And Roger Moore, already a trifle old for the part at 51, could still be vigorous and funny when he needed to. As both bad guys and audiences learned long ago, you can't beat James Bond.
PG / 1979 / CBS/Fox

▲ THE MORNING AFTER

When you first see Jane Fonda as a bleached blonde in this brittle murder mystery, you want to shout hallelujah. If there was any star in need of new packaging, it's Fonda, and she had indeed pushed herself all the way off the pedestal. The result was her most compelling and corrosive performance since *Coming Home*. When Fonda plays a wanton woman it's a novelty act, and she could coast on that surprise in this film, where she plays an alcoholic movie actress who wakes up in bed with a dead man. Fonda, however, goes further, mining the brazenness and bitterness in this misfit. For a change, she seems to inhabit a heroine instead of assessing her. As etched by Fonda, this character is the de facto granddaughter of Norma Desmond in *Sunset Boulevard*—a loser who won't admit she's lost. "They were grooming me to be the next Vera Miles," brays Fonda at her unlikely lover, a down-and-out California cop whom Jeff Bridges comfortably portrays. His racial slurs are emasculated by Fonda's clever comebacks in James Hick's street-smart script. It's all capably directed by Sidney Lumet, who usually works in New York City instead of the alleyways of Los Angeles. *The Morning After* is distressingly full of convenient confidences that torpedo too many mysteries. Then, too, once this has-been dyes her hair back to its natural shade, the movie suddenly seems to adopt the Vidal Sassoon theory of salvation: With your real hair color, you'll become the real you. In a gratuitous coda, Fonda climbs back up into the pulpit to deliver a sermonette about alcoholism. It mars the film, but not her performance. Slight as it is, *The Morning After* does practice what it preaches. This is a drama about redemption in which one of our best actresses at long last redeemed herself.
R / 1987 / Karl-Lorimar

▲ MOSCOW ON THE HUDSON

New York has enjoyed a featured role in most of Paul Mazursky's movies. Never has it played the contradictory and complex part it does in this melancholy comedy. A troupe of Soviet circus performers visiting Manhattan on a cultural exchange encounters a forbidden wonderland of surrealistic sights: break dancers on the streets, billboards promoting designer underwear, and hotel shower caps that the Russians refer to as giant prophylactics. During a frantic excursion to Bloomingdale's, the circus saxophonist, Robin Williams, decides to defect. What follows is Mazursky's meditation on instant assimilation and Manhattan as a land of golden opportunity. "You don't have to thank me—you have to pay me," says Williams's Cuban lawyer. As usual Mazursky is a sly commentator with a puckish point of view: Befriended by a black security guard at Bloomingdale's, Williams makes his first American home in the Harlem flat of his pal's family. Despite the freshness of Mazursky's vision, the film's second half indulges in a patronizing golly-gee patriotism. When customers in a coffee shop erupt into a recitation of the Declaration of Independence, the film turns into a mushy pledge of allegiance. Whenever Mazursky falters, though, Williams' performance steadies the film. Williams is a master at misfits, and this is perhaps his most controlled and most creative movie performance. Stripped of his old Morkish shtick, Williams still finds the humor as well as the pathos in his character's plight; he proves himself a substantial dramatic actor. Watching one of America's top comics convincingly transform himself into a troubled Russian immigrant is this movie's most delightful and satisfying culture shock.
R / 1984 / RCA/Columbia

▲ THE MOSQUITO COAST

"Look around you, Charlie," says Harrison Ford to his son as they drive down a fast-food freeway, "this place is a toilet." Two hours later, this adaptation of Paul Theroux's novel has traveled from Middle America to Latin America, but it still hasn't gone anywhere. In a polemic masquerading as an adventure, Ford flounders as an eccentric inventor who forsakes his homeland and takes his wife and four kids to an area of Honduras known as the Mosquito Coast. In the jungle he wants to be emperor of his own kingdom but instead becomes what poet Wallace Stevens called the Emperor of Ice Cream, a nowhere man in a no-man's land. As chronicled in Theroux's novel, the journey to the Mosquito Coast was a metaphysical expedition into the power of a patriarch; in Paul Schrader's reactionary, moralistic screenplay, it's an outing with the Swiss Family Pat Robertson. The labored script makes the same point time and again—the self-proclaimed realist is just a different breed of impotent romantic. Peter Weir's passionless direction doesn't make up for the monotony, reflecting nothing like his brilliantly framed compositions of Amish farmlands in *Witness*. His images look as if he hasn't caught any of Ford's back-to-nature fever, which is imperative. Meanwhile, Ford is being confounded by one of the most problematic roles any movie actor ever faced. There's supposed to be a trace of humane motivation and a touch of tragedy in this deluded fellow, but forever sweaty and smug, Ford only plays him as one of those wackos on a radio call-in show at four in the morning. As the narrator, River Phoenix, the tough kid in *Stand By Me,* makes exquisite use of his deadpan face, but he's one of the film's few pleasures. When the movie reaches a painful and pathetic conclusion, you're just relieved to depart from *The Mosquito Coast*.

PG-13 / 1986 / Warner

▲ MOTEL HELL

Ever since that rainy night in 1960 when Janet Leigh walked into the Bates Motel, travelers have been alert to the idiosyncrasies of the nation's roadside innkeepers. Here we went again with a new loony, that old cowpoke Rory Calhoun, looking craggily handsome at 58. He seems to be a benevolent hotelier who also makes the best smoked meat in town. His goofball sister, Nancy Parsons, helps him with the secret recipe, which turns out to include human flesh from bodies the pair raise in the garden. Despite a preponderance of gore, the film is respectably shot and edited, and Calhoun does justice to an often ridiculous script. There is one scene right out of *Night of the Living Dead* that indicates how effective genuine horror can be. Also, while in most chillers any female under 95 is fair game, here is a non-

sexist approach in which everybody gets it, regardless of gender.

R / 1980 / N/A

▲ THE MOUNTAIN MEN

In Hollywood them varmints what make movies about Indians and white men on the frontier take a heap of killing, as this throwback demonstrates. In these permissive days, of course, the heroes (Charlton Heston and Brian Keith) swear more, cavort with naked women, and fight dirtier. Down deep, though, they're like Clark Gable in *Across the Wide Missouri,* Gary Cooper in *Unconquered,* or Spencer Tracy in *Northwest Passage*—clever, noble, lovable, and able to beat up fifteen or twenty Indians at a time. (That's fortunate, since they get into a battle every six or seven minutes.) There is also one of those svelte, sexy young Indian women, Victoria Racimo (of Irish-Filipino descent) who arrives in what looks like designer buckskins and starts nuzzling the white guys. The two main "red men" are Stephen Macht, as the squaw-beating warrior who loses Racimo to Heston and becomes apoplectic, and the old villain, Victory Jory, 77, as a chief. While there are a couple of affecting scenes between Heston and Keith, most of the film—written by Fraser Clarke Heston, the young son of guess who—is superficial and preposterous. Only the Jackson Hole, Wyoming, location, featuring the Grand Teton Mountains, emerges with reputation enhanced. Too bad both the movie and the mountains can't be given back to the Indians.

R / 1980 / RCA/Columbia

▲ MOVERS & SHAKERS

Movers & Shakers assembles Walter Matthau and Vincent Gardenia as aging, mediocre Hollywood producers, Charles Grodin as a hypochondriac and blocked screenwriter, Bill Macy as a lunatic director, and Steve Martin as a face-lifted matinee idol of yesteryear. Even it if weren't sharply satirical, at least it could have been funny. But this is a case of disappointed expectations. The movie starts with the deathbed promise Matthau makes to his mentor, Gardenia. Gardenia wants

Matthau to "make something great, make something about something," and he wants it to be titled *Love in Sex,* after a best-selling how-to manual. Matthau hires the ingratiating Grodin and a spacy Macy to figure out what such a film might be about. Grodin and Macy decide *Love in Sex* should be Up, Happy, and Romantic, but they write no dialogue and shoot no scenes, since their own personal relationships are on the rocks. Tyne Daly overanxiously plays Grodin's frustrated, humorless wife. Gilda Radner whines and shrieks her way through her role as Macy's overbearing, violent girlfriend. (She does supply the film's only really funny sight gag when, on her way to an appointment, she nervously places facial tissues under her bare arms to absorb perspiration.) After months of creative desperation, Matthau, Grodin, and Macy finally seek out the advice of legendary celluloid lover Fabio Longio —Steve Martin in a powdered pompadour and rubbery makeup. Martin's simpering advice is that "women want to conquer as well as feel conquered." He should know, since his live-in girlfriend turns out to be a negligee-and-feathers-bedecked Penny Marshall, who outwhines and outshrieks even Radner. The women in *Movers & Shakers,* portrayed as irredeemable harridans or sexual piranhas, are typical of this movie's insipid, outdated humor. Screenwriter Grodin and director William Asher (known for his 1960s beach movies, for example, *How to Stuff a Wild Bikini*) don't seem to realize that jokes about "boggy" prostates, bulk-rate face-lifts, and male befuddlement over women aren't enough to make a movie, not even a movie about Hollywood.

PG / 1985 / MGM/UA

nice gimmick is the shameless use of identical sets for both pictures. Many of the players also perform double duty—notably a gruff but lovable George C. Scott and the engaging Broadway veteran Barry Bostwick. This is, by definition, a highly derivative movie, but it succeeds where other send-ups, like *The Cheap Detective,* failed. Enjoy, Enjoy.

PG / 1979 / CBS/Fox

▲ MOVING VIOLATIONS

Neal Israel and Pat Proft, who co-wrote this movie about a school for violators of traffic laws, also co-wrote *Police Academy.* Enough for the humor-in-pedagogy notion. They rely in this case on sight gags involving vehicles careening downhill out of control, which make an excellent metaphor for their movie. The film's star is John Murray, who is Bill's brother and just asking to be told, "Get out of here, you younger sibling." He made a classically wrongheaded decision to try to imitate his brother, right down to the way Bill slouches when he's doing one of his super-laid-back reaction lines. At best John is only a poor copy. (By comparison John Belushi's brother Jim established his own style early in his movie career.) The rest of the cast is slighted, though Sally Kellerman and James Keach have time to embarrass themselves as a corrupt judge and a cop. Only Jennifer Tilly, as a ditsy NASA physicist, engenders any goodwill. Her appeal is considerable, but even she can't stifle the yawns for more than a few frames.

PG-13 / 1985 / CBS/Fox

▲ MOVIE, MOVIE

Producer-director Stanley Donen brought off a delicious parody of the Depression-era movie—a mini-double feature (plus coming attractions)— all in 105 minutes. It opens with an up-from-the-canvas boxing story titled *Dynamite Hands,* followed by *Baxter's Beauties of 1933,* a backstage musical à la Busby Berkeley. Both offer a feast of mixed metaphors and cleverly rearranged movie clichés. *Dynamite* is funny—Rocky comes to mind—and *Beauties* is a positive delight. One

▲ MR. MOM

If you laughed when Dustin Hoffman folded the egg-sopped bread to make French toast for his son in *Kramer vs. Kramer,* you'll love all 92 minutes of *Mr. Mom.* It's a little more than an expansion of that dunce-dad image but with a Reagonomics-working-woman hook. Michael Keaton plays a high-level auto plant engineer laid off in Detroit; Teri Garr, the dutiful mom of their three suburban kids, lands a job as an ad exec assigned to a sinking tuna account. (Her boss,

Martin Mull, obviously hires her because he's mulling over a hot after-hours campaign of his own.) The film, directed by Stan Dragoti—he of *Love at First Bite,* the 1979 cocaine bust in Frankfurt, and, formerly, Cheryl Tiegs—exploits the reverse sexism of *Tootsie* (the notion that a man can make it only in drag.) That's leavened, though, by Keaton's endless series of house husband headaches. A partial list involves: diapers, a vacuum cleaner named "Jaws," a kitchen fire, and exploding popcorn poppers. Garr underplays her part nicely. But it's Keaton's kinetic energy, ever-undulating eyebrows, and wise-guy humor that carry the whole potentially dismal project. Try to get beyond the obvious dumb implausibilities: Would Garr, in fact, clean up the junk food debris from her first round-table meeting with ad executives "out of habit"? And if Keaton is really an engineer, would a front-loading washer really throw him that far? Writer John (*National Lampoon's Vacation*) Hughes has, however, loaded this film with some invention: Keaton's riotous game of food-coupon poker with The Girls ("I'll see your Tender Vittles . . ."); his addiction to daytime soaps; the microwaving of socks to dry them; the ironing of his son's lukewarm grilled cheese. Focus on the moments—not the muddled sexual polemics—and *Mr. Mom* can relieve people of all sexes of the tedium of their daily routines, domestic, professional, or otherwise.
PG / 1983 / Vestron

▲ MRS. SOFFEL

There's a fascinating couple in *Mrs. Soffel* but, unfortunately, it isn't Mel Gibson and Diane Keaton. Toward the end of an illicit escapade, the lovers played by Keaton and Gibson take shelter in the isolated farmhouse of an elderly married couple. Although they're peripheral to the plot, Paula Trueman and Les Rubie convey the charged chemistry of a convincing twosome. The same cannot be said of the stars, even though this is a love story with extraordinary potential. Based on a real incident in turn-of-the-century Pittsburgh, *Mrs. Soffel* chronicles the perilous attraction between a prison warden's repressed wife and an infamous inmate. But even after Keaton helps her lover escape and flees with him and his brother, she and Gibson play as if there

were still bars separating them. Although both are persuasive in scenes with other characters, they never connect with each other, which may explain why the film delivers so little sense of liberation even after Keaton escapes her suffocating household. Director Gillian Armstrong, usually an inventive filmmaker, here sinks in a quicksand of period details and dark-as-night cinematography. Ron Nyswaner's script is humorless, and Armstrong's monotonous staging of the jailhouse scenes undercuts the incubation of passion that is the core of the movie. Despite its possibilities, *Mrs. Soffel* mainly induces indifference.
PG-13 / 1985 / MGM/UA

▲ MURPHY'S LAW

Break out the body bags. Charles Bronson is back, this time as a divorced cop who is framed and then arrested for a string of murders. Before he can be tried, he escapes from jail to hunt for the real murderer. Bronson picks up an unlikely sidekick, a foul-mouthed street punk played with pluck by Kathleen Wilhoite, who seems to have cast a spell over the perennially wooden actor; he appears more genuine than ever in their bantering scenes. Bronson can afford to kick back in *Murphy's Law* because for once someone else—a psychotic played by Carrie Snodgress—bumps off most of the cast. Snodgress, acting with too much gusto and too little menace, has a death wish for Bronson and others who collared her for a crime a decade earlier. Director J. Lee Thompson, a veteran of six Bronson films, deftly orchestrates the violent segments. The pace lags periodically, but true-blue Bronson buffs will get their money's worth.
R / 1986 / Media

▲ MURPHY'S ROMANCE

You looked at the thoroughly charming and heartfelt performance that James Garner gives here and you thought, what a waste. After three decades and thirty-seven movies, this marvelous actor is still best known as TV's *Maverick* and *Rockford,* with only one picture (1964's *The*

Americanization of Emily) that can be called truly memorable. Then, at 57, Garner found this role of a lifetime and a well-earned first Oscar nomination as Best Actor. He is Murphy Jones, a shrewd, sassy widower who runs a drugstore in a small conservative Arizona desert town. Murphy loves his backwater burg but doesn't quite fit in. When a divorcee, played by Sally Field, comes to town with her 12-year-old son (Corey Haim), Murphy helps her battle prejudice against women, enabling her to get a loan to convert her ranch into stables so that she can board horses. Cracker-barrel corn, you say? Maybe so. But veteran director Martin (*Norma Rae*) Ritt and screenwriters Harriet Frank, Jr., and Irving Ravetch wisely put the emphasis on the beguiling romance that develops between Garner and Field. Neither rushes the relationship. He's still bruised from his wife's death; she's bristling from her former husband's irresponsibility. Besides, Garner is sensitive about his age and about a paunch that is no match for the muscled torso of Field's young ex, who shows up to win back his wife and son. Brian (*The Young and the Restless*) Kerwin is wonderful at showing the sexy and shiftless sides of this perennial Peter Pan. But when Field and Garner look at each other at a church bingo game, they generate more feeling than Streep and Redford managed with all Africa as a backdrop. Without the pressure of having to save the union or the farm (and win another Oscar) Field relaxes into a sunny and seductive performance. She and Garner play off each other beautifully. When Field drags him to see a *Friday the 13th* flick at the local theater, he walks out in disgust. "I haven't been to a movie since the Duke died," says Garner sheepishly. Neither have a lot of people. This unabashedly old-fashioned romance—untrendy, unadorned and plain irresistible—helped to bring them back.
PG-13 / 1985 / RCA/Columbia

setback: "Dear diary, nothing ever happens." But before you start fidgeting, the girl is played by an enchantress named Margaret Langrick, without a trace of movie-kid mugging. Langrick had never acted before. She won the role because she was a Vancouver neighbor of writer-director Sandy Wilson, previously a documentary filmmaker. Wilson felt a kinship with Langrick, whom she strongly resembles, and since Wilson's story is largely autobiographical . . . Well, you get the point. Langrick (called Sandy in the film) lives on a ranch in the Okanagan Lake region of British Columbia. Pretty scenery, sure, but limited for a teenager longing to rock 'n' roll in fast cars. One day her 17-year-old cousin from California (a James Dean look-alike) roars into town in a cherry red Caddy, epitomizing the glamour of the States and everything that Langrick thinks she's been missing. Toronto actor John Wildman, playing the cousin with a teasing sexuality, takes Langrick and her giggling girlfriends on a speed run in the convertible and a raucous skinny-dip that both terrifies and excites them. Langrick is gaga until she learns that her idol is afraid to face a girl back home whom he may have made pregnant. The film won six Canadian Oscars (called Genies), including Best Picture. Chauvinism may have been a factor. Langrick's final acceptance of home over flashy packaging must taste sweet to Canadians long dominated by American pop culture. This is not a great film, though the small pleasures it offers are not to be sneered at. In the era of *The Breakfast Club* and *Ferris Bueller,* where teens trade one-liners and wear their psyches on their sleeves, it's gratifying to find a film with an eye for what kids keep inside. *My America Cousin* rings with laughter and truth—a rare, welcome combination.
PG / 1986 / Media

▲ MY AMERICAN COUSIN

You might fear the worst about this $1.5 million (the low budget means no stars) Canadian film. Yes, it is another meditation on youth coming of age. And yes, it is set in the '50s, a maddening movie cliché for a time of innocence. The film's first line, spoken by a 12-year-old girl, is another

▲ MY BEAUTIFUL LAUNDERETTE

Something exhilarating was afoot in British movies in the mid-'80s. Young filmmakers were beginning to examine the London working class with a vigor unfelt since the glory days of *Room at the Top, This Sporting Life,* and *A Taste of Honey* a quarter of a century before. *My Beautiful Launderette,* about the conflict between street

punks and Pakistani immigrants in south London, makes most American teen films look like sitcom fodder. Written by playwright Hanif Kureishi, then 29, the son of an English mother and Pakistani father, the film stars Gordon Warnecke as an ambitious 18-year-old Pakistani trying to make peace with his adopted country. His journalist father, played with mournful dignity by Roshan Seth, sees little hope in the future. But Warnecke's businessman uncle, acted with verve and wit by Saeed Jaffrey, imbues the boy with a sense of hustle. Warnecke sees a chance of creating Utopia by turning a rundown launderette into a neon-lit social club. He enlists the help of his loutish male lover, astonishingly well acted by Daniel Day Lewis in a role strikingly different from that of the aesthete he portrayed in *A Room with a View*. For all the high-spirited wit conveyed by the actors under Stephen Frears' lively direction, the film's vision is bleak. But here is a truly exciting and original film that opens up a world most of us know only from headlines.
R / 1986 / Karl-Lorimar

▲ MY BODYGUARD

Tony Bill spent most of his career playing second lead to the likes of Frank Sinatra (in *Come Blow Your Horn*) and Warren Beatty (in *Shampoo*) before he began producing a string of fine movies including *The Sting* and *Hearts of the West*. In this quiet debut as a director, he showed he had learned a thing or two about the business. The story is simple: After a new teenager in town (Chris Makepeace) is shaken down for protection money by the high school bully, he hires a bodyguard—a huge classmate the other kids whisper once actually killed a man. Naturally, Makepeace and his protector (Adam Baldwin) become fast friends, and the bully (Matt Dillon) gets his comeuppance in the end. The story is affectingly told. Martin Mull, as Makepeace's harried hotel manager father, and Ruth Gordon, his hilariously eccentric grandmother who tries to pick up out-of-towners at the bar, splendidly complement the boy's earnestness. As a result, Bill's first directorial effort didn't change him into Ingmar Bergman, but it turned into an unpretentious winning film.
PG / 1980 / CBS/Fox

▲ MY BRILLIANT CAREER

It's easy to see why this adaptation of a 1901 novel by Miles Franklin swept six of the 1979 Australian Academy Awards. Actress Judy Davis didn't win, but she is superb as a free-spirited teenager who longs to escape her family's poverty and become a writer. Director Gillian Armstrong and screenwriter Eleanor Witcombe illustrate effectively the barriers the girl faces. She even wonders at times if she wouldn't be better off settling for bourgeois domesticity. The continent is distant, the backdrop strange, but, as American women will deduce, the problems are very familiar.
G / 1980 / Vestron

▲ MY CHAUFFEUR

We hadn't seen Bo Derek for a while. Could it be that she had opened an underground acting school, with a faculty of Charo, Ali MacGraw, and Mamie Van Doren? How else to explain Deborah (*Valley Girl*) Foreman, the substarlet who plays the lead in this limp farce? Surely she could not be this bad an actress by accident; she must have studied at the feet of the immortals. Foreman portrays a free-spirited young woman who gets a job driving for a snobbish limousine company. She drives a little, but what she does mostly are cute reactions. It's as if Phyllis George at her most ingratiating were suddenly revved up to triple charm power. Writer-director David Beaird seems to have the attention span of a gnat. The wit too. A mildly clever opening sequence, in which Foreman gets the job offer while working as a dishwasher, appears to have exhausted Beaird's imagination. The rest of the movie just drones on, through grating bits by Howard (TV's ''Head of the Class'') Hesseman, a scene that trashes the talents of the comic magicians Penn and Teller, and numerous lifeless transitions. Sam (*Flash Gordon*) Jones, as a rich man's son, bares most of his hunky self and is not humiliated too much. The sound track has some nice rock 'n' roll by an L.A.-based group called the Wigs. Other than that, there's no humor, style, or pace. There's not even anything to satisfy the voyeurs, except some fleeting nudity. Things are not real slick here, folks.
R / 1986 / Vestron

▲ MY DEMON LOVER

Sort of a cross between *Teen Wolf* and *The Exorcist,* this film tries to be both cute and scary and succeeds at being neither. Scott Valentine is cast as the title character, who isn't much different from his "Family Ties" character, Nick. (He even manages to get in a "Heyyy.") A Greenwich Village derelict, he had a curse cast on him as a kid by a Romanian woman who caught him fooling around with her daughter. Whenever he gets sexually aroused, he literally turns into a monster. Unfortunately all the women around wear low-cut blouses, spandex pants, and miniskirts. Then appears Michelle Little, who dresses like Annie Hall and says things like, "I'm a woman of the '80s. I can risk my life in armed combat, I can have empty sex with strangers, and all I want is to be loved." When Valentine meets her, he falls immediately in love. All he wants is to be cured. Performing a really noble deed will lift the curse, though it then will leave his body—stay with us here—and enter the person to whom he feels closest. Little, of course, says to him, "I've never felt so close to anyone before." The opportunity for a noble deed is supplied by a slasher who is terrorizing women. Valentine, who blacks out when he undergoes transformation, worries that he might be the villain. But it's obvious who the real culprits are: director Charlie Loventhal and debuting screenwriter Leslie Ray. Ray says she conceived the script just after ending a horrible relationship and giving up on men. So here's the apparent moral: All men are monsters unless they're in love, and even then they hurt women. Thanks, Leslie, we needed that.

PG / 1987 / N/A

▲ MY DINNER WITH ANDRE

A movie like no other, defying categorization, but a must for viewers interested in adventurous experimentation. Directed by Louis (*Atlantic City*) Malle, the film takes place almost entirely inside a small, elegant Manhattan restaurant. The camera sticks to one table where a playwright, played by playwright-actor Wallace Shawn, talks to a friend he hasn't seen in half a decade. The friend is an avant-garde director, played by actor and avant-garde director Andre Gregory. As Gregory weaves lyrical tales of transcendental experiences from Scotland to the Sahara that make Shirley MacLaine look like a timid stay-at-home, Shawn listens quietly. Finally he explodes in a passionate and hilarious defense of common sense and more common comforts. For nearly 2 hours these two sparring partners will hold you in thrall. Skeptics are advised to rent the video at once and see how conversation can be comedy, drama, mystery, adventure and, yes, even a movie.

PG / 1982 / Pacific Arts

▲ MY FAVORITE YEAR

Richard Benjamin hit on a smashing idea to mark his transformation from actor to director—recreate the golden age of "live" television. The year is 1954, when Sid Caesar, Carl Reiner, and Milton Berle were the kings of comedy and such brash young writers as Mel Brooks, Neil Simon, and Woody Allen fed them the jokes. Benjamin, who was an NBC page at the time, doesn't appear onscreen himself, but he sets up the '50s Manhattan atmosphere exactly right, from the Rockefeller Center studios to the Stork Club nightlife. And with newcomer Mark Linn-Baker as a writer, Joe Bologna as top banana, and Peter O'Toole as a boozing matinee idol doing a guest shot on their show, the elements are set to mesh. Benjamin and screenwriters Norman (*Blazing Saddles*) Steinberg and Dennis ("Welcome Back, Kotter") Palumbo are fatally perfunctory about structure, pace, and characterization. Many of the sight gags, some older than the 1950s, are blah when they should be boffo. Nevertheless, the actors do a lot to retrieve the project, except for Linn-Baker, who tries haltingly to substitute a genial grin for grit. Lainie Kazan is fat and sassy as Linn-Baker's Jewish mama, and Bologna's send-up of Sid Caesar is a withering, wicked caricature. Still, it's the triumphantly mannered O'Toole who walks off with the picture. Whether he's swilling Scotch to allay his fear of the live TV camera, unapologetically using a ladies' room, or excusing his behavior by declaiming, "I am not an actor—I am a movie star," the Oscar-nominated O'Toole performs with an irresistible nippy panache. In a film of only flickering fun, he's the light that never fails.

PG / 1982 / MGM/UA

N

▲ THE NAME OF THE ROSE

You can't argue with the facts: Umberto Eco's 1980 novel of heresy and murder in a 14th-century Italian monastery sold an astonishing four million copies in twenty-four languages. Of course, no figures exist showing how many readers actually understood Eco's philosophical, theological, and epistemological allusions, often rendered in great gobs of untranslated Latin. Those who didn't comprehend it all were probably holding out for a movie version that would get right to the juicy parts. What emerges on-screen is definitely more whodunit than who-thunkit, though the use of Aristotle's *Poetics* as a key clue may still confound viewers weaned on Mike Hammer. Still, for a good while the film moves along as a gripping, grandly atmospheric detective story. Sean Connery is superb, bringing reserves of strength and welcome humor to the role of Brother William of Baskerville, a Franciscan Sherlock Holmes determined to unmask the culprit in the bizarre deaths of seven monks. Christian (*The Legend of Billie Jean*) Slater is wonderfully appealing as his Watson, a 16-year-old novice in whom the older monk sees his younger self. After a young peasant girl (Valentina Vargas) seduces Slater in one of the hottest love scenes of recent years, Connery delivers a teasing lecture on carnal pleasures that turns out to be the film's last sign of playfulness. That's when director Jean-Jacques Annaud, of *Quest for Fire* fame, loses his sense of pace and balance. There is too much of William (*Prizzi's Honor*) Hickey, who overacts shamelessly as a doomsaying mystic. There's too little of F. Murray (*Amadeus*) Abraham in fine, vigorous form in the role of the heretic-burning inquisitor. Instead Annaud substitutes gory torture scenes for the real drama, a battle of wits that Connery and Abraham could have delivered with zest. Worse, the film has none of the novel's passion for the power of the word. Annaud's monks are all grotesques borrowed from a Fellini nightmare; there's nary a glimpse of the dedicated transcribers who might make an audience care about the fate of their lives and immortal souls. Those unfamiliar with the book may nod off before Connery gets his man. For them it's a case of *Haec Rosa te fecit obdormire*—most of this *Rose* is a doze.

R / 1986 / CBS/Fox

▲ NATIONAL LAMPOON'S ANIMAL HOUSE

We know it made a bundle, spawned a rash of imitations, put John Landis on the map as a director, and made a star of John Belushi, but what we have here is far from a classic comedy. This one-gag movie—on early '60s fraternity life—wears thin somewhere between the toga party and the umpteenth make-out session on the bluff. It does, however, feature Belushi as the raunchiest member of the Delta house, whose charter the school's evil dean wants to get revoked. Belushi runs through a whole anthology of comic styles here but fails to generate as many laughs as, say, his samurai bit on TV. All the classic campus archetypes from bouffant-coiffed cheerleaders to wimpy new pledges are here, though Donald Sutherland as an ersatz hip English prof and Stephen Bishop as a guitar-playing folkie contribute funny cameos. It's fun, too, spotting stars of tomorrow in supporting roles: There's Tom (*Amadeus*) Hulce, Karen (*Raiders of the Lost Ark*) Allen, and Kevin (*Footloose*) Bacon. Somehow this first film effort by *National Lampoon* magazine (three staffers wrote the script) is reminiscent of stale beer. As Belushi cracked when he was expelled: "Seven years of college down the drain."

R / 1978 / MCA

▲ NATIONAL LAMPOON'S EUROPEAN VACATION

The notion that he's Chevy Chase and we're not has come to be more and more appealing. At least none of us was responsible for the string of sour comedies in which he participated. This one is almost grim. It's a disappointing sequel to *National Lampoon's Vacation* and includes Chase as well as his "wife," Beverly D'Angelo, from the original with two new teenagers, Dana Hill and Jason Lively. They are supposed to be having a less than idyllic time on their European trip, but they overplay considerably. These whiney, unlikable actors often seem barely dutiful in their approach to dialogue that is, admittedly, about as funny as oatmeal. The only imaginative bit opens the film, when Chase and his family win their trip on a "Family Feud"-like TV show where greed and foolishness are the entertainment. John Astin sends up Richard Dawson's smoochy emcee, lusting after nubile female contestants. Once Chase and company get to Europe the best to hope for is a muddled travelogue. Chase is his smirky self, pausing after every line as if he's waiting to hear the laugh. Director Amy Heckerling and co-writer John Hughes seem to have agreed that when their imaginations failed, they would use a car crash scene. There are many car crash scenes.

PG-13 / 1986 / Warner

▲ NATIONAL LAMPOON'S VACATION

Thanks largely to Chevy Chase's zaniness and comic timing this is a very funny movie. Chase, whose career has taken more than a few pratfalls since his "Saturday Night Live" days, plays an all-American boob—a father driving his family on a cross-country road trip all preplanned down to the minute. Their destination: the Walley World amusement park. The trip is a series of mishaps and goofs. Chase, wife Beverly D'Angelo, and their kids, Dana Barron and Anthony Michael Hall, visit a cousin (Randy Quaid) who likes to barbecue Hamburger Helper without the hamburger. Then they pack up old Aunt Edna, who wants to visit her son en route. Only one problem—Aunt Edna (Imogene Coca) dies in the car. So Chase, worried about getting to Walley World on time, decides to strap her to the luggage rack and drop her off at her son's house with a note. Directed by SCTV veteran Harold Ramis, the movie strikes one discordant note (lifted directly but inappropriately from *American Graffiti*): Every once in a while supermodel Christie Brinkley, making her movie debut, pops up driving a red Ferrari, flirting with Chase for no apparent reason. When she finally lures him into a motel pool, it seems wildly out of place—the only reason for the scene is to show her in a bathing suit, which isn't reason enough. The ending is on the wishy-washy side, too, as if to say, "Gee, aren't we all having a good time?" In this case, though, that is precisely the truth.

R / 1983 / Warner

▲ NATIVE SON

There's a star-making role at the center of this drama, but unfortunately it didn't make a star of Victor Love, the young actor who inhabits—or in this case inhibits—the title role. In Richard Wright's 1940 novel about racism and retribution in Chicago, Bigger Thomas was the embodiment of oppressed youth and repressed rage. But Love isn't incendiary—and without passion he can't achieve the pathos of Wright's book, which, after all, detailed an American tragedy. Brought into a wealthy white household as a chauffeur, Bigger accidentally kills the daughter who has befriended him. As he goes on trial, so does the American class system. Director Jerrold Freedman treats the classic novel as a classic. The movie has no life or voice of its own, but neither does it properly honor Wright's work. The novelist painted Bigger as the pawn in a cruel panorama, but Freedman deals mainly in close-ups and redundant claustrophobia—perhaps the necessary evils of a $2.5 million budget. In an all-star cast that includes Oprah Winfrey as Bigger's mother and Geraldine Page as the family cook, it is the two performers with the least sympathetic roles who most skillfully interpret Wright's characterization. As Bigger's beloved victim, Elizabeth McGovern gives her most incisive performance. Wearing a coy smile with her white gloves, she clearly understands the condescension that this woman markets as compassion. Playing her communist boyfriend, Matt Dillon strips away his mannerisms. It's surely some of the best work of these young actors, and when this couple takes Bigger out on the town, where he experiences a night of inadvertent humiliation, the movie is temporarily in sync with Wright's vision of anguish and ambivalence. Watching *Native Son* when these two are absent from the screen, you feel certain that junior high school students everywhere will admire it. They should, since it seems to have been fashioned solely for them.

PG / 1986 / CBS/Fox

▲ THE NATURAL

As a simplistic fairy tale, this baseball film has a couple of wonderful moments. In one, Robert Redford, a young bumpkin pitcher on his way to a major league tryout, runs into a sneering Ruthian big league slugger, Joe Don Baker, at a country fair and strikes him out. The other is the movie's climactic scene, where Redford is at the plate with the season on the line, blood seeping through his shirt, his magic bat broken, and the forces of corruption, who have bet against his team already, gloating over their apparent victory. Who could avoid rooting for Redford in that situation? Those involving moments are, however, separated by long stretches of listless, murky, rarely entertaining exposition. As whimsy, the film is rarely funny. As drama, it is amok with clichés. And as a baseball movie, it is full of gaffes: A pitcher winds up when he should be stretching; a ball park that is supposed to be Wrigley Field in Chicago is nowhere near a major league stadium (the action sequences were all shot in Buffalo); most of the players are inept (two ex-pros, Joe Charboneau and Sibby Sisti, have tiny roles). Redford himself is convincing enough, and the cast includes Robert Duvall, Glenn Close, Kim Basinger, Wilford Brimley, and Richard Farnsworth. But putting those actors in a clumsy film such as this is like putting Mike Schmidt, Eddie Murray, and Wade Boggs on a semipro team in Punxatawney, Pennsylvania. Cinematographer Caleb Deschanel engages in the cinematic equivalent of overmanaging too. Every other scene, for instance, seems to be in silhouette or just plain in the dark. The film, based on Bernard Malamud's 1952 novel, is also enigmatic. Redford is shot early in the film by a mysterious woman, Barbara Hershey. Then he reappears sixteen years later as a middle-aged rookie, with no explanation of where he's been. Lightning flashes every once in a while, suggesting divine intervention—not by the commissioner of baseball either. And Close seems to have a mystical, other worldly demeanor. Overall, while it would ordinarily take ten Tab Hunters to get one Robert Redford in a trade, this movie makes you long for the fantasy and fun of *Damn Yankees*. The scouting report on *The Natural* has to read: lots of tools but no heart.

PG / 1984 / RCA/Columbia

▲ NEA

Raunchy but charming, this film by French director Nelly Kaplan manages to be all about pornography without falling into the category itself. It concerns a brooding 16-year-old virgin (played with great range by lovely Ann Zacharias) who turns her sexual fantasies into an erotic novel called *Nea*. What she hasn't learned from the books she shoplifts, she gleans from studious voyeurism until eventually she is compelled to seek out firsthand experience. She finds a cooperative subject in a handsome publisher, Sami Frey. Alas, what began as a wicked, lighthearted sexual comedy thereupon descends into muddled melodrama. For the audience, it's a case of enjoyment interruptus. (In French with subtitles.)
R / 1978 / RCA/Columbia

▲ NEAR AND FAR AWAY

Sweden never had cowboys or Indians. The country was not a major factor in the world wars. It isn't disputed Mafia turf. So it's no wonder Swedes turn out so many movies about people who stand in front of blank walls and think bleak thoughts. This one, the first directing job for filmmaker Marianne Ahme, is about a young therapist, played by Lilga Kovanko with resignation. Her burden is a young man who refuses to talk and has two basic moods—pout and tantrum. He is not an appealing character but she is, and the film has something to say about how difficult it is for people to communicate. The subject is one the Swedish are adept at. (Anyway, who would believe *Gunfight in Matsknutsgardarana?*) (In Swedish with subtitles.)
Unrated / 1978 / N/A

▲ NEIGHBORS

In this fitfully funny movie, based on Thomas Berger's sharply satirical novel, wild man John Belushi plays a dull suburban type who comes home from work, eats dinner with his bored wife (Kathryn Walker), and watches television. Then Dan Aykroyd, all bluster and fast-mouth (the part you'd expect Belushi to play) and looking like a '50s greaser with dyed blond hair, moves in next door with his ravishing wife, Cathy (*Raging Bull*)

Moriarty. He cons Belushi out of his car, cadges dinner money, and the two men have a mud wrestling match. Moriarty accuses Belushi of making a pass at her, then he turns to arson and brings down the house in more ways than one. Badly directed by John (*Rocky*) Avildsen, the film never finds a comfortable comic tone. But Belushi, in his last film, worked hard to show he could play successfully against type. His actor's discipline—he never broke character—proved he might have surprised us all with better material. *Neighbors* stands as a reminder of Belushi's potential and a measure of what was lost with his untimely death.

R / 1982 / RCA/Columbia

▲ THE NESTING

It may be true that sex, or the fear of it, lies at the core of all good horror movies. This film pays homage to that well-worn conceit but seems curiously shy about pushing it to dramatic effect. The result: a watered-down version of the usual haunted house story. Newcomer Robin Groves plays a novelist suffering from a variety of ailments: writer's block, fear of men, and agoraphobia (fear of being in open spaces). She moves alone to a place in the country. Naturally, it's a strange, octagonal-shaped house in the middle of nowhere. Soon everything goes wrong: She begins to have odd dreams; the owner of the house takes one look at her and has a heart attack; she's even attacked by the handyman. What's going on? The house used to be a brothel, and all the whores were murdered one night by a group of neighborhood thugs. Ghosts are a-slink. Groves, as the neurotic, obsessed writer, is wholesomely sexy. John Carradine, as the landlord, is as usual wasted. Sadly, this also marks the last appearance of Gloria Grahame, the sultry blonde in many early '50s films, who has a cameo as the brothel's madam.

R / 1982 / Warner

▲ NEVER CRY WOLF

A government biologist at Project Lupine in the Arctic arrives to study the behavior of wolves in the wilderness. Soon he is alone, sliding around the ice, and munching mouse sandwiches to survive. Charles Martin Smith, the nerd in *American Graffiti,* eventually becomes transformed from fearful scientist to unofficial protector of the wild pack. As might be expected from cinematographer-turned-director Carroll (*The Black Stallion*) Ballard, this drama is rife with memorable images: blue mountains at dawn, frozen wastelands punctuated by the sight of a lone man, and Smith running naked with a herd of wolf friends. Despite the visuals, the film is uninvolving, perhaps because Ballard, a whiz with the camera, is less skilled at narrative drive. In his debut feature, *The Black Stallion,* the boy-meets-horse adventure tale compensated. Here he resorts to that desperate device, voiceover narration. Smith can't save him either, he doesn't have the presence to carry a feature. *Never Cry Wolf* was an early attempt by the Disney studio to beef up its image. For both the studio and Ballard, the film was a nice try but a disappointment.

PG / 1983 / Disney

▲ NEVER SAY NEVER AGAIN

It's not a rap against Roger Moore to say that this film seemed to bring James Bond back to life. Sean Connery did, after all, define the character. In this, Connery's first Bond film since *Diamonds Are Forever* in 1971, he restores the temper, the vague nastiness, the passion to Ian Fleming's agent. (In fairness, some Bond purists argue that Moore's cooler, more detached portrayal is closer to Fleming's 007.) The plot is a little too familiar—it is only a slightly updated version of 1965's *Thunderball,* in which a SPECTRE operative steals two nuclear weapons and holds them for ransom. Bond in this case is brought out of retirement to handle the situation. That fits in nicely with the return of Connery who, at 53, looked noticeably older but still more than fit (and still possessed of an Oscar caliber hairpiece). He is also surrounded by some first-rate acting. Klaus Maria Brandauer, the great Austrian actor, plays the sadistic SPECTRE agent. It's the kind of performance that should be shown in acting classes—understated, tense, and full of intelligence; he becomes one of the screen's most convincing psychotics. Barbara (*Masada*) Carrera has a great time as Brandauer's equally insane henchwoman; she never has trouble looking sexy, and she throws herself into the evil of this part with delicious abandon. Kim (*Fool for Love*) Basinger is gorgeous and bright as Brandauer's more or less innocent mistress. Irvin (*The Empire Strikes Back*) Kershner directed, with occasional lapses into near slapstick but far greater attention to his actors and less to effects than had been typical of later Bond films. It doesn't hurt that the wry script by Lorenzo (*Flash Gordon*) Semple, Jr., takes itself with exactly the right degree of seriousness. At one point former chorus boy Connery and Basinger are doing a tango—quite a spiffy one at that—when he reveals to her that Brandauer has been using her. "Your brother is dead," Connery whispers in her ear. "Keep dancing." Welcome back, Mr. Bond.

PG / 1983 / Warner

▲ NEWSFRONT

In Australian director Phillip Noyce's offbeat, nostalgic look at newsreels, the action takes place during the late 1940s and early 1950s and centers on a Sydney movie news company. By cutting back and forth between real events and the private lives of his fictional characters, Noyce affectively weaves a narrative of a decade marked by the end of World War II and the Melbourne Olympics in 1956. There's a good sense of how public events sometimes influence private lives—in one scene, a cameraman's wife leaves him largely because of his leftist politics. If the slow pace of the movie is bothersome, it's probably meant to remind us of those long-ago days before TV speeded everything up.

PG / 1979 / Embassy

▲ NEW YORK, NEW YORK

Robert De Niro delivers a fine-tuned performance as a flakey '40s sax player who conceals a violent personality beneath a slapstick exterior. Liza Minnelli, his Garlandesque singer-wife, belts out old-time big-band hits ("The Man I Love") and four new Kander and Ebb (*Cabaret*) songs with expected gusto. But despite fine support from Mary Kay Place and an evocative "Honeysuckle Rose" from Diahnne Abbott (Mrs. De Niro), director Martin Scorsese lets nostalgia mortis set in. Too many cocktail table conversations in too many sepia-tinged dance halls induce a stupor that doesn't lift until the credits crawl. For purists, the video features cut footage including the "Happy Endings" musical number. Additional note: No one, including Oscar voters, made much

of the rousing title song until Sinatra recorded the tune years later and made it a standard.

PG / 1978 / CBS/Fox

▲ NIGHT CROSSING

The fact that this is a true story of two families' flight in a hot-air balloon from East to West Germany deprives it of some potential nail-biting suspense. (The production also comes from the Walt Disney studios, where unhappy endings are anathema.) Yet it is a well crafted, honest film directed by Delbert Mann. Political polemics are minimized in favor of focusing on the families, one headed by John Hurt and Jane Alexander, the other by Beau Bridges and Glynnis O'Connor. Hurt is superb as a grim, ingenious electrician who builds the balloon's heating system; Alexander plays her usual fretful Earth Mother/devoted wife. At one point she conscientiously cleans house before fleeing, though only the police will be coming there. Bridges, however, with his all-American looks and voice, seems absurdly out of place, like some beach-movie refugee who surfed over the Berlin Wall. Klaus Lowitsch's nasty, snooping policeman provides all the villainy needed.

PG / 1982 / Disney

▲ NIGHT GAMES

French director Roger Vadim became the GM of sex symbols, having turned out Brigitte Bardot, Catherine Deneuve, and Jane Fonda in earlier model years and thrown his heart so much into his work that he had a child with Deneuve and made Mrs. Vadims of the other two. Another product off his assembly line was the star of this film, Cindy Pickett, a Houston-bred actress, late of the TV soap "The Guiding Light." She doesn't measure up to her predecessors on a number of counts, including acting ability. And Vadim in his second Hollywood film didn't help by putting her in a movie with no visible plot. It's about a California housewife turned so frigid by a childhood rape that she screams anytime any man—including her wealthy husband, Barry Primus—looks at her. This affliction leads Primus to go to London by himself, leaving Pickett with some execrable supporting actors and a few Vadim fantasies that are more ludicrous than sexy. The only interest lies in minor mysteries: Who's the character in the strange get-ups who keeps ravishing Cindy? If she's so rich, why can't she afford underwear? Did Fonda really start like this? R / 1980 / Embassy

▲ NIGHTHAWKS

Sylvester Stallone still looked like a one-punch performer in this feeble dud about two New York cops (Sly and Billy Dee Williams) assigned to track down an international terrorist (Rutger Hauer) in Manhattan. Stallone seemed to have whittled his thug shtik down to one vacant expression with moronic diction to match. "Dat," Stallone triumphantly tells his partner, "is dem standing over dere." Not that David Shaber's script provides many lines better dan dat. "Goddammit," Stallone mumbles after seeing Hauer murder a woman hostage in cold blood, "he killed her." Lindsay Wagner, as Stallone's ex-wife, and Persis Khambatta, as Hauer's sultry accomplice, are both wasted in throwaway roles. Worse, Shaber and director Bruce Malmuth made Hauer the screen's first designer terrorist, a gorgeous, finely tailored Teutonic hunk whose passion for bombing crowded urban areas is matched only by his taste for discos. Not even a desperation dip in the East River to escape his pursuers can dampen Hauer's *Gentlemen's Quarterly* flash. He emerges for a final showdown with his white crewneck sweater totally dry. The film, however, remains thoroughly all wet. R / 1981 / MCA

▲ A NIGHT IN HEAVEN

How about *An Afternoon in Purgatory? An Evening in Limbo? A Day in the Pits? Flashdunce?* No title would be idiotic enough to reflect the mindlessness of this film about a college student/male stripper who seduces his speech professor. Christopher ("Dallas") Atkins plays the student. He was, of course, the most boyishly good-looking type in Hollywood. His voice didn't quite seem to have changed, though, and the closest he comes to sensuality is that of a rutting Mouseketeer. Then, too, he is to acting what Helen Hayes is to playing middle linebacker. The usually splendid Lesley Ann (*Victor/Victoria*) Warren sinks to the level of her leading man's performance. Trying to portray a sensitive middle-aged woman whose husband's neglect has made her vulnerable, she frets, blushes, sobs, and all but gnaws on the camera lens. Carrie (*The Fury*) Snodgress plays Atkins' waitress mother as if she were auditioning for a paper towel commercial, and Deney Terrio, the preening host of the syndicated TV series "Dance Fever," also has a small role, though not small enough. Director John (*Rocky*) Avildsen did at least help screenwriter Joan (*Nashville*) Tewkesbury prove that women writers are the equal of men when it comes to writing doltish films. R / 1983 / Key

▲ A NIGHTMARE ON ELM STREET

It didn't lead to any picnics on Fourth and Main either. Director Wes Craven includes two moments of comic relief. In one, a teenage girl, haggard from lack of sleep, looks in a mirror and exclaims, "Wow. I look twenty." In the other it is revealed that the featured monster is named "Freddie Krueger." Other than that, Craven goes for the scare 91 minutes out of 92. Freddie, who shows up in the nightmares of four teenagers the same evening, is a cadaverous-type guy who wears a plaid shirt and has long, stilettolike appendages on the ends of his fingers, as if he had an overimaginative manicurist or perhaps an excessively iron-rich diet. He is out for blood, which he gets in vast, gushing quantities, though he himself seems to be filled with what looks like antifreeze. Craven (then 35) is something of a generational turncoat. All his adult characters have the intelligence and courage of cantaloupes. John Saxon, the John Carradine of his era as far as B pictures go, plays a police detective. Ronee Blakely seems to be half asleep as Saxon's alcoholic ex-wife. It's their daughter, Heather Langenkamp, who is Freddie's main adversary. Langenkamp is quite impressive; if this were a different movie, her acting ability would probably have attracted some attention. But then in this kind of movie it's not the actors' sweat and tears the audience cares about; it's only the blood. R / 1984 / Media

▲ A NIGHTMARE ON ELM STREET, PART 2: FREDDY'S REVENGE

For anyone wondering how scary this sequel to the dreadful 1984 chiller is, its frightening moments include an attack by a berserk parakeet, a toaster that catches fire, and some exploding beer cans. Pretty terrifying, eh? Freddy Krueger, the original *Nightmare*'s villain, is back with his steel fingernails. Sometimes he is invisible, sometimes he's not. Sometimes he makes lightning, sometimes he makes snakes appear. Sometimes he just closes doors. His main antagonist is played by Mark Patton, with an intensity better reserved for *King Lear.* The director, Jack Sholder, has written and directed for PBS. For this he deserves to be boiled in oil or, worse, forced to watch his own tedious, humorless mess three or four times in a row.

▲ 'NIGHT, MOTHER

It's hard criticizing this earnest screen version of Marsha Norman's 1983 Pulitzer prizewinning play about a mother's futile eleventh-hour attempt to keep her daughter from suicide. In a scant 90 minutes onstage, the blazingly intense acting duo of Kathy Bates and Anne Pitoniak laid two lives bare in a small-town living room and left audiences reeling. But what soared onstage sinks onscreen with a resounding thud. Screenwriter Norman decided to stick to two characters on one set in transposing her play to film. That forced first-time feature director Tom Moore (who staged the Broadway original) to compensate by racing his camera around the small house like a kid at an Easter egg hunt. The effect is more intrusive than energizing. A worse problem is the miscasting. Sissy Spacek, Oscar winner for *Coal Miner's Daughter,* is one of our ablest actresses. Without her early commitment to do the role, the movie might never have been made. But she's all wrong for the character. The daughter is an epileptic whose handicap has made her ashamed and bitterly antisocial. Abandoned by her husband and delinquent son, she lives with her wheedling, widowed mother. Bates, who created the daughter role and whose performance ranks with the theater's greatest, portrayed an overweight, pasty-faced house flower with a no-bull intelligence. The characterization made believable her arguments to end her own misery. Outdoorsy to her toes, Spacek is so cuddly cute that you ache to save her, which defeats the daughter's case and the play's point. As the mother, Anne Bancroft is surprising effective at first. She offsets her striking lack of resemblance to Spacek by

adopting a near-flawless match for Sissy's down-home twang. And she gets laughs. Searching her mind for something cheerful (revealingly, more for her sake than her daughter's), she suggests, "Let's call a taxi and go to the A&P." Bancroft emotes vigorously, but she seems unwilling to play the mother's cruel, clutching side. Eyes flashing fire, she wants to be Mother Courage. The result is only half a performance in a movie that's merely a pale shadow of a powerhouse play.
PG-13 / 1986 / MCA

▲ NIGHT OF THE JUGGLER

Everything about this prolonged chase movie is illogical, including the title. Except for ten minutes or so, it takes place in bright sunshine, and there is no juggling, although that might have been a relief. The film starts promisingly as a psychotic sewer worker, Cliff (*Lenny*) Gorman, kidnaps the cherubic daughter of ex–New York cop James Brolin in Central Park. Problem is, he nabbed the wrong girl (he was looking for a real estate developer's daughter), and there follows a farfetched odyssey through Manhattan as Brolin tries to rescue his child. Considering the ease with which he overpowers street gangs, pornhouse bouncers, and the entire NYPD, it ought to be a snap. The onetime sidekick to Dr. Welby even defies medical science, sprinting about on an injured leg that necessitated crutches only minutes earlier. Gorman is convincingly crazy but undone by inane dialogue. Director Richard Butler, a veteran of six Disney movies, handles action sequences capably enough, yet the project is a nonstop assault on credibility. Credibility loses.
R / 1980 / Media

▲ THE NIGHT OF THE SHOOTING STARS

The Raviani brothers, who directed 1977's *Padre Padrone* and co-directed this movie, start out with an intriguing situation. At the end of World War II, the townspeople of San Martino, Italy, are divided: some are for the retreating Germans, others for the advancing Americans. Late one night the pro-Americans steal out of town to look for their liberators. Their adventures along the

way are the real meat of the story. In the climactic sequence the pro-Fascists and the pro-Americans fight it out in a beautiful wheat field. There are other striking scenes. In a touchingly erotic moment, an older villager and a married woman with whom he has been in love for forty years finally sleep together in a farmhouse. Lyrical and compelling, the film haunts the heart and the conscience. (In Italian with subtitles.)
R / 1983 / MGM/UA

▲ NIGHT SHIFT

Ron Howard, then 28, was still burdened by his images as the ageless Opie of "The Andy Griffith Show" or as Richie Cunningham of "Happy Days." Directing this film about prostitution and mortuary science vaulted him at last into the R-rated world, even though the hookers and the morgue in *Night Shift* are a facade for an amiable, sitcommish comedy. Henry Winkler, whose film career never made people forget the Fonz either, stars as a meticulous, self-effacing morgue attendant. He eagerly shows a picture of his plain, neurotic fiancée to everyone, explaining, "The picture doesn't do her justice. She's suffering from water buildup." His "mother goes to a séance every Friday night since my father died just so she can still yell at him." Winkler remains appealingly apologetic in the face of life's degradations. But as the film bounces along and the character becomes more indignant, he loses his charm. Then newcomer Michael Keaton, on the other hand, is consistently pleasing as the wacked-out hustler who talks Winkler into running a call girl service out of the morgue. And a pre-"Cheers" Shelley Long is a thorough delight as a happy hooker. The writers, TV veteran Lowell ("Laverne and Shirley") Ganz and Babaloo Mandell, add enough eccentrics and offbeat situations to keep things interesting. This is a penny candy film, bereft of significance but not lacking in charm. And Aunt Bee needn't have worried, it didn't deserve this rating.
R / 1982 / Warner

▲ 9½ WEEKS

For a moment let's forget who's at fault for this sad-sack sex saga and praise instead one participant who isn't to blame. Her name is Kim Basinger. For a while, most people knew her as

the blond Georgia peach in the ads for Revlon and Clairol. Then she quiet modeling to do star spots on TV (*Portrait of a Centerfold*) and in movies (*Never Say Never Again*) that crudely capitalized on her looks. She proved there was more by providing the only comic zing in *The Natural* and *The Man Who Loved Women*. In 1985, as Sam Shepard's emotionally bruised half sister in *Fool for Love,* Basinger surprised detractors with an acclaimed dramatic performance that showed she was ready to make a real run at stardom. Not even *9½ Weeks* could stop her, though the film is dumb enough to crush a lesser actress. Basinger plays a newly divorced art gallery assistant who wants nothing more of love until she meets Mickey (*Year of the Dragon*) Rourke, a commodities broker with a penchant for sadomasochistic games. Adapted from a 1978 novel by Elizabeth McNeil (supposedly based on her own experiences), the movie is crowded with 9½ weeks' worth of sex scenes meant to represent the height of cinematic daring. Phooey. Compared to the lion's roar of *Last Tango in Paris,* *9½ Weeks* manages at most a mouse's squeak. Rourke brandishes a riding crop in one scene and never uses it. Basinger dresses as a man to meet him at Manhattan's Algonquin Hotel and looks merely silly. When, as a prelude to sex, they spill the gooey contents of Rourke's refrigerator over their bodies and onto the kitchen floor, you think only of who's going to clean up the mess. The erotica dished out here by director Adrian (*Flashdance*) Lyne sparks with all the excitement of a soggy sweat sock. And this from a movie widely heralded as "too dirty to release." Scenes of Basinger handcuffed to a bed and swallowing Seconal pills with Rourke were deleted to avoid an X rating. But no one spared us Rourke moping around like a truant messenger boy or clunky dialogue or tricky camera techniques that grow tiresome. Against this flow of piffle, Basinger makes a valiant try at finding the heart of a woman in thrall to her own dark impulses. Her honesty earned her something her colleagues in this fetid enterprise didn't deserve: another chance.
R / 1986 / MGM/UA

▲ 1918

You can't help rooting for this small, spare movie. At first glance the subject seems like box-office suicide: A small-town Texas family copes with a

world at war and an influenza epidemic that killed more Americans than died in battle. Try selling that to the *Porky's Revenge* crowd. The main attraction for a young audience is the presence of Matthew Broderick. Broderick is both funny and touching as a teenager who says he's eager to fight in Europe yet gets homesick if he travels as far as Galveston. But his role is basically a supporting one. Nothing about *1918* smacks of a star vehicle. The film is a family affair. Two-time Oscar winner Horton Foote wrote the screenplay (part of a cycle of nine Texas plays he began in the late 1970s). One of them, *Valentine's Day*, marked Matthew Broderick's stage debut in 1979. He co-starred in that production with his late father, James, and dedicates his performance in *1918* to him. Foote is writing about his own family, Texas pioneers who helped settle the state and build its character. Filmed in Waxahachie, Texas (as was *Places in the Heart*), this is clearly a labor of love. To make it more so, Foote's wife Lillian is one of *1918*'s producers. Son Horton, Jr., and daughter Daisy serve as performance assistants. And daughter Hallie Foote has the pivotal role of a young Texas wife (based on her grandmother) who loses her baby and almost her husband to the flu. Her performance is a triumph of strength and sensitivity. Hallie Foote plays a woman whose parents (sharply defined by Rochelle Oliver and Michael Higgins) have brought her up not to give vent to her emotions and doubts. Even her husband (William Converse Roberts) cannot express his own fears about leaving his family to go to war—it would lead to public disgrace. Foote does nothing to dramatize these characters or their situation. There are no bloody death scenes (the carnage is only talked about), no special-effects tornadoes, and no knuckle-wrenching monologues. What Foote delivers are real people coping with the worst that life has to offer and carrying on. Arid realism to some. But those who are weary of hyped-up teen sex comedies will find *1918* an authentic piece of Americana.
PG / 1985 / CBS/Fox

▲ **1984**

The best and perhaps only reason for cheering this film version of George Orwell's classic novel is Richard Burton. In this, his last screen performance, Burton acted with stunning resourcefulness. Despite his health problems, the Welsh actor's resonant voice never lost its power to stir. The rest of the film rarely rises to Burton's sterling standard. Writer-director Michael Radford eschews dealing with the ways time had or had not fulfilled the events Orwell prophesied thirty-five years before. Totalitarianism in the form of Big Brother hasn't blanketed the world, but the age of computers, television monitoring, surveillance, and the nonlanguage of Newspeak is here. Radford, however, makes no use of existent technology, one of the few feasible reasons to remake the original 1956 film. *1984*'s bleak landscapes and overall malaise destroy our interest in hero John Hurt's fight to insist that two plus two equals four. Hurt plays this beleaguered employee of the Ministry of Truth as a walking cadaver whose battle is lost before the film begins. His love scenes with a surviving sensualist (Suzanna Hamilton)—tremendously moving in the book—fail to provide even a spark, and the incessant caterwauling of a Eurythmics song called "Sexcrime (Nineteen Eighty-Four)" doesn't help. Only Burton, as an Inner Party member who befriends and then betrays Hurt, comes through with real dramatic intensity. But Radford sacrifices even this marvelous actor to an obsession with graphic violence (rats chewing on a human face) that renders the last third of the film virtually unwatchable. Endless scenes of Hurt being stretched on a rack offer little besides an apt metaphor for the film: George Orwell's novel of ideas being tortured in a numbing chamber of horrors.
R / 1985 / USA

▲ **1941**

It's never been considered a vintage year. But if you thought December 7 was a disaster, wait until you see what happened six days later! Imagine, as director Steven Spielberg did, that a Japanese submarine is sighted off the coast of California. All hell breaks loose, right? As a study in excess, this so-called "comedy spectacular" is rarely rivaled in recent American cinema. There are a few laughs, yes—for $33-plus million (in 1979 dollars), one expects a little aisle-rolling. But more often, scenes are simply interminable, such as one marathon dance-hall brawl. Some sequences exist solely for one throwaway joke—like the tank that hurtles through a paint factory and then a turpentine factory, emerging good as new. No one in the huge cast has much screen time, though John Belushi, as a loony daredevil pilot, and Warren Oates, playing a paranoid general, manage to stand out. Spielberg falls back shamelessly on his previous movies (the best bit is ripped off from *Jaws*); nor is he above borrowing from *Star Wars* or *The Russians Are Coming*, either. All that might be forgiven if this attempt at humor achieved anything like the sheer terror of *Jaws*'s or *Close Encounters*'s sense of awe. The only sense here is of extravagant waste of time, money, and talent.

PG / 1979 / MCA

▲ 1900

Bernardo (*Last Tango in Paris*) Bertolucci's 4-hour saga of Italian life in the 20th century is alternately brilliant and boring. Robert De Niro plays the patrician son of a Po valley landowner, and Gerard Dépardieu is his best friend, a peasant who works the land. The story traces their relationship from childhood through the turbulent years of Fascism, socialism, and finally, the bitter aftermath of World War II. Dominique Sanda is dazzling as the young wife, Burt Lancaster blustery as the patriarch, and Donald Sutherland vicious as the Blackshirted foreman of the family estate. As always, Bertolucci uses his camera like a paintbrush—and some of the lushest, most erotic scenes ever splash across the screen. Unfortunately, this epic grinds to a yawning close with some mindless breastbeating about the virtues of Marxism. (Dubbed in English.)

Unrated / 1977 / N/A

▲ 9 TO 5

As office workers beset by a sexist boss, Jane Fonda, Lily Tomlin, and Dolly Parton come up with a feather-headed farce about what they call the "pink-collar ghetto." Fonda, playing against type, is a dowdy housewife who joins the work force when hubby dumps her for his own Girl Friday. Tomlin is the office veteran, always passed over in favor of less talented men. And Dolly, bless her, is the stacked sec who spends her time picking up pencils for her leering boss (Dabney Coleman, in a delectable piece of bad-guy ham-

ming). When he gets too boorish to bear, the women take their revenge. Director Colin (*Foul Play*) Higgins and co-scenarist Patricia Resnick sometimes coagulate the plot with sitcom slapstick. But Tomlin, recovering neatly from her *Moment by Moment* fiasco, was inventive, Fonda exhibits refreshing reserve, and Dolly dazzles with her tangy one-liners. Threatening to go for her gun, she warns the boss: "I'll change you from a rooster to a hen with one shot." While the subject merits more subtlety, *9 to 5* does get in a good word for equal jobs, equal pay, and day-care centers. In this case a hoot instead of a hammer proves effective propaganda.

PG / 1981 / CBS/Fox

▲ NOBODY'S FOOL

Crassly patronizing and not nearly funny enough to compensate for its offenses, this diatribe against small-town life was written by playwright Beth (*Crimes of the Heart*) Henley. Based on a screenplay she wrote in 1977, when she was 25, the picture has the tone of a piece of sophomoric fiction written by someone from a rural town trying to prove how sophisticated she has become. Rosanna Arquette plays a forlorn country girl who is ostracized because she got pregnant and stabbed her boyfriend when he wouldn't marry her. The townspeople in the film (shot in Prescott, Arizona) are portrayed as heartless, slack-jawed bumpkins. Eric (*Runaway Train*) Roberts, as a stage-lighting man in town to work on a summer theater project, is the cosmopolitan who will take Arquette away from all that. Arquette and Roberts, two of today's most attractive young actors, have a palpable rapport that Henley and first-time feature director Evelyn Purcell waste. Henley seems to have forgotten the distinction between simple and simpleminded, making Arquette seem almost retarded at times. Her mother, Louise Fletcher, is uncaring. Her brother, J.J. Hardy, is an obese slob. Her boss, played by Arquette's real father, Lewis, is a tyrant. The plot centers on whether Arquette will go to Los Angeles with Roberts when he leaves, but the resolution seems obvious, given the option of staying in a place where everybody acts like Pappy and Mammy Yokum, without their folk wisdom.

PG-13 / 1986 / Karl-Lorimar

▲ NO MERCY

Don't be fooled by the hot-paced first fifteen minutes of this mystery thriller. Despite the fancy cast and New Orleans scenery, you are hurtling toward the abyss of pretension. Richard Gere had himself another expensive clinker. The only thing remotely interesting about his performance as a tough Chicago cop is that he looks older, plumper, and more human than usual. Gere has come to New Orleans to track the killer of his cop buddy. His only lead is a gorgeous blonde—a heart stopper, he calls her—played by Kim Basinger, one of the few still gainfully employed actresses who could almost match Gere's record for flops. While Basinger looks lovely (her lips may be the poutiest and most provocative in screen history), she is hopelessly playing a Cajun sold into sex slavery as a child. Faced with torture and abuse, she never looks more than mildly miffed, like a yuppie who can't find the right shade of lip gloss at Bloomingdale's. Holland's Jeroen Krabbe, eager to kill Gere for stealing his woman, plays the villain of the piece. But the real culprit is screenwriter Jim Carabatsos, who switches from unprintable vulgarity to jaw-dropping symbolic excess. We are meant to see Gere as a modern-day Orpheus descending into Hades to save Eurydice. The final shoot-out, filmed like a surreal *High Noon* by director Richard Pearce, provides the film's only laughs, welcome if unintended. The phony-baloney set is the same one used to represent Chinatown in 1985's major fiasco *Year of the Dragon*. Ah, memories.
R / 1986 / HBO/Cannon

▲ NO NUKES

More than a film compendium of a series of concerts at New York's Madison Square Garden and the following outdoor rally at Battery Park, this is a large-scale, mostly successful screen test for several rock performers. Oh, the message is there all right, laboriously laid out in song, story, speech, and Three Mile Island film clips. But the audience got a bigger bang out of music from Crosby, Stills & Nash, the Doobie Brothers, John Hall, Bonnie Raitt, Jesse Colin Young, and Gil Scott-Heron. Four additional rockers come off especially strongly. Jackson Browne offers a pounding, dramatically motivated "Running on Empty." Dueting "Mockingbird," James Taylor and Carly Simon, then still married, exude the kind of erotic eye contact last seen with Bogie and Bacall. And the pre-superstar Bruce Springsteen, in one riveting set, demonstrates how to fill a stage, not just occupy it. He is his own three-ring circus. For these musical highlights, try *No Nukes;* for unbiased illumination on the nuclear energy dilemma, turn elsewhere.
PG / 1980 / N/A

▲ NORMA RAE

A low-key story about union organizing in an Alabama cotton mill, this film restored the good name of labor movement movies. Its main asset is the presence of three previously underappreciated actors. Sally Field, as a working mother struggling to raise two children alone, richly earned the Oscar she won for the film, with a performance that was passionate but not mawkish. Escaping the yoke of "The Flying Nun" wasn't easy, but Field made the break clean with this achievement. Beau Bridges, who becomes her second husband, is convincingly baffled by her increasing liberation. (In one scene he berates her for neglecting the housework, and she responds by throwing a whole, uncooked chicken and a head of cabbage into the same pot.) And Ron Liebman brings off a challenging role as an organizer from New York who confronts small-town southern hostility and teaches Field some Yiddish slang in his spare time. The movie is quiet, unpretentious, and often moving. Martin Ritt directed with considerable subtlety.
PG / 1979 / CBS/Fox

▲ THE NORSEMAN

"The Six-Million-Dollar Man" in mothballs, Lee Majors moved over onto the big screen, with a less-than-rollicking adventure story under the then family banner, Fawcett-Majors Productions. Majors plays the stuffy leader of a band of Norsemen seeking his father, the king, a blind blond played implausibly by Mel Ferrer. Small wonder Majors seems uptight—the search goes on in what is obviously Florida, where the Norse, in wool leggings and metal helmets, ply steamy Everglades-like waterways in their Viking ship and chase

near-naked Injuns. One scantily clothed maiden (Sonny Bono's then lady Susie Coelho) aids them, for unexplained reasons, and after it's over leaps bravely aboard their Norway-bound ship with no fear of freezing. Majors's mustache and helmet can't disguise his mechanical origins. When he runs—you guessed it—he's still in slow motion.
PG / 1978 / Vestron

▲ THE NORTH AVENUE IRREGULARS

Imagine *Death Wish* or *Walking Tall* in the hands of Walt Disney. Implausible as it may seem, this comedy (based on a true story) recalls both those cynical films, even if corruption is relatively benign in the Disney world of crime. There are no guns, vice, or bad language. Recruited by the activist minister of the North Avenue Presbyterian Church, a spunky band of suburban housewives goes undercover to fight mob-run crime in their community. Amusingly inept at first, the ladies eventually triumph in a demo derby of a finale in which no one gets more than a bump on the noggin. Edward Herrmann is charmingly earnest as the preacher, but the best laughs are provided by loopy Barbara Harris and Ruth Buzzi, who attacks her cameo with maniacal glee. The film is an imaginative variation on the reliable Disney formula that ridicules, then vanquishes, evil; it reassures us that good can find new ways to triumph.
G / 1979 / Disney

▲ NO SMALL AFFAIR

You know something's wrong with a coming-of-age comedy when you'd rather see the teenage hero with the prostitute who propositions him than with the love he pines for. In this boy-meets-older-woman brief encounter, a gawky 16-year-old, Jon Cryer, becomes infatuated with a down-on-her-luck 20ish club singer, Demi Moore. But given the unpleasantness of their topsy-turvy affair, the reasons for it are no small mystery. As played by Moore, this songstress is an unlikable cross between Tovah Feldshuh and Cyndi Lauper. Strident, selfish, and self-pitying, she lives in a highly decorated but incredibly cluttered loft, wears mismatched antique clothes, and bamboozles everyone. As with certain Goldie Hawn clunkers, this script considers kookiness an aphrodisiac. The more oddball and abrasive Moore is, the further in love with her Cryer falls. In the tradition of May-December movie romances, *No Small Affair* represents de-evolution. The movie caresses all the clichés that *Risky Business* avoided: piranha women, passive guys, horny older brothers out of Philip Roth fiction, and caricature moms. Although Cryer's innocent-puppy demeanor works against the offensiveness of the proceedings, director Jerry Schatzberg either encouraged or permitted Cryer to ape Matthew Broderick, who was once signed for the role. The bittersweet conclusion of this affair is intended to suggest that this hapless hero has received an adult education. Instead, you think what he needs is a remedial lesson in romance.
R / 1984 / RCA/Columbia

▲ NOTHING IN COMMON

Tom Hanks was one of the most bankable, likable, and funny young comic actors around. He could turn a mediocre comedy into a good one; to wit, *Volunteers*. But the Shakespearean-trained actor was saying he would like to get away from comedy. A third of the way through this movie, he makes his departure. The drama comes in when Hanks' mother, played by Eva Marie Saint, walks out on husband Jackie Gleason after thirty-six years of marriage. They each turn to Hanks for support, disrupting his life and driving him nuts in the process. Things start getting heavy when Saint says, "It took every ounce of courage to walk out that door." The movie completes its 180-degree turn when Gleason becomes seriously ill. There are some touching scenes between Hanks, who makes the switch to the dramatic look easy, and Gleason, who in his last film is splendid as a cantankerous, unsympathetic womanizer. Still, the movie is best in its pure Hanksy-panky first half. The architecture of the Chicago locations and a pleasing sound track help supply the atmosphere as Hanks, an advertising executive, tries to woo a new client and the client's daughter, sexy Sela (*The Man Who Loved Women*) Ward, at the same time. And director Garry (*The Flamingo Kid*) Marshall seems more at home with the comedy. As Ward says to a befuddled Hanks

after a one-night stand, "It was nice, but let's not make a Wagnerian opera out of it."
PG / 1986 / HBO/Cannon

▲ NOTHING PERSONAL

The grains of a cute romantic comedy á la *Foul Play* were there: Suzanne Somers as a sexy-smart lawyer in aid of frumpy-hip professor Donald Sutherland, who's devoted to saving the baby seals from extinction on the Alaskan coast. The winsome twosome's improbable adventures en route to truth, justice, and the American way are so deftly mangled, though, that all the funny situations are thrown away. The guilty parties apparently are director George Bloomfield and editor George Appleby, as well as scriptwriter Robert Kaufman. Count it as a lost opportunity for puncturing academics, ecologists, bureaucrats, and capitalists. Nothing personal, Donald and Suzanne.
PG / 1980 / Vestron

▲ NUNZIO

Nunzio (David Proval) is a retarded innocent abroad delivering groceries in a tough section of Brooklyn. Italian family sagas being what they are, Nunzio of course has a protective mama (Morgana King, inescapably typecast by *The Godfather*) and a street-smart but loving brother, James Andronica. Andronica proves to be the most sympathetic fellow in the picture, not surprisingly perhaps since he wrote it. He leaves Proval to bumble about as neighborhood stooge, when the poor boy isn't swooping around in a cape pretending to be Superman. The audience suffers through a movie that, while sweet (a heavy sex scene was trimmed to lighten the rating), has little action and little characterization. Nunzio may think he's Superman, but Andronica seemed to think he was Stallone.
PG / 1978 / N/A

O

▲ OBLOMOV

The novel *Oblomov* is one of the most treasured but, outside the Soviet Union, least read masterpieces in 19th-century Russian literature. Written by Ivan Goncharov, an eccentric contemporary of Dostoyevski, it chronicles the ho-hum life of a gentleman landowner gone to seed, who tries to snooze his way through most of the book's 485 pages. "Lying down was not for Oblomov a necessity, as it is for a sick man or for a man who is sleepy," wrote the author. "It was his normal condition." In this Soviet screen version, the passive hero (played by Oleg Tabakov) goes from bed to worse once he is coaxed from his couch by his bubbly best friend. He is dragged on a dizzying round of social visits in snowbound St. Petersburg and falls helplessly in love with a simpering virgin, Elena Solovei. So unstrung is he by this happiness, he abandons her and seeks refuge in his well-worn bunk. The performances are inspired, the cinematography is lyrical and, though no film could match Goncharov's understated, biting narrative, director Nikita (*A Slave of Love*) Mikhalkov makes a graceful attempt. Like Oblomov himself, this movie turns out to be a Russian sleeper. (In Russian with subtitles.)
Unrated / 1981 / N/A

▲ THE OCTAGON

The title must refer to an eight-sided Hollywood plot line none of whose obtuse angles ever intersect, at least until the blade-glinting, teeth-gnashing finale. The hero is Chuck Norris, the real-life black belt superstar and successor (pardon the sacrilege, fans) to Bruce Lee as moviedom's master of handmade mayhem. He plays an ex-karate champ who takes on a secret corps, training mercenaries in the "Ninja" tradition of silent killing. The trainees dress in Darth Vader garb and hone their skills by piercing cantaloupes with three-pronged hooks. Never fear. Norris knows his way around orthopedic nightmares like this film. He has a great bod, and he shows a balletic savagery in his high kicks and lethal punches. But he'll never get a black belt for dramatic wallop. He is an unmussable blond, blue-eyed Good Guy in a world otherwise divided between bad guys and worse guys. He's almost too nice, in fact—like a Redford of martial arts. Only one lady seduces him, Ninja-trained defector Carol Bagdasarian, and then only after confessing she's never hurt anyone, except a guy years earlier who "set fire to my hog." The dialogue is often as painful as a flying kick to the dictionary. Norris's archenemy prepares for their battle by flailing two mini-machetes around with moves from a *Dance Fever* contest. So many scenes take place in the dark that much of this film could be shown with no bulb in the projector.

R / 1980 / Media

▲ OCTOPUSSY

Let's get the standard objections out of the way: Yes, in this, the thirteenth film in the James Bond series (not counting the spoofy *Casino Royale*), there is a lot of casual violence. The leering sexism is relentless from Maurice Cinder's silhouetted opening credits, in which obviously naked women cavort with obviously clothed men. Yes, some of the gimmicks are a little tired by now, and there is some faltering here in the pacing that keeps the eyes and ears so involved the brain has no time to ponder the implausibility of it all. All that said, this is still a marvelous film. Roger Moore, in his sixth Bond movie, does his raised-eyebrow take to perfection. The film, set in sumptuous locations in India, looks and sounds wonderful; it is full of bright colors and brightly recorded sounds. (It is no coincidence that the same production designer, Peter Lamont, has done eleven of the Bond films.) Such familiar faces as Lois Maxwell (Moneypenny), Desmond Llewelyn ("Q"), and Walter Gotell (Gogol, the Russian general) return, as does Maud Adams, the first woman to have two major roles in Bond films, having been disposed of by Christopher Lee in 1974's *The Man with*

the Golden Gun. Kristina Wayborn, who plays Adams's right-hand woman, is an attractive newcomer, and Louis Jourdan makes a superb villain. Tennis pro Vijay Amritraj handles a substantial part decently, and Michaela Clavell, novelist James's daughter, makes a token appearance. The plot has to do with a berserk Soviet general who wants to set off a nuclear bomb in Western Europe and make it seem like an accident, so antiwar forces will demand unilateral disarmament and cede power to the USSR. Director John Glen, who debuted with the twelfth Bond film, *For Your Eyes Only,* maintains the kinetic magic for the most part. While this film is not up to the level of *Goldfinger* or *Live and Let Die,* it is still first-class escapist entertainment.

PG / 1983 / CBS/Fox

▲ AN OFFICER AND A GENTLEMAN

You've seen it all before. Soldier in training falls for girl. She wants marriage, he doesn't. Result: heavy combat. *An Officer and a Gentleman* is a 1980s version that doesn't tamper much with the formula, but it does revitalize it, thanks to the erotic teamwork of Richard Gere and Debra Winger. Gere, usually an actor of catatonic drabness (*Yanks, American Gigolo*), delivers his first passionate screen performance. He plays the son of a whoring sailor (his mother is a suicide), a social climber who sees thirteen weeks of agonizing training at Washington State's Port Rainier Naval Aviation Officer Candidate School as his way to self-esteem and fortune. Winger, realizing her *Urban Cowboy* promise, is a "Puget Deb"— one of the local mill girls who hang out around the Puget Sound base hoping to hook an upwardly mobile meal ticket. The sexual grappling of Gere and Winger is realistically graphic, but director Taylor Hackford and screenwriter Douglas Day Stewart also wisely concentrate on subtle changes in Gere's character under the prodding of Lou Gossett, Jr., who plays a nail-hard drill instructor. Gossett, who was Fiddler on TV's "Roots," is one of those rare actors who can make you feel the emotion that's making him sweat. His performance is Oscar caliber (and darn if he didn't win the thing). But Gere and Winger also earn the thanks of film lovers for reviving the love story in a movie era increasingly dominated by technology and special effects. They have taken

a Silly Putty plot and molded it into a form that shows flair, intelligence, and heart.
R / 1982 / Paramount

▲ OH, GOD!

In the gospel according to Saint Carl (director) Reiner, God is a withered old gent who frets about having made avocado pits too large, wears Topsiders, and bears an uncanny resemblance to George Burns. Burns, sans cigar, is excellent as the Big Guy, and John Denver makes an amiable nonsinging film debut as the bewildered supermarket manager chosen to spread the Good Word. There are lots of funny moments, but the seriocomic handling of some arcane theological questions doesn't succeed in either the sacred or profane realms. It's as if Reiner wanted to be taken seriously but not *too* seriously.
PG / 1977 / Warner

▲ OH, GOD! BOOK II

Why God, in His infinite wisdom, would choose to visit Earth twice within three years and manifest Himself in southern California both times is beyond comprehension. So is almost everything else about this sappy sequel to the successful 1977 film. George Burns is back as the Man Upstairs, and he is as delightful. This time around, He's looking for a good advertising slogan and enlists the aid of an 11-year-old schoolgirl, played by a girl named simply Louanne, who has a serious case of the cutes. After rejecting suggestions like "God is bullish on humanity" and "Let God put you in the driver's seat," the Supreme One settles on the direct approach: "Think God!" It's hard to argue with the message: It's just that the medium leaves so much to be desired. With five screenwriters and Gilbert Cates as director, the sequel seems hopelessly contrived and desperately unoriginal in comparison with the story according to Carl Reiner's 1977 film.
PG / 1980 / Warner

▲ OLD BOYFRIENDS

Joan Tewkesbury established her name by writing such Altman movies as *Nashville* and *Thieves Like Us,* but this, her first effort as director, was disappointing. Talia Shire, cast in a string of tough roles after *Rocky,* plays an emotionally disturbed L.A. woman who seeks out old lovers in hopes of understanding her past. One is Richard Jordan, whom she discovers making movies and living alone with his child (played by his real-life daughter Nina). Another is John Belushi, making his dramatic debut (he's raunchy but effective) as a lascivious bandleader in pursuit of Talia again. When she finds out her first love was killed in Vietnam, she decides to take up with his younger brother, Keith Carradine. Tewkesbury absorbed much of Altman's ability to capture spontaneity but none of his genius for telling a good story. The result is a baffling movie that leaves the heroine—and the audience—searching vainly for a reason to stay with it.
R / 1979 / CBS/Fox; Embassy

▲ OLIVER'S STORY

What can you say about the inevitable follow-up to a silly and very successful movie about a girl who dies tragically at 25? That the sequel is not as bad, not as tear-jerking, not as long as the original? That Candy Bergen gives a (marginally) better performance than Ali MacGraw? That Ryan O'Neal should stop looking so tortured and enjoy himself for a change? This movie is basically a commercial afterthought by Erich Segal and Paramount, and not a very bright one at that. Nothing happens. No one cares. We learn an awful lot about the garment industry. At the end O'Neal stares soulfully at Boston's Charles River, resolving to start anew. He was apparently thinking: "I will not star in *The Rest of Oliver's Story.* I will not star in . . ."
PG / 1979 / Paramount

▲ ONCE BITTEN

Once Lauren Hutton was one of America's top models and acting in such ambitious films as *American Gigolo* and *A Wedding.* That's what makes this film—an adolescent vampire comedy—so sad; instead of laughing, you cringe with sympathetic humiliation when Hutton, as a vampire looking for male virgins, starts nibbling on Jim Carrey's thigh. As Hutton's gay servant, Cleavon Little minces in the most stereotypical fashion. Howard Storm, who wrote and directed for such TV series as "Mork and Mindy" and "The Bob Newhart Show," might have found his ideas for the tone of this movie—and maybe a few of the jokes—written on high school locker-room walls.

PG-13 / 1985 / Vestron

▲ ONCE IN PARIS . . .

In a movie about an American screenwriter (Wayne Rogers) who is sent to Paris to doctor a sick script, one wishes that art would imitate art. Producer-director-writer Frank Gilroy's script certainly could have used a bit of surgery. Rogers—in a nicely understated departure from his best-known role, *M*A*S*H*'s wisecracking Trapper John—is in one of those midlife crises that seem to befall movie characters who have been married eight years with two wonderful children and never a thought for another women. Not, at least, until someone slinky like Gayle Hunnicutt comes along. The script did allow for a fine acting debut by Jack Lenoir as a strange, chummy chauffeur. (He was never heard from again, however.) The picture of charm one minute and darkly suspicious the next, he creates what interest there is.

PG / 1979 / Media

▲ ONCE UPON A TIME IN AMERICA

An epic about a gang that rises from New York's Jewish ghetto in the 1920s, this film is like a kosher *Godfather*. An Italian, Sergio Leone, directed it, obviously intending his move from the spaghetti Westerns to matzo ball "Easterns" to be a major statement. The movie does have its moments, and there were a few hundred more of them scattered on the Ladd Company's cutting-room floor. The studio trimmed the film from Leone's original 227 minutes to 144 for U.S. release to cut down on the violence and cater to Americans' presumed limited attention spans. (An expanded version—82 minutes longer—was later released.) The film, photographed by Tonino Delli Colli, is striking to look at, especially its New York street scenes, which were shot in Manhattan, Montreal, and a back lot near Rome. The acting is stunning. Robert De Niro, who turns understatement into a spectacle, and James Woods

play the gang leaders. They're supported brilliantly by three relative newcomers: Bill Forsythe, Larry Rapp, and James Hayden. (A remarkable combination of melancholy sweetness and strength, Hayden died at 29 of an apparent drug overdose while appearing on Broadway in 1983.) Elizabeth McGovern, as the dancer De Niro pines for, and Tuesday Weld, as a hooker, are powerful too. The youngsters cast as the principals in early scenes are also remarkable, especially Scott Schutzman, Rusty Jacobs, and an intense young model, Jennifer Connelly. All of this cinematic beauty and talent goes for naught because of the absurd cuts and plot turns in the shorter form. Characters come and go with no explanations, time sequences get tangled, and there's no chance for tension to build. Once upon a time in Hollywood, what may or may not have been a masterpiece got shredded into fragments.

R / 1984 / Warner

▲ THE ONE AND ONLY

Henry Winkler is sure he's the One and Only. Trouble is, nobody else realizes it except Kim Darby, the love of his life. Even she begins to wonder when, after failing as a Broadway actor, Winkler turns to pro wrestling and hangs out with an assortment of freaks and hustlers. One of them is a lascivious midget who suffers a lot of short jokes; he is portrayed with (presumably heartfelt) sympathy by three-foot five-inch Herve Villechaize, who had yet to ship out to "Fantasy Island." Actor-director Gene Saks (better known as Bea Arthur's husband) adds some nice New York wisecracking as a tough promoter. For all its sweetly poignant story line, this Carl Reiner film is hilarious, and Winkler, as a swish superstar in blond wig and pink tights, is wonderful.

PG / 1978 / Paramount

▲ ONE FROM THE HEART

The previous films of Francis Coppola had never been known for innocence, sweetness, or romance. To fill the gap, the director risked his reputation, his fortune, and his own Zoetrope Studios on this $26 million musical. His reputation muddled through; if Coppola had done only the *Godfather* films, his place in film history would be assured. This, though, is a misguided, unmagical pastiche, a full-fledged fiasco. Thanks

to Dean Tavoularis's snazzy studio sets and the neon blaze of Vittorio Storaro's photography, *One from the Heart* glitters, but it is assuredly not gold. Set in a fantasyland Las Vegas on the Fourth of July, Armyan Bernstein's inane screenplay tells of a bored couple, played by Frederic Forrest and Teri Garr. They declare their own independence by having affairs with others—he with a gorgeous circus acrobat (Nastassia Kinski) and she with a Desi Arnaz-type lounge entertainer (Raul Julia). There is a jazzy score by Tom Waits, sung by Waits and Crystal Gale on the sound track, but they never appear, and the effect is finally alienating, like watching a film while plugged into Walkman earphones. Vincente Minnelli's old MGM musicals often used stylized sets, but he decorated them with illustrious stars like Astaire, Kelly, and Garland. Coppola built a handsome home for a movie, but left it essentially uninhabited. Are audiences to be attracted by their love for art direction? This film left moviegoers still waiting for the day when Coppola would open his heart without losing his head.
R / 1982 / RCA/Columbia

▲ ONE ON ONE

In Hollywood college sports movies, the college cheerleader has almost always won her letter-sweater hero and he has won the Big Game. In this case a slinky senior tutor, Annette O'Toole (who had yet to face *The Cat People*) overcomes her loathing of "animals" and takes naive freshman basketball star Robby Benson way beyond the lessons of Soc 101. Despite the film's didactic handling of college shamateurism (the script was coauthored by Benson and his father Jerry Segal), it is at least partly redeemed by Benson's sensitive portrayal of a five-foot ten-inch mortal among giants.
PG / 1977 / Warner

▲ ONE SINGS, THE OTHER DOESN'T

Once labeled "the Founding Mother of the new French cinema" for *Cleo from 5 to 7* and *Le Bonheur,* director Agnes Varda refracted through a feminist lens her own tale of a fourteen-year friendship between two women. Often honest, revealing, and moving, it is also tendentious—as in the lyrics to the consciousness-raising songs Varda wrote for the sound track—and pat, especially in the epilogue when the women wind up blissful. Valerie Mairesse is particularly effective in one of the two lead roles. (In French with subtitles.)
Unrated / 1977 / RCA/Columbia

▲ ON GOLDEN POND

The direction of this film, by Mark (*The Rose*) Rydell, is maddening; every shot, from gleaming pond to floating loons to concerned faces, shouts, "Look how sensitive I am!" The Oscar-winning screenplay, by Ernest Thompson from his own Broadway hit, is full of stilted characters and contrived incidents. Yet the moviegoer can hardly fail to be affected, thanks to an emotional center provided by two of Hollywood's most glorious actors, Katharine Hepburn and Henry Fonda. Hepburn might well have made this film with Spencer Tracy had he lived, though it then would probably have been too intimate to watch. She and Fonda had never even met before *Golden Pond,* yet as an aging couple trying to come to terms with death, they manage together to transcend the material. Their gestures, looks, and touches say what their clumsy dialogue cannot. Hepburn, then 72, was still a powerhouse, and Fonda, then 76 and a year from his death, invests this role with an anger and wit he had rarely shown before; it is a proud performance. Jane Fonda, appearing with her father for the first time, has an impossible task as an estranged, bitter daughter with no saving graces. Even her character doesn't deserve such a doltish boyfriend as Dabney (*9 to 5*) Coleman portrays. Fifteen-year-old Doug McKeon, as Coleman's son, undergoes a number of drastic personality changes before he finds that the meaning of life has something to do with fishing with Fonda. The movie itself deserves neither honor nor affection. In it, however, Henry Fonda and Hepburn (who both won Oscars) earn our deep respect and, in that peculiar relationship Americans have with celebrities, our love.
PG / 1981 / CBS/Fox

▲ ONLY WHEN I LAUGH

Neil Simon onscreen can run hot (*The Goodbye Girl*) or cold (*Seems Like Old Times*), but with this astonishingly sharp rewrite of his 1970

Broadway flop, *The Gingerbread Lady,* the king of one-liners sizzles. Out of some achingly familiar plot threads—alcoholic actress rehabilitates and renews her relationship with daughter—Simon made a fine, deeply felt film. As the self-described "38-year-old wino," Marsha Mason (then Mrs. Simon) gives nepotism a good name. Her performance has sensitivity, sass, and a disarming lack of sentimentality. Kristy McNichol is first-rate as the kid, as is James Coco as a gay actor buddy. But Joan Hackett is a particular joy as a rich, killingly chic neurotic who weighs herself in ounces and "dresses for depression." Occasionally Simon falls into his joke-for-joke's-sake pattern. But the actors (Mason, Coco, and Hackett were all Oscar nominated), with the help of TV director Glenn Jordan in a remarkably nuanced film debut, always restore the emotional balance. The result is superior Simon, with the slickness happily replaced by heart.
R / 1981 / RCA/Columbia

▲ ON THE NICKEL

Ralph Waite, Dad Walton himself, cast himself aptly here as a down-and-outer on Los Angeles' Skid Row. A recovered alcoholic offscreen, he lent a deeply felt performance to an otherwise slim story. It's about a reformed wino (Donald Moffat) who is having trouble adjusting to life on the wagon. He finds himself inexorably drawn back to "the Nickel," L.A.'s Bowery, by concern for a dying friend (Waite). Produced, directed, and written by Waite, this intensely personal statement evinces his empathy for the derelicts. Yet the film is painful to endure—not only because the winos are portrayed as such a wretched lot but also because the pace is dreadfully slow. Only in its final scenes does it come to life. Though an affecting title tune sung by raspy-voiced Tom Waits frames the film perfectly, it is not a telling experience.
R / 1980 / Vestron

▲ ON THE YARD

Ex-con Malcolm Braly's 1967 prison novel has been transformed into a handsomely photographed, impressively acted, but awkwardly plotted movie. The screenplay, also by Braly, tells of a tough young "top con" (Thomas Waites)

locked in a brutal power struggle with prison officials who are intent on breaking his hold over the other inmates. As the new arrival who runs afoul of this deadly system, John Heard is stunningly effective, and veteran Mike Kellin puts his hangdog looks to good use as Waites's dumb but dutiful sidekick. The movie tries to turn funny toward the end with an escape attempt by balloon that seems painfully out of place. Still, it was a creditable first effort for director Raphael Silver, whose only previous film ventures were as producer of wife Joan Micklin Silvers's *Hester Street* and *Between the Lines.*
R / 1979 / Media

▲ OPERATION THUNDERBOLT

Israel's dramatic 1976 rescue of hostages being held by terrorists in Uganda was reenacted in two American TV movies, but this full-length Israeli feature was the best version. Huge troop planes fly in low, commandos rush to free the hostages, and the terrorist kidnappers are gunned down in their tracks. The film takes a hard pro-Israel stance—not surprising, since most of the cast are Israelis and their government cooperated fully in its making. Twelve of the original ninety-one hostages play themselves, and the best moment comes when they recreate the tumultuous reunion with their families after being flown home.
PG / 1977 / MGM/UA

▲ ORCA

Jaws meets *Moby Dick*. Richard Harris plays a sea dog who hunts a maddened killer whale (*orcinus orca*) despite the trembly-lipped qualms of marine biologist Charlotte Rampling. Before it's done, the anthropomorphic monster destroys a flotilla of fishing boats and most of a town—not to mention swallowing a $12 million budget. Kids may love the silly plot and wondrous shots of whales doing wheelies in the sunset. Everyone else can reminisce about Marineland.
PG / 1977 / Paramount

▲ ORDINARY PEOPLE

Robert Redford made his debut as a director with this somber but memorable adaptation of Judith Guest's 1976 best-seller about a suburban Chicago

family torn apart by the accidental death of the elder of their teenage sons. He got an Oscar for it. In many ways Redford's film heightens the impact of the book, leaving audiences weeping and thoughtful. The story is simple. The surviving son blames himself for his brother's death; the parents are savagely divided. A psychiatrist tries to help the boy. The film ends with no loose ends neatly tied; the ambiguity is powerful. Throughout there is a feeling of voyeurism, of watching real people trying to cope with tragically real problems. Alvin Sargent's screenplay lapses once in a while into psychiatric clichés but is otherwise lean and good. Director Redford drew skillfully on a brilliant cast. Timothy Hutton, at 19, was a marvel as the guilt-ridden son who finds comfort in analyst Judd Hirsch's therapy and in the arms of Elizabeth McGovern, then a stunning newcomer. As the tax attorney father trying to hold the family together, Donald Sutherland is a model of compassion, but the film's hard edge comes from Mary Tyler Moore in a disciplined performance as the unforgiving mother. Photographed without camera tricks to hide the age lines, MTM brings dignity to a role that seems excessively unsympathetic. It is an extraordinary achievement in an unforgettable film.
R / 1980 / Paramount

▲ THE OSTERMAN WEEKEND

People who like to read Robert Ludlum's espionage novels are people who like to unravel masses of tangled string. From page to page it is always difficult to tell who is alive or dead, not to mention whose side they are or were on. Chronic complication may be one reason this was the first of Ludlum's thirteen novels to be made into a movie; most people who see it should have the plot figured out by, say, mid 1997. Burt Lancaster seems to be a CIA chief. John Hurt seems to be a CIA agent (though he has a British accent and keeps calling himself an FBI agent). Rutger Hauer seems to be an American talk-show host, though he's as convincing in the part as Don Meredith would be playing a West German chancellor. Dennis Hopper, Chris Sarandon, Craig T Nelson, Helen Shaver, and Cassie Yates seem to be traitors ripe for exposure by Hauer, Hurt, and Lancaster. The big showdown takes place at a weekend party at Hauer's house in Los Angeles. Afterward, Hauer delivers what seems to be a sermon on the evils of watching TV. Are you following all this? In his first film since *Convoy* in 1978, Sam Peckinpah got to engage in some characteristically violent scenes at the end. But this is perhaps his least idiosyncratic and least entertaining movie; it's run-of-the-mill spy stuff.
R / 1983 / Thorn/EMI

▲ THE OTHER SIDE OF MIDNIGHT

Tougher editing would have improved this overlong (nearly 3 hours) sob opera based on the best-selling novel by Sidney Sheldon. John (*Audrey Rose*) Beck is sufficiently reprehensible as a caddish World War II pilot, and Susan Sarandon is splendid as his victimized wife. But French actress Marie-France Pisier (*Cousin, Cousine*) is exhausting as the vengeful sexual predator Noelle Page. She pants through a sequence of graphic love scenes that border embarrassingly on the comic. It's enough to give heavy breathing a bad name.
R / 1977 / Image

▲ THE OTHER SIDE OF THE MOUNTAIN, PART TWO

In Part One (released in 1975) Jill Kinmont, an Olympic skiing contender, took a fall in 1955 and was paralyzed from the shoulders down. In the continuation of her true story, Marilyn Hassett is again convincing and affecting as Jill—eighteen years after her accident. She is still a quadriplegic but has tried to live a full life. The only thing lacking is a man, and on a summer vacation she meets one, truck driver Timothy Bottoms. They fall in love, despite the obvious difficulties. Jill, however, is as frail psychologically as she is physically. She learns that this man, too, like two earlier boyfriends and her father, will die. Pull out the hanky you used for Part One, if it's dry yet.
PG / 1978 / N/A

▲ OUR WINNING SEASON

Who needs another *American Graffiti,* especially a bad one? Scott Jacoby plays a high school runner who can't win. But when a close friend is killed in Vietnam, he gets inspired and, well,

261

you know the rest. There are lots of familiar '60s scenes; hanging around the hamburger joint, necking at the drive-in, and playing chicken with souped-up cars. Some young actors gave promising performances, especially Jan Smithers as the sister who falls in love with the doomed friend and Dennis Quaid as the buffoonish pal. But director Joseph Ruben and writer Nick Niciphor don't help them. Wait till next year.

PG / 1978 / N/A

▲ OUT OF AFRICA

Every year at Oscar time critics and the public look for a film champion—one that makes it respectable to go to the movies again. Something with the lofty, literary patina of a *Gandhi* or *A Passage to India* works best, no matter how tedious or timid at the core. In 1985, *Out of Africa* was the pearl before which we swine were meant to grovel. And we did, or at least the Academy did, awarding the film the Best Picture Oscar. The cast, headed by Meryl Streep and Robert Redford, not to mention top director Sydney (*Tootsie*) Pollack and the $30 million budget, commands attention. And the subject matter oozes integrity. This is the tale of Karen Blixen (Isak Dinesen was her nom de plume), a Danish aristocrat who ran a coffee plantation in Kenya from 1914 to 1931. Nothing remarkable there except that when Blixen returned to Denmark she wrote a magical memoir called *Out of Africa*. Dinesen's rarefied prose resisted film adaptation until screenwriter Kurt (*Absence of Malice*) Luedtke availed himself of Judith Thurman's excellent 1982 biography of Dinesen. That book told of the writer's 1914 marriage of convenience to Bror Blixen, a philandering Swedish baron from whom she contracted syphilis, and her doomed love affair with the dashing British hunter and aviator Denys Finch-Hatton. Impressed? Don't be. Luedtke and Pollack bought these high-priced literary sources only to chuck them for a conventional, largely fictionalized movie romance. Streep, adding Danish to her growing list of accents (does anyone remember what she really sounds like?), makes a game, sharp-witted Dinesen. But the script gives her little chance to relate to the plantation, her African servants, or the proud Kikuyu tribe Dinesen described with such yearning. Instead, Streep spends most of the film's 155 minutes going ga-ga over Redford, who is crushingly miscast as Finch-Hatton. Since Redford does not use an English accent or do anything to suggest the Oxford-educated, poetry-spouting son of an earl that was Finch-Hatton, the filmmakers have thrown out every reference to the man's background. So Dinesen's grand passion is no longer for someone who shared her ardor for words that distilled the essence of a continent. Now it seems directed at an aging American pretty boy who strikes movie star poses and takes her flying but won't marry her. Worse, when her lover dies in a plane crash, Streep's Dinesen must deliver a tearjerking graveside eulogy. Such misdirection diminishes Dinesen and devitalizes the film. The subject of the Streep-Redford sexual chemistry is difficult to discuss because none is discernible. Streep gets more going with the devilish Blixen, expertly played by Klaus Maria Brandauer, who provides the only vulgar life in the film. Call *Out of Africa* a gorgeously photographed view of Dinesen's lost world. But don't call it art.

PG / 1985 / MCA

▲ OUT OF BOUNDS

Anthony Michael Hall, star of *The Breakfast Club,* possesses the most vacant eyes in Hollywood. And he's got a great open-mouthed, dumbfounded expression that quickly became his trademark. If *Out of Bounds* weren't so misguided and misdirected, this thriller could have taken wonderful advantage of Hall's talents. At 18, he was cast as an Iowa farm boy who inadvertently gets caught up in drug dealing and double-dealing when he takes the wrong bag off the luggage carousel after arriving in Los Angeles. The premise of an adolescent *North by Northwest* fits Hall well; that vacant look of his is ideal for just about any fish-out-of-water scenario. But *Out of Bounds* misunderstands that expression; it's the look of a suburban teenager who has already seen too much, not too little, of the world. Thematically it would have been more novel to reverse the situation in Tony Kayden's script—envision Hall as a seen-it-all city slicker who stumbles upon unlikely corruption in the cornfield. Although director Richard Tuggle traverses the back streets and nightclubs of Los Angeles, he shows no talent for innovation in using his locations. Neither does he have the playfulness or sense of dislocation that Brian De Palma might have brought to the material. Although Tuggle wrote and directed *Tightrope,* one of Clint Eastwood's best and most perverse efforts, he settles for violent surprises and mundane tableaus this time. How often do we have to see punkers strutting down the sidewalk or cops giving chase to the wrong man? Contrived and condescending, *Out of Bounds* degenerates into what is primarily a cautionary tale about checking your luggage tags at the airport.

R / 1986 / RCA/Columbia

▲ OUTLAND

Picture a mining town complete with swinging saloon doors and happy hookers. A badge-wearing do-good marshal, Sean Connery, tangles with the evil mine operator, Peter Boyle, and suddenly it's *High Noon.* That's the basic plot, with a difference: When Boyle brings in two hired guns for the big shoot-out, the stagecoach they arrive on is the afternoon space shuttle. Con-Am 17, the mining town, only feels like Dodge City—it looks like the U.S.S. *Enterprise* in drydock. This is a Western set on Io, one of Jupiter's moons, in a future century. It's outlandish, conceptually as well as geographically, but the whole idea is charming, and it works. Director Peter Hyams, who showed his flair for this kind of fanciful adventure in *Capricorn One,* handles it expertly here. The special effects are as good as in *Star Wars,* and the acting is top-drawer. Longtime Broadway actress Frances Sternhagen is especially appealing as a warmhearted but cynical doctor who becomes Connery's ally. As they prove Io is big enough for both of them, you'll be cheering.

R / 1981 / Warner

▲ OUTRAGEOUS!

What's so "outrageous" about two looneys—a schizophrenic young woman and an aspiring female impersonator—setting up house together and trying to survive in a not-altogether-sane-world? What is outrageous is that this fast, funny, fresh first effort from director Richard Benner wins you over completely. Craig Russell, a closet Tallulah Bankhead, steals the show with first-class impersonations of, among others, Bette Davis, Mae West, and Barbra Streisand. It's a crummy name for a classy, if little noted flick.

PG / 1977 / RCA/Columbia

▲ THE OUTSIDERS

With 1982's disastrous *One from the Heart* behind him, director Francis Ford Coppola appeared, at least, to be headed back in the right direction. This effort is an enterprising mix of the real and the highly improbable, which is both the film's blessing and its curse. An adaptation of S. E. Hinton's novel about minunderstood youth, the film presents a view of mid '60s Tulsa through its warring street kids: the greasers and the "socs" (pronounced "so-shes," the well-to-do teens from the other side of town). Ensuing relationships are overtly borrowed from the Jets and Sharks, not to mention the Capulets and Montagues. There's an accidental death, an all-out rumble, and two characters who try to step beyond the boundaries set by their comrades. The film focuses on C. Thomas (*Soul Man*) Howell, who is impressive as a 14-year-old greaser named Ponyboy. Though the dialogue goes off on florid tangents, especially in corny sequences between Howell and his best friend, played by Ralph (*Karate Kid*) Macchio, both young actors communicate a certain measure of "gold"—a word used to express the innocence of youth in a Frost poem they refer to. As the lead greaser, Matt Dillion brings frustrated anger back to the character. The film's drawbacks include the underuse of Diane (*Six Pack*) Lane as the soc who befriends Howell, as well as the inappropriately jubilant score composed by Coppola's father, Carmine. But for those willing to see virtue in its eccentricity, the film seems a strangely refreshing slice of between-the-coasts America.

PG / 1983 / Warner

▲ OVER THE TOP

Starring Sylvester Stallone—who got a reported $12 million up front—and directed by Menahem Golan, *Over the Top* is also as predictable as Stallone's previous bombastic hits. Stallone plays a truck driver who is estranged from his wife and whose hobby is arm wrestling. This doesn't leave much time for his twelve-year-old son, nicely done by David Mendenhall. In fact Dad hasn't seen the boy in ten years. So the son is naturally shocked when Stallone comes to pick him up at his graduation from an Eastern military school. Mom, Susan Blakely, is dying, and decided it would be a good time for father and son to get to know one another as they drive cross-country to visit her in the hospital. Mendenhall, an intellectual little twit, is furious. He wants an answer as to why Dad never so much as sent him a birthday card. "Do you really think you can make up ten years in two to three days?" he asks. Mendenhall starts to behave like a normal kid when Stallone teaches him how to drive a truck, arm wrestle, and "lose like a winner." But of course Stallone never really loses when it counts. Although he's gunning for the World Arm Wrestling Championship, his real opponent is his millionaire father-in-law, Robert Loggia, who views the boy as his own. Though the cast does a fine job serving the vehicle—Stallone—the script has enough holes in it to drive an eighteen-wheeler through. Nobody explains why a millionaire's daughter married a truck driver or why Stallone left her. And somehow only Stallone knows the no-fail arm wrestling move that inspired the title.

PG / 1986 / N/A

P

▲ PADRE PADRONE

A Sardinian peasant boy is forced by his tyrannical father to live in stark isolation until the age of 20. Then he enlists in the Italian army—and so begins a chain of events that climaxes in his fight for freedom from his brutal *padrone*. (The title translates "father, master.") Based on the autobiography of Italian author Gavino Ledda, this tough, uncompromising film won both the Grand Prize and the Critics Prize awards at 1977's Cannes Film Festival. Though some scenes are definitely not for the squeamish, this is a richly rewarding film. (In Italian with subtitles.)

Unrated / 1977 / RCA/Columbia

▲ PALE RIDER

In his first Western sine 1976, Clint Eastwood cast himself as a miracle. This sober effort to resuscitate the genre has a 14-year-old girl praying for deliverance in a California canyon where an evil land baron, lugubriously named La Hood, is trying to run out a settlement of honest prospectors. As the girl beseeches God, the camera focuses on a black-hatted man astride a white horse. Dressed like a preacher, and a devil of a shot, this mysterious, possibly mystical, certainly mythical figure answers the girl's prayers. Soon he is righting all wrongs that befall the unfortunate citizens of Carbon Canyon, and since it appropriates a quote from the Book of Revelation, the movie suggests that this spirit of salvation is, in fact, Death. That's the problem with *Pale Rider*—Eastwood plays a symbol, not a character. From right-wing iconoclast in the '70s to Reagan-era emblem, Eastwood onscreen and off has always proved an inadvertent archetype. That's the source of his appeal—the guy who steadfastly stands for his own values and unexpectedly ends up standing for everyone else's too. But *Pale Rider* (which Eastwood produced and directed) needlessly hypes Eastwood and his myth, as if Clint weren't already capable of energizing an audience with just the whites of his eyes. Eastwood is the one star who need not do an advertisement for himself. Unlike Lawrence Kasdan's superior *Silverado,* this script never marries the classic Western to contemporary sensibility. Eventually this *Shane* with skirts degenerates into a monotonous series of showdowns with the cliches showcased instead of skewered. Despite his careful compositions, Bruce Surtees's autumnal, dark cinematography demonstrates what's wrongheaded about *Pale Rider*—it's an attempt to revive the Western by fashioning an elegant elegy for it.

R / 1985 / Warner

▲ PARADISE

It's a rare film indeed that can be compared unfavorably with *The Blue Lagoon,* but *Paradise* out trashes even that ankle-deep wallow on teen sex. This time New York model Phoebe Cates, then eighteen, and Willie Aames, of TV's "Eight Is Enough," don the peekaboo fig leaves discarded by Brooke Shields and Christopher Atkins. On a caravan leaving Baghdad for Damascus, circa 1823, Phoebe and Willie are thrown together when their elders are slaughtered by marauding Arabs led by a dark-eyed sheik (Tuvia Tavi) with a lust for Phoebe's virginal flesh. The kids escape, finding solace and love in a lush desert oasis. Filmed in Israel, *Paradise* at least looks good. Cates has a lithe figure, flawless skin, and diction bad enough to make Shields sound like Helen Hayes. Aames, a moony Malibu type, adjusts his loincloth a lot, especially while watching Phoebe shower, which she does with scrupulous attention to erogenous zones. These two innocents shed inhibitions almost as fast as clothes, learning sexual technique from the monkeys. Since the orangutans are played by Doc and Eve, the two pros who showed Bo Derek how to do it in Tarzan, Phoebe and Willie are in good paws. The script and direction, however, are in the none-too-firm grasp of Stuart Gillard, best known as head writer on "The Donny & Marie Show." Contemplating the sheik's perverse desires, Phoebe moans: "If he just kills me, I'll be lucky." As fates worse than death go, this movie itself is far more insidious.
R / 1982 / Embassy

▲ PARADISE ALLEY

Since this is a virtual home movie, it opened Sylvester Stallone to even sharper accusations of egomania: He writes, directs, stars, and even sings the title tune. But if Stallone demonstrates any skill in *Paradise Alley,* it is his casting. Sure, he planted his brother Frank and then manager Jeff Wald in minor roles, but where it counted he got the real article. An ex-pro fighter in his screen debut, Lee Canalito delivers a marvelously adept performance as a handsome, slow-witted but sensitive hulk of a wrestler in the 1940s. Sly and Armand Assante play Canalito's two brothers, who use his skill in the ring to escape the rough Hell's Kitchen area of Manhattan (where

Stallone himself grew up). The main actors play off one another well. But the love interests (Anne Archer and Sly's own one-time flame Joyce Ingalls) are poorly resolved in the script, and the Rockyesque final bout is overlong. Whatever it was Stallone was trying to sell, the public wasn't buying. Stallone's directing debut, drubbed by the critics, faced a box-office drought.
PG / 1978 / MCA

▲ PARDON MON AFFAIRE

A solidly married executive is smitten by a beauty in a red dress and sets out after his first affair, abetted by three cronies. Director Yves Robert, who did *The Tall Blond Man with One Black Shoe,* has produced a funnier cousin to *Cousin, Cousine,* whose star, Victor Lanoux, appears here—can it be?—as a loutish philanderer who never learns. This film later was transposed in Hollywood into *The Women in Red.* (In French with subtitles.)
PG / 1977 / Embassy

▲ PARIS, TEXAS

A man is found wandering in the Texas desert. His brother comes to claim him. The man is in shock. Four years earlier, after his wife abandoned him, he left his son, age three, with his brother and went off into the wilderness. Now the man, who can barely talk, must build a relationship with his son. The two leave for Houston to find the boy's mother. That's all that happens. No one dies. No one is physically abused. No one even utters a four-letter word. But *Paris, Texas,* directed by Wim Wenders and written by playwright-actor Sam Shepard with L. M. Kit Carson, may be the most disturbing film ever about the roots of family relationships. Shepard's words and Wender's images blend in a magical poetry. Harry Dean Stanton, character actor extraordinaire in such films as *Christine* and *Straight Time,* moved up to the star class of Robert Duvall and Jack Nicholson with his mesmerizing performance as the father. Paris, Texas, where his parents conceived him, is where he wants to be. The scenes in which Stanton uses home movies to reconnect with his boy, superbly played by then eight-year-old Hunter Carson (the son of Kit

Carson and actress Karen Black), have a wrenching poignancy. And Nastassja Kinski comes alive on screen as never before as the mother. Working in a bizarre brothel, where the customers pay for talk, not sex, Kinski speaks to men through a mirror. With the glass separating them, Kinski and Stanton relive the agony of their lives in a shattering half-hour scene. This is daring, demanding filmmaking, with a haunting ending. Every element enriches the whole, including strong performances by Dean Stockwell and Aurore Clement as the boy's caring relatives, Robby Muller's stunning photography, and Ry Cooder's evocative music. Though *Paris, Texas* is long (150 minutes) and sometimes maddeningly self-indulgent, few movies cut so clear a path to the heart.
R / 1984 / CBS/Fox

▲ PARTNERS

Nobody would make a film today in which all the blacks were dumb, subservient shufflers or all the women were helpless, poor-little-me darlings. But this film takes exactly that approach to homosexuals, and it is as insulting to straight people's intelligence as it it to gays' sexuality. Ryan O'Neal and John Hurt are the heroes— O'Neal as a tough homicide detective and Hurt as a gay police clerk. They are ordered to team up and pretend to be lovers to help catch a gay model's murderer. The mismatched team has been a staple of detective mysteries at least since Holmes and Watson, and this notion could work too. But *Partners* director James Burrows, a veteran of TV's "Taxi," turning out his first feature here, and screenwriter Francis (*La Cage aux Folles*) Veber make *Cruising* seem a model of understanding and intelligence by comparison. Almost every gay character in the film is a raving queen. Even Hurt, ordinarily a marvelous actor, is ghastly, playing his character as a mincing, simpering, hand-on-hip stereotype. O'Neal is called on only to look handsome, which he is terrific at, and disgusted, which he doesn't do quite so well despite the head start the script gives him. Even the murder plot is feeble and ineptly set up. Burrows and this movie ought to get back in the closet.
R / 1982 / Paramount

▲ THE PASSAGE

The only excuse for this film was that it gave Anthony Quinn a chance to check off one more category on his ethnic-roles list by portraying a Basque. (That left him only fifteen or sixteen short of having done the whole U.N.) He plays a shepherd guiding the family of a scientist (played in surly fashion by James Mason) out of occupied World War II France, through the Pyrenees into Spain. They are pursued by a tirelessly fiendish SS officer who says things like "They hate me because I wear a black uniform." In that hopeless role, Malcolm McDowell overacts outrageously. In a similar 1940 movie, James Stewart and Margaret Sullavan tried to ski away from the Nazis, two of whom were youthful Robert Young and Robert Stack. That film was called *The Mortal Storm;* it's a better bet by far than this bad trip.
R / 1979 / N/A

▲ A PASSAGE TO INDIA

Such productions as *Gandhi, The Far Pavilions, The Jewel in the Crown,* and *Heat and Dust* well established the notion that the British occupation of India was foolhardy. This adaptation of E. M. Forster's 1924 novel plays that theme once again in a movie more interesting for its style than its content. Director David Lean already had among his credits *The Bridge on the River Kwai, Doctor Zhivago,* and *Lawrence of Arabia,* and *Passage* is full of his trademark vistas, which are often breathtaking. There are striking performances too. Dame Peggy Ashcroft won a Best Supporting Actress Oscar portraying a model of controlled anxiety as a woman in India visiting her petty bureaucrat son. Indian actor Victor Banerjee symbolizes ambivalence as a doctor who loathes the English even as he tries to become more like them. Judy Davis, as Ashcroft's prospective daughter-in-law, James Fox, as a college professor with a conscience, and Sir Alec Guinness, as an Indian mystic, are all fascinating. The movie seems very long, however, at 163 minutes, and the climax, involving Banerjee's trial for attempting to rape Davis, is a tempest in a Darjeeling pot. Ultimately this film is too much like the British mentality its creators deplore; there are

moments of real elegance and dignity, but there is too much pomp and not enough circumstance.
PG / 1985 / RCA/Columbia

▲ PASSION

Many movies by Jean-Luc Godard, the great French director, are rich with movie allusions: *Breathless, Contempt,* and *Weekend* among them. The passion here is the passion of filmmaking. The story line focuses on the lack of a story line for a movie in the making. Hanna Schygulla plays herself—a German actress trying to make sense out of the chaos around her. She flirts with the director (Jerzy Radziwilowicz), a Polish emigré whose heart belongs to Solidarity. Isabelle Huppert plays a strange, stuttering factory girl who is having an affair with the same director. Why? Lots of questions are left unanswered, that one among them. If you don't stop to think about this film but enjoy the flow of images, it moves along nicely. Just don't try to explain it to your friends. (In French with subtitles.)
Unrated / 1983 / N/A

▲ PATERNITY

Burt Reynolds called this trendy comedy about a bachelor who wants a son but no wife "the story of my life." But for all Burt's flash, talent, and eagerness to please, this groggy flick is an assembly-line product that never meets its obligation to a loaded, potentially explosive subject. Reynolds, as the manager of Madison Square Garden, sets out to find a surrogate mother, motivated by the desire for a son "who will say I was here." His search leads him first to Lauren Hutton, then to a woman with braces on her teeth whom he rejects because he doesn't want a child "who looks like Jaws II." Then he hits on waitress Beverly D'Angelo, she of the requisite "healthy breasts." After legally settling on the number of impregnation attempts and a fee ($50,000), the two strangers go at it—mostly standing up, since Burt thinks that's how you make a boy. Well, guess what? Right, they fall in love. Unhappily, the story's stronger satirical implications then go out the window. A director with the right touch, like Alan Pakula in Reynolds's *Starting Over,* might have fleshed out the gags in the Charlie Peters script. But comic David Steinberg, in his directorial debut, showed neither the technique nor the inclination to midwife the movie's potential. What should be sly is merely smug. Reynolds has an undeniable built-in charm, D'Angelo a buoyant wit, and Paul Dooley, Norman Fell, and a smashing Elizabeth Ashley provide a wealth of comic reserves. But for the most part, *Paternity,* which aims for pertinence, settles for platitudes.
PG / 1981 / Paramount

▲ PAULINE AT THE BEACH

It might have become *Beach-Blanket Bingo à la Plage,* but French director Eric (*Claire's Knee*) Rohmer has instead fashioned this film into an involving, if slightly pedantic fable about the possibility—no, make that the certainty—of self-deception when it comes to romance. The story is best described as a love quadrangle. A teenager just budding into womanhood, Amanda Langlet, and her older cousin, Arielle Dombasle, arrive at a beach on the northwest coast of France. Dombasle, recently separated from her husband, is clearly on the make; she first puts the moves on an old friend she meets windsurfing, then drops him for a mysterious stranger. Meanwhile, the younger cousin has fallen for a boy her own age, and their own mating dance begins; lots of awkward groping, following by a tumble in bed with clothes on thank you. Soon the mysterious older lover gets caught cheating on Dombasle. Then he disappears just as quickly as he turned up. The moral seems clear: Young love, even in its innocence, can often be wiser. Dombasle, an aspiring director in her own right, is sensational. While she had a small part in Rohmer's *Le Beau Mariage,* in this film she gets to show off real talent as a comedienne. Because of her restraint and Rohmer's, the film, while talky in spots, creates images that linger long after the lights have gone up. (In French with subtitles.)
R / 1983 / Cinémathèque

▲ PEE-WEE'S BIG ADVENTURE

With his red bow tie, white shoes, and childishly self-satisfied smile, Pee-Wee Herman poses as the essence of '50s nerdiness. But as his stand-up comedy routines and talk show appearances

Pee Wee's Big Adventure: Pee Wee, a madcap Peter Pan for the '80s, is an acquired taste many are still waiting to acquire, but his film debut proved box-office dynamite despite the brickbats.

suggest, Pee-Wee isn't so much a character of the '50s as a comment on that era. That is one problem with Herman's first movie: You can't sustain a comment through a full-length film. Making his feature debut, director Tim Burton attempted to fashion a cinematic equivalent of Herman's sensibility—a movie filled with kitschy sets, vibrant-colored costumes, and overdone music. When a bully steals his bike, Pee-Wee goes on a cross-country search to retrieve it. But unlike the heroes of most picaresques, Pee-Wee is no smarter at the end than he is at the start. In effect that means he is just another one of the movie's silly props. Herman is trying to turn attitudinizing into comic performance art. But in this case he hasn't developed his stand-up posture into a fleshed-out character. Herman's idiosyncrasies sabotage the comedy; when Pee-Wee lets loose his little-boy laugh because he's enchanted with his surroundings, he cheats the audience out of its own laughter. And as the film lurches from situation to situation, it looks increasingly calculated to

evoke comparisons to Buster Keaton and Charlie Chaplin, who reign over a pantheon Pee-Wee hasn't yet approached. There's something misguided about a Pee-Wee Herman comedy that gets its best laugh out of Lone Star locals singing "Deep in the Heart of Texas."
PG / 1985 / Warner

▲ PEGGY SUE GOT MARRIED

No one should ever mistake this giddy, romantic comedy for a classic. Mixing *Back to the Future* zap with *Our Town* sap, the film feels patched together. But after a quartet of tortoise-laced fiascos (*Cotton Club, Rumbleship, The Outsiders, One from the Heart*), director Francis Coppola steps lively this time. Delivering a performance of depth and conviction is the ever-dazzling Kathleen (*Prizzi's Honor*) Turner. In a role originally meant for Debra Winger, Turner plays Peggy Sue, an ex-prom queen attending the reunion of

her 1960 high school class. Portraying a slightly dumpy housewife is a stretch for the potently sexy Turner, even with unflattering costumes and some added poundage. But the actress finds the heart of a character who is distraught because her TV pitchman husband and childhood sweetheart, played by Nicolas (*Birdy*) Cage, has ditched her for a younger woman. Spotting her errant hubby at the reunion sends Turner into a faint that propels her backward twenty-five years with the chance to alter her future. She shocks her stuffy parents, Don Murray and Barbara Harris, by guzzling the family booze supply. She stuns the school nerd—splendidly played by Barry (*Fame*) Miller—with her descriptions of computers, panty hose, and jogging shoes, and surprises boyfriend Cage, an aspiring singer, with a song she promises him will be a big hit. (She's right: It's the Beatles' "She Loves You.") But when Turner tries some liberated '80s sexual thinking on Cage and the school poet, played by Kevin O'Connor, things backfire. So does the movie, which turns mawkish and unbelievable in its final quarter. Another nagging problem is the casting of 30ish actors, who don't seem to be convincingly 18 or 43. As Turner's buddy, Joan Allen (so fine as the menaced blind woman in *Manhunter*) is a brilliant exception; Cage, a dud as a romantic hero for any decade, is not. No use denying that *Peggy Sue Got Married* has its share of problems. But when Coppola clears the way for Turner to mine the veins of rude humor in this Arlene Samer–Jerry Leichtling screenplay, the film proves to be spirited fun.
PG-13 / 1986 / CBS/Fox

▲ PENNIES FROM HEAVEN

An ambitious and often brilliant experiment, this downbeat movie musical earned plaudits from some critics and potshots from others. There seemed to be no middle ground. The public stayed away in droves. Video now gives *Pennies* another chance to win an audience. The chance is deserved. Director Herbert (*The Turning Point*) Ross attempted to make a 1930s musical with 1980s sensibilities. Busby Berkeley's movies were designed to help the viewer forget the Depression; *Pennies* creates the opposite effect by dwelling on poverty and gloom. Based on Dennis Potter's British TV series (which starred Bob Hoskins),

the film tells the story of a struggling sheet-music salesman, played with expected comic resourcefulness and astonishing musicality by Steve Martin. To escape his boring job and loveless marriage to Jessica (*Stardust Memories*) Harper, Martin fantasizes a happier life with the help of period songs which he lip-syncs with gusto on the sound track. But Potter doesn't allow audience sympathy for this loser, who impregnates innocent Bernadette Peters (a lovely performance) and sends her off callously into a life of vice. Along the way, Peters teams up with a sordid pimp, played by Christopher Walken, who stops the show with a spectacular dance number. And so the movie goes, contrasting the period's musical cheer with a sordid reality that ends in murder and a hanging. Near the end, Martin and Peters dream themselves into an Astaire-Rogers movie where life can be transformed by art, if only momentarily. *Pennies* was not built to warm the heart but to excite the imagination in ways few musicals ever do. By all means, give it a go.
R / 1982 / MGM/UA

▲ PERFECT

The cast is a rousing good company; there's a zip in the pace and zing in the dialogue, and John Travolta—playing a *Rolling Stone* reporter—delivers one of his best performances. But *Perfect,* based in part on Aaron Latham's 1983 *Rolling Stone* cover story on the fitness craze, is not nearly as consistently caustic as it could be. Latham had an angle on health spas: He thought the clubs had become the singles bars of the '80s. The movie, written by Latham and director James Bridges, attempts to raise larger issues, including the ways reporter and subject are compromised when objectivity is lost. This happens when Travolta falls for Jamie Lee Curtis, playing an aerobics instructor with a bad past history, and tries to leave her out of his story. Curtis has the kind of body cameras understandably worship, and her fierce intelligence shakes out every grain of truth she can find in the script. Some of *Perfect,* the part about how Travolta charms and cheats his way into the spa story, is sassy, scathing fun. The part that attempts to turn Travolta into a torchbearer for journalistic ethics is cannily camouflaged hot air. This is done through Travolta's parallel assignment, an interview with a businessman involved in cocaine smuggling. "You do serious stuff too?" says Curtis, clearly awed. When Travolta won't surrender his tapes to a federal court, we're supposed to be awed too. The sanctimonious subplot is artificial enough to get an audience giggling. But when *Perfect* drops its pretensions, it's maliciously on target. Jann Wenner, the real-life editor of *Rolling Stone* and *Us* magazines, offers a devastating send-up of himself. He plays a pudgy, penny-pinching, perpetually hung-over celebrity chaser ("Mikey Douglas is in town"). Wenner is one of *Perfect*'s pluses. So are Marilu Henner and Laraine Newman. Newman, expertly walking the line between hilarity and heartbreak, is a spa regular known as "the most used piece of equipment in the gym." Bridges and Latham show us the cruelty of that remark by transforming what Wenner calls "California airheads" into recognizable human beings. Travolta sees the humanity too, but Wenner doesn't publish Travolta's feelings, only the facts. In the film's most powerful scene, Curtis, Henner, and Newman silently gather around the just-published story, their faces a mirror of how words can wound. *Perfect* is far from perfect, but in scenes like this one it comes very close.

R / 1985 / RCA/Columbia

▲ A PERFECT COUPLE

There's no historical analysis, social satire, or reflection on man's violent nature in this work from the usually serious-minded director Robert Altman. *A Perfect Couple* is only a romantic little rock musical and only very entertaining. The "couple" is the middle-aged son of a tyrannical Greek antique tycoon and an aging backup singer in a communal rock group. The man is played by Paul Dooley, a gifted star of stage and commercials, and the woman is gaunt Marta Heflin, an ex-singer who is theater-trained herself. They're both full of marvelous idiosyncrasies. So is the rest of the cast: Belita Moreno is especially beguiling as Dooley's sister. A band called Keepin' 'Em off the Streets plays the appealing soft rock score, most of which it wrote. Altman adds all his best touches—a relaxed feel, believable dialogue, and a recurring phantom character, here a nauseatingly lovey-dovey couple. The result is, within its limited ambitions, a perfect film.

PG / 1979 / N/A

▲ THE PERILS OF GWENDOLINE

Writer-director Just Jaeckin claimed *Gwendoline* was a departure from his customary soft porn— he did *Emmannelle*—into the realm of adventure-fantasy. But the pervasive smuttiness here indicates that this leopard hasn't changed any spots. The film is a chintzy exploitation in which *Romancing the Stone, Raiders of the Lost Ark,* and many ladies' blouses are ripped off. The movie is based on a forty-year-old "adult" comic strip by the late bondage illustrator John Willie. Jaeckin's plot involves the tribulations of an explorer's daughter, Tawny Kitaen, and her female sidekick, Zabou. They embroil an unshaven adventurer, former model Brent Huff, in their search for Kitaen's father. If the script ever made any sense, it was lost in the process of dubbing dialogue from the native languages of the multinational cast into English. Kitaen and her often-bared body are shamefully exploited. At one point the questing, and by this time thirsty, trio is caught in a downpour. Huff, of course, can only think of one way to collect some water: "Hurry. Take off your clothes. Unless you want to die of thirst." There is also an underground city populated by Amazons who wear black leather breast-plates and G-strings. This pandering metropolis is located in the forbidden land of Yik-Yak. Claptrap. Throw this dog a bone.

R / 1985 / Vestron

▲ PERSONAL BEST

Title notwithstanding, producer-director-screenwriter Robert Towne fell dismally short of his own personal best. He wrote *The Last Detail* and *Chinatown,* but in his directorial debut, he seems to have put together this film about female Olympic pentathletes from news clips about women's sports and body building. He shows us that women want to win as much as guys do, they talk dirty, they flex their pecs, they take drugs, and they pair off in lesbian affairs. It's around one such relationship that the film is structured. Leggy Mariel (*Manhattan*) Hemingway and an older seductress, played by 1976 Olympic hurdler Patrice Donnelly, are the lovers. Beyond the bed scenes, there doesn't seem to be much affection between the women, though; when Donnelly's competitive zeal causes Hemingway to escape to

a male lover, it's hard to mourn their breakup. Mariel acts mostly by sniffling and whining at Donnelly. Of the cast, only Scott Glenn (the ex-con heavy in *Urban Cowboy*), as the women's coach, stands out. Towne uses clichéd slow-motion track-and-field footage, pans up female thighs and groins, and lingers on high-toned muscles as if he had sculpted them. His attempts at pumping irony into the script by gender role reversals—apparently to justify lesbianism—are flaccid. The beefy male Olympians are gratuitously emasculated, reduced to ironing clothes, carrying beach umbrellas to protect themselves from the sun, and shaking pom-poms on the sidelines while the girls play touch football. The sound track over one sequence says it all: It's the Doobie Brothers' "What a Fool Believes."
R / 1982 / Warner

▲ PHANTASM

For those who think *Remembrance of Things Past* is a homage to the horror films, this is a wonderful time to be an American: Thanks to video cassettes, your house can be crawling with new monsters every day. This wildly uneven creation is one of the more interesting exercises in cheap thrills. A nearly one-man project by a young unknown named Don Coscarelli, *Phantasm* is all about what happens when the undertaker gets carried away. Bodies disappear, little hooded monsters snarl and bite, a metal ball with teeth tries to drain everyone's blood, and a severed finger literally takes on a life of its own. There's really no plot, only special effects and some stunning, weirdly beautiful photography. An interesting performance is turned in by Angus Scrimm, a pseudonym for old horror movie actor Rory Guy, who plays the funeral director with unabashed glee. Director Coscarelli meant all the mayhem in fun, but the rating board humorlessly assigned the film an R. By present-day standards of gore, it's very good-natured.
R / 1979 / Embassy

▲ THE PHILADELPHIA EXPERIMENT

This was strike three for young actor Michael Pare. His debut film, *Eddie and the Cruisers,* died a quick death at the box office. His second,

Walter Hill's rock 'n' roll fable *Streets of Fire,* was rapidly extinguished. This one was put out of its misery soon too. A goofy sci-fi mishap all too similar to the 1980 film *Final Countdown* leads to ludicrous action and hackneyed dialogue. Even the likable Nancy Allen looks adrift. Pare and buddy Bobby Di Cicco are sailors recruited for a 1943 government project that attempts to render U.S. ships invisible on enemy radar. In the process their destroyer gets thrown into a time warp. They land in 1984 and, in Pare's case, into the arms of Allen. Meanwhile, the same scientist who conducted the World War II experiment is still at it, forty years later. Now an opening in hyperspace threatens to vacuum up the whole planet. Pare looks stoic—or bored—as always, though he manages to squeeze out a tear to show he has a vulnerable side when it comes to matters apocalyptic. Allen relies on a quavery voice and a childlike expression. Glowing visual effects, under the direction of Max Anderson, are everywhere, though they aren't nearly distracting enough to save the film.
PG / 1984 / Thorn/EMI

▲ PICNIC AT HANGING ROCK

Obviously designed to ride the crest of interest created by his *Last Wave,* this Peter Weir film (that's Weir, as in weird) got its U.S. release in 1979. That *Picnic* was then the largest grossing picture in Australian history says something—it's hard to tell what—about the moviegoers Down Under. It is the supposedly true story of three schoolgirls and a teacher who disappeared without a trace on Valentine's Day, 1900. Weir did not so much photograph this tale as paint it onto the screen with rich, luxurious brush strokes reminiscent of *Elvira Madigan*. At times, however, the pace is so languid it borders on listless, and much of the meaning seems to lurk just below the surface. The players aren't at fault. Veteran British actress Rachel Roberts is appropriately stern as the school's headmistress, and Anne Lambert gives a stunning performance as one of the ill-fated girls. Without revealing the denouement (or lack therof), suffice it to say it's unsatisfying. Weir makes beautiful and daring movies, but this one is longer on style than substance.
Unrated / 1976 / N/A

271

Peggy Sue Got Married: Kathleen Turner's performance as a bitter divorcee who gets a chance to relive her youth remains the only reason to recommend this rather slight, overrated comedy.

▲ A PIECE OF THE ACTION

Take a dash of *Blackboard Jungle,* add a generous measure of *To Sir, With Love,* serve it up in the Chicago slums, and you have a pretty good idea of what's going on in this well meaning but rather silly film directed by Sidney Poitier. The plot focuses on Poitier and Bill Cosby getting tangled up with the Mob while doing volunteer work at a black community center. As director, Poitier is far from subtle. But as an actor, he works well with the always good-natured Cosby. Loads of action, a lively Curtis Mayfield score, and a few genuinely touching moments struggle to hold their own against soggy social commentary.

PG / 1977 / Mastervision

▲ PINK FLOYD THE WALL

Don't expect a concert version of the 1980 album of the same name. Not one of the four-member rock group Pink Floyd appears, though lead singer and songwriter Roger Waters is credited with the skimpy screenplay, and the sound track is Floyd music, which blares and bludgeons, revealing that each incident is "just another brick in the wall." The story revolves around Pink, a self-destructive rocker (Bob Geldof of the Boomtown Rats and honored organizer of aid programs to Africa) who sits around an L.A. hotel room conjuring up images from his life and nightmares. Played with seductive insolence by Geldof, Pink is hardly a laugh a minute. His thoughts are mostly of war, dismemberment, drugs, groupie sex, and suicide. Geldof doesn't act, he gives an exhibition—but it's an effective one. The film, however, would depress a hyena. Director Alan (*Midnight Express, Fame, Shoot the Moon*) Parker piles on enough wretched excess to make Ken Russell seem constricted. The few genuinely erotic moments come from artist Gerald Scarfe, whose animated plants display the film's only sexual gusto. For all its visual and aural zap, sitting through the entire 95 minutes qualifies as an unnatural act for all but the most self-confident masochists.

R / 1982 / Vestron

▲ PIRANHA

Screenwriter John (*Return of the Secaucus Seven*) Sayles and director Joe (*Gremlins*) Dante had a low-budget ball sending up the *Jaws* films with this off-the-wall satire. Your everyday piranha is a lethal enough genus, but the variety in this movie is an especially voracious mutant strain. When Heather Menzies and Bradford Dillman, the Olivier of minor movies, discover that hundreds of the little devils have escaped from a testing tank, a Texas river becomes a red sea. Though *Piranha* doesn't exactly venture into uncharted waters, it is a sufficiently scary horror film for those who don't get or aren't interested in getting the in-jokes. Still, listening to an assistant tell a resort director, "Excuse me, sir, but the piranha are eating the guests," makes for a wickedly funny good time.
R / 1978 / Warner

▲ THE PIRATE MOVIE

The most notable act of piracy associated with this film is that of the cashiers who rake in money from people at the video rental stores. The movie is a badly photographed, recorded, choreographed, directed, written, and acted "modernization" of Gilbert and Sullivan's 19th-century operetta *The Pirates of Penzance*. (The film starring Linda Ronstadt, Kevin Kline, and Rex Smith, which was based on the New York Shakespeare Festival's hit production of the classic, was much preferable, if imperfect. See below.) The basic plot remains the same, but the film is presented as the heroine's dream: She conjures up a young pirate who wants to make an honest living. They fall in love, keeping a battle between the buccaneers and a skittish constabulary from getting serious. The original work was pre-camp camp; this updating has all the flavor of a lettuce sandwich. The heroine, the endearing Kristy McNichol, is trapped in a role with such laugh lines as "It's a bitch" and "Up yours." She's also handicapped by the fact that her leading "man," Christopher (*The Blue Lagoon*) Atkins, is prettier than she is. Director Ken (*The Longest Day*) Annakin throws in slow motion, speed-up sequences, and weird photographic effects at random. Every thirty seconds the script has a sight gag having to do with poking, stabbing, or kicking someone's groin. It is a measure of how bankrupt everyone's imagination was that just before the closing credits, two outtakes of McNichol being cute between scenes appear. There are modern soft rock songs, and the Gilbert and Sullivan score is pillaged; even the wonderfully lickety-split *The Very Model of a Modern Major General* is rewritten to include references to the Beatles, and it is badly performed by Australian actor Bill Kerr. (The film was shot and largely cast in Australia.) This film is not a treasure, but it ought to be buried.
PG / 1982 / CBS/Fox

▲ PIRATES

This film, directed by Roman (*Chinatown*) Polanski, is a tedious succession of listless battles between effete Spanish sailors and a scruffy bunch of buccaneers led by Walter Matthau. Matthau is a peerless comic actor. But even he can't get much out of this movie, except for one scene where the grandees force him to eat a boiled rat, and he toys with it delicately as if it were pheasant under glass. Cris Campion, a young French musician, plays Matthau's stalwart assistant, and Charlotte Lewis, another in Polanski's string of nubile protégées, is a noblewoman in constant distress. The script—calling it vapid would be offering a compliment—was co-written by Polanski and his frequent collaborator Gerard Brach. The 1976 pirate spoof *Swashbuckler* with Robert Shaw and James Earl Jones was a classic by comparison. It makes this film worse that Polanski is such an accomplished director. It looks like a movie and it sounds like a movie, yet there's not really anything to see or hear.
PG-13 / 1986 / USA

▲ PIRATES OF PENZANCE

Linda Ronstadt can sing gloriously. This film version of Gilbert and Sullivan's operetta, which Ronstadt did on Broadway for producer Joe Papp, makes that clear. Sadly, it also reveals Linda cannot as yet walk, talk, smile, gesture, or otherwise act convincingly in front of a camera. Her squeaking a line like "Oh, Frederick, in the calm excellence of your wisdom" is enough to set G&S spinning. Debuting film director Wilfred Leach, who staged the play in Central Park and on Broadway, lost much of the stage production's go-for-it spontaneity too. This is not the fault of the performers, most of whom appeared in the Broadway version. Kevin (*Sophie's Choice*) Kline, with his acrobatic wizardry as the pirate king, again dazzles. So do George Rose, as the fast-talking major-general, and Rex Smith, with his sweet crooner's voice. *Pirates,* thanks largely to William Elliott's orchestrations, still delights the ear. But Leach shows little subtlety. What should be gossamer (and was onstage) is rendered all too solid and earthbound onscreen.

G / 1983 / MCA

▲ PLACES IN THE HEART

Remarkably poignant, this drama of Depression-era Texas boasted Sally Field's finest performance since *Norma Rae*—and she earned her second Oscar with it. Field plays a sheriff's widow struggling to run a cotton farm and support her two small children. Even when the plot veers into *Perils of Pauline* conventionality, with its mortgage foreclosures, tornado, and brutal cotton harvest. Field never strikes a false note. Director Robert Benton succeeds best when he concentrates on character and the small details that reveal it. One simple scene—Field in a bank learning how to write a check—has more impact than a storm of special effects. Happily, there are many such scenes, including an opening and closing (not fair to give away here) that demonstrate an audacity rare in a director of Benton's refinement. No filmmaker could wish for a better cast. John Malkovich is superb as a blind boarder Field takes in for extra cash, touching in a manner that never begs for sympathy. Just as authentic is Lindsay Crouse as Field's sister, a beautician whose husband, Ed Harris, has been philandering with her best friend, Amy Madigan. With this small-scale but brilliant performance Crouse redeemed her strident work in *Daniel* and *Iceman*. Harris and Madigan (real-life husband and wife) are first-rate in less carefully defined roles, and Danny Glover brings amazing directness and gallantry to what might have been a clichéd part as a black farmhand. Benton could have added more grit, but in an era of machine-age movies, why quibble with a film that scores an emotional bull's-eye?

PG / 1984 / CBS/Fox

▲ PLATOON

No sane person should want to get any closer to war than this film, which won the 1986 Best Picture Oscar. Focusing on a 25th Infantry Division platoon in Vietnam, it is often as emotionally grueling as such great war films as *All Quiet on the Western Front, A Walk in the Sun,* and *The Jungle Fighters.* Writer-director Oliver Stone, who enlisted at age 21 and fought in 1967–68 with the 25th Infantry near the Cambodia border, recreates the war with unnerving honesty. The sounds, the light, the texture are right. So is the withering sense of fear, the instant cynicism that the war generated, and the looks of anger and terror on the faces of Vietnamese youths who never had a childhood. In one evocative scene the platoon enters a village just after having lost two men. It is never clear whether the villagers are Vietcong or North Vietnamese sympathizers; it is clear that everyone on both sides has been seized by the war at its most unreasoning. Stones' ability to make the ensuing atrocities understandable is probably his biggest achievement. What keeps this film from being the masterpiece it might have been is Stone's implicit lack of respect for his audience. If ever a story could speak for itself, this is it, yet Stone seems unconvinced that anyone will get this message—that this was a confused, hopelessly vicious war on both sides. He hammers it out with voiceovers and on-camera philosophical debates that merely remind viewers that it's only a movie after all. He also fails to answer a crucial question: What makes Tom Berenger such a remorseless killer? Berenger plays a super-hard-core platoon sergeant, a peerless soldier gone bad. Yet Stone never provides a clue as to whether the war fed on Berenger's ruthlessness or created it. Berenger himself is faultless, as is most of Stone's cast. Notable are Charlie Sheen, the new man whose letters to grandma supply the voiceovers, Willem Dafoe, Keith David, Forest Whitaker, and Reggie Johnson. Retired Marine Captain Dale Dye, who served as technical adviser, plays a credible company commander. The actors' contribution is even more significant than usual since they have to compete with Stone's philosophical grandstanding. That they succeed so well is to the director's credit too, of course. There is more than a little greatness in this movie, which garnered a truckload of Oscar nominations. Perhaps it is only fitting

that Stone's film, like the war it depicts, should be riven at its heart with ambivalence.
R / 1986 / Vestron

▲ PLAYERS

This is a tennis movie, but the real competition, waged in lingering close-ups, focuses on who is more adorable—coy Ali MacGraw or sincere Dean-Paul Martin. (The plot details how her inspiration puts him into the Wimbledon finals, though she proves elusive as a lover.) They are both gorgeous, of course, though Martin, Dean's son, bares his muscular if bald chest every other scene while MacGraw, inhibited by the PG rating, can only undo a button or three. Neither, alas, is an overpowering actor, rendering laughable such already insipid lines as "Everything about you is my business," "I can't believe this conversation," and "It's over." (Reports that parts of the film were improvised were all too believable.) Martin, who in a real life was a tennis pro and pilot who died in a 1987 plane crash, tends to overact on the court, flopping and diving so much he looks like a tennis player imitating a porpoise, or vice versa. Only the guy who plays borrish Ilie Nastase is totally convincing, and that's because it *is* Ilie Nastase.
PG / 1979 / Paramount

▲ PLENTY

David Hare's angry and very British play about the corruption of England's wartime ideals in the moral rot of peacetime emeges as an unqualified screen triumph thanks, oddly enough, to an American actress (Meryl Streep) and an Australian director (Fred Schepisi). Streep is fiercely intelligent and sexier than she's ever been on-screen. She plays an altruistic Englishwoman who fought with the French Resistance, marries a diplomat (splendidly done by Charles Dance of *The Jewel in the Crown* fame), and goes mad as post-World War II society fails to live up to her exacting standards. At first it's off-putting to hear Streep trot out the la-de-dah English accent she used with mixed results in *The French Lieutenant's Woman* to play a character meant to symbolize Britain's decline. Wisely, though, Streep and Schepisi, the master stylist of *The Chant of*

Jimmie Blacksmith, emphasize the human drama over the loftier implications in Hare's acidly brilliant script. As a result, *Plenty* is warmer, wittier, and finally more emotionally devastating than it was onstage. Pop music stars Sting and Tracy Ullman are astonishingly fine as, respectively, Streep's lower-class lover and friend. Sam Neill and Ian McKellen contribute vivid cameos. But if anyone comes near to stealing the show from Streep it is John Gielgud who, at 81, delivered his finest screen performance as a senior official in the Foreign Office. In the movie's best scene— a wickedly funny dinner party in which both Streep and Gielgud lose control—these two pros put on an electric display of acting prowess.
R / 1985 / Thorn/EMI

▲ POLICE ACADEMY

If after graduation those beasts from *Animal House* had decided to go into police work, they would have ended up in this movie. It does for police schools what *Stripes* did for Army basic training—trashes it. The film stars Steve Guttenberg and Kim Cattrall as two of a motley group of recruits enticed to a police academy by a new mayor's attempts to broaden the force. (The city is never named though the movie was shot in Toronto.) G. W. Bailey is the training sergeant, in a tonsil-baring, hyper-disciplinarian role straight out of the Jack Webb–Lou Gossett handbook. The other recruits include ex-pro footballer Bubba Smith, Dave Graf, and Michael Winslow. The sharp-eyed will recognize Debralee Scott from TV's "Mary Hartman, Mary Harman" and porn queen Georgina Spelvin in small roles. But the funniest bits go to George Gaynes, so terrific in *Tootsie* as the actor with the crush on Dustin Hoffman's female alter ego. Gaynes plays the academy's absentminded commandant and is a perfect foil for a film that dotes on demolishing authority figures. Hugh Wilson, the main writer-director on TV's "WKRP in Cincinnati," directed the film as his first feature. He sinks to that now-standard ploy: having a male character peek at shapely young women taking showers, as if this in itself is funny. But the movie is generally good-natured and, for this kind of thing, tasteful. Nobody should be arrested because of it, anyway.
R / 1984 / Warner

Pennies From Heaven: This ambitious and, yes, depressing musical about the Depression flopped at the box office—so did the real-life romance of its stars Steve Martin and Bernadette Peters.

▲ POLICE ACADEMY 2

It's almost an insult to a modern comedy to say that it is not either all-out tasteless or mean spirited. But this sequel, like 1984's original *Police Academy,* is good-natured without sacrificing its punch lines. Steve Guttenberg is still the focus of his unobtrusively likeable class of now-rookie cops. But Bubba Smith, Michael Winslow (the one who can mimic all kinds of noises), David Graf, Marion Ramsey, and Bruce Mahler are back too. They're all assigned to a gang-troubled precinct commanded by Howard Hesseman. George Gaynes again plays the academy superintendent who evinces a beaming lack of connection to the real world. There's also a marvelous performance by San Francisco comic Bob Goldthwait. He plays the gang leader, a giddy vegetarian psychopath who talks in a steady slur, as if he were a cross between Pee-Wee Herman and Marlon Brando in *On the Waterfront.* Jerry Paris, a veteran of TV's "Dick Van Dyke Show" and "Happy Days," directed. The jokes are obvious, running to such things as substituting epoxy for the shampoo of a despotic watch commander. But not many movies these days offer so many amiable, guilt-free guffaws. **PG-13 / 1985 / Warner**

▲ POLICE ACADEMY 3: BACK IN TRAINING

All that stands between this movie and nonexistence is the variegated appeal of its cast, still more or less intact from the original. Steve Guttenberg, Bubba Smith, Marion Ramsey, Michael Winslow, David Graf, George Gaynes, Leslie Easterbrook, and company are all likable enough, and each has a funny riff or two. But director Jerry (TV's "Happy Days") Paris and screenwriter Gene (*King Solomon's Mines*) Quintano offer them almost no support. The only chances for laughs in the film come from Guttenberg's ingratiating womanizing, Smith's calm displays of supermanic strength, and Winslow's goofy imitations—the best moment is Winslow doing a badly dubbed character in a martial arts movie. Bob Goldthwait, who played a gang leader in *Police Academy 2,* becomes a recruit this time and has cleaned up his diction a little, though his basic mode of communication is still a giggling howl. Model Shawn Weatherly—star of the unintentionally hilarious TV "docudrama" series "oceanQuest"—is comely as Guttenberg's new conquest. All the characters seem to be milling around waiting for something to happen, and it never does. The plot has to do with a competition between police academies. But by the time the film gets to its drawn-out finale, everyone, Guttenberg and Smith especially, seems to be tired of the whole project. It's easy to sympathize with them.

PG / 1986 / Warner

▲ POLTERGEIST

Things have rarely gone bump in the night so effectively as in this haunted-house fable directed by Tobe (*The Texas Chainsaw Massacre*) Hooper and coproduced and co-written by Steven (*Close Encounters*) Spielberg: The film is set in the normal suburban California home of a normal couple, JoBeth Williams and Craig T. Nelson, and their normal kids, Dominique Dunne, Oliver Robins, and Heather O'Rourke. But as soon as the ghostly apparitions appear, well, forget normal. While not many movies insist on the suspension of disbelief that *Poltergeist* demands, skepticism vanishes quickly. For *Poltergeist* is more than an entertaining spook show. It's also touching, funny, and human. To give any of the plot away would be a gross disservice. (Small children who think the objects in their rooms take on scary shapes when the lights go out, however, should be kept away from *Poltergeist* at all costs.) Though the film avoids the blood and guts endemic to the genre, it is nonetheless a goosepimpler. The performances are all first-rate, and tiny Heather will melt the hardest heart. *Poltergeist* is a film to steel yourself for. Hooper and Spielberg worked long and hard to bring the ghost story to its fullest potential. They succeeded.

PG / 1982 / MGM/UA

▲ POLTERGEIST II

No movie creature, however fearsome, is as invulnerable as a box-office monster. That explains the return of the little terrors who seemed to have gotten their comeuppance at the end of *Poltergeist*

in 1982. Directed by Brian (*Breaking Glass*) Gibson, this sequel is on the dutiful side, essentially reprising Tobe Hooper's (and Steven Spielberg's) original. Once again an overpossessive demon is stalking an Arizona couple, Craig T. Nelson and JoBeth Williams, and their children, Heather O'Rourke and Oliver Robins. It's a helpful touch to have the original cast back to portray the family. They're all accomplished players, and so are such added performers as the late Julian (*The Cotton Club*) Beck, as the demon in human form, Will (*One Flew Over the Cuckoo's Nest*) Sampson, as a heroic Indian medicine man, and Geraldine Fitzgerald, as Williams' psychic mom. The cast, in fact, lends a lot more substance to the proceedings than was provided by Gibson and writers Mark Victor and Michael Grais. Sampson, for instance, has to muster all his considerable supply of dignity to get anything other than guffaws when he counsels the family, "Band together; that will prevent you from crossing over into the other dimension." (Even Fitzgerald, however, can't help but seem on the dotty side when she appears in an ethereal, gauzy outfit that makes her look like the ghost of the Good Witch of the North.) The movie works best when it's played for laughs. Nelson, doing a sort of restrained Chevy Chase imitation a lot of the time, says at one point that his suspicions of Sampson aren't really racist: "I got nothing against those people. I read *Bury My Heart at Wounded Knee*." But the electrical storm effects, icky fiends, and stomach-turning shocks are routine by this time, and while small children might easily be disturbed by some of the gorier sequences, the film will bore a lot more people than it scares.

PG-13 / 1986 / Warner

▲ POLYESTER

Having offended eyes and ears with such shockers as *Pink Flamingos*, Baltimore's underground filmmaker John Waters moved on to noses with this film. Walter Reade tried to make movies with appropriate scents back in 1959; Mike Todd, Jr., countered with Smell-O-Vision. Both used expensive air-pipe systems. Waters's process, Odorama, succeeded out of sheer tackiness, using a cheap piece of cardboard with ten numbers keyed to numerals that flash onscreen. The audience scratched the appropriate digit and got the same whiff as leading person Divine, the three-

hundred-pound transvestite starring in her fifth epic for Waters. Numbers two, six, and nine (the smells range from pizza to old gym shoes) were perilous. But don't shy away from the film. You don't have to use an odor strip at home, and the writer-director kept *Polyester* within the bounds of respectable bad taste. The result was the funkiest fun since *Animal House* and *Airplane!* Divine sweetly plays a typical suburban housewife plagued by a cheating husband, a murderous mother, a nympho daughter, and a son with a fetish—he stomps women's feet in shopping malls. Divine suffers every possible humiliation (her husband uses a bullhorn to tell the neighborhood of her stretch marks) until she meets Tab Hunter. Looking half his age (then 49), Tab owns a highbrow drive-in that shows triple bills by esoteric French screenwriter Marguerite Duras. Tab's and Divine's love scenes are inoffensively depraved, all part of Waters's pungent satire of an American gone mad. The acting by Hunter and Waters's Baltimore regulars really does stink, which is purposeful. *Polyester* may not be for every nose, but it smells like a hit.
R / 1981 / N/A

▲ THE POPE OF GREENWICH VILLAGE

Petty crooks taking a shot at the big time is not exactly an original subject, but Vincent Patrick's 1979 novel, *The Pope of Greenwich Village,* had genuine crackpot verve. The movie, from Patrick's own script, too often confuses busywork with energy. It also seems constructed from scrap parts. Yet the actors and the atmosphere of New York's Little Italy provide glue enough to create an emotionally compelling package. Mickey Rourke and Eric Roberts are marvelously matched in the leads. Rourke, with enough shirts and shoes to make a pimp envious, plays a failed Greenwich Village maitre d' ripe for a big score to impress his WASP girlfriend, Darryl Hannah. His entree into the world of crime is his hustling cousin (Roberts), a bag of bones and nerves hot for any get-rich-quick scheme. When the boys pull a safecracking job, they find themselves on the wrong side of mobster Burt Young, a sadistic godfather who likes to hack off fingers to discourage ambitious punks. Martin Scorsese directing Robert De Niro and Harvey Keitel in *Mean Streets* handled a similar story with pungent assurance. But the task is beyond *Pope* director

Stuart Rosenberg, who keeps slamming through the picture as if he didn't trust the material enough to shape it. The blitz effect is hard on the actors, especially the otherwise striking Roberts, whose performance sometimes spins out of control, along with the film. The veterans fare best: Ken McMillan is superb as an old safecracker, and Geraldine Page is shrewd as a cop's iron-willed mom. With more careful handling *Pope* might have been something extraordinary. Still, fired by Rourke and Roberts, it's an absorbing show, delivering in dazzle a lot of what it lacks in depth.
R / 1984 / MGM/UA

▲ POPEYE

"What am I?" chants Robin Williams, the squinty-eyed sailor man in Robert Altman's musical version of the durable E. C. Segar comic strip. Williams has an idea, so do Altman, screenwriter Jules Feiffer, and composer Harry Nilsson. Unfortunately, no two of them have the same idea. As a result, *Popeye* is a mess, even if it's often charming. The real spinach is Shelley Duvall's performance as the spindly Olive Oyl. Whether snappish or swoony, as in her rapturously funny "He Needs Me" number, Duvall hits the right notes. That can't be said for Nilsson's dull-to-derivative score, with tunes memorable only for lyrics consisting of endlessly repeated titles ("He's Large," "I'm Mean," "I Yam What I Yam"). The other magical performer is Wesley Ivan Hurt (Altman's then 23-month-old grandson) as the ever-smiling "orphink Swee'pea." He doesn't just steal scenes from veterans like Ray Walston and Paul Dooley; it's a grand larceny. Williams takes longer to get rolling. There's the weight of those bulbous latex-and-foam rubber forearms for one thing. Williams does finish in full vigor, though, and the movie picks up in its second half when Altman's "morality tale" subtext gives way to fun for the devil of it.
PG / 1981 / Paramount

▲ PORKY'S

There's a temptation to dismiss *Porky's* swiftly, but the enormous box-office success of the film and its two sequels to date makes *Porky's* one of the most humiliating cultural artifacts of the 1980s. Set in a high school in south Florida, circa 1954,

the plot focuses on six teenage boys—"the dirty half-dozen"—who'll stop at nothing to make their sex fantasies a reality. They peep at girls in the shower room, hire a hooker, and create lots of prophylactic jokes. The film's humor would need a crash course to reach even the sophomoric level. The Porky's of the title is a redneck roadhouse where Sheriff Alex Karras keeps the customers from killing one another. The acting is better than the movie deserves. Susan Clark (Mrs. Karras) has a funny bit as a whore named Cherry Forever. Writer-director Bob (*Tribute*) Clark, himself a former Florida high schooler, said he's been waiting to make this movie since he decided to become a filmmaker. On the egregious sexism of such ambitions, Hollywood planted the seeds of ruin.
R / 1982 / CBS/Fox

▲ PORKY'S II: THE NEXT DAY

The first line of dialogue comes from Dan Monahan, the star—of the first *Porky's,* that is. He awakes and shrieks, "I got laaaaiiiid!" That imbecilic bit of self-congratulation indeed goes a long way toward explaining the whole reason for being (if not the $110 million gross) of the original. Be grateful that Bob Clark, who directed, co-wrote, and helped produce II (he wrote and directed *Porky's*), mercifully tried to move his Florida high schoolers at least some distance beyond their juvenile sexual obsessions. This story is focused mainly on a white-haired local evangelist trying to rally his Righteous Flock, the school board, and city and county commissioners against Angel Beach High School's "Evening of Shakespeare." He thinks it will turn out to be lewd and degenerate. In the first confrontation the principal backs the kids; he and the evangelist, Bill Wiley, quote the Bible as well as the Bard to prove either can be construed as gospel for either side. The whole scene actually is only a setup for the principal to yell, "Get the Flock out of here." If that line doesn't jackknife you at the waist in guffaws, stay away. It's one of the funnier ones. There is an attempt at a sympathetic story by Roger E. (*The Lathe of Heaven*) Swaybill and Alan (*Cat People*) Ornsby. The schoolboy Romeo, a Seminole, is beaten by some Indian-baiting local Klansmen. So Monahan, Kaki Hunger (his frizzy, scrawny laidee), and even rival jerks in school all gang up to take on the KKK, whose members turn out to be pretty tight with—surprise—the county commissioner, the preacher, and the city fathers. Even the tyrannically uptight girls' gym teacher, actress Nancy Parsons, flees the Righteous Flock in the end. It is not exactly deep praise to say *The Next Day* benefits from its broader comedic basis and is more enjoyable than the original. What it doesn't do is more important: Unlike *Porky's,* the sequel does not crassly—and thoroughly—insult the intelligence of the people who pay to see it.
R / 1983 / CBS/Fox

▲ PORKY'S REVENGE

This movie's title may suggest a comeuppance. No such luck. That fun-loving group of Florida high school kids is still in charge, and they still have nothing on their minds but gratuitous sex and every bad joke that goes with it. In fact this third film in the series seemed to pay tribute to the qualities all too common to the quick-thrill, teen film genre: sexism, exploitation, and grossness of all kinds. Once again our heroes, including Dan Monahan, Mark Herrier, and Tony Ganios, when not ogling every bit of flesh that saunters by, are up against Porky (Chuck Mitchell), who now owns a riverboat casino/brothel and grill. A thin plot about throwing a state basketball championship game is intertwined with a shotgun wedding between one of the kids and Porky's well-endowed, Daisy Mae-ish daughter, Wendy Feign. Meanwhile, former Playboy Playmate Kimberly Evenson, as a Swedish exchange student, shows off her own endowments while saying things like "Ja, ja, play" and "Ja, ja, movie." A couple of teachers engage in drawn-out scenes of sexual psychodrama. The rest of the movie is so reminiscent of vapid, early '70s, made-for-TV stuff that it's not surprising to note that James ("Welcome Back, Kotter") Komack directed. At times the film verges on self-parody, which would be a welcome change.
R / 1985 / CBS/Fox

▲ THE POSTMAN ALWAYS RINGS TWICE

"You're scum," Jessica Lange snarls to Jack Nicholson near the climax of this relentlessly seedy version of James M. Cain's 1934 novel. It's about a Depression drifter who lusts for the

Poltergeist: Heather O'Rourke learns that there are disadvantages to being the one in the family with the supernatural powers when she tries to turn down an invitation to a spirited get-together.

seductive young wife of a Greek roadhouse owner and then joins her in mercilessly killing the husband they've cuckolded. The book was banned in Boston, and Hollywood shied away from making a film version until 1946, when Lana Turner and John Garfield were teamed as the doomed lovers. The result was a smashing rat-a-tat-tat film oozing glamour and sex. This time director Bob (*Five Easy Pieces*) Rafelson and playwright-turned-screenwriter David Mamet slowed the pace to a crawl, letting a lot of the excitement seep out. The film's squalid Twin Oaks diner, just outside L.A., is set in a gray land illuminated only by lightning flashes of passion and violence. Much was made of the graphic couplings of Nicholson and Lange, especially their first encounter on a kitchen table. Yet seedy proved decidedly unsexy. Nicholson plays his loser with unforced urgency. But whatever is worth stealing in this picture is purloined by Lange in the performance that finally made audiences forget she was the insipid blonde pursued by King Kong the Younger. Alternately erotic, murderous, and childlike, she occupies her complex character

with mesmerizing conviction. Bravos for Lange; boos for the picture.
R / 1981 / CBS/Fox

▲ **POWER**

Richard Gere is livelier than usual in this dumb but entertaining gloss on the wicked ways media wizards package political candidates. Don't look for an incisive probe into the methods of real-life campaign handlers such as David Garth and Pat Caddell. Gere's Peter St. John is a fantasy figure, gifted with an unlined face, great money, terrific suits (no actor fills a Dunhill better), a private jet, and a high-tech office. His assistant, played by Kate (*Indiana Jones*) Capshaw, obligingly wiggles out of her tight skirt whenever the boss calls for some quick dictation in the shower. At least director Sidney Lumet pumps up the picture with all the pizzazz, if not the passion, he brought to the similarly themed *Network*. Gere, in a role originally set for Burt Reynolds (until he dropped out), finally found the perfect outlet for the smug self-involvement that makes most of his other performances insufferable. His work here has the tone of a buzz saw's nasty burr. So does David Himmelstein's dialogue. Himmelstein, once a press aide to former Massachusetts Sen. Edward Brooke, showed a keen ear for the cadence of hustle. *Power* is at its best on the run, watching Gere trying to win a Senate seat for a tongue-tied millionaire (Fritz Weaver), keep in office a freshly divorced woman governor (smartly done by Michael Learned), and cope with a ruthless lobbyist (Denzel Washington). Whenever Lumet slows down so that Gere can moon over his ex-wife (Julie Christie is wasted in the role) or bemoan his lost ideals with old boss Gene Hackman, *Power* poops out. Worse is all the blather about selling images instead of issues, a fault the movie all too clearly shares with its alleged targets. By the end, when Gere finds redemption by giving young pol Matt Salinger (J.D.'s son, in a striking debut) the old "to thine own self be true" speech, the only recourse is to stuff popcorn in your ears. R / 1986 / Karl-Lorimar

▲ PRACTICE MAKES PERFECT

Funny thing about French films: They make it seem nothing in the world should be taken seriously, no matter how bad it is. In Philippe de Broca's movie, Jean Rochefort plays a philandering concert pianist whose nightly encores seem to be catching up with him. There's the beautiful wife he ignores, Nicole Barcia (who won the French Oscar for her performance). As Rochefort's ex-wife, for whom he still lusts, Annie Girardot is marvelous, as always. And lovely Catherine Alric plays an empty-headed girlfriend. As a farce, the film is light and bright. But de Broca lapses into heavy-handed moralizing. His film is recouped only by a climax that's happy, if not quite parfait. (In French with subtitles.) Unrated / 1980 / N/A

▲ PREDATOR

With a title like that and a cast headed by Arnold Schwarzenegger and Carl Weathers, Rocky's old sparring mate, this movie is not likely to attract people looking for the new *Blithe Spirit*. And those who like action movies and are not easily offended by relentless implausibility and violence will find *Predator* fast, flashy, and as distracting as a whack in the head with a brick. Schwarzenegger plays the leader of a commando unit that specializes in rescuing hostages. These are ruthless guys: One of them totes a machine gun that in real life would be heavy enough to give a rhinoceros a hernia, if you could find a rhinoceros stupid enough to carry it. Arn has lots of scruples, though. He notes self-righteously that his men don't do assassinations or offensive missions, and you half expect him to snarl, "And we don't do landscaping or small-appliance repair, either." Weathers, as a CIA operative, orders Schwarzenegger and the boys into a Latin American jungle to rescue two hostages being held by guerrillas. There's a murky subplot here about an invasion of someplace by someone, but never mind. What matters is that the commandos blow the guerrillas away. And why not? There are six commandos, and only three thousand or so guerrillas, none of whom could shoot straight enough to hit a wall if he were standing on the floor of the Grand Canyon. But this isn't Arnold's lucky day. He and his men happen on a spot frequented by a creature from outer space. This character is sort of invisible and likes to tear humans to pieces and turn them into people tartare, without any scallions or raw egg, either. It eventually boils down, of course, to a confrontation between Schwarzenegger and the creature, during which, suffice it to say, Arnold absorbs enough punishment to destroy a midsize city. Director John (*Nomads*) McTiernan follows a shoot-first-and-forget-about-the-questions policy but uses his pyrotechnics and special effects adroitly. Especially effective are the shots from the monster's point of view. The creature seems to "see" using an infrared technique, which sets up a nice gimmick during the shoot-out. Schwarzenegger, considerably slimmed down, has little to do but flex, glare, and shoot. He manages to be likable nonetheless. That may be because even though there's little overt humor—only a couple of bad dirty jokes—he never seems to take things too seriously. Somehow you know that no matter how barbarically crude and violent Schwarzenegger gets, what he would really like is to be home eating strudel and reading some Schopenhauer. R / 1987 / N/A

▲ PRETTY BABY

To say this is the best Brooke Shields film of all time is not exactly a rave, of course. But it is an often fascinating movie, the first made in the U.S. by Frenchman Louis Malle. The movie was controversial because Brooke, then just 12, played the daughter of a whore (Susan Sarandon) in the Storyville red-light district of New Orleans, circa 1917. Brooke isn't all *that* grown up by the time she's turning tricks too. And that is what's troubling, particularly because of a full frontal nude scene. Keith Carradine plays E. J. Bellocq, a real-life photographer of the era who survives through his sensitive portraits taken inside bordellos. The handsome, re-created portraiture provides some redeeming value.

R / 1978 / Paramount

▲ PRETTY IN PINK

Years from now Molly Ringwald may well be the only survivor of Hollywood's dalliance with the Brat Pack. Unlike her peers Ringwald is uncompromising in front of the camera. She consistently delivers the sort of direct, seemingly spontaneous performances that are the essence of screen acting. With the persistence of an ace detective, Ringwald finds the contrariness in her characters; she can track down the sinner in a saint and the dork in a teenage do-gooder. Unfortunately she gets straightjacketed in this movie by a script that settles for black-and-white pronouncements instead of the delicate shades of gray that Ringwald employs. She is cast as a high school senior who has her heart destroyed and social status imperiled by a rich, handsome, fickle classmate played by Andrew McCarthy. He's a Romeo with a credit card, and she's a junk-shop Juliet. Beneath the slick MTV veneer of this movie beats the trashy heart of a '37 tearjerker—Stella Dallas at 18. Video director Howard Deutch, who was making his feature debut, even costumes his characters in old-time movie clichés: The rich kids always wear solids, while the poor kids favor mix-and-match combos. Haven't these filmmakers looked in on any homerooms lately? Dressing differently, which brings Ringwald peer-group grief in this movie, makes you a hero in high school these days. Alas, Ringwald's male co-stars treat her equally poorly. As the Brooks

Brothers cad, McCarthy peddles one expression—the hangdog pout of a passive patrician; Jon Cryer, Ringwald's comrade in kookiness, who's infatuated with her, pilfers Matthew Broderick's mannerisms—as he did in *No Small Affair.* With the likable Broderick in the role, the puppy love triangle would have had equal sides and tension. Screenwriter John Hughes, who directed Ringwald to near perfection in *The Breakfast Club* and *16 Candles,* tailored this script to her talents, but the gesture has backfired. Giving a performance streaked with a subtlety and sensitivity absent in the script, Ringwald exposes the facile sentiment of Hughes's vision. Then 18, she already faced a professional dilemma that usually plagues only the most seasoned movie star. Shining brightly, she unwittingly shames a movie meant to showcase her.

PG-13 / 1986 / Paramount

▲ PRICK UP YOUR EARS

If you want to be surprised by an altogether astonishing British import, this is a perfect choice. Director Stephen Frears teamed up with screenwriter Alan Bennett to make this film of John Lahr's 1978 biography of playwright Joe Orton. Back in the 1960s, Orton shocked and stimulated theater audiences with his plays *Entertaining Mr. Sloane, Loot,* and *What the Butler Saw.* For using humor to expose hypocrisy, Orton was widely touted as a successor to Oscar Wilde. But on August 9, 1967, Orton, then 34, was bludgeoned to death by his lover, Kenneth Halliwell, who then killed himself by swallowing twenty-two Nembutals. A trite, tawdry film could have been made from this on the order of, say, Bob Fosse's grim *Star 80.* Instead, Frears, Bennett, and Lahr filmed Orton's story as Orton might have done it, brimming with spirit, wit, and outrage. And in Gary Oldman, who plays Orton, they discovered an actor of ferocious talent. Oldman finds the carnal and verbal audacity in Orton and, more surprisingly, the insecurity. When he meets Halliwell at the Royal Academy of Dramatic Art (they are both acting students), it is the better-educated Halliwell who teaches Joe about literature and art. Orton instructs the terrified Halliwell, hauntingly played by Alfred Molina, about the joys of cruising public urinals. They move into a claustrophobic one-room flat in North Lon-

don and quit acting to find even less success as writers. They're separated in 1962, when both do six months in prison for defacing library books, and Orton begins writing on his own. On the outside, a leading theatrical agent, Peggy Ramsay, offers encouragement. As Ramsay, Vanessa Redgrave, sexier and looser than she's been in years, is deliciously comic. While she conducts Orton into a world of celebrity (he's signed to write a movie for the Beatles), homebody Halliwell is ignored. His neurosis festers. Oldman and Molina find the hilarity and the horror in this familiar situation. Indeed, Frears handles all his large cast with startling expertise. Julie Walters, the tarty treasure of *Educating Rita,* is unforgettable as Orton's mother, and Wallace Shawn and Lindsay Duncan mine every telling detail from brief roles as biographer Lahr and his wife, Anthea. But it's Oldman who holds you in thrall and inspires you back to Orton's plays for another jolt from a voice too quickly silenced. *Prick Up Your Ears* makes watching movies once more something to get excited about.
R / 1987 / N/A

▲ PRIEST OF LOVE

D. H. Lawrence, who lived from 1885 to 1930, was a giant of English literature, but today he is read mostly on college campuses. The once startling candor with which he treated sex in such books as *Women in Love* and *Lady Chatterly's Lover* seems almost tame. Perhaps to make up for the modern era's neglect of the author, and possibly because producer-director Christopher Miles has a strong background in British TV, the movie has an episodic, almost documentary feel. Ian McKellen, who starred in *Amadeus* on Broadway, portrays the tortured, tubercular Lawrence, who lures a German noblewoman (Janet Suzman) away from her husband and three daughters. They traipse all over Europe, often hounded by local bluenoses, and end up living in Taos, New Mexico, as wards of an American patroness (played winningly by Ava Gardner). The scenes in *Priest of Love* (the phrase is from one of Lawrence's letters and refers to himself) are brief, the pace is swift. A visit to the popcorn counter could deprive a moviegoer of five years of the author's life. It is an odd movie; the performances are uniformly splendid and the locations authentic, but it sac-

rifices emotion for information. For a perceptive view of Lawrence's later life, see the movie; for a glimpse into his heart, read his books.
R / 1981 / N/A

▲ PRINCE OF THE CITY

A New York City cop decides to blow the whistle on corruption within the force, touching off a disastrous chain of events that ends in betrayal and death. Sound familiar? It's the basic premise of *Serpico,* directed by Sidney Lumet, who also did this film. But that's where the similarities end. *Serpico* was taut, gripping and superbly acted by Al Pacino. This movie's 2 hours and 47 minutes are muddled and egregiously overacted by Treat Williams, who plays the cop. He's the leader of a special investigative unit, nicknamed the "princes of the city" because of their autonomy within the police force. Screenwriter Jay Presson Allen and Lumet don't give Williams much to work with either. We never know why he becomes an informant—a motivation crucial to the film's dramatic tension. One bright spot is Lindsay (*Slap Shot*) Crouse, who plays Williams' wife. She sees her husband has chosen a dangerous path, but she's helpless to stop him. And Jerry Orbach, who plays one of Williams' partners, is terrific. The movie is based on the true story of a recently retired New York cop, Bob Leuci. Better you should read the book and then rent *Serpico.*
R / 1981 / Warner

▲ THE PRISONER OF ZENDA

Anthony Hope wrote the novel in 1894, and its cinematic possibilities were exploited as early as 1913. In this fifth film version, it turned to spoof. The story is a classic (and hackneyed) confusion-of-identity piece. When the mad King of Ruritania (cameoed by Peter Sellers) falls from his balloon into a well, his foppish son Rudi (Sellers again) inherits the throne. Rudi's brother (Jeremy Kemp) plots to seize the crown, but loyalists discover a London cabby look-alike for Rudi (guess who). The predictable prince-and-pauper misidentity is lightened by some bawdy slapstick and another history-making accent from Sellers as Rudi. The movie lags at times, though Sellers's real-life fourth wife, Lynne Frederick, is gorgeous as Princess Flavia. And Sellers himself was almost invariably a joy.

PG / 1979 / MCA

▲ PRIVATE BENJAMIN

Her husband dies while making love to her on their wedding night. To get over the trauma, Judy Benjamin, played by Goldie Hawn, takes the improbable step of enlisting in the Army. Howard Zieff directed this delightful satire about a character transformed from an immature, dependent girl—gushing she "would have been Mrs. Alan Bates (in *An Unmarried Woman*) so fast he wouldn't know what hit him"—into a bare-knuckled, assertive woman who decks her new boyfriend (Armand Assante) when he dares call

her stupid. Barbara Barrie is an ever-sympathetic mother, Sam Wanamaker is Goldie's overbearing Jewish father, and Mary Kay Place is her basic training buddy. The chemistry of these stereotypes somehow works, even for Eileen Brennan as a thin-lipped, neurotically aggressive captain and for Robert Webber's gung-ho Colonel "Thornie." These are caricatures to be sure, but *Private Benjamin,* later turned into a TV series, is a wonderfully campy, feminist answer to "Gomer Pyle."

R / 1980 / Warner

▲ A PRIVATE FUNCTION

Maggie Smith and bathroom humor aren't the most likely matchup, but combining the two is only the most perverse of the many perverse

Private Benjamin: Goldie Hawn scores her biggest comedy hit playing a Jewish American Princess dragged kicking and screaming into maturity by some decidedly unpampering Army treatment.

notions that enliven *A Private Function.* This comedy joins the lunatic sensibility of a Monty Python sketch with the leering and scatological jokes of those West End comedies beloved by British theatergoers. Although it features Betty the Pig in a prominent role, what really distinguishes this film is its social conscience. Set in a small English town in 1947, it concerns the humiliations of postwar food shortages. Members of the upper crust of the town have hidden away their own "unlicensed" pig for a reception celebrating the marriage of Princess Elizabeth to Prince Philip. Their plans are thwarted by the town's timid chiropodist, Michael Palin, who accidentally discovers Betty. At the urging of his social-climbing wife, Smith—"It's not pork, Gilbert, it's power," she hisses—he steals the pig. Despite the gross-out nature of the movie, its real subject is not gluttony or even greed but the prison of propriety. Written by Alan Bennett, who was part of the Beyond the Fringe comedy troupe, and directed by Malcolm Mowbray, this movie is as angry about the class struggle as any modern English drama, but seldom has indignation been so imaginatively packaged. Palin and Smith, who were well matched in *The Missionary,* again work together marvelously. His deadpan and her hauteur play off each other with the precision of a metronome. Smith also enjoys an inventive foil in Liz Smith, who plays her dotty mother. Maggie proves herself a high priestess of low comedy. No matter how outrageous the material gets, she never condescends to her character's provincialism, which is the soul of this satire. That is the ultimate perverse irony of *A Private Function.* By embracing the crassness of the material, Maggie Smith shows just how classy an actress she is.

R / 1985 / Thorn/EMI

▲ PRIZZI'S HONOR

While Young Turks in Hollywood fret themselves into a frazzle trying to duplicate last year's hot model in space hardware or teen titillation, director John Huston remains a rambunctious risk taker. The legend behind such classics as *The Maltese Falcon, The Treasure of the Sierre Madre, The African Queen,* and *The Man Who Would Be King,* Huston never considered making a sequel to any of them. Why should he, as long as there's a chance to be different? *Prizzi's Honor,* a daring, deliciously demented black comedy based on Richard Condon's surreal 1982 novel, allows Huston to be different with a vengeance. His coarse vitality is irresistible. You can almost see him grinning wickedly behind the camera. Jack Nicholson, one of the few names in movies these days that guarantees a good time, stars as a Brooklyn Mafioso. Never mind that Nicholson's accent would baffle Brooklynites; he makes it work. The way he stiffens his upper lip is nifty too, giving him a Bogart air. Add this to his rogues' gallery of unforgettable characters. He plays a trusted, if none too bright, enforcer for a Mafia don, deftly overplayed by William Hickey. Hickey's striking but malevolent granddaughter, Anjelica Huston, was jilted by Nicholson four years earlier. Anjelica, the director's daughter and Nicholson's longtime real-life lady, plays this small but telling role (a sort of modern-day Lucrezia Borgia) with career-making panache. She won a Best Supporting Actress Oscar for it. Confronting Nicholson at a family wedding, she is obviously cooking up a rematch. But Nicholson's eye is taken by a gorgeous unknown guest, played by Kathleen Turner with enough come-on carnality to singe the screen. Turner is glorious, the sexiest presence in movies of the '80s and a prodigious actress to boot. Nicholson follows this paragon to L.A. where she tells him she works as a tax consultant. But he finds he has linked up with a free-lance hit woman. So Nicholson asks himself: "Should I ice her or marry her?" Why, after all, can't two killers wed, set up house, and plan a family between planning jobs? Says Nicholson to Turner: "I look at you. I see what I want to see. That's what love is." Nicholson and Turner, a magical screen pair, make something wonderfully credible and inexplicably touching of this bizarre coupling. They are two cobras with a nesting itch, and they mine the script (by Condon and Janet Roach) for every satirical poison dart aimed at the evil in everyday America. There is no sadism in their violence, only greed—which makes their actions more shocking and human. *Prizzi's Honor* is overlong and overwrought, with the most convoluted plot since Bogie and Becall cut their way through the muddle of *The Big Sleep* forty years before. But thanks to Huston and his superb cast, the film is also outrageously entertaining.

R / 1985 / Vestron

▲ PROJECT X

In the beginning there was *E.T.* and it begat many lesser sci-fi brethren—all with the same story. First there is a secret, then an engaging young man accidentally discovers the secret, and then the military-industrial complex tries to hush up the truth, terrible or otherwise. In the case of this Matthew Broderick comedy the secret involves the effects of radiation on laboratory chimpanzees. That's a slightly hairy, hoary variation on the theme, but this is still another young-idealist-saves-the-world-from-itself adventure. So as a public service we offer the following guide on how to differentiate *Project X* from its many predecessors. In *War Games,* Broderick looked less bored and more boyish. There is no cute and cuddly robot, as in *Short Circuit.* There is no mermaid, as in *Splash.* Come to think of it, this movie could use a robot and a mermaid. Some such monkey business could camouflage the familiarity in Stanley Weiser's secondhand script. Director Jonathan (*Heart Like a Wheel*) Kaplan, however, is a tedious moralizer. He likes to photograph the doomed animals in slow motion as they shoot accusatory looks at their tormentors. Broderick, too intelligent an actor to be charmed by these proceedings, looks embarrassed. Despite him and the other primates, *Project X* is really an exercise in movie de-evolution.
PG / 1987 / N/A

▲ THE PROMISE

In this shameless tearjerker the alleged tragedy centers on a car crash involving a young engaged couple, Kathleen Quinlan and Stephen Collins. When they regain consciousness, his mother, who opposes the marriage, offers to pay for plastic surgery on the girl's mangled face if she will forsake the son. The girl is the sort who wants to bury beads under a rock as a marriage ceremony, but she accepts the bribe. After that, the plot is afflicted with a case of rampaging coincidence plus atrocious performances by a nostril-flaring Beatrice Straight as the impossibly wicked mother and an egregiously inept Michael O'Hare as Collins's seemingly moronic best friend. Collins and Quinlan muddle through, though their roles are hopelessly clucky and sappy, respectively. When they get together in the end, the only feeling aroused is relief. Such a cluck and such a sap deserve each other.
PG / 1979 / N/A

▲ PROM NIGHT

Prom themes are usually something like "Summer Rhapsody" or "Dancing in the Dark." The high school soiree in question is called "Disco Madness," but "Romance and Getting Hacked to Pieces" would be better. A killer is loose, out to avenge a childhood prank that turned ugly. He also seems to have something against kissing, since the sexier-minded victims go first. For all its gore (plenty) and stereotypes, though, this is an involving entry in the maniac-stalks-teens school of scare films. Canadian director Paul Lynch effectively uses the inherently nightmarish qualities of disco music and mounts a couple of tense hide-and-seek chases. Jamie Lee Curtis, at the peak of her victim period, is a comely and feisty heroine; Eddie Benton as the bad girl and Joy Thompson as the lovable one are appealing too. Lynch eventually gets hoisted on his own axes, shards of glass and butcher knives, lapsing into soft-focus photography, slow motion, and fades to black at all provocations. Still, this isn't a bad film to watch with a date, especially if you go someplace nice afterward.
R / 1980 / MCA

▲ PROPHECY

Rarely has a horror film been so stylishly photographed. Director John Frankenheimer unreels a tale about cataclysmic pollution produced by a Maine paper mill and at the same time evokes memories of such noble monsters as *Jaws, The Beast from 20,000 Fathoms,* and *Creature from the Black Lagoon.* Alas, every horror director sooner or later shows his menace on camera, and when it looks like this one—clumsy, disgusting, and cheap—the thrill is gone. Frankenheimer doesn't take it too seriously, though. He plays when-is-it-coming games with the audience before the monster whacks victims out of the county with a forehand that would make it a top seed at Wimbledon. The cast (including Robert Foxworth and Talia Shire) has little to do, but it is shameful in a movie which pays lip service to the Indian rights movement that the chief activist of the Maine tribe is played by Armand Assante, who looks, talks, and is Italian.

PG / 1979 / Paramount

▲ PROTOCOL

Goldie Hawn's success as a comedienne has depended largely on her playing against the dumb blonde stereotype. Here she plays to the type, and the results are disastrous. She is a Washington, D.C., cocktail hostess who accidentally thwarts the assassination of a Middle Eastern dignitary, gains instant media celebrity, and is enlisted by the State Department as a goodwill ambassador to the diplomat's home country. Never mind that the U.S. is trying to negotiate a military treaty with the country. Never mind that Goldie is being used as bait. "The Emir wants to be shown a very good time," she is told by a sniveling protocol officer. What's a girl to do? Goldie's reaction is to read the Declaration of Independence to visiting dignitaries and lounge around the Lincoln Memorial, ostensibly to soak up patriotic spirit. Meanwhile, the State Department crowd is being portrayed as the most venal bunch of bureaucrats alive, save for Chris Sarandon, who falls in love with Goldie because she "always tells the truth." Their alleged romance is so incidental that it seems an afterthought, and Goldie seems oddly sexless. This is a dumb, dizzy, and dispassionate blonde. The movie has the look of something worked on by a committee—try a little romance here, a little slapstick there, some patriotic fervor there. What's surprising is that such talent was involved in the making of the movie. It was written by veteran screenwriter Buck Henry and directed by Herb Ross.

PG / 1985 / Warner

▲ THE PSYCHIC

Jennifer O'Neill's once promising film career (begun with *Summer of '42*) fizzled into a series of B movies, of which this is perhaps the most dismal. As the American wife of a rich Italian, she starts to have scary visions of torture and death—her own, it turns out. Naturally, everyone around her thinks she's nuts, so O'Neill must solve her own murder before it happens. As long as the action focuses on her desperate struggle, it's fine. But there are so many subplots and dramatic culs-de-sac that things quickly bog down. For those who can sit through the initial bone-crushing gore, the twist at the end is at least a shock. O'Neill herself goes through as many costume changes as there are scenes and is at least gorgeous to see. Too bad the rest of the movie isn't as enjoyable to look at.

R / 1980 / N/A

▲ PSYCHO II

The opening of this sequel to Alfred Hitchcock's classic 1960 shocker is a pip—brilliantly shot and absolutely terrifying. No wonder. It is, in fact, footage from the original *Psycho,* in which Anthony Perkins, as Norman Bates, dresses up as his mother and stabs Janet Leigh in the shower. *Psycho II* director Richard Franklin, an Australian whose dubious credits include the murky thrillers *Patrick* and *Road Games,* is betting his work can stand up in comparison. He loses. Though the film (in color instead of the original's black and white) captures much of the *Psycho* look, it completely lacks Hitchcock's mastery at suspense buildup and black humor. Tom (*The Beast Within*) Holland's script picks up the original story twenty-two years later. Norman is released from a mental institution and goes back to run the Bates Motel, now a rundown hot-bed establishment. While working as a part-time cook's helper at a local hash house, Norman meets a pretty waitress, Meg (*The Big Chill*) Tilly, and invites her to use the spare room at the old Bates house. Before long Tilly gets the urge to shower and, well, it would be dirty pool to give away more, except to say that the ensuing murders are more *Friday the 13th* sledgehammer than *Psycho.* It's nice to have Perkins back as Norman, even if he indulges in a bit too much eye-rolling. Back from the original too, are Vera Miles, who has aged gracefully, and the late Mrs. Bates, who hasn't. The authorities exhume her because Norman feels that knowing she is dead "would be a great load off my mind." *Psycho II* may succeed intermittently as spoof, but only Hitchcock buffs will experience true horror at this unfortunate return to the scene of the crime.

R / 1983 / MCA

Prizzi's Honor: Life a pair of crocodiles bumping into each other on a river bank, hit-persons Kathleen Turner and Jack Nicholson meet, fall in love, and find they're two of a kind.

▲ PSYCHO III

Alfred Hitchcock's stunning 1960 original made the world safe for maniac movie murderers. The entertaining first sequel in 1983 was part homage to the original, part send-up. This, however, is an aggravated case of overkill. Tony Perkins not only returned to play the schizophrenic Norman Bates, he directed this time, from a screenplay by stage actor Charles Edward Pogue. Norman having reverted to his homicidal tendencies at the end of number II, there weren't many directions a new plot could take, and this film indeed goes nowhere. We're right back at the Bates Motel for what amounts to a classy slice-and-dice chiller. There are a couple of sly touches, though one of them—Perkins, dressed in murderous drag as his own mother, is mistaken for the Virgin Mary—will not seem amusing to everyone. Mostly, however, this one is played for its scary moments, all of which pale beside the memory of the terrifying original. Perkins even uses some footage from Hitchcock's often-cited scene in which Janet Leigh is killed in the shower, as if to invite invidious comparisons. As Norman, Perkins still does all that twitchy, halting business. Diana (*Silkwood*) Scarwid adopts an intriguing beatific demeanor as a woman who wanders into the motel. And in the movie's best development, Jeff (*Silverado*) Fahey plays a drifter who is nearly as insane as Perkins and far less scrupulous. The violence is overly graphic, though, and the dialogue only routine. Like a lazy relative, the movie seems to be sponging off the success of its forebears.
R / 1986 / MCA

▲ PURPLE HEARTS

It's corny, predictable, and often laughably improbable, but this love story set in Vietnam does have a lovely, affecting performance by Cheryl Ladd and the kind of stroll-off-into-the-sunset romance they don't put in films anymore. Ladd, doing her best to fight the curse of "Charlie's Angels," is understated and touching as a nurse who falls in love with Ken Wahl, a doctor with a penchant for ending up in the middle of terrible battles. The hunky Wahl has the acting ability of something carved from the trunk of an oak. There are helpful supporting performances, though, by Stephen Lee, as Wahl's best friend, Annie McEnroe, and Lee Ermey, a real-life Marine veteran of Vietnam, as the gunnery sergeant of a decimated battalion. (He showed up more substantially in Stanley Kubrick's *Full Metal Jacket*.) Director Sidney Furie showed in *The Boys from Company C* that he has a feel for the intensity and energy of war, though he also co-wrote a screenplay that forces Ladd to utter such threadbare lines as "He's not dead. If he was, I'd know it." There's nothing political about this movie. It does serve as reminder to movie fans, however, of how enjoyable it can be to cheer for two people in love.
R / 1984 / Warner

▲ PURPLE RAIN

Whenever Prince performs the songs he wrote for this rock musical, it's clear that he has the makings of a movie star. He has the brash directness and the hip-swaying sexuality that the camera craves. The main problem with *Purple Rain* is that sometimes Prince stops singing. The movie interupts its fifteen numbers for a self-pitying pretentious story about the Kid, as Prince's character is called, who has an innovative musical act nobody appreciates and a violent home life nobody would want. At the local nightclub he is taunted by the crass dandies who share the stage with him; at home he is haunted by the sight of his black father beating his Italian mother. After the Kid similarly abuses his girlfriend, she warns him, "Like father, like son." Essentially *Purple Rain* is an insidious instance of the MTV-ization of American movies. The musical numbers could easily exist as videos. Prince hoards all his ex-pressiveness for his songs. Without music to tell him which postures to play with, he is nearly immobilized and he tries to sustain a character with one acting device, a pouty lip. As the lady friend, Apollonia Kotero can throw back her hair with the best of them, but the character is just an ornament. Worst of all, the movie's misogyny rivals that of the most outrageous antiwomen videos. Crudely directed by Albert Magnoli, the film uses physical abuse to connect with the audience. It looks for laughs when a guy throws a woman in a dumpster and for tears when the Kid slaps his lover around. Simplistic, superficial, and surprisingly sentimental, *Purple Rain* is everything Prince's music is not.
R / 1984 / Warner

▲ THE PURPLE ROSE OF CAIRO

Anyone looking for a bad word about this Woody Allen film should read no further. *The Purple Rose of Cairo* is pure enchantment—84 bracing minutes of wit, wisdom, and romance. The only thing missing is Woody himself, since he chose to write and direct and leave the acting to others. Like all of Allen's choice work *Purple Rose* is deceptively simple. Mia Farrow, flat-out fabulous in a role that fits perfectly, plays a Depression-era waitress in New Jersey with no escape from her abusive husband, Danny Aiello, except at the movies. Director Herbert Ross went over some of this territory with Steve Martin and Bernadette Peters in 1981's *Pennies from Heaven*, but Allen doesn't settle for that film's easy cynicism. He admires the Farrow character's pluck and shares her love for those films. In an inspired movie within a movie, Allen and his superb camerman Gordon Willis create a '30s black-and-white period film (called *The Purple Rose of Cairo*) that Farrow watches continuously in the darkness of the theater. It's everything that her life is not. The hero, played by Jeff Daniels, is a handsome young adventurer enjoying a madcap Manhattan weekend in the company of sophisticates, hilariously played by Zoe Caldwell, Edward Herrmann, Van Johnson, and Deborah Rush. Farrow falls hard for the Daniels character, and when he steps offscreen to claim her, havoc ensues. To say more would spoil the surprise. But Pirandello was rarely this much fun. Special praise must go to Daniels, Debra Winger's jellyfish husband in

Terms of Endearment. He earned star status here in a difficult dual role. He is wonderfully endearing as the fictional hero thrust into a real world of power, sex, and money for which his rigidly moral Production Code values have hardly prepared him. Daniels also plays the far-from-noble actor who created this hero onscreen, and it's as this inflated ego that Allen aims his sharp-est salvos. Within the confines of this charming comedy, Allen is wrestling with matters that concern him most: the heart's propensity to be wounded and art's power to heal. Funny and touching in fresh, unexpected ways, *The Purple Rose of Cairo* has the scent of an enduring classic.

PG / 1985 / Vestron

Q

▲ QUARTET

Since the life-size mannequins in this painstaking look at the decadent side of Paris in the 1920s are always claiming to be "bored, bored, bored," it's hard to work up much interest in the talk, talk, talk spewed out in Ruth Prawer Jhabvala's adaptation of the late Jean Rhys's 1929 novel. Rhys, a former chorus girl and lover of author Ford Madox Ford, turned to writing to overcome her loneliness and fear of poverty. Her heroine is a crushed-petal type set adrift in the seedy cafe society of Montparnasse when her husband is sent to jail. This frightened girl, played by the intelligent and luminously lovely Isabelle Adjani, is the most believable character in the film. Those brilliant actors Maggie Smith and Alan Bates portray the English couple who take in the poor waif, but—aha—only so Bates can have his wicked way with Adjani in the guest room while Smith suffers in silence. Bates, it appears, is an aging rogue who's done this kind of thing before, resulting in one girl's suicide and his own nervous breakdown. Patient Maggie just keeps clearing the guest room. Director James Ivory tracks the protagonists through jazz clubs and porn parlors of not-so-Gay Paree, exhibiting the same exhausting attention to detail he displayed in his 1979 adaptation of Henry James's *The Europeans*. For Ivory, the sight of a dirty curtain blowing in the breeze can often be a substitute for characterization. Those who prefer real life to still life may find themselves more in agreement with Bates's final summation: "It's all so abominably sordid and pitiful."

R / 1981 / Warner

▲ QUEST FOR FIRE

Popular entertainment's portrayal of prehistoric man is usually of two varieties. In one, the cave dwellers inhabit a kind of antediluvian Club Mediterranee, where females who look like *Playboy* centerfolds run around in designer leopard skins and the males resemble all-pro linebackers. In the other version, primitive life is portrayed as a sitcom where Fred Flintstone or Ringo Starr banters with dinosaurs. This remarkable film, however, is different. Directed by Frenchman Jean-Jacques Annaud, whose *Black and White in Color* won the Best Foreign Film Oscar in 1976, it is a serious attempt to recreate what early human life must have been like. It centers on a small tribe that loses its caves and its campfire to marauding enemies. (The promise is that before man learned to make fire, he had to preserve flames ignited by lightning.) The tribe leader, played by Everett McGill, spends the rest of the film trying to recover the fire. This is not a heroic adventure. McGill and his tribe are dirty, cold, hungry, tired, and afraid. After the opening sequence, there is no narration and no subtitles. But McGill and the rest of the unknown cast—notably Rae Dawn Chong (daughter of comedian Tommy Chong)—do a marvelous job of communicating, using a crude language created by novelist Anthony Burgess and gestures devised by anthropologist Desmond Morris. There are excesses. At one pont McGill and Chong triumphantly engage in new mating techniques, as if they have come upon a stone-tablet edition of *The Joy of Sex*. In another scene, McGill subdues a herd of mammoths simply by offering them

grass. Overall, though, the mood is of suffering and indomitability, and it's convincing. If nothing else, this daring film will give you a new respect for those creatures who became us.
R / 1982 / CBS/Fox

cameras on bicycles, then maneuvering his cyclists through treacherous city traffic. But in the end, even his stylish photography cannot save this movie from spinning its wheels.
PG / 1986 / RCA/Columbia

▲ QUICKSILVER

This film is nothing more than a contrived remake of *Footloose* with bicycles. It's no coincidence that the two movies have the same producers and star. In this one, Kevin Bacon plays a reckless stock options trader who loses everything in an afternoon gamble, including his lust for the market. He abandons high finance to take a job with Quicksilver bike messengers, where he will have nothing to worry about except his own survival. Life in the bike lane brings Bacon to the side of cute Jami (*Square Pegs*) Gertz, but the two seem to backpedal in a confusingly vague plot in which Rudy (*The Enforcer*) Ramos, as a cartoonish tough guy, enlists Gertz to deliver a series of suspicious packages. What's inside? We never know. *Quicksilver* is best when it shifts gears to the biking scenes. Olympic cyclist Nelson Vails, a former bike messenger, who plays a cameo role, also served as a technical adviser. Cinematographer Tom (*The Breakfast Club*) Del Ruth creates striking visual sensations by mounting

▲ QUINTET

The title of director Robert Altman's self-indulgence suggests harmony, but nothing could be more misleading. *Quintet* is, instead, a game, a deadly backgammon of the future where loss is death. The pentagon (get it?) is a recurring visual note and the basis for a ridiculous pseudophilosophy—the five sides represent birth, maturing, dealing with guilt, aging, and death; the central space represents the void. The vestigial plot concerns a citizen of an ice-bound planet, Paul Newman, seeking—no joke—the meaning of the five-sided game obsessively played by a degenerating society. It is literally going to the dogs (packs of Dobermans nibble on frozen corpses throughout the film). Newman searches through decaying concrete corridors festooned with icicles and powdered with snow. While fabulously Kafkaesque, the sets cannot redeem a picture that doesn't so much chill viewers as bore them to death.
R / 1979 / Key

R

▲ RABBIT TEST

In this tasteless, offensive, and (worst of all) humorless movie, Billy Crystal (then the house homosexual of TV's "Soap") gets raped at a USO party and becomes the world's first pregnant man. Instant celebrity follows. The President of the U.S. (George Gobel) deploys him on a global goodwill mission, but leaders of the overpopulated nations try to do him in. Cast members Crystal, Gobel, Paul Lynde, Roddy McDowall, and Imogene Coca try to shtick out the disaster. Producer-director Joan Rivers learned her lesson

and returned to the talk show circuit after her *Rabbit* died.
PG / 1978 / CBS/Fox

▲ RACING WITH THE MOON

Elizabeth McGoverns's smile is the closest thing to sunshine the movies have managed in years. And she can act: Just watch her in *Ordinary People* or *Ragtime*. Sean Penn has displayed an astonishing versatility. But neither has ever left so indelible a mark on an audience's emotions as

they do in this rapturous, old-fashioned love story. In a small California coastal town in 1943, Penn, a gravedigger's son, and buddy Nicolas Cage are biding their time before joining the Marines. Cage leches after every skirt he sees, but Penn is fixated on McGovern, a newcomer he takes for a "Gatsby girl" since she lives in a mansion. Director Richard Benjamin handles the courtship scenes with disarming freshness. And the period details— USO dances, movie newsreels, air-raid drills— are irresistible. There is little of the ghastly nostalgia of *Summer of '42,* though that 1971 hit was filmed on some of the same lovely Mendocino locations. First-time screenwriter Steve Kloves, at 23, created plot complications (an abortion, a poolhall fight) too archly obvious to have much bite. But his ear for dialogue is finely tuned, and Penn and McGovern make the script sound even better. Cage is also solid, and Carol Kane, as a local hooker, steals all her scenes. One wonders where Kane finds her costumers in such a doggedly decent town. But *Racing with the Moon* is so puppy-dog likeable you go along with it. This film has a plaintive richness that sticks in the memory.
PG / 1984 / Paramount

▲ RAGGEDY MAN

Jack Fisk is a first-time director whose debut was graced by the gifted Sissy Spacek. She happens also to be his wife. Spacek plays Nita, a mother of two who leaves her do-nothing husband and is forced to work as a phone operator to support the young'uns in rural Texas. It's a lonely life until she meets a Navy man on furlough, beautifully played by Eric Roberts. Their brief fling lights up her life, but when the dust settles she's turned into the town outcast, hounded by two lecherous bullies. If the movie ended with Spacek's proud resolve to buy herself three bus tickets to shake off the town's scarlet fetters, it would have packed a wallop: Her weary struggle to survive and protect her children is compellingly believable. But scriptwriter William Witliff can't leave well enough alone. Sissy has to be rescued from the bullies' sexual attack by the town's token eccentric, the Raggedy Man, played by Sam Shepard. It's a plot convenience at best, designed to provide the one ironic twist that would tie everything together. But it doesn't work; the plot, like the title character, is too raggedy. It's an honest failure, though, and a creditable debut for Fisk behind the camera. Spacek is riveting; the 1940s set design and Ralf Bode's cinematography are simply glorious.
PG / 1981 / MCA

▲ RAGING BULL

Extraordinary, electric, perverse, brilliant—they are puny words to describe Robert De Niro in this unflinching biography of Jake La Motta, the middleweight boxing champ of 1949 to 1951. De Niro gives a performance of such intensity and physical punishment that even the Oscar he won seemed insufficient recompense. To prepare for the role, the actor trained for a year with La Motta, then 59. De Niro not only mastered his speech, behavior, and boxing style, but even gained fifty-six pounds to show the champ's physical decline as a pathetic burlesque comic in the 1960s. Using La Motta's 1970 autobiography as a base, director Martin Scorsese and writers Paul Schrader and Mardik Martin crafted a ferocious and sometimes funny look at a Bronx street kid who could never confine his fury to the gym. Aided by Michael Chapman's superb black-and-white photography, Scorsese keeps his 128-minute film at a fever pitch. The fight scenes are the best ever filmed and only slightly more brutal than La Motta's emotional flareups with family, friends, and the Mob. As La Motta's sultry second wife, a tall, blonde newcomer, Cathy Moriarty, at 20, seemed a Lana Turner with a Bronx accent. She also manifested an indelible screen presence. Joe Pesci, as Jake's beleaguered manager brother, is splendid too. But it is De Niro who dominates this movie, seeming to tear his performance out of his own soul. At the end, La Motta sits before a mirror, fat and 50ish, rehearsing a monologue from *On the Waterfront* for his club act. Suddenly we understand what the line about "a one-way ticket to Palookaville" really means. The scene, like the entire film, is painful to watch—and impossible to forget.
R / 1980 / CBS/Fox

▲ RAGTIME

They said it could only go wrong (ignore those who said it did), but things went spectacularly right with Milos Forman's supremely elegant distillation of E. L. Doctorow's 1975 best-seller about America in 1906. Forman and screenwriter Michael (*Hair*) Weller utilize only a few crucial threads in Doctorow's vast weave of fictional and historical characters. Emma Goldman, Theodore Dreiser, and Sigmund Freud are out; Houdini is barely in. But what remains is faithful in spirit to Doctorow's view of a small-town family that finds itself propelled into a 20th-century exploding with civil, political, and sexual conflict. "Never play ragtime fast," Scott Joplin, the master of the genre, once advised, and Forman kept his 2-hour and 27-minute film carefully measured yet constantly enthralling. The archetypal family—Mother, Father, Younger Brother (they're never given names)—is beautifully delineated by Mary Steenburgen, James Olson, and Brad Dourif, but the entire cast is exceptional. In his last feature, James Cagney, then 82 and gloriously unretired after a break of twenty years, plays a ramrod New York police commissioner with a wicked top-of-the-world twinkle that makes even a tossed-off insult ring with his old "you dirty rat" thunder. And at least two new stars were born. As the black piano man Coalhouse Walker, Jr., who initiates the film's climactic act of terrorism, Howard E. Rollins has the fire, dignity, and sex appeal of a young Poitier. Elizabeth McGovern, Tim Hutton's girlfriend in *Ordinary People,* is the pliable, unprincipled Evelyn Nesbit. She was a notorious beauty whose jealous husband, Harry K. Thaw (Robert Joy), shot down her architect lover, Stanford White—played by a surprisingly adept Norman Mailer. The deliciously lovely McGovern, then 19 and Oscar-nominated for her role, does a long, drunken nude scene with a shocked boyfriend and two lawyers that's both unselfconsciously erotic and funny. Hats in the air as well for the sets, costumes, photography, and Randy Newman's richly evocative score. For Forman, this is not just another credit in an admirable career (including *One Flew Over the Cuckoo's Nest* and later *Amadeus*) but a work of imperishable heart.

R / 1981 / Paramount

▲ RAIDERS OF THE LOST ARK

An inspired, all-star collaboration of director Steven (*Jaws*) Spielberg, producer George (*Star Wars*) Lucas, and screenwriter Lawrence (*The Empire Strikes Back*) Kasdan, this film is a volcano of creative ideas in full eruption—the modern high-action adventure against which all others are now measured. Lucas wanted to do a film about a daredevil archeologist set in the 1930s and modeled on that era's cliffhanger serials. With the help of Philip Kaufman, who directed 1978's *Invasion of the Body Snatchers,* he sketched a plot that pits his hero, Harrison Ford, against the Nazis. They're searching for the Ark of the Covenant—a golden chest, lost since 980 B.C. and said to contain the broken tablets of the Ten Commandments. Since biblical lore suggests the ark will be recovered at the true Messiah's coming, Hitler is hot to have it. "He's a nut on the subject," a U.S. Government agent announces. Ford, armed only with a bullwhip and his sharp-tongued lady-love (Karen Allen), sets out to save the ark for democracy. Historical fact does not figure prominently in these proceedings, but fun does. Spielberg has staged the most exultantly good-humored, head-on, rousing series of traps and escapes since Pauline was eluding her perils. Cheers, too, for Ford's satirical approach to macho, Allen's Jean Arthur-ish zest, and the venomous villainy of Paul Freeman and Ronald Lacey. But the show actually belongs to Lucas and Spielberg. They lavish mint-fresh inventiveness on every frame and raise movie escapism very near the level of art.

PG / 1981 / Paramount

▲ RAISE THE TITANIC

The irresistible drama surrounding the sinking of the unsinkable liner remained undiminished long after it went down off Newfoundland. To capitalize on that interest, Britain's lord of the pot-boilers, Lew Grade, reportedly spent $33 million on this semi-epic. It's adapted from Clive Cussler's best-seller, which hypothesizes a monumental co-incidence. On board the *Titanic,* it seems, was a load of a rare ore that now can be used to build an impregnable antimissile system. As Richard Jordan, the hero in charge of the raising, admits, "I'm not going to say it will be easy." But the process itself is interesting, and there are a few predictable crises, though nary one giant octopus shows up. Richard Jason, Jason Robards, and David Selby are accessories in this film. They dryly crack out snippets of dialogue, included just to tie together the special effects. The effects, credited to production designer John De Cuir, are mostly convincing, and John Barry's often balletic music is reminiscent of his evocative James Bond scores. A romantic subplot involving Anne Archer is irrelevant—though she is a lovely and substantial presence—and some plot turns don't bear scrutiny. Outdated by the real discovery of the *Titanic*'s remains in 1986 (no powerful ore was on board), this remains a diverting, seaworthy adventure film.

PG / 1980 / CBS/Fox

▲ RAMBO: FIRST BLOOD PART II

Despite the promiscuous violence of *Rambo*, the pivotal scene isn't one of the film's many battles or killings. When John Rambo, the unstable veteran that Sylvester Stallone created in the original *First Blood*, returns to Vietnam on a top-secret mission to search for prisoners of war, he finds a camp that is a hellhole. Between trees hangs a bearded skeletal prisoner strung up as though he's been crucified. With a flick of his ever-ready, frequently caressed fifteen-inch knife (the most lovingly photographed of the many phallic symbols in the movie), Stallone cuts down this Jesus-in-the-jungle. Jesus may save, but Rambo saves Jesus. It's that kind of brazen deification of the macho ethic that makes Rambo more insidious and dangerous than a mere *Rocky Goes to the Killing Fields*. This film equates violence with manliness to a degree that might make even Brian De Palma blush. In fact, director George C. Cosmatos invents a new success ethic in this situation: You're only as masculine as your last murder. And because the sparse script by Stallone and James Cameron unfolds with none of the plot or imagination that brightened Cameron's solo effort, *The Terminator*, masculine mythmaking provides just about the only diversion in *Rambo*. After Stallone is double-crossed by an American government official who doesn't expect him to

Rambo: Sylvester Stallone's box-office bonanza about a one-man killing machine tracking MIAs in Cambodia might be an insult to Vietnam vets if the whole thing wasn't such a dumb, cartoonish joke.

find any prisoners, he explodes in an orgy of spitting gunfire and spent bullets—complete with an orgasmic cry of relief. Before he walks off, Stallone proclaims that all veterans just want "for our country to love us as much as we love it." Stallone might have found the audience more receptive to that sentiment if his character hadn't just run amok. Violence isn't simply a purifying act for this guy; it also succeeds in making him articulate. Until his climactic burst of brutality, he hasn't spoken more than two sentences. Then suddenly, he's a grandstanding spokesman for soldiers everywhere. As Stallone departs, the rescued Christ figure bestows on him a nod of thanks. The gesture provides what is apparently the real message of the movie: Even God owes one to Sly.

R / 1985 / Thom/EMI

▲ RAN

Prepare to be astonished. In this film, the famed Japanese director Akira (*Rashomon, Seven Samurai*) Kurosawa realized his ten-year dream to fuse King Lear with his own tantalizing meditation on Japan's 16th-century feudal past. The result is an action epic to dwarf anything from Lucas or Spielberg. Ran is the work of an old man (Kurosawa was 75 when it appeared). But try to find a young director to match this vigor and assurance. Kurosawa—whose beloved wife of thirty-five years died during filming—has the reputation of an autocrat, barking orders at extras or sitting out the weather until nature comes around to color the sky the way the sensei (Japanese for master) wants it. But look at the visual splendor he gets: emerald pastures, crystalline air, red and yellow armies cutting through cold, gray dawn. He can make one thousand soldiers seem three times as strong and do the same for his $11.5 million budget (highest ever for a Japanese film). He can break your heart as a son's treachery drives a once distinguished lord (Tatsuya Nakadai in a powerfully underplayed performance) to madness. He can risk casting a transvestite rock performer named Peter (the Japanese Boy George) as the lord's fool and come off with a character so alive he nearly jumps off the screen. He can mix violence and eroticism to shame Brian De Palma: When one of the lord's scheming sons is killed by his brother, the dead man's wife (the stunning Mieko Harada) jumps

the assassin. She cuts his throat with a dagger and then lasciviously licks the blood as a prelude to passion. Forget that this subtitled film is nearly 3 hours long. It moves. *Ran* (Japanese for chaos) also demonstrates that adventure and art can come in the same package. It ranks as a towering achievement in any language. (In Japanese with subtitles.)

Unrated / 1985 / CBS/Fox

▲ RAW DEAL

Nobody knocks 'em dead like Arnold Schwarzenegger. Think about it. Stallone, Eastwood, and Chuck Norris have to work at pumping up their images with camera chicanery. Not Arnold. The Big Guy (his six-foot two-inch frame looms, onscreen and off, as one bulging two-hundred-and-twenty-pound bicep) is his own best special effect. This time the omnipotent killing machine of *Conan* and *Commando* is hunting smaller game. Playing an undercover ex-FBI agent, Schwarzenegger merely takes on two warring Mafia families in Chicago. "You've done a hundred years of police work in a single afternoon," says one stunned cop after Arnold's climactic one-man rampage. That final shoot-out is a corker, but action fans may wilt while they're waiting. For most of the movie Arnold strains to do the impossible (for him): act. British director John Irvin, who guided Glenda Jackson and Ben Kingsley through Harold Pinter's *Turtle Diary*, couldn't do much with Schwarzenegger. The script has more holes than the bodies of Arnold's victims and enough inept dialogue to prompt giggles. Meanwhile, such tasks as trying to twist his Austrian-accented tongue around a sentence containing the words "molested," "mutilated," and "murdered" are too much for Arnold. The love scenes are worse, though Kathryn Harrold is gorgeous and underrated, as ever. (Harrold had the similarly unenviable task of trying to probe for the heart of another legendary jumbo, Luciano Pavarotti, in *Yes, Giorgio*.) Tarted up here as a gangster's moll, Harrold unshirts our hero in her bedroom and hungrily eyes that Mr. World chest, only to watch him pass out from too much champagne. Irvin may be trying to kid the fact that Schwarzenegger can't play love scenes, but better to leave the romance out altogether. The funny thing is, though the movie's a dud, you keep rooting for Schwarzenegger. With material that doesn't strain his capabilities, he can be effectively endearing (*Stay Hungry*) or terrifying (*The Terminator*). He isn't much of either here, and that's the real raw deal for video fans.

R / 1986 / HBO/Cannon

▲ THE RAZOR'S EDGE

Memo to Bill Murray: Hey, pal, what a great idea to show you're as good an actor as a comic by doing a big budget ($13 million) drama. You don't see Chevy, Dan, or Gilda taking those chances. But Bill, why *The Razor's Edge?* The book was not one of W. Somerset Maugham's best: all that blather about a disillusioned World War I vet trying to find the path to salvation by renouncing wealth and going to India to study with a high lama. You must have known you'd look silly in those Tibetan hats. The first film version, in 1949, was pretty heavy going. Tyrone Power played your role then. Audiences were used to old Ty playing hangdog. But Bill boy, you're the funnyman from "Saturday Night Live," *Ghostbusters,* and *Tootsie.* You've got to get folks adjusted gradually. Why not a juicy supporting part in some hotshot flick with Meryl Streep or Bobby De Niro? Look what *Silkwood* did for Cher. A 2-hour-and-30-minute epic with you in almost every scene seems a bit much for starters, don't you think? Those were some nice changes you put into John Byrum's script, trying to make the character funnier than Maugham wrote him. I liked the bit with the monkey and the organ grinder. But it seemed strange that you were playing in a hip '80s style while the rest of the actors were doing period performances. Sometimes you looked like you just dropped in from SNL. Those dramatic scenes, like when your girl, played by sexy Theresa Russell, got her throat cut—were you supposed to be thinking deep thoughts when you let your face go all blank like that? Get outta here. You looked like a potato. The only impressive scene was the one you did with your dying buddy—the one you once said you wrote to say good-bye to Belushi. The rest looked like you weren't trying. The word is you and Byrum rode around the country writing the script in noisy bars to get real vitality into the picture. Maybe you guys should have picked a library. And by the way, what made you hook up with Byrum anyway? Do you know what movies Byrum has directed or scripted? Nobody does, man, that's the trouble. They're turkeys like *Mahogany,* the one that nearly stopped Diana Ross's movie career cold. What good were pro actors like Catherine Hicks, Denholm Elliott, and James Keach if Byrum was going to force them to act hysterically? But look at the brighter side: You got to England, France, and India to shoot the movie, so it wasn't a total loss.

PG-13 / 1984 / RCA/Columbia

▲ REAL LIFE

Offbeat, off-the-wall, and only occasionally off-base, this is an original and insidiously funny film. Directed and co-written by sometime stand-up comic Albert Brooks, it starts as a parody of the 1973 TV documentary *An American Family,* the saga of the Louds. But in this case the film crew—headed by Brooks, playing himself—is an onscreen part of the documentary, even though Brooks constantly tells his subjects to ignore him. (When the wife of the subject family, on the verge of a breakdown, tells Brooks, "I'd like to be alone," he says, "Okay, can we come with you?") Though some of the Brooks film quickies that ran on "Saturday Night Live" seemed inane, here, with time to work on mood and characters, he quietly devastates Americans' fascination with the mass media. He's helped by Charles Grodin, who as the husband is marvelously confused. Grodin tries at one point to react calmly when his wife (TV veteran Frances Lee McCain) announces that she's suffering her period on camera ("I have terrible cramps, I'm bleeding profusely, and I want to vomit on the table"). This is the perfect movie for those who suspect cinema verité is more cinema than verité.

PG / 1979 / Paramount

▲ RE-ANIMATOR

The Cannes Film Festival has gotten excited about some pretty weird things in its time but none odder than this gore-mongering chiller, which was unofficially named Best Science Fiction Film of 1985's extravaganza. Okay, as movies about severed heads living independent lives go, this is the greatest of all time. The lighting and photography are exceptionally good for this sort of

movie, too, which is to say the lights are on and the camera is in focus. Director Stuart Gordon, an alumnus of Chicago's innovative Organic Theater, obviously has a sense of style to go with his abysmal lack of restraint. The cast is bright and witty enough, especially Jeffrey Combs as a mad young scientist working on a serum that can revive the dead, and David Gale as a mad old scientist who learns about the serum and thereupon loses his composure and head in rapid succession. (At one point Combs scoffs at Gale, "Join the sideshow. You're a talking head. Who'll listen to you?") Barbara Crampton, playing a coed, looks good with her shirt off. With all that, it's pretty hard to admit to actually liking a film in which one character ends up being strangled by the intestinal tract of another and skulls are crushed with monotonous frequency. Most people will find this movie about as tasteful as a worm sandwich. (Also available in an unrated version.)
R / 1985 / Vestron

▲ RECKLESS

From the first smoldering look, you know that Aidan Quinn is trying to be James Dean. That he almost succeeds is a tribute to him, though certainly not to this movie, a pale imitation of Dean's classic *Rebel Without a Cause*. Quinn, in his breakthrough role, plays a scruffy, dead-end kid: He drives a motorcycle, he likes to play chicken, and he mumbles enough to make Marlon Brando sound like a speech therapist. Daryl Hannah is the beautiful blonde from a good home: She drives a white Cadillac and, naturally, is fatally drawn to bad-boy Quinn. They finally get it on the boiler room of the local high school after hours. It's pretty hot stuff: Hannah couldn't act much at this point (*Roxanne* was 3 years away), but she looks good. Directed by James Foley, the movie kicks into high gear when Quinn reveals he has an emotional life beneath his pout. It seems his mother abandoned his drunkard father, wonderfully portrayed by Kenneth McMillan, and Quinn has never forgiven either of them. When his father is killed in a mill accident (the movie was shot in the same grimy West Virginia mill town used for *The Deer Hunter*), Quinn torches their house, jumps on his bike, and rumbles off in search of Hannah. Teen melodrama, anyone?
R / 1984 / MGM/UA

▲ RED DAWN

Some high school students in Colorado are sitting in history class when some Russian and Cuban paratroopers land outside their window as part of a nationwide invasion by Soviet-bloc forces. When their teacher walks out to investigate, he's shot. Wham! What a beginning to this movie by John Milius, director of the first *Conan*. That's about all there is to the movie, though: one orphaned idea. Some of the boys flee to the hills to form a guerrilla resistance group. But they do nothing other than run an occasional raid on an enemy tank or troop column. Their female companions—Lea Thompson and Jennifer Gray—are superfluous. Their only function is to cry, an act denied to the boys. Patrick Swayze as the boys' leader and Charlie Sheen as his younger brother share one astonishing scene in which one of their group is executed for being a spy. But Harry Dean Stanton is wasted as the brothers' father; so is Ben Johnson as a kindly townsman. Only Ron O'Neal, as a Cuban colonel whose conscience gradually brings him over to the kids' side, is able to arouse much interest.
PG-13 / 1984 / MGM/UA

▲ REDS

Producer-director-star Warren Beatty (he's also co-writer with Trevor Griffiths) set himself a gargantuan task—to show the 1917 Russian Revolution through the eyes of American journalist John Reed, who witnessed the events and came back to write *Ten Days that Shook the World*. The $33.5 million film, which runs 3 hours and 20 minutes, also details Reed's romance with Louise Bryant, a writer and feminist. Diane Keaton, very fine as Bryant, is the film's emotional center. Married to a dentist, she meets Reed and seduces him; later, when Reed's cronies such as anarchist Emma Goldman (Maureen Stapleton in an Oscar-winning supporting role) and editor Max Eastman (Ed Herrmann) snub her, Bryant drifts into a sordid affair with playwright Eugene O'Neill, done to a cynical turn by Jack Nicholson. Bryant finally rejoins Reed in Russia, and together they vow to bring the revolution home. It's here, when the film is at its most doctrinaire, that *Reds* collapses. Beatty and Keaton, once involved offscreen, make the love story compelling, that is until she starts chasing him in a fictionalized trek across the frozen tundra. In the film's heavy second half, Beatty plumbs the American Communist Party while political theory flies so thick that the uninitiated will find their eyes glazing over. Beatty's device of using real witnesses to the period, everyone from Rebecca West to George Jessel, was inspired and probably helped him win his very undeserved Oscar as Best Director. Hitchcock and Orson Welles never won, but Beatty does! It's an outrage. Yet *Reds* has its moments, for Beatty made a passionate, if not always coherent, thrust at illuminating a crucial period of history.

PG / 1981 / Paramount

▲ RED SONJA

The title sounds as if this movie is about a communist spy or maybe a new flower. No such luck. It's about Sylvester Stallone's then-future wife, Brigitte Nielsen. She plays a warrior maiden on a mission of revenge in the days of swords, magic, and low-cut warrior-maiden outfits. Arnold Schwarzenegger is the warrior boyfriend who wrestles with killer machines and does the heavy lifting. Sandahl Bergman is a wicked queen, Paul Smith is a jester, and Ernie Reyes, Jr., is a boy prince. All the other actors are so awful they make Schwarzenegger seem pretty good. The romantic chemistry between Arn and Nielsen, though, is what you would get if you fixed up a dumpster with a mulberry bush. But that's hardly the point, which is mayhem. Heads are lopped off, landslides rumble, lava flows, people leap on one another, and swords clang relentlessly. It seems fitting that when they kiss, Schwarzenegger and Nielsen almost miss; she ends up kissing his chin while his nose bores into her forehead.

PG-13 / 1985 / CBS/Fox

▲ REFORM SCHOOL GIRLS

This B flick about babes behind bars, directed by Tom De Simone, was inspired—if that's the word—by such cult favorites as *The Concrete Jungle* and *Chained Heat*. Indeed De Simone was responsible for *The Concrete Jungle* and the sim-

ilar *Prison Girls*. This film could have been fun, and it does start out sassy enough. At the Pridemore Juvenile Facilities, the monster matron (played by the buxom Andy Warhol star Pat Ast) munches on chocolates and checks out her newest novitiates. "My name's Edna, but the girls just call me Eddie," she sneers. The rest of the movie never becomes the we're-bustin'-out-of-this-genre send-up you want it to be. Instead it gets bogged down in gross-out bathroom humor. And not many people are going to get laughs out of a scene that centers on stomping a kitten to death. The dialogue has its camp hoots—"Your time's just been doubled, sweetie" . . . "Yeah, and so's your chin!" And it's almost nostalgic to see those prison stereotypes, such as the ice witch of a warden (Sybil Danning, who has played so many similar roles straight in these low-life films that she rivals Linda Blair as Queen of the Junkpile). But the film's one true inspiration is to cast nihilist rocker Wendy O. Williams as the foul-mouthed cellblock leader. Playing what must be the eldest juvenile offender on record, Williams emotes by gnashing her teeth, flexing her tattooed biceps, and bulging out of her underwear. When she turns Terminatrix and goes on a demolition derby rampage inside the reformatory, the film heats up. Unfortunately, it also ends. You're as likely to want to bother with this movie's credits as you are with those of roller derby reruns.

R / 1986 / New World

▲ REMEMBER MY NAME

Geraldine Chaplin plays a recently released ex-con who travels to southern California to find her ex-husband, Tony Perkins. He has since remarried, but soon they are in each other's arms, if only for a moment. That is the story, but director Alan Rudolph takes too long to tell it. Rudolph may have been too much under the influence of Robert Altman, whose company produced both this film and Rudolph's previous *Welcome to L.A.* Where Altman's eccentric style works for him (usually), Rudolph's imitation is elliptical and vague. There are saving graces, especially the fine blues score by Alberta Hunter and an often affecting performance by Berry Berenson, who plays Perkins' second wife (she got practice as his Mrs. in real life).

R / 1979 / N/A

▲ RENALDO AND CLARA

Bob Dylan's home movie is great when he's singing, but it's boring otherwise. Shot during his 1975–76 Rolling Thunder tour, it combines superb concert footage with bits of fact and fantasy about his offstage life. Most interesting are glimpses of his then-wife Sara, who looks remarkably like her husband. In one intriguing scene, she and Joan Baez (an old flame, of course) pretend to vie for his affections, leaving the Tambourine Man decidedly rattled. The rest of the film is baffling, including the title. (We can guess who Renaldo is, but which woman is Clara? And why those names?) The film also features poet Allan Ginsberg, Ronee Blakely, and assorted crazies picked up on the road—so those who can't sit through all four hours will know what they missed.
R / 1978 / N/A

▲ RESURRECTION

A car accident leaves Ellen Burstyn clinically dead. For several minutes she is "on the other side," awash in bright light and familiar old faces. Through the miracle of modern medicine, she recovers to find she has somehow acquired the gift of healing. Screenwriter Lewis John Carlino, who directed *The Great Santini*, convincingly suggests how such a gift might be as much a curse as a blessing. Yet director Daniel Petrie seems unsure whether he's making a sci-fi movie or an affecting drama. The result is an uneasy compromise saved only by remarkable performances. Stage veteran Eva Le Gallienne is moving as Burstyn's grandmother, and playwright Sam Shepard plays the son of a religious zealot with dark intensity. At the heart of the film is Burstyn—she is intelligent, compassionate and, when necessary, humorous. As an ordinary woman attempting to cope with an extraordinary power, Burstyn proves again that she is no ordinary actress.
PG / 1980 / N/A

▲ THE RETURN OF MARTIN GUERRE

High in the French Pyrenees, in a small farming village, there is rejoicing. Years after deserting his young bride, Martin Guerre, one of the vil-lage's sons, has returned to claim his wife and his father's land. But doubts are soon raised about the identity of the man who says he is Guerre. The matter goes to court—and the courtroom drama, which takes up most of the last half of this movie, is stirring indeed. The opening credits tell us that the story is true, that it happened in 1549, and that director Daniel Vigne used as extras real villagers who live not far from where the events took place. Gerard (*The Last Metro*) Dépardieu, one of France's most versatile actors, plays Guerre with charming loutishness. As his wife, Nathale (Truffaut's *The Green Room*) Baye is demurely chaste. The story lags at times, but other sequences more than make up for it, as in one remarkable flashback to the couple's wedding night when the villagers all but dance around the matrimonial bed. As a period piece, the movie is fascinating, with the 16th century recreated against a background as lush as a painting. The film has emotional power, too, with sentiment swinging finally to Dépardieu, whether or not he is the real Martin Guerre. (In French with subtitles.)
Unrated / 1983 / Embassy

▲ THE RETURN OF THE JEDI

Is Darth Vader really Luke Skywalker's father? Who is Luke's twin sister? Will Princess Leia and Han Solo finally get it on—or at least agree to go steady? Is Yoda getting senile (he is 900, remember)? Yes, everybody's favorite space saga turned, indeed, into a kind of intergalactic soap opera in this third installment. The distraction is welcome. Like *Star Wars* and *The Empire Strikes Back,* this film is a lot of fun—colorful, energetic to the point of being manic, good-humored, and full of marvelous invention. There is, for instance, a huge new villain called Jabba the Hutt, a cross between Edward G. Robinson and an overripe three hundred-pound avocado. There are some great effects involving what look like flying snowmobiles zooming through a forest. There is also a cuddly new teddy-bear-like tribe called the Ewoks. But too much of what happens is too familiar: the laser battles, the death star, the light swords, the nonacting by Mark Hamill and Harrison Ford, though Carrie Fisher seems to have matured. George Lucas, who co-wrote the film with Lawrence (*Raiders of the Lost Ark*) Kasdan, includes his customary salutes to old films, but

Return of the Jedi: Carrie Fisher seems to be facing a future as Mrs. Jabba the Hutt until the usual heroes are rounded up to save her—and the day—from the Empire's perfidy.

there's also an early scene involving a lot of particularly weird-looking creatures that is too reminiscent of the bar scene in *Star Wars*. It's as if Lucas is now at the point of paying homage to himself. (Richard Marquand, best known for TV's "Search for the Nile," directed but he said having Lucas so involved was "like directing King Lear with Shakespeare in the next room.") Even C-3PO and Yoda, who has one of the most florid death scenes since Greta Garbo in *Camille,* were getting a little tiresome. Worst of all, Hamill is badgered to give himself to "the dark side" by the Emperor, played by British stage actor Ian McDiarmid. After a while McDiarmid's prating about the inevitability of evil's triumph sounds like a stuffy father saying, "I know you don't believe it now, son, but someday you're going to be a Republican." There's more violence than usual, too, and some obvious sexual innuendo when Jabba captures Fisher, chains her up, and puts her into a harem outfit. Six parts were supposedly still left in Lucas's planned nine-part Star Wars series, but the next one was supposed

to be set chronologically before *Star Wars,* so the cast gathers at the end of Jedi for what amounts to a curtain call. Lucas is too smart to go beating a dead Wookie. It was fun, George; now let's get on with something else.
PG / 1983 / CBS/Fox

▲ THE RETURN OF THE SECAUCUS SEVEN

Preceding and in some ways outdoing *The Big Chill,* this film by John Sayles is a wise, witty, fresh look at a group of '60s student activists bumping aging psyches against present-day realities during a reunion in New Hampshire. It's familiar territory, botched in such previous films as *A Small Circle of Friends* and *The Big Fix,* but Sayles, the author of the books *Union Dues* and *The Anarchists' Convention,* combines acute observation with kinetic imagery. (He cut his movie teeth writing two Roger Corman epics, *Piranha* and *Battle Beyond the Stars.*) His most

impressive directorial debut was filmed in twenty-five days for $60,000 with a cast of unknowns. Especially noteworthy is Jean Passanante's multifaceted performance as a radical-turned-political flack. Her scenes with Gordon Clapp, as a strait-laced outsider, achieve an uncommon vibrancy.
Unrated / 1980 / RCA/Columbia

▲ REUBEN, REUBEN

Actor Tom Conti's reputation derived mostly from Broadway, but his hilarious, touching, Oscar-nominated performance as the boozed-out, womanizing poet hero of this film boosted his reputation as a virtuoso screen actor. Conti plays a poet not unlike Dylan Thomas: He is giving readings in a small New England town when he falls in love with Kelly McGillis, a much younger woman who forgives him his wicked ways. The movie was written by Julius J. Epstein, who won an Oscar in 1942 for *Casablanca*. Conti is wonderful to watch: stealing tips from restaurants his wealthy patrons take him to, confounding local citizens with ribald innuendoes, and often drinking himself into a stupor. McGillis, then 20, made the kind of debut actresses dream of, displaying the clean-cut sexuality of a Grace Kelly; *Witness* and *Top Gun* were yet to come. (The title role is played by an exuberant English sheepdog who figures in the Conti-McGillis meeting.) *Reuben, Reuben* was directed by Robert Ellis Miller, who shows a restraint that's all too uncommon.
R / 1984 / CBS/Fox

▲ REVENGE OF THE NERDS

Even as a summer throwaway, this college comedy about nerds, those born-to-be-victimized souls, was pitifully thin. It's a wonder an image shows up on the screen at all. When the ending turns messagey—we all have something of nerdhood within us—the movie becomes worse than nothing. It's like trying to enjoy eating a Twinkie while someone keeps insisting that its main asset is its nutritional value. The movie is competently enough acted by, among others, Robert Carradine, Anthony Edwards, Curtis Armstrong, and Julie Montgomery. But the screenwriters, first-timers Steve Zacharias and Jeff Buhai, take themselves too seriously: Buhai even said, "We tried to write almost an anti-Nazi movie." They just trot out

collegiate clichés—ugly computer whizzes, egotistical football players, gorgeous and mindless cheerleaders—as if merely putting them onscreen is funny. Director Jeff Kanew apparently had no better ideas. The jocks just bluster and the nerds grovel, until the inevitable turnaround. The only fun comes when the nerd types modify their hopelessly out-of-style outfits into a punk look for a rock skit in the college carnival. Set your alarm for about 72 minutes into the picture if you want to catch that scene.
R / 1984 / CBS/Fox

▲ REVENGE OF THE PINK PANTHER

The serenely incompetent Inspector Clouseau is on the case again for this fifth and—for star Peter Sellers—final chapter. While Sellers is routinely brilliant in most vignettes, director Blake Edwards seems to operate on the theory that any sight gag worth doing (revolving doors, tray-carrying waiters, and the old car-off-the-pier trick) is worth doing at least twice. The film is fine for Panther lovers, and co-star Dyan Cannon proves a delightful foil, but it is not the pick of the litter—1964's *A Shot in the Dark* remains the peak.
PG / 1978 / CBS/Fox

▲ REVOLUTION

Suggested resolution for Hollywood producers: Find a good movie for Al Pacino. The fine actor who gave us electrifying performances in the two *Godfather* movies as well as *Serpico* and *Dog Day Afternoon* then went on a losing streak for nearly a decade. *Bobby Deerfield, And Justice for All, Cruising, Author! Author!, Scarface*—and then this abomination. What made Pacino choose this incoherent treatise on the war that won America its freedom from Britain? Perhaps on paper Robert (*The River*) Dillon's screenplay hinted at an intriguing idea. The film would look at the revolution through the eyes of a New York fur trapper (Pacino) and his young son. Conscripted into service, the two fight a battle they never wanted and end up maligned by their own country. As directed by Hugh (*Greystoke*) Hudson, *Revolution* is a mess. Nothing seems authentic, especially Pacino's Scottish accent, which is worse than the Charo number he tried as a Cuban hood

in *Scarface*. And try to get your bearings as the film jumps from Valley Forge to Philadelphia with absurd abandon. Nastassja Kinski keeps popping up as a sort of early USO girl, aging nary a minute as the years fly by. Poor Donald Sutherland is saddled with the role of a redcoat officer whose main occupation seems to be procuring young drummer boys for himself and his pederast pals. When Pacino's son falls victim to one of Sutherland's sadistic foot-beating tortures, we watch Pacino and a group of friendly Indians cauterize the wounds with nauseating explicitness. This was usually the point where the walkouts started in theaters. To avoid walkouts or worse among family members in your own home, avoid this one at your local video store.
PG / 1985 / Warner

▲ RHINESTONE

Ordinarily, there's barely enough room on a movie screen for Sylvester Stallone and his ego, let alone anyone else. Well, Sly, meet Dolly Parton. Parton is such a powerful screen personality that her shimmery, sweet-natured energy more than matches Stallone's sullen, macho introversion. The contrast between them is fascinating. It also fits the story line. Parton is trying to teach New York cabby Stallone to be a country singer so that she can win a bet and get her contract back from Ron Leibman, for whom she performs in indentured servitude at his urban cowboy bar. Stallone is hardly a natural comedian, but he tries so hard to be endearingly corny that he's impossible to resist. Even though director Bob Clark's main previous credit was *Porky's*, the humor in this film is relatively restrained. The breast jokes are kept to a minimum, even though Parton has never looked more fetchingly voluptuous. And the barnyard humor when she takes Stallone back to her Tennessee farm stays more or less in good taste. There's also a very funny parody of a country song, "The Day My Baby Died," written by Clark, co-screenwriter (with Stallone) Phil Alden Robinson, and Mike Post. Parton wrote the rest of the classy country score; it's frustrating that she never really gets to sing a complete song alone, although her duet with Sly on "Stay Out of My Bedroom" is high-spirited. Richard Farnsworth adds a masterpiece of upstaging as Parton's father, speaking so gently you have to strain to hear him; how else could an actor make

his presence felt in this kind of company? Leibman is also effectively sleazy as the club owner. Stallone seems to get an inordinate number of close-ups, and there's a jarring, unnecessary plot twist at the end. But this is a charming movie, spunky and full of surprising fun. It's as if a mixture of lasagne and grits turned out to be the hit of the picnic.
PG / 1984 / CBS/Fox

▲ RICH AND FAMOUS

Back before the enlightenment, they'd have called this a woman's picture. Actually, it's a glamorous, old-fashioned soap opera directed by the late George Cukor, then 82, for the not-to-be-sniffed-at purpose of giving Jacqueline Bisset and Candice Bergen a chance to look great while acting their hearts out. Playing pals from Smith College, class of '59, the intellectual Bisset graduates into serious writing, the flighty Bergen into marriage and motherhood. All is well until Bergen, jealous of her friend's achievements, writes a novel, a trashy best-seller, that catapults her into riches and divorce. The plot spans twenty years as the two fight and reconcile while wearing almost fifty of Theoni Aldredge's most dazzling costumes. Bergen has rarely been this good. *Starting Over* suggested she had hidden comic resources; *Rich and Famous* confirms it. Bisset's task, though, is more trying. Her role is meant to showcase the feminist revolution, which here seems to mean that mature women have an inalienable right to bed teenage boys. In one scene Bisset takes a wet-behind-the-ears street hustler (Matt Lattanzi, later wed to Olivia Newton-John) back to her hotel suite for a quickie. As a naked Lattanzi thrusts his pelvis at her, Bisset looks embarrassed, and one cringes that Cukor, the director of *Little Women*, should have to watch this strained kinkiness, let alone direct it. The men are all studs or saps: Hart Bochner's *Rolling Stone* reporter is moronic enough to give that publication grounds for a suit. All is brighter when the screenplay sticks to the ladies. Bette Davis and Miriam Hopkins played the leads in 1943's *Old Acquaintance*. They didn't need the sleaze, and neither do Bisset and Bergen. When they're going at each other for the sheer, bitchy, movie-queen fun of it, *Rich and Famous* is a pleasure indeed.
R / 1981 / MGM/UA

▲ RICHARD PRYOR: HERE AND NOW

Richard Pryor stands up and tells a New Orleans audience that he hasn't taken drugs or gotten drunk in seven months. "I was tired of waking up in my car doing ninety," he cracks. That's the most printable of his routines in this, his third and by far best, concert film. It's brilliant exposition of Pryor's raunchy, no-holds-barred sense of humor. He talks about his bathroom habits, the difference between black and white women, herpes, meeting Ronald Reagan in the White House, a visit to Africa. His language is, shall we say, graphic, but in context, it's strangely inoffensive. In an apparently unplanned segment, someone in the audience (the concert was shot at the Saenger Performing Arts Center in New Orleans in August) hands him a glass with a crab in it. Pryor puts the tiny creature on a stool and talks with it about the problems of life in the spotlight. It's so affecting you don't know whether to laugh or cry. A lot of material will seem familiar—his old man from the South bewildered by modern civilization or his drunk trying to find a comfortable position to lie down in. But Pryor constantly works and reworks the territory he knows best—his own experience and psyche, and ours. In a brief prologue, he is interviewed backstage before the show. He says, rather somberly, that he knows the audience is rooting for him when he goes out onstage. That certainly seems to be the case in this film, and that may be part of Pryor's comic genius. He takes you in. Listening to him is like listening to an eccentric, vulnerable friend.
R / 1983 / RCA/Columbia

▲ RICHARD PRYOR LIVE ON THE SUNSET STRIP

As this film begins, cinematographer Haskell Wexler's camera focuses, ironically, on the sign at the entrance to the Chateau Marmont hotel in Los Angeles, where John Belushi died. Richard Pryor went to the very edge of a similar fate. If he returned with more suffering in his eyes and was noticeably more given to sermonizing, he is still an acute observer of human foibles, a randy raconteur, and a resourceful actor. This film, edited from two celeb-studded SRO concerts at the Hollywood Palladium includes bits about a Mafia type who owned a club where Pryor ap-

peared, a kinky assignation with a Playboy bunny, heartbreak, and making *Stir Crazy* with Gene Wilder at the Arizona State Penitentiary. ("We were there six weeks; it was strange—eighty percent black. What is strange is that there are no black people in Arizona.") He uses his near-fatal burning accident for laughs too. "Fire is inspirational," he muses. "They should use it at the Olympics. I did the one hundred-yard dash in 4.3." Now, he says, "I act like I ain't been burned up, and they (other people) do too. They sneak a peek. 'Nice tattoo you got . . . all over your body.'" Pryor's agony is, once again, our ecstasy.
R / 1982 / RCA/Columbia

▲ THE RIGHT STUFF

Based on Tom Wolfe's book about the original seven Project Mercury astronauts, this film has flight scenes that are exhilarating, often giving the audience the feeling of being in the cockpit. The acting, by an ensemble cast, is uniformly splendid. Director-writer Philip (*Invasion of the Body Snatchers*) Kaufman can claim credit for those virtues. But he's also to blame for the film's simplistic attitudes, stupid mysticism, and cheap shots at the public, the press, and government officials. The movie tells two stories. One is about test pilot Chuck Yeager, the first man to break the sound barrier; he is played, with the right John Wayne touches, by playwright-actor Sam Shepard, who won an Oscar nomination. The other story is about the astronaut program. Wolfe's point was to contrast the solitary courage and enterprise of men like Yeager with the illusions built around the astronauts. Kaufman muddies that idea; his astronauts come out as buddy-buddy heroes facing a hostile world. It's not the actors' fault. Scott Glenn as Alan Shepard, Ed Harris as John Glenn, Dennis Quaid as Gordon Cooper, and Fred Ward as Gus Grissom portray the roles Kaufman has written in a natural, convincing style. (Veronica Cartwright as Mrs. Grissom and Pamela Reed as Mrs. Cooper are striking too.) But Kaufman, in addition to playing fast and loose with the truth, injects jarring elements. Lyndon Johnson, for instance, is depicted as a dolt; there's a fiendishly hypocritical NASA official, but Kaufman lacks the courage to use the official's name. (He was presumably alive and, unlike Johnson, able to defend himself.) There is

The Right Stuff: Mercury astronauts *(from the left)* Scott Glenn, Scott Paulin, Charles Frank, Fred Ward, Dennis Quaid, and Ed Harris face some bumpy rides.

also some lengthy nonsense (the film runs 3 hours and 11 minutes) about aborigines and Sally Rand. And there is a bizarre fascination with bodily functions (separate incidents involve urine samples, sperm samples, and bowel movements). All this dims the film's triumphs. Kaufman made a big, small-minded movie.
PG / 1983 / Warner

▲ RISKY BUSINESS

Tom Cruise plays an upstanding Chicago high school senior with proud parents, membership in the Future Enterprise club, and aspirations to attend Princeton. When his folks go away on vacation, the boy is left in charge of the house, not to mention the Porsche. That may be an adolescent's dream, but in director Paul Brickman's shrewdly observed, sexually charged comedy, wish fulfillment has some hilarious, nightmarish consequences. The house is invaded by new-comer Rebecca De Mornay, a $300-a-night hooker who won't leave. Mom's beloved crystal egg is stolen; Dad's Porsche ends up at the bottom of Lake Michigan. Ever enterprising, the son solves his problems with a one-night-only business venture that pairs up a houseful of his buddies with De Mornay's colleagues. The story may sound unseemly, but in fact Brickman (no relation to Woody Allen's pal Marshall) fashioned a sweet-tempered, affectionate look at growing up good-hearted and guilt-ridden. As did his script for the 1977 cult comedy *Handle with Care* (also known as *Citizens Band*), with Candy Clark and Paul Le Mat, this one delights in the quirky behavior of ordinary people; it's a sure-footed, accomplished directorial debut. Brickman gets able assistance from his two leads. A pre-*Top Gun* Cruise ex-udes a basic decency that keeps smarminess at bay and credibility at hand. De Mornay provides the right combination of spunk and spark; she's the smarter sister of hooker Nancy Allen in *Dressed to Kill*. *Risky Business* is an invigorating, first-class affair: It manages to make coming of age a witty proposition.

R / 1983 / Warner

▲ RIVER'S EDGE

One of the best and boldest American movies of recent years hardly qualifies as escapist entertainment. Loosely based on several real-life, teen-kills-teen cases, the script, by newcomer Neal Jimenez, bravely takes on a knotty theme: numbness of feeling. The film begins with a distant shot of a teenage boy (Daniel Roebuck) sitting calmly on a California river bank. As the camera moves closer we see the nude body of a girl beside him. Strangulation marks discolor her throat. The boy's expression is blank. Later he tells his friends what he has done. They follow him to the scene, doing little more than peering at the corpse of the girl they once called a friend. The group's leader, flamboyantly and forcefully played by Crispin Glover (Michael J. Fox's father as a teen in *Back to the Future*), urges them to help the boy evade the cops. No one weeps for the dead girl. Her former pal, strongly acted by the lovely, lone Skye Leitch (daughter of '60s folksinger Donovan), wonders why she can't feel emotion when "I cried when that guy died in *Brian's Song*." Glover seeks advice from the town drug connection, played with customary demented urgency by Dennis Hopper. Living alone—except for a life-size sex doll—Hopper recalls shooting his own girlfriend out of jealousy. "Did you love her?" he asks the teen killer, who answers with chilling apathy, "She was okay." In the context of the film Hopper's crime of passion is more comprehensible than Roebuck's cold-blooded execution. Much of the picture's power comes from the way Jimenez and director Tim Hunter show how the behavior of peers and parents has helped to suppress the kids' feelings. One of the group, sharply characterized by Keanu Reeves, has a mother who accuses him of stealing *her* marijuana. The film's final scene offers no pat answers, just the sight of a few human beings struggling to find some moral bearings. *River's Edge* may often be crude and disorganized, but here is a different kind of youth picture: one that matters.

R / 1987 / N/A

▲ ROADIE

Travis W. Redfish likes his beer straight from the pitcher and prefers Milk Duds casseroles to health salads. He's just a good old boy from Texas, who also happens to be "the world's greatest roadie," a dubious distinction if ever there was one. (A roadie, in case you've forgotten, is a rock functionary who drives semis, sets up equipment, runs errands, and bounces overzealous fans for touring musicians.) As portrayed by rock heavy Meat Loaf, Redfish is pure delight, innocent, and irresistible. In his first starring role he doesn't sing a note and still steals the movie. Not that there's much to steal. Coyly billed as "the story of a boy and his equipment," the movie has plenty of paraphernalia but no notion of how to use it. Director Alan Rudolph signed on Hank Williams, Jr., Alice Cooper, and Blondie to lend musical authenticity, yet there is no semblance of a story line, apart from an unlikely love affair between Loaf and a tiresome groupie, Kaki Hunter. "Everything works if you let it" is a recurring slogan in the script, but this movie suggests at least one exception.

PG / 1980 / MGM/UA

▲ THE ROAD WARRIOR

"For reasons long forgotten," the narrator intones, "two mighty warrior tribes went to war—and touched off a blaze which engulfed them all. Their world crumbled. Men began to feed on men. Only those mobile enough to scavenge, brutal enough to pillage would survive." Against the backdrop of that post-nuclear-war scenario, Australian director George Miller fashioned a stylish sequel to his 1979 *Mad Max* about a sort of samurai warrior of the next Dark Ages. Mel Gibson, the New York-born actor who became a star in his adopted home Down Under (and *People*'s Sexiest Man Alive in 1985), is again the loner who saves a man's life in exchange for a tank of gas, then finds himself in an embattled outpost of civilization that has one last chance to thwart an attack by a gang of subhuman invaders. Miller managed to summon up a hellish, surreal quality that is haunting and provocative. The sets, costumes, makeup, special effects, and stunts are all first-rate, as is Gibson's performance. With the 1985 sequel, *Mad Max: Beyond Thunderdome*, Miller and Gibson have created a unique action trilogy that has moved from cult status to a raging video store popularity. If you only have time to see one, make *Road Warrior* your pick. But be warned: This is not family entertainment. Despite its occasional outbreaks of humanity, this is an unapologetically violent picture.

R / 1982 / Warner

▲ ROCKY II

This sequel to the 1976 box-office smash was good news for *Rocky* fans. Sylvester Stallone reassembled the same cast and crew (except Sly himself replaced John Avildsen as director) and told basically the same story, picking it up with the last round of Rocky's fight against Apollo Creed (Carl Weathers). Then Rocky retires, can't find work, and is shamed back into the ring. Talia Shire recreates her role as Adrian, marrying Rocky and producing a son named, naturally, Rocky. As the battered old manager, Burgess Meredith is still blustering, though Burt Young, as Adrian's crazy brother, puts on a coat and tie and acts a little more subdued. Stallone touches the familiar bases: the pet shop, punching carcasses at the meat-packing plant, training on the Philadelphia streets and, of course, the bounding run up the steps of the art museum. The fight scenes are beautifully choreographed and shot, with a surprise climax. One might have said this was the sequel to end all sequels, but one would have vastly underestimated Rocky's staying power. . . .

PG / 1979 / CBS/Fox

▲ ROCKY III

. . . Indeed. Number 3 followed just three years later. Sure it was corny. So you expected *King Lear?* Any foot-dragging about seeing yet another chapter in the life of boxer Rocky Balboa dissolved as soon as that driving Bill Conti theme started pumping under the credits and Sylvester Stallone, flexing his muscles as actor-writer-director, yelled his first "Yo, Adrian." What's new? Not much. In *Rocky,* in 1976, Stallone lost the title. In 1979's *Rocky II,* he won it. In *Rocky III,* he works to keep it. With designer suits to match his hairstyle and newly trim physique, Rocky has made a good life for wife Adrian (Talia Shire) and Rocky Jr. (Ian Fried), but brother-in-law Burt Young and trainer Burgess Meredith don't like what fame has done to him. When

faced with new rival Clubber Lang, played with fire-breathing brio by former Muhammad Ali bodyguard Mr. T, Rocky asks former opponent Carl Weathers to teach him street fighting. The training scenes, filmed in downtown L.A., are fun, and a sequence with Stallone being wrecked by a pro wrestler named Hulk "Thunderlips" Hogan is a howl. Rocky is the role Stallone was born to play (it may be the only one), but he joined underdog heroics and humor so unerringly that criticism is kayoed. We're clearly a long way from *Rocky Takes a Dive.* . . .

PG / 1982 / CBS/Fox

▲ ROCKY IV

. . . Indeed. Much, much further adventures of boxer Rocky Balboa settled one burning issue: Sylvester Stallone does better video workout routines than Jane Fonda. Let's face it, when you pay to see a *Rocky* film it's mainly for the privilege of watching Sly ripple as he totes that barge and lifts that bale in training to beat one more impossible foe. In each successive *Rocky* film, took something more drastic to drag the reluctant hero back into the ring. This time Sly is motivated to redeem the death of old nemesis-turned-friend Carl Weathers, who is done in by the preternatural punching of a Russian played by Dolph Lundgren, a six-foot five-and-a-half-inch, two-hundred-and-forty-pound Swede heretofore best known as the suitor of disco singer Grace Jones. Yep, Stallone is back defending the American way against the Commies, this time without his headband. Stallone ultimately travels to the Soviet Union to battle Lundgren before a hostile crowd presided over by the Politburo. As usual he absorbs forty-seven times his weight in punishment, winning over the Soviet people with this display of courage and will. His vacuous post-bout speech indicates why boxers with seventy-five professional bouts are rarely called upon as public speakers. But then if—or should we say when—there's a *Rocky V,* it's unlikely to be about the world debating championships.

PG / 1985 / CBS/Fox

▲ ROLLERCOASTER

Other than the witless title (rather as if *Rocky* had called itself *Boxing Ring*) and the irritating Sensurround effects (which TV sets thankfully can't yet reproduce), this is a tense, admirable film

about an extortionist who threatens amusement park owners by blowing up rides. Director James Goldstone shows a Hitchcockian sense of menace and a mordant appreciation for detail. The effective cast includes George Segal (a safety inspector), Timothy Bottoms (the bomber), Richard Widmark (expertly playing an officious FBI agent), and the Revolution roller coaster at Magic Mountain Park near Los Angeles.
PG / 1977 / MCA

▲ ROLLING THUNDER

One of the first movies about Vietnam features William Devane, convincing as a returned POW who witnesses the brutal murder of his wife and son, then seeks revenge. Tommy Lee Jones looks appropriately shell-shocked as his sidekick, but the real sneak attack in this film is the marvelously gritty performance of Linda Haynes as the girl who goes along for the ride. Based on a story by Paul Schrader, the film has a climax that's predictably violent—and the moral, if any, is drowned in a sea of blood.
R / 1977 / Vestron

▲ ROLLOVER

Jane Fonda and Kris Kristofferson try to save the world from an apocalyptic cash crunch when they uncover a plot by Arab moneymen to pull all their deposits from American banks (rather than "roll it over," in financial jargon, by reinvesting in the U.S. economy). Alas, they can't even save this luxuriously trashy, abrasive film from an apocalayptic plausibility crunch. Fonda is an ex-actress who takes over her husband's giant petrochemical firm when he is murdered. Kristofferson is a banker who helps secure her rise with a $500 million loan and shows some fancy moves among the sheets, balance and otherwise. Director Alan J. Pakula is usually right on the money (Klute, Parallax View, All the President's Men), but this is just a horror film: The monster is capitalist greed. David Shaber's screenplay offers either fast-paced Wall Street patois that is infuriatingly esoteric or lines like these, from Kris: "The world is full of deals" and "We're playing with the end of the world." It isn't easy, either, to go along with Fonda's politics here since her movie production company is using a profit-making (she futilely hoped) $15 million epic to decry profit.

At the end a worker in the bank's frenzied trading room is near tears when she screams, "Gold is up to $2,000!" She's crying for a hero. Can the monetary system come to the rescue? Will anyone understand what's happening if it does?
R / 1982 / Warner

▲ ROMANCING THE STONE

Born of the success of Raiders of the Lost Ark, and somebody's memories of those schlocky '30s and '40s cliff-hangers, this rollicking, tongue-in-cheek romance adventure stars Michael Douglas and Kathleen Turner. The man-eating crocodiles, the hair-raising jungle chase, the ride over the waterfall—all this is the stuff of pulp movies in the best tradition, and Romancing the Stone, despite a few stray bits of plot and dialogue, is in that tradition. It's also a lot of fun. Turner plays a romance novelist who cries at the end of her own books. She is a rather plain New York career woman whose only romantic entanglement seems to be with her cat. Then things start happening: Her sister is kidnapped by thugs in Columbia, Turner's apartment is ransacked, and she flies to South America with the ransom, a treasure map everyone seems to want. Douglas, a drifter, meets Turner when she is about to be attacked by the bad guys in the jungle. Their chemistry is not exactly Tracy and Hepburn, but things do heat up eventually. Danny De Vito is embarrassingly hammy as one of the bumbling bad guys; the movie would have been better without him. But the screenplay by rookie writer Diane Thomas (a waitress in Malibu when she wrote it) lampoons a lot of pop icons. Watch for the copy of Rolling Stone Douglas discovers in the fuselage of a wrecked plane ("The Doobie Brothers broke up," he moans while poor Turner is fighting off a poisonous snake). Turner is terrific, Douglas is fine, and the action is slam-bang. Add lots of laughs and it all works out just right.
PG / 1984 / CBS/Fox

▲ A ROOM WITH A VIEW

There's a revivifying charge of greatness in this movie. And the best part is, you don't anticipate it. From producer Ismail Merchant, director James Ivory, and screenwriter Ruth Prawer Jhabvala, the trio behind such book-to-film translations as Henry James's The Bostonians and Jean Rhys's

Risky Business: Rebecca De Mornay teaches Tom Cruise some less than orthodox techniques of free enterprise as he goes straight from high school into the, uh, personal-services business.

Quartet, you expect a puppy-dog faithfulness to source that often crosses the line from stately to plodding. This time they blew the dust off the pages. Working from E. M. Forster's less than celebrated 1908 novel, written when Forster was 29 (with the triumphs of *Howard's End* and *A Passage to India* ahead of him), the filmmakers have uncovered a masterful comedy of manners. Oh, the snob appeal is still in evidence, but there's nothing stuffy about this one. *Room's* structure is deceptively simple. A young Englishwoman, played by Helena Bonham Carter, visits Florence, chaperoned by her spinster cousin, acted with anguished grace by the incomparable Maggie Smith. Disappointed that her pension is run by a Cockney and that her room is facing a courtyard instead of the Arno, Bonham Carter

complains she might as well be in London. Forster's point about the English, of course, is that they are always in England, closed off to any new culture afforded them. Bonham Carter meets handsome, headstrong Julian Sands, a young Britisher traveling with his vulgarian father, Denholm Elliott. Bonham Carter gets more than she bargained for, first witnessing a bloody stabbing in a piazza and later being passionately kissed by Sands in the erotically lush Italian countryside. Shaken, she returns home and gets engaged to a prig, brilliantly acted by Daniel Day Lewis in such marked contrast to the punkish lout he played in *My Beautiful Laundrette* that he walked off with several year-end awards as Best Supporting Actor. That's when Sands and his father make a last attempt to save her. Director Ivory displays

a keen understanding of the hypocrisy festering beneath the elegant surfaces of Edwardian society. The comic highlight is a telling scene in which the rigidly costumed Bonham Carter and her mother come upon Sands, Bonham Carter's brother (Rupert Graves), and a plump minister (Simon Callow) frolicking naked and innocent in a muddy pond. The sterling cast, indeed, could not be bettered. But special praise must go to Smith and Elliott, whose alchemy turns small roles into bold and memorable characterizations. With faultless assurance and ingenuity, the Merchant-Ivory-Jhabvala team made it all come together this time in one of the best literary adaptations ever filmed.
Unrated / 1986 / CBS/Fox

▲ ROSELAND

New York's famous Roseland Ballroom is the setting for this bittersweet trilogy about love-on-the-hoof. In the first episode a nostalgic widow (Teresa Wright) hopes in vain that a gruff, unpolished widower (Lou Jacobi) can replace her deceased husband—on the dance floor and off. The second segment plots the romantic involvement of a smoothie (Christopher Walken) with two attractive older women (Helen Gallagher and Joan Copeland) and a young, on-the-rebound divorcee (Geraldine Chaplin). Finally, in the funniest and most poignant vignette, a pair of elderly contestants (Lilia Skala and David Thomas) try desperately to win a dance contest just once before they die. Despite uniformly excellent performances, director James Ivory allows the segments to melt into one another in a way that muddles an otherwise enjoyable film.
Unrated / 1977 / Vestron

▲ ROUGH CUT

In 1936 Cary Grant made a film, *Big Brown Eyes*, about a detective chasing a jewel thief. It was no artistic triumph but didn't ruin anyone's career. In 2024 or so, people may be saying the same thing about this harmless romantic caper starring Burt Reynolds. It's another spin on the gentleman diamond robber theme, whose style, wit, and tension were pretty well exhausted by the time of the original *To Catch a Thief* and *The Pink Panther*. *Rough Cut* director Don Siegel is responsible for a varied, admirable range of work—

including the first *Invasion of the Body Snatchers*, Elvis's *Flaming Star*, and *Dirty Harry*. Here he overdoses on close-ups of Reynolds, who plays the thief, and Lesley-Anne Down, his elegant if reluctant moll. They're both gorgeous, but once Burt has gone gamely through his arsenal of lovable expressions and Lesley-Anne has run out of possible hair styles, their faces are left up on the screen looking huge and uneasy. Yet David Niven, then 70, added class as a Scotland yard inspector in a vendetta against Reynolds, and there are a couple of mildly surprising twists. If this isn't a diamond in the rough, it's at times a tolerable imitation.
PG / 1980 / Paramount

▲ ROUND MIDNIGHT

Dexter Gordon was a sorcerer on the tenor sax for forty years and more than eighty LPs. Then in 1986, at 63, he made his feature film debut as a troubled black American jazz musician and delivered the performance of the year. There is more astounding news. Far from boring the non-jazz buff, the musical sequences, shot in long takes, become an integral part of the drama. Director and co-screenwriter Bertrand (*A Sunday in the Country*) Tavernier loosely based his story on the real experiences of Francis Paudras, a young Frenchman who met the legendary jazz pianist Bud Powell in Paris in the late '50s and tried in vain to save his American idol from self-destructing on alcohol. Tavernier, unimpressed with actors faking musical prowess (such as Robert De Niro in *New York, New York*), insisted on a real musician for the role. After combing the market, he seized on Gordon—like Powell, a pioneer of the bebop jazz era of the '40s, but unlike Powell, one who kicked a problem, heroin, to make a major comeback in 1976. A tall (six feet five inches), elegant man with a shambling gait, Gordon speaks slowly, in a rhythmic rasp that runs the scale from self-mocking to mournful. "I'm tired of everything except the music," he tells French actor François Cluzet, playing the fan who holds nothing more dear than his idol's salvation—not even his job, a possible reconciliation with his wife, or the care of his young daughter, beautifully acted by 12-year-old Gabrielle Haker. To the musically obsessed Cluzet, Gordon is a god. Constantly watched by his employers lest he slip out for drinks, Gordon's jazzman is a human shell until he takes the stage. There, every fiber of his body becomes attuned to the beat, his fingers show a surgeon's precision, his arms an interpretive dancer's grace. Tavernier is right: This can't be faked. Along with Cluzet, we are enthralled—and later enraged. After a few drinking binges that land Gordon in the hospital, we lose patience with Cluzet for sacrificing so much for a man who won't save himself. Still, the selfishness in the Samaritan helps the film skirt false nobility for something more truthful and telling. By trying to rescue the artist, he is rescuing his art and, Cluzet thinks, sharing in art's immortality. Credit must go to the musical tapestry woven by such jazz greats as Herbie Hancock, Billy Higgins, and Pierre Michelot, as well as superb acting cameos by Lonette (*The Cotton Club*) McKee as an old flame of Gordon's, newcomer Sandra Reaves-Phillips as his watchdoglike friend, and especially Martin Scorsese, director of *Raging Bull*, as a hustling club owner. Above all there is deserved Oscar nominee Dexter Gordon, evoking the highs and lows of the bebop era with stunning virtuosity. The result is spellbinding entertainment.

PG-13 / 1986 / Warner

firefighter Rick Rossovich, a tongue-tied hunk who can't find the vocabulary to ask for a date. Martin helps Rossovich by writing for him rapturous love letters that deliver Roxanne to the wrong man's bed. Not for long, though. This new Cyrano has a happy ending. Director Fred (*Plenty*) Schepisi gives the movie a lush romantic atmosphere that allows Martin to build character as well as jests. Martin is trying something ambitious here: to make a romantic farce in which laughs don't undercut the love story. His footing isn't always sure. He lets syrupy music and sight gags polute the poignancy of the famous balcony scene in which, hidden in the dark, he can finally speak to Roxanne of his love. And Martin never develops the rapport he starts to establish with his bumbling firemen or with matchmaker Shelley Duvall, who was a welcome sight back on the screen after five years of producing TV fairy tales. But if Martin sometimes trips up, he deserves a salute for trying something different instead of taking the easy path to box-office booty (read: Eddie Murphy in *Beverly Hills Cop II*) by trotting out a sequel to one of his hits. *Roxanne* has the exuberance of fresh comic thinking.

PG / 1987 / N/A

▲ ROXANNE

They say most comics long to play Hamlet. Perhaps as a warmup, Steve Martin took on Cyrano de Bergerac, the swashbuckling soldier hero of Edmond Rostand's poetic tragedy set in 17th-century France. In updating the piece for the 1980s, Martin—doubling as star and screenwriter—dumped most of the sob stuff and added his own brand of inspired silliness. The result, purists be damned, is a romantic lark that soars with Steve Martin's wittiest and warmest screen performance. Martin's C. D. Bales is a Washington State fire chief leading a troop of misfit volunteers. Like Cyrano, C.D. is a man with a heart the size of his schnoz—that is to say, prodigious. (Michael Westmore designed the nose, which is, well, hugely funny.) In the film's comic high point Martin takes on a barroom heckler with a barrage of his own nose insults. But his humor barely masks the inadequacy he feels around women, who revel in his wit yet are repelled by his nose. C.D. loves a beautiful astronomer named Roxanne, played with surprising exuberance by the usually bland Daryl Hannah. She lusts after

▲ RUDE BOY

Though redeemed by several blazingly performed songs by the Clash, this woefully disjointed film does not do for punk rock what *The Harder They Come* did for reggae: illuminate the musical milieu and make the musicians' and fans' dedication comprehensible. The vague plot concerns a loutish London kid who hooks up with the Clash as a roadie. Variously late, drunk, and clumsy with equipment, he seems to serve the band only as a pathetic target for physical and verbal abuse. Their continuing tolerance for each other is baffling and, finally, depressing. But then the characters are so bogged down in anomie they make the ghouls in *Night of the Living Dead* look like Keystone Kops. Only the concert scenes—which throb with anger, desperation and instrument-flailing violence—make very much sense. Directors Jack Hazan and David Mingay may have been trying to illustrate the social disaffection that gave punk rock its raison d'etre, but instead they succeeded only in turning out a numbing, alienated movie.

R / 1980 / N/A

▲ RUMBLE FISH

Another backward step for Francis (*The Godfather, Apocalypse Now*) Coppola. Film historians may mark 1982 as the year Coppola stopped directing movies and began to settle instead for decorating them; his *One from the Heart* was a virtually plotless romance shot on a flamboyantly fake studio set. Strike One. Early in 1983 Coppola blew up S. E. Hinton's troubled-youth novel *The Outsiders* until its simple story exploded under his epic visuals. Strike Two. Then, with *Rumble Fish* (another tale of wayward youth from a Hinton book), Coppola created an existentialist teen-gang movie set in an unidentified city in the unspecified near future. To that already bleak symbolic load he adds endless shots of clouds, smoke, and assorted blight that all but crush the life out of the central characters. They are Mickey (*Diner*) Rourke as the Motorcycle Boy—the leader of the pack—and Matt (*Tex*) Dillon as the kid brother who lives in Rourke's shadow. Rourke, color-blind and half deaf from too many rumbles, sees the world like "a black-and-white TV screen with the sound off," which is also how Coppola apparently sees his film. Not even the talented Dillon and Rourke can make anything of impossible roles. Dennis (*Easy Rider*) Hopper as the boys' drunken father and Diane (*The Outsiders*) Lane as Dillon's girl fare better in small parts because they don't bear the weight of Coppola's more eccentric flights of fancy. In one scene Dillon's spirit rises from his body and flies over the neighborhood listening to imagined reactions to his death. Rourke must spout philosophy about pet-store fish; he wants to set them free. Get the parallel? Coppola shoots the fish in color (the rest of the film is in black and white) in case you miss the point. Such self-conscious tricks would be understandable in a film student. They're unforgivable in Coppola. *Rumble Fish,* for all its technical polish, is a definite Strike Three.
R / 1983 / MCA

▲ RUNNING SCARED

This buddy comedy about two cops in Chicago is an efficient, entertaining time killer without a glimmer of originality. Gregory Hines and Billy Crystal work undercover, dress funky, talk dirty, and play tough (see: Eddie Murphy's *Beverly Hills Cop*). Each takes turns playing straight man for the other's guy's jokes (see: Richard Pryor and Gene Wilder's *Stir Crazy*). Their base is a bustling police precinct where they have to cope with a curmudgeon captain (Dan Hedaya), jealous rivals (Steve Bauer and Jonathan Gries), and heavy caseloads that have wrecked their respective marriages (see: TV's "Hill Street Blues"). The jobs they bungle are played for laughs (see: all the *Police Academy*s), but when they mishandle a syndicate drug bust (see: *Scarface*), their livid boss boots them off the case (see: *Dirty Harry*). That's when the boys take off for an enforced vacation in Key West, which allows them plenty of time for biking, swimming, lusting, and listening to music that turned up on the sound-track album and in some MTV videos (see: nearly every big-studio movie of the last few years). They're soon back on the beat, of course, to participate in a spectacular car chase staged on Chicago's elevated train tracks (see: *The French Connection*). What makes the familiarity fun for much of the time is the puppyish charm of the two stars, though director Peter (*2010*) Hyams can't always hide the calculation behind the cuteness. Crystal promises to be the next "Saturday Night Live" alumnus to make the grade in flicks. His comic timing is expectedly marvelous, but the surprise of his performance is the emotion he brings to the scenes with his ex-wife, touchingly played by the gorgeous Darlanne (*To Live and Die in L.A.*) Fleugel. Hines also does well, though this song-and-dance master is frittering away his formidable talents in a film that ignores them. *Running Scared* is no more than a serviceable job of packaging, further sad evidence the the new-model Hollywood comedy is manufactured almost entirely out of retooled tooled parts.
R / 1986 / MGM/UA

▲ RUSTLERS' RHAPSODY

Fortunately for a lot of reputations, this Western spoof bit the dust quickly in the theaters. Tom Berenger, sinking in a quagmire of bum jokes, plays Rex O'Herlihan, a singing cowboy presumably modeled on Roy Rogers, since Rex always wears white, shoots only at the gun hand, and possesses the libido of a slug. In the opening scene (shot in black and white) we're told by the narrator that O'Herlihan starred in fifty-two cowboy movies between 1938 and 1947. What if those films had been made today? asks the irritating, disembodied voice. Then the picture widens, fills with glorious color, and the action (filmed in Spain) commences. Mel Brooks pulled off this sort of revisionist ranchiness in *Blazing Saddles,* but writer-director Hugh Wilson is no Brooks. It's hard to figure out what Wilson is doing, except telling his actors to smirk a lot after delivering a line, to allow time for the audience to laugh. Here's a sampling of the thigh slappers: At a saloon, Berenger, wanting to appear tough, orders ''warm gin with a human hair in it.'' Our hero is taunted with the name ''Prairie Fairy,'' and even another good guy, played by the Duke's son, Patrick Wayne, questions Rex's status as a ''confident heterosexual.'' The gay subtheme doesn't stop at one-liners. Andy Griffith returns to movies after ten years to play a villainous colonel with a beautiful daughter (former model Sela Ward) and a yen for his cowboy henchmen. G. W. Bailey overacts shamelessly as the town drunk. Fernando Rey (a glory in the cinema of Bunuel and Wertmuller) rolls his eyes like a clown for hire as a railroad baron. Marilu Henner is onscreen so briefly as a saloon gal that charitable viewers might forget she was in the movie at all. For the rest, forgiveness comes hard. The producer was David Giler, who once turned out such estimable entertainments as *Alien* and *The Parallax View.* Couldn't he have put us all out of our misery? They still shelve movies, don't they?

PG / 1985 / Paramount

▲ RUTHLESS PEOPLE

As soon as you see Bette Midler in this rowdy and raunchy comedy, you know the title is a misnomer. *Tacky People* would be more accurate.

As a kidnapping victim who has just been dumped in a basement, Midler makes an entrance that elicits gasps from the audience. She pokes out of a sack with her red hair flying, eyes popping, and venom spewing. Midler looks like a she-devil from outer space, and she's dressed like the most *nouveau gauche* belle of Bel Air, which she is. In this cunning '80s update on O. Henry's *The Ransom of Red Chief,* two kidnappers, Judge (*Beverly Hills Cop*) Reinhold and Helen (*Supergirl*) Slater, are saddled with a witch nobody wants. Midler's sleazo husband, Danny De Vito, would rather cavort with his mistress, Anita Morris, than put up the money to get his wife back. But these desperate characters suffer more from an excess of tastelessness than ruthlessness. Besides being funny, *Ruthless People* is entertainment with an edge. Dale Launer's script (his first produced screenplay) is spiked with clever commentary on the poodle culture. In fact, like *Handle with Care* this is a low-down comedy that accommodates high-minded insights. And Launer's well-structured script apparently inspired the filmmakers to keep their minds on the material for a change. Directed by Jerry Zucker, Jim Abrahams, and David Zucker, the trio responsible for *Top Secret!* and *Airplane!,* this comedy marks a satisfying advance over their previous work. This time they don't keep interrupting themselves with gratuitous asides or movie allusions. While the cast performs uniformly well, it's Midler who surprises most pleasantly. In *Down and Out in Beverly Hills,* Midler looked reined in and uncomfortable. Here she gives a bawdy, clownish performance that captures some of the energy of her stage persona. At its considerable best, *Ruthless People* is a riotous anomaly: very good farce about very bad taste.

R / 1986 / Touchstone

S

▲ SAINT JACK

When a director falls flat on his face again and again, it becomes embarrassing, but Peter Bogdanovich didn't let this washout stop him.

Based on a novel by Paul Theroux, the movie tells, haltingly, of an American in Singapore who runs a whorehouse against brutal Chinese competition. The movie is largely incoherent and amateurishly shot and acted. Ben Gazzara as the American is so wooden he's absolutely unsympathetic, as are most of the other characters. Worse, whole scenes seem to have been shot out of focus—as if they came from a film school student rather than a seasoned movie director. Bogdanovich was the wunderkind of American films after he directed *The Last Picture Show* in 1971 at 31. His next property, *What's Up Doc?*, with Barbra Streisand and Ryan O'Neal was so-so. He never really impressed anyone again until *Mask* in 1985.

R / 1979 / Vestron

▲ SAME TIME, NEXT YEAR

Alan Alda—no "M*A*S*H"'er but a happily married accountant—picks up a young and happily married Ellen Burstyn one evening when they're loose from their respective spouses. They spend a weekend together so ecstatic, we're to believe, that they arrange to meet once a year—but never in between—same time, same place, in spite of their changing personalities, divorces, deaths in the family, and fierce guilt. The premise was contrived but successful as a play; as a movie it just creaks. And while both Burstyn and Alda are charming, the onus of carrying a movie with only two characters and no change of scenery is a hopeless chore. Slowly, too slowly, pass the years.

PG / 1979 / MCA

▲ SGT. PEPPER'S LONELY HEARTS CLUB BAND

Like a box of candy left on the beach, this movie is a gooey, sugary mess. But buried in the glop are a few nuggets. The opening sequence—when the band (Peter Frampton and the Bee Gees) is introduced to Heartland, U.S.A.—is full of exuberant promise. Sandy Farina delivers a glorious "Here Comes the Sun," and Billy Preston high-steps his way through a brilliant version of "Get Back." Comic Steve Martin is deliciously diabolical as Maxwell Edison, and George Burns, in the film's only nonsinging part, is warm and witty. But Frampton and the Brothers Gibb, while able enough songsters, can't act a smidgen or get through faking it. Henry Edwards's comic-book screenplay bobs uncertainly from high camp to lowest humor. Unlike the Who's "Tommy," "Sgt. Pepper"—the Beatles' greatest album and the source of most of the score of this film—was never intended to be a rock opera. *Saturday Night Fever* producer Robert Stigwood paid a bundle for the rights to the music, and of course those songs are just as magical as they were when the album appeared in 1967. But you can't buy class. Just imagine the movie that could have been—with, say, Richard (*A Hard Day's Night*) Lester directing and four Liverpool lads as the leads.

PG / 1978 / MCA

▲ SASQUATCH

Also known as Bigfoot—a huge, hairy, apelike beast—Sasquatch is a kind of second cousin to the Abominable Snowman. Since there are people who believe such a creature really exists in remote areas of the Pacific Northwest, this film purports to dramatize sundry encounters with him in British Columbia. If you run screaming from the screen, it will only be in disgust at the amateur acting, shoddy dubbing, and tiresome use of third-rate animal photography as filler. Old Sas and his friends—who seem to resemble bears with Ernest Borgnine's face—should have gotten a lawyer to sue for defamation.

G / 1978 / United

▲ SATURDAY NIGHT FEVER

In his first big movie role, John Travolta starred as the king of a Brooklyn disco in this *American Graffiti* of the big-city '70s. *Fever,* though, has a sharper edge. Travolta (whose real mother and sister also appear briefly) plays a nice Italian kid—during the week. Weekends he cuts loose on dance floors, but after a gang bang, gang fight, and a suicide cramp his style, he wants out. Karen Lynn Gorney, a gal with a make-something-of-yourself drive, seems to be his ticket. Travolta's sad-eyed sensuality is appealing, and Donna Pescow as the girl he leaves behind is fine. The Bee Gees' music charged the atmosphere that director John Badham set up so skillfully. Travolta and the film galvanized the disco scene into an imperishable artifact of the 1970s. (A PG-rated version in 1979 eliminated some of the rougher language and more obvious sex scenes.)

R / 1977 / Paramount

313

▲ SATURDAY THE 14TH

Nice title. Nice idea: Parody the recent epidemic of gruesome chillers in which young women are stalked and savaged. Lousy movie, though. The film puts Richard Benjamin and Paula Prentiss in an inherited mansion, along with vampires, monsters, and evil forces but not many jokes. (The best is that the TV set receives only reruns of "The Twilight Zone," and a Rod Serling voice murmurs in the background.) This is not a parody, just another haunted-house spoof, and not done nearly as well as *Abbott and Costello Meet Frankenstein,* Polanski's *The Fearless Vampire Killers,* or even 1941's *Spooks Run Wild,* with the Bowery Boys and Bela Lugosi.
PG / 1982 / Embassy

▲ SATURN 3

An aging agronomist, Kirk Douglas, and his nubile assistant, Farrah Fawcett, are happy as hamsters in their subsurface nest in one of Saturn's moons. Then Frankenstein comes to outer space. The malevolent (as usual) Harvey Keitel plays the mad scientist, a computer programmer who unloads his gear and builds a monster-robot-gone-mad. The robot's lust for Farrah and hatred for Kirk are more laughable than scary, except when he starts smashing dogs and cutting off hands in scenes the camera dwells on excessively. The dialogue is a riot, and, but for a few moments of *Alien*-like suspense, the story meanders off into the void. Blame it on Stanley Donen, who in better days directed *Singin' in the Rain* and *Two for the Road.*
R / 1980 / CBS/Fox

▲ SAY AMEN, SOMEBODY

George T. Nierenberg, best known for his tap-dancing film *No Maps on My Taps,* produced and directed this warmly adoring documentary on two pioneers of black gospel music: Willie Mae Ford Smith and Thomas Dorsey. The film is a series of recollections—intercut with singing and close-ups on grainy black-and-white photos—that reconstruct anecdotally the roots of black gospel.

Smith, often filmed at home with family members around a dinner table, recalls when churches told her to "take that coonshine" music out of religious settings. Dorsey, a onetime blues pianist, said once he heard "the voice of God was speaking and said, 'You need a change.' " Later his young wife and baby died only days apart in 1932, and Dorsey says, "I started singing right then and there." Also on camera singing or speaking are Mahalia Jackson, the O'Neal Twins, and the Barrett Sisters. But the film belongs to the magnificent Dorsey and Mother Smith. She tells her grandson—who is not entirely in favor of his young wife's aspirations to sing gospel—that if a woman can bear kids, keep house, and do dishes, "how come she can't take the Word and carry it?" In another scene she tells a young male singer that his cheeks should act to enrich and hold the tone in his voice. As he begins again, she pushes in her own big cheeks with her index fingers and says, "Don't forget to step on the pedals." The last sequence—when Dorsey and Smith lead a national convention of gospel choirs and choruses—is profoundly moving, with delegates swooning and fainting to the music. And Dorsey, leaning on his walker, moves slowly down a hotel corridor wearing a white robe embroidered in red and quietly singing his classic "Precious Lord." "I won't be through with my work," he says at the end, "until God takes my voice."
G / 1983 / Pacific Arts

▲ SCANNERS

This Canadian horror flick could suitably be described as a mindblower, though your latest meal is more precisely at stake. The title refers to a small group of weirdos whose brain waves are capable of controlling and—in one spectacularly revolting scene—demolishing a scannee's brain. Naturally there are good scanners and bad ones, and the latter seek to rule the world. Patrick McGoohan and Jennifer O'Neill admirably survive the scanning—and the humorless scripting by Canadian director David Cronenberg—but Stephen Lack's performance is simply scan-dalous. Cronenberg brings to this film an undeniably entertaining visual flair (he did the 1986 remake of *The Fly*)—and an interesting sci-fi conceit—

but the deadening dialogue and good versus evil plot all but obscure these virtues.
R / 1981 / Embassy

▲ SCARFACE

What becomes a 3-hour endurance test of a movie begins brilliantly. Al Pacino is a young thug arriving in Miami with 125,000 other Cubans in the 1980 boat lift. In short order, Pacino and his buddy, subtly played by newcomer Steven Bauer, have hitched their wagons to Miami cocaine kingpin Robert Loggia. Director Brian (*Dressed to Kill*) De Palma, art director Ed Richardson, and visual consultant Ferdinando Scarfiotti create a Miami of vulgar richness. And Michelle Pfeiffer, undefeated by the fiasco of *Grease 2,* makes one of the sexiest entrances in screen history as Loggia's mistress, a hot number who'd rather powder her nose with cocaine than respond to Pacino's advances. The premise is explosive. And why not? *Scarface* is an updating by screen writer Oliver (*Platoon*) Stone of the 1932 classic directed by Howard Hawks, written by Ben Hecht and starring Paul Muni as a gangster loosely based on Al Capone. The new *Scarface,* though, goes nowhere. Pacino's hyper performance soon becomes tiresome. His Cuban accent vacillates disconcertingly between a Desi Arnaz model and a Charo. The language, with constant use of what Neil Simon once referred to as "the f word," soon becomes an assault. Characterization and plot go out the window. Arms are cut off by chainsaws. By the third hour everything is out of control. Pacino, now the big shot, snorts from a Mount Everest of coke piled atop his desk; it covers his nose and eyelashes. He rejects Pfeiffer ("yer womb is polluted") and faces incestuous longings for his sister, vividly portrayed by Mary Elizabeth Mastrantonio. The bloodbath that ends the film is an insult to everything De Palma had done before. There is no style to this violence; everything seems to be in service of an Oscar-stalking Pacino performance. His acting isn't acting; it's shameless showing off. So is the movie. Compare the original's way of handling a murder. When George Raft, in the Bauer role, is killed by Scarface, all the camera shows is the coin that Raft customarily tosses in the air falling to the ground. In the De Palma/Pacino version, it's a graphic gore-a-thon. The new *Scarface* ends with

a dedication to Hawks and Hecht; it's the film's final, unforgivable obscenity.
R / 1983 / MCA

▲ SECRET ADMIRER

How many new ideas can come from the time-worn premise of love letters mistakenly falling into the wrong hands? None from David Greenwalt, the director of this film, a sex farce with all the heart of an answering machine. High schooler C. Thomas Howell is smitten by Val Gal Kelly Preston and receives a love letter he believes came from her. He writes back. Of course the correspondence goes through Lori Loughlin, his best friend, and the actual author of the first letter. A series of conventional mishaps leads to a frantic, romantic quadrangle between Howell's parents, played by Dee Wallace Stone and Cliff De Young, and Preston's parents, played by Leigh Taylor-Young and Fred Ward. The plot is so thin that the fine cast is made to seem moribund. Howell is one of the few young actors around who successfully plays his age. Loughlin, who spent three and a half years getting kidnapped as Jody Travis on "The Edge of Night," is a fresh film personality. But this appealing couple is thrust into an environment filled with grating characters unworthy of the attention they get onscreen. Wallace Stone and Preston whine endlessly; Cory Haim, as Howell's obnoxious little brother, steals money from family members; even Taylor-Young's and De Young's fumbling attempt at infidelity gets wearisome. *Secret Admirer* should have been a totally clandestine affair.
R / 1985 / Thorn/EMI

▲ THE SECRET OF MY SUCCESS

Although he's the new boy in town, he looks very familiar. Just arrived in the big city, he immediately witnesses a robbery, eyes the girls in their summer dresses, and uses terrorist tactics on the roaches in his apartment. He may have arrived from Kansas, but he comes across more like a refugee from American movies circa 1963. *The Secret of My Success* is a retro comedy given a yuppie make-over to differentiate it from its obvious forefathers, which range from *How to Succeed in Business Without Really Trying* to *The*

Apartment. The result, half boardroom farce and half romantic fairy tale, would be dreary were it not for its star, *Back to the Future*'s Michael J. Fox. He plays the go-getter who insinuates himself into a Manhattan corporation run by a distant and distasteful uncle, Richard Jordan. Unc is having an extramarital affair with the woman of his nephew's daydreams. In an earlier era she would probably have been a secretary. In this version she's a Harvard MBA, in the person of Helen Slater. The serviceable script by *Top Gun* perpetrators Jim Cash and Jack Epps, Jr., written with A. J. Carothers, doesn't capitalize on the comedy targets that inhabit the corporate culture. But ironically, if this movie weren't such a slapdash, ramshackle comedy, it probably wouldn't showcase Fox as well as it does. He's the center of attention, right down to his skill at the lost art of the double take. Like Jack Lemmon or Robert Morse in those '60s comedies, Fox is an island of innocence even when he's playing office politics. That's just as well, since in true yupscale tradition, the hero is more defined by his hedonism than his heroism. A midtown Manhattan setting invigorates director Herbert Ross, who finds a kind of romance in the cacophony of the city, particularly as it is shot by cinematographer Carlo Di Palma. Ross also populated the movie with a number of curious background characters, including the smashing Margaret Whitton as Jordan's horny wife, Carol-Ann Susi as Fox's bumbling secretary, and playwright Chris Durang as a corporate bozo. Without Fox, though, this comedy could be mostly an eminently disagreeable apologia for greed and ambition. What preserves the charm is that Fox, unlike most leading men these days, doesn't seem afraid to be affable.

PG-13 / 1987 / MCA

▲ SECRETS

The purpose in the belated release of this 1971 film was obviously exploitation: It includes Jacqueline Bisset in a five-minute nude scene. The plot is elemental. Bisset, her husband (Robert Powell), and their young daughter, impressively played by Tarka Kings, all enjoy separate romantic flings on the same day. The surprise is not that Bisset is exquisite (she is) but that the movie,

far from being a hot number, is a low-key meditation on the nature of love.

R / 1978 / Prism

▲ THE SEDUCTION

Morgan Fairchild of TV's "Flamingo Road" made her big-screen debut as an L.A. anchorwoman who is stalked, mostly through a Mount Palomar-size lens, by photographer Andrew Stevens. He is your typical Beverly Hills sex maniac: He blow-dries his hair in front of a three-paneled mirror, buys his love object flowers and an engagement ring when what he really needs is more developing fluid, and could be a cover boy for the *Preppy Pervert Handbook*. Andy's sex drive, however, seems lodged inside his quivering nostrils. He doesn't need to seduce anyone. He needs to sneeze. Director David Schmoeller must have seen a lot of films like this. *The Fan, Don't Answer the Phone,* and *Tattoo* come to mind, since virtually every scene in *The Seduction* seems familiar. For the most part the acting is lackadaisical. Vince Edwards is the sleepy-eyed police captain reluctant to bring Stevens in. Stevens can't hold a straightjacket to Bruce Dern when it comes to demented intensity. And if Fairchild can act, you can't tell by this.

R / 1982 / Media

▲ SEEMS LIKE OLD TIMES

A comedy with more than one dog is usually short on inspiration. This Neil Simon effort requires about a dozen of them. They all belong to Goldie Hawn, an attorney with a weakness for lost souls—canine and human. She's married to Charles Grodin, a stuffy nominee for Attorney General, but when her mutt of an ex-husband, Chevy Chase, shows up on the lam for a bank-robbery frameup, she takes him in for a dose of T-bone and sympathy. This is the sort of film where Goldie's Mexican maid warns, "ju'd better wear slippers, the dog's beeen on the stairs again." That, alas, is about the level of humor in a surprising lemon from Simon's assembly line. The cast itself is abundantly appealing. Hawn is an adorable dingaling, Grodin always works wonders with scraps, and Chase's irony helps deflect the goo. Nonetheless, theirs is a losing battle with a script thrown to the dogs.

PG / 1981 / RCA/Columbia

▲ **SEMI-TOUGH**

If, because of Dan Jenkins's funny novel, you think this movie is about pro football, surprise. The game action is limited pretty much to brief flashes. The rest of the time the story revolves around some silly people who are into an EST-like consciousness-raiser called BEST. Only when Jill Clayburgh is onscreen is there much to watch. As the woman the pro footballers Burt Reynolds and Kris Kristofferson are scrimmaging over, she creates some zany moments that recall Jean Arthur's best comedies. Too many scenes are random, though, and there is something grim about watching a pair of middle-aged men try to get by as cute jocks. The title should have been *Butch Reynolds and the Touchdown Kris.*

R / 1977 / CBS/Fox

▲ **THE SENDER**

The minute he walks in the joint (a very laid-back loony bin) and begins telepathically distributing thoughts that arouse nightmarish visions of rats, roaches, and fires, you know this kid is a real big sender. What you don't know is what in the world is going on. The plot, written by Thomas (*Carny*) Baum, is a Freudian's delight, concerning a 20-year-old man, Yugoslavian-born Zeljko Ivanek, who is followed around by his mom, Shirley Knight, or maybe it's only a ghost of his mom. She seems to have the idea that he's a Christ figure, and Ivanek does, indeed, project the gaunt, hollow-eyed look popularized by actors who have portrayed movie Jesuses. Sensitive shrink Kathryn (*Yes, Giorgio*) Harrold is sure she can figure out a way to help him, even though the mental hospital already has one patient who thinks he's the Messiah. Director Roger Christian, meanwhile, fills the screen with blizzards of ominous presences and illusory scares. He won an Oscar for set decoration on *Star Wars,* but this is a rat's nest of a movie in more ways than one. There's one striking scene when Ivanek, in the

process of undergoing electroshock therapy, transmits his surge of pain to the treatment room staff, sending all of them into a balletic slow-motion frenzy. But even that turns out just to be in everyone's mind. None of the goings-on restore anyone's faith in either mental institutions or moviemakers.

R / 1982 / Paramount

▲ **THE SENTINEL**

Poor Cristina Raines may have wished she was anywhere else as she wandered through the gore of this satanic schlock. It was a droll notion to utilize a Brooklyn brownstone as the gateway to hell. But that's it for subtlety. The cast, including Ava Gardner, Jose Ferrer, John Carradine, and Christopher Walken, had to wade through a lot of noxious yuck to collect their salaries. A highlight is corpse-noshing, the latest in pop demonology.

R / 1977 / MCA

▲ **SEPTEMBER 30, 1955**

An offbeat little movie—named for the day James Dean died in his silver Porsche—this is not about the actor himself but about a young college student in Arkansas who ties his life to Dean's screen persona. The boy apes his hero—bongos, red "Rebel" jackets, motorcycles, and all—earning a friend's suggestion that like his role model he is "sick, affected, and weird." Dean's death sends him into a day of mourning that ends tragically when a girlfriend's prank backfires. As the Dean disciple, Richard Thomas gives an intelligent performance, although it is a pale imitation of Dean's own sexually charged presence. Susan Tyrell is suitably hysterical in her standardized sleaze role. And Dennis Quaid (then known primarily for being Randy's brother) is impressive as Thomas's pal. Still, Leonard Rosenmam's sound track, echoing the music he wrote for *East of Eden* and *Rebel Without a Cause,* recalls how memorable Dean's own films were and how forgettable, for all its interesting experimentation, this one is.

PG / 1978 / N/A

▲ SERIAL

It's so easy to goof on California's Marin County, man. Like, it's the kind of space where a shrink, played by Peter Bonerz, can give a kid a Gay Bruce doll to work through his hostilities. And a hot tub isn't something you draw in a bathroom— it's for when you're feeling hassled. So this movie's vibes—taken from the Cyra McFadden satire—are so negative that they're really a kick. Martin Mull is this dude who has not mellowed out. He's into the most bizarre behavior, like wearing suits, fearing orgies, hating lentil loaf, and despising minister Tom Smothers, who does the most pair-bondings. Mull's wife, Tuesday Weld, can't really relate to him—after all, she has had her consciousness raised by pals like Sally Kellerman in her women's group, and their daughter has joined a love cult. Director Bill Persky's dizzyingly intercut vignettes of life in the bike lane are a riot. So is the movie. Awesome, really.

R / 1980 / Paramount

▲ THE SERPENT'S EGG

Berlin in the '20s. Thousands live on the edge of despair, haunting sleazy debauched cabarets. Sound familiar? David Carradine is an alcoholic circus acrobat. Liv Ullmann is a valiant cabaret performer and sister-in-law. Unfortunately, Liv is no Liza, and *Egg* is a rotten *Cabaret*. Cacophony, brutality, and death surround the couple, but Ullmann can only struggle with wooden dialogue while Carradine is just wooden. Neither engages in sympathy. This is one of those Ingmar Bergman movies where the unrelieved anguish leaves one wondering why, if the director had to exorcize his demons, he should subject audiences to them. This movie is only for thrill-seekers who want to see Liv with chartreuse hair.

R / 1978 / Lightning

▲ SEVEN SAMURAI

It was an event when Japanese director Akira Kurosawa's 1954 masterpiece on the absurdity and inevitability of war and humanity's apparently indestructible ability to survive was released on video. It demonstrates why the starkly beautiful black-and-white film is often cited by cinema buffs as one of the greatest ever made. (It inspired the less classic *The Magnificent Seven,* which starred Yul Brynner and Steve McQueen.) The story is set in 16th-century feudal Japan. A farming village is pillaged at every harvest by marauding bandits. The desperate villagers hire seven samurai warriors to protect them, offering only food and shelter as pay. The warriors are led by wise Takashi Shimura, the swaggering, buffoonish Toshiro Mifune, and devastating swordsman Seiji Miyaguchi. Much of the film shows how these three leaders rouse the villagers from their nearly suicidal hysteria and gloom, training them to face the climactic invasion and its terrifying odds. Kurosawa's cinematography, capturing the eloquent faces, the feudal period textures, the look and sound of torrential rains, the farmers constantly scurrying through the dust, provides haunting touches. In one breathtaking scene, Mifune treads in a shallow stream toward a flaming waterwheel as a dying mother hands him her infant. In another, he races barefoot down a steep slope through a forest like a slalom skier. The last-stand combat, filmed in monsoon rains, with horses and falling bodies slapping up dense mud, must rank as one of the greatest battle scenes on film. Mifune and Shimura, who were part of Kurosawa's ad hoc repertory company, are magnificent. Kurosawa himself so influenced major American directors that George Lucas and Francis Coppola helped finance Kurosawa's 1980 color film *Kagemusha* when he couldn't raise enough money in Japan. *Seven Samurai* remains in a class by itself. (In Japanese with subtitles.)

Unrated / 1954 / Embassy

▲ SEXTETTE

Even at 85, nobody did Mae West better than Mae West. *Sextette* was a boudoir musical, based on one of her 1920s stage plays. It concerns a movie superstar whose sixth honeymoon is constantly interrupted by ex-husbands, lovers, business managers, singing waiters, the entire United States Athletic Team, and an international summit meeting. Groping across the generations, the cast includes Ringo Starr, Tony Curtis, George Hamilton, Alice Cooper, Dom De Luise, and Timothy Dalton (1987's James Bond), plus Mae's contemporary, George Raft. Edith Head's costumes push everything out and up, and West herself is shot through so much gauze that at times she seems lost in smog. In a career that was hardly lacking in campiness, West, in her last film, outdid even herself.

PG / 1978 / Media

▲ SHANGHAI SURPRISE

What this movie needs isn't criticism but a stake through the heart. Now this nerve-numbing killer has risen up from the box-office ashes to appear on cable TV and at the local video store and siphon off your time, money, and wits. No one is safe. The first reaction, before torpor sets in and audience members acquire the look of glaze-eyed zombies, is disbelief. That can't be Madonna playing a frumpy '30s-era missionary. The Madonna of those stylish pop songs, videos, and the 1985 film hit *Desperately Seeking Susan* is a sexy, sassy vamp. The lifeless Barbie doll here cannot walk, talk, or say a line without sounding as if she were reciting by rote from a cue card. And that can't be her real-life husband Sean Penn playing a seedy opportunist hired by this mis-sionary to help recover an opium cache. (The mission needs the drugs, lost during the Japanese occupation of China, for medical use.) The Penn of such films as *Bad Boys, Fast Times at Ridgemont High,* and *At Close Range* is an actor of skill and sensitivity. The Penn here is a clod. Aping the young Clark Gable, in tattered shirt and scruffy beard, Penn succeeds only in looking like a twerpy teen in Daddy's clothes. The thud, thud, thud heard by the audience are the stars' attempts at humor, action, and romance falling flat. Under the circumstances, those self-satisfied smirks the Penns keep flashing at each other are maddening. Why didn't Penn, infamous for decking camera-men, zap into action here where it might have done some good? Jim Goddard, of TV's "Ken-nedy" and "Reilly: Ace of Spies" miniseries, is listed as director. Again incredulity. No profes-sional could deliberately make actors look this bad. The dialogue, credited to John Kohn and Robert Bentley, seems improvised by students just beginning a class in English-as-a-second-language. When the jokes, which range from racist to bathroom, fail to liven things up, the

Shanghai Surprise: Sean Penn and Madonna tried to follow the distinguished path of the Burtons, the Lunts, the Oliviers, and other distinguished acting marrieds. This movie fiasco proves they couldn't.

filmmakers throw in a rickshaw chase or a close-up of exploding bodies. A Shanghai surprise, the script explains, is a slick piece of packaging that contains a bomb. Since the description also applies to this movie, perhaps the MPAA, as a service to viewers, should replace its PG-13 rating for *Shanghai Surprise* with a new and more helpful classification: HO, for Hands Off.
PG-13 / 1986 / MGM/UA

▲ SHARKY'S MACHINE

Sometimes little treasures show up in the unlikeliest places. This would seem to be a routine Burt Reynolds cops-and-robbers movie, with a familiar plot: A high-class hooker embroils a leading candidate for governor in murder and corruption. But Reynolds directs the film with uncommon style, using tight close-ups and a moody lighting that add texture to even the most mundane scenes. Playing an Atlanta police sergeant who is demoted to the vice squad and stumbles onto the scandal, he acts with more nuance than he had since *Deliverance*. He also draws uniformly splendid supporting performances from, among others, Earl Holliman as the politician, Vittorio Gassman as the inevitable Mr. Big, Henry Silva as a hit man, Darryl Hickman as a cop on the take, and Bernie Casey, Charles Durning, Brian Keith, and Richard Libertini as Reynolds's cohorts. They and screenwriter Gerald Di Pego (he wrote the TV movie *A Family Upside Down*) manage to turn even minor characters into personalities. Reynolds winds up in a pat romance with the hooker—played nicely by Rachel Ward—and there's a little too much wisecracking. Violence and obscenity, though never arbitrary, are frequent. But this is mostly a film of energetic, gratifying surprises, down to the final cleverly paced shoot-out.
R / 1982 / Warner

▲ SHEENA

A jiggly jungle epic, this film offers an excess of star Tanya Roberts' bare flesh—more than usually permitted in a PG flick. The rest is woeful acting, wobbly direction, and a series of one-line hooters. At least the animals seem authentic (except for Sheena's steed, a horse painted like a zebra since real zebras are too difficult to ride). The spectac-ular Kenya scenery helps compensate, but director John Guillermin and screenwriters David Newman and Lorenzo Semple, Jr., have been at this kind of thing too long. Their plot gimmick has Sheena trying to save her tribe's land from a greedy prince. The film plods after thirty minutes, the just right length of the 1955 TV series that had all the tacky verve this 117-minute feature lacks. Irish McCalla, the original TV Sheena, became a successful painter after the show was cancelled. Tanya's friends should have sent her some brushes.
PG / 1984 / RCA/Columbia

▲ SHERMAN'S MARCH

Calling *Sherman's March* a home movie is a bit like labeling Proust a diarist. Still, the most enchanting moments in Ross McElwee's "nonfiction film" are so mundane and idiosyncratic that you're surprised—then delighted—to see them outside the confines of a family rec room. Pat, a real-life effervescent ingenue, demonstrates her cellulite exercises; Deedee shyly unveils the powdered milk she's stockpiling for Armageddon. Wini looks up from milking the cow in her island hideaway to declare that "the only things that really matter are sex and linguistics." Such scenes end up mixed with readings from Gen. William T. Sherman's Civil War diaries, monologues on nuclear war, and the odd glimpse of Burt Reynolds. The film began in 1981 when McElwee—an alumnus of the MIT graduate film program—set out to retrace Sherman's Civil War devastation of the South. En route to his native North Carolina, McElwee, then 33, was jilted by his girlfriend. He began to brood about the state of his love life. Then he began to film it. Sherman had to take a supporting role in McElwee's awkward encounters with new women and pensive post-mortems with former lovers. Despite the potential for Bergman-style psychodrama, this mission never became so earnest that McElwee couldn't detour off into such sideshows as the mountain retreat of some rock-ribbed survivalists. ("What we're trying to do here," one member explains, "is get back to 'Little House on the Prairie.' ") Car breakdowns, history lessons, and histrionics are all layered in with a novelist's skill and an unflagging sense of humor. While it has few obvious laugh points, *Sherman's March* generates a low chuckle throughout its 2-hour and 30-minute length.

It is a sound that both recognizes the familiarity of the all-American material and marvels that anyone had the wit, patience, and humanity to capture it on film.
Unrated / 1986 / N/A

▲ SHE'S GOTTA HAVE IT

Black sexuality onscreen, or the lack of it, inspired Spike Lee, then 29, a graduate of New York University's film school, to write, direct, produce, and co-star in this exuberantly erotic romance. Lee shot the film with an unknown all-black cast over twelve days in Brooklyn. He did not let a shoestring budget of $175,000 force him to skimp on imagination. Here's a movie (luminously photographed in black and white by Ernest Dickerson) that crackles with energy and racy wit, pun intended. Tracy Camila Johns stars as a graphic designer juggling three lovers. Straight arrow Tommy Redmond Hicks wants marriage. Macho model John Canada Terrell wants a hot-looking mirror image. Lee himself (in a blissfully funny performance) plays No. 3, a skinny bike messenger who wants only to keep this goddess interested. So much cinematic invention has been lavished on this film it sometimes spins out of control, but Lee's joy in making movies informs every frame. No director in 1986 made a more exciting feature debut.
R / 1986 / Key

▲ THE SHINING

Stanley Kubrick, a director who had done just about everything else, tried for the ultimate horror film with this adaptation of Stephen King's novel—and almost achieved it. Jack Nicholson plays a struggling writer prone to bouts of drinking and depression. To get away from it all, he packs up his wife (Shelley Duvall) and young son and takes a job as caretaker of a lodge in the Rockies. Slowly, surely, he goes mad—and the movie flails off into an orgy of psychological terror. Nicholson is, as usual, superb, and Duvall makes the most of her natural wide-eyed innocence. Young Danny Lloyd is also compelling as the son, who it turns out has the gift of ESP—the "shining" of the title. But Kubrick has tried to mix a lot of classic horror elements, with only mixed success. He proves a master at creating a sense of impending dread through music, shadow, and startling camera angles. Toward the end, though, the movie takes a curious twist, with a clumsily introduced time warp that seemingly implicates the lodge itself as a cause of Nicholson's madness. Still, nobody ever claimed to have fully understood all the goings-on in Kubrick's epic *2001* either. Suspend disbelief. *The Shining* is like a near-miss auto accident: You don't know how scared you really were until you start shaking a few hours later.
R / 1980 / Warner

▲ SHOOT THE MOON

From the moment Albert Finney walks out on Diane Keaton, his wife of fifteen years and mother of their four school-age daughters, *Shoot the Moon* reverberates with little jolts of recognition for anyone whose life has been touched by divorce. The film's subject is the shock, pain, and adjustment of the first month of a couple's separation, and despite the obvious emotional engineering, nothing feels pat. Bo (*Melvin and Howard*) Goldman's caustic, honest screenplay can also be prankishly funny, as when the kids must cope with Karen Allen, as the stylish divorcee Finney moves in with, and Peter Weller, as the sexy contractor Keaton takes to her bed. The three younger children are excellent, but Dana Hill (of TV's "Fallen Angel"), as the troubled, back-talking eldest, rakes the heart. Director Alan (*Fame*) Parker keeps the film's melodramatic moments under firm control and elicits remarkable work from his two stars. Keaton is Annie Hall matured, sexually spirited and possessing a fiery new edge. As for Finney, after three recent film fizzles (*Wolfen, Looker, Loophole*), the delight he takes in such meaty material is almost palpable. "You always had such a pretty smile," he says to Keaton, momentarily forgetting that he has just erased her from his life. The longing and loss in that remark is the essence of the film: a hardboiled counter-valentine for the '80s.
R / 1982 / MGM/UA

▲ SHORT CIRCUIT

There's a singular original moment in this defiantly derivative comedy. Discovering an apparent alien being on her premises, Ally (*St. Elmo's*

The Shining: Jack Nicholson has a field day scaring the bejesus out of wife Shelley Duvall and son Danny Lloyd in the Stanley Kubrick horror show that proves even more eerily effective on video.

Fire) Sheedy exclaims delightedly, "Oh, my God! I knew they'd pick me." Obviously, this young woman has seen too many creature features. Obviously, so too have the makers of *Short Circuit.* This movie doesn't just lift from *E.T.* or *Star Wars;* it rips off all the rip-offs of those two blockbusters. Everything is calculated to reward pop-culture consciousness. As Sheedy soon learns, the alien is a runaway robot. On its trail are a likable inventor, Steve (*Cocoon*) Guttenberg, and his sidekick, Fisher (*The Flamingo Kid*) Stevens, as well as the requisite military-industrial buffoons and bullies. Although the film poses as a humanistic fable, it treats humans like joke machines. The robot gallivants around like the Alan Alda of automatons; sensitive and sincere, it interrupts a chase to ponder the beauty of a butterfly. Meanwhile, the actors mechanically sputter wisecracks. In one particularly vulgar se-

quence, the robot proves its humanity by laughing at an anti-Semitic joke. "Spontaneous emotional response!" glows Guttenberg. Director John Badham, who helped perpetuate the high-tech movie trend of the '80s with *WarGames* and *Blue Thunder,* is such a sterile moviemaker that his films look secondhand even when they're trend-setters.

PG / 1986 / CBS/Fox

▲ SHORT EYES

The brutal impact of this prison film makes all those Big Houses that Cagney, Bogie, and Raft did time in seem like day camps. The actors here are less glamorous, but Bruce Davison (the rat-lover in *Willard*), Jose Perez, Nathan George, Shawn Elliot, and Joe Carberry and a number of

real ex-convicts (notably Tito Goya) are uniformly devastating. The story, by Miguel Pinero, is about how a cell block with its own peculiar system of justice copes with a newcomer in for child molesting—a "short eyes" in prison jargon. (Pinero, who served five years in Sing Sing for armed robbery, wrote the movie from his own play and has a small role.) Shot in the Tombs, Manhattan's notorious Men's House of Detention, the film is claustrophobic, intense, and unrelievedly harrowing.
R / 1977 / Lightning

▲ SID AND NANCY

The punk movement in the late '70s had its dog-collared, spike-haired teenage followers shouting rebellion and slam-dancing to often unintelligible music. This film, directed by Alex (*Repo Man*) Cos, doesn't try to explain the phenomenon, yet it remarkably captures the outrageousness of a subculture doomed to self-destruction. It is a nightmarish love story about two of punk's best known figures: Sid Vicious, bass player of the British group the Sex Pistols, and Nancy Spungen, his American groupie girlfriend. The story begins and eventually works its way back to the 1978 night that Vicious, played by British stage actor Gary Oldman, allegedly stabbed and killed Spungen, potently played by New York actress Chloe Webb. (Vicious later died of a heroin overdose.) In between they fight, swear, make love, cope with fame, take heroin, visit Nancy's white-bread family, cut Sid's chest with a razor, and laugh a lot. The film is filled with a dark kind of energy and grotesque wit. Oldman plays Vicious as awkward, insecure, and violent; Webb's Spungen is tantrum-prone yet has a streak of generosity. They both seem very real, though neither will generate much sympathy. They seem only misbegotten, misunderstood, and misdirected. Then again, they probably would have wanted it that way.
R / 1986 / Embassy

▲ SIDEWINDER 1

Vroom, vroom. This is not about snakes. It is about hogs—many, many motorcycles but mainly one called the Sidewinder. Vroom, vroom. The

nonstop footage of motocross (the cross-country motorcycle races) probably exceeds the saturation point for even hard-core dirt bikers. Vroom, vroom. In between races, Alex Cord as a cycle tycoon turns in perhaps the worst performance in the movie, which is saying something since Marjoe Gortner is in the cast too. Hssssssssssss. Snakes would have been better.
PG / 1977 / N/A

▲ THE SILENT PARTNER

Elliot Gould has a basset hound's mug and range of expressions to match. Here his lugubrious presence weighs down an otherwise sprightly film about a Toronto bank teller who empties the till with the unwitting help of a conventional robber. The screenplay is full of understated humor and a spider's web of crosses and double-crosses, most of them provided by a deliciously evil Christopher Plummer as the frustrated thief. Director Daryl Duke had plenty of time to work on the plot; his only previous feature credit was the underappreciated *Payday*, made in 1973.
R / 1979 / Vestron

▲ SILENT RAGE

Silent Rage, an apt description of Chuck Norris's dramatic presentation, was his sixth film but the first done with a major studio (Columbia). It shows. The production values are much better than those in his previous martial arts epics—*The Octagon, An Eye for an Eye,* and *A Force of One.* The script, for once, is not laughable, and the acting is good, especially Ron (*Baker's Dozen*) Silver as a scientist with a conscience and Stephen (*Animal House*) Furst as Chuck's droll sidekick. There's even a convincing romantic interest between Norris and Toni (*I'm Dancing As Fast as I Can*) Kalem. Of course, none of this really matters to hard-core Chuckles fans. They get their money's worth. The bulk of the film is violent foreplay leading up to the showdown between Chuck, a Texas sheriff, and a seemingly indestructible villain, Brian Libby. The latter is a sociopath who has had his genetic makeup altered so that he is an insurance company's dream come true—bullets don't stop him, neither does sulfuric acid injected into his bloodstream, nor fire, nor a four-story fall to asphalt, nor being hit by a Jeep. Even Chuck can't finish him off, which left the door wide open for a sequel Norris never seemed to get around to.

R / 1982 / RCA/Columbia

▲ SILKWOOD

Since her death in 1974, Karen Silkwood has become a symbol of the antinuclear-power movement. An employee at Oklahoma's Kerr-McGee nuclear plant, Silkwood, then 28, was on her way to a meeting with a *New York Times* reporter when she was killed in an auto accident. It was said that she was carrying papers documenting dangerous conditions at the plant. The papers were never found, but her estate successfully sued Kerr-McGee and was awarded $10.5 million. Director Mike (*The Graduate*) Nichols and screenwriters Nora Ephron and Alice Arlen have remolded the story in terms more human than propagandistic. As played by Meryl Streep, Silkwood is a sassy, slightly promiscuous, resolutely average woman caught up in extraordinary circumstances. Nichols wisely gives Streep the screen time to fill out the character: a Texas-born mother of three who loses custody of her kids to her common-law husband and moves to Oklahoma to start over again. In the two years before she dies, she enjoys an on-off relationship with a fellow worker (Kurt Russell) and a nonsexual friendship with a lesbian roommate, played by Cher in a performance that surprised those who

Silkwood: Meryl Streep and Cher try to sort out their personal emotions in the midst of a bitter dispute involving an accident at a nuclear-power facility.

thought of her as merely a leftover pop icon. Cher inhabits her role (reportedly a composite of several women in Silkwood's life) with ease and beguiling naturalness. Streep must work harder to stay life-size. The Texas accent, the cheap wardrobe, and the behavior (Karen likes to flash a bare breast now and then to shock her co-workers) come off as cosmetic touches at first. But Streep generates tremendous emotional power as Silkwood steals documents to prove her case against the company. The scenes in which Streep's skin must be scrubbed after being "cooked" (exposed to radiation) are harrowing. The film seems false in making the plant managers stereotypical bad guys and unconvincing when it tries to argue the case of Silkwood's martyrdom, but it soars magnificently when it confines itself to the drama of one woman's courage in renouncing complacency for action.
R / 1983 / Embassy

▲ SILVERADO

Here's a Western for people who think they hate Westerns. They don't, of course. It's just that they haven't seen one done right in years (Clint Eastwood's *The Outlaw Josey Wales* in 1976 had been the last in a long, great line including *High Noon, The Searchers, Shane, Rio Bravo, Butch Cassidy and the Sundance Kid,* and *The Wild Bunch*). *Silverado* contains elements of each of these classics, slyly and affectionately refurbished by director Lawrence Kasdan, who co-wrote the invigorating script with his brother Mark. Kasdan's riskiest notion, and one that pays off handsomely, is casting theater-trained actors to play out his 1880s frontier tale. Kevin Kline and Scott Glenn are two confused cowboys who come to the outlaw town of Silverado (the film was shot near Santa Fe) looking for their place in the world. Both have a yen for pretty homesteader Rosanna Arquette. Kline runs the saloon owned by corrupt sheriff Brian Dennehy, and Glenn must settle a score with an evil cattle baron, Ray Baker. When the bad guys kidnap a small boy and beat his mother, the heroes join forces with Danny Glover, as a sinned-against black man, and Kevin Costner, as Glenn's sex-and-trigger-happy brother. Kline, Glenn, and Glover have never been better, and Costner showed the spark of a future star. The 132-minute film teems with scene-stealing supporting characters. Dennehy, Jeff Goldblum

(as a gambler), and Monty Python's John Cleese (as a Limey lawman) may be the most unlikely villains in shoot-'em-up history. Amid these macho fireworks, the women fight a losing battle for screen time. Arquette makes a strong first impression and then vanishes. Kasdan also loses his verve with an offbeat flirtation between Kline and a saloon hostess, brilliantly played by Linda Hunt. This astonishing actress packs more wit, style, and sassy self-assurance into her tiny frame than a wagonload of starlets. "What can I do you for, stranger?" she teases Kline from her perch behind the bar. Alas, Kline's kisses are reserved for his horse, leaving a promisingly unconventional love story unplumbed. But why nitpick? With its sweeping vistas, spiffy shoot-outs, and surefire performances, *Silverado* is a lalapalooza.
PG-13 / 1985 / RCA/Columbia

▲ SILVER BEARS

Columbia had planned to release this film in November 1977 but withdrew it to concentrate the studio's resources on the megapromotion of *Close Encounters*. They might as well have put off this version of Paul Erdman's 1974 novel about international silver trading for another thirty or forty years. Maybe by then it will seem funnier. Tom Smothers is wasted. A pre-"Moonlighting" Cybill Shepherd reaches a comedic low that the grim *At Long Last Love* only hinted at. Michael Caine and Louis Jourdan simply look embarrassed. So will you if anyone hears you watched this crashing bore.
PG / 1978 / USA

▲ SILVER BULLET

As werewolf movies go—and the woods have been full of them for years—this is relatively tolerable. It was written by Stephen King from his short novel *Cycle of the Werewolf*. If it seems at times that King might have dashed the screenplay off while delivering phone books to make a little extra money, it is literate and occasionally funny, with a minimum of severed heads. The movie is also given substance by two winning performances. Corey Haim, then 13, is appealing as a wheelchair-bound boy who comes upon the werewolf, shoots it in the eye with a fireworks rocket, and comes to understand that these crea-

tures aren't the sort to let bygones be bygones. Gary Busey, as Haim's ne'er-do-well uncle, adds some quirks to his standard skeptical adult role. The werewolf's civilian identity is tipped off too early, though. Moreover, Carlo Rambaldi—the effects wizard who created *E.T.*—got carried away. He crafted a werewolf that reportedly was able to smile and wink, when all it does onscreen is glare in a humorless manner. In fact, this is a pretty mean-spirited character all around, with none of the saving graces of the misunderstood werewolves of the past. It would be unfair to tip off the ending, but the title does not stem from a cameo appearance by the Lone Ranger.
R / 1985 / Paramount

▲ SIMON

Simon says: "I'm a toaster." What nonsense! Simon says: "No more children named Free, Moonbeam, Sky, Rain." What sense. Written and directed by frequent Woody Allen collaborator Marshall Brickman, this movie is loaded with sensible-sounding nonsense, reminiscent of (though not as funny as) *Sleeper*. The idea is promising: A group of heavy thinkers at the Institute for Advanced Concepts wonders how earthlings would react to an extraterrestrial visitor. So, quick as a computer can find a Columbia psychology professor named Simon Mendelssohn, he is transformed into a zany outer-space creature played by Alan Arkin. Max Wright is marvelous as a mad scientist. Brickman tees off on modern-day annoyances like Hawaiian music in elevators, diet books, and drivers who block intersections. However, some jokes fall dreadfully flat, e.g., a commune that worships "the sacred box" and takes its Scripture from *TV Guide*. Brickman's barbs generally are amusing, but the sum of the parts doesn't quite constitute a comic whole.
PG / 1980 / Warner

▲ SINBAD AND THE EYE OF THE TIGER

Patrick Wayne, the Duke's son, swashbuckles through an Errol Flynn part, while Taryn Power, Tyrone's daughter, is somehow credible falling in love with a baboon (actually, a metamorphosed prince). The facsimile beasts in this amiable $5 million yarn roam the landscape thanks to a stop-

motion technique called Dynarama that has a legacy of its own. The process traces back to *The Beast from 20,000 Fathoms* in 1953.
G / 1977 / RCA/Columbia

▲ SITTING DUCKS

Contributions are hereby solicited for the National Fund to Prevent Henry Jaglom from Making Another Movie. Since he won praise for helping edit *Easy Rider*, Jaglom has been struggling to make it as a director—no, make that *auteur*. His surrealistic *A Safe Place* (with Tuesday Weld and Orson Welles) and *Tracks* (with Dennis Hopper) sold very few tickets here, but did sell a few gullible critics and European moviegoers on his talent. With this quacker, however, he proves only one thing: A movie does not have to be expensive, flashy, and filled with stars to be pretentious and boring. Jaglom's cast of second-line actors meanders through a listless, silly plot about two men who abscond with some Mob money. The single delight is Jaglom's wife, Patrice Townsend, charming and sexy in a well-scrubbed, wide-eyed way. She could have been a substantial actress if she ever appeared in a real movie.
R / 1980 / Media

▲ SIX PACK

A lot of good singers try acting. A few—Crosby, Sinatra, Streisand, Bowie, and Midler—have a natural affinity for the camera and the gift of never being boring. On the basis of *Six Pack,* his feature film debut, Kenny Rogers was not among the lucky ones. Playing a down-at-the-heels stock car driver who hooks up with half a dozen cute, cussin' urchins, the lethargic Rogers is clearly dependent on audience goodwill to see him through. He's not above stacking the deck either. The script (by Mike Marvin and Alex Matter) and direction (Daniel Petrie)—overseen by Kenny's own Lion Share Productions—are geared to make the star irresistible. Shucks, the kids love him. And the women, in particular the gorgeous Erin Gray (of TV's "Silver Spoons"), can't keep their lithe bodies off him, despite his persistent paunch. Even his varmint racing rival, Terry Kiser, can't help admirin' him. Except for a credit song,

"Love Will Turn You Around," this is a straight acting job for Rogers, who can't find an equivalent acting gimmick for the throaty rasp that carries such conviction in his best music. Rogers and the movie keep pushing smarmy, sitcom emotions. There is a sharp, intuitive performance by Diane (*A Little Romance*) Lane, then 17, as the only girl among the kids. But the moral seems to be: Kenny, don't take your beard to Hollywood.
PG / 1982 / CBS/Fox

▲ SIXTEEN CANDLES

For his first feature, screenwriter-turned-director John Hughes, who wrote *Mr. Mom,* came up with a promising premise: In the chaos surrounding her older sister's wedding, Molly Ringwald turns 16, and the occasion passes unheralded by her family. In effect, this noisy contemporary comedy is a consolation party—a celebration of adolescent angst. But as the party-giver, Hughes proves to be an absentminded host. Midway through the movie he loses track of the guest of honor, gets seduced by secondary characters, and allows a sly character comedy to degenerate into yet another beer-and-chased-cars affair. In the process, Hughes also sabotages the considerable talents of Ringwald. She is an unaffected young actress of enormous spunk and ingenuity. But this part is much too passive for her; because Ringwald is such a self-possessed presence on-screen, her shyness and humility aren't convincing. You know the actress could conjure up a snappy comeback, even if the character cannot. In fact, all that passivity lets Anthony Michael Hall, who plays a geek with an eye for Ringwald, pilfer the film. Of course, Ringwald is suffering from the obligatory crush on the senior-class stud (Michael Schoeffling), and the results are just as predictable. As a director, Hughes doesn't show much faith in his screenplay: Instead of letting his characters and dialogue stand on their own, he punctuates scenes with redundant musical punch lines, such as the themes from TV's old "Peter Gunn" and "The Twilight Zone." Despite occasional low-comedy hijinks that raise a few laughs, *Sixteen Candles* is more rowdy than rousing. Still, it was a box-office bonanza and made Hughes the Neil Simon of teen angst.
PG / 1984 / MCA

▲ SIX WEEKS

A movie is in trouble when its saccharine plot centers on the incipient death of a 12-year-old girl. A movie is in trouble when it casts Britisher Dudley Moore as a politician running for Congress in southern California. A movie is in trouble when it uses Mary Tyler Moore as an austere, rigidly stylish woman mulling over an affair with a married man while in emotional turmoil over her daughter's refusal to take treatments for leukemia. A movie is in trouble when the dying daughter, as played by Katherine Healy, oozes precocious piety from every pore. A movie is in trouble when it ladles out a soupy piano score to heighten the gloom. A movie is in trouble when, as in this one directed by Tony Bill and written by David Seltzer, it almost makes the audience wish the supposedly sympathetic child would hurry up and expire.
PG / 1983 / RCA/Columbia

▲ SKATEBOARD

A ghost of a fad past, this film is ostensibly about a hustler (Allen Garfield) who gets himself out of hock to gangsters by putting together a money-making skateboard team. It was, however, mainly an excuse for the big wheels of the sport to show off what were known in the skateboarding trade as "rad" or "radical"—that is, breathstopping maneuvers. Skateboard pros Richard Van Der Wyk, Tony Alva, and Steve Monohan do just that, but Ellen Oneal and teen heartthrob Leif Garrett hold their own too. Surprisingly, the rest of the movie isn't bad either: The dialogue is honest, and there is a refreshing lack of superimposed adult moralizing. People who remember the sport or noted its comeback in the late '80s may even find the movie earns that ultimate nod—super rad.
PG / 1978 / N/A

▲ SLAP SHOT

Player-coach Paul Newman incites his third-rate hockey team into storm-trooping maniacs. His dialogue is nearly as blue as his eyes, but the team and the movie end up winners. Here's another box-office reject that deserves to find a new life on video. Newman's performance, which failed to win even an Oscar nomination, remains one of the best of his career.

R / 1977 / MCA

▲ SLAVE OF LOVE

Despite the title, this Russian work is not an X-rated porno flick. Rather, it's about a group of filmmakers caught in postrevolutionary turmoil. A cameraman tries to smuggle out footage of the secret police; he's caught, killed, and the whole company suffers. Some scenes are stunning: lazy, sun-drenched afternoons in the Crimea; a lyrically bloody assassination in a quiet town square; and a runaway trolley car pursued by soldiers on horseback. But most compelling is the knockout performance of star Elena Solovey, who plays a self-centered actress drawn into a real-life drama infinitely more complicated than anything she ever played on screen. (In Russian with subtitles.)

Unrated / 1978 / RCA/Columbia

▲ SLOW DANCING IN THE BIG CITY

What a shame such a great title was wasted on such a lousy film. Paul Sorvino, a fine actor, plays a hard-boiled New York newspaper columnist with a more than passing resemblance to Jimmy Breslin. When not chasing down sappy human interest stories, he falls in love with a beautiful ballerina, Anne Ditchburn, in real life a dancer with the National Ballet of Canada. That she can't act is the least of the movie's problems. The screenplay by Barra Grant, Bess Myerson's daughter, is trite and weak on character development. By the climactic final scene, when Ditchburn insists on performing despite a crippling leg injury, the audience is long since off its toes. This was director John Avidsen's first outing after *Rocky;* he returned one movie too soon.

PG / 1979 / N/A

▲ THE SLUGGER'S WIFE

Neil Simon did something courageous and, as it turned out, foolhardy with this film about a two-career marriage between an Atlanta Braves outfielder, Michael O'Keefe, and his rock singer wife, Rebecca De Mornay: He wrote a script that doesn't sound like Neil Simon. Perhaps he was responding to past criticism that even his most artful stage comedies—*The Odd Couple, The Sunshine Boys, Chapter Two*—sound artificial when transferred to the screen. But that light-hearted literate artifice, exemplified in the screen pairing of, say, Marsha Mason and Richard Dreyfuss in *The Goodbye Girl,* is what makes Simon an original. In *The Slugger's Wife* Simon left his personality at home, leaving O'Keefe and De Mornay to play what might be called "the flat couple." The plot is determinedly old hat, with O'Keefe unable to hit homers unless the little woman is in the stands. All the modern trappings (high-tech discos, rock songs, a not-so-happy ending) can't disguise the fact that these are 1950s characters trapped in a 1980s time warp. Little wonder then that director-turned-actor Martin Ritt steals the picture as the veteran Braves manager, a throwback who gets Simon's only good lines. "You know what makes really good champagne?" he snarls after a bad day. "Winning." Let the record book show that O'Keefe and De Mornay bear the burden of the plot and of Hal Askby's sluggish direction with game good humor. O'Keefe does not make a very convincing slugger; with that swing he couldn't hit his grandmother if she walked across the plate. But he conveys a real sense of love and loss. De Mornay—an actress with looks and smarts—makes that dismay understandable. Terrific as the tart with the heart of a cash register in *Risky Business,* De Mornay can make a cliché sound freshly minted. It's a gift that comes in handy in *The Slugger's Wife.*

PG-13 / 1985 / RCA/Columbia

▲ SMOKEY AND THE BANDIT

Remember when Burt Reynolds and Sally Field were in love and made cute little smoochy movies together? It was only a decade ago, before Sally went her own way, married somebody else, and won two Oscars. But *Smokey,* the first of their four films, has taken on a nostalgic appeal now. The stupid plot, about smuggling a truckload of Coors out of Texas, is meant to be ignored. As is everything else except jolly Jackie Gleason as the dumb, blubbery sheriff leading the posse of patrol cars. But through the haze of car chases, Burt and Sally really did get something going onscreen. Whether trading insults about musical

tastes (he likes country, she prefers Sondheim) or appreciative glances, they had something the film didn't. Real heat.
PG / 1977 / MCA

▲ SMOKEY AND THE BANDIT II

Burt Reynolds and Sally Field again squandered their formidable talents in this dim-witted sequel that again involves cars, cussin', CBs, and concrete cowboys. The 1977 *Smokey* grossed an amazing $250 million—even as it grossed out city-slicker critics. *Smokey II* is a pointless carbon copy. Abetted by Jerry Reed in his eighteen-wheeler, Bandit Burt and Sally (again a runaway bride) are back revving up a black Trans Am with sheriff Jackie Gleason in frustrated pursuit. This time their cargo is a pregnant elephant. As before, the humor is cheap and verges on obscene when zany Dom De Luise plays a gynecologist pressed into service as a veterinarian. Gleason gets extra mileage by playing two lawmen brothers—Reggie, a mountie, and Gaylord, a Texas patrolman who arrives with his braided boyfriend PT (for "Perfect Ten"). Director Hal Needham's feel for vehicular mayhem helps the pace, but *Bandit II* quickly runs out of gas.
PG / 1980 / MCA

▲ SMOKEY AND THE BANDIT III

It was sad to see an entertainer of the quality of the late Jackie Gleason in an exploitive, boring film like this one. The first two movies in this series will never be mistaken for *Hamlet* but at least had some virtues: Burt Reynolds's charm and wit and the flashy car chases of director Hal Needham. This bottom-of-the-rain-barrel enterprise, directed by Dick (TV's "The Gambler") Lowry, has only Gleason, glumly reprising his role as the southern sheriff with an accent that sounds like a cross between Brooklyn, Atlanta, and someplace incomprehensible—Bulgaria, maybe. The jokes are a succession of smarmy references to genitals, body wastes, and sex. This film's only hint of vitality is Jerry Reed, also an alum of the earlier *Smokey*s, who gets to drive the Banditmobile and be more or less a hero. Colleen (*They All Laughed*) Camp reads her leaden lines with the animation of a zombie; Mike Henry, as Gleason's dim-witted son, is about as funny

as a turnip; comedian Pat McCormick and singer Paul Williams, as a long-short father-son team who lure Gleason out of retirement for a cross-country race, just look foolish. The road scenes are routine. Even the vehicles aren't appealing.
PG / 1983 / MCA

▲ S.O.B.

In 1970 Blake Edwards starred his wife, Julie Andrews, in *Darling Lili*, which went way over budget and didn't enhance Edwards's reputation among Hollywood money men. He eventually climbed back to favor with the *Pink Panther* series and *"10"*, but he obviously stayed angry. *S.O.B.* is a poison pen letter to the industry, a film of undisguised hatred. Edwards's sense of the funny sank to sour insults, with ugly characters like a transvestite studio head (Robert Vaughn), a lesbian agent (Shelley Winters), and a back-stabbing columnist (Loretta Swit). The movie's only redeeming feature is the acting. Robert Preston is a raffish delight as a Malibu quack with a drug connection, William Holden (in his last performance; he died the same year) plays an aging director with a penchant for teenagers, and Larry (J.R.) Hagman is the epitome of yes-man sleaze. Guilty of overkill is Richard Mulligan as the Edwards figure, a producer driven mad by the rejection of his $40 million family musical. He labors to turn his G-rated project into a porn triumph, and the scene where Mulligan tries to convince his prissy mate (Andrews) to bare her breasts is a howl. Julie has rarely thrown herself into a role with such abandon. "I'm going to show my boobies," she asserts, and does so. For the record, they're lovely. The film is not.
R / 1981 / CBS/Fox

▲ SO FINE

The only thing praiseworthy in this slapstick sitcom with four-letter words, exhausted jokes, and no characterization is the daring it took to title such a feeble farce *So Fine*. Ryan O'Neal, whose charm grows less palpable and more processed with each film, stars as a college prof on leave to help Dad, Jack Warden, save the family dress business from loan sharks. There's a nifty notion of satire in Andrew (*The In-Laws*)

Bergman's screenplay: O'Neal outdoes Brooke and her Calvins by inventing designer jeans with see-through holes in the derriere. The subsequent buttock-flashing TV ad campaign has a breezy bite to it. But Bergman, in his directing debut, can't keep the rhythm going. Instead, he belabors O'Neal's pursuit by hot-blooded Mariangela Melato, the Italian spitfire of Lina Wertmuller's *Swept Away*. Melato is certainly lively, but her role as the adulterous wife of bad guy Richard Kiel, the seven-foot two-inch, 335-pound giant from the James Bond flicks, reduces her to a sexual sight gag. At one point she complains to O'Neal that her husband is "how you say, not al dente enough in bed." *So Fine* is, how you say, similarly limp.

R / 1981 / Warner

▲ A SOLDIER'S STORY

All hail Adolph Caesar, an astonishing actor who brought this film version of Charles Fuller's Pulitzer prizewinning *A Soldier's Play* to gritty life. Though some Hollywood slickness seeped in, in his first major movie role Caesar (who died two years later) was always on target and at the center of this drama set at an Army base in Louisiana near the end of World War II. He plays an aging, bantam-weight bundle of muscle and malice, a drill sergeant contemptuous of his white superiors for keeping his black platoon functioning as a base-ball team and out of the war. He's scornful, too, of the subservient men under him. Twisted by self-hatred, exacerbated when he drives a "yas-sah-boss" soldier (touchingly played by Larry

A Soldier's Story: Howard Rollins added his star power to the film version of Charles Fuller's honored play about murder on a military post, but the result is more earnest than exciting.

Riley) to suicide, Caesar is a ticking time bomb of racial tensions. The film opens with his murder (the killer is not revealed until the climax) and continues in flashback as a black Army attorney, played with movie-star handsomeness and stinging intelligence by Howard Rollins, interrogates black and white suspects on the base. Director Norman Jewison encouraged Fuller, who wrote his own screenplay, to emphasize the whodunit aspects of the story. As a result, much of the play's trenchant observation about prejudice within the black community is compromised for the sake of conventional movie narrative. But the sergeant is a character that nags at the conscience, and, thanks to Fuller's writing and Caesar's performance, the power of this *Soldier's Story* is impressive.
PG / 1984 / RCA/Columbia

▲ SOMEBODY KILLED HER HUSBAND

Somebody also killed this picture's chance to be a solid romantic thriller, but it wasn't Farrah Fawcett-Majors (that's what she was called until she and Lee Majors divorced). Her acting is creditable, and her "Charlie's Angels" look is refined to an appealing sensuality. Farrah is cast as an unhappily married mother who falls instantly in love with toy salesman Jeff Bridges, doing a Richard Dreyfuss *Goodbye Girl* number. The lovers discover her husband stabbed, and to establish their innocence they begin a search for the killer. Several grisly murders later, they're still searching, but the audience has stopped caring. The movie's problem may be a result of trying for too much—suspense, amour, and comedy. Or perhaps it is the television flavor of Lamont Johnson's direction (he's in fact a TV pro who also did *The Last American Hero* and *Lipstick*). As Farrah's first serious venture onto the big screen, the film is interesting as a historical footnote, nothing more.
PG / 1978 / N/A

▲ SOME KIND OF HERO

With the notable exception of his two brilliant concert flicks, Richard Pryor has lavished his formidable talents on some astonishingly weak movies. *Some Kind of Hero* is no exception. The screenplay by James Kirkwood and Robert Boris,

based on Kirkwood's novel, is an incoherent mix of comic and dramatic moods. Pryor, home from six years in a North Vietnamese prison camp, finds his wife, Lynne Moody, living with another man. His mother, Olivia Cole, is the victim of a stroke, and his bookstore business is in ruins. When his Army back pay is withheld by red tape, he decides on a life of crime for which he is hilariously unsuited. Director Michael (*Those Lips, Those Eyes*) Pressman offers mostly misdirection to a strong cast, including Margot Kidder as a $200-a-night Beverly Hills call girl, Ray Sharkey as a fellow POW, and Ronny Cox as a sympathetic Army colonel. Characteristically, Pryor carves out solo moments that shrewdly separate him from the rest of the picture. Whether he's gently feeding a rat in his prison cell ("Hey, brother") or standing silently outside an apartment door listening to his wife and daughter professing familial love for another man, Pryor proves equally adept at humor and heartbreak. The rest of the movie tries to get by on borrowed inspiration: a bank robbery from *Take the Money and Run*, a suitcase mixup from *What's Up, Doc?*, a homecoming scene from *The Deer Hunter*. That it succeeds at all is due to Pryor's wizardry at bringing dead scenes to life.
R / 1982 / Paramount

▲ SOMETHING WICKED THIS WAY COMES

The Walt Disney conglomerate was trying to shake its image as a maker of goody two-shoes movies, but that's exactly what this one is, despite some fancy special effects at the end. Two boys, wonderfully played by Shawn Carson and Vidal Petersen, are growing up in a beautiful, bucolic town in the Midwest. Suddenly they get a strange feeling something eerie is about to happen. That something is a carnival, and with it comes the malevolent Mr. Dark. The curious boys sneak under the tent after the show to see Mr. Dark doing some strange things to people— he makes them disappear, he makes them revert to childhood, he makes them go blind. Pretty nasty stuff. Then Mr. Dark sees the boys—and the chase is on. Dark, played with a Dracula-like leer by Jonathan (*Brazil*) Pryce, enlists the help of the beautiful but evil Dust Witch, played by sexy Pam Grier, late of *Fort Apache, the Bronx*. Their showdown with good comes late at night during a raging thunderstorm. Yes, this is a morality tale—the good guys and the bad guys, although one problem is that the film never makes clear why the bad guys are bad. Even Jason Robards, who plays the sympathetic father of one of the boys, seems a bit befuddled by it all. Those who have read the 1962 Ray Bradbury novel on which the film is based know the villains represent Evil with a capital E. Bradbury hoped François Truffaut would direct this film, which might have given it more emotional strength. Steven Spielberg and Sam Peckinpah were interested too, which might have made it more exciting. But Jack Clayton ended up with it, his first film since 1974's *The Great Gatsby*. His climactic scenes, after a slow, almost agonizing start, are all special effects, and here the Disney technologists are clearly light-years behind such modern-day wizards as Spielberg and George Lucas. The sky rolls ominously, the ghosts fly all over the place, the glass shatters—today's moviegoers have seen it before. This is the kind of spooky movie that would have been considered pretty scary in the 1950s; now, unhappily, it's just boring.

PG / 1983 / Disney

▲ SOMETHING WILD

Pay the video rental fee for this whirligig of a movie at your own risk. You enter a fun house and exit through a chamber of horrors. But director Jonathan (*Swing Shift*) Demme provides a hell of a ride. The "something wild" of the title is Melanie (*Body Double*) Griffith. A cunning cupcake, she meets a yuppie exec (Jeff Daniels) at a New York diner and offers him a lift back to his office. Instead she speeds the scared nerd to New Jersey. They wind up at a hot-sheets motel where she handcuffs him to a bed for a sexual workout that leaves him panting for more. Just when you think you've got the plot figured, Demme and screenwriter E. Max Frye throw in a toolbox full of monkey wrenches. Daniels doesn't tell Griffith he's divorced; she doesn't tell him she's setting him up. Griffith, suddenly gentle, goes home to visit her mother and introduces Daniels as her husband. Then they attend her tenth high school reunion, where her real ex-husband (Ray Liotta, in a smashing performance) shows up. Hubby is an ex-con, and he involves Daniels in armed robbery. What had started as a carnal comedy shifts into violent domestic drama.

Those who stick with the switch will be rewarded with a powerhouse piece of filmmaking. Griffith proves equally expert at tickling the funny bone and touching the heart. And Daniels is without peer at showing the frustrations gnawing at the average Joe. But the movie belongs to Demme. His best films, including *Citizens Band, Melvin and Howard,* and the Talking Heads concert film, *Stop Making Sense,* speak eloquently of the dislocation in American life. There are no villains, just people fighting to belong to something. Tak Fujimoto's camera shows how divorce dots the country with half-empty houses; Daniels's suburban home, stripped of all but mementos of the family that was, looks like a war zone. Once again Demme has made a comedy suffused with melancholy. Once again he resists easy categorization with a quirky, personal film that says something disturbingly funny about the way we live. Don't ask how he gets box-office-minded Hollywood to support his risk taking. A simple hallelujah will suffice.

R / 1986 / HBO/Cannon

▲ SOMEWHERE IN TIME

Somewhere in time there may have been a place for movies like this one. But not here, not now. To be fair, the story, while preposterous, has some charm. (It was adapted from his novel *Bid Time Return* by sci-fi veteran Richard Matheson, who earlier wrote *The Incredible Shrinking Man.*) While seeking inspiration for a new drama, a young playwright (Christopher Reeve) falls helplessly in love with a picture of a turn-of-the-century actress (Jane Seymour) and wills himself back in time to find her. Most of the film is shot at the splendid old Grand Hotel on Michigan's Mackinac Island. The setting and Seymour are entrancing. Reeve, though, spends much of his screen time awkwardly carrying on conversations with himself. Perhaps the fault lies with director Jeannot Szwarc who, if his other credits (*Bugs* and *Jaws 2*) are any indication, had more experience handling lower forms of life than actors.

PG / 1980 / MCA

▲ SOPHIE'S CHOICE

On the printed page, William Styron's bestselling novel was at once overwhelming and overwrought. Director Alan (*Klute*) Pakula's faithful film version (he also wrote the screenplay—his first) shows the same strengths and weaknesses. But in Meryl Streep, Pakula found an actress to make such criticism seem nitpicking. Playing Sophie, a Polish-Catholic survivor of Auschwitz who takes refuge in Brooklyn from the dark secrets of her past, Streep dominates the screen with her uncanny emotional range, an unerring Polish accent, and a radiant carnality that cuts through the chilly remoteness of some of her past screen roles. In this, her eighth film, Streep earned an Oscar and validated the praise that had been heaped on her since her 1977 debut in *Julia*. As Nathan, the anguished Jew who befriends and berates Sophie in an all-consuming passion, Kevin Kline, of Broadway's *Pirates of Penzance,* acts a difficult role with charm and subtle menace. The scenes in which he nurses Streep back to health are among the loveliest romantic interludes ever committed to film. The pair's dependence on each other is almost palpable, heightening the harrowing violence of the film's latter half. Pakula's direction, especially in the concentration camp scenes, abounds in understated, assured touches. His inspiration deserts him only with Stingo, the book's young southern writer, who as the movie's narrator spouts Styronisms ("In making love she was beating back death") better left unspoken. Though Peter (*Dragonslayer*) MacNicol plays the role impeccably, Stingo's comical attempts to lose his virginity seem gratuitous in a film that runs 2 hours and 37 minutes. No matter. Streep and Kline, embodying their characters in a way that goes beyond performing, obliterate the excesses on their straight and stirring journey to the heart.

R / 1983 / CBS/Fox

▲ SORCERER

Director William Friedkin's first film after *The Exorcist* was not, despite the title, another satanic saga. Rather, four desperadoes trapped in a corrupt South American country undertake a suicide mission to drive two nitroglycerin-loaded trucks through two hundred miles of mountain, desert, and rain forest. Roy Scheider repeats the taut performance he gave in Friedkin's *The French Connection,* but he and the rest of the international cast are overwhelmed by the blood and bullets of the special effects department. Something in this melodrama (based on 1953's *The*

Wages of Fear with Yves Montand) explodes every couple of minutes. *Sorcerer* itself remains a dud.

PG / 1977 / N/A

▲ SOUL MAN

On the surface the premise of this film is as contrived as a tabloid headline: An overprivileged, underfinanced white student, C. Thomas (*The Hitcher*) Howell, takes super-tanning pills to win a minority scholarship to Harvard Law School. Howell, who initially makes as convincing a black as Al Jolson, takes getting used to. Then there's the predictability of practically every plot twist—Howell falls in love with a beautiful black student, Rae Dawn Chong, while keeping his identity a secret. But hold on. Despite its drawbacks, *Soul Man* becomes a charming, funny comedy, and prerelease worries to the contrary, director Steven (*House*) Miner's film succeeds at being antiracist. (There were protests anyway, especially from Harvard students.) In one scene Howell has dinner with an upper-crust Boston family; while they eat, the family members visualize him variously as an angry slave, an angrier pimp, and Prince. The message throughout is clear, but coproducer Carol Black's script is less pedantic than that of 1970's *Watermelon Man,* in which a bigoted and white Godfrey Cambridge awakes to find he has changed color. Howell and Chong, whose subtlety works well against the film's broad comedy, make an impressive duo. Arye (*Exterminator II*) Gross, too, is terrific as Howell's fast-talking roomie. The supporting cast also includes James Earl Jones as a gruff, demanding professor, Max (*Alf*) Wright as a neurotic analyst, comedian Jeff Altman as a slow-witted building superintendent, and even First Son Ron Reagan as a lily-white jock.

PG-13 / 1986 / New World

▲ SOUP FOR ONE

The main character is short and weird. He is supremely ill-equipped for the swinging singles scene he is surrounded by in Manhattan. He is sensitive and funny, and he has a tall friend who revels in the opportunities life sends his way. Woody Allen and Tony Roberts it isn't, though.

Saul (*Ticket to Heaven*) Rubinek and Gerrit Graham it is, and thanks to them, *Soup for One* sometimes succeeds. Rubinek, a Canadian, plays a newswriter for an underground cable TV station. He describes one of his typical blind dates as "an ex-addict from Queens who had herself surgically altered to resemble Janis Joplin." But he's also a hopeless romantic who carries in his wallet a police artist's sketch of his dream girl. The suave Graham is a news anchorman. He corrals Rubinek into a singles weekend at a hotel in the Catskills, where the shy friend is vigorously seduced by SCTV's Andrea Martin. There he also meets an approximation of his dream girl, Marcia ("Welcome Back, Kotter") Strassman. Strassman owns a roommate referral service, and her father is an adult bookstore owner who is having a Beethoven's Birthday Sale. ("Did you ever see so many men in raincoats looking for a bargain?" he asks.) So the film is funny. It is also by turns, broad, tasteless, tacky, and achingly familiar.

R / 1982 / Warner

▲ SOUTHERN COMFORT

Anyone who has ridden the rapids of the Chattahoochee River will find this familiar territory indeed. Comparisons with *Deliverance* are inevitable, since this film is about nine Louisiana National Guardsmen who get lost on maneuvers in the bayous and run afoul of the native Cajuns. Missing, however, is the tremendous tension that existed between hunter and hunted in *Deliverance*. The screenplay basically boils down to two questions: Who will be the next to go, and how grisly will it be? (One standard clue is the higher the star billing, the longer the character is likely to last.) The performances are uniformly good. Keith Carradine strikes the right chord as a wisecracking Guardsman who is forced to take charge, and Powers Boothe, who won an Emmy for his portrayal of the Reverend Jim Jones, does a splendid job of speaking softly and carrying a big knife. As he proved in *The Warriors* and *The Long Riders,* director Walter Hill has a keen visual sense. He captures the brooding bayou country and seldom-glimpsed Cajun subculture effectively. Yet it is the story itself that finally fails to live up to its exotic surroundings.

R / 1981 / Embassy

▲ SPACEHUNTER: ADVENTURES IN THE FORBIDDEN ZONE

Peter Strauss, in his first feature since starring on TV's "Rich Man, Poor Man" series, played a space salvage pilot in the Harrison Ford mold—handsome, surly, and invincible. Molly Ringwald, is atrocious as his whining, sulky sidekick. (John Hughes surely came to her rescue with *Sixteen Candles, The Breakfast Club,* and *Pretty in Pink.*) Together they set out to track down three women who have been kidnapped by the evil Overdog (Michael Ironside), a half-man, half-machine who presides over something called the Forbidden Zone, a kind of mausoleum for space derelicts. Strauss and Ringwald make the usual trip over the usual bleak terrain and meet the usual alien monsters: flying vultures, mutant children who throw hand grenades, gorgeous but deadly Amazones. Of course, they all end up in a big showdown with Overdog. The dialogue is idiotic, the sound too loud, and the acting, with the exception of Strauss, terrible. The movie's low point may be when Overdog, strapped to some kind of cherry-picker device, grunts and drools as one of his cronies undresses a woman prisoner. The impression is that the makers of this movie—Lamont (*Cattle Annie and Little Britches*) Johnson directed it—have tried to touch all the bases. They've succeeded only in making a kind of *Valley Girl Meets George Lucas,* with a little soft-core porn thrown in.

R / 1983 / RCA/Columbia

▲ A SPECIAL DAY

With her Fascist husband and six children gone for the day—to celebrate Hitler's prewar pact-signing visit to Rome—working-class housewife Sophia Loren finds something better to do than wash the dishes in the sink. Lonely and unfulfilled, she meets up with solitary neighbor-across-the-court Marcello Mastroianni for a brief bittersweet interlude. Both Sophia, as fetchingly haggard as in *Two Women,* and Marcello, as an aging gay, deliver sensitive performances. But for all the ambitious themes of Fascism, feminism, and homosexuality, the film, written and directed by Ettore Scola, remains insubstantial. (In Italian with subtitles.)

Unrated / 1977 / N/A

▲ THE SPECIAL EDITION: CLOSE ENCOUNTERS OF THE THIRD KIND

Whatever the motivation, this reissue of Steven Spielberg's 1977 sci-fi hit with a beefed-up ending is far superior to the original. True, much remains the same. Richard Dreyfuss's scary encounter at the railroad tracks, the kidnapping of Melinda Dillon's child, and the swooshing spaceships in the night are as they were. But Spielberg has wisely shortened the time it takes to get everyone to the mountain for the big encounter with the alien mothership. The special effects at the end are even more dazzling: Not only do we get a closer look at the friendly space creatures with their kidnapped earthlings, but there's a glimpse inside the saucer itself. Spielberg has been criticized for employing pyrotechnics at the expense of human drama; here he has made a film that is religious in its hope. The notion of movie ''special editions'' is not to be encouraged: Why go to Spielberg's next film, since it may just be an imperfect first draft? In this one case, however, the revised version merits a second look.

PG / 1980 / RCA/Columbia

▲ SPIES LIKE US

The most fitting moment in *Spies Like Us* is also the film's most damning. In the middle of the shenanigans perpetrated by bumbling intelligence agents Dan Aykroyd and Chevy Chase, Bob Hope suddenly saunters into a tent in Pakistan brandishing a golf club. ''Mind if I play through?'' he asks. Hope's cameo makes perfect sense: *Spies Like Us* tries to imitate the kind of freewheeling, globe-trotting, buddy-buddy comedy that Hope and Bing Crosby made with so much skill forty years ago. Watching Aykroyd and Chase ghost-walk through this mundane effort, it's hard to remember that they were anywhere near the cutting edge of comedy. It's even harder to accept this soggy white-bread humor knowing that Aykroyd co-wrote the script with Babaloo (*Splash*) Mandel and that it was directed by John Landis, who once showcased the ''Saturday Night Live'' sensibility in *National Lampoon's Animal House*. As Chase's graying temples and Aykroyd's new second chin attest, these comics are no longer

young, and they're doing something they never did in their younger days. They're playing it safe.

PG / 1985 / Warner

▲ SPLASH

Here's one of the comedy catches of the '80s: a fantasy about a man and a mermaid that's inventively naughty and nice. Tom Hanks, in a career-making role, plays a Manhattan wholesale-produce market owner who is bored with his love life (though his brother, John Candy, is still having a lively leer of it). Hanks retreats to Cape Cod to think through his life. He falls off a boat and is rescued by a gorgeous blond creature, Daryl Hannah, who quickly splashes back into the sea. Later, back in New York, the mermaid comes looking for her man—her tail magically replaced by delectably long legs. She can't speak, except for phrases she picks up from a bank of department store TV sets, but she hooks Hanks. The plot complications include a villainous marine scientist played by Eugene Levy, who thinks a squirt of water will zap the girl's legs back into a tail. Okay, the idea's been used before, in 1948's *Mr. Peabody and the Mermaid*. Some of this film is silly sitcom stuff. But Candy is so full of low-comedy life, he's a riot just standing there. And the romance at the heart of the movie glows. Hanks proves a thoroughly charming hero. Hannah showed a major talent in her first crack at comedy; she's a beauty with a rambunctious Carole Lombard bounce. The real triumph, though, belongs to director Ron Howard, the gawky TV kid from ''The Andy Griffith Show'' and ''Happy Days.'' At 30 he proved himself a filmmaker to reckon with, giving this sunny, unpretentious picture unexpected poignancy. It is nearly on a par with such accomplished contemporary comedies as *Tootsie*.

PG / 1984 / Touchstone

▲ SPLIT IMAGE

Human drama fairly bursts from stories about middle-class kids caught up in religious cults. That's the trouble. Movies on the subject often let the headlines do the work for them. The result here, as in the Canadian film *Ticket to Heaven*, is affecting but skin deep. College freshman

Michael (*The Great Santini*) O'Keefe has looks, athletic talent, and rich parents (sharply etched by Elizabeth Ashley and Brian Dennehy) who ignore him. When Karen (*Raiders of the Lost Ark*) Allen picks him up, the weekend in the country she promises turns out to be more than he bargained for. Allen is a member of Homeland, a celibate youth cult run by Peter Fonda. After a few days O'Keefe is hooked. How? The film never reveals. Though O'Keefe (himself a member of a religious cult while going to high school in New York's Westchester County) is convincing, he can't fill gaps left by director Ten (*North Dallas Forty*) Kotcheff and three screenwriters. James (*The Onion Field*) Woods, as a deprogrammer hired by O'Keefe's parents, saves the movie. He is an odious marvel, using every cheap trick to get his man and his fee. Before he's buried in scare-show tactics, Woods suggests the power of the movie that might have been.

R / 1982 / Embassy

▲ SPRING BREAK

Fort Lauderdale hosts its annual Sun Belt Woodstock for Airheads and the Whitebread Generation. About a quarter million horny college kids spend a week screaming "go for it" at one another and checking out boobs and buns. Let's see. What is this throwaway film's most fully realized moment? The bellyflop contest? The wet T-shirt or He-shirt contest? The teeny bikini contest? Is it when the star, Perry (*Cattle Annie and Little Britches*) Lang, sniffs his reeking armpits and runs for the deodorant? Awesome! Director Sean (*Friday the 13th*) Cunningham and writer David Smilow could have saved some money and just released the screen test and casting calls for this ghastly project.

R / 1983 / RCA/Columbia

▲ THE SPY WHO LOVED ME

In the tenth Bond saga, Roger Moore battles an evil shipping mogul (Curt Jurgens) who kidnaps nuclear submarines and threatens to blow up the world. Along the way he meets a ravishing Russian agent (Barbara Bach) for a little romantic détente in such exotic spots as Egypt and Sardinia. The usual gimmicks (supertankers, submersible cars, etc.) abound and are gorgeously photographed, especially underwater. Richard Kiel as Jaws, a shark-eating man with steel teeth, achieved a certain fame from the film, as did Carly Simon's version of the theme by Marvin Hamlisch, "Nobody Does It Better."

PG / 1977 / CBS/Fox

▲ STAND BY ME

Though this movie is based on a novella, *The Body*, by scaremeister Stephen King, it's not another one of his chillers. Filled with childhood nostalgia about such pastimes as hanging out in tree houses, it's more like a Norman Rockwell painting. The film, directed by Rob (*The Sure Thing*) Reiner, opens with narrator Richard Dreyfuss, in a cameo as a successful writer, reflecting on the recent death of one of his boyhood friends and the first time he saw a corpse when he was twelve. The rest of the film is a flashback to that summer of 1959. His memory takes him—in the form of Wil (*The Buddy System*) Wheaton, then 15—on a trip through the scenic Oregon countryside, beautifully captured by cinematographer Thomas (*The Breakfast Club*) Del Ruth. The scenes are punctuated with an evocative sound track full of such oldies as the Monotones' 1958 hit, "Book of Love." Wheaton and the three kids who join him on the trip constantly trade wisecracks; Dreyfuss points out that "finding new and preferably disgusting ways to describe a friend's mother was always held in high regard." There's an antagonistic relationship between Wheaton and his jock father, played by Marshall Bell. (Reiner has acknowledged strengthening this part of the story by basing it on his own youth as the son of actor-director Carl Reiner.) Wheaton's pals have their own problems at home, and they all touchingly seek refuge and reassurance in one another. By the end of the movie, when Ben E. King's rousing 1961 title song kicks in and Dreyfuss laments that he's never had friends like the ones he had when he was twelve, it's hard to resist joining him in pining for those exhilarating, if not always carefree, summer days.

R / 1986 / MCA

▲ THE STAR CHAMBER

Question: If the bad guys are getting off these days because the courts are too lenient, what can be done? Answer: Kill them. That's the premise of this paranoid suspense thriller by Peter Hyams, who also directed *Capricorn One,* another paranoid suspense thriller. It almost works. Michael Douglas, looking very unhappy and intense, plays a Los Angeles superior court judge. He becomes increasingly angry as case after grisly case (a child murder, the slaying of helpless old women) is dismissed on legal technicalities. Enter Hal Holbrook, a crusty superior court judge. He reveals that a small group of judges have taken matters into their own hands. Called the Star Chamber (after an arbitrary and tyrannical 15th-century tribunal in England) they mete out extralegal punishment by hiring executioners. Douglas, though first sputtering all kinds of idealistic patter, joins up. Then he discovers that two men who he was sure had molested, tortured, and killed a young boy are in fact innocent. He appeals to Holbrook to stop their execution, which had been ordered by the Star Chamber, but Holbrook tells him it's too late. Douglas enlists the help of honest cop Yaphet (*Blue Collar*) Kotto and tries to get to the men before the murderer does. It makes for a thrilling chase scene, but there's something wrong. Douglas's own complicity makes him less than a sympathetic hero. And since in the end he can't accept the Star Chamber's solution to crime, where does that leave him? In limbo, like the audience. Director Hyams' sleek, slick movie is emotionally unsatisfying. Everyone, in one way or another, turns out to be a villain.
R / 1983 / CBS/Fox

▲ STAR CRASH

What began as a halfhearted galactic rip-off, starring Marjoe Gortner and Caroline Munro as a couple of space-smugglers-turned-heroes, emerges as an unconsciously funny film. Munro has a strange way of flaring nostrils, eyes, and mouth at the same time while saying lines like "Fantastic!" and "This is incredible." Marjoe, reacting to his nonsense role with a pout, shows practically no expression—less, in fact, than the inevitable charming robot. The special effects are

a guffaw too. Ray guns look like French horns, one space station resembles an orbiting Cuisinart, and Munro's outfits could only have been created by Frederick's of Hollywood. There is also the sci-fi world's first giant female aluminum foil monster—topless yet. *The Sound of Music*'s Captain Von Trapp, Christopher Plummer, is in the cast, and when he says "There's one thing we haven't tried" against the villains, one expects him to burst into a lethal chorus of "Edelweiss."
PG / 1979 / Embassy

▲ STARDUST MEMORIES

"I especially like your early, funny films," sasses a fan to Woody Allen in this mordant but mercilessly witty self-portrait of an artist coming apart. Allen plays a frustrated filmmaker, much like himself, who made his reputation in comedy but longs to do despair. (Allen tried and fell short in *Interiors*.) At a weekend seminar in a New Jersey resort hotel, the characters of his life come to taunt him in a surreal daydream. For a unique artist like Allen, the form of the film is strikingly unoriginal. After Bob Fosse's *All That Jazz,* do we need another version of Fellini's *8½?* Allen's answer: yes. Though the film is self-indulgent and often cruel (his fans in the film are like Diane Arbus photographic misfits), Allen's eye for the absurd is unerring. He has written telling scenes for the three main women in his life, played by Charlotte Rampling, Marie Christine Barrault, and Jessica Harper. All three are talented and beautiful, Rampling extravagantly so. If the film lacks anything, it's a generosity of spirit—just the flaw Allen seems to find in himself. At the end he retreats, alone, to the strains of Cole Porter's "Easy to Love." Easy to love he isn't. But for his uncompromising intelligence and humor, Allen, as always, repays the effort to understand him.
PG / 1980 / CBS/Fox

▲ STAR 80

Not a pretty picture. Writer-director Bob (*Lenny, All That Jazz*) Fosse doesn't really specialize in pretty pictures. But he outdoes the ugliness and himself this time. In 1980 *Playboy* centerfold-turned-actress Dorothy Stratten was murdered by her estranged husband, Paul Snider. Before

shooting himself, Snider sexually attacked Stratten's mutilated corpse. Fosse does not skimp on the graphic details. Stratten's story was told in 1981's TV movie "Death of a Centerfold," starring Jamie Lee Curtis. Fosse is not interested in just telling it again. His *Star 80*—that was the license plate on Snider's car—told from Snider's point of view, is basically a scathing attack by Fosse on the American success ethic. The film is based on Teresa Carpenter's Pulitzer prizewinning *Village Voice* article, "Death of a Playmate," in which Snider is characterized as a cheap hustler who picked up Stratten, a high school kid working at an ice cream stand, and turned her into Bunny material. Fosse contends that Snider was pushed over the line when Stratten became a success and he was passed by. He points a finger at Hugh Hefner, who ostracized Snider. He also aims at a character who seems to be director Peter Bogdanovich (though he is called Aram Nicolas, probably trying to avoid a suit), who fell in love with Stratten during the making of her third and last film, *They All Laughed,* and urged her to leave Snider. From the look of the evidence, Hefner and Bogdanovich gave Stratten solid advice. But Fosse prefers to show the effect of a freeze-out on the volatile Snider. Could their rejection have pushed Snider to murder? Fosse doesn't let up on it for a minute. Unfortunately, he uses the same techniques (interviews, flashbacks) he used in *Lenny.* And his point seems questionable at best. What Fosse has in his favor are some superb performances. Mariel (*Personal Best*) Hemingway has never looked lovelier or more vulnerable; without great lines or sufficient dramatic motivation, she makes us feel the tragic senselessness of Stratten's death. Cliff Robertson etches Bunny boss Hefner with just the right touch of smarmy charm, and Carroll (*Baby Doll*) Baker leaves a striking impression as Stratten's mother. But the film belongs to Eric (*Raggedy Man*) Roberts. In a scarily sensational performance, he gets deep inside Snider's skin. Still, this is a film that's disturbing at best, and it leaves a terrible taste in the mouth.
R / 1983 / Warner

▲ STARMAN

Women generally don't fare well in sci-fi films. They're either screamers to be rescued or schemers to be stopped. Even Princess Leia is often a bystander. But in its own backhanded way, *Starman* condescends to women more than any sci-fi movie outside of *The Stepford Wives,* in which suburban spouses turn out to be robots. This adventure insists that the cure for a lady's grief, loneliness, and even sterility is not an extramarital but an extraterrestrial affair. Despite nifty special effects and an '80s sex scene, *Starman* is a '40s weeper given a high-tech twist. This is a real star-crossed romance: The forbidden love is between Karen Allen, a young Wisconsin widow, and an alien who assumes the shape of her dead husband, Jeff Bridges (who won a surprising Best Actor Oscar nomination). Although not of this world, the starman acts as though he's read too many Alan Alda interviews: He bears a striking resemblance to the New Man of the '80s—sensitive, warm, forgiving, and considerate in bed, he's a real Mr. Goodstar. He also comes on like Mister Rogers from Planet Nine, spouting observations that reassure the audience. "You are a strange species, not like any other," he explains. "You are at your best when things are at their worst." Director John Carpenter apparently still hadn't gotten *Christine,* his last film, out of his system. As government officials try to capture Bridges, Carpenter dwells on his car chases. And for a filmmaker who has given his horror films a distinctive signature, Carpenter surprisingly relies on Spielbergesque touches: wind chimes that announce the alien's arrival, blue lights in the living room, a spaceship climax at an isolated western location. Even the overlong chase that dominates the film seems paraphrased from Spielberg's *Sugarland Express.* Although *Starman* wants to suggest *E.T. in Love,* it ends up more like *E.T. in Hock.*
PG / 1984 / RCA/Columbia

▲ STARSHIP INVASIONS

Considering the other-worldly box-office success of *Star Wars* and *Close Encounters,* it was no surprise that filmmakers madly tried to clone them. But this piece of trash has neither the naive low-budget charm of the UFO films of the '50s nor the technical wizardry of high-tech box-office biggies. To top it off, you've seen it all before—the Bad Aliens are out to colonize the earth and the Good Aliens want to defend "the progress of civilization." Pointy-chinned

Robert Vaughn just seems to want to say "uncle" to the whole thing.

PG / 1977 / N/A

▲ STAR TREK: THE MOTION PICTURE

Deadlier than the Klingons! More insidious than a planet of neo-Nazis! As confusing as the force that created an evil Captain Kirk! Yes, Trekkies, it's *The Attack of the Special Effects Men.* Even Spock can't stave off the worst disaster since Cancel Date 1969. To be sure, the effects—masterminded by John (*Star Wars*) Dykstra, Douglas (*Close Encounters*) Trumbull, and an army of technicians—aren't bad. Even if the *Enterprise* still looks as though it ought to be plugged in and used to dry hair, there are spectacular light shows, computery sounds, and, of course, all those undersides of things passing above. What makes "Star Trek—The TV Reruns" (and later *Star Trek* films) so endearing, however, is not hardware but the chemistry among William Shatner, Leonard Nimoy, DeForest Kelly, and James Doohan. In this feature-film reunion, they're allowed little time with each other, so busy is director Robert Wise making sure every gizmo gets lovingly photographed. There are also two new characters. Stephen Collins, the *Enterprise*'s replacement skipper, resents it when Shatner (now *Admiral* Kirk), resumes command against a cosmic menace—after all, he's younger than Shatner, more up to date, and much better looking. So is Collins's love interest, Indian actress Persis Khambatta. They're the focus of a flashy ending that is half ingenious, half inane.

G / 1979 / Paramount

▲ STAR TREK II: THE WRATH OF KHAN

As the *Enterprise* sets off on a training mission into outer space, it's Admiral Kirk (William Shatner) who wonders if the escape pods are in place. But non-Trekkie moviegoers might put the same question to themselves when the lights go down. There may be only one reason to stick around beyond the first ten Trekkie in-jokes as the *Enterprise* heads ever so slowly toward a confrontation with its nemesis, Khan. That is to see if Ricardo Montalban, hilariously miscast as the contemptible villain Khan, will warp-speed from the depths of hyperspace back to "Fantasy Is-land." Only Herve Villechaize in a Darth Vader costume could have seemed more out of place. The gray-thatched Montalban, in a short-sleeved, open-chested sweater, gold chains, amulets, and a studded wristband, looks like a heavy metal rocker who's been touring the intergalactic road a few light-years too long. There are some new faces, including the sultry Kirstie Alley and Merritt Butrick, cast as a scientist. But they, Shatner, Leonard Nimoy, and everyone else act with little expression. Director Nicholas (*Time After Time*) Meyer's pacing and Jack Soward's script are leaden, and the special effects seem subpar in the post-Star Wars era. Devout Trekkies will want to know whether the rumors are true that Spock reaches the end of his space logs this trip. But the merely curious are warned. If *Star Trek: The Motion Picture* showed little of the *Enterprise* of the culty TV series, this sequel is at times a flat-out Khan-job.

PG / 1982 / Paramount

▲ STAR TREK III: THE SEARCH FOR SPOCK

No other film of the high-tech space-epic era has done such a satisfying job of making sure that its special effects are kept in their place: supporting a story line that is full of human—not to mention Vulcan—emotions. Written by Harve Bennett and directed by Leonard Nimoy (old Spock himself, in his first feature directing job), it makes deft use of the relationships that had been built up among the *Enterprise*'s crew during its long TV history and the two previous, largely lamentable features. The original crew—William Shatner, De Forest Kelley, James Doohan, Walter Koenig, George Takei, and Nichelle Nichols—is back, cruising around the universe trying to find out if Spock really died in *Star Trek II*. There are some new faces: Robin Curtis as a young officer, Christopher Lloyd as a vile Klingon, and Dame Judith Anderson as a Vulcan priestess. But they're only incidental. The film focuses tightly on the *Enterprise*'s old gang. This wasn't a bunch of spring chickens anymore; Shatner was 53, Kelley, 64. There are moments when a more apt subtitle might be *The Search for a Good Toupee*. But their age is part of the movie's charm. The affections and tensions among the characters are by this time almost all unstated, the way they are in a real family. It certainly helps to be, if not a card-carrying Trekkie, at least familiar with the basic plot lines. It's useful to know, for example, of the bickering between Spock and Dr. McCoy (Kelley) or the Lone Ranger–Tonto relationship between Spock and Captain Kirk (Shatner). But the movie has enough warmth and energy to involve anyone who likes adventure films—especially those full of feeling as well as firepower. **PG / 1984 / Paramount**

▲ STAR TREK IV: THE VOYAGE HOME

To most people, the *Enterprise* is an old aircraft carrier, and warp factor is what happens to your records when you leave them out in the sun. To Trekkies, however, they're universal terms of endearment. It hardly matters what the context is, which is just as well, given the mess *Star Trek IV* is in. The plot picks up where *The Search for Spock* ended, with the crew returning to Earth to stand trial for the crimes they committed in tracking down everyone's favorite Vulcan. Luckily for them there's a giant, cigar-shaped alien probe that is "ionizing the atmosphere and vaporizing the oceans" of the Earth in an attempt to communicate with the now-extinct humpback whale. It's never clear why the probe wants so badly to speak to the whale. The crew (all the principals from the TV series are still around) returns to the 20th century to find two humpbacks, thereby setting up a lot of *Back to the Future* humor and a potential romance between William Shatner and Catherine (*Peggy Sue Got Married*) Hicks. She plays a biologist at an aquarium near San Francisco, acting with such cartoonish earnestness you just hope she's camping it up. The film often seems to be sending itself up, in fact, with overwrought bumper-sticker sloganeering about whales and nuclear power. True Trekkies will devour every Spockism and Kirk command, but others will feel as entertained as they would if someone told a joke in a foreign language they didn't understand. **PG / 1986 / Paramount**

▲ STAR WARS

Second only to *E.T.* as the all-time box-office champ, director George Lucas's space fantasy incorporates *Flash Gordon, 2001, Planet of the Apes,* and *20,000 Leagues under the Sea* and tops them with enough ingenious, Oscar-winning special effects (laser sabers, holographic recordings, air cars) to animate an Arthur C. Clarke anthology. Mark Hamill, Harrison Ford, Carrie Fisher, and Alec Guinness lead the good rebels against the evil Galactic Empire abetted by Darth Vader (voiced behind that black mask by James Earl Jones). Still, it was R2D2 and C-3PO, a Laurel and Hardy team of robots, who most captured the public's fancy. It spawned two sequels, 1980's *The Empire Strikes Back* and 1983's *Return of the Jedi,* not to mention toys, books, comics, videos, posters, drinking cups, and bedsheets. Lucas, like Disney before him, managed to turn movies into industry without losing the magic. May The Force stay with him. **PG / 1977 / CBS/Fox**

▲ STAY AS YOU ARE

In this, her film debut, Nastassja Kinski, then 18, is powerfully seductive and—from the scant evidence provided—it was clear she is a natural actress too. The trouble is that there's hardly any plot and no real dialogue between Natassja and co-star Marcello Mastroianni, 55. So what if Kinski may be his daughter from a long-ago affair. The possibility is raised, then forgotten in time for a barrage of unabashed lovemaking. Poor Marcello is exhausted; not so Kinski, who takes off her clothes early and does, indeed, stay as she is most of the way. (In Italian with English subtitles.) **Unrated / 1979 / Warner**

▲ STAYING ALIVE

See John strut. See John dance. See John hustle his way into the chorus of a Broadway musical. So much for plot development. In director-screenwriter Sylvester Stallone's sequel to *Saturday Night Fever,* variations on one basic sequence appear again and again: John Travolta, back as Tony Manero, makes a date with his wholesome American dancer-girlfriend, Cynthia Rhodes, gets sidetracked and snubbed by the show's snooty British star (Finola Hughes), then returns to the sweet thing, who cries a perfect tear as she takes him back. Stallone's monotonous screenplay, coauthored with Norman Wexler, who wrote *Saturday Night Fever,* shamelessly pillages the clichés of '40s and '50s movies: The rich are rotten, an underdog can come out on top, don't forsake your hometown roots and, most important, listen to your mother whenever you're in trouble. Surprisingly, this time Stallone doesn't deliver his specialty: a nemesis for the hero. There's no villain for Travolta to vanquish and consequently no emotional catharsis in the climax. The songs, by the Bee Gees and Sly's brother Frank, keep horning in on the action; neither the characters nor the drama has any room to breathe. By contrast with *Fever,* the dancing is pedestrian, almost clunky. Travolta seems to have traded the charm he had in the original for a massive dose of egotism brought about by his new muscled body, courtesy of Stallone's *Rocky* regimen. He may look like a god, but he acts like a goon. Give us the old Tony Manero any day. Here is a movie caught in the time warp: a slick MTV video that celebrates Eisenhower-era morality. For viewers of *Staying Alive,* the problem is staying awake.

PG / 1983 / Paramount

▲ ST. ELMO'S FIRE

Posing as a kind of *Medium-Size Chill,* this ensemble comedy takes an emotionally charged moment—that purgatory between college graduation and assimilation into the Real World—and mutilates it. Living in Washington, D.C., seven friends are four months out of Georgetown. Ally Sheedy and Judd Nelson face-off as an upscale couple whose romance is poisoned by pal Andrew McCarthy's infatuation with Sheedy. Demi Moore vamps as the group's token virgin, whom Rob Lowe is determined to deflower. Emilio Estevez is saddled with an improbable subplot about his obsession with an older woman. But *St. Elmo's Fire* never gets the everyday details right, let alone the emotions. These kids drink brandy instead of beer. They live in exotic apartments suited to Hollywood art directors. When Sheedy sighs, "I wish everything could be like it was— all of us friends," the audience laughs. What are these people pining for—the distant past of four months ago? Director Joel Schumacher, who co-

St. Elmo's Fire: This cinematic yawn shows a marked lack of chemistry among Brat Packers Ally Sheedy, Judd Nelson, Emilio Estevez, Demi Moore, Rob Lowe, Mare Winningham, and Andrew McCarthy.

wrote the anecdotal script with newcomer Carl Kurlander, proved with *The Incredible Shrinking Woman* that he's a set decorator masquerading as a moviemaker. His film is also intolerant of anyone who isn't a yuppie. Bag ladies, welfare mothers, and Koreans, among others, are indiscriminately insulted. The script ambushes its actors too. Only Sheedy, McCarthy and, particularly, Winningham acquit themselves admirably. Lowe's preening sabotages his character. The conspicuously mediocre Nelson, as an ambitious congressional aide, overplays as much as he did in *The Breakfast Club*. As the jealous lover in the juvenile *Jules and Jim* subplot, he shouts at Sheedy, "Wasted love!"—and you're reminded of high school Strindberg. *St. Elmo's Fire* comes off as an expensive edition of *Let's Play Dress Up*.

R / 1985 / RCA/Columbia

▲ THE STEPFATHER

A man, with no distinguishing features save the beard he's now shaving meticulously in the bathroom mirror, whistles a bit of "Camptown Races," dresses, and leaves his home. With no more than a passing glance he walks by his wife and stepchildren, their bodies mutilated and lifeless in the family parlor. Then he's off, putting a jaunty spin on his whistle, in search of a new widow with children and another chance to commit murder. So begins one of the most marrow-chilling of movies. Credit director Joseph Ruben and crime novelist and screenwriter Donald Westlake with knowing how to grip an audience without resorting to constant bloodletting. Terry O'Quinn (Debra Winger's boss in *Black Widow*) is sensationally effective as the stepfather whose rage is sparked whenever his idealized vision of family life goes askew, a psychopath posing as an average Joe. With his bright sweaters to offset his rigidly bland personality, O'Quinn could have stepped off a Father's Day card. The film focuses on O'Quinn's latest identity, as a real estate salesman who marries the widowed Shelley Hack. She has a 16-year-old daughter, played with likable orneriness by Jill Schoelen. The teenager doesn't like her new dad. She sees through his attempts to buy her affection with a puppy and suspects something sinister when she catches him throwing a tantrum in the basement. Helped by her therapist (Charles Lanyer), Schoelen finds herself heading for a fearful confrontation. Ruben works

the eerie give-and-take in these daughter-stepfather scenes with a finesse that recalls Joseph Cotten and Teresa Wright in Hitchcock's 1943 classic, *Shadow of a Doubt*. To reveal more would be a cheat. *The Stepfather* is a rare find in this gore-glutted era, a terrifying thriller that plumbs the violence of the mind.

R / 1987 / N/A

▲ STEVIE

Glenda Jackson has made a career of portraying tense, chilly women, but this time, as the eccentric English poet Stevie Smith, she injects unexpected warmth and empathy into a part that could have been sterile. Mona Washbourne, as her fussy, supportive aunt, gives one of the most witty and moving performances in screen history. That neither won an Oscar remains a shame on the Academy. The only other actors with substantial roles are the gifted Trevor Howard and Alec McCowan. While matters get a trifle claustrophobic (the camera rarely leaves the poet's house), director Robert Enders has turned Hugh Whitemore's play into a surprisingly affecting movie. If there's any justice, *Stevie*'s availability on video will bring this little-seen and undervalued film a new life.

R / 1978 / Embassy

▲ STICK

For the first ten minutes or so, director-star Burt Reynolds gets the tone of this film version of Elmore Leonard's gritty 1983 crime novel exactly right. You can almost smell the seedy side of Florida rotting in the sunshine. And the bearded Reynolds, as a just-released con with a conscience, has the big, sad, and quiet quality the part calls for. Reading the credits is reassuring too. That's where you learn that Leonard, a long neglected writer whose twenty-fourth novel, *Glitz*, at last won him best-seller status, collaborated (with Joseph C. Stinson) on the script. Regrettably, from the look of things, Reynolds sent Leonard home after that first promising scene. In any case, few movies have ever disintegrated as fast as *Stick*. If the first ten minutes prove Reynolds could have done it well if he wanted to, the remaining ninety-nine seem to prove he didn't care. When *Stick* shaves his beard and takes a job as chauffeur to a loud-mouthed millionaire, George Segal, the movie switches gears. It lapses into farce curdled by the kind of hyped-up violence (severed hands, black magic torture, etc.) whose inspiration is desperation. Segal hams shamelessly, as does Charles Durning, playing a sadistic drug smuggler. They're not bad, just inappropriate. Candice Bergen is wasted as Reynolds's absurdly conceived love interest. There's something sad about watching a man as talented as Reynolds grinding a filet mignon project into hamburger for no apparent purpose. This is the kind of ain't-I-a-tough-guy? vanity production Frank (*Tony Rome*) Sinatra and Dean (*Matt Helm*) Martin tried to foist off as fun in the 1960s. Plagued by well-publicized health problems during the filming (unmotivated exercise sequences are used to explain the star's dramatic weight loss from scene to scene), Reynolds may indeed have had a difficult time doing this picture. Like the pro he is, he tries not to let the strain show. What does show in *Stick* is Reynolds's lack of faith in himself to be more than a movie star. The man who contributed so much to such admirable films as *Deliverance, Semi-Tough, Hooper, Starting Over, The Man Who Loved Women,* and *Sharky's Machine* is better than that.

R / 1985 / MCA

▲ STILL OF THE NIGHT

Considering the exalted reputations of Meryl Streep, Roy Scheider, and writer-director Robert (*Kramer vs. Kramer*) Benton, it's disappointing that all they're doing here is cribbing from Hitchcock. Nothing wrong with that in theory: With his perversely teasing style, Brian (*Dressed to Kill*) De Palma has made it pay off handsomely. Benton, however, approaches the master hat in hand, and Benton's classy style is too cautious to generate much heat. Scheider is cast as a Manhattan shrink, newly divorced. He finds himself strangely haunted by Streep, who's having an affair with one of his patients, Josef Sommer. When his patient turns up stabbed to death, Scheider starts to do some private sleuthing. Streep, who works in a Madison Avenue auction house, arouses his suspicions along with his passion. Scheider is sterling throughout, and his scenes with his shrink mother, beautifully done by Jessica Tandy, suggest the more affecting movie that might have been. But when Benton

switches his and the plot's focus to the mysterious Streep, the is-she-or-isn't-she-the-mad-slasher theme seems mildewed and monotonous. Streep tries valiantly—even desperately (she fidgets madly with her hair and does a near-nude scene with a Chinese masseur)—to keep the attention of the audience riveted, and the strain shows. There's certainly an actress here, but no role. Benton is so self-consciously fancy about atmosphere that he loses track of character and plot. The film dips a toe into some of Hitchcock's greatest works, especially *Vertigo, Notorious, Suspicion,* and *Spellbound,* and predictably, in view of the context, those remain the real jewels. *Still of the Night* is pretty but transparently paste.

PG / 1982 / CBS/Fox

▲ THE STING

No one back in 1973 seemed very surprised that this zippy flick about the ultimate con job managed to win the Best Picture Oscar over *American Graffiti, The Exorcist,* and Bergman's *Cries and Whispers.* Nothing like the passing of time to provide perspective. Or perhaps it's just impossible for anyone to resist Newman and Redford's oozing camaraderie. Scott Joplin's music and director George Roy Hill's ability to avoid taking things too seriously also help a lot to make this stylish entertainment. But seven Oscars was overkill. Amazingly, this froth remains the only time that Redford has received an Academy award nomination for his acting.

PG / 1973 / MCA

▲ THE STING II

The closest this sequel comes to the good-natured cleverness and bright spirit of its progenitor is a few bars of the *Sting* theme, Scott Joplin's "The Entertainer," which are played over the opening credits. After that, this is just another sorry attempt to capitalize on the popularity of a big hit. The heroes again are a pair of sympathetically drawn drifters, but instead of Paul Newman's eyes, sly and sparkling blue, there are Jackie Gleason's, tired and bloodshot; instead of Robert Redford's smile, cheery and smart, there is Mac Davis's, wan and disinterested. The plot involves another complicated scam, this one centering on a fixed boxing match featuring Davis. While a

lot of the fun of the original came from the audience's being conned along with the villains, there are so many twists here that they become almost predictable. The movie's only moments of flash come from Teri Garr, as a snappy con woman, and Jose Perez (who played God in the PBS production of *Steambath*), as a dedicated hitman working for Oliver Reed. Director Jeremy Paul (*The Chosen*) Kagan and scriptwriter David S. Ward, who wrote the original *Sting* screenplay, probably faced an impossible task; the Newman-Redford chemistry can't really be duplicated. But they could have turned this film in a different direction instead of turning out a clumsy counterfeit that is a real-life con game against the hapless video buyer or renter.
PG / 1983 / MCA

▲ STIR CRAZY

The situation seems ripe for humor, as Richard Pryor and Gene Wilder are accused of robbing a bank dressed up as big-league ball park woodpeckers. Unhappily, the movie promises more than it delivers. Sidney Poitier has directed some cheerfully slapdash comedies (*Uptown Saturday Night* and *Let's Do It Again*), but this one is curiously cold. Two scenes, however, almost compensate. In one, an elegant dinner party turns wonderfully wacky when the kitchen help mistakes waiter Pryor's marijuana for oregano. The other highlight recalls the moment in *Silver Streak* when Pryor instructed Wilder on how to act soulful. Here Pryor, jailed for the first time, attempts to convince the inmates of his toughness by strutting around boasting, "We bad; we very bad." If Pryor fares better than Wilder, both are ill-used. The film's final third, a prison break, is played straight, which is a waste of comic talent that is close to criminal.
R / 1981 / RCA/Columbia

▲ STRAIGHT TIME

One of Dustin Hoffman's rare flops (until he hit the jackpot with *Ishtar*), this film involves an ex-con who bungles his attempt to go straight. There's a careening car stunt on an L.A. freeway, a glass-shattering jewelry story heist, and a bunch of bare-bottomed men in the jailhouse shower, but all to little purpose. Hoffman's intensity and the loveliness of Theresa Russell as his naive girlfriend aside, they are a distinctly unsympathetic pair. With few laughs and only a weak pass at the psychology of the recidivist, *Straight Time*, directed by Ulu Grosbard and based on Edward Bunker's novel *No Beast So Fierce*, is unrelievedly grim. Woody Allen treated the same subject better—and, needless to say, funnier—in *Take the Money and Run*.
R / 1978 / Warner

▲ STRANGE BEHAVIOR

No one claimed this was another *Psycho*. But compare it to any other low-budget horror film and Michael Laughlin's directorial debut is impressive. Formerly a little-known producer, Laughlin proves mastery of his genre by using fine camera work as he delivers the requisite series of slayings (the victims are teens in a Midwestern college town) and believable special effects (read: blood). In fact, despite the constraints of a thirty-one-day shooting schedule, he rises far above the level of, say, *Friday the Thirteenth Part II*. For one thing, the story (written by Laughlin and then 25-year-old William Condon) holds together well enough to make us care whodunit. Indeed, the script is sometimes funny (in a campy, *Rocky Horror Picture Show* kind of way) and sometimes touching. Creep-film veteran Fiona Lewis, as an evil psycho professor, has the best part. Louise Fletcher (Nurse Ratched of *One Flew Over the Cuckoo's Nest*) is, unfortunately, wasted on an unimportant role, and Michael (*Manhattan*) Murphy mostly spins wheels as the police chief. But as his son, Dan (*Wise Blood*) Shor is perfect. Not everything about this film is good, but more things work than anyone would have expected.
R / 1981 / RCA/Columbia

▲ STRANGE BREW

As a change of pace in the sophisticated humor of SCTV, Rick Moranis's and Dave Thomas's "Great White North" routine was a perfect brief television bit. Sure enough, as a movie, it is still a perfect television bit. The Moranis-Thomas characters are the McKenzie brothers, country bumpkins who host a Canadian TV show devoted

largely to burping, discussing the all-encompassing vitures of beer, doughnuts, and back bacon, and insulting each other—their "Take off, eh" and "Hoser!" entered the vernacular. That can be awfully amusing for five minutes and awfully tedious for ninety. The subplot of the film, directed and written (with Steven De Jarnett) by Moranis and Thomas, involves a megalomaniac brewmeister, Max Von Sydow (let's hope Ingmar doesn't see this, Max). He is putting drugs in beer served to inmates of a mental institution so he can control them and eventually take over the world. The execution of that sappy idea is as gaseous as its conception. Moranis and Thomas are spontaneous and likable, and co-star Lynne (*The Amateur*) Griffin is a beauty. The McKenzies, though, quickly wear out a welcome. The film mainly makes clear again the skill that went into those 1940 films by another media crossover, Bob Hope. In, say, *The Ghost Breakers* or *My Favorite Blonde,* he stayed in his basic radio character but was surrounded by amusing actors and snappy plots. It's not as easy as it looked, is it, boys?
PG / 1983 / MGM/UA

▲ STRANGE INVADERS

Take a few notions from the *Invasion of the Body Snatchers,* a couple more from *Close Encounters of the Third Kind,* and add a touch or two of Hitchcock paranoia—from, say, *The Thirty-Nine Steps.* That, in effect, is what director Michael (*Strange Behavior*) Laughlin and writer William Condon did in concocting this amiable if pointless movie about aliens from space who take over a small Illinois town. Though the film's gimmicks are hardly novel, it does have a likable cast. Paul (*Melvin and Howard*) Le Mat plays an entomology professor whose ex-wife and daughter are threatened by the creatures. Nancy (*Blow Out*) Allen, offhandedly funny and charming, is a sensationalist tabloid reporter who has made up a story that's too close to the truth. Louise (*One Flew Over the Cuckoo's Nest*) Fletcher is a government official from an agency that made some sort of pact with the aliens when they first landed twenty-five years ago. Kenneth Tobey, a hero in such '50s space monster films as *The Beast from 20,000 Fathoms,* plays one of the creatures. Nobody is likely to dress up as a Strange Invader for Halloween, and you don't care whether they phone home. But as a breezy diversion, this film is not a bad video for a slow Saturday night.
PG / 1983 / Vestron

▲ A STRANGER IS WATCHING

In *Friday the 13th,* director Sean Cunningham's 1980 low-budget shocker, a spike is driven through the back of a man's neck and emerges bloodily in front. In *A Stranger Is Watching,* Cunningham has the spike go in the front of the neck and come out the back. So much for artistic development. Cunningham took Mary Higgins Clark's suspenseful, densely plotted best-seller about a psycho who holds a child and a female newscaster hostage in the catacombs beneath Grand Central Station and turned it into a horror show. Fans of the genre are bound to stand in awe of Cunningham's imagination in killing off most of his cast. Despite some impressive on-location photography, admirers of Clark's nifty novel will be less enthusiastic. Unlike the book, the film doesn't build, it bludgeons. With no time for characterization, Kate (*Mrs. Columbo*) Mulgrew as the newscaster, Shawn Von Schreiber, then 10, as the kidnapped girl, and James Naughton as her harried father are no more than efficient puppets. Rip Torn, however, enlivens the villain role. Whether he's eating egg salad with his fingers, lasciviously lifting Mulgrew's skirt, or tossing an old lady on the tracks, Tom is a hiss-worthy bad guy. In one scene, just before knifing an old man, he cheerfully gives his paperboy a big tip. Nobody's perfect.
R / 1982 / MGM/UA

▲ STREAMERS

Robert Altman, who directed some of the finest films ever, including *M*A*S*H* and *Nashville,* later started approaching has-been status. He has not made a commercially or critically successful picture since 1977's *3 Women.* He finally resorted to working on the cheap to bring plays to the screen. Whether he gets by (*Fool for Love*) or falls on his face (*Beyond Therapy*), Altman seems constricted by the theatrical environment. In *Streamers,* based on David Rabe's 1976 play about four soldiers preparing to go to Vietnam, Altman pumps up the dramatics so much he destroys much of the play's subtle terror. He has better luck with his relatively unknown cast. After auditioning hundreds of men, Altman picked Mitchell (*The Lords of Discipline*) Lichtenstein as a homosexual recruit who is alternately vilified, kidded, and propositioned by the other three, Michael (*The Wanderers*) Wright, Matthew (*Private School*) Modine, and David Alan Grier, best known for his role as Jackie Robinson in Broadway's *The First*. They are all superb in grueling roles that encapsulate the traumatic effects Vietnam had on this country. (Two drunk sergeants, played by George Dzundza and Guy Boyd, provide black comic relief.) The disturbing realism of the story and its violent conclusion also kept this film from becoming as popular as *M*A*S*H*. As Altman said, "That film was 1969. I'm telling the same war story now, but it just isn't funny anymore."

R / 1983 / Media

▲ STREET SMART

A dubious title for a dumb movie. Assuming a know-it-all attitude about how the underworld and the media operate in the Big Apple, the plot actually is naive. Directed by Jerry Schatzberg from a script by David Freeman, the film is as authentic as the Montreal locations that stand in for Manhattan. We're asked to buy Christopher (*Superman 1, 2, 3,* and *4*) Reeve as a street reporter for a weekly magazine something like *New York*. Trying to pander to the sleazy tastes of his editor, camped to a fare-thee-well by Andre Gregory, Reeve sells a story idea about twenty-four hours in the life of a pimp. But there's a hitch: No pimp will talk with him. Even a hooker, pertly played by theater actress Kathy Baker, tells him lies about working free-lance. In despair he uses his own uptown girlfriend, Mimi Rogers (who later became Mrs. Tom Cruise), as a lure. But Reeve just can't procure any procurers. So he does the next best thing—as the *Washington Post*'s Pulitzer prizewinner (and loser) Janet Cooke did—and makes up the story. In no time Reeve is a media sensation, moving from print to TV as the new Geraldo Rivera of the evening news. Then an assistant district attorney, played by Jay Patterson, thinks that Reeve's phony pimp is the very real killer (a scary Morgan Freeman) he's trying to indict for murder. Patterson demands

that Reeve turn over his nonexistent notes. Reeve wrestles with his conscience. We know this because he furrows his brow a lot. The chucklehead then sleeps with the hooker, apparently not having heard of unsafe sex. His excuse to Rogers is: "It didn't mean anything. It just kinda happened." Many trashy movies of this ilk, at least the unpretentious ones, get off the hook with audiences on a similar plea bargain. In this case the court does not recommend leniency.

R / 1987 / N/A

▲ STREETS OF FIRE

Director Walter Hill, fresh off the box-office success of *48 Hrs.,* fashioned what he called a "rock 'n' roll fable," but it looked a lot like a long MTV video. Diane Lane plays a rock singer with more than a little resemblance to Joan Jett. During an especially rowdy concert in some unnamed town—the setting looks like a cross between Chicago and postwar Berlin—she's kidnapped by a gang of bikers. Enter her ex-boyfriend, Michael Pare, who looks like a junior Sylvester Stallone and talks like him too. He is persuaded to go get his ex, and the love story begins. The streets are almost always wet and nobody smiles except when they're threatening violence, which means they get to smile a lot. The dialogue veers all over the place, ranging from such tried and stupid lines as "Let's get out of here" to hard-boiled 1940s detective talk—the women are called "skirts," the wimpy guys are dubbed "Shorty." (SCTV veteran Rick Moranis, in a straight role, plays one of the wimps in an occasionally grating fashion.) The film is often very funny, whether it's supposed to be or not. But the most compelling reason to see it, aside from its gorgeously sleek, wet look, is Amy Madigan, who plays Pare's sidekick. With her frizzy blond hair, baseball cap, and rough mouth, she generates a palpable appeal. The rock music by Ry Cooder effectively deepens what is already a palpably dark mood, and Hill clearly threw himself into this chancy project. He comes quite close to pulling it off too. He doesn't quite set the streets on fire though. Let's just say that there's a lot of smoke where this movie should have been.

PG / 1984 / MCA

▲ STRIPES

Bill Murray stars in this film about Army basic training, and it features John Candy and Harold Ramis. Director Ivan Reitman coproduced *Animal House*. Do not, however, except a devastating satire on the military; this film is so innocuous that the Defense Department let Reitman use Fort Knox, Kentucky, to make it. There's no point of view, and the characters—a snarly drill sergeant, an inept captain, unbelievably gorgeous WACs—come out of the screenwriter's instant plot kit. *Stripes* is like the bumbling-but-lovable-recruit comedies done before, and much better, by Abbott and Costello, Martin and Lewis, and Robert Walker in the old Private Hargrove series. Murray is great in small doses, but as the film wears on he seems more sour and insecure than funny. Candy, as an earnest lummox, and Ramis, who has a nice way with a throwaway line, fare better. Reitman, though, wastes opportunities. In one, Murray whips his platoon into shape for a parade—a nice twist, yet the parade is carried off halfheartedly. KP for all these guys.
R / 1981 / RCA/Columbia

▲ STROKER ACE

There are times when Burt Reynolds seems like the Cary Grant of the '80s. Then there are times, such as in this movie, when he seems like the Andy Devine of the '80s. This is yet another automobile-oriented comedy directed by Hal (*Smokey and the Bandit*) Needham, who is wonderful with stunts, chases, and races but breaks down when it comes to things that don't have pistons and cylinders, such as actors or actresses. Reynolds plays a stock car driver who is competing under the sponsorship of a ruthless fast-food chicken merchant played by Ned Beatty. To say Reynolds takes on his role halfheartedly is to exaggerate his apparent interest; he doesn't throw away his lines so much as he seems to let them dribble out. Jim Nabors, as Reynolds's ace mechanic, lapses back into his *Gomer Pyle* persona, rolling his eyes two or three hundred times. If the constant stock shots of racing crowds haven't made clear how desperate the situation is, the closing credits do—they're accompanied by a series of outtakes, which are even less interesting than the film itself. *Stroker* has a couple of

redeeming features, however. One is Beatty, who blusters, fumes, huffs, and puffs enough to make his character amusing. He is a first-class actor. The other is Loni Anderson, Burt's offscreen lady, playing her first feature role. She is marvelously fresh and attractive, and the big screen makes the most of her appealing qualities.
PG / 1983 / Warner

▲ STROSZEK: A BALLAD

A pathetic, oft-jailed Berlin street musician (Bruno S.) emigrates to Wisconsin with this streetwalker girlfriend (Eva Mattes) and an eccentric old man. All three discover America holds little worth making the trip for. That is the plot, but the film's real strength lies in director Werner Herzog's ability to convey his characters' moods visually. Haunting background music by Chet Atkins and Sonny Terry deepens the enjoyment of this lyrical film. (In German with subtitles.)
Unrated / 1977 / N/A

▲ STUNTMAN

Peter O'Toole's reputation as one of the screen's most eccentric personalities was enhanced by this strange, episodic story of a movie director gone mad—or so it seems. It's hard to tell. The story line is deceptively simple: A stuntman on a movie set is accidentally killed, endangering the whole project. Enter Steve Railsback, who is fleeing the law for an unspecified reason. O'Toole, as the director, learns Railsback is a fugitive and offers him a deal: If he'll take the place of the dead stuntman, O'Toole will shield him from the law. What follows is a rollercoaster movie-within-a-movie that will test the attention span of even the most patient viewer. Barbara Hershey plays a sexy, unstable leading lady who beds down with Railsback and seems part of O'Toole's sinister determination to coax him into increasingly dangerous stunts. The movie is by turns ridiculous, stunning, and baffling as director Richard Rush, whose previous credits included *Hell's Angels on Wheels,* keeps up a manic pace. O'Toole performs the film's most accomplished stunt, a roaring, off-the-wall performance that holds it all together—if only for a while.
R / 1980 / CBS/Fox

▲ SUCCESS

William Richert co-wrote (with Larry Choen) and directed this goofy, uneven comedy, and along with his far superior *Winter Kills,* it is becoming a cult favorite. A far easier case could be made for *Winter Kills,* a dark, fast-paced spoof of a Kennedyesque assassination. Both films star Jeff Bridges and stunning ex-model Belinda Bauer. *Success* has its amusements but doesn't really go anywhere. Bridges works for a Munich-based credit card company run by Ned Beatty and has married Beatty's outrageously narcissistic daughter, Bauer. When they go to a party, Bridges sees her at a mirror making eyes at herself and over-dubs, "I wasn't the only one who couldn't keep his eyes off her; she couldn't either." Beatty is an insulting, demanding father-in-law who sees Bridges as good for nothing. To break out of this wimpy image, Bridges takes on an alter ego. As "Mac," he works out daily with his mistress-instructor Bianca Jagger and roughs up his wife. He tortures her, too—by demanding that she cook for him. She, of course, falls in love with "Mac," while he uses his new disguise to pull off a $5 million heist. At that point the plot falls apart under the weight of its own convolutions. The pacing bogs down, and the gags run too far apart to keep things moving. Bauer's deadpan bimbo beauty could make her a fine comedienne, but Bridges is barely more than cute. As for Jagger's pseudo-smoldering brand of androgyny, it looks much more charismatic on her ex-husband.
PG / 1983 / N/A

▲ SUDDEN DEATH

Exploitive, misogynist, stupid, and boring, this movie is also gratuitously violent and unqualifiedly lamebrained. Its emotional highlight is the poignant theme song: "Sudden death/Sudden death/No time/For regrets." In the depressing tradition of *Death Wish* and *Ms. 45,* it is about a New York woman who, after being raped and beaten, sets out for revenge. Denise Coward plays the vigilantette; the rest of the cast has done a similarly admirable job of keeping their existence secret from the movie-going public. In fact, there are fewer familiar people on the entire list of credits than might be found in, say, a random selection of names from the Kearney, Nebraska,

phone book. Those folks in Kearney could undoubtedly make a better movie too.
R / 1985 / Media

▲ SUDDEN IMPACT

Clint Eastwood's meal ticket role—that of the brutal San Francisco detective Harry Callahan—is hardly a one-shot proposition. But it's certainly a one-note character: Harry can be violent, more violent, and turn-on-the-blood-making-machine violent. So much for emotional range. In this fourth film in the series, Harry is assigned to track down a killer in the San Francisco Bay area. Sandra Locke (Eastwood's real-life love) has been avenging the gang rape of herself and her sister in a small northern California town by systematically eliminating the rapists. When Harry goes to the town for some R & R, he meets Locke and, because they share a taste for mayhem, romance blossoms. Taut at the beginning, even funny, the movie deteriorates when Eastwood, who also directed, launches an endless series of shoot-outs. One gun battle can be exciting, a half dozen become tedious. If Meathead, the bulldog who pals around with Eastwood, wanted to be the new Lassie, he picked the wrong film. This is something only a gunsmith could love.
R / 1984 / Warner

▲ SUMMER HEAT

Very quiet, slow-moving, and yet oddly absorbing, this film about a romantic triangle in a tobacco town in 1937 could have been called *The Postman Who Always Rings Twice Goes to North Carolina.* In a high-tech era, *Summer Heat* depends on the eye for detail of its Virginia-born writer-director Michie Gleason and a cast headed by three impressive young actors. Anthony (*Top Gun*) Edwards and Lori (*The Falcon and the Snowman*) Singer play a struggling young farm couple who have a little daughter (acted with consummately pudgy appeal by 22-month-old Jessie Kent). The third point in the triangle is a hired hand portrayed by Bruce (*Re-Animator*) Abbott. He is a Sam Shepard-kind of nouveau he-man. No male chauvinist, he's no Mr. Sen-

sitivity, either, and isn't above using disgraceful means to get to what he considers honorable ends. This is a movie of images, not language, so the actors convey much of the story—quite movingly in Singer's case—with their faces. Gleason closes in on those faces, on leaves of tobacco, on a doll in a child-size casket, on the sweat running down a lover's back. It's as atmospheric a film as *Body Heat* or *Days of Heaven,* on which Gleason was producer Bert Schneider's assistant. (Her only previous directing job was on the obscure *Broken English.*) Adapted from Louise Shivers's novel *Here to Get My Baby Out of Jail,* the film also gives B-movie veteran Clu Gulager the chance of a career as Singer's mortician father, and he creates a complicated character in not a lot of screen time. The ending takes a melodramatic turn into a too-pat resolution. The mood is never broken, though, nor is the sense of a conspiracy among the capricious forces of passion, desperation, and love.
R / 1987 / N/A

▲ SUMMER LOVERS

As sappy and ultimately evanescent as the holiday romances it celebrates, this film is about a ménage à trois on the Greek island of Santorini involving two young American tourists, Peter Gallagher and Daryl Hannah, and a French archaeologist, Valerie Quennessen. It is really more of a ménage à deux et demi. Gallagher, now best known for his role on TV's "L.A. Law," has a sleek body and a handsome face decorated by the bushiest eyebrows since Groucho Marx. But he is overwhelmed by the women. Hannah, now best known as the mermaid from *Splash,* shows a disarming sweetness. And Quennessen, little known (unfortunately) for the 1979 film flop *French Postcards,* is a rare beauty, with luminescent blue eyes, a gently angular face, and a near-tangible screen sensuality. She is also an actress of some subtlety deserving of far more mature roles than this. Writer-director Randal (*Grease, Blue Lagoon*) Kleiser has no touch with actors, though he does keep his camera in the proximity of a lot of unclothed and gorgeous young bodies for most of the film. That's as close as this movie gets to any naked truths.
R / 1982 / Embassy

▲ SUMMER RENTAL

Although John Candy may be one of the funniest film presences around, you couldn't tell it from this, the first comedy in which he had the lead. In fact, *Summer Rental* might easily be mistaken for a Jack Lemmon movie from 1965. Straitjacketed in the role of a put-upon suburban father, Candy embraces the middle-class martyr pose that has been Lemmon's mainstay. As an air-traffic controller on a Florida vacation with his family, Candy even endures a series of Lemmon-like humiliations. He fumes when denied a table at a fancy restaurant. He huffs when threatened with eviction from his rental cottage. He puffs when bullied by a rich creep (Richard Crenna), whom he challenges to a climactic (and murderously uncinematic) sailboat race. But since he's a sponge for suffering, all the huffing and puffing doesn't let Candy deliver what he does best: a madman's revenge. Even when the script does give Candy his due, it saddles him with sentimentality. "We're not out of this yet," he assures his defeated family during the race. Who wants to watch John Candy be Robert Young? This star vehicle owes its few clever moments to performers other than the star. The only decent joke involves a neighbor who flashes her breast implants to any interested party. As directed by Carl Reiner, the movie never has any momentum. The only original touches of this sourpuss comedy are also its most odious: *Summer Rental* may qualify as the first film to highlight a Frisbee-to-the-groin gag.
PG / 1985 / Paramount

▲ SUPERGIRL

Supergirl is very much like her cousin Superman. She fights evil reflexively, the way most people swat mosquitoes. She does quick costume changes, though she must take a gallon of bleach into the phone booths with her, since she goes from mousy brunette in her civilian togs to sex-bomb blonde when she Supes up. And she has the basic arsenal of bending-steel-with-the-bare-hands power, though in this case she also has the power to bore just about anyone into submission. Directed by Jeannot Szwarc, this movie has some flashy effects and is never offensive in its violence or its language. It is merely bland. Helen Slater, who plays Supergirl, is sweetly pretty. But she's far

less charismatic than Faye Dunaway, who plays a small-time carnival charlatan turned archvillainess by a magic device. Dunaway is all glaring eyes and flaring nostrils. This is her standard, later career fiend-level performance, and she and Peter Cook, who is her devilish suitor, are the main sources of fun. (Peter O'Toole shows up briefly as a sort of guru.) As an antisexist message, the film shows the kids that females can be superwhatevers. But as entertainment, it's about as much fun as watching a hunk of kryptonite glow for a couple of hours.
PG / 1984 / USA

▲ SUPERMAN

A lot of money was spent making The Man fly onscreen—between $38 and $78 million, depending on whom you believe and how much went for the preplanned first sequel. But for once extravagance paid off. The production is lush, from opening credits to knockout special effects and locations. As Superman, Christopher Reeve doesn't just soar, he reseals the San Andreas Fault and voyages among the stars. The script is delightful—camp but not too cute. The actors manage to be more than comic-book characters, especially villain Gene Hackman (as that archenemy Lex Luthor) and Jackie Cooper (as Perry White). Marlon Brando was paid millions to be pedestrian in the extreme as Supie's dad, but Reeve is terrific. As Clark Kent, he turns out to be not only mild-mannered but funny, too, while his high-altitude alter ego is Kryptic as well as tender with Lois Lane (Margot Kidder). While Reeve was doomed in a way by his own success—eight years and three sequels later he was still the Man of Steel—it wasn't a terrible way to go. The ending, truncated to make way for Superman II, is unsatisfying, and the effects sometimes run amok, but it is, after all, a fable. The good guy wins big and with style—make that a capital "S."
PG / 1979 / Warner

▲ SUPERMAN II

That old adage about the sequel never being as good gets blown away like the planet Krypton in Superman II. The novelty is gone and so, for better or worse, is Brando, but this film is much

better. The special effects, with nip-and-tuck rescues from Niagara Falls to the Eiffel Tower, provide the giddy sensation of daydreams fulfilled. This time Christopher Reeve's Man of Steel is up against those three archvillains (Terence Stamp, Jack O'Halloran, and Sarah Douglas) Papa Brando dispatched to a cosmic void in the original Superman. Possessed of extravagant powers, these meanies, with the help of the still devious Gene Hackman, attempt to humble Supie. Director Richard (A Hard Day's Night) Lester, replacing the axed Dick Donner, hadn't lost his waggish style. The big surprise, though, is how beautifully the love story comes through. Reeve still seems blissfully right as Superman (there's a disarming tickle in his performance) and hopelessly smitten with Margot Kidder's sassy Lois Lane. When he reveals his love and true identity to her, it's one of those magic movie moments, more potently erotic for being so restrained. Then Supermom Susannah York declares her son must give up his powers to have Lois, inciting a pull-out-the-stops romantic wallow. Superman II is irresistible.
PG / 1981 / Warner

▲ SUPERMAN III

Always most intriguing when he reveals a touch of flawed humanity, the Man of Steel had his best moment in Superman II when he finally cast off his superego and bedded down with Lois. In Superman III, he goes one step further, metamorphosing into a Scotch-guzzling, unshaven sleazeball. In one scene he breaks bottles in a dive by supersonically tossing beer nuts, then jets off to wreak havoc upon the world. The Superman-goes-psycho bit (he's driven temporarily insane by a chunk of doctored kryptonite) is the centerpiece of the film, directed by Richard Lester and written by David and Leslie Newman, who also collaborated on numbers 1 and 2. Richard Pryor is the delightful villain of the movie, a fired restaurant worker who discovers he has talent for high tech. His services are commandeered by boss Robert Vaughan, a multinational bad guy who quotes Attila the Hun and won't rest till he's conquered the world. The plot juxtaposes the Pryor-Vaughan villainy and Clark Kent's blossoming romance with hometown girl Lana Lang, played with sexy vulnerability by Annette O'Toole. (Lois Lane, in the guise of

Superman: In his first scheduled flight as the newspaper nerd who turns into the Man of Steel, Christopher Reeve zooms off to defend truth, justice, and the sequel way.

Margo Kidder, appears only briefly. Kidder had talked herself out of the film in a dispute with the producers, but later compromised on a cameo.) Lester and Co. keep things moving with sight gags and shrewd satire of the 1980s computer culture. Christopher Reeve turns in a wonderfully playful performance as the schizo hero, grinning wickedly during his super stupor as he straightens up the Leaning Tower of Pisa and blows out the Olympic flame. The film loses most of its spark three-fourths of the way through, bogging down in an endless, metaphysical junkyard battle between Superman's good and evil sides and finishing with the requisite scene of mass destruction. Still, if not as exhilarating as *Superman II, Superman III* is surprising and boisterously witty.
PG / 1983 / Warner

▲ THE SURE THING

Just when you think this is another run-of-the-corridor college comedy, along comes a sharp-tongued, lovable young actor, John Cusack, to splash ice water on your weary eyes. An amiable product of the Bill Murray/Tom Hanks school of situational lunacy, Cusack earned a cozy spot for himself, even in the current overpopulated world of young male stars. As a fun-loving Ivy League freshman who falls in love with bookworm cum laude Daphne Zuniga, Cusack glides along serving up one-liners. He makes a play for a girl, for instance, with the promise of "a sexual encounter so intense it could conceivably change your political views." He feigns insanity to confuse a lecherous good old boy intent on having his way with Zuniga. He tenderly talks about wanting to have a son named Nick ("the kind of guy who doesn't mind if you puke in his car"). Throughout, Cusack has the presence and timing to pull off the strangest of deadpans with panache. Otherwise, director Rob Reiner, who took a questionable 180-degree turn from the originality of his brilliant 1984 satire, *This Is Spinal Tap,* does a pedestrian job with the standard tale of the mismatched pair who inevitably get together. The bright spot: Zuniga has a spirited charm to match her soulful face. Viveca Lindfors, as a hip English professor, and Lisa Jane Persky and Tim Robbins, as nerds who pass time on a cross-country auto trip with bad renditions of every known show tune, offer a little support. The sound track is solid, with original music by Tom Scott. The film lapses too often into the predictability endemic to the genre, but anyone stricken with an irresistible urge to see another movie about teenage tribulations could choose worse.

PG-13 / 1985 / Embassy

▲ THE SURVIVORS

Two men are sitting in a cheap diner in New York City. One of them, Robin Williams, is moaning that he has just lost his once lucrative salesman's job. The other, Walter Matthau, is out of work too; his gas station blew up. Then in strides Jerry Reed; he's been fired from his job as a mob hitman and has to resort to common stickups. The fun is supposed to start here, but what could have been an amusing comedy about the tribulations of the unemployed turns out to be as funny as a two-hour wait in a soup kitchen. Director Michael (*The Bad News Bears*) Ritchie and screenwriter Michael (TV's "Taxi") Leeson turn the plot into a pallid chase, with Reed in pursuit of Williams and Matthau because he knows they have seen his face. Williams, in desperation, joins a survival training course. Matthau just wants to hide out. If that sounds like the movie is all over the lot, it sounds right. Williams displays his customary energy, complete with self-generated sound effects. Matthau is laconic, and Reed has some nicely turned moments—a seemingly calm conversation while he holds a loaded gun to Matthau's head, for instance. Kristen Vigard, then 19, is appealing as Matthau's daughter. But the film is too unfocused; it's not something the cast will ever feature on their resumes.

R / 1983 / RCA/Columbia

▲ SUSPIRIA

Allegedly a thriller, this Italian import is about as scary as a bowl of cold ravioli—and not much more interesting. Jessica Harper plays a young dancer who arrives at a ballet school in Germany run by Joan Bennett, who made a sadly dumb choice if she was looking for a comeback vehicle. The school is actually the lair of a moldering old witch, however, and some listless mayhem ensues. The film, directed by Dario Argento, has a grating sound track that randomly rises to a painful pitch. The title is never explained; it may be Italian for "pretty boring."

R / 1977 / N/A

▲ SWAMP THING

It's the old story: Boy meets girl, boy loses girl, boy turns into a plant. Based on DC Comics characters, *Swamp Thing* opens with the arrival of Adrienne Barbeau at a remote research laboratory. (The actual location was Charleston, South Carolina.) Someone is sabotaging experiments involving recombinant DNA. Can vegetable cells be fused with an animal's to create aggressive plants? Or will a monster result? Louis Jourdan, in a mood to rule the world, shows up and attempts a takeover of the lab. Barbeau escapes with some crucial notes and flees into a bog, where she meets her old scientist boyfriend. He has gotten recombined and is no longer much in the looks department—he resembles a descaled, vegetarian version of the Creature from the Black Lagoon. But as plants go, he's affectionate. So they go off together, hand in stalk, to face Jourdan, who ends up drinking some stuff he hopes will change him into a kind of supercabbage. Suffice it to say, he could have had a V-8.

PG / 1982 / Embassy

▲ SWANN IN LOVE

Proust scholars may carp. Those who have spent the better part of a lifetime plowing through the Master's seven-part *Remembrance of Things Past* may fault director Volker Schlondorff's version of a fragment of the novel. But *Swann in Love*'s clumsier literary contrivances are forgivable because it is so ravishingly photographed. (Could fin de siècle Paris ever have been as lovely as Sven Nykvist's camera sees it now?) Jeremy Irons plays Swann, a French Jew who has managed to infiltrate high society without overcoming the feeling that he's an outsider. When he inexplicably falls for Ornella Muti, a former prostitute his friends can't abide, his world begins to crumble. The film follows a twenty-four-hour period in Swann's life, with an epilogue showing how he eventually comes to ruin. One scene in which

Irons and his coachmen pursue Muti through the night to the Paris opera (the coachmen's contempt for their master is barely contained) captures Proust's world. At other times Schlondorff and co-screenwriter Peter Brook blunder badly, approaching the material with hats in hand. At these moments the camera merely stares, while the characters recite awkward lines and the rest of us admire the furniture. Muti can't begin to plumb the depths of the woman who is Swann's poisonous passion, but Fanny Arant and Marie-Christine Barrault are first-rate as society queenpins. French matinee idol Alain Delon, nearly disfigured by makeup, brilliantly creates the tortured homosexual Baron de Charlus, and though Irons's British-accented French won't please purists, not since Olivier's Healthcliff days has an actor matched piercing intelligence with such imposing good looks and physical grace. While Stallone flexes and Gere grunts, Irons may single-handedly bring back the romantic leading man. (In French with subtitles.)

R / 1984 / Cinémathèque

▲ THE SWARM

Producer Irwin Allen, that master of disaster, this time had a bee in his bonnet. A gigantic swarm of African killer bees descends on the American Southwest and wreaks unholy havoc. The plot is preposterous, and the dialogue belongs in comic strip balloons. There are so many performers (thirteen) that several members of the all-star cast have only three or four lines before they buzz off. Henry Fonda alone escapes mortification. Michael Caine, Katharine Ross, and Richard Chamberlain are around too. But the real disappointment is the bees—they simply aren't scary. From a distance the swarm looks like dirt on the camera lens, and up close the little devils act like what they are—harmless and busy bugs. This is one Bee-picture that's really a D-picture.

PG / 1978 / Warner

▲ SWEET DREAMS

Jessica Lange checked in with another incandescent performance in this film biography of Patsy Cline, the country singer who died in a 1963 plane crash en route to her home in Nashville. Cline was on the verge of a major crossover career, and thanks to her legacy on record, including such hits as "I Fall to Pieces," "Crazy," and "Sweet Dreams," she has achieved cult status since her death. Lange, bedecked in wigs and glitter, is sultry, nervy, delicate, and altogether amazing as Cline. No singer, Lange mouths the words while Patsy's throaty wail (from various recordings) flows heartbreakingly from the sound track. Lange's lipsynching is expert, but its the way she (not the script) gets at what's burning inside her character that makes the film more than a country version of TV's "Puttin' on the Hits." Still, Sweet Dreams is haunted by a ghost that undercuts it at almost every turn. The ghost is not Cline's but that of Coal Miner's Daughter, the superb 1980 film in which Oscar winner Sissy Spacek acted and sang the role of Loretta Lynn, Patsy's protégée (Cline was wonderfully acted and sung then by Beverly D'Angelo). With an evocative screenplay by Tom Rickman, Daughter uncovered the country roots that inspired Lynn to build an original musical style. Sweet Dreams deals only with the last six years of Cline's life, and Robert Getchell's script skimps on musical passion in favor of the achingly familiar domestic variety. Much of the film is taken up by Cline's bickering with her lusty, abusive second husband, Charlie Dick, played by Ed Harris, a fine actor who may have impersonated one too many cheatin' rednecks (Places in the Heart, Swing Shift, Alamo Bay). Director Karel Reisz leans hard on the Lange-Harris sexual chemistry. They have it to spare, but their big scene (a slow dance to a Sam Cooke number on a car radio) seems a direct lift from the more erotic Harrison Ford–Kelly McGillis scene in Witness. Cline deserved more for her life story than a downhome remake of A Star Is Born. But in Jessica Lange she at least found an actress to memorialize her tang and tenacity. For that reason Sweet Dreams—sour notes and all—stands as a tribute to both their talents.

PG-13 / 1985 / Thorn/EMI

▲ SWEET LIBERTY

Nitpick if you like over the blah parts, but it's more fun to just give in and enjoy writer-director-star Alan Alda's otherwise sharp and sassy comedy about moviemaking. In his first film since 1981's over-40 favorite, *The Four Seasons,* Alda plays a divorced college professor in a small North Carolina town. Having sold the movie rights to his Pulitzer prizewinning novel on the American Revolution, the prof must now face a Hollywood invasion. His genteel southern hamlet (actually Long Island's swanky Hamptons, where Alda has a home) is deemed the perfect shooting location. Things get imperfect fast. Alda's first encounter is with the screenwriter, a toadying hack with the wardrobe of an L.A. used-car salesman and mouth to match. British actor Bob (*The Cotton Club*) Hoskins plays him in a burst of comic inspiration. "Step on me, curse me, use me," he tells Alda, desperate to be associated with anything approaching real literature. The main obstacle to quality is the whiz-kid director, played by Saul (*Against All Odds*) Rubinek, who sees historical fact as a low priority compared to teen audience demand for nudity and *Animal House* mayhem. Alda, learning that the way to win at movies is through the egos of its stars, flatters the film's womanizing hero (saucily done by Michael Caine) and plays up to leading lady Michelle (*Into the Night*) Pfeiffer's penchant for accents and accuracy. The delectable Pfeiffer delivers a wickedly funny send-up of the kind of actress who'd bed or betray anyone to improve her performance. Alda is on to something here about the corrupt ways movies make their magic. But as in his 1979 political satire, *The Seduction of Joe Tynan,* Alda fails to go far enough. He falls instead into safe sitcom gentility. One subplot about his aged, crackpot mother (Lillian Gish) is irrelevant; another, involving his romance with a fellow teacher, Lise (*The Hunger*) Hilboldt, pushes cute to the cringe level. But why kick? Alda may be stroking his hard-won mainstream audience with one hand, but he's jabbing it into awareness with the other. That subversive hand deserves more exercise. When Alda uses it, *Sweet Liberty* is a fresh, frisky charmer.

PG / 1986 / MCA

▲ SWEET REVENGE

A dog 'n' cat comedy in which Sam Waterston, sincere buttoned-down lawyer, tries to reform a street-smart auto klepto, Stockard Channing. (With the aid of movie newcomer Franklyn Ajaye, who specializes in radios and tape decks, she has been cleaning out the parking lots of Seattle.) Some hotter wiring between the principals would have helped, but this is still a lively film with an engaging cast.

PG / 1977 / N/A

▲ SWING SHIFT

The advance word on this film spelled trouble: The opening kept being delayed, and at least two screenwriters (Nancy Dowd and Robert Towne) had their names removed from the credits. When the film finally showed up, it was hard to understand the fuss. Director Jonathan Demme turned out a fresh, funny, moonbeam of a movie about the women who went to work in defense plants when their men went to war in 1941. The period details are convincing, and the stirrings of feminism among the women are unexpectedly moving. Goldie Hawn, rarely as sexy or scintillating, also shows new depths as the wife of Ed Harris. When hubby goes to sea, Hawn takes a job at a Santa Monica plant and finds herself wooed by a 4-F (for a bad heart) worker, extraordinarily well played by Kurt Russell, Goldie's real-life love. They fall in love *first,* then go to bed. (There's real proof that this, bless it, is a period film.) Hawn's singer-turned-riveter pal, acted with Eve Arden zest and Joan Crawford glamour by Christine Lahti, helps Hawn deceive the neighbors by pretending Russell is her boyfriend. But Lahti is really carrying a torch for gruff dance-hall owner Fred Ward. What could have been a mawkish 1940s-style soap opera becomes something more delicate and deceptively complex. Demme never turns his characters into clichés. There are no bad guys. Harris is touching as the wronged husband. Hawn's loneliness, Russell's frustration, and Lahti's bitterness are all presented without a breath of ill will. These are decent people who don't need the cutting edge of one-liners to work their way into the heart of an audience. Though *Swing Shift* was a box-office dud, it stands as American moviemaking at its lyrical, buoyant best.

PG / 1984 / Warner

T

▲ TABLE FOR FIVE

How can a divorced father whose three children live with their mother show them he still loves them? When he is hampered by his incompetence, a devoted stepfather's appeal, and myriad external complications, he can suffer a lot. And Jon Voight does plenty of that in this sometimes wrenching, sometimes dumb film. He has a number of quietly touching scenes with the children— played with understatement, happily, by Roxana Zal, then 13, Robby Kiger, then 9, and Saigon-born Son Hoang Bul, then 15, effectively sullen as Voight's adopted Vietnamese son. But the movie is full of preposterous turns of event, not the least of which is the cruise to the Mediterranean that Voight, as a ne'er-do-well schemer, can somehow afford to take the kids on. That forms the set for the drama. There's an admirable supporting cast: Marie Christine (*Stardust Memories*) Barrault, as the French divorcee Voight woos, with incredible ease; Richard Crenna, as the good-hearted but self-righteous stepfather; and Millie Perkins, as Voight's ex-wife. Like Voight and the children, though, they are the victims of director Robert Lieberman, making his first feature after a career noteworthy mainly for his McDonald's commercials, and writer David Seltzer, who may have jerked one too many a tear, having scripted *The Other Side of the Mountain* as well as *Six Weeks*. Instead of gaining momentum, the film just loses plausibility until all the plot twists braid themselves together too neatly, ending up like a bad wig with nary a strand out of place
PG / 1983 / CBS/Fox

▲ TAI-PAN

With some movies, you're forever checking your watch; with Tai-Pan, you'll be checking your calendar. Adapted from James Clavell's 1966 novel, this $25 million time-warp epic honors all the traditions of clunky spectacles from thirty years ago. In this account of the founding of Hong Kong in the mid 1800s, you have your big brawny hero, a renegade who will be brought down by his own greed. You have your native girl, who will stand by and sleep by her man. You have your cast, or in this case castes, of thousands, who persevere through typhoons and terrible dialogue. You have trouble. As a history lesson, the ostensible purpose of Clavell's narrative, this is a cartoon lecture. As a romance, it's as sexist as it is sentimental. As travelogue, the kind of thing that usually gives these ventures some redeeming value, it's second-rate compared to anything at Disney's Epcot Center. Besides the audience, the only real victim of this exercise is Bryan Brown, still a movie star waiting to happen. Likeable, rugged, and idiosyncratic, Brown has yet to find his vehicle. Although director Daryl Duke shaped *The Thorn Birds* into one of TV's most compelling melodramas, he hasn't found a consistent style here. With its cumbersome narrative and clumsy pacing, *Tai-Pan* makes it look as if Duke hasn't seen a movie since *The Greatest Story Ever Told*.
R / 1986 / Vestron

▲ TAKE DOWN

The students of working-class Mingo Junction High want to beat their arch-rivals, snooty Rockville, just once—at anything. Wrestling is their last hope, but Mingo doesn't even have a team until a sorry-tailed bunch of losers gets together in desperation. Shot on a sneaker-string ($1.8 million) in American Fork, Utah (starring many local high schoolers), *Take Down* was the first independent film distributed by Walt Disney Productions in twenty years and the first PG ever. (The rating is due to some locker-room language.) Director Keith Merrill, whose documentary *The Great American Cowboy* won a 1973 Oscar, creates a mood that's real without being artsy-gritty and wrings individuality from his amateur actors. But this film is, as they say at graduation, not an end but a beginning. Kevin Hooks and Lorenzo Lamas were part of the talented young cast. The hunky Lamas showed he could act as

well as project a "lean-on-me" quality reminiscent of the young Gary Cooper.
PG / 1979 / Unicorn

▲ TANK

"This will be our last post, so let's just tough it out," Shirley Jones advices her son, C. Thomas Howell, and husband James Garner. That advice would be helpful to anyone who plans on watching this confused movie. Garner is a career Army noncom trying to coast through his last assignment at a small southern post (the film was shot at Fort Benning, Georgia) until he can retire to life on a fishing boat. But screenwriter Dan Gordon throws every southern stereotype imaginable in his way. The most offensive of them is G. D. Spradlin, a racist sheriff who arrests young Howell. Garner then battles the sheriff throughout the film with the help of a World War II Sherman tank. The premise may sound amusing, but director Marvin J. Chomsky has interspersed a preposterous plot development with scenes of child abuse that are shockingly inappropriate to the comic tone of the movie. Then, too, there is sadistic behavior from the sheriff and sappy, *Ordinary People*-style family confrontations. The usually wry Garner seems listless, as though he's constantly in pain. And when the film tries to be sentimental, it's only ludicrous. Are we supposed to be moved? Thanks, but no, Tanks.
PG / 1984 / MCA

▲ TAPS

There is probably an allegory about Vietnam in this film about the boys at a military academy who take over their school to protest its sale to real estate developers. Or maybe it's a parable of militarism. Or a treatise on fanaticism and honor. Maybe it's all of the above, which would be fine if that were clear. Instead, as events escalate into a predictable confrontation with the National Guard, the movie too often seems to be about nothing more than boys planning war. It is not the cast's fault. You expect George C. Scott, in a small but telling role as the academy superintendent, to be good. But the young actors are a splendid surprise. Timothy (*Ordinary People*) Hutton brings dignity and strength to his part as the cadet leader. He's supported by such teenage

newcomers as Sean Penn and Tom Cruise (whatever happened to them?) It's fun watching all this young talent before their press agents told them they were stars. These young men often manage to arouse compassion at the same time that the script and the direction by Harold (*The Black Marble*) Becker are arousing disdain.
PG / 1982 / CBS/Fox

▲ TARGET

For all the money, talent, and skill expended, not to mention the excitement engendered, this slam-bang spy thriller ultimately shakes down as a disappointment. That's too bad, for the idea had promise. The ever resourceful Gene Hackman (this was his fortieth film, and it's hard to recall a bad performance) stars as a Dallas lumberyard owner, a slow, steady type with a college dropout son, played by teen idol Matt Dillon, and a sexy wife, Gayle Hunnicutt. When wife takes a European vacation that hubby's too busy to share, Dad is left home alone to try to communicate with his alienated boy. Hackman's playful glint, Dillon's becoming modesty, and director Arthur Penn's stylish intensity combine to make these early scenes touchingly real. And when the plot jolt comes (Hunnicutt is kidnapped, and father and son rush to Paris for the rescue), the audience is hooked. There's fun too when Milquetoast Hackman reveals his hidden past—he's an ex-CIA agent with a stash of 007 tricks and a lost love in the exotic person of Russian actress Victoria Fyodorova. We're flabbergasted, along with Dillon, as the old man rips into action. Right here, though, *Target* stumbles onto a mine field of plot improbabilities. Penn's high-speed pacing helps only briefly. Car chases, lurking shadows, trigger bombs, and last-minute rescues, however well staged, are still overused, B-picture conventions. The Hackman-Dillon relationship had led us to expect more than standard hokum.
R / 1985 / CBS/Fox

▲ TARZAN, THE APE MAN

"I'm still a virgin; what are you?" asks Bo Derek's Jane of Miles O'Keeffe's uncomprehending Ape Man. With lines like that, it's no wonder Tarzan finds it more sensible just to yell. Despite the claims by the estate of creator Edgar

Rice Burroughs that Bo and her director-husband John Derek profaned him in this $5.5 million mom-and-pop production, Tarzan isn't around long enough to make an impression. He isn't even seen the first hour. Then he swings in, bundles Bo off to his tree house, and stares at her like a mooning Malibu lifeguard. Though Derek keeps the setting in 1910, he and screenwriters Tom Rowe and Gary Goddard insinuated feminist attitudes into Jane so that she can seem an early free spirit beset by sexist double standards. Her adventurer father, woefully overplayed by Richard Harris, orders her around and nurses thoughts of incest. "I wallow in myself," says hambone Harris, who might be speaking for the director. Without success, Derek tries to make the film lofty instead of capitalizing on the jungle fantasy with which *Tarzan* made its bundle in past incarnations. His photography is unyieldingly pretentious (the focus isn't soft, it's marshmallow), and his slow-motion effects in action scenes are infuriating. When all else fails, he ogles Bo. Whether swimming in the nude, frolicking topless with the animals, or teaching Tarzan a new way to count to ten, she's admittedly enough to make a monkey out of any man. The movie died on the vine but could have made a terrific calendar.

R / 1981 / MGM/UA

▲ TEACHERS

CLASS REPORT: *What This Work Is About:* It's about, like, a public high school where the teachers don't teach and the students don't study and Nick Nolte doesn't give a damn. It's about JFK High where the best substitute teacher is a mental hospital outpatient. It's about 105 minutes. *What the Themes Are:* Nick Nolte should give a damn. Students can transform teachers into real people again. *What This Work Tells Us:* If you're lucky, your most boring teacher will croak right in the classroom. *What I Learned from This Assignment:* A movie can be funny, black, and biting one moment and pretentious, ponderous, and silly the next. Even a strong cast, which includes Lee Grant and Ralph Macchio, can't salvage a rickety script. Director Arthur Hiller should not make JoBeth Williams strip in a school corridor just because screenwriter W. R. McKinney can't think of a better climax. Judd Hirsch does strange

things with his nostrils when he loses his temper. Nick Nolte has done enough hangover scenes.

R / 1984 / CBS/Fox

▲ TEEN WOLF

Michael J. Fox plays an ordinary, small-town high schooler in the throes of an out-of-the-ordinary adolescence, sprouting strange chest fur and clawlike fingernails. Yep, he is a natural-born werewolf, but one whose interests turn more to chasing girls and winning the school basketball championship than chomping on passersby. Suddenly he finds athletic ability, power, and celebrity, the wolf emerging as his alter ego much as the Buddy Love character did in Jerry Lewis's *Nutty Professor.* Fox's performance is remarkably controlled. His natural comic ability adds a little flair to every situation. Veteran character actor James Hampton is wonderful as Fox's knowing father, himself a chummy sort of werewolf in tortoise shell glasses and graying whiskers. Susan Ursitti and Jerry Levine also fare well. Ursitti is the "nice" girl whom Fox overlooks while pursuing the proverbial dumb blonde (Lorie Griffin); Levine is the fast-talking, enterprising buddy who sees the marketing possibilities in the wolf—T-shirts, buttons, banners. Director Rod Daniel doesn't quite have the light touch of John Landis, who directed 1982's *An American Werewolf in London.* But this combination of wolf and Fox is well-intentioned, harmless fun, and it's got *I Was a Teenage Werewolf,* the lycanthropic skeleton in Michael Landon's closet, beat by a mile.

PG / 1985 / Paramount

▲ TELEFON

Charles Bronson would have been a great silent movie star: He is so good at action and so bad at the speaking parts. In this feeble effort a renegade KGB clerk flips out and threatens to trigger fifty-one Russian spies living in America. So far so good, but when Bronson, as the Russian super-agent sent to stop him, tries to suave it up à la Cary Grant, he becomes laughable. At least Lee Remick, a lovely double agent, has the good sense to play it for jokes from the start. Bronson seems familiar with only two acting devices—pulling a trigger and throwing a punch. They're not enough to get him or anyone else through this.

PG / 1977 / MGM/UA

▲ TELL ME A RIDDLE

Okay. What takes 90 minutes, is depressing, and leaves you feeling empty? No, not a tax audit or eating at a bad Chinese restaurant but this singularly bleak movie about two people growing old together unhappily. Melvyn Douglas and Lila (*Zorba the Greek*) Kedrova both deliver affecting performances as the oldsters, and talented Brooke Adams, who plays their granddaughter, brightens up the screen whenever she appears. But even Brooke can't rescue a screenplay as grim as this one. The movie has a washed-out look, too, and the camera work is uncertain at times. Director Lee Grant, best known for her Oscar-winning performance in *Shampoo,* brought in her first film for under $2 million, which is commendable. The dreary result isn't.

PG / 1981 / Media

▲ TEMPEST

In his seven previous films, including *An Unmarried Woman* and *Harry and Tonto,* director Paul Mazursky had often been unorthodox, but until this film he never quite seemed incompetent. He turned the plot of Shakespeare's play into a sort of tragicomedy with modern characters and settings. The tedious result, which runs nearly 2 hours and 30 minutes, is naturally loaded with generous borrowings from the Bard, but most moviegoers won't care a whole lot about that. What they will see is a mixed-up story of a New York architect, John Cassavetes, who leaves his actress wife, Gena Rowlands, to move with Susan Sarandon to a lush Aegean island. There Raul Julia, portraying a Puerto Rican-accented Caliban, sings *New York, New York* to the sheep and makes a pass at Cassavetes's teenage daughter, played by future star brat Molly Ringwald. Meanwhile, the architect discovers that he has supernatural powers, including the ability to conjure up a magnificent storm. Sarandon is as appealing as she was in *Atlantic City,* and Rowlands and Cassavetes are certainly first-rate actors. Mazursky and his wife Betsy turn up in a party sequence. And there are some funny moments, many of

them at a swanky, ultrastatus party. But mostly the humor is stale, the situations are clichéd. Those seeking a cinematic spin-off of Shakespeare's play might more profitably check out the 1956 film *Forbidden Planet.*

PG / 1982 / RCA/Columbia

▲ TENDER MERCIES

Here is a small, shining gem of a movie that sneaks into your heart with the insinuating potency of a great country song. Robert Duvall stars as a boozy, burned-out C&W singer-songwriter tentatively taking a few reticent steps back into music and life. Drinking and whoring had wrecked his first marriage, to a country queen (Betty Buckley), who retaliated by cutting him off from their daughter. His salvation is the love of a widow, played by luminous newcomer Tess Harper, who runs a shabby motel-gas station in Texas with the help of her young son (Allan Hubbard). Buckley, of Broadway's *Cats* and *The Mystery of Edwin Drood,* is bitchy and brilliant in a difficult role, and Ellen (*Diner*) Barkin etches a tough and touching portrait of the now grown daughter. Although Horton Foote's tense screenplay does bear some resemblance to the life of Nashville's onetime first couple, George Jones and ex-wife Tammy Wynette, don't expect a film à clef. *Tender Mercies* is about one man's emotional comeback, and Duvall gives it everything he has, which is saying a great deal. His beery singing voice is a revelation (Duvall himself wrote two of the appealing songs), and his unfussy, brightly burnished acting is the kind for which awards were invented (deservedly, he won the Oscar). Credit for the film's many grace notes must also go to director Bruce (*Breaker Morant*) Beresford, whose feel for character and atmosphere is unerring. That Beresford is Australian only makes the singular American quality of this accomplished, authentic film more remarkable.

PG / 1983 / Thorn/EMI

▲ TENTACLES

A man-eating octopus (its admirably varied diet includes shapely women and bouncing babies) is meandering around off sunny San Diego. Naturally, endangered residents ignore the warnings of John Huston, who unconvincingly plays an

agitated seaside reporter. Shelley Winters, his funny, fat sister, is buoyant, and Henry Fonda, as the amoral corporate exec, is firm of chin. Murky, however, is why Fonda and Huston would have lent themselves to such squishy nonsense.
PG / 1977 / Vestron

▲ 10 TO MIDNIGHT

First, take a story about a battle-weary cop who wages a personal war against street crime and makes it seem that the way of the vigilante might not be so bad after all. Next, hire a graying Charles Bronson to play the cop. Finally, use a publicity campaign that has *Death Wish III* written all over it. Sounds like enough to discourage viewers away in droves, doesn't it? Surprisingly, this film creates a taut, suspenseful game of psychotic cat-and-mouse and even steps aside to comment on the loopholes in our legal system. There are four solid performances. Bronson skillfully underplays the role of an embittered cop on the trail of a slasher who preys on women. Lisa (*An Officer and a Gentlemen*) Eilbacher, as Bronson's estranged daughter, and Andrew Stevens round off the trio of believable good guys. Gene (*Night Games*) Davis, as the murderer, brings the countenance of a schoolboy to his vengeful character, a manic depressive who is not the most fun date on campus. Israeli filmmakers Menahem Golan and Yorma Globus, responsible for such dubious ventures as 1981's *Enter the Ninja* and 1982's *Death Wish II,* are the executive producers of this perhaps accidentally substantial film. J. Lee (*The Guns of Navarone*) Thompson directed and, without skimping on the sex or violence, made this a film that offers some exposition along with the exploitation.
R / 1983 / MGM/UA

▲ THE TERMINATOR

The title character of this film speaks English with a terrible accent, never says more than one sentence at a time, is as expressive as a rhino, and moves as gracefully as an anvil with legs. In other words, he was born to be played by Arnold Schwarzenegger. His role is that of a murderous robot who looks like a human, or at least as much like a human as Arnold does. A nuclear war has

been started by computers to rid the world of human beings; during ensuing mop-up operations a man leads a human uprising, and the irritated computers send Arnold back through time to 1984 to wipe out the leader's mother before he's even born. A human soldier, Michale Biehn, makes the time trip, too, to try to save the woman. It was foolish to wait until halfway through the movie to explain all of this. But the plot device seems logical in context, and things move so fast there's no time to analyze anything too closely. Linda Hamilton, who plays the mother-to-be, is appealing, and Biehn is a fresh face. The most impressive credit of director/co-screenwriter James Cameron was that he had seen *2001* (more recently he had directed *Piranha II*). He keeps things under control nicely, though, right through the final confrontation. It wouldn't be fair to give too many details. Suffice it to say that Arnold has a run-in with a hydraulic press, and in any realistic sequel he'd have to be playing a waffle iron.
R / 1984 / Thorn/EMI

▲ TERMS OF ENDEARMENT

The year of 1983 produced films more ambitious (*The Right Stuff*), more profound (*Fanny and Alexander*), and more stylish (*Zelig*), but none better charted the course of the human heart than *Terms of Endearment*. Based on the 1975 novel by Texas writer Larry McMurty, it traces the relationship of mother and daughter from the daughter's birth to her bout with cancer as a 30-year-old mother of two. Give up the idea right now, though, that this is a mawkish weepie out of the *Love Story* mold. *Terms* earns the laughter and sobs it provokes, thanks to career-crowning performances from Shirley MacLaine and Debra Winger as the mother and daughter. MacLaine, in her Oscar-winning role, eschews any hint of vanity or showbiz gloss as the fading Texas widow whose love for her daughter is not enough to reconcile their differences. The parent-child relationship has rarely been as wittily examined. Nothing Winger had done previously, including *Urban Cowboy* and *An Officer and a Gentleman,* prepared us for the virtuoso work she exhibits here; she is stunning. The screenplay by James Brooks, the creator of the ''Mary Tyler Moore Show'' and ''Taxi,'' is a model of economy and taste and, in his directorial debut, Brooks proves

The Terminator: Arnold Schwarzenegger, looking even more inhuman than usual, is a robot sent back from the future more or less to cause as much havoc and be as murderous as possible.

himself a master with actors. He chalked up a couple of Oscars, including the coveted Best Picture prize. Jack Nicholson is devilishly funny in his Oscar-winning role as MacLaine's next-door neighbor, a former astronaut she tries to distract from the jailbait nymphets he keeps chasing. Among the excellent supporting cast, Jeff Daniels, from Broadway's *Fifth of July,* is first-rate as Winger's unfaithful teacher husband, and John Lithgow is wonderfully touching as a shy bank officer Winger takes up with in retaliation. But it's MacLaine and Winger, forging a truce from a lifetime of hostilities, whose performances burn in the memory. Their final exchange of looks—no dialogue—packs an emotional reso-

nance that is shattering. Many movies are called unforgettable. *Terms of Endearment* is literally that.

R / 1983 / Paramount

▲ TERROR IN THE AISLES

Whatever is in the aisles, there seems to be slush in the brains of the people who made this non-movie. Misdirected by Andrew Kuehn and written by Margery Doppelt, both makers of coming attractions, it is an all-but-random compilation of clips from films that include *Midnight Express, To Catch a Thief,* and *Klute,* along with such

hard-core horrors as *The Thing with Two Heads, Konga,* and *Friday the 13th, Part II.* Between clips, which are meshed in a bewildering string and almost never identified, Donald Pleasence and Nancy Allen read idiotic transitions; their lines are uniformly without wit or insight. ("These are the movies that create our nightmares . . . or is it our nightmares that create the movies?") A couple of brief excerpts from an interview with Alfred Hitchcock are idly dropped in —he's the only person interviewed—among interminable shots of flashing knives, spurting blood, and sweating faces. The only thing this movie proves is that even the scariest scenes, when taken out of their tension-building context, are less likely to prompt tingling spines than droopy eyelids.
R / 1984 / MCA

▲ TERROR TRAIN

Amtrak won't look so bad after a 97-minute trip on this iron hearse. A college fraternity hires an old steam train for an all-night costume party, which turns ugly when an unknown murderer begins dispatching revelers in increasingly grisly fashion. The movie works better as a mystery than as a bloodcurdler, with several unusual plot twists before the killer is revealed. Veteran Ben Johnson lends a professional touch as the kindly engineer. Plucky Jamie Lee Curtis survives another cinematic encounter with an ax-wielding psycho. The script is uniformly bad, and novice director Roger Spottiswoode sets everything in distracting shadows, as if to hide the production's shabbiness. Two particularly dreadful moments stand out: an inane discussion about recreational vehicles and a scene in which Johnson attempts to dance with a lady in a wheelchair. Even hard-core chiller freaks won't want to get railroaded into catching this train to nowhere.
R / 1980 / N/A

▲ TESS

Previous Roman Polanski movies such as *Repulsion, Rosemary's Baby,* and *Chinatown* bordered on the perverse. In this one, based on Thomas Hardy's sprawling 19th-century novel *Tess of the d'Urbervilles,* Polanski plays it relatively safe, and the film is relatively boring. The adaptation is a faithful (3-hour) version of the story of a young Englishwoman victimized by the men in her life, beginning with a distant cousin who rapes her. The title role features Nastassja Kinski, then 20, the daughter of German actor Klaus Kinski and reportedly a former flame of Roman's. Though she seems to be playing dress-up in the period costumes, Kinski has an exquisite Bergmanesque beauty. The Oscar-winning photography is also gorgeous, evoking the misty English countryside (though most of the movie was shot in France). It was good, too, to see Polanski, always a fascinating director, back at work— even on what is more a succession of still lifes than a real fleshed-out movie.
PG / 1980 / RCA/Columbia

▲ TESTAMENT

Testament possesses the virtues of a PBS production: It's tasteful, discreet, intimate, and sensitive. Unfortunately, those qualities are not necessarily virtues when the subject at hand is the aftermath of a nuclear attack. In a suburb north of San Francisco, Jane Alexander, a mother of three, struggles to maintain her houshold, even though she knows fallout will prove fatal to nearly everyone. By keeping the camera basically on one family and town, director Lynne Littman, in her first feature, is aiming for the heart more than the mind. There are some unexpectedly touching moments, as when Alexander's doomed daughter asks her mother what lovemaking is like. But unlike ABC's brutally explicit *The Day After,* this film is ever polite. We are spared violence, physical suffering, and panic in the streets. Worse, the film treats its children not as characters but as sentimental symbols. When grade school students stage *The Pied Piper of Hamelin,* the we-are-leading-our-kids-to-destruction message is more than clear. Alexander (Oscar-nominated as Best Actress) bestows this drama with quiet dignity; she can make the most banal monologue moving. And Littman, then married to director Taylor (*An Officer and a Gentleman*) Hackford, has a knack for intimate moments. But what you want with this kind of story is the Big Picture. Even those who agree with the film's pacifist politics are not likely to find any of that kind of power in it.
PG / 1983 / Paramount

▲ TEX

With 1982's *Tron,* the Disney studios used video games to get at the hearts and pockets of the Pac-Man generation. They met with limited success. That same year, with *Tex,* they took a different, more personal route and, if nothing else, proved even young men do not live by silicon chips alone. Based on S. E. Hinton's 1979 novel about two Oklahoma teenage brothers getting by without a mother (she's dead) or a father (he rides the rodeo circuit), *Tex* is the kind of film bound at first to strike most as wholesome, ho-hum, adolescent pandering. Nothing like it. First-time director Tim Hunter and co-screenwriter Charlie Haas (they co-wrote the 1979 gang film *Over the Edge*) captured both the grace and grittiness of Hinton's prose. Sex, drugs, violence, and racism have rarely reared their heads in a Disney film. That they do so here, realistically, is a credit to all concerned. Playing the title role—a shambling 15-year-old with few interests past his horse, his girl, and practical jokes—Matt Dillon is a revelation. His macho hood roles in *Little Darlings* and *My Bodyguard* earned him teen hunk status. In *Tex,* his face shows the play of thought in fresh, unexpected ways. Dillon, then 18, finds humor and honesty in the role with a disarming lack of guile. Jim Metzler, as Dillon's ulcer-ridden older and smarter brother, is also excellent. When the plot lurches into melodrama, the actors always wrench it back on track. *Tron* was an ambitious first attempt by Disney to change with the times. *Tex*—by showing that you cannot do it solely by computer—was its first triumph.
PG / 1982 / Disney

▲ THANK GOD IT'S FRIDAY

How soon they forget. *TGIF*'s production notes claimed this was "the first major film to utilize . . . a contemporary disco nightclub for its principal setting." Oh, really? Maybe the producers (Motown and Casablanca Record and Film Works) were simply jealous that they lacked John Travolta, the Bee Gees, and a plot. *TGIF* has a cast of characters aiming *Nashville*-style toward a Friday-night dance contest. The music is hardly memorable (except for Donna Summer's glorious "Last Dance," which won an Oscar). The hoofing is neo-two-step compared to *Saturday Night Fever*'s footwork fireworks. The movie was bad enough to help kill disco. It's notable now only for marking the film debut (in a minor role) of an extraordinary actress: Debra Winger.
PG / 1978 / RCA/Columbia

▲ THAT CHAMPIONSHIP SEASON

More than a decade ago Jason Miller's *That Championship Season* finished first on Broadway, earning Miller a Tony award and a Pulitzer Prize. The play, about the boozy twenty-fourth reunion of a Scranton, Pennsylvania, high school basketball team that had been state champion, was a mordant treatise on success. But it took Miller a long time to get a film version going, and he turned to acting (*The Exorcist, Monsignor*) instead. Producers were afraid his intimate drama could never be opened up for the screen. The boys with the bucks were right. The film is a faithful adaptation. But the playwright Miller was not well served by first-time director Miller, whose reverence for his own words created a static, stifling environment. What's left is a handful of fine actors struggling to break through stage conventions. Stacy Keach and Martin Sheen are solid as two brothers with a grudge. Bruce Dern is less psychotic than usual as the mayor who doesn't know he comes off like Bugs Bunny on TV. And Paul Sorvino (the only cast member who appeared in the play) adds sexist wit as a rich strip miner with a yen for married women—"They don't yell, tell, or swell, and they're grateful as hell." The powerhouse performance comes from Robert Mitchum as the bigoted, dying coach who does his best to keep his 40ish boys, "my real trophies," in arrested adolescence. Through the long dark night of beery confessionals, these actors can only suggest the sparks this drama gave off onstage. There it belongs, and there it should have stayed.
R / 1983 / MGM/UA

▲ THAT OBSCURE OBJECT OF DESIRE

Not quite so murky in its intentions as Luis Bunuel's past films, this, his last offering, shows the Spanish director still fascinated with psychological sleight of hand. Fernando Rey is a wealthy Frenchman who can have anything—except what he really wants, a Spanish girl who is so elusive and has moods so changeable that Rey is never quite sure just whom he is pursuing. Neither is the audience: Different actresses play the two incarnations of the girl—Carole Bouquet and Angela Molina. Between them, they convincingly portray the classical tease. (In French with subtitles.)

R / 1977 / N/A

▲ THAT'S DANCING!

So you say you hate motherhood, the flag, apple pie, baseball, milk, kittens, and rules against litterbugs, eh? Well then, you won't be able to stand this no-hassle package of unadulterated enjoyment descended from *That's Entertainment!* A few quibbles can be made. Many great routines—Gene Kelly's ''Singing in the Rain,'' for instance—were used up in *T.E.* or *T.E.II.* Among the narrators who connect clips of movie dance sequences are Sammy Davis, Jr., and Mikhail Baryshnikov, whose careers were not notably enhanced by films. The narration, written by director Jack Haley, Jr., tends to be obvious: ''Without movement, there would be no dancing.'' Some footage from Michael Jackson's ''Beat It'' video is tacked on at the end, as if to appease the younger generation. But what's crucial in this kind of anthology is that the clips run long enough to be representative, and Haley is diligent about that. A long sequence is devoted to the daffy, astonishing choreography of Busby Berkeley. There's a satisfying amount of Fred Astaire. There are even clips from *Saturday Night Fever,* *Flashdance,* and *Fame,* though nearly all the other excerpts date from before 1960. Seeing these performances, in or out of context, is always a joy.

G / 1985 / MGM/UA

▲ THAT'S LIFE!

With time left in the decade, it may be premature to label this emotional slop bucket from director Blake (*Victor/Victoria*) Edwards the worst major movie of the '80s. But it's surely a strong contender—up there with Coppola's *One from the Heart,* De Palma's *Scarface,* and Friedkin's *Cruising*—as the marker of a leading filmmaker's fall from success into wretched excess. Edwards, a past master of comedy (*Breakfast at Tiffany's,* *The Pink Panther*) and drama (*Days of Wine and*

Roses), used his own mid-life crisis as raw material. Working out of his Malibu beach house on a self-financed $1.5 million budget, he used a script he co-wrote with—and we don't make these things up—his analyst, Milton Wexler. Edwards even considered playing the lead, an architect coming apart just as his clan gathers to celebrate his sixtieth birthday. Instead, Edwards anointed his friend Jack Lemmon, who in lieu of a performance trots out a repertory of bughouse mannerisms that Tony Perkins might envy. Julie Andrews, the real-life Mrs. Edwards, plays Lemmon's wife. Her real daughter, Emma Walton, and his real daughter, Jennifer Edwards, play two of their children. Their son is played by Chris Lemmon, Jack's real son. Lemmon's wife, Felicia Farr, has a role as a nympho fortune-teller. Sally Kellerman plays a scatterbrained neighbor. Her husband is the film's executive producer. The nepotism goes on and on, as does this loathsome movie. Trapped with this self-pitying bunch, any sensible house guest would dive out a window and swim for Catalina. Lemmon thinks he's impotent, until the fortune-teller lifts his spirits and leaves him with crab lice (his squirming in church is used as an alleged source of humor). Lemmon whines that he'll never be Frank Lloyd Wright. The unmarried daughter (Walton) whines about her uncaring boyfriend. The pregnant daughter (Edwards) whines because her vain dad doesn't want the baby to call him grandfather. Mercifully, the lovely Andrews doesn't whine; she suffers in silence while awaiting results of her throat biopsy (an alleged source of suspense). There hasn't been a more repugnant crowd since the last *Friday the 13th* picture, and this time Jason isn't handy to dispatch the worst offenders. Edwards said making this film helped cure his depression. If so, he did it by transferring his ailment to his audience.

PG-13 / 1986 / RCA/Columbia

▲ THAT WAS THEN . . . THIS IS NOW

Emilio Estevez wrote the screenplay of this movie and plays the young punk who is its focus. He's more impressive as an actor than as a writer. For one thing, the dialogue is full of clunkers. For another, the film hinges on Estevez's moodiness, but we don't find out the reason for his rage— his dad shot his mom in an argument over him— until toward the end. This is supposed to be a film about growing up. Yet it becomes such a one-dimensional caricature of adolescent angst that it's hard to care what happens to Estevez. That's true even when he starts to unravel and his best friend, newcomer Craig Sheffer, deserts him to spend time with Kim Delaney. Despite some moving moments between Estevez and Sheffer, dull performances by Sheffer and Delaney don't help. This was the fourth S. E. Hinton novel about brooding youth to be turned into a movie. *Tex* was directed by Tim Hunter, *The Outsiders* and *Rumble Fish* by Francis Coppola. Christopher Cain did this one. None of them need have bothered.

R / 1985 / Paramount

▲ THEY ALL LAUGHED

But is it with or at Peter Bogdanovich, the writer and director of this unrelentingly frothy romantic comedy set in Manhattan? Ben Gazzara and John Ritter are private eyes who enjoy their work too much when they are hired to follow two wandering wives. Ritter's lovesick pursuit of Dorothy Stratten is more often a grating, WASPy Woody Allen shtick—except for one inspired roller-skating sequence. Gazzara's gumshoeing leads him into a subdued, richer bond with an underused Audrey Hepburn. Freckled top model Patti Hansen isn't bad as a cabby in her first film, but Colleen (*Apocalypse Now* and *Smile*) Camp is annoyingly mannered as a bitchy motor-mouth country singer who has designs on every man she spots. But even if this movie were funnier, it would be hard to laugh much, knowing that the lovely Stratten was shotgunned in a 1980 murder-suicide by her jealous estranged husband, in part because she and Bogdanovich had become close during its filming. For that story see Bob Fosse's 1983 film *Star 80*.

PG / 1982 / Vestron

▲ THIEF

Although the title may conjure up images of Cary Grant suavely cat-burgling on the Riviera, forget it. True, this is the story of a professional diamond thief, but so much for similarity. The heists are all bloodless, businesslike affairs. Shot largely in Chicago, this film provides an unromantic look at the dealings and double-dealings of the underworld, and there is not one good guy. James Caan, in his best work in years, played the title character with a steely single-mindedness. Tuesday Weld is excellent as his wife, the only vulnerable person in the movie, though her relationship with Caan is slighted, as is every other personalizing quality in the film. (Willie Nelson appears briefly in a curious cameo as a master thief.) Writer and director Michael Mann, whose previous credits included the Emmy Award-winning prison film *The Jericho Mile* and who later created "Miami Vice," has a strong sure hand, and *Thief*'s pounding pace is accentuated by Tangerine Dream's pulsating score. This is a powerful piece of moviemaking, lacking just one vital ingredient—heart.

R / 1981 / CBS/Fox

▲ THIEF OF HEARTS

Imagine an acting class that is giving a dramatic reading of, say, the Kearney, Nebraska, phone book. Nobody might want to see the work performed again, but the actors' skill can still be admired. That kind of reaction is the best this film can hope for. It's about a burglar who burgles the journals of a woman and finds her fantasies are much livelier than her life with her twerpy husband. Burglar meets girl, burglar loses girl, etc. Steven Bauer, who got the same sort of going-down-with-the-ship exposure in *Scarface*, plays the thief with some intensity. Canadian actress Barbara Williams as the wife and TV actor John Getz as the husband protect their reputations. David Caruso, who plays Bauer's psychopathic partner, is as palpably evil as Richard Widmark in *Kiss of Death* in 1947. This cast, though, gets no help from director Douglas Day Stewart. The story suggests fantasies are best left unlived.

R / 1984 / Paramount

▲ THE THING

A twelve-man American research team in Antarctica finds that a neighboring camp run by Norwegians has been devastated. Then a dog

from the deserted camp starts to run amok. Pretty soon some kind of monstrous force begins to invade the Americans' bodies. Yes, from there in the ice emerges a new version of the 1951 thriller of the same title. Both films are based on John W. Campbell, Jr.'s 1938 science fiction story *Who Goes There?* This one is directed by John (*Escape from New York*) Carpenter. He makes effective use of his chilling locations (in Alaska and Canada) as well as special-effects makeup by Rob (*The Howling*) Bottin and Ennio Morricone's subtle, doom-announcing synthesizer score. But a little more subtlety would have souped up the suspense. Kurt Russell plays the laconic hero, a role that did not make Kenneth Tobey the biggest of stars in the first version. Russell got luckier with other parts, especially *Silkwood* with Meryl Streep, and marriage to Goldie Hawn. You'll get luckier by skipping this remake and sticking to the original, available on Nostalgia Merchant Video.
R / 1982 / MCA

▲ THINGS ARE TOUGH ALL OVER

No one has mined the pits and peaks of the hopeless doper more than the comedy team of Cheech and Chong, both on records and in their zany films (*Up in Smoke, Nice Dreams*). Their lode of drug jokes seemed to be getting exhausted, though, and the labored measures they take to fill the void this time indicate that the boys' imaginations had been numbed. Two major devices are tip-offs to the uninspired plot. First, this is yet another on-the-road comedy—Cheech and Chong leave Chicago for Las Vegas in a car that, unbeknownst to them, has $5 million stuffed under a seat. Second, the boys play both themselves and the Arab brothers Slymand and Habib, who own a cartel of businesses all named Mecca. These sheiks are the not-so-rightful owners of the $5 million. The two sets of protagonists spend a lot of time just wandering around the desert, narrowly missing each other, and the only change of pace is when C&C are picked up hitchhiking by a corny comedian (Rip Taylor, playing himself). His jokes are even worse than the rest of the film—for example, "I just made a killing in the market: I shot my butcher." The movie's ending sets a new standard for feckless afterthoughts; a voiceover announces that the Arabs

have turned Cheech and Chong into pornographic movie stars. Where are Abbott and Costello when you really need them?
R / 1982 / RCA/Columbia

▲ THE THIRD GENERATION

The prolific Rainer Werner Fassbinder was one of the leaders of the new German cinema. In this feature, he took on the young terrorists plaguing Europe—and made mincemeat of them. The movie opens with a plot to kidnap a wealthy industrialist in Berlin. The gang planning the abduction is composed of malcontent, perhaps slightly psychotic men and women who think terrorism is a game. That, Fassbinder seems to be saying, is precisely what makes them so dangerous. Gradually they realize there is an informer in their midst, but not until some of them have been killed and maimed. The director's usual stock company is on hand, headed by Hanna Schygulla, who was so wonderful in Fassbinder's *The Marriage of Maria Braun*. She is the industrialist's scheming secretary. As always, the beauty of a Fassbinder film is in the telling—the camera work is stunning, the color and the music superbly complement the story line, and the director's chilling sense of irony is apparent. (In German with subtitles.)
Unrated / 1980 / N/A

▲ THIS IS ELVIS

No Presley fan could imagine a more sympathetic documentary than this collection of news footage, home movies, TV, film, and concert clips pieced together by Malcolm Leo and Andres Solt. Thanks to the cooperation of his manager, Col. Tom Parker—who once was quoted as saying, "I owned twenty-five percent of Elvis alive, and I own twenty-five percent of him dead"—rare film of the King at home in Graceland was made available. His wedding and honeymoon with Priscilla and their celebrations of the birth of their daughter Lisa Marie are shown too. Parker's participation is otherwise a mixed blessing. The film glosses over the singer's drug addiction and the pressures that left him a doughy, overweight mess before his death at 42. The narration is mere padding, and the attempt to bridge gaps with four Elvis stand-ins (Paul Boensch III, David Scott, Dana MacKay, Johnny Harra), ranging in age from 10 to 42, is disorienting. Still, the sight of Elvis onstage mesmerizes. Even at the end, his bloated body bathed in sweat, he invested a tune like "Are You Lonesome Tonight?" with grace and feeling. *This is Elvis* burnishes the legend but only just brushes the man.

PG / 1981 / Warner

▲ THIS IS SPINAL TAP

It's billed as a "Rockumentary by Marty Di Bergi." But it's fiction, not a documentary. And "Marty Di Bergi" is Rob Reiner, the film's director, co-writer, narrator, and co-star as a rock filmmaker. He focuses on a comeback attempt by a '60s heavy-metal rock band, Spinal Tap. In a style reminiscent of Martin Scorsese's *The Last Waltz,* Reiner does takeoffs on practically every rock cliché there is, with often hilarious results. As the leaders of the group, co-writers Michael McKean, Christopher Guest, and Harry Shearer deftly satirize the scream-and-shake school of pop rock, deadpanning their way through a script that goes from subtle humor to slapstick. The band plays to empty houses, fights over girlfriends' influence, and battles about "artistic differences" ("There's a fine line between stupid and . . . clever," Guess says to Reiner). The tiny Shearer gets trapped in an onstage fiberglass prop. The aging, bleached-blond idol McKean attempts to lead the group in an a cappella version of *Heartbreak Hotel* at Elvis Presley's gravesite. But Guest stands out as the misunderstood member of the group—when he's not working on a piece of his "Mach" music (Mozart mixed with Bach), he's complaining about the dressing-room food (the rye bread doesn't fit the cheese). The trio also wrote all the group's songs—"Sex Farm" and "Hell Hole," for instance—and performs them with great comic panache. There are cameos by such familiar faces as Billy Crystal, Ed Begley, Jr., David Letterman's band leader Paul Shaffer, and Howard Hesseman. This is a very funny movie—not as funny, perhaps, as some real-life heavy metal bands are unintentionally, but very funny.

R / 1984 / Embassy

▲ THOSE LIPS, THOSE EYES

The title does not mean that after his *Dracula,* Frank Langella stopped being a neck man and moved upward. There isn't a single nibble in this sometimes wryly amusing look at a Cleveland summer stock company grinding out operettas like *The Desert Song.* The time is 1951, and screenwriter David Shaber, himself a straw hat veteran, seems bent on recapturing the thrill of his brush with the theater. Langella helps. Even if his rendition of "Indian Love Call" could set Nelson Eddy spinning, he's astonishingly adept at light comedy. Engagingly goofy, the pre-*Amadeus* Tom Hulce plays a hick awestruck by Langella's matinee-idol panache. Glynnis O'Connor, as an adulterous lady in the troupe, and Jerry Stiller, as a harried father, do wonders in support. But director Michael Pressman buries his small, nice details under overwrought theatrics. What film, especially one so delicate, could survive lines like "I can touch up my hair but not my life"?

R / 1980 / MGM/UA

▲ THREE AMIGOS

About fifteen minutes into a packed Manhattan theater showing of this comedy starring Steve Martin, Chevy Chase, and Martin Short, a young woman turned with disgust to her date—who was howling uproariously—and said, "What a stupid movie." She was right. But you could understand his reaction. The star trio, playing silent-screen actors who get mistaken for real heroes by Mexican peasants, had actually earned that laugh. (It would be uncharitable to give the joke away since there are so few in the movie.) For the rest, this painfully forced farce coasts along—or tries to—on goodwill. Martin, Chase, and Short have all been so good before, especially on TV's "Saturday Night Live," that just seeing them sparks a smile. What might have been a decent five-minute SNL sketch has been stretched so thin it's lifeless. Martin, as co-screenwriter (with composer Randy Newman), fills in with anachronistic gags about light beer, genital japes, and sophomoric word play. Mere repetition of the phrase "a plethora of pinatas" is supposed to be the summit of literary gamesmanship. John (*The Blues Brothers, Spies Like Us*) Landis directed with his

customary heavy-handed comedy touch and encouraged his cast to giggle at their own inane shenanigans. It's like watching Sinatra and the Clan in Rat Pack movies of the 1960s: infuriating.
PG / 1986 / MCA

▲ THREE FOR THE ROAD

At only 88 minutes, this movie is still an hour and a half too long. The only thing it has going for it is Charlie Sheen, and he seems to be just going through the motions. Sheen plays a junior aide to a tyrannical U.S. senator, Raymond Barry. Barry is embarrassed by the high school pranks of his daughter, Kerri Green, and asks Sheen to drive her to a reform school in the South. Green, so good in *Lucas,* is woefully miscast as the troubled teen. It's impossible to believe that this adorable little thing could ruin her dad's campaign. She is so miscast that whatever potential there might have been for an interesting romance between her and Sheen is frittered away, though director B. W. L. Norton tried to force the notion anyway. Sheen starts to feel sorry for Green when she tells him she hasn't seen her mom, Sally Kellerman, in eight years. So he takes her to see Kellerman, setting up a cynical dad versus loving mom clash. Sheen got into this wreck before *Platoon* was released. So just consider it a youthful mistake.
PG / 1987 / N/A

▲ 3 WOMEN

In one of the most haunting movies of the 1970s, Sissy (*Carrie*) Spacek rooms with kindhearted loser Shelley Duvall, her co-worker in a Desert Springs bathhouse for arthritics. They are joined by the spaced-out Janice Rule, who paints lizardlike figures on the bottoms of swimming pools. Duvall is impressive, and the drugged pace is vintage Robert Altman, reminiscent of *Nashville* or *California Split.*
PG / 1977 / CBS/Fox

▲ THRESHOLD

The timing was phenomenal: a film about the world's first human to receive an artificial heart. The subject, however, was not Dr. Barney Clark

but a 20-year-old woman, played by Mare (*St. Elmo's Fire*) Winningham. The graphic realism of the film is reminiscent of documentary. Yet this is a drama, a fact that almost gets lost amid the clinical precision. Donald Sutherland is cast as an acclaimed heart surgeon frustrated by the limits of traditional operating procedures. Jeff Goldblum is the intense young biologist obsessed by his experiments with artificial hearts. They are researching the problem when Winningham appears. She is desperate; all standard operations have failed. Symbolism is abundant, from Winningham's feeling of emptiness after her heart is removed to Goldblum's self-serving quest for glory, which destroys his sense of humanity. But the film, for the most part, avoids overwrought emotionalism. Sutherland's interpretation of the surgeon is marvelous; he spent two days interviewing and observing cardiac surgeon Denton Cooley to prepare for the role. Yet his technical concerns didn't prevent him from adding restrained touches of humor to his performance. That makes his character a most convincing and sympathetic one. Goldblum's biologist has an appropriate otherworldliness, and Winningham conveys an appealing mix of uncertainty and bravado. Director Richard (*Woodstock*) Pearce's documentary experience is in evidence, while James Salter's original screenplay creates a tense hospital atmosphere. It might spoil the film to reveal its ending, but however the operation turns out, *Threshold* is a huge success.
PG / 1983 / CBS/Fox

▲ THUNDER AND LIGHTNING

Why are David Carradine and Kate Jackson racing through the Florida Everglades in a '57 Chevy? They're chasing after some poison moonshine, that's why. Kate's dad (Roger C. Carmel) is in the soft drink business as a cover for manufacturing the stronger stuff, and the Syndicate wants to take over his still. When Carradine, playing a small-time moonshine runner, sets out to recover a bad batch of Dad's brew, he becomes the latest entry on the mob's hit parade. The movie is one long chase scene, with Everglades airboats and the *de rigueur* smashed crates of squawking chickens.
PG / 1977 / Key

▲ TICKET TO HEAVEN

The Reverend Sun Myung Moon's Unification Church newspaper damned this movie as "a truly Archie Bunkeresque view of the phenomena of religious conversion," and it's easy to see why it would make cultists nervous. Canadian actor Nick Mancuso plays a young man getting over a broken romance who flies from Toronto to San Francisco to visit a friend. There he is sucked into a Moonie-like group, aided by the comely Kim Cattrall. Though the film is based on John Freed's 1980 book *Moonwebs,* about the Unification Church, this group is called the Heavenly Children. The young man's psychological defenses are quickly broken down, and he becomes a hollow-eyed, wasted member of the cult. Mancuso's transformation is startling—in one scene, having briefly escaped, he desperately wolfs down a forbidden hamburger and milkshake and then, out of guilt, induces vomiting to rid himself of the offending food. Equally good is Saul Rubinek, as a concerned friend who tries to rescue Mancuso. The most chilling sequences involve R. H. Thomson as a tall, sometimes brutal deprogrammer who locks Mancuso in a "safe house." Though sometimes didactic and cliched, this first feature by Canadian director Ralph Thomas has a raw power that makes it work as both message and drama.
PG / 1982 / MGM/UA

▲ TIGHTROPE

Don't hoot, cackle, throw things, or accuse any reviewers of losing their grip, but Clint Eastwood deserves credit for an astonishingly risky performance in this film. Eastwood had played variations on his granite-faced image before, especially in 1980's underrated *Bronco Billy,* but this time the effect is unsettling and unforgettable. As a New Orleans homicide detective, Eastwood is a man about to lose control. His wife has left him, and except for custody of his two young daughters (Jennifer Beck and Alison Eastwood, Clint's real daughter and a natural actress), his job is all he's got left. A series of sex slayings precipitates a crisis. Lonely and sex-starved himself, Eastwood starts seeking more than information from the whores he questions. When several of these women turn up dead soon after he beds them, he starts questioning his own sanity. (How to reconcile the loving father with the man who likes to handcuff hookers to bedposts?) A rape-crisis therapist, played with snappy authority by Geneviève Bujold, tries to help, but Eastwood must grapple with the killer and his conscience alone. *Tightrope* is not a perfect movie. The plot wobbles and the climax is a bloody, horror-movie cliché. But director Richard Tuggle, an Eastwood protégé who wrote *Escape from Alcatraz,* wisely kept the violence to a minimum and his star at stage center. The result is an eloquent character study from an actor who once talked with bullets. There's hope for Hollywood yet when a Clint Eastwood at 54 can summon the emotional resources of a major actor.
R / 1984 / Warner

▲ TILL MARRIAGE DO US PART

Knowing a good thing when they see it, American distributors fell all over themselves to dig up old Laura Antonelli movies to release here when she became hot in the late '70s. After *The Innocent* and *Wifemistress,* the beautiful, bountiful Italian actress indeed emerged as a Bardot-like phenomenon. In this 1974 comedy she played an innocent young bride who concludes she has mistakenly married her half brother. What follows is an erotic romp in which she alternately tries to suppress her carnal desires and to fulfill them, mainly with a leering, lusty chauffeur. There are some hilarious set pieces, and as her rich husband, Alberto Lionello is scandalously funny. With veteran French actor Jean Rochefort adding a perfect touch as a lovesick suitor, the film is a clever comedy that survived better than Antonelli's career did. (In Italian with subtitles.)
R / 1974 / Vestron

▲ TIME BANDITS

A number of Monty Python alumni worked on this film. Terry Gilliam directed and wrote the screenplay with Michael Palin, who's also in the cast, as is John Cleese. There are some Pythonesque plot touches too: an ogre who has a hard time being terrible because he has a bad back, a devil who wants to get into computers, a God who wears a baggy three-piece suit and has a neatness complex. This is less a comedy, however, than a child's nightmare crossed with *The*

Wizard of Oz, which it openly parallels in many ways. Young Craig Warnock plays a boy thrown in with a gang of dwarfs traveling through time looking for riches to plunder. They run into a lot of grim surrealistic sets, gruesome violence, including someone eating a live rat, and such characters as Robin Hood (Cleese), King Agamemnon (Sean Connery), and Napoleon (Ian Holm), as well as the Supreme Being and the Evil Genius (Sir Ralph Richardson and David Warner). Palin and Shelley Duvall also appear in two separate scenes as skittish lovers, once in medieval times, once on the *Titanic*. If this sounds meandering, it's more so on screen. The little people who play the dwarfs—Kenny (R2D2) Baker is among them—provide the film with some odd flashes of emotion. But the ending is enigmatic and the moral, if there is one, is hidden. This is an enterprising project in free-form cinema; it's just not very entertaining.
PG / 1981 / Paramount

▲ TIMES SQUARE

"Presenter" Robert Stigwood may have figured he could use this low-budget, new wave rock musical to sell sound track albums. There was a two-record set that featured Joe Jackson, the Talking Heads, Patti Smith, the Ramones, et al. But the album got no help from this implausible picture. Teenager Trini Alvarado decides to run off with a juvenile delinquent girlfriend (Robin Johnson), chucking private schools and servants for a home on an abandoned pier and a job in a grubby Times Square disco. Tim Curry is funny as a flaky deejay whose listeners establish the girls as minor new wave stars. As the Sleaze Sisters, they advertise by dropping TV sets from high-rises. While Curry makes things interesting, most of the script by Jacob Brackman, a composer who co-wrote Carly Simon's "Haven't Got Time for the Pain," is silly.
R / 1980 / Thorn/EMI

▲ THE TIN DRUM

Gunter Grass's *The Tin Drum,* about a child who defies the horrors of Nazism by refusing to grow up, has often been praised as Germany's finest postwar novel. Still, great books often make disappointing movies. But director Volker Schlondorff, with Grass's collaboration on the screenplay, created a magical and stirring film that captures the spirit of the book. The movie's parable about the dark side of human nature is rendered both more charming and more chilling by the use of a child as the protagonist, Oskar; David Bennent, then 13, with his large, sunken eyes and stubborn mouth, was brilliant. The film thoroughly deserved the Oscar it won for best foreign film. (In German with subtitles.)
R / 1980 / Warner

▲ TIN MEN

For starters this is the best comedy film ever made about the aluminum-siding business. It's also a comedy with a sober undertone, one of those clouds with the silver lining turned inside out. Subtly written and directed by Barry Levinson, it is a kind of sequel to his *Diner,* set in Baltimore in 1963. Danny DeVito and Richard Dreyfuss are two siding-salesmen—"tin men" to people in the trade. They meet when they have a car accident; each blames the other and a peculiar vendetta develops. Dreyfuss finds DeVito's car and smashes its headlights; DeVito finds Dreyfuss's and shatters the windshield. Dreyfuss escalates things by seducing DeVito's wife, Barbara Hershey; DeVito tells him he's glad to be rid of her. Both Dreyfuss and DeVito give striking performances—natural, wry, and convincing. DeVito in particular, provided with a role that doesn't force him to mug constantly, creates a realistically rounded character. The supporting cast is engaging too. Hershey is quite touching as she finds herself falling in love with Dreyfuss. Comedian Jackie Gayle and J. T. Walsh are especially strong among the small crowd of people playing salesmen. In one scene in the diner, DeVito and his cronies argue about *The Ed Sullivan Show*—whether it's more entertaining to see the jugglers who spin plates on sticks or Señor Wences. Beneath the frivolous surface, though, the plot is disquieting. DeVito's life is falling apart. The IRS is after him, he's in a selling slump, and a government commission is about to investigate the often-fraudulent siding-sales practices. Dreyfuss too is ill at ease about his life. "I've had a lot of training in deceit," he says. "It's an occupational hazard." The whole film, in fact, seems like a rumination on honesty—when it works and when it doesn't. Its wit and intelligence suggest, as have all Levinson's films (even the erratic *The Natural*), that he is trying to communicate with his audiences, not put something over on them.

R / 1987 / N/A

▲ TO BEGIN AGAIN

Winner of the 1982 Oscar for Best Foreign Language Film, this movie may not make much sense to those unversed in the history of the Spanish Civil War, but it is beautiful to see. The background: In 1939 the democratically elected government of Spain was overthrown by right-wing Gen. Francisco Franco, whose totalitarian rule survived until he died in 1975. Many Spaniards (and others who fought with the Republicans) vowed never to set foot in Spain until Franco was dead. This movie is about one returning Spaniard, a Nobel Prize winner for literature, played by Antonio Ferrandis. He arrives in his hometown of Gijon, a lovely port city, after collecting the prize. He visits an old sweetheart and rekindles their romance. He sees a friend, a doctor, and reveals a terrible secret—the reason for his return to Spain. This small-scale yet highly charged personal drama, played out against a political backdrop, is plainly shot and plainly acted, which is its strength: Ferrandis walks with a poise that dignifies the whole movie. The farewell scene between him and his doctor friend is touching, as is the parting of the lovers. At first the sound track is obtrusive; it seems determined to manipulate your every emotion, with either Cole Porter's "Begin the Beguine," the lovers' favorite song when they were young, or Johann Pachelbel's majestic "Canon," a kind of elegy for time gone by. Still, the music grows on you. So does the film. (In Spanish with subtitles.)

PG / 1982 / N/A

▲ TO BE OR NOT TO BE

No; to remake or not to remake, that is the question. Ernst Lubitsch, the Berlin-born director who became a success in Hollywood in the '20s, first made this film in 1942. Starring Jack Benny and Carole Lombard, it was a broad farce about a Polish actor and actress who end up fighting the Nazis. Benny was an underappreciated film comedian, and Lombard was a wry, gorgeous

actress who was impossible not to like. There wasn't anything profound about the movie, but it was sunny and possessed the naiveté of many wartime productions. In this film, Mel Brooks and Anne Bancroft redid the story with Tim (*Animal House*) Matheson in the old Robert Stack role as a heroic Polish pilot and Alan Johnson making his directorial debut. Johnson is best known for staging musical numbers in previous Brooks films (including "Springtime for Hitler" in *The Producers*). So it's not surprising that the highlight of this movie is its opening sequence, in which Brooks and Bancroft do a spiffy vaudeville version of "Sweet Georgia Brown," all in Polish. As for the rest, there's some standard Brooks shtick, a lovely performance by Bancroft, and Charles Durning doing an Oscar-nominated turn as an oafish Nazi. There's also a nice, if obscure, tribute to Benny: In one scene there's a "Kubelski St." (Kubelsky was Benny's real name.) But little has been added to the Lubitsch version. People who haven't seen the 1942 film should find this one funny enough. Those old enough to remember the war will also remember the days of priorities. They may well ask, "Was this film necessary?"

PG / 1983 / CBS/Fox

▲ TO LIVE AND DIE IN L.A.

Samuel Goldwyn once said that he wanted a movie that "starts with an earthquake and works its way up to a climax." He would have been proud of this MGM/UA thriller. In the opening sequence an Islamic terrorist strapped with explosives blows himself to bits after he's caught by Secret Service agents. The rest of the movie moves at a similar gut-busting pace. As director William Friedkin showed long ago with *The French Connection* and *The Exorcist,* he knows from relentless pacing. While this was his first film, actor William Petersen showed he can handle a pulse-pounder too. He plays a Secret Service agent whose longtime partner is killed investigating a counterfeiter, portrayed with sinister verve by Willem Dafoe. Shot on the outskirts of Los Angeles, the film has a textured seediness. Its theme is phoniness—not only in the counterfeit money but also in the relationship between Petersen and his informant-girlfriend, Darlanne Fluegel, and in Hollywood itself. In the end the only thing that's real is the bond between part-

ners. Based on the 1984 novel by Gerald Petievich, himself a Secret Service agent, this is a little like *The Maltese Falcon* updated with some touches of "Miami Vice." (The British band Wang Chung did the score.) The date and time keep flashing up on the screen for no apparent reason, and the language is a little too like Mickey Spillane: "If you're looking for a pigeon, go to the park." But the movie, edited by Bud Smith, zips by too quickly for quibbles.
R / 1985 / Vestron

▲ TOM HORN

Steve McQueen had a history of getting out of tight spots, from *The Great Escape* to *Papillon,* but he was trapped in this one-horse Western. As executive producer and star, McQueen was reportedly attracted to the project by the title character's impressive real-life resume—Indian tracker, Roughrider, cavalry scout, and Pinkerton detective. Why, then, did screenwriters Thomas McGuane and Bud Shrake concentrate on the last two years of Horn's life? The audience must accept him as "a legend in his own time" with little supporting evidence. Apart from picking off a few cattle rustlers with nifty long-range rifle work, Horn gets by largely on reputation. After a de facto four-year absence from the screen (his *Enemy of the People* was barely released), McQueen delivered an economical, understated performance, while the Arizona locations and lovely Linda Evans, in her pre-"Dynasty" period, provide some stunning scenery. Still, as directed by William Wiard, this movie is an easy target because it moves so-o-o-o slowly.
R / 1980 / Warner

▲ TOOTSIE

A classic that ranks with the best Hollywood comedies ever made. Dustin Hoffman plays a mostly unemployed New York actor with a reputation for being difficult. When his agent, sassily portrayed by *Tootsie*'s whiz of a director, Sydney Pollack, tells him no one will work with him, Hoffman sets out to prove otherwise. Disguised as a woman, Hoffman auditions for a TV soap and wins the role of a hospital administrator despite some reservation on the part of the soap's egomaniac director, Dabney Coleman. Compli-

cations ensue when he falls for the soap's star, Jessica Lange. She mistakes that look in his eye for lesbianism, while her smitten father, Charles Durning, sees it as directed at him and offers Hoffman a ring. Makeup turns Hoffman into a convincing woman, though his five o'clock shadow makes her something less than a 10. Despite the sound of it, though, *Tootsie* is not just *Some Like It Hoffman* or even *Dustin/Dustina.* Hoffman does more than wriggle into girdle and heels; he gets inside a woman's character. Part of *Tootsie*'s considerable achievement is that the humor is aimed at Hoffman's struggle with makeup and clothes, never at the woman he plays—a southerner with a compassionate heart and a feminist edge. Hoffman himself comes to realize this woman "is the best part of me." Resourceful screenwriters Larry (*M*A*S*H*) Gelbart and Murray (*Luv*) Schisgal never falter; they combine an accurate, affectionate tribute to actors with a zany send-up of soaps and a stylish romantic comedy. And what performances! Bill Murray, Coleman, and Durning are expert farceurs. Teri (*One from the Heart*) Garr shines as a frazzled, too-often-rejected actress. And Lange's delectable way with a wisecrack led to an Oscar as Best Supporting Actress. But Tootsie belongs to Hoffman, who gives it a triumphant freshness that is at once funny, elating, and emotionally satisfying. Movies just don't come better, funnier, or more touching than this deserved smasheroo.
PG / 1982 / RCA/Columbia

▲ TOP GUN

Talk about timing. The jangle of jingoism in the air made a box-office bell ringer out of this Navy recruiting poster disguised as a movie. Ronald Reagan, who may have reigned supreme in 1957's *Hellcats of the Navy,* had to shove over for Tom Cruise. Cruise plays Maverick—read: Lt. Pete Mitchell—a hotshot fly-boy. He's graduated to Top Gun—read: the Navy's elite Fighter Weapons School. It's located in Fightertown, U.S.A.—read: near San Diego. Clearly the Navy has a nickname fetish. Maverick's world involves his pal Goose (Anthony Edwards), an RIO—read: Radar Intercept Officer; his chief pilot competitor, Iceman (Val Kilmer); his base commander, Viper (Tom Skerritt); and his female instructor in astrophysics (the gorgeous Kelly McGillis) who, being a civilian, doesn't get a nickname.

Tootsie: A classic comedy with Dustin Hoffman at the peak of his form as an out-of-work actor who dresses like a woman to win a part on a TV soap opera and finds out instead about becoming a man.

There is also his F-14 Tomcat, a $36-million jet that can climb thirty thousand feet in one minute. What's most frightening about the movie is that its background is not fabricated. Founded in 1968 to improve Navy fighter pilot effectiveness, the Top Gun school soon raised the Vietnam conflict's early three-to-one kill ratio (three enemy planes shot down for every U.S. jet) to twelve to one (the U.S. ratio in World War II was fifteen to one). With Pentagon approval, an ex-Top Gun instructor and a former Top Gun pilot worked as technical advisers to this film. So naturally our side looks pretty tough. From his Learjet perch, British director Tony (*The Hunger*) Scott shot some thrilling aerial sequences. Propaganda con-

cerns aside (the climax involves a rescue mission in undisclosed enemy territory), the movie is swift, spiffy, and shamelessly entertaining. The story's the same arrogant-hero-learns-humility-and-wins-the-war-and-the-girl pap that John Wayne cut his teeth on, but the young cast fairly bursts with high spirits. Edwards, making something freshly funny and touching out of his clichéd best-buddy role, is outstanding, and McGillis, the Amish widow in *Witness,* deserves a medal. Tarted up in stiletto heels and tight skirts more appropriate for Frederick's of Hollywood than flight school, McGillis still manages to let her natural warmth shine through. She makes the film a lot sexier than *Rambo.* But it's Cruise who

keeps the movie at full throttle. Whether he's coming on to McGillis or riding shotgun in a sleek F-14 cockpit, Cruise has a cocksure camera face that holds an audience in thrall. "I feel the need," he says, winking conspiratorially, "the need for speed." Whatever else it doesn't do—read: scratch the surface—*Top Gun* meets that need by delivering 2 hours of pure pow.
PG / 1986 / Paramount

▲ TOP SECRET

Airplane! was filled with dumb jokes, yes. But it was filled so full of them that it seemed a work of comic genius. Once it got you laughing, it didn't let you go. *Top Secret,* by the same film-makers—Jim Abrahams and brothers David and Jerry Zucker—never grabs you. If *Airplane!* had a laugh a second, *Top Secret* has one an hour. It is about some fascist-communist (ideology doesn't matter much in comedy) East Germans who want to reunite their fatherland and then, one presumes, take over the world. All that stands in their way is a singing, skeet-shooting surfer, played by Val Kilmer, whose biggest previous role was Cher's real-life boyfriend. Kilmer comes to East Germany and falls in love with Lucy Gutteridge, an imprisoned professor's daughter. (That does sound almost bad enough to be good.) There are a few good sight gags, too (muscle men in drag playing East German women athletes, for instance) but not nearly enough. If *Top Secret* were edited to its proper length, it might be okay, but who wants a one-minute movie?
PG-13 / 1984 / Paramount

▲ TOUGH ENOUGH

Despite the clichés, the overworked theme, and its absolute predictability from start to finish, *Tough Enough* still manages some charm, thanks to its star, Dennis (*Breaking Away*) Quaid. Quaid is a struggling country singer whose artist's soul recoils at his job as a tree trimmer. Broke, with a wife and child at home, he enters an amateur boxing contest in hopes of winning $100,000, national exposure, and a possible recording contract. The film proceeds, with Rocky-like steadfastness, according to Hollywood plan. There are moral dilemmas, a mercenary promoter (in a terrific, gravelly performance by Warren Oates

in one of his last roles), even the climactic Big Bout. All of which would be pretty tiresome if it weren't for Quaid. His energy and humor give his scenes spontaneity, and his exchanges with his young son (Christopher Norris) are delightful, particularly one in which Quaid sings a rousing "lullaby" called "The Jungle," written by Quaid himself. (He's an appealing singer too.) Film newcomer Carlene Watkins, as Quaid's concerned wife, is a little too self-conscious to seem natural. Stan ("Roots: The Second Generation") Shaw, though, shows an energy that matches Quaid's. He becomes Quaid's trainer, and their scenes together brim with contagious enthusiasm. Director Richard (*Tora! Tora! Tora!*) Fleischer gives the film a light, unassuming spirit; he doesn't take anything too seriously. But it is Quaid who really commands attention.
PG / 1983 / CBS/Fox

▲ TOUGH GUYS

The first thing you notice is the way they wear their fedoras. Under those hats Kirk Douglas and Burt Lancaster don't look as if they are striking poses; they look strikingly poised. Unfortunately, the comedy that enshrines them is never as civilized as its co-stars. As famous train robbers released after thirty years in jail, Douglas and Lancaster face a brave new world that is a kaleidoscope of pop-culture curiosities. Lancaster bemoans that he's relegated to life in an old folks home. Douglas just moans, after an oversexed aerobics teacher tests his stamina. Although *Tough Guys* pleads for compassion for the elderly—"I'm beginning to think old is a dirty word," says Lancaster—this shrill comedy never practices what it screeches. Instead, director Jeff (*Revenge of the Nerds*) Kanew treats his old-timers like newcomers in a crass teen exercise. With the fedoras and flattering close-ups, Kanew seems to be trying to canonize his stars, but most of the time the film degrades them. Douglas doesn't really need to moon the audience at this point in his career. Those kicks to the groin don't do much for his art either. In their seventh film together Douglas and Lancaster display an infectious camaraderie, although both have played the out-of-step social misfit before in better movies—Douglas in *Lonely Are the Brave,* Lancaster in *Atlantic City.* These veterans manage to maintain dignity while sidestepping the bird-dropping jokes.

Watching *Tough Guys*, though, is like seeing someone receive a life achievement award and a pie in the face at the same time.
PG / 1986 / Touchstone

▲ THE TOY

Richard Pryor is an out-of-work reporter who finds employment as a part-time maintenance worker in the sprawling empire of a Louisiana tycoon named U.S. Bates, played by Jackie Gleason. When Gleason's unloved, friendless little son, Scott Schwartz, comes home from military school to spend a week, he encounters the buffooning Pryor in a sporting goods store. The kid, instructed by Daddy to buy anything he wants, selects Pryor—and Gleason's yes-men pay him off and ship him home to the mansion. It's an utterly preposterous setup, and indeed, the first half of the script by Carol (*Annie*) Sobieski and directed by Richard (*Superman*) Donner is full, for the most part, of sight gags. (The kid dumps buckets of mush on Pryor's head; Pryor takes a low blow from a boxing robot.) And there are more than enough dumb double entendres, such as referring to the kid as "Master Bates" and having Gleason's third wife, the balloon-chested Teresa Ganzel, drawlingly call him "You-ass" instead of "U.S." Meanwhile, of course, Pryor and the kid end up discovering brotherly bonds of love, and the movie's second half is largely about Pryor's helping the kid reach out for Gleason. "If you love him and need him," he instructs the boy at one point, "tell him." The last twenty minutes—when they unite at last against the corrupt, power-mad Gleason—are oddly endearing and warmhearted. Pryor turns out to be unexpectedly sweet and even lovable here. Gleason was still the screen's most amusing Fat Cat character. But as the 9-year-old brat who at once learns to cry and love, Schwartz steals *The Toy* from his comedic elders.
PG / 1983 / RCA/Columbia

▲ TRACKS

In another early attempt to win moviegoers' hearts and minds with a Vietnam story, Dennis Hopper, shaved and short-haired, plays an Army sergeant accompanying the body of a buddy home for a hero's burial. The journey is across country by train, where most of the action takes place, and Hopper meets an assortment of characters: a land salesman doubling as a government agent, an antiwar activist disguised as a lounge-car lizard and, finally, a sweet young college girl (Tyrone Power's daughter Taryn), whom he seduces. About halfway through, the camera suddenly begins recording Hopper's fantasies—including a brutal rape scene—and the film seems to reel out of control. But director Henry Jaglom, who had trouble getting distribution in the U.S. (though his almost incoherent previous film, *A Safe Place*, had a cult following) knows exactly what he's up to. He made a film about nightmares, personal and societal, and it succeeds at being painfully disquieting.
R / 1979 / Monterey

▲ TRADING PLACES

Just when you might have given up on Dan Aykroyd (after *Neighbors* and *Dr. Detroit*), along came this satisfying comedy. *Trading Places* made it respectable again to enjoy one of our truly gifted comedians. Make that two of our truly gifted comedians, since Aykroyd's fellow "Saturday Night Live" alum, Eddie Murphy, co-stars. Aykroyd plays a detestably prissy wimp who runs a Philadelphia brokerage house for his wicked uncles, brilliantly sketched by Ralph Bellamy and Don Ameche. Murphy is a ghetto-issue hustler who cons Christmas shoppers by pretending to be a blind, legless vet. Ameche and Bellamy, who love to debate the relative importance of upbringing versus heredity, engineer a role exchange to satisfy a dollar bet. Will Aykroyd, stripped of privilege, degenerate? Can Murphy, if given a lavish home, a limo, a butler (the deft Denholm Elliot), and proper training in trading pork belly futures, step into Aykroyd's handmade shoes? It's all outrageously contrived, and only surprising restraint by director John (*Animal House*, *The Blues Brothers*) Landis makes it work. The writing (Timothy Harris and Herschel Weingrod) is superb too, leaving the two funnymen free to do inspired, textured portrayals. Aykroyd is by turns infuriating and winsome as he loses his credit, banking privileges, and fiancee, the striking Ralph Lauren model Kristen Holby. But he finds a tough-talking, warmhearted pal in a hooker, played with disarming appeal by Jamie Lee Curtis. Murphy, meanwhile, adroitly and hilariously modulates his street wisdom and vulgarity into a high-class-white life-style. Getting out of such a convoluted, farcical plot on acceptable terms isn't easy. But Landis's climax works to perfection, as the two pawns pay back the uncles with a scam at the frozen orange juice exchange. One unseen star is Bonnie Timmerman, the film's casting director, who concocted one of the most entertaining cast chemistries in recent memory.

R / 1983 / Paramount

▲ TRAIL OF THE PINK PANTHER

While it's dedicated to Peter Sellers, who died in July 1980, this film is an exploitive insult to him and the classic comedy character he created, Inspector Jacques Clouseau. It is composed of outtakes and excerpts from real Clouseau films, stitched together with a lame excuse for a script, written by Panther series director Blake Edwards, his son Geoffrey, and Frank and Tom Waldman. (It is a measure of their desperation that they resort to three separate urination jokes.) In the new footage, Joanna Lumley plays a TV reporter who goes on a vain search for Clouseau's beleaguered boss. David Niven and Capucine reprise the suave thieves they played in the series' first film, 1963's *The Pink Panther*. And Burt Kwouk, as the martial artist-manservant Cato, attacks Lumley as well as flashing back to his wonderful battles with Sellers. The only even marginally funny new bits involve Richard ("Soap") Mulligan, who does a passable Sellers imitation as Clouseau's father, and the opening credits, in which the Panther gets transmogrified into a Pink Pac-Man. Edwards, who in a magazine interview once referred to Sellers as a "monster" who was impossible to work with, seemed to be letting greed make a monkey out of one of the movies' most beloved characters.

PG / 1983 / CBS/Fox

▲ TRENCHCOAT

The opening shot of Margot Kidder shows her hands on a typewriter; in Robert Hays's first scene, he's trying to hustle a stewardess at cruising altitude. Is director Michael Tuchner, who did the TV version of *The Hunchback of Notre Dame,* trying to hint he's dealing with the high-flying comedy potency of *Superman I* and *II* and *Airplane! I* and *II?* Sorry, Mike, *Trenchcoat,* despite its, pardon the expression, flashes of off-beat humor, has trouble just getting off the ground. Kidder is a court stenographer who's dying to write a novel. So she flies to Malta in search of some experience—and gets caught in a web of multinational terrorism involving two murders and some pilfered plutonium. Hays, ostensibly an M.D., eventually reveals a clandestine identity once he and Kidder are hot on the trail. The story starts out low-key, but by the last half hour the plot, craftily unfurled by writers Jeffrey Price and Peter Seaman, does pick up pace. Kidder looks great even in her nebbishy comedic gags; Hays plays his deadpan hunk about as unimpressively as he could and still register on film. Best scene: After receiving a shot of sodium pentathol from some kidnapping Arabs, Kidder gets out of that jam. But then she finds herself unwittingly betraying what has been a heartily sublimated love interest in Hays, after he picks her up and takes her on a picnic. Kidder survives enough close calls to inspire her novel, with material for a short story or two left over. All of that cliff-hanging also serves to enliven the proceedings, and it almost makes you forget how long the film takes to really get going.

PG / 1983 / Disney

▲ TRIBUTE

What can you say about a 51-year-old Broadway press agent who's dying? That he'll do anything for a laugh. That he's great at parties but can't keep a wife or sustain a relationship with his son. Bernard (*Same Time, Next Year*) Slade said it in a play that managed a six-month run on Broadway despite a plot that seemed a cross between *Willie the Weeper* and *Smilin' Through*. This adaptation suffers from the same weaknesses. The film, like the play, features another overwrought performance from Jack Lemmon as the manic crowd pleaser who, as son Robby Benson charges, "uses the whole world as a straight man." Slade's script and Bob Clark's direction only encourage Lemmon's tendency to histrionics. Naturally, he earned another Oscar nomination, though *The China Syndrome* revealed his finer shadings in a richer context. *Tribute* is merely a chance for an actor to show off.

PG / 1980 / Vestron

▲ THE TRIP TO BOUNTIFUL

A warm heart beats at the core of this film, even if its pulse is sometimes so slow you'd need a stethoscope to detect any signs of life. Adapted by Horton (*Tender Mercies*) Foote from his 1953 TV script and play, the movie stars Geraldine Page as an aging woman living in Houston with her wimpy son and his shrewish wife. That they're supposed to be too poor to take Page on a visit to Bountiful, her girlhood home, is only one of the plot's implausibilities. It centers on Page's "escape," during which she encounters Rebecca (*Risky Business*) De Mornay, whose serviceman husband has just gone overseas. Page, who finally won her Best Actress Oscar after eight nominations, manages to make touching what is often a hackneyed story, balancing her sentimentality with a petulant streak. Her climactic scene back home, confronting the ghosts of her past, offers one of the best movie cries in years. Still, Foote's script does ramble with dialogue about Texas bird life and train schedules. John (*After Hours*) Heard, who plays the son, also overdoes the blandness. De Mornay provides some brightening and Carlin (*Sixteen Candles*) Glynn, as Page's daughter-in-law, is effectively bitchy. While director Peter Masterson in his first feature sometimes seems to be aiming for a golden-agers' *The Last Picture Show,* the film's doggedness and Page's, is hard to ignore.

PG / 1986 / Embassy

▲ TRON

For the money that Walt Disney Productions spent on this film, they could have bankrolled America's video-game fanatics through 100 million rounds of Donkey Kong or Pac-Man and left everyone a lot happier. The attempt by first-time director Steven Lisberger to visualize what the insides of a computer might look—and act—like is imaginative, ambitious, and original. It is also, however, noisy, needlessly disorienting, and boring. The plot involves a computer games whiz, Jeff Bridges, whose bonanza idea has been stolen by another programmer. Bridges is left trying to break into a huge computer electronically for evidence of the theft and is finally absorbed into the device itself by the ill-tempered Master Control Program. Once inside, Bridges finds a lot of

The Trip to Bountiful: Geraldine Page *(right)* takes a time out from her nostalgic journey to her girlhood home to offer some advice to fellow traveler Rebecca De Mornay.

computer programs in the shape of people he knows on the outside. One of them, Tron, is the duplicate of a good-guy programmer, Bruce Boxleitner. Good luck to all in trying to tell Bridges and Boxleitner apart; their looks and acting styles are so similar they could be clones—but that's another movie. They encounter all kinds of special effects, many generated by Disney computers. A few of them are dazzling, such as a high-velocity battle between two three-man teams on what appear to be motorcycles; it is the only sequence in the movie that captures the speed and fascination of video games. Most of the effects, though, are no less or more interesting than looking through a kaleidoscope, and too often the rules of games Bridges plays are left unexplained, so there is no drama, only puzzlement. It's impossible to care about the characters, despite fleeting attempts at humor—the Master Control Program, for instance, sounds like a Hollywood gangster when it snarls, "When someone pushes me, I push back." Too many films had already been made about computers run amok—*The Forbin Project, Demon Seed* and, of course, *2001*—for that notion to carry this film. Seeing it is like spending two hours in a hardware store gussied up with streamers and flashing lights. It's different, but it's not entertainment.
PG / 1982 / Disney

▲ TROUBLE IN MIND

At first you may not know what to make of this brilliantly bonkers mood piece, but hang in there. Writer-director Alan Rudolph, on a roll after the equally pungent *Choose Me* and *Songwriter,* sends out waves of giddy, charged-up romanticism that exert a tidal pull. Set in a surreal urban landscape called Rain City (the location was actually Seattle), the film follows an ex-cop, played by Kris Kristofferson, who has just been sprung after two years in the slammer. Kristofferson, never more life-battered or roguishly sexy, is the classic man alone. When he wanders into Wanda's Cafe, which is run by the sassy, man-hating Genevieve Bujold, he could be Jim Arness seeking refuge at Miss Kitty's or Bogie trying to heal his emotional wounds at Rick's Cafe in Casablanca. When Bujold rejects Kristofferson's pent-up passions, he turns to the luminous Lori Singer, who steals his heart and every scene she's in, as a doe-eyed innocent freshly arrived from the country with

her husband and infant son. As the hick husband, Keith Carradine is both scary and flamboyantly funny. Corrupted by the city, where he eagerly embraces the underworld, Carradine starts affecting punk hairdos and wearing eye shadow that, by film's end, give him the look of a space creature—the weirdest of this weird lot. This is no small accomplishment, considering that Carradine's nemesis, a crime boss, is portrayed (in his first male role) by the female impersonator Divine. Playing a tough guy so nasty that "he made dice out of his mother's knucklebones," Divine emerges as jovially malevolent. If Rudolph sometimes comes unglued along with his characters, his creation is nonetheless hot-blooded, haunting, and howlingly comic. Besides top-notch performances, the movie boasts a seductive, otherworldly look, a dazzling Mark Isham score (with Marianne Faithful growling the classic blues title song and a Kristofferson original called "El Gavilan") and dialogue that shames the purplest passages in Hammett and Chandler. Says the irresistibly loony Bujold to Kristofferson and Singer: "Between the two of you there's almost a whole person." Rudolph successfully mines such lines for laughs while trying to elicit a kinship with the oddballs in question. His picture is a strange brew and, on analysis, mostly moonshine. But *Trouble in Mind* packs a moonshine's combustible kick. Proceed at your own risk.
R / 1986 / Charter

▲ TRUE CONFESSIONS

This is a movie of surprises, all of them pleasant. The stars, Robert De Niro and Robert Duvall, are two of the screen's most explosive actors. Not so here; this film, adapted from John Gregory Dunne's 1977 novel, is stunning, largely because De Niro and Duvall (both memorable in *The Godfather, Part II*) so masterfully underplay their roles. The setting is Los Angeles in the late 1940s. De Niro, an ambitious young Catholic priest, is wheeling and dealing his way up the church's local hierarchy. Duvall, all twitchy and full of restrained rage, is his older brother, a cop, and the family black sheep. He is assigned to investigate the grisly murder of a young woman who was a porno movie actress. The victim turns out to have had connections with some unsavory characters who know his priestly brother. The movie, directed by Ulu (*Straight Time*) Grosbard

and photographed by Owen Roizman, has a gauzy, almost dreamlike quality reminiscent of Roman Polanski's *Chinatown*. The script, by Dunne and his novelist wife Joan Didion, also helps. It's beautifully structured, allowing De Niro and Duvall to convey the tension that exists between two people who clearly love each other but don't quite know how to say it.
R / 1981 / MGM/UA

▲ TRUE STORIES

Like most of David Byrne's music as singer, songwriter, and guiding intellect of art-rock's Talking Heads band, his nonconcert film debut as an actor, writer, and director is both haunting and hilarious. What it isn't is mainstream moviemaking. The existential setting is a made-up town called Virgil, Texas, which Byrne visits as narrator. Despite his Western garb, the gaunt, chicken-necked Byrne (born in Scotland, raised in Baltimore) resembles a new wave Brother from Another Planet. The resulting feeling of dissociation helps us see afresh, in a series of vignettes and songs, the shopping mall mentality. Byrne drew his characters from supermarket tabloid clippings. There's a fat, forlorn bachelor (beautifully played by John Goodman), the laziest woman in the world (Swoosie Kurtz), a couple (Spaulding Gray and Annie McEnroe) who talk only through their children, and a woman (Jo Harvey Allen) who claims she wrote all of Elvis's songs. Byrne rarely stoops to making sport with easy targets. Instead he finds surprising dignity, even courage, in the commonplace. Watching the gifted Byrne invest his ideas and music in characters so alien to himself is a movie weird pick-me-up.
PG / 1986 / Warner

▲ TUFF TURF

In still another teenage rite-of-passage flick, James Spader plays a prep school outcast who has to prove himself against the students of Lawson High, a Los Angeles school where most of the kids seem to be majoring in switchblade. He quickly falls for the chain-wearing, tight-jeaned, spike-heeled Kim Richards. Thus begins the usual new-kid-on-foreign-turf adolescent romance. The resulting ego clashes lead to fight scenes of re-lentless, almost unwatchable violence that all but nullify the sympathetic performances the young cast provides. This production also borrowed liberally from such films as *Rebel Without a Cause, West Side Story,* and even *The Karate Kid.* If Spader lacks the introspective moodiness of James Dean, his performance is forceful. Richards, too, shows the potential to break out of the child-star syndrome; she maintains an enticing reserve despite the burden of her routine sex-kitten role. The sound track, featuring the music of such people as Southside Johnny, Marianne Faithful, and Lene Lovich and slick onscreen stage performances by Jack Mack and the Heart Attack, is driving without being overbearing. The film is schizophrenic, though, alternately winning and abhorrently violent. Director Fritz Kiersch misses whatever chance he had to rise above his picture's all-too-plentiful competition for the teenage audience.
R / 1985 / New World

▲ TURK 182!

The theme of this film seems to be hell hath no fury like an angry young man scorned, especially when he has a can of spray paint and is interested in a career in graffiti. Timothy Hutton stars as a New Yorker who decides to fight city hall on behalf of his brother, Robert Urich. An apolitical working-class Brooklyn eccentric who dresses in loud print shirts and drives a World War II motorcycle, Hutton can't hold down a job. That's okay because he's really an aspiring artist. But then Urich, a gung-ho fireman nicknamed "Turk," is interrupted while drinking with his buddies one night by news of a building burning across the street. Though he rescues a little girl, he is disabled in a two-story fall. Later, heartless city officials deny him a pension, saying he broke regulations by appearing drunk at the fire. That sends Urich into a manic-depressive tailspin. Hutton launches a one-man graffiti war, trying to undermine Robert Culp's mayoral campaign. Thus, he becomes a folk hero known only as "Turk 182" (the "182" is Urich's badge number). Apparently director Bob Clark thought he could hang a movie on such implausible plot machinations. Nothing redeems *Turk 182!* Not the embarrassingly feeble script by Denis and John Hamill (brothers of writer Pete) and James Gregory Kingston. Not the acting performances. Though

Hutton competently portrays the loony, impulsive boy-hero, Urich brings all the depth of a "Vega$" episode to his role. Culp humorlessly plays the petty autocrat. Peter Boyle, as a half-crazed detective, reprises his *Young Frankenstein* shtick without the makeup or the humor. And the earnestly saccharine Kim Cattrall seems an afterthought as Hutton's love interest. This movie about two Brooklyn brothers deserves a round of Bronx cheers.

PG-13 / 1985 / CBS/Fox

▲ THE TURNING POINT

There are two fascinating matchups in this often enthralling film. It marked the screen debut of both Mikhail Baryshnikov and a beautiful and talented 20-year-old ballet newcomer, Leslie Browne. But the story centers on the relationship between two women—an aging ballerina (played by Anne Bancroft) and her best friend (Shirley MacLaine), who gave up a promising dance career to run a small ballet school in Arizona and raise a family. Bancroft and MacLaine turn in moving performances, as do supporting actresses Martha Scott and Alexandra Danilova.

PG / 1977 / CBS/Fox

▲ TURTLE DIARY

Delicate, detached, and paced a tad slower than the speed of one of its title characters, this curio of a movie is an instant write-off for the Chuck Norris action crowd. A writer of children's books, played by Glenda Jackson, meets a repressed bookstore clerk, played by Ben Kingsley, while they watch giant sea turtles through glass at a London aquarium. They resolve to free these marine reptiles from their thirty-year captivity. With a minimum of fuss and bother, they do so and then return to their separate lives. That's it for plot. What's left is characterization, and screenwriter Harold Pinter (working from Russell Hoban's 1975 novel) gave his two accomplished actors delicious dialogue on which to feast. The patented Pinter pauses, during which emotional earthquakes can rumble between the simple exchange of "Yes" and "I see," are very much in evidence. But the Pinter menace is missing this time. There are scenes when Master Harold actually verges on sentimentality. It will take a little

getting used to, but as Pinter warms to his curious couple, so will you. On leave from her intense stage roles, Jackson displays a welcome tenderness that makes this her most appealing performance in years. And Kingsley, miles from the world of *Gandhi,* is dazzling. Through the tiniest gesture or flicker of an eye, he lets us see what is whirling through this quiet man's brain and feel the longing in his heart. The film is too slight to add up to more than an oyster appetizer before the red meat entree. But this oyster yields two pearls in Kinglsey and Jackson. For those willing to dig, *Turtle Diary* proves an unexpected treasure.

PG-13 / 1986 / Vestron

▲ TWICE IN A LIFETIME

Twice in a Lifetime was compared with such Oscar winners as *Ordinary People* and *Terms of Endearment.* Hardly. Impeccable writing, directing, and casting kept those emotional family dramas from toppling into the pit of soap opera. *Twice,* which might just as well have been titled *Search for Tomorrow,* unabashedly dives right in. Absorbing, yes; but beware of confusing contrivance with craft. Gene Hackman and Ellen Burstyn play a working-class, suburban Seattle couple in a boring thirty-year marriage. He's a well-meaning slug; she's a couch potato, happy with game shows and buying presents for her grandchildren with the spare bucks she earns sweeping up in a beauty salon. Hackman's fiftieth-birthday celebration precipitates a crisis. At his favorite pub he meets a barmaid, played by the gorgeous, savvy Ann-Margaret. Don't ask why she falls for Hackman. It's simply a given in Colin Welland's patronizing screenplay, with which the formidable cast fights a losing battle. Soon the taciturn Hackman is whispering come-ons to A-M: "You're my round, sweet-smelling female." After the initial shock Burstyn accepts the end of her marriage. She dyes her hair blond and attends a male strip show. Accepting, too, is the couple's younger daughter, nicely done by Ally Sheedy. Older married daughter Amy Madigan, however, is furious, dragging her mother and young child along to challenge her father and his girlfriend with a loud, public outburst. Director Bud Yorkin doesn't have the hounds of hell yapping along at Madigan's heels, but he throws in everything else. There hasn't been a confron-

tation scene like this since the early talkies, when Mom regularly sent Junior to the barroom to shame Poppa back home. Madigan is undeniably strong but irritatingly one-note. One waits in vain for someone to shout back, "Grow up!" The same vain hope applies to waiting for the movie to dig beneath its intriguing surface.
R / 1985 / Vestron

▲ TWILIGHT'S LAST GLEAMING

A bomb bursting in air. A silly leftist general (Burt Lancaster) commandeers a very casually defended SAC missile base, and you keep wishing he'd blow up the world so you could go cut the grass.
R / 1977 / Key

▲ TWILIGHT ZONE

Somewhere, in whatever different dimension he's inhabiting these days, the late Rod Serling is probably mad as hell. Eight years after his death, the Hollywood hotshots finally made a movie version of his famed TV scare series. And they botched it. Divided into four segments, three based on stories for the series, the film boasts top technical talent and four name directors. Things begin promisingly with a prologue featuring Dan Aykroyd and Albert Brooks driving on a deserted road at night, reminiscing about old "Zone" TV episodes. Written and directed by John (*Trading Places*) Landis, the prologue leaves a delicious tingle. But Episode One, also directed by Landis, leaves only a bad taste. Vic Morrow stars as a bigot who finds himself punished by being tossed to the Nazis, the Ku Klux Klan, and a GI patrol in Vietnam. Everything about this episode is oppressive, even without the memory of the helicopter accident that decapitated Morrow and killed two Vietnamese children during filming. In Episode Two, directed by Steven Spielberg, Scatman Crothers has the power to give some retirement-home oldsters a chance at childhood again. The Spielberg whimsy, so effective in *E.T.*, is chokingly sticky this time. Episode Three takes a scarier turn as Kathleen Quinlan is kidnapped by a boy, Jeremy Licht, with mind-control powers à la *Carrie*, and taken to a house run by the

child's rules. Director Joe (*The Howling*) Dante pulls out some eye-popping special effects, but the story runs out of steam. Episode Four is best, with John (*The World According to Garp*) Lithgow playing a passenger who thinks he sees a monster trying to rip an engine off the wing of the plane he's on. Australian director George (*The Road Warrior*) Miller works visual wonders in a confined space, and Lithgow gives a sensational performance. The rest of the episodes bypass imagination in their fixation on a more lucrative dimension: the box office.
PG / 1983 / Warner

▲ TWINKLE, TWINKLE KILLER KANE

There are two reasons why this is probably the finest large-scale American surrealist film ever made: (1) It is about the only large-scale American surrealist film ever made (*Slaughterhouse-Five* is the closest contender); (2) it is oddly enticing, often funny, superby acted, and ingeniously written and directed by William Peter (*The Exorcist*) Blatty. The movie is set during the Vietnam era in a castle in the Pacific Northwest. American servicemen are being treated there for failures of nerve. One thinks he's Superman. Another tries to walk through walls, and when he can't, pounds them with hammers, "to set an example for the other atoms." A third wants to stage *Hamlet* with an all-dog cast, featuring a Great Dane. Into this *Marat/Sade* spin-off enters a Special Forces colonel, an expert in hand-to-hand combat who has been assigned as "chief psychiatrist." (His name, Killer Kane, comes from the 1930s Buck Rogers serial villain, who lobotomized his enemies with special helmets.) Despite a flurry of war metaphors and religious parables, the plot unravels, thanks to Stacy Keach, who plays Kane; Scott Wilson, as an astronaut who aborted a moon mission; Ed Flanders, marvelously effective as a real doctor in frenetic surroundings; and Jason Miller, the old exorcist himself, as the Shakespearean. The film, also known as *The Ninth Configuration*, is talky and its ending discordant, but it has momentum and some nicely staged confrontations. One, between Keach and a motorcycle gang leader, belongs in a textbook for directors on how to build tension. *Kane* is pretentious—also challenging and fascinating.
R / 1980 / New World

▲ TWIST AND SHOUT

Denmark, 1964. The height of Beatlemania. A teenage rock 'n' roller named Bjorn (Adam Tonsberg) spies a beautiful girl named Anna (Camilia Soeberg) across a crowded dance hall. Love at first sight. Erik (Lars Simonsen), Bjorn's best friend, is preoccupied with his mentally ill mother, puritanical father, and his own infatuation with a local debutante named Kirsten (Ulrikke Juul Bondo). Kirsten likes Bjorn. Bjorn gets Anna pregnant and must pay for an abortion. Bjorn and Erik grow up. On paper, the plot seems impossibly trite. Danish director Billie August and some powerful young actors, however, made this a most affecting coming-of-age film, one that was chosen Best Picture at the 1985 European Film Festival. For one thing, August paid extraordinary attention to detail. Half smiles, tiny gestures, and quick glances enrich each scene as we follow Tonsberg, completely consumed by his first love. "Sometimes I miss you even though we're together," he tells Soeberg, a softer-featured Amy Irving whose acting, especially during a harrowing abortion scene, is captivating. August balances the film's hard edge with an eye for human, humorous foibles. When Soeberg must leave him for three days, for instance, Tonsberg's imagination—as seen through August's camera—races with scenes in which she is slobbered over by practically every sailor in Denmark. Jan Weincke's photography, which includes idyllic Danish holiday scenes that look like Christmas cards come to life, is icing. It may sound familiar, but *Twist and Shout* is worth reliving. (In Danish with subtitles.)
R / 1986 / HBO/Cannon

▲ TWO OF A KIND

Let's put our cards on the table: John Travolta and Olivia Newton-John were obviously trying to duplicate their box-office success in *Grease* when they teamed up for this fantasy comedy. The plot was supposed to be daring because the stars were playing amoral moderns this time, not '50s teenagers. Both are thieves. Olivia—for shame!—actually says a four-letter word and tugs at Travolta's pants, but there's nothing here that Doris Day couldn't have done with Rock Hudson in an earlier day. The plot: If Olivia and John can reform with the help of a cheering section of angels (Charles Durning, Beatrice Straight, and Scatman Crothers), God (the voice of Gene Hackman) won't destroy the world. John and Olivia were clearly hoping for another *Heaven Can Wait,* but what they got is closer in quality to *Heaven's Gate.* The execrable script and direction by John Herzfeld make it impossible for the stars to bluff their way through on charm alone. With such a rotten deal, *Two of a Kind* looks more like a pair of dull jokers.
PG / 1984 / CBS/Fox

▲ 2010

When we left the vessel *Discovery* in Stanley Kubrick's epic *2001: A Space Odyssey,* Keir Dullea was floating somewhere in outer space, his shape changing from astronaut to old man to embryonic baby. This is a sequel, also based on an Arthur C. Clarke novel, and for a while it promises to be as good as the original. Roy Scheider plays a space agency head who is approached by a Russian scientist: The Soviets are about to launch a probe to find *Discovery,* and they want Scheider to accompany them since they don't have the know how to deal with the ship once they locate it. Though the U.S. and Russia are close to going to war over Honduras, Scheider agrees to participate. He is joined by John Lithgow, playing an engineer with a fear of heights. (When they dock up with *Discovery,* Lithgow's heavy-breathing trip between the two spacecraft is hilarious.) Bob Balaban is the inventor of *Discovery*'s renegade computer, HAL 9000. It is his job to get HAL to pilot *Discovery* home. There is also the big black slab to be dealt with, the one that caused all the trouble in the first movie, and in the eeriest sequence Scheider is visited by what appears to be the ghost of Dullea. With all this promising material, though, producer-director-writer-cameraman Peter Hyams lets the film dissipate. He wastes British actress Helen Mirren as the head of the Soviet crew. And his climax, a kind of cosmic Christmas card celebrating peace, seems unfinished. This movie could have benefited from another half hour to tie up the loose ends.
PG / 1984 / MGM/UA

U

▲ UNCLE JOE SHANNON

Burt Young, the crazy brother in *Rocky,* wrote this hopelessly sappy sob opera. He also stars as a trumpet player on the rise until he loses his wife and son in a tragic fire. The predictable slide into booze and despair follows. Then he meets a young boy who needs an operation and in no time at all he has rehabilitated himself and become the great men we knew he was all along. The music by Bill Conti, also an old *Rocky* hand, is good, as is the photography by Bill Butler (a concert sequence with Burt on trumpet—jazz star Maynard Ferguson does the actual playing—is sensational). But Young overdoes it as a slob with a heart of gold, à la Ernest Borgnine, and the tearjerking that results from his stabs at being touching is almost unwatchable.
PG / 1979 / N/A

▲ UNCOMMON VALOR

In 1983, ex-Army Colonel Bo Gritz tried to steal into Laos to rescue American POWs who he insisted were still being held captive. He failed, and in fact never produced any hard proof that Americans were still being held. This film is the story of what might have happened had he succeeded. Gene Hackman, an ex-Army colonel who believes his son is a POW, rounds up some of his son's buddies for the mission. Fred Ward is a freaked-out combat veteran, Harold Sylvester is a helicopter pilot-turned-hospital administrator, Tim Thomerson another ex-helicopter pilot whose wife cheats on him, Reb Brown a muscle-bound surfer and former explosives expert, and Randy "Tex" Cobb is a real-life former boxer making his movie debut as a drugged-out biker. After a promising beginning, the plot becomes confusing, with the actors milling about. By the time they get to the rescue attempt, complete with blazing guns, blown-up bridges, and some sensational helicopter footage, the movie has turned into a routine adventure whose only focus is violence. Despite the emotionally charged nature of the material and the movie's blatant appeal to

jingoist fantasies, it is just another project that probably shouldn't have been attempted in the first place.
R / 1984 / Paramount

▲ UNDER FIRE

Nick Nolte is a photographer who takes pictures so reflexively he can hardly finish making love before he begins snapping artsy shots of his dozing lady. Gene Hackman is a *Time* foreign correspondent who is being courted by a TV network in New York. Joanna Cassidy is a freelance writer who is a terrific reporter, in addition to being the object of both men's affections. Years ago they would have made a vigorous, charming triangle, much as Clark Gable, Walter Pidgeon, and Myrna Loy did in 1938's *Too Hot to Handle.* In this politically heavy-handed movie, the triangle is grim and tense. That's not to say the film lacks excitement. Cassidy's performance is enough to maintain interest all by itself. She's bright, aggressive, funny, beautiful. Nolte is expressive in his stoic way, and Hackman handles his relatively small part with typically pungent style. As the film begins, the three of them are covering the civil war in Chad, but they quickly end up in Nicaragua at the height of the Sandinista rebellion in 1979, Nolte and Cassidy are particularly cold-blooded journalists. "I don't take sides," Nolte says at one point, "I take pictures." Yet the two of them align themselves on the side of the Sandinistas against Gen. Anastasio Somoza's repressive regime. Nolte even takes a picture for the rebels' propaganda purposes, leaving Hackman to decide how he will treat his friends' violation of journalistic ethics. The directorial debut of Roger Spottiswoode, whose writing credits include *48 Hrs.,* the film is full of moving moments; one comes when Nolte first realizes he has been used by a French intelligence agent, played with reptilian finesse by Jean-Louis Trintignant. ("Hill Street Blues" Rene Enriquez, as Somoza, and Ed Harris, as a ruthless mercenary, add powerful support.) But the movie is

also burdened by a series of ludicrous coincidences and a blatant bias toward the Sandinistas. The ending's pat resolutions defy credibility. But the film, which was shot in Mexico, has so much emotional energy and visual texture it transcends the clichés to which it often resorts. This is a film to see. Argue about it later.
R / 1983 / Vestron

▲ UNDER THE CHERRY MOON

It's all but impossible to take this film seriously. For one thing, "a film by Prince" sounds like a German shepherd's home movie. For another, in his first directing try Prince seems to have been trying to wrap up an Oscar for lifetime achievement in narcissism. Playing a lounge pianist-gigolo on the Riviera, he flounces, primps, preens, leers, flirts, and minces through what amounts to a nearly nonstop close-up. The tone is set by the opening shot in which he shows himself seated at a piano wearing a garish shirt and a sequined flapper's cap: He looks like a silent movie vamp with a mustache and too much eye makeup. There are moments when he seems to be sending himself up. At one point he says he's floating, and his co-star, the Julie Andrews-like newcomer Kristin Scott-Thomas, says, "It would be easy to float with a head as inflated as yours." But it would take eleven boxcars full of Jerry Lewis movies to disarm the self-adoration *Cherry Moon* suggests. It's all in black and white—in homage to the '40s romantic movies Prince admires—and while he wrote all the music, he performs only briefly onscreen. The basic plot has him falling in love with a rich socialite, Scott-Thomas. Her father, sternly played by Steven (*Rambo*) Berkoff, questions his daughter's taste in men. Predictable consequences ensue. As a director, Prince demonstrates an eye for intriguing images, yet he does not always notice when his actors' attention wanders. Scott-Thomas's eyes sometimes roll as if she's about to faint. And the script by Becky Johnston takes a thudding, melodramatic turn at the end of what has been a romantic comedy. Like Elvis Presley, Prince has the charisma to carry an atrocious movie—real fans just want to see him—but even Elvis never got so carried away with himself that he thought he could direct.
PG-13 / 1986 / Warner

▲ UNDER THE RAINBOW

Anyone who thinks it could be wildly amusing to watch 150 midgets mill around for 90 minutes should see this movie. All others should wait for yet another rerun of *The Wizard of Oz*. The sadly wasted idea for this would-be comedy comes from Oz lore, expanding on the reports that the little people brought to Hollywood in 1938 to play Munchkins and flying monkeys spent their spare time indulging in pint-size revelries. The film's cast of characters includes a midget Nazi spy (Billy Barty), a Secret Service man guarding a European duke (Chevy Chase), MGM's liaison with the little people (Carrie Fisher), and a semi-sauced house detective ("Tonight" show writer Pat McCormick). None of them are funny, and Chase even seems wan and disinterested. Fisher looks better than she ever did as Princess Leia—she spends half this movie running around in her underwear—but she has nothing much to do or say. One commodity in abundance is sexual innuendo—breast fondling, groin injury shtick, and even some fleeting nudity. Director Steve (*The Buddy Holly Story*) Rash tolerates some atrocious acting. If ever a movie got short shrift, this one is it.
PG / 1981 / Warner

▲ UNDER THE VOLCANO

Director John Huston fashioned something quite extraordinary from Malcolm Lowry's acclaimed 1947 novel about a British ex-consul trying to drink himself to death in Cuernavaca in 1938. The book was basically the consul's interior monologue, the action being confined to one twenty-four-hour period—November 1, Mexico's Day of the Dead. The film also holds to that structure, a liability Huston turns into an asset. Huston, at 77, was in full vigor and at home with the material. He lived and worked in Mexico (his *Treasure of the Sierra Madre* was shot there). He seemed to know its ways and understand the consul from the inside. To Huston, the diplomat's drinking is heroic, an act of retaliation against himself, his wife's infidelity with his brother, and a decadent civilization rushing toward war. Huston imbues the film with a firebrand's fervor. The consul is a roaring drunk—funny, infuriating, touching, but never pathetic. It's the best role of

Albert Finney's career, and he seizes it with passion. In one brilliant, unnerving scene, Finney lets loose his demons in a soul-destroying torrent of words. This is a master actor's performance. Anthony Andrews is a bit too stiff-upper-lip as the brother; Jacqueline Bisset makes the wife a figure of strength and beauty. But the film belongs to Finney and Huston, who play it like the fulfillment of a life's ambition. Even when Guy Gallo's screenplay falters (there is too much self-conscious metaphor), Finney and Huston make *Under the Volcano* poetic, powerful, and richly rewarding.
R / 1984 / MCA

▲ UNFAITHFULLY YOURS

In this funny remake of a funny 1948 Preston Sturges film, Dudley Moore plays a famous orchestra conductor who has just married a much younger woman, Nastassja Kinski. (Rex Harrison and Linda Darnell were the 1948 principals.) When he begins to think she has been seeing another man, his jealousy consumes him to the point that he suspects one of his best friends and plots to kill him. Moore, whose films have been erratic, is wildly in form, especially when he gets looped on tranquilizers and tries to carry out the planned murder. His gift for comic timing has never been better exploited. Kinski, who has appeared to struggle in many of her roles, shows a surprising subtlety as a comic actress and looks gorgeous. As Moore's manager, Albert Brooks becomes a good straight man, and Armand Assante deftly plays a womanizing violinist. Richard Libertini, as Moore's Italian butler and cook, is hilarious hacking up an eggplant while describing what he would do to an unfaithful wife. Director Howard Ziell's style is brisk. A few confusing plot turns are a minor fault in such an otherwise effective comedy.
PG / 1984 / CBS/Fox

▲ UNION CITY

Maybe—just maybe—Deborah Harry can act, but she may be eligible for Social Security before anyone knows for sure. Playing herself in the good-natured *Roadie,* Harry became vapid the moment she stopped singing. In *Union City,* she

is at least cast intriguingly. She's the drab wife of an irritable accountant, Dennis Lipscomb, as well as the nascent love interest of the superintendent of her apartment building, Everett McGill, a Jack Palance type. Despite her tantalizing, Betty Boop mouth, Harry is as warm as wet matches. At one point she steps into the hall, beckons to some neighbors, and says, "Hi, come have coffee. I just made bread pudding too." An EKG machine would be hard-pressed to detect any vital signs. This may be because writer-director Mark Reichert, in his first feature, concentrated on Harry's husband's rage at the daily disappearance of milk from the doorstep. Hubby, in fact, is ready to commit murder over it. The plot comes from a mystery by '40s writer Cornell Woolrich, whose stories have been used by Hitchcock (*Rear Window*) and Truffaut (*The Bride Wore Black*). But Reichert's style—which pays muddled homage to Brian De Palma and Elia Kazan—is overly brooding. The photography is so unremittingly dark that Reichert apparently equates the '50s with the Cro-Magnon era, which isn't fair, especially to the Cro-Magnon era.
R / 1980 / RCA/Columbia

▲ AN UNMARRIED WOMAN

Jill Clayburgh made the jump to star in this marvelous film, portraying a woman whose husband suddenly walks out. While trying to piece her life together, she sees a shrink (played with convincing quirks by real-life shrink Penelope Russianoff), takes a lover, and soon finds out that being alone isn't all that scary. Michael Murphy is sympathetic as the confused husband, Alan Bates sexy and winning as the new man in her life, and Lisa Lucas perfect as the daughter. Director Paul Mazursky's sensitivity and wit shine through, but the film belongs to Clayburgh, whose character became a kind of role model for unhappy wives.
R / 1978 / CBS/Fox

▲ THE UNTOUCHABLES

Whoever would have expected to look fondly back upon Walter Winchell's snarly narration or Robert Stack's stiff-as-a-concrete-slab acting as federal agent Eliot Ness? This overdone remake

by director Brian De Palma has just that nostalgia-inducing effect; keeping the cartoonish good guy–bad guy basis of the old TV "Untouchables" and dressing it up with color film and the mixed blessing of modern techniques for depicting violence. No director today is more adept than De Palma at pacing, framing, cutting, angling. But he insists on trotting out his tricks even when there's no reason for them. In one scene Kevin Costner, as Ness, and the small group of cops he has enlisted to help him fight Al Capone are seated around a circular table. De Palma takes his camera in a 360-degree, unbroken tour around the perimeter, as if he's a skater doing a compulsory figure eight. In another scene he demonstrates that he has seen the silent Russian classic *Battleship Potemkin,* with a drawn-out bit involving a baby buggy going down a flight of steps in the middle of a gunfight. While De Palma's idol, Alfred Hitchcock, used lots of gimmicks too, they were rarely so obtrusive. In this case De Palma wastes whatever chance there might have been to give this film some substance. Sean Connery, as a veteran Chicago cop recruited by Costner, seems constricted. Robert De Niro, as Capone, gives an animated performance, but it's nothing Rod Steiger or Neville Brand (the TV Capone) hadn't done already. Capone still seems like a caricature, as does Ness. Costner is saintly when he's not mowing people down, yet he has little human dimension. The film eventually becomes a series of shoot-outs, like De Palma's last excursion into organized crime, *Scarface.* Unlike *Scarface,* this film never really gets ugly or boring. But from a director of De Palma's resources—both aesthetic and, these days, financial—it's fair to expect something more than just not being bored.
R / 1987 / N/A

▲ UP IN SMOKE

Cheech and Chong's drug-joke comedy made a mint, much to the surprise of critics and tastemakers. By the time Cheech Martin appears onstage at a rock concert in a tutu and Mickey Mouse ears, any pretense of a plot has been forgotten. It's a series of wild skits centering around the duo's scrapes with the law and their lust for drugs. In one sequence, the pair light up a joint the size of a baseball bat and Cheech turns into a raving loony while driving through L.A. Another scene has the boys unwittingly smuggling a truck made entirely out of marijuana across the Mexican border. Stacy Keach adeptly (especially in consideration of his own troubles with drug laws) plays the cop in hot pursuit. All of it is managed by Lou Adler, the rock producer, in his debut as a director. Very foul-mouthed and scatological the film will probably not be very funny anymore for those who see the burgeoning drug use among young people as a scant source of laughter.
R / 1978 / Paramount

▲ UP THE ACADEMY

Ron (*Kaz*) Leibman is the big star. He has the most lines. He plays the film's central character. Yet he dissociated himself from it; his name never appears in the credits or promotion. That may be the smartest thing Leibman ever did; *Mad* magazine, the director Robert Downey, and Barbara Bach should have been so smart. The movie is basically *Animal House Goes to Military School,* but if *Mad*—dabbling in film for the first time—were parodying it, the title would read something like *Down the Drain*. Leibman, as a sadistic commanding officer, is solemnly intense; he seems to be in a melodrama. Downey, who directed the satirical hit *Putney Swope,* resorts to voiceover narration and a rock-filled sound track to cover huge gaps left in the action by screenwriters Tom Patchett and Jay Tarses. (In better days, they wrote many of the finest scripts for "The Mary Tyler Moore Show." Bach, a gorgeous woman and decent actress—as she was in *The Spy Who Loved Me*—is barely seen. Worse, the teenage newcomers who play the students are consistently unappealing. The whole package is what *Mad,* in its old glory days, would have dismissed as a furshlugginer potrzebie.
R / 1980 / Warner

▲ URBAN COWBOY

As a contemporary Texan who punches clocks at a petrochemical plant instead of cows and raises a nightly ruckus at the Houston honky-tonk Gilley's, John Travolta dances a mean Western jig and fights villain Scott Glenn like a young John Wayne. With the help of Madolyn Smith and Debra Winger (who sexily strutted away with the picture and turned herself into a star), Travolta also generates extraordinary erotic heat for a PG movie. But even Travolta, photographed with excessive attention and doing his damnedest to block a Stetson around his Brooklyn persona, cannot subdue all the pretensions of the screenplay by director James Bridges and Aaron Latham, whose *Esquire* article inspired the film. Bridges squanders a full third of the movie showing his star and the studs at Gilley's trying to keep up their testosterone levels by riding a menacing mechanical bull. The West has changed, the film suggests solemnly, as if Sam Peckinpah had never existed, and Bridges's bull is forced to bear more symbolic weight than Kubrick's monolith in *2001*. The bull and the film just barely survive the strain.

PG / 1980 / Paramount

▲ USED CARS

There have been a lot of lemons among Hollywood's car movies, but surprisingly, this vehicle is not among them. While it may not soar to the comic heights of *Airplane!*, the raunchy laughs click along with the regularity of highway markers. Robert Zemeckis and Bob Gale, who created the underappreciated *I Wanna Hold Your Hand* in 1978, wrote this screwy screenplay, and Zemeckis directed with a free hand. The story bears about as much scrutiny as most of the so-called automobiles being peddled in the movie, but it revolves loosely around the rivalry between two used-car dealers, Kurt Russell and Jack Warden. Russell is a convincing con man, as well as an engaging actor, and Warden adds another blustery triumph to his impressive list of credits. You'd be crazy to buy a used car from either one of these hucksters, but their pitch is irresistible.

R / 1980 / RCA/Columbia

V

▲ VAGABOND

Just because this film is French and stars teen sexpot Sandrine Bonnaire (who made a sensational debut at 15 in 1982's *A Nos Amours*), don't expect a Gallic *Pretty in Pink*. Writer-director Agnes (*One Sings, the Other Doesn't*) Varda has capped a distinguished twenty-two-year career as filmmaker and documentarian with this bleak look at a woman alone. Bonnaire plays Mona, an 18-year-old drifter hitchhiking through the French countryside in winter. We see her first in a ditch. Bundled in rags, her hair matted, her face and fingernails encrusted with dirt, she has frozen to death. The film then unfolds in flashbacks as Varda introduces the people (farmers, maids, mechanics, ditchdiggers) whom Mona met during the last months of her life. The film is a fiction based on the screenwriter's reaction to the very real situation of the no-hope vagrants who die on the road each year. Withholding easy and comforting answers, Varda wants the audience to

squirm, to challenge responses to this new breed of homeless rebel. It's not that they can't come in from the cold; they don't want to. Though Mona stays distant and even hostile to those who give her help, we see a break in her facade twice. It happens with a kind Tunisian field worker (Yahaoui Assouna) and again with an old woman, beautifully played by Marthe Jarnias, with whom Mona shares a sip of sherry and a burst of giggles. The effect is heart-piercing. *Vagabond* is daring in concept and overwhelming in the human devastation it depicts. Bonnaire, who won the Cesar (the French Oscar) for her stunning performance, provided a character to haunt our waking nightmares. "I want spectators to define themselves vis-à-vis Mona," says Varda. "For example, would you give Mona money or a ride or let her sleep in your car?" It's a measure of *Vagabond*'s success that such questions keep nagging long after this remarkable film is over. (In French with subtitles.)

Unrated / 1986 / Pacific Arts

▲ VALENTINO

Ballet virtuoso Rudolf Nureyev is way out of joint as Valentino, the silent screen Romeo of the 1920s. Although his posturing, twirling, and tapping are bearable, his cardboard characterization of the foppish Italian romantic peels off the screen. There isn't a scintilla of sexual tension between Valentino and his dancer-turned-designer wife, Natasha, played by Michelle Phillips. They revolve about each other like orbiting planets, finally colliding in a "passionate" nude love scene that crunches like burnt toast. The rococo decor and costumes can't carry the movie; for Nureyev, it was indeed a *faux pas*.
R / 1977 / N/A

▲ VALLEY GIRL

How boring can a movie be when it's about a teenage girl whose biggest problem is deciding with whom to go to the junior prom? The answer: to the max boring. Like, gag everybody with a spoon before they can say, "I want to rent this one, please." Directed by Martha (*Not a Pretty Picture*) Coolidge, the film seemed dated from the outset, probably because the Valley Girl phenomenon, spawned by the peculiar middle-class non-culture of California's San Fernando Valley, had, thank goodness, already been beaten into the ground. Still, an amusing film could have been made from this passing fad. But this one isn't it. Deborah Foreman stars as the Valley Girl and Nicholas Cage as the boy from Hollywood who falls for her. Theirs is a huge philosophical confrontation, since she is into consumer chic while Cage wears old clothes, doesn't hang around shopping centers, and has a friend with magenta hair. Foreman has lots of smirky, smug chums; Cage knows some black people and swears. Her friends smirk awhile, he swears awhile, then they kiss and he takes her home. You could cut the dramatic tension with a thread from an angora sweater. Meanwhile, most of the actors portraying parents—Colleen (*They All Laughed*) Camp as Foreman's mother, for instance—seem as young as the kids. They also seem universally stupid, especially Frederic (*The Rose*) Forrest, who plays Foreman's ex-flowerchild dad as if he is improvising his lines while mentally figuring out his income tax. The sound track includes some good rock 'n' roll; the high point of the movie is Josie

Cotton doing her tune "Johnny, Are You Queer?", which tells you how bad things are. The only positive thing about *Valley Girl* is its reminder not to wax too nostalgic over childhood. Being 16 can get mighty tedious too.
R / 1983 / Vestron

▲ VENOM

The ads for this one were effusive and then some: "the mystery of *The Birds*," "the danger of *Psycho*," "the evil of *The Omen*," "the terror of *Jaws*." That's known as the hard sell—and this movie needs it. A young boy living with his rich American parents in London goes to the local pet store to pick up a snake he has ordered. By mistake, he takes a deadly African mamba home in a box. When he gets there, he finds some nasty kidnappers waiting. When one of them accidentally shoots a curious cop, the house is quickly surrounded by Scotland Yard. The only question is, who will collar the bad guys first, the police or the snake, which by this time has been let out of the box. The silly plot wastes a lot of good actors, including Nicol Williamson as the hard-boiled cop trying to smoke the kidnappers out, Klaus Kinski as the menacing kidnapper, and Oliver Reed as his trigger-happy sidekick. Susan George is the snake's first victim, and the late Sterling Hayden is the kindly grandfather trapped in the house with the boy (Lance Holcomb). But the movie really belongs to the snake, which slithers through the heating ducts of the house in search of something to eat. The snake hisses constantly—and intelligent audiences will too.
R / 1982 / Vestron

▲ THE VERDICT

In a three-decade-plus film career, Paul Newman had been nominated for an Oscar five times—for *Cat on a Hot Tin Roof, The Hustler, Hud, Cool Hand Luke, Absence of Malice*—but the Academy had never seemed able to see past those bedazzling blues to the intelligent, passionate actor behind them. The *Verdict* won him a sixth nomination and while the Oscar went to Ben Kingsley in *Gandhi*, it set Newman up for his *Color of Money* triumph. He plays a chiseling, alcoholic Boston lawyer using a hospital mal-

The Verdict: Paul Newman turns quietly noble as a Boston lawyer who tries to rebuild a dissipated career by taking on a very unlikely case involving a suit against a powerful hospital.

practice suit as a last shot at regaining his integrity. There's nothing he can do about his looks (then 57, he was still staggeringly handsome), but Newman captures the corruption and moral fatigue eating at his character. To watch an actor who can make millions coasting (as he did in *Towering Inferno*) take such a daring gamble with his star image and come up aces is exhilarating. Except for a few lapses of logic and some melodramatic moments in the courtroom, David Mamet's script from Barry Reed's novel is unusually incisive. And director Sidney (*Network*) Lumet works his customary magic with actors. James Mason, nominated as Best Supporting Actor, is brilliant and bitingly funny as Newman's high-priced legal adversary; Milo O'Shea makes a canny old hoot of the judge; Lindsay Crouse (Mrs. Mamet) is unforgettably moving as a key witness; and Jack Warden, as Newman's ex-partner, may well be the best character man in the business. Even chilly Charlotte Rampling, whose role seems cosmetically attached to give Newman a love interest, finds ways to make it more. *The Verdict* is a film manufactured out of old parts but put together by experts in a way that demands fresh attention and respect.

R / 1982 / CBS

▲ VERTIGO

Some still think of Alfred Hitchcock as merely a maker of thrillers, good for a few chills and little more. They are wrong. The film that best makes the case for Hitchcock's genius is this masterpiece, given a revival in 1984. It stars James Stewart and Kim Novak, hardly darlings of the high culture set. But *Vertigo* is as complex, mesmerizing, and memorable as anything from Bergman, Fellini, or Renoir. Such fine directors as François Truffaut, Brian De Palma, and Robert Benton have tried unsuccessfully to recreate its spell. Set in San Francisco, the film casts Stewart as a detective with a fear of heights. He's trailing a rich client's wife—an elegant blonde named Madeleine (played by a stunning Novak)—who seems preoccupied with death. For most of the film Hitchcock employs little dialogue, just Bernard Herrmann's haunting score, as Stewart follows Madeleine through an art gallery, a church, and a graveyard. The effect is hypnotic. When he sees Madeleine jump from a church bell tower, Stewart, paralyzed by vertigo, is powerless to help her. Later he meets a trashy shopgirl (Novak again, this time in a brunette wig) and tries to recreate her in Madeleine's image. There is no trick surprise ending; the director unravels the mystery two-thirds of the way through the film. Hitchcock's concern is obsession, the romantic's insistence on imposing illusions on reality. (Hitchcock himself, deserted by Grace Kelly when she became a princess, vainly tried to fashion other actresses in her image.) *Vertigo*, a neurotic dream world profoundly visualized, is Hitchcock's most personal, disturbing film and, not coincidentally, a work of art.

PG / 1958 / MCA

▲ VICTOR/VICTORIA

In 1981's *S.O.B.*, writer-director Blake Edwards had his wife Julie Andrews go topless. This time Edwards dresses Julie as if she were a man in drag (she looks a bit like David Bowie). Fans of the old chaste Julie may well shudder at the thought of what might be next, but others will find *Victor/Victoria* one of her strongest roles. It is also Edwards's best work since the early *Pink Panther* films. Gone is the bilious spirit that marred *S.O.B.* Instead, Edwards has devised a good-natured burlesque of sexual confusion. The setting is Paris, circa 1934, where out-of-work opera singer Andrews hooks up with a homosexual cabaret performer (Robert Preston). His plan is to dress Julie as a man and promote her as the world's best female impersonator. The ruse works

until Julie falls for a macho Chicago gangster (James Garner at his deadpan best), who believes she's a man and questions his own sexuality. Garner's chorus girl moll, played by Lesley Ann Warren in Jean Harlow style, is even more puzzled. Meanwhile, Preston is enjoying an affair with Garner's beefy bodyguard, former Detroit Lions tackle Alex Karras. Despite the theme, the effect is more roguish Disney than R-rated decadence. Preston portrays a mature gay without lapsing into caricature or condescension. His friendship with Andrews is poignant, and an early restaurant scene in which they bilk a waiter out of two dinners is great film farce. There are faults: The film is overlong at 2 hours and 13 minutes and is plagued by a sometimes cloying Henry Mancini score; and, as always, Edwards tends to beat his punch lines into the ground. But *Victor/Victoria* combines high and low comedy without missing a laugh in between. Andrews, Preston, and Warren all won deserved Oscar nominations. But in a year of cross-dressing flicks, *V/V* was clearly outclassed by *Tootsie*.

PG / 1982 / MGM/UA

▲ VICTORY

This film shows Sylvester Stallone at his worst. Trimmed down forty pounds from his fighting weight, Sly is still Balboaesque—he makes his character seem like a conceited creep in a film that demands, and otherwise gets, more subtle acting. The story concerns a soccer game in 1943 between the German national team and the best players among Germany's prisoners of war. Max Von Sydow gives a vivid portrayal of the gentlemanly Nazi major who suggests the game and Michael Caine is convincing as the British coach who takes up his challenge. Except for Stallone, playing an American goalie, the POW team is manned by real pro soccer players, including Pelé (unbelievably acrobatic in some slow-motion sequences) and Britain's Bobby Moore. There are also a half-dozen Eastern Europeans; in one moving scene they are delivered to Caine, near death, from concentration camps. Director John Huston offers several prison camp sequences that have the tense, gray face of reality. It's hard for one film to be *Stalag 17*, *The Great Escape*, and *The Longest Yard* at the same time, however. Huston repeatedly cuts the best dramatic scenes short to leave time for soccer. But the game, which oc-

Victor/Victoria: In this stylish Blake Edwards farce Julie Andrews plays a cabaret entertainer who pretends to be a man pretending to be a woman and still manages to attract James Garner.

cupies the last twenty minutes or so, is the thing. The rest is mostly halftime drivel.

PG / 1981 / CBS/Fox

▲ VIDEODROME

Before this film drowns in a tide of bloody gore and drippy foolishness—and it doesn't take long—there are some signs of biting black satire on the influence of television in modern society. James (*The Onion Fields*) Woods plays the owner of a small cable TV station in Toronto that caters to an audience craving soft-core porn and violence. Woods is anxious to give them "something that'll break through, something tough," and decides he has it when one of his engineers intercepts a satellite signal from Pittsburgh showing programs consisting of nothing but murder, torture, and dismemberment. It seems indeed to be his lucky day, especially when he goes on a talk show and meets Deborah Harry (brown-haired but, yes, that Deborah Harry), the masochistic hostess of a local call-in show called "Emotional Rescue." Woods is a fine actor, Harry is an entrancing presence, and the idea is involving. Then writer-director David Cronenberg, as he did later with *The Fly,* lets the movie dissolve in an idiotic succession of grotesque effects—holes opening in Woods' stomach, TV sets coming alive, bodies splitting open. These may or may not be hallucinations resulting from a broadcast signal that causes brain tumors in viewers and drives them crazy in pursuit of some never-quite-defined villainy. It's never clear who's doing what to whom; it's only clear that blood and guts are spilling out of people—not to mention TV sets—every minute or two.

R / 1983 / MCA

▲ A VIEW TO A KILL

The strain was indeed starting to show on 007 as incarnated by Roger Moore. When it comes to reeling off a sly Bondism, Moore, at 57, was as

smooth as ever; the same couldn't be said, however, for either his skin or his gait. There's nothing that says James Bond can't have a wrinkle or two or lose that extra step, but this script (unlike the Sean Connery's *Never Say Never Again* in 1983) doesn't allow for such intrusions of reality. Bond is apparently supposed to be as ageless as ever. Screenwriters Richard Mailbaum and Michael Wilson seemed to be wearing out a little, too, which is understandable since they had worked on eleven Bond films between them. The opening sequence, always a Bond highlight, is unexceptional. It features a snow sequence far too much like the dazzling chase that began *The Spy Who Loved Me*. This film also has little in the way of new gimmicks or hardware, and even its best action scene, a chase involving a fire truck, pales beside memories of, say, the beautifully planned and photographed boat pursuit in *Live and Let Die*. Director John Glen knows a great location when he sees one—Paris and San Francisco, to name a couple—but has a harder time striking sparks with his cast. One exception is singer Grace Jones, who, with her panther's look, makes an ideal villain—in a class with Gert Frobe as Goldfinger or Richard Kiel as Jaws. Ex–"Charlie's Angel" Tanya Roberts shows far less vitality as Moore's romantic interest. Roberts still hadn't shaken her New York accent, and she still had trouble with any line more complex than "Look out, James!" Christopher Walken is amusingly laconic as the main villain—a standard psychopathic Bond foe, in this case one who is out to corner the world microchip market. But this movie drags in too many places, and it would be a shame to let the Bond films deteriorate like a heavyweight fighter who refuses to admit he's losing it. That's why it wasn't a bad idea for Moore to hang up his martini shaker after this film, leaving to Timothy Dalton his license to kill, smooch, and quip so entertainingly.
PG / 1985 / CBS/Fox

▲ VIOLETS ARE BLUE

If you're going to make a blustery, bittersweet romance, you don't cast Sissy Spacek and Kevin Kline in the leads. Although fine actors, both are really best at miniatures. They specialize in everyday people, and despite its small-town setting, *Violets Are Blue* is a tearjerker operating on overdrive, in need of overblown star perfor-

mances. After all, this is a movie with a climax cribbed from *Casablanca* and a syrupy score suitable for *A Summer Place*. Naomi Foner's skeletal script grafts an '80s career-woman plot onto a '50s star-crossed-lovers situation. Once upon a time, Spacek and Kline were high school sweethearts, and they frolic through an embarrassing prologue to make that point. (Kline, then 38, and Spacek, then 35, can hardly pass for teenagers.) Soon they part paths and values. She becomes a globe-trotting photojournalist. He becomes editor of the local paper in their hometown of Ocean City, Maryland. Fifteen years later, Spacek swoops into town to rekindle romance, which doesn't much please Kline's wife, wonderfully sketched by Bonnie Bedelia. You have to be immediately wary of any movie that establishes a romance with a montage set in an amusement park. This project, however, was probably doomed from the start. Spacek is better playing the sort of gullible woman who might sob through a showing of *Violets Are Blue* than she is at fleshing out the superworldly heroine. And Kline suggests a man with dulled ambitions by dulling his responses as an actor. These are quiet actors to start with, but they've been directed to give performances that border on mute. Only Bedelia colors her character with the idiosyncrasies that resemble real life. As a wife devoted to domestic duties, she confesses to Spacek, "I'm beginning to like the smell of paint thinner." Directed by Spacek's husband, Jack Fisk, who collaborated with his wife on *Raggedy Man*, this movie asphyxiates on its reverence for the common folk. Instead of celebrating the virtues of ordinary people, *Violets Are Blue* is inadvertently condescending. Small-town life has never been made to look so suffocating or mundane as it does under Fisk's admiring gaze. Besides undercutting its own good intentions with bad execution, *Violets Are Blue* is something a movie romance should never be: It's smaller than life.
PG-13 / 1986 / RCA/Columbia

▲ VIOLETTE

Somewhere here there's a good story struggling to get out. But French director Claude (*La Femme Infidele*) Chabrol has substituted psychology for plot. Isabelle Huppert, so good in *The Lacemaker*, plays a young Parisienne in the 1930s who leads a strange double life—Daddy's little girl by day, a ruby-lipped floozy by night. Her relationship with her bourgeois parents, meant to be the focus, is poorly defined. So when she decides to kill them, the impact is dissipated. Huppert is sad-eyed and occasionally brilliant—she shared best actress honors at Cannes with Jill (*An Unmarried Woman*) Clayburgh for this role. The parents are played by veteran actors Jean Camet and Stephane Audran (Chabrol's real-life wife). What Hitchcock would have made chilling, though, Ghabrol renders tiresome. (In French with subtitles.)

Unrated / 1978 / N/A

▲ VISION QUEST

A Hollywood hybrid, this is a jock movie arguing that it is every American male's inalienable right to go for it. At the same time it's a coming-of-age movie that believes a young man's virginity is best dispensed with through the aid of an experienced older woman. *Vision Quest* could get annihilated in the cross fire of formulas, but it doesn't. Although it religiously honors the touchstones of both genres, director Harold Becker's film insists on finding something fresh in the formulas. When high school wrestler Matthew Modine decides to face down a state champ in another weight class as a personal challenge, he disrupts the camaraderie of his team. And when newcomer Linda Fiorentino, an aimless but fearless 21-year-old, moves into the house Modine shares with his father, a mechanic, he must ponder his sex drive as well as his takedowns. It's that impertinent, imperfect love affair that gives the movie its conflict and chemistry. As the boy and young woman try to side-step sex and each other, the movie manages to be funny and feisty about adolescent affection. As the tunnel-visioned hero, Modine finally found a role that really suited his quirky talents. In his previous outings, he came on like an ethereal, asexual refugee from the Vienna Boys Choir. But this movie gives him a much needed counterpoint and foil in Fiorentino, who neutralizes the clichés of her role with integrity. Modine and Fiorentino give their scenes together a nervous tension and an honest humor that is momentarily mesmerizing. Becker, however, doesn't do anything to showcase effectively those performances or the clever script that novelist Darryl Ponicsan adapted from Terry Davis's first novel. Becker doesn't have a tremendous

aptitude for sports movies—he doesn't even show the scoreboard at crucial moments—and he doesn't give the relationship between Modine and Fiorentino breathing room. But the two stars transcend the formula even when his direction doesn't.

R / 1985 / Warner

▲ VOICES

Modest but moving, this film is a romance between a young deaf woman, Amy Irving, and a struggling rock singer, Michael Ontkean. Though Ontkean suffers from the Paul Michael Glaser overearnestness syndrome, he's ruggedly good-looking. Irving, whose real-life older sister has taught the deaf, conveys with considerable subtlety the confusion and pain of feeling constantly on the outside. She also suggests the angular beauty of the young Lauren Bacall. Director Robert Markowitz, in his first feature film, dwells on her face too much, and the segments when he cuts off all sound, simulating deafness, seem out of place. He did, however, stage a marvelous scene for Viveca Lindfors, as Irving's overconcerned mother, and for the most part kept a sweet story from turning into saccharine.

PG / 1979 / N/A

▲ VOLUNTEERS

Compulsively impudent and indiscriminately malicious, *Volunteers,* with Tom Hanks and John Candy as the leads, achieves what no other recent comedy has: It hits every target it takes on. Always smart and occasionally smart-alecky, it is a hip, '80s version of a Bing Crosby–Bob Hope *Road* movie. Like the Crosby-Hope collaborations, it doesn't let coherent plotting get in the way of an insatiable need to satirize—in this case, the Camelot days of the Kennedy era. Just out of Yale and into trouble, Hanks decides to trade places with a Thailand-bound Peace Corps volunteer to escape a gambling debt. As the 1963 paragon of prep ("I'm very rich, and I have certain rights"), Hanks is appalled to encounter among his self-righteous colleagues Tom Tuttle from Tacoma, as Candy constantly introduces himself, and Rita Wilson, who reads *Profiles in Courage* the way some women read *Peyton Place,* that is, in bed. This unholy trinity is assigned to

A View to a Kill: In his last appearance as James Bond, Roger Moore gets to grapple with Tanya Roberts as well as miscellaneous villains, including Grace Jones.

build a remote bridge with the help of some remote villagers. When *Volunteers* rhapsodizes about "doing the right thing for the right reason," it threatens to sputter. But the contrivances don't intrude because the movie seldom aspires to do anything more than amuse. Sporting an incongruous white dinner jacket in the jungle and assuming a lockjawed delivery, Hanks dashes off a wonderfully perverse Cary Grant impersonation. Candy looks as if he's having fun onscreen

for the first time since *Splash.* Although director Nicholas Meyer hadn't trafficked in comedy before, he handles it as craftily as he does the idealism of the early 1960s. He even gets fresh laughs out of "Puff the Magic Dragon." Beyond its slapdash surface, *Volunteers* provides a public service: It demonstrates that a comedy can prove altogether entertaining without being either vulgar or pretentious.

R / 1985 / Thorn/EMI

▲ WALK PROUD

Cute, wholesome, all-American Robby Benson as a Chicano? That bit of casting is a blow from which this film about gang wars in the L.A.

barrio never recovers. Benson tries to take his character beyond the limits that a swarthy tan, breathy Mexican accent, and comical swagger impose on him. The plot is an updated *West Side Story,* with Sarah Holcomb as a WASPy upper-

class girl who falls for him. But the bang is strictly Hollywood, and first-time director Robert Collins fails to produce any visual impact.
PG / 1979 / N/A

▲ WANTED DEAD OR ALIVE

Rutger Hauer plays a modern-day bounty hunter who lives in a high-tech loft and loves to dress in leather. He also likes big guns, and when he sets out after an Arab terrorist, who specializes in blowing up Los Angeles movie theaters, he's like a blond, beefy Rambo. Maybe there was never any chance to make much of this, but the script is just plain stupid, never giving enough information about Hauer's character to suggest why anyone should care about him. (The closest it comes is to note that he is supposed to be a descendant of Josh Randall, the character Steve McQueen played on a '50s TV series.) This is an action-adventure film, and despite some scary stuff at the beginning—Hauer saves some Vietnamese grocers from robbers—the movie just grunts along to the predictable climax. Ex-rocker Gene Simmons kisses off his terrorist role with an appropriate glower. Robert Guillaume is a friendly CIA agent who discovers that his colleagues are setting Hauer up. About the only sympathetic character here is newcomer Mel Harris, who plays Hauer's flight-attendant girlfriend. There is more intelligence and warmth behind those eyes than in all the rest of this moribund film. When the best thing you can say about a movie is that it reminds you of *Cobra,* it is a sorry project indeed.
R / 1986 / New World

▲ WARGAMES

It's hard to imagine a better plot for a goodtime movie. A 17-year-old high school computer jock, while trying to master a new video game called Global Thermonuclear War on a terminal in his bedroom, accidentally taps into the Pentagon's missile-launching system and comes within a byte of starting World War III. Director John (*Blue Thunder*) Badham does the concept justice with this tightly suspenseful yet frequently amusing film. The sets are spectacular in themselves, especially a replica of the Pentagon's NORAD control center that looks as if it alone should have

cost $13 million—the film's entire budget—to construct. But Badham's biggest asset is Matthew Broderick, who made his film debut in *Mac Dugan Returns* and already had a Tony for his role in *Brighton Beach Memoirs* on Broadway. Broderick carries the film comfortably on his 21-year-old shoulders; he is the perfect nerd-in-shining armor. Co-star Ally Sheedy (Sean Penn's girlfriend in *Bad Boys*) is a more talented Brooke Shields, and there is some real heat in the exchanges between her and Broderick, though nothing little kids shouldn't see. The supporting cast includes the deft John (*Slaughterhouse Five*) Woods and Dabney (*Tootsie*) Coleman, who is as reliable as a character actor as there is in films today. The only drawback is that the film's anti-nuke message seems a bit heavy-handed at times. It is hard, though, to imagine any message being more entertainingly delivered.
PG / 1983 / CBS/Fox

▲ WARLORDS OF ATLANTIS

A band of explorers and greedy central casting cutthroats drop in on a bunch of rubbery beasts who inhabit the fabled underwater continent. The film is set in the late 19th century, but Doug McClure, the designated hero, wisecracks with a kind of disco posturing and surf's-up accent that are eighty years out of synch. That's hardly the worst of it though. Maybe it's the stock footage of herky-jerky monster fights. Or Cyd Charisse showing up in a teased wig as the high priestess of Atlantis. No, it's hard to beat the climactic scene, where the inevitable giant octopus—battered enough to be the very beast that gave Jon Hall a hard time in *South of Pago Pago* (1940)—begins whacking the explorers' ship with the gold totem they were trying to steal. Nothing here will win any awards from the Atlantis Chamber of Commerce.
PG / 1978 / N/A

▲ WARNING SIGN

While there are one or two dumber movies on the shelf, none does such a thorough job of trashing a talented cast as this high-tech, low-brow thriller. Sam Waterston, in particular, should have been ashamed to collect his check; he seems

totally enervated as a Utah county sheriff whose jurisdiction becomes the focus of a biological warfare scare. Kathleen Quinlan, Yaphet Kotto, and Richard Dysart seem only slightly more animated. Quinlan plays an inept security guard locked inside a genetic engineering plant when some klutz spills a bit of stuff that turns people into homicidal zombies. Kotto heads an inept government team that comes swooping in to contain the contamination. Dysart is the inept semimad scientist who started the whole business. Director Hal Barwood and Matthew Robbins are the inept screenwriters who created such dialogue as the line Waterston delivers when a scientist accuses him of being reluctant to enter the contaminated plant: "It's different with you; germs are your job." Everyone is so inept, in fact, it's tempting to root for the bugs. By the end, only one real bit of suspense remains: How does it happen that Quinlan remains healthy when everyone else inside the plant seems to be turning into extras for a *Living Dead* sequel? Cynics will suggest it's because she is the only name actress in the movie. Robert Wise's 1971 film, *The Andromeda Strain*, covered the same ground with lots more style and plausibility. But then the people in Hollywood were never ones to let sleeping dogs lie, let alone contagions.
R / 1985 / CBS/Fox

▲ THE WARRIORS

The first five minutes of this movie are stylishly choreographed and visually arresting. A subsequent letdown is only natural. Director Walter Hill clearly likes his scripts lean, a predilection that served him well in *Hard Times*, failed miserably in *The Driver*, and falls somewhere in between here. The Warriors are a gang of Coney Island toughs who make the long subway trip to the Bronx for a meeting of the city's gangs, only to be wrongly accused of assassinating a would-be messiah. The chase is on as the Warriors try to outwit and outhit cops and rival gangs. Michael Beck and David Patrick Kelly (as the real assassin) stand out in a cast of unknowns, but the real star is nighttime New York—dark, menacing, and slightly surreal. Although it's harnessed haphazardly, this film throbs with the city's raw energy.
R / 1979 / Paramount

▲ WARRIORS OF THE WASTELAND

This ghastly little number is a must for any Fred Williamson retrospective. Otherwise, it can be dismissed faster than you can say the name of its producer, Fabrizio de Angelis. It is a thinly disguised, made-in-Italy version of that classic post-Armageddon adventure fantasy, *Road Warrior*. Williamson, Timothy Brent, and George Eastman tool around a nuclear-war-devastated landscape in what seem to be used-car-lot rejects remodeled with help from the James Bond Special Effects Handbook. Williamson and Brent are free-lance good guys. Eastman heads a homosexual cult dedicated to eradicating all humanity, though why George and the boys don't start with themselves is a question of some philosophic import. Anna Kanakis provides the heterosexual romantic interest; luckily for her, the holocaust doesn't seem to have caused any shortage of eye makeup. Enzo Castellari directed; this was easily his most moving, emotion-packed movie since *Seven Winchesters for a Massacre*.
R / 1984 / Thorn/EMI

▲ WATER

Michael Caine makes movies almost as often as other people go to them. He began 1986 with one of his best, *Hannah and Her Sisters*, followed with *Sweet Liberty*, *Half Moon Street*, *The Whistle Blower*, and *The Fourth Protocol*. However well or bad these films turned out, you could always count on Caine. In *Water*, a Monty Pythonesque political satire, he plays Baxter Thwaites, governor of Cascara, a forgotten British colony in the Caribbean. When the gov isn't testing the local marijuana crop or warding off his hysterical Guatemalan wife (deliciously overplayed by Brenda Vaccaro), he's dictating futile pleas for financial aid to Margaret Thatcher. It seems Cascara is a wasteland. The inhabitants are descended mostly from shipwreck victims (the national anthem is a hymn to the breaststroke that brought them there) or from the local minister (Fulton MacKay), who provided the women of his parish with more than spiritual comfort. But Caine sees his chance to end the island's tropical torpor when an American oil company's long-abandoned drilling well starts spewing out water. Not just any water. This lemony fizz is a match for Perrier. Suddenly business interests from America and Cuba are

inciting a revolution to cadge bottling rights. With the help of ecologist Valerie Perrine, Caine sides with the natives against Whitehall's avaricious minister, hilariously played by Leonard Rossiter of TV's "The Rise and Fall of Reginald Perrin." Sneers Rossiter (and no one sneered better) to Caine: "You've become the Patty Hearst of the British Diplomatic Corps." If only laughs like this weren't so often followed by boredom. Director and co-writer Dick (*Bullshot*) Clement can't keep *Water* above the ragtag level. But Hand-Made Films (whose co-founder George Harrison does a singing cameo) should be celebrated for financing films (*The Long Good Friday, A Private Function*) that don't play it safe. And while we're celebrating, let's raise one to Caine—an actor who is never less than a class act.
PG-13 / 1986 / Paramount

▲ A WEDDING

By staging a lavish wedding involving two huge families and following it through to the honeymoon, director Robert Altman created the same kind of cinematic encounter group that served him so well in *Nashville*. The cast lists fifty featured actors, from veterans (Lillian Gish, Viveca Lindfors) to Altman repertory players (Geraldine Chaplin, Nina van Pallandt) to new recruits (Carol Burnett, Lauren Hutton, and Mia Farrow). Young Desi Arnaz, Jr., and Amy Stryker play the bridal couple. The performances are almost uniformly impressive, but this is a director's film sustained by his vision of the collision of high comedy and wrenching tragedy in everyday life. The denouement becomes rather overwrought, as if Altman had suddenly decided the movie was too static and needed some melodrama (for example, a gratuitous car crash). Still, he conducts his players like a maestro, and the result is a classic impression of American life.
PG / 1978 / N/A

▲ WEIRD SCIENCE

For his first joke, director-writer John Hughes resorts to having his heroes lose their pants. *Weird Science* never recovers from the lame vulgarity of that beginning, nor does it try to. In this high-tech version of *Bride of Frankenstein,* two teenage outcasts, using a computer, create their

idea of the ultimate woman. When she appears in their midst alive and aroused, she engenders the pair's conversion from geeks to cool guys. Despite the situation's possibilities, Hughes doesn't pursue the consequences of adolescent wish fulfillment. In such earlier films as *The Breakfast Club* and *Sixteen Candles,* he displayed an admirable empathy for his youthful characters, but this time he took empathy too far. He's interested only in the same things as his 15-year-old heroes: good times and rock 'n' roll. Consequently, Kelly Le Brock, who plays the dream woman, is really nothing more than an ornament. She's treated like an early Jackie Bisset. Nor do her creators fare any better. As the wise guy of the pair, Anthony Michael Hall is so bossy he can't ply his ingratiating vulnerability. As his cohort, Ilan Mitchell-Smith possesses an oddball warmth that gives the movie its only emotional verve. *Weird Science* is a perversion of the high-concept movie: It's all concept, no execution. Audiences can tell the difference if Hollywood cannot.
PG-13 / 1985 / MCA

▲ WELCOME TO L.A.

A comely cast (Keith Carradine, Sally Kellerman, Geraldine Chaplin, Lauren Hutton, Sissy Spacek) couples and uncouples in what looks like producer Robert Altman's *Nashville-West.* Actually, it was something more. The film marked the debut of writer-director Alan Rudolph, who perfected an original and bizarre style with 1984's *Choose Me* and 1986's *Trouble in Mind.*
R / 1977 / CBS/Fox

▲ WETHERBY

Things are not what they seem in this quietly devastating meditation on British repression from playwright David Hare, in an impressive film debut as screenwriter and director. As the film opens, Vanessa Redgrave, as a schoolteacher in a middle-class Yorkshire town, is acting the perfect dinner hostess to a handful of friends in her cottage. Among the guests is a crasher, young Tim McInnerny. Redgrave and her guests all assume he is an invited extra. This being Britain, no one presumes to pry. They should have, for when the young man returns to confront Redgrave alone and next day, he brings a gun. The ensuing

violence leads to the uncovering of a secret full of menace. At times, Hare's film evokes Harold Pinter too overtly, but Hare hasn't merely filmed a play. The movie exerts a real pull as a police detective, Stuart Wilson, interrogates the parties involved, including a neighboring couple, expertly played by the English stage actors Ian Holm and Judi Dench, and McInnerny's girlfriend, icily done by Suzanna Hamilton. The key to the mystery lies with Redgrave and a long-ago affair shown in flashback. In these scenes the young Redgrave is portrayed by her daughter, Joely Richardson, showing every sign of a stunning future. Redgrave, as ever, is luminous—finding just the right gesture and nuance to lay a character bare. Literate, provocative, and disturbing, *Wetherby* strikes like a bolt of lightning.
R / 1985 / MGM/UA

▲ WE WILL ALL MEET IN PARADISE

Lightly, lightly, and lots of laughs—that's the formula in French director Yves Robert's sequel to *Pardon Mon Affaire*. Jean Rochefort plays a husband who suspects his wife is cheating but botches his own attempt to do the same. His three buddies compound the confusion. Victor Lanoux is loutishly charming as a tennis-club owner who loves kids; Claude Brasseur plays a car salesman with an AM-FM sex drive; and Guy Bedois is wonderfully *fou* as a doctor whose heart still belongs to Mommy. There are some very funny moments, even though a few of the jokes fall flat. (In French with subtitles.)
PG / 1978 / N/A

▲ WHEN NATURE CALLS

A low-budget send-up of all things Hollywood, this film harkens back to those mid '70s cult comedies *The Groove Tube* and *The Kentucky Fried Movie*—crude, often hilarious views of films and TV by hip Baby Boomers. *When Nature Calls* (subtitled *You've Gotta Go*) presents several movie trailers leading to an hour-long feature, complete with an intermission and a charity collection drive. A parody of 1981's *Raging Bull* has its moments, as does the feature section, "The Outdoorsters"—a takeoff on the *Wilderness Family* series. Funny, too, is a testimonial for the Society for the Prevention of Jerry Lewis,

in which spokesman G. Gordon Liddy—yes, that G. Gordon Liddy—pleads. "We've got to stay ahead of the Russians. . . . We've already lost France." Writer/director Charles Kaufman saturates the film with one-liners; at ten jokes a minute, some are bound to hit. Cameos by Myron Cohen, John Cameron Swayze, and Morey Amsterdam, to name a few, add little. But the ultimate failing of this film is that it lacks the fundamental element of its predecessors: It's not really outrageous. When he falls back on a Bo Derek gag, Kaufman seems more desperate than the people he's parodying.
R / 1985 / Media

▲ WHEN TIME RAN OUT . . .

Time isn't the only thing that ran out on this film; imagination, humor, and money also seem to have been in short supply. After paying for Paul Newman, Jacqueline Bisset, William Holden, and the rest of an all-star cast, producer Irwin Allen apparently didn't have much cash left for special effects. The result is a tepid tale about a volcanic eruption on a Polynesian island. Director James Goldstone is stymied by a not-so-Sterling Silliphant and Carl Foreman screenplay; its highlights are the interminable crossing of a rickety bridge over a fake lava flow and a scene where the stars cling precariously to the kind of crumbling cliff found only on a Hollywood sound stage. Close-ups of Bisset (her T-shirt is dry) and exteriors shot on Hawaii's Kona coast make for magnificent scenery, and Newman struggles gamely. But even he sounds foolish uttering lines like "They may cancel tomorrow." This is the kind of disaster film that makes you muse about one called *Revenge of the Bored Audiences*.
PG / 1980 / N/A

▲ WHEN YOU COMIN' BACK, RED RYDER?

Grown-up child evangelist Marjoe Gortner certainly let his light shine in here: He conceived the movie version of the Mark Medoff play, produced it, starred in it, and married guest star Candy Clark. But for all the egocentrism, Gortner (whose acting gigs have mainly been B movies and TV guest spots) does have charisma as the flipped-out hippie who holds a group of people hostage in a diner. Obviously visualized as an

Easy Rider-type cult picture, *Red Ryder* is heavy on sex (Clark as the sweetheart has a nice body, but do we really need to watch Hal Linden having an orgasm?), drugs (actually the picture is shot as if it were a bad acid trip), and cars. Peter Firth manages to trade in his British accent for a southern drawl as a short-order cook, graveyard shift. Audra Lindley is painfully right as his faded mom and newcomer Stephanie Faracy equally so as his fat girlfriend. Unfortunately for Marjoe, the piece seemed dated even when it came out.
R / 1979 / N/A

▲ **WHERE THE BOYS ARE '84**

Watching this inane remake of the 1960 spring break comedy, one mostly wonders what happened to girls of that camp classic. Well, wonder no more: Delores Hart became a cloistered nun in Connecticut. Paula Prentiss, who suffered a nervous breakdown in 1964, became the wife of director Richard Benjamin, the mother of two, and a much-missed presence on the screen. Connie Francis fought a long battle against physical and mental problems. And Yvette Mimieux split from her husband, director Stanley Donen. Somewhere in those epilogues lies the plot of a terrific pop movie. *Where the Boys Are '84,* which features Lisa Hartman, Lorna Luft, Wendy Schaal, and Lyne-Holly Johnson, doesn't begin to qualify for that distinction.
R / 1984 / Key

▲ **WHERE THE BUFFALO ROAM**

Orson Welles was "Citizen Kane," and Robert Redford and Dustin Hoffman were natural as Woodward and Bernstein, but who could handle *Rolling Stone* "Gonzo" journalist Hunter S. Thompson? Right, Bill Murray. After months of research that allegedly included an expense account tab for $10,000 or so of Thompson's beloved Wild Turkey bourbon, the cast was primed to do justice to the crazed crusader. The trouble is that the movie can't decide if it's trying for laughs or social statement, and the commentary by Peter Boyle as the lawyer-turned-revolutionary, Karl "Brown Buffalo" Lazlo, is wearisome. Art Linson directed. Somebody needed a good editor, and for once it wasn't Thompson.
R / 1980 / MCA

▲ **WHERE THE RIVER RUNS BLACK**

As a visual experience this film is a triumph, with its spectacular sunsets and intensely colored vistas of the Brazilian rain forest. As a story it is an often laughable combination of *The Emerald Forest, The Wild Child, Greystoke,* and an episode of *Flipper.* The plot centers on a boy born to a strange woman who lives alone on the banks of the River Negro. The boy is conceived when a missionary priest happens upon the woman, makes love to her, and then paddles off in his canoe. The priest is promptly attacked by an anaconda that seems made of papier-mâché and behaves as if it thinks it's a kangaroo rather than a snake, leaping out of the water to demonstrate the wages of sin to the clergyman. The boy, played by Alessandro Rabelo, then 10, grows up to be a good swimmer and a pal of the local dolphins. They even save him from a crocodile. (If the croc gives a wooden performance, it may be because it seems to have been carved, not hatched.) When his mother is murdered by a passerby, the boy ends up in a city many miles away—with a priest, Charles Durning, who knew his father. The city is clearly undergoing an epidemic of coincidences because Rabelo immediately finds the murderer, a politician in the middle of a big campaign. The film ends in a crescendo of implausibilities, most of which involve Rabelo's mystical relationship with the dolphins. Director Christopher (*That Was Then . . . This Is Now*) Cain wisely chose a cinematographer with vision, Juan (*At Close Range*) Ruiz-Anchia, and shot the film on location in Brazil, but screenwriters Peter Silverman and Neal Jimenez left him up the Amazon without a plot.
PG / 1986 / Playhouse

▲ **WHICH WAY IS UP?**

A takeoff on Lina Wertmuller's *The Seduction of Mimi,* this funny if vulgar film stars Richard Pryor. He demonstrates his versatility by playing three roles—Rufus, "the dirtiest old man in the world," Leroy Jones, "the sex-starved fruit picker," and Reverend Thomas, a preacher who treats the women's choir like his private harem. Marilyn Coleman, the reverend's wife, is hilarious as a horny piano teacher who suc-

cumbs to Pryor's advances. *Which Way Is Up?* is no downer.
R / 1977 / MCA

▲ WHITE NIGHTS

Mikhail Baryshnikov stands alone on the darkened stage of Leningrad's Kirov ballet. He turns on the house lights and gazes at the splendor of the empty theater where, before defecting to America, he enjoyed his first triumph. He begins to move, first with the grace of a tentative fawn, then in a series of gravity-defying leaps. The dance is a solitary act of love and defiance to the Mother Russia that both nurtured and constricted him. Nothing in this screenplay by James Goldman and Eric Hughes approaches the anguish of that wordless scene. Without Baryshnikov, this handsome suspense thriller (made in Finland to simulate the summer "white nights" of Russia's midnight sun) would be cracker-jack entertainment. With him, however, the film is touched with greatness. In a story reminiscent of his own defection eleven years ago, Baryshnikov performs brilliantly. And director Taylor Hackford takes him farther. What if this Russian defector, on a 747 flight from London to Tokyo, should crash-land (the scene is stunningly staged) in Siberia? As this plot tells it, the dancer is captured and forced for propaganda reasons to rejoin the Kirov for a special performance. A contrivance, yes, but forgivable when it's this compelling. Unfortunately Hackford pours on the improbables. A KGB officer, acted with poisonous charm by Polish director Jerzy Skolinowski, puts Baryshnikov in the custody of a black American tap dancer, Gregory Hines, who defected to Russia as a protest against Vietnam and now regrets it. Hines and his Russian translator wife, the hauntingly lovely Isabella Rossellini, will figure in a climactic escape. But first the audience has to endure endless subplots. They involve Hines's and Rossellini's interracial marriage; a rekindling of Baryshnikov's affair with a Russian woman (Helen Mirren); and the schemes of Baryshnikov's agent (tartly done by Geraldine Page) to publicize her client's plight. Forgive these too. No matter how clumsy the process of getting the two leads together, when they dance it's worth it. The score, from Bach baroque to Phil Collins pop, brings out the breathtaking best in both Baryshnikov and Hines, and their tap duet is particularly sublime. You can wait around and hope, but you won't see a dance team like this again.
PG-13 / 1985 / RCA/Columbia

▲ WHO IS KILLING THE GREAT CHEFS OF EUROPE?

Some $180,000 was reportedly spent on culinary effects for this epicurean extravaganza (overseen by real-life chef Paul Bocuse). None of it was wasted, as the movable feast travels from Venice to Maxim's in Paris to London's Cafe Royal. It all begins when Robert Morley—a gourmand who fires a secretary for eating peanut butter—is forced to diet. Immediately thereafter a succession of chefs are killed in the style of their own specialties (including pressed duck). Each had planned a fling with dessert chef Jacqueline Bisset and received a suspicious visit from her ex-husband, George Segal, whom she divorced because of his fast-food enterprises. So it's not long before it looks as if Bisset may be on the murderer's menu herself. Wildly improbable, the movie is like a mousse au chocolat—hardly nutritional but a delight while it lasts. And Morley is a jolly and jowly delight in the performance of his life.
PG / 1978 / N/A

▲ WHO'LL STOP THE RAIN

This Vietnam-theme film, based on Robert Stone's brilliant novel *Dog Soldiers,* is sadly disappointing. Nick Nolte is the ex-Marine who smuggles heroin into the U.S. It's hard for a friend, played by Michael Moriarty, a journalist who lost his moral compass in the horror of the war. When Nolte makes the delivery to Moriarty's pill-popping wife (Tuesday Weld) in Berkeley, he's jumped by crooked narcs. Except for the stunning finale and solid acting, the film lacks the book's emotional punch.
R / 1978 / Key

▲ WHOLLY MOSES

The plot involves an idolmaker who thinks he has been chosen by God when he overhears the burning bush talking to Moses. The cast features Dudley Moore, Laraine Newman, and James Coco, with substantial cameos by Richard Pryor, John Ritter, John Houseman, Dom De Luise, and Madeline Kahn. The director is Gary Weis, a one time "Saturday Night Live" filmmaker. If it sounds like a satirical promised land, well, thou shalt not take anything for granted when it comes to movies. The script (by Weis's buddy Guy Thomas) is witless except for an occasional sight gag such as Coco sweeping up a plague-load of frogs. The pace is tedious, and the actors seem to be waiting to be told what to do next. Newman, particularly, is ill-served, looking gaunt and off her comic rhythm. This is absolute sacrilege in comedy terms as well as religious.

PG / 1980 / RCA/Columbia

▲ WHOSE LIFE IS IT ANYWAY?

"This hospital will kill no quadriplegic before his time," sasses Richard Dreyfuss to his doctors after an auto accident has doomed him to life in a hospital bed. Such gallows humor was the core of the Broadway hit that won a Tony for British actor Tom Conti and raves for Mary Tyler Moore when she replaced him. In this film version, Dreyfuss gives a touching performance despite a rabbity laugh and mannerisms that make one cringe. Director John (*Saturday Night Fever*) Badham tries to open up a basically one-set play and does everything but mount his camera on roller skates, even adding a silly nude ballet dream sequence. The sideshows unnecessarily damage Brian Clark's play. Still, the script, by Clark and Reginald Rose, has its own carefully constructed power. When Dreyfuss asks that his life-support systems be disconnected, he confronts hospital chief of staff John Cassavetes and statuesque doctor Christine Lahti, who cries a lot, for all her medical training. Then, with the help of a lawyer (Bob Balaban), Dreyfuss successfully argues his case before a judge (Kenneth McMillan). In these sequences, when the fine cast is allowed to play the material as written, the film triumphantly regains its grip on itself—and on our minds and hearts.

R / 1981 / MGM/UA

▲ WHY WOULD I LIE?

Why, indeed? It would be fibbing to say that this movie is powerfully directed, expertly acted, and filled with insights about the human condition.

Still, it's light, funny, and affecting. Treat Williams is at his most engaging as a Spokane, Washington, social worker who resorts to "fabrications," as he calls them, because they are more interesting than facts. He becomes obsessed with returning an adorable orphan (Gabriel Swann) to his real mother. Lisa Eichhorn, a conquest of Treat's, radiates warmth in a role more complex than it first appears. Director Larry Peerce, an expert at tugging the old heartstrings (he did *The Other Side of the Mountain*), plies his trade again here. Saccharine? Yes. Oversimplified? Yes. Truth to tell, it's refreshing too.

PG / 1980 / N/A

▲ THE WICKED LADY

Michael Winner, who made his reputation directing such action films as *Death Wish, Chato's Land,* and *Firepower,* turned to a period piece here, and the period seems to be the Age of Flouncing, Baleful Stares, and Goofy Plots. The setting is more or less 19th-century England, where Fay Dunaway steals her best friend's fiancé, falls in love with another man on her wedding day, becomes a highwaywoman, takes on still another lover, poisons a family retainer, bullwhips a romantic rival, and plots to murder her husband. Now is that wicked or is that wicked? As it turns out, it's not wicked or funny either, just silly. Dunaway acts the heck out of the lame script by Winner and Leslie Arliss, flaring her nostrils, widening her eyes, and leering rapaciously. Watching her is like watching a Porsche stuck in the mud; she's just spinning her wheels. The members of the estimable supporting cast, including Glynis Barber, Alan Bates, Denholm Elliott, and Sir John Gielgud, don't embarrass themselves too much. Winner is typically voyeuristic—nude women, interrupted in mid-sexual encounter, scamper around an awful lot of scenes. But few peeping Toms have real vision, and Winner's no exception.

R / 1983 / MGM/UA

▲ THE WICKER MAN

This is an eerie basket case of a British movie about a sex-obsessed religious cult on an island off Scotland. Produced in 1973, it was only released in the United States in 1980, presumably

to exploit the then new notoriety of Britt Ekland. She is pleasant enough in a peripheral role, even if her brogue is less convincing than her nude seduction dance. More important, though, is the seducee, a straitlaced cop searching for a missing girl; he's played with wide-eyed zeal by British TV star, and later American TV's "Equalizer," Edward Woodward. And Christopher Lee, in one of his sardonic villains-will-be-villains performances, is the island's high priest and orchard owner. That business enables Woodward to say, "Killing me won't make your apples grow," an example of the strange wit that makes this perverse, sometimes perverted film intriguing. The script is by Anthony Shaffer, who, with previous credits like *Sleuth* and Hitchcock's *Frenzy,* obviously knows his apples when it comes to perversion.
R / 1973 / Media

▲ WIFEMISTRESS

Unlikely as it seems, this is a film produced, written, and directed by Italian males that celebrates feminism—and does so effectively. Marcello Mastroianni plays a neglectful husband who is often away form home on business. As his long-suffering young wife, Laura Antonelli is marvelous, not to mention ravishingly beautiful. When Marcello mysteriously disappears, she feels so liberated she takes a lover (Leonard Mann), assumes control of the family wine business, and finds she can easily compete in a man's world. When Marcello returns, of course, her new-found identity is tested, with unexpected results. Director Marco Vicario, supported by the lush photography of Ennio Guaranieri and a melodramatic score by Armando Trovaioli, makes his point. Italian men may never be the same. (In Italian with subtitles.)
Unrated / 1979 / RCA/Columbia

▲ WILDCATS

So how much do you love Goldie Hawn? If it's enough to spend 107 minutes watching her be, by turns, gritty, warm, vulnerable, loving, vulgar, wistful, defiant, grateful, defeated, triumphant, and cute, this is your kind of movie. But not much else goes on in this film about a Chicago teacher who decides she wants to become a football coach and ends up with a team at a tough, inner-city school. The plot is tediously predictable and the dialogue, by Ezra (*A Small Circle of Friends*) Sacks, is banal. Comic Nipsey Russell, as the principal of Hawn's school, has a lively moment or two, and there's a decent bit by college wrestling champion Tab Thacker, who at four hundred pounds could play Meat Locker to William Perry's Refrigerator. The movie, though, is almost all Goldie. She was even desperate enough to do a brief nude scene. She's likable but the film is never involving, up to and including the Big Game climax. Since the director was Michael (*Fletch*) Ritchie, it may not be entirely coincidental that the movie often seems to be a lame descendant of his *The Bad News Bears*.
R / 1986 / Warner

▲ THE WILD GEESE

Here's a movie that combines suspense with intelligence and is reminiscent of those guts-and-guns classics *The Magnificent Seven* and *The Guns of Navarone*. Once again a hand-picked band of professionals sets out on a mission against all odds. In this instance, the venue has been updated to present-day central Africa. Richard Burton and a high-priced squad of mercenaries (code-named Wild Geese) attempt to rescue a native leader who dreams of racial harmony in his country but has been deposed and awaits execution by a military dictator. The cast (also including Richard Harris and Roger Moore) is in fine, vigorous form. Andrew (*Shenandoah*) McLaglen directs the action sequences with a sure hand, and Reginald Rose's screenplay is full of unexpected wit and warmth. The film is a trifle long and the mercenaries tend to be lionized, but why quibble? This is a superior action film.
R / 1978 / CBS/Fox

▲ THE WILD LIFE

Meanwhile back at the campus another troupe of trendy adolescents is trying to deal with trendy adolescent problems. This teenage school comedy at least has a look and feel different from those of other films of the *Animal House* genre. The intriguing lead characters are young Eric Stoltz, who gets his first taste of life after high school by moving into an apartment with an improbable

roomie, Christopher Penn, a bleached-blond high school wrestler. Stoltz underplays the frustrated nerd opposite Penn, a solid challenger to brother Sean as a heartthrob. Penn knocks heads with his buddies when he's happy and shrugs off life's lesser moments with a breezy "It's casual." Lea Thompson and Jenny Wright are haplessly harried as the estranged girlfriends of the duo, and Ilan Mitchell-Smith rounds out the core cast as a mischievous 15-year-old obsessed with the '60s. Screenwriter Cameron Crowe, who wrote the slicker if more frivolous *Fast Times at Ridgemont High*, and director Art Linson, who produced *Fast Times* and directed *Where the Buffalo Roam*, barely scratch the surface of the ideas they touch upon. There are the usual teenage high jinks, the raucously destructive climactic party scene, and the obligatory pop sound track. But Crowe and Linson seem to be striving for something semi-serious, and their film never finds its focus.
R / 1984 / MCA

▲ WILD STYLE

In 1980 Charlie Ahearn, a white filmmaker with only minor documentary work to his credit, wandered into the predominantly black and Hispanic South Bronx to make a musical featuring rap music and break dancing. Spending less than $300,000, he returned with this half-fictionalized, half-spontaneous film that is filled with energy and feeling for the urban streets. The scanty plot concerns a graffiti artist, George Quinones, who in real life went by the pseudonym of Lee when depositing his spray-painted "works" on the New York City subway. With the help of a promoter played by artist-rapper Fred "Fab 5 Freddy" Brathwaite and a newspaper reporter played by Patti Astor (actually Brathwaite's gallery manager), he tries to bring his talent out of the ghetto. Most of the scenes seem unstructured, but Quinones, who is essentially playing himself, has some presence. The rapping, by the Cold Crush Bros. and the Fantastic Freaks, among others, is infectiously rhythmic. And the dancing, by Rock Steady Crew (the *Flashdance* breakers), Electric Force, and Loose Bruce and Polly G., is a hyperactive version of all those '30s and '40s tap-dancing routines. If rap-break movies never really hit the main stream, it wasn't Ahearn's fault.
R / 1984 / World

▲ WILLIE AND PHIL

Unexpectedly bracing, this Paul Mazursky film about two men (Michael Ontkean and Ray Sharkey) in love with the same woman (Margot Kidder) may seem to be an American copy of *Jules and Jim*. But Truffaut's 1962 classic, with its morbid denouement, was a link to the great romances of the past. Mazursky, as he showed in *An Unmarried Woman* and *Harry and Tonto*, is a determinedly modern filmmaker. This story, which spans the 1970s, speaks of a Me Generation for whom threesomes are not shocking; suicides over love go against the grain. Kidder's Jeannette (a babe out of Kentucky but not in the woods) is eager to embrace the new morality. Conservative Willie and Phil (a teacher and a photographer) are not. The comedy and pathos come in watching them pretend. Following her lead, they dope, debauch, drop out, and go looking for themselves. Only Jeannette likes what she finds. Kidder's work is the best of her career, and Ontkean and Sharkey deliver career-making performances. But the triumph is Mazursky's. With wicked wit he shows us the darkest side of a life in which the Juliets don't think love is worth dying for. For true romantics this is a real horror show.
R / 1980 / RCA/Columbia

▲ WINDOWS

"Why don't you ever smile?" Elizabeth Ashley asks Talia Shire. The answer is obvious: There is nothing in this dreary movie to smile about. Although it's billed as a romantic thriller, the thrill is gone once the only plot twist is revealed, which is instantly. In a discomfiting opening scene Shire is sexually assaulted in her Brooklyn Heights apartment. The audience learns that her psychopathic lesbian neighbor, Ashley, is behind the attack, and the rest of the story is a drag as Shire and her police detective boyfriend, Joseph Cortese, painfully catch on. Shire, then and still best known as Miss Godfather and Mrs. Rocky, does all she can with the thankless role of a timid woman fighting a stutter. Cortese is a handsome and pleasant new actor with an unfortunate first major role. But Ashley—normally a marvelously resourceful actress—is almost laughable here with her heavy-breathing mannerisms. The fault probably lies with first-time director Gordon Willis,

a fine cinematographer (*All the President's Men, Manhattan*) who knows how to paint a picture but can't bring this one to life.
R / 1980 / N/A

▲ WINTER KILLS

There's a talented cast, an intriguing idea, and Oscar-winning (*Close Encounters*) cinematographer Vilmos Zsigmond behind the screenplay and direction by William Richert. Jeff Bridges plays the stepbrother of an assassinated President who bears more than a passing resemblance to JFK. He accidentally discovers a conspiracy behind the killing—and thus sets off on a trail of murder and deceit. John Huston, as the womanizing father of the late President, plays it for laughs. Twitchy Anthony Perkins is the manager of the family fortune. Eli Wallach simpers as a Jack Ruby-like nightclub owner. And Sterling Hayden portrays a right-wing industrialist. Belinda Bauer, whose steamy sex scenes with Bridges probably led to the R rating, gets noticed. Political conspiracy plots (this one is based on Richard Condon's novel) need suspense and believability. Far more than the later, all too similar *Flashpoint, Winter Kills* delivers.
R / 1979 / Embassy

▲ WISDOM

The previous film Emilio Estevez wrote, *That Was Then . . . This Is Now,* was so bad, you'd think he'd have tried to master screenwriting before he tried directing. So much for wisdom with a small w. As director, writer, and star at 23, Estevez is audacious, but this movie turns as fast as a square wheel. Estevez plays the title character, a combination Robin Hood and Pretty Boy Floyd. Having stolen a car while in high school, he can't get a decent job and complains that "you make one mistake, and society never lets you forget it." So he becomes a criminal. But after hearing about the bank foreclosures of farmers on TV, he decides to be "a criminal for the people, not against them." He arms himself with a submachine gun and Molotov cocktails and storms into banks blowing up mortgage files. He and accomplice Demi Moore soon become national heroes. Estevez, however, didn't set out

to make a point about the banking system. He wanted to make a statement about the way we idolize movie stars and people like subway vigilante Bernhard Goetz instead of those Estevez considers real heroes, such as Vietnam vets. The message is never clear until the FBI catches up with the fugitives and there's some real pathos to contend with. Yet even this is diminished by a monumentally sappy ending that only Bobby Ewing could love. If it's true, as Estevez has said, that he can learn from even a bad movie, he was a much wiser man after this project.
R / 1987 / CBS/Fox

▲ WISE BLOOD

"JESUS CALLED," reads the epitaph on a headstone adorned with a sculpted telephone, its receiver off the hook. It is just such delightfully offbeat touches that makes this John Huston film a wonder. Based on the 1952 novel by Flannery O'Connor, it chronicles an army vet (Brad Dourif) who returns to find his hometown in the Deep South all but deserted. So he heads for the big city, Macon, Georgia, aiming "to do things I ain't never done before," such as establishing a street-corner religion called the Church of Christ Without Christ. Director Huston satirizes religious hypocrisy, deploying Ned Beatty and Harry Dean Stanton as unsavory evangelists. With eyes that could bore a hole in any soul, Dourif (the stuttering Billy in *One Flew Over the Cuckoo's Nest*) is marvelously intense in his central role. At times the sheer eccentricity of this movie obscures its message, but then Huston—whose work includes *The Maltese Falcon, Treasure of the Sierra Madre,* and *Prizzi's Honor*—has never been one to stand by convention.
PG / 1980 /MCA

▲ WISE GUYS

Director Brian (*Body Double*) De Palma, who had injected a lot of tangential wit into most of his previous films, deserves some credit for having the enterprise to make a full-fledged comedy. Well, make that a slightly-fledged comedy. Danny (*Jewel of the Nile*) De Vito and Joe (*Johnny Dangerously*) Piscopo play New Jersey hoodlums who are held in such low esteem that their main jobs are to start their boss's car to check for bombs and do the gang's grocery shopping. When they try a scam that ends up with their owing the boss $250,000, they find themselves running for their lives. De Vito and Piscopo do a decent neo-Abbott and Costello. But neither De Palma nor debuting writer George Gallo give them much to work with. The few funny bits are like oases in a desert, separated by agonizingly long dry stretches. (The best line comes when Dan Hedaya, who plays the mob boss, gathers his thugs to consider revenge against De Vito and Piscopo. "Do we really hurt them by killing them?" he muses. The henchmen ponder this for a while and one finally murmurs, "It's a start.") For the most part, though, De Palma is not as funny trying to be as he was unintentionally with *Scarface*.

R / 1986 / CBS/Fox

▲ THE WITCHES OF EASTWICK

It would take black magic to make sense out of this overheated film version of John Updike's 1984 best-seller. Updike's novel, set in a cozy Rhode Island town during the Vietnam era, was a playfully malicious joke on feminism. Three divorcees form a coven (read: support group) and find they can make their enemies—mostly the wives of the men they sleep with—cough up insects and feathers. Soon after, the Devil moves into Eastwick in the guise of a hairy, foul-mouthed millionaire. He invites the witches over for some tennis and later group sex in his hot tub before inciting them to more dastardly deeds. Updike's restrained wit kept the horror fanciful and the satire rooted in reality. The film, clumsily written by Michael Cristofer (who gained an ill-gotten Pulitzer for his heavy-handed play *The Shadow Box*), totally misses the point by setting the story in the '80s and taking the witchcraft literally. Worse, director George Miller—the action master of the Mel Gibson *Mad Max* movies—behaves as if he's remaking *The Exorcist*. His actors' main task is to spew vomit or get spewed upon. At other times he resorts to *Friday the 13th* scare tactics and monster-movie effects. Why pay Updike $250,000 for the movie rights to a book no one wanted to film? Miller leads a marvelous cast astray. Cher, Michelle Pfeiffer, and Susan Sarandon make lovely, sympathetic witches, which is precisely what they should not be. They are now victims of that old devil—man—instead of strong women flexing the new and dangerous muscles of independence. That leaves the task of providing the fun to jumping Jack Nicholson, who had been working toward playing Satan since he filmed *The Shining* back in 1980. He snorts. He cackles. He bugs his demon eyes, lolls amorously on his belly, and rages like a rhino when he's crossed. In one memorable scene he even irons his shirts like an overworked housewife while watching "The Price Is Right" on the tube. While nothing he does has anything to do with Updike, it's a helluva performance. But it can't save this movie from damnation.

R / 1987 / N/A

▲ WITHOUT A TRACE

Based on Beth Gutcheon's 1981 *Still Missing* (Gutcheon also wrote the screenplay), the plot centers around the disappearance of a 6-year-old Brooklyn schoolboy. The story strongly resembles the case of Etan Patz, a 6-year-old Manhattan boy who vanished while walking to school in 1979. Some reviewers found Gutcheon's book exploitive, but onscreen most criticism was allayed, thanks to producer-turned-director Stanley R. Jaffe's handling of the material. Canadian Kate (*Eleni*) Nelligan plays the boy's mother with clarity and chilly strength. Maintaining an outward calm through police interrogations, media interviews, false leads, panicky friends, and a despairing estranged husband (David Dukes), Nelligan lets us hear the screaming inside. Matching her is Judd ("Taxi") Hirsch as a police detective who hangs onto Helligan's slim thread of hope. Stockard Channing, Dukes, and Keith McDermott offer fine support. But even Nelligan and Hirsch can't keep the movie from overstating the big emotions. The mawkish ending is pure TV drivel.

PG / 1983 / CBS/Fox

▲ WITNESS

From its brutal opening moments in a Philadelphia train station to its meltingly romantic conclusion outside an Amish family farm in Pennsylvania's Lancaster County, *Witness* is a spellbinder. As he proved in *The Year of Living*

Dangerously, Australian director Peter Weir (this was his American debut) is a master at mixing the exotic and the mundane in a way that holds an audience in thrall. A young Amish boy, beautifully played by Lukas Haas, then 8, witnesses a murder in a railway restroom. Suddenly he and his widowed mother—Kelly McGillis—are swept up in a big-city nightmare of cops and corruption. Their rescuer is a detective played by Harrison Ford. His finely shaped performance is a marvel. Was there a real actor all along behind the one-dimensional heroes of *Indiana Jones* and the *Star Wars* trilogy? Hiding out among the Amish until he can finger the guilty parties, Ford's Philly cop finds himself inside a nonviolent world that hasn't changed in two hundred years. The Amish scene, long a Lancaster County tourist attraction, was new to movies, and Weir (assisted by his brilliant cameraman, John Seale) saw it with a poet's eye. With their Spartan life-style (no radio, TV, telephone, car, central heating, not to mention anything by Gucci), the Amish are a plain people but far from unfeeling. McGillis, a radiant actress, is courted by a local farmer, played by ballet's Aleksandr Godunov with a brio that suggests big film potential. And her own attraction to outsider Ford has a lyrical urgency. One night, helping Ford repair his car, McGillis hears the radio crackle with a Sam Cooke oldie ''(What a) Wonderful World.'' As Ford starts singing and moving to the kind of arousing backseat music that has been forbidden to her, McGillis is caught up and transformed. Two worlds collide and, for a moment, mesh. It's a great love scene worthy of a time capsule. This is a movie for grownups—no special effects, aliens, or randy teenagers. *Witness* settles for being superbly crafted, erotically charged, and hugely entertaining.
R / 1985 / Paramount

▲ THE WIZ

Take the *Wizard of Oz,* put some psychological spin on it, relocate to an all-black urban context, and then forget all about Judy Garland, Ray Bolger, Jack Haley, and Bert Lahr. The result was a long-running Broadway musical but a complicated property to adapt back to the screen. Director Sidney (*Network*) Lumet was clearly successful at casting: Michael Jackson as the Scarecrow (before anyone heard of an LP called *Thriller*) is a wow. Good, too, are Nipsey Russell

as the Tinman and Ted Ross as the Lion, as they scamper through an inner-city vision. A couple of scenes deftly use terrifying aspects of New York—a subway with menacing tile pillars, trash cans with teeth. But in the song-and-dance extravaganzas the almost $20 million budget seems ill-spent; the stage choreography and erratic cinematography don't help much either. Diana Ross, playing Dorothy as a 24-year-old repressed schoolteacher, sings well, but her acting is a little overwrought. Still, the other actors (notably Richard Pryor as the Wiz and Lena Horne as Glinda the Good) are sharp, and the story is eversweet. If ever a whiz there was, *The Wiz* isn't one because it's overproduced, but there are worse ways to spend 133 minutes.
G / 1978 / MCA

▲ THE WIZARD OF BABYLON

Before he died in 1982 at 36 of a drug overdose, Rainer Werner Fassbinder had established himself as the most important German filmmaker since World War II. He was certainly one of the most prolific directors, with forty-one films to his credit in just thirteen years. This documentary, shot in the Berlin studio where Fassbinder was making what would be his last movie, *Querelle,* is his final testament—and a fascinating one. Fassbinder was fat, disheveled, and painfully shy. But his presence was overpowering, whether he was working or ruminating on fame, death, love, homosexuality, Jackie Onassis, Andy Warhol, or the Oscars. There are also interviews with the three actors in *Querelle*—American Brad Davis, France's legendary Jeanne Moreau, and Franco Nero, a preening egomaniac if there ever was one (''I'm the only actor in Europe who takes chances,'' he says with a straight face). But the core of the film is a twelve-minute interview with Fassbinder, made just ten hours before he was found dead. This segment, in which Fassbinder chain-smokes and wheezes throughout as if in a stupor, was originally cut from the film by a court order after Fassbinder's mother protested, but it was restored. There is a problem with the narration—it's hard to tell at times if the voice is Fassbinder's or someone else's. And when he is actually shown directing a scene, there is no translation from the German. The film does, though, achieve a starkly explicit personality. It is, by turns, moody, fascinating, boring, enig-

matic, and revealing—much like Fassbinder himself. (In German with subtitles.)
Unrated / 1983 / N/A

▲ WIZARDS

Animator Ralph Bakshi (*Fritz, the Cat*) creates sci-fi landscapes that make you want to say Hello, Dali! But despite hordes of cartoon characters and what is for the raunchy Bakshi a cleaned-up act, the *Wizards* aren't very magical. This is the kind of cartoon that when your mom yelled, "Turn off the TV, it's time for dinner," you didn't mind.
PG / 1977 / Playhouse

▲ WOLFEN

Clearly these are not your standard monster wolves. They can disappear at will. They tear out people's throats in a blink. They outwit computers. And what really drives them crazy is not secret potions, nonbelievers, or even full moons but urban renewal. Yes, they are part of an ancient species who've survived modern times by hiding in big-city slums gobbling up stragglers. So they get testy when they see renovation in the South Bronx, for instance. Albert Finney, who plays a New York cop, was so impressed by this theme that he didn't like the movie referred to as a horror feature. True, his character, in confronting the beasts, doesn't call for a bazooka or try to mollify them with dog biscuits. He instead pulverizes an architect's model of a new housing project to show his heart's in the right place. But this movie is no more about ecology than *Them!* was about nuclear physics. It's a slick, tense chiller with eerie visual and sound effects. There are precise, cynical performances by Finney, recent Juillard grad Diane Venora as a psychologist cop, and then newcomer Gregory Hines as a morgue technician. Director Michael (*Woodstock*) Wadleigh provided his first feature with a scary pace and sharp, witty dialogue. The violence, with severed limbs and heads, is excessive; there's also real footage of a python eating a rat. And one Indian character shows how close to nature he is by running around New York naked, baying at the moon. That doesn't make him a wolf, and it doesn't make this a sociopolitical treatise either.
R / 1981 / Warner

▲ THE WOMAN IN RED

When it comes to criminal waste of time and talent, it would be hard to top this would-be romantic comedy. Gene Wilder wrote, directed, and stars in it as a married, middle-aged advertising executive going through a pro forma mid-life crisis. Gilda Radner has a bit—she's scandalously underemployed—as a woman in Wilder's office who thinks she's going to benefit from the crisis. Stevie Wonder wrote and performs most of the sound track songs, which are more like fragments. (Having access to the ability of Stevie Wonder and trashing it in this way ought to be a capital offense.) The supporting cast includes Charles Grodin, Judith Ivey, Joseph Bologna, and as the woman in red whose appearance galvanizes Wilder's adulterous impulses, Kelly Le Brock, a stunning English-born model who in real life was married to the film's producer, Victor Drai. Despite all that it has going for it, the movie is spurious in the extreme. The only affecting moment comes in a brief scene where Wilder, having learned that his old crony, Grodin, is gay, attempts to comfort him. But that's like finding a pinhead-size dollop of caviar in a bathtub full of Jell-O. The film drones on through all the clichés of infidelity to a resolution that isn't emotionally, morally, or comedically satisfying. It's all on the order of 86 minutes of foreplay that leads to a limp, sweaty handshake.
PG-13 / 1984 / Vestron

▲ THE WORLD ACCORDING TO GARP

The better the book the worse the movie. The film version of John Irving's 1978 best-seller does nothing to disprove that axiom. Director George (*The Sting*) Hill and screenwriter Steve (*Breaking Away*) Tesich have transformed Irving's unbridled, character-packed amalgam of hilarity and horror into a slick, tame Hollywood package. T. S. Garp (Robin Williams) is the bastard son of a nurse who once cozied up to a dying but libidinous World War II turret gunner for the sole purpose of conceiving a child. Growing up at a New England prep school, Garp becomes a wrestler, dog-biter, and lover, then a husband, father, writer, and battler of the "Under Toad," a force that threatens to destroy his life. (The term comes from his son's malapropism for "undertow.")

Casting Robin Williams as the sanity-seeking Garp can hardly be called inspired. He plays so hard against his Morky, zonked-out image, it's like watching an actor in a straitjacket. Then newcomer Glenn Close, late of Broadway's *Barnum,* fares much better. As Garp's beautiful, maddening mother, whose feminist autobiography outsells her son's serious work, she is believable, touching, and an Oscar nominee. (She lost to *Tootsie*'s Jessica Lange.) The rest of the cast, including Mary Beth Hurt as Garp's adulterous wife and John Lithgow (also Oscar-nominated) as a pro football tight-end-turned-transsexual, fight a losing battle against a script that veers between broad visual effects and literary stodginess. Only an infant Garp, tossed repeatedly in the air during the opening and closing credits, fully lives up to Irving's novel. The baby reflects what the movie most lacks: a free spirit.
PG / 1982 / Warner

▲ THE WORLD'S GREATEST LOVER

Toadish Gene Wilder seems a wildly inept choice to play the title role, and that is only one reason this film is so funny. Another is Carol Kane, leaving the waify roles she played in *Hester Street* and *The Last Detail* to become a resourceful comedienne as the wife of a man who wants to become a new Valentino. Wilder, who also directed, still carries as big a slapstick as the other alums of the Mel Brooks school of comedy but at his best walks a lot more softly. While Dom De Luise's borderline hysteria and the gay gags are tiresome, any film whose hero accidently floods the sunken living room of his hotel suite

and then uses it as a swimming pool has to win you over.
PG / 1977 / CBS/Fox

▲ WRONG IS RIGHT

Remember *1984, Dr. Strangelove, Goldfinger, All the President's Men,* and *The China Syndrome?* Now imagine someone edited together snippets of all those apocalyptic films, plus a dozen or so more. That gives an idea of what this miasma is like. Columbia Pictures said screenwriter-director Richard (*Looking for Mr. Goodbar*) Brooks based his screenplay "on his own observations of the state of the world today." If so, Brooks was not be very optimistic. His hero is a traveling TV reporter, played as a self-loathing opportunist by Sean Connery. He is mainly a vehicle for cynical jabs at TV, politics, business, the CIA, the military, religion, revolution, Watergate, Vietnam, and everything else less innocuous than the Campfire Girls. There are the sudden death of an oil kingdom's leader, a nuclear bomb threat by terriorists, a silly President (played by George Grizzard) and his silly opponent (Leslie Nielsen), and frequent clumsy references to television's ratings mania. There is excessive gory violence. What is the point of all this? Nothing is what it seems—unless it seems to be an illusion. In a closing shot, Connery suddenly takes off his hairpiece and looks into the camera, as if to say, "See, this diatribe against illusions was itself an illusion." But then, were the other "illusions" not illusion? Even where wrong is often right, confused is never clear.
PG / 1982 / RCA/Columbia

X

▲ XANADU

Olivia Newton-John's encore—after Grease—was this awkward musical fantasy that dooms the Australian songbird to play a muse, one of Zeus's nine daughters. Over the centuries she has in-

spired the likes of Shakespeare and Beethoven; now she's concentrating on Gene Kelly, an unhappily retired clarinetist, and Michael Beck, a commercial artist tired of selling out. Her magic brings both men together as owners of Xanadu, a tacky roller disco that combines the big-band sound of the '40s with new wave. Musically, the two mix like oil and water, but Olivia is oblivious. She has a worse problem: Beck has made her love him—a no-no for immortals. So much for plot. What should have been a goddess-on-earth soufflé (à la *One Touch of Venus*) becomes in the hands of director Robert Greenwald the flattest, most annoyingly artsy musical this side of *The Wiz*. No amount of flamboyant lighting, animation, and opticals can disguise the dead space at the film's core. It's not Olivia's fault; she warbles fetchingly (even on wheels), and her sweet-tough upper register makes the purest gossamer of songs like "Magic" by John Farrar and "Xanadu" by the Electric Light Orchestra's Jeff Lynne. Seeing the great Kelly dance again is also an unmitigated pleasure—his soft-shoe with Olivia to "Whenever You're Away from Me" brings the movie fitfully to life. But he dances too little—and he is not onscreen enough. The rest of the film, muse or no muse, is sadly uninspired. **PG / 1980 / MCA**

Y

▲ THE YEAR OF LIVING DANGEROUSLY

Australian director Peter (*Gallipoli*) Weir's supercharged movie, based on C. J. Koch's 1978 novel, assaults the conscience through the senses. The year is 1965, the place Indonesia, a country besieged by poverty and political unrest. Enter Mel (*The Road Warrior*) Gibson in a smashing, fiercely wrought performance as an Aussie journalist out to make a name for himself by exploiting the situation. He meets Sigourney (*Alien*) Weaver, a British Embassy attaché with access to secret documents, and uses her. In the hands of a director like Costa-Gavras, the film might have been a treatise on the evils of imperialism. But Weir is infinitely more daring. No sooner does he plunge Gibson into this Third World hotbed than he starts throwing things. Images, hallucinatory and horrific, crowd for attention—hookers cruising a graveyard, diplomats and press gorging on oysters a stone's throw from a starving crowd, a mass assassination briefly glimpsed at an airport. In this feverish atmosphere, Weir eroticizes and personalizes his politics. Gibson and Weaver start at a sexual white heat that allows for little emotional growth. Their awakening is precipitated by a Chinese-Australian cameraman named Billy Kwan, a dwarf who remains the only character tall enough to see over the issues to the real face of Asia. Gibson's betrayal of the idealistic Kwan is an essential piece of the film's mosaic. As played by the extraordinary New York actress Linda Hunt, Kwan is a character of such exemplary humanity that gender seems irrelevant. (Weir chose Hunt for the male role after testing a series of actors. "We've disturbed something between what is male and female," he said.) Hunt won a much deserved Oscar for a portrayal that tears at the heart. Gibson and Weaver are wonderful to watch together. Still, it's Weir probing to find the timeless underpinnings of injustice that makes this film a pertinent, prodigious achievement. **PG / 1983 / MGM/UA**

▲ YEAR OF THE DRAGON

Optimists will note that director Michael Cimino saved $20 million or so on this movie. While it took him $40 million to make *Heaven's Gate,* he managed to trash this equally chaotic, foolish film for a reported $18 million. Be grateful for small favors, because that's all you're going to get. The story, taken from a 1981 novel by Robert Daley, concerns as impossibly ruthless young gang lord in Manhattan's Chinatown and the impossibly determined cop who is out to clean up one hundred years' worth of crime in a couple of days. All right, so it's a little like *The Godfather Meets Fu Manchu*. But Cimino and screenwriter Oliver Stone turned a workable idea into a cinematic version of chop suey. Nothing that happens is remotely plausible. The cop, played

with noble but ultimately futile intensity by Mickey Rourke, can hardly take a step without running into a wild shoot-out, knifing, garroting, or brawl. In his quieter moments he just discovers bodies. The Hong Kong-born John Lone, as the ambitious gangster, is so relentlessly evil he makes the devil seem like a pretty nice fellow; at one point Lone has to brandish the head of a rival he has just disposed of. It's an embarrassingly bad scene, and not just because the head looks like a sack of potatoes with hair. The Japanese-Dutch model Ariane, then 21, plays a glamorous Chinese-American TV newscaster who gets involved in an unconvincing affair with the slovenly Rourke. Hers may be the worst performance since Mamie Van Doren's in *Sex Kittens Go to College.* The only thing that seems right is the crowded, uneasy Chinatown atmosphere (though the film was shot mostly on sets in North Carolina). That's hardly enough to redeem a movie that is often so inept it's funny. Mike, have you thought of driving a bus or becoming a piano tuner or otherwise doing something useful?
R / 1985 / MGM/UA

▲ YELLOWBEARD

The cast of this pirate spoof includes Monty Pythonites Eric Idle, John Cleese, and Graham Chapman, plus Peter Boyle, Marty Feldman, Madeline Kahn, Tommy Chong, Peter Cook, Martin (*Endless Love*) Hewitt, Cheech Marin, Kenneth Mars, James Mason, Stacy (*Halloween III*) Nelkin, and Susannah York. They all average about a laugh apiece, which, if it doesn't make this film a treasure chest of humor, does make it funnier than most modern film comedies. Chapman has the title role as a totally ruthless buccaneer. He's perfectly willing to cut off the head of his own son (Hewitt) because it bears a treasure map tattooed on it by Kahn, who's usually referred to as "Mrs. Beard." When Chapman and Hewitt set off after the buried loot, everybody else in the cast follows after them. The pace more than drags at times. And there's a lot of foolish swordfighting and tedious slapstick en route to the treasure island, which is ruled over by Marin, a monarch of vague antecedents who is variously called "Your Vapidity," "Your Ruthlessness," and "Your Offensiveness" by his chief aide Chong. (The movie establishes, if nothing else,

that Cheech and Chong don't have to resort to cheap drug jokes to get laughs.) The level of the verbal humor is exemplified by one of Cleese's bits. As the Cockney "Blind Pew," he tells the stuffy Idle, who portrays a secret agent of Queen Anne, that his lack of sight isn't really incapacitating, protesting, "I've got acute 'earing." Idle impatiently replies, "I don't care about your jewelry." Chapman, Cook (Dudley Moore's unfortunately all-but-forgotten partner), and Bernard McKenna did the writing. Newcomer Mel Damski directed. Students of the genre will, in any case, prefer 1948's *The Pirate,* which sent up swashbuckling films in more timely, stylish fashion, and had music, with Gene Kelly and Judy Garland to boot. (Parents should note that while *Yellowbeard* is rated PG, it has a smattering of female nudity and some annoying smutty jokes.)
PG / 1983 / Vestron

▲ YENTL

Barbra Streisand's *Yentl* is the kind of movie they weren't supposed to make anymore—sweet, simple, and emotionally satisfying. Derived from an Isaac Bashevis Singer story, *Yentl* tells the tale of a young Jewish woman living in Eastern Europe at the turn of the century who must disguise herself as a man in order to study the Talmud. Streisand was the first to know a plot like that doesn't exactly jump off the page and shout box office. She spent fifteen years trying to get it on the screen before becoming the first woman in movie history to produce, direct, write, and star in a film. While Oscar ignored her efforts and Hollywood wags dubbed the $14.5 million project *Tootsie on the Roof,* the analogy ignores Streisand's heartfelt personal vision—she dedicates *Yentl* to her teacher-father Emanuel who died when she was only fifteen months old. In the film Yentl's scholar-father, who is played beautifully by Nehemiah Persoff, must teach his daughter the sacred books in secret. When he dies, Yentl is forced to continue her quest for knowledge alone. The parallel between Yentl and Streisand makes that parallel both touching and telling. This is no *A Star Is Born* vanity production; Streisand leans heavily on the members of her crew and her co-stars, and they deliver. Cameraman David (*Chariots of Fire*) Watkin suc-

Yentl: Barbra Streisand (with Mandy Patinkin and Amy Irving) disguises herself as a man to get an education in Talmud in this underrated film version of Isaac Bashevis Singer's short story.

ceeds in giving the film a burnished beauty. And the acting is first-rate. Mandy Patinkin contributes a star-making performance as the student Yentl loves. But he, in love with the luminous Amy Irving, sees Yentl as a man. Director Streisand handles this triangle with humor and surprising restraint. In a Shakespearean twist Streisand and Irving marry, and the subsequent love scene between the two is moving and tasteful to boot. Streisand's generosity as a writer and director enhances her own performance—along with *Funny Girl* and *The Way We Were,* this is her best acting. And her voice, flowing like eiderdown over the score by Michel Legrand and Marilyn and Alan Bergman, has never sounded lovelier. The thirteen songs, sung by Streisand as interior monologues, sometimes slow down the action, and her climactic number rings too much of *Funny Girl* and Broadway brass. These are minor faults. Streisand gives *Yentl* a heart that sings and a spirit that soars.

PG / 1983 / CBS/Fox

▲ YES, GIORGIO

Kate Jackson turned down the chance to play Luciano Pavarotti's adulterous lover in this romantic comedy with music that marks the superstar Met tenor's film debut. Wise woman, that Kate. Pavarotti's extra-large talent may shatter glass and concert box-office records, but as a leading man he's a bust. Kathryn Harrold, late of NBC's soap "The Doctors," is as lovely as Jackson, but she was stuck with a hopeless role that calls for her to be indifferent to Pavarotti's voice but gaga over his body. Huh? Pavarotti has an engaging manner, but as a lover he weighs in on the far side of Orson Welles. Norman Steinberg, a former Flip Wilson comedy writer, adapted Anne Piper's novel about a married Italian opera star who gets involved with a sexy lady doctor on his American tour, and maybe that's why the dialogue is full of unintentional howlers. "You are a thirsty plant—Fini can water you," Luciano tells Harrold lasciviously. After he informs her that he won't leave his wife, Harrold retorts, "Part of you isn't enough." Given his girth, what more does she want? Their relationship culminates in a free-for-all fight that, like the entire movie, has all the snap of limp fettuccine. What attracted director Franklin (*Patton*) Schaffner to take on this misguided attempt to turn Pavarotti into the new Mario Lanza is anyone's guess. Chances are he is simply a devoted opera buff. If so, he should have let his star just sing. When Pavarotti caresses "Ave Maria" or turns his glorious voice loose on an aria from *Turandot*, he hits all the right notes. The rest falls flat.

PG / 1982 / MGM/UA

▲ YOR, THE HUNTER FROM THE FUTURE

Okay, so this film is moronic, but you have to admire it for sheer gall. On the theory that there's always an audience for (a) musclemen adventure fantasies and (b) *Star Wars* rip-offs, Italian director Anthony M. Dawson (real name: Antonio Margheriti) combined the two in a single production. The resulting story line is incomprehensible; it has to do with the strong, fair-haired hero who is caught in a time warp and must fight his way out of the Stone Age to return to his own high-tech society somewhere in the far distance. Little-known American actor Reb Brown has the title role. He is equally invincible with stone ax or death ray, depending on circumstances, and makes the transition through the countless millennia with nary a change in expression or loin cloth. French actress Corinne Clery, fetchingly togged in a prehistoric off-the-shoulder-number, heads a female supporting cast that takes turns lusting after Brown's sleek, unbruisable physique. The blatantly imitative special effects range from monster lizards to Darth Vader look-alikes, and the dialogue runs to lines like "This is no place for man or beast" and "My destiny carries me elsewhere." If you're lucky, yours will too.

PG / 1983 / RCA/Columbia

▲ YOU LIGHT UP MY LIFE

Reach into your southern California cliché bag and what do you get? This schmaltzy, overorchestrated concoction of freeways, aspiring starlets, recording studios, and one-night stands. Writer-director Joe Brooks is best known for his slick advertising jingles (Pepsi-Cola, Dr. Pepper) and perhaps should have been content with his residuals. But Didi Conn gives a delightfully unrestrained performance as a third-rate comedienne trying to make it as a singer-songwriter. The title tune became a huge, if often maligned, hit—and won an Oscar—but the rest of this low-budget musical comedy is pure corn. It's a tip-off that the winningest character is a clam.

PG / 1977 / RCA/Columbia

▲ YOUNGBLOOD

Eric Nesterenko, a former National Hockey League player, plays Rob Lowe's father in this movie. He also served as the film's hockey consultant. From the look of the resulting series of donnybrooks, the producers would have been better off retaining Muhammad Ali. After a promising beginning, with some funny lines and cute banter between Lowe and Cynthia (TV's "Fame") Gibb, *Youngblood* becomes anemic real quick. Lowe plays the title character, a 17-year-old New York farm boy whose only career choices are to spread manure the rest of his life "or play hockey in front of twenty thousand people at Madison Square Garden." Opting for the latter, Lowe goes to Canada to try out for the mythical Hamilton Mustangs. He is obviously Rookie-of-the-Year material. In his first week he makes the team, makes love to the coach's daughter (Gibb), and makes a lot of enemies. The league he plays in seems more like a training ground for Saturday night wrestling bouts than the NHL. Lowe, who gets slapped around more than the puck, asks Gibb, "Where else can I get beaten up every day by a bunch of prima donna Canadians?" Frustrated, he quits. But cue the *Rocky*-like sound track for the pep talk and training scenes back at the farm, and you guessed it. Lowe returns for the championship game and, well, you guessed it again. The end of this movie is so unimaginative that writer-director Peter (*Hot Dog: The Movie*) Markle, a former Yale hockey player, should get a misconduct penalty.

R / 1986 / MGM/UA

▲ YOUNGBLOOD

Lawrence Hilton-Jacobs of a then-hot TV show, "Welcome Back, Kotter," is top-billed and performs convincingly as a Vietnam vet who returns to run a street gang, the Kingsmen. But the real star is young Bryan O'Dell as a teenager intent on becoming a Kingsman—the good boy in what amounts to a ghetto morality play. He shows remarkable range—from confronting his unsympathetic mother to impressing the gang by cutting the badge off a rival gang member's jacket to being scared witless at the start of a rumble. The film has a tough kind of street humor, a strong cast, and an effective score by the rock group War; it rises far above the usual jive school of black exploitation.

R / 1978 / MGM/UA

▲ YOUNG DOCTORS IN LOVE

Garry Marshall, who created TV's "Laverne & Shirley," "Happy Days," and "Mork & Mindy," directed this as his first feature film, and it should surprise no one. *Young Doctors* is light, funny, lightning-paced and (unshackled by TV's mores) bawdy. Similar in spirit to *Airplane!*, this film relies on ensemble acting, visual gags, bedpan jokes, and pratfalls to achieve its scattershot effect. The plot ostensibly involves a group of young doctors new to hospital life. That affords Marshall an opportunity to pair off his large cast sexually and to spoof every TV medical show from "Ben Casey" to "General Hospital." There are cameo appearances from some soap opera players, among them Steven ("The Young and the Restless") Ford, Stuart Damon, Kin Shriner and Jackie Zeman (all from "General Hospital"), and Susan ("All My Children") Lucci. Among the featured actors, only Dabney Coleman as the hectored hospital administrator and Harry Dean Stanton as a crazed pathologist are energetic enough to rise above Marshall's frantic plot line, though Saul Rubinek as the pathologist's lackey has his moments. Marshall, like Mel Brooks, is irrepressible, and—also like Brooks—when he errs, it is most often in exhausting a good idea.

R / 1982 / Vestron

▲ YOUNG SHERLOCK HOLMES

Splendid is the word for this captivating entertainment. Who'd have guessed there was any life left in Conan Doyle's master sleuth? There was the traditional Holmes: fourteen films with Basil Rathbone starting with 1939's *The Hound of the Baskervilles*. Since then the old boy has been served up as a 1954 TV series, a 1965 Broadway musical (*Baker Street*), and even as pure camp (Gene Wilder's *The Adventure of Sherlock Holmes's Smarter Brother* in 1976). But none till this one could match the elegant contours and stylish snap of the Rathbone originals. Screenwriter Chris Columbus's notion of Holmes as a schoolboy is inspired. And the folks at Amblin Entertainment (the Steven Spielberg film factory) wisely let special effects complement rather than crush characterization this time. *Young Sherlock Holmes* is the thinking teen's *Goonies*. We meet Holmes, still a bit gangly, in school, along with his chubby new roommate, John Watson. Two newcomers, Nicholas Rowe, then 19, as Holmes, and Alan Cox, 15, as Watson, deliver wonderfully engaging performances. And director Barry Levinson, after the ham-handed symbolism of *The Natural,* shows here (as he did in 1982's *Diner*) the wonders he can work with young actors. It's fun, and often moving, watching Holmes trying not to let his yearnings for a young woman (the ravishing Sophie Ward) interfere with his thinking. The mystery, about a cult that kills its victims with poison darts, might be a shade too elementary were it not for the visual wizardry. The hallucinations in which everything from a brass coat hanger to a roast goose takes on monstrous life are irresistibly scary. An attack by a trayful of French pastries merits special notice. Affectionately conceived and expertly executed, *Young Sherlock Holmes* respects its viewers.

PG-13 / 1985 / Paramount

Z

▲ ZAPPED

When 1992 rolls around and the class reunion is held for 1982's spate of high school films (*Porky's, Class of 1984, Fast Times at Ridgemont High, Homework*), reserve a small table by the kitchen for *Zapped!* It is a smarmy vehicle designed to showcase teen idols Scott ("Happy Days") Baio and Willie ("Eight Is Enough") Aames. Baio plays a nebbishy student who, through a lab accident, acquires telekinetic powers. Being an earnest scientific genius with dreams of receiving grants to continue his research in botany, how does he put his newfound talents to use? By fixing baseball games, foiling fraternity bullies, and popping open the sweater of cheerleader Heather ("Fall Guy") Thomas, of course. To set objects in motion, Baio must glare at them and crook an eyebrow; much of his performance comes straight from the Elizabeth ("Bewitched") Montgomery School of Twitching. Aames is convincing as a slick teenage Lothario. This film, a kind of *Son of Flubber* flavored with "Our Miss Brooks," is so thin that the late Scatman Crothers, who encourages Baio to cure his cancer so that his wife will let him eat salami again, almost steals the show. The funniest scenes (and that ain't saying much) involve Baio's domestic life. His father, Roger Bowen, drinks prune juice and rum when he isn't snoring on the couch, and the ditsy mother, Marya Small, races around brandishing a crucifix once she has had a look at her son's telekinesis. *Zapped* climaxes at the prom (where else?), as Baio strips the student body of its formal wear. If the title hadn't been used, this could have been called *The Nude Bomb*.

R / 1982 / Embassy

▲ ZELIG

Fast, funny, high-spirited, and strikingly original, this is, if such a creature exists, a perfect film. Written and directed by Woody Allen, it succeeds, as the best works of art do, on many levels. The basic story is in the form of a documentary about a 1920s misfit, Leonard Zelig, whose desperation to be liked by everyone else is so overwhelming he develops the ability to emulate whomever he is with: When he's with someone fat, he becomes fat; when he's with a trumpet player, he comes a trumpet player. The KKK, intones the narrator Patrick Horgan, considers him "a triple threat, because he's a Jew who can turn into a Negro or an Indian." Zelig, played by Allen, becomes a national figure and is nicknamed the Human Chameleon; a dance is named after him ("make a face just like a lizard/feel that beat down in your gizzard"). He becomes a human exhibit; only his faithful psychiatrist, Mia Farrow, really cares about him. The documentary style is beautifully mimicked—"Monty Python" never did it better. And the "old" black-and-white footage of Zelig, interspersed with real vintage film of such figures as Hitler and William Randolph Hearst, seems amazingly realistic. Allen and Farrow are marvelous. As '20s characters in '20s newsreels, they subtly achieve major triumphs of acting. Even the extras seem to have exactly the right wide-eyed, nervous, uncomfortable look of people in the real newsreel footage of the era. Such living figures as author Saul Bellow and psychoanalyst Bruno Bettelheim appear as themselves, commenting on Zelig as if he were a real person, sending Warren Beatty's pretentiousness in *Reds* up to the stratosphere. This alone makes for a comedy film of enormous production. (Director of photography Gordon Willis, production designer Mel Bourne, and editor Susan Morse, all longtime Allen colleagues, clearly had something to do with this success too.) But there is much more. Allen is obviously making statements about conformity, celebrity, artistic responsibility; many of the comments seem directed at himself and his own work, which had been vacillating between the obvious comedy that made him a success—which his fans seem to want—and the more serious but usually less entertaining impulses behind *Interiors* and *Stardust Memories*. Whatever interpretations one prefers, you can't ask for much more from a movie than that it gives you a lot to laugh about while it's unreeling and a lot to think about afterward.

PG / 1983 / Warner

▲ ZORRO, THE GAY BLADE

Former pretty boy George Hamilton was a one-man growth industry for a while. A delightful Dracula in 1979's *Love at First Bite,* he triumphed as a zany Zorro in this riotous reworking of the hoary legend. It seems that the Zorro of old has passed on his mantle to his son Don Diego, Jr., who assumes it with zeal, vowing to "help the helpless, befriend the friendless, and defeat the . . . feetless." Then an inquiry forces Don to turn the cape, mask, and villain-skewering over to brother Ramon (who has changed his name to Bunny Wigglesworth), a swishbuckler if ever there was one. "There is no shame in being poor," says the dandified Ramon (also played by Hamilton), "only in dressing poorly." It's all great campy fun, thanks largely to Hamilton's winning performance. In addition, he's more than ably supported by lovely Lauren Hutton, randy Brenda Vaccaro, and nasty Ron Leibman. Director Peter (*The Changeling*) Medak keeps things moving at a lively clip.

PG / 1981 / CBS/Fox

CHILDREN'S MOVIES

A

▲ AN AMERICAN TAIL

This enigmatic animated film, mixing the ingenuous and the trite, is at once a heartwarming adventure and a ponderous morality tale. Taking place in 1885, the story follows wide-eyed Fievel Mousekewitz (whose affectingly emotive voice is that of 7-year-old Phillip Glasser). He is a little rodent separated from his family after fleeing Russia for America—where ''the streets are paved with cheese.'' Washing ashore in a bottle in New York harbor, he desperately searches the Lower East Side for the sound of his father's violin and comes upon a sometimes interesting, if derivative, array of characters. There's a rodent Artful Dodger named Tony Toponi (the voice of Pat Musick), a Fagin-like rat (John Finnegan), and even a French pigeon (Christopher Plummer) who is supervising work on the Statue of Liberty and sounds like a flighty Maurice Chevalier. Best are the voices of Madeline Kahn, who as a society matron-anticat activist reprises the Dietrich accent she used in *Blazing Saddles,* and Dom De Luise, delightful as a lovable, bushy-tailed pussycat named Tiger. Director Don Bluth, who left the Disney studios and released *NIMH* in 1982, creates such a heightened sense of reality you almost forget you're watching animation. The cobblestoned streets of 19th-century New York are dank, shadowy, and scary. Most scenes are short, suiting small attention spans. The musical numbers have some drawn-out lyrics, though ''Somewhere Out There'' is a first-rate ballad. Still, as a simple tale, *Tail* is effective. It's when Bluth (perhaps influenced by executive producer Steven Spielberg) goes for Greater Meaning that things get muddy. There are overworked devices—a corrupt Tammany Hall politician, a pretty Irish suffragette—and a confusing scene about the changing of mice names at Ellis Island. There are references to religious prejudice that are likely to confuse as much as they enlighten. While the kids may have a good time, Mom and Dad will have to pay attention so they can explain later what it all meant.

G / 1986 / MCA

▲ THE ARISTOCATS

Forgive the heresy, but you can hold off on rushing to watch this Walt Disney full-length animated feature. It's a seat squirmer for all ages. The plot, about a rich lady who decides to leave her millions to her cats, plays like an adult joke. The animation, the result of eighteen months of labor to evoke turn-of-the-century Paris, is too sophisticated. Looks, however impeccable, mean little if the characters don't run lickety-split to your heart as they did in *Snow White, Pinocchio, Dumbo, Bambi,* and the last great Disney animation, 1961's *101 Dalmatians.* In this film the felines have none of the zip-a-dee-doo-dah of the canines in *Lady and the Tramp.* Eva Gabor does the voice of the Duchess, French mother of three syrupy-cute kittens denied their inheritance by a catnapping butler. Gabor explains all this in a Hungarian accent more goulash than Gallic. No wonder the kids watching are likely to wage a fidget revolt. But don't blame Uncle Walt. He was dead for four years when the inheritors of his studio tried to prove they could work the same magic without him. Not with *The Aristocats* they couldn't. Meow.

G / 1970 / Disney

B

▲ THE BAD NEWS BEARS GO TO JAPAN

In the beginning, after all, there were Three Bears, so it was perhaps inevitable that the producers of the *Bad News* bunch would say, "One more time." The third *Bears* saga proved that they don't travel well. The raggedy baseball squad is up this time against a strictly disciplined and perfectly outfitted Japanese team to whom honor, of course, is more important than winning. The U.S. manager (Tony Curtis) is desperate to win and recruits three oversized ballplayers to help out. This was perhaps Curtis's most delightful performance since *Some Like It Hot*. But Burt Lancaster's writer son Bill (who batted out the original *Bears* in 1976, skipped *Breaking Training* in 1977, and then rejoined the lineup) served up warmed-over porridge that only the littlest cubs are likely to find just right. It was the last of the series due to lack of interest at the box office, as in Three Bears and You're Out.
PG / 1978 / Paramount

▲ BENJI THE HUNTED

In today's movie marketplace family entertainment has become a loaded label. For Yuppie singles the words have the peal of a leper's bell. Parents pretend the phrase precisely describes what they want for their kids but yawn (justifiably) at the thought of sitting through what passes as G-rated fare. Younger kids force-fed on an ickky-poo diet of *Care Bears* flicks soon mature into cunning older kids. When dropped off by elders at the local video store to pick up, say, *The Chipmunk Adventure*, they begin to wander into the tempting forbidden zone of *Beverly Hills Cop II* or *The Untouchables*. Who can blame them? Except for the occasional Disney revival or a clever Muppet movie, family entertainment has come to mean something barren of fun or excitement. *Benji the Hunted*, the fourth feature film starring the Captain Marvel of mutts, changes all that. Not merely the best and most ambitious of the series (*Benji, For the Love of Benji*, and *Oh! Heavenly Dog* preceded it), number 4 has the spirit and quality of Disney's remarkable true-life adventures. It seems fitting that Joe Camp, the former Texas ad exec who created the *Benji* films, signed with Disney to distribute this new film. (The Disney organization was not involved in any of the previous *Benji* projects.) As writer-director, Camp hit on a potent plot for his canine hero. After a fishing accident separates him from his trainer, Frank Inn, Benji swims to shore in the wilds of the Pacific Northwest and finds himself playing protector to a group of orphaned cougar cubs. Camp takes a big risk in telling most of the story without dialogue. Luckily, Benji's eloquent eyes and actions are more than up to the task. Doggone it, at the risk of barks from Lassie lovers and Rin Tin Tinophiles, Benji delivers the most winning dog performance ever committed to film. Who needs human actors when you have Benji to rescue his charges from a black timber wolf and a jaw-droppingly huge Kodiak bear. Eagles, rabbits, a raccoon, an owl, and a frog also figure in the vigorously staged action, gorgeously filmed in the mountains and backwoods of Oregon and Washington. And do have a hanky ready for the farewell scene. *Benji the Hunted* has the humor and heart to make family entertainment once again mean something that all ages can cheer.
G / 1987 / N/A

▲ THE BILLION DOLLAR HOBO

Released by an Atlanta-based outfit called the International Picture Show Company, this children's film at times looks amateurish and is burdened by a dizzingly complicated plot—something about dognappers trying to steal a rare breed (a Shar-pei) being given to the U.S. by China. But Tim Conway gives a helping paw to the film's real star, London the German shepherd (sometimes known, by his trainer anyway, as the "World's Greatest Intellectual Dog"). London jumps into moving trains and climbs ladders and turns on lights while Conway looks befuddled. That results in a film that may make children squeal with excitement and giggle at the jokes— which is, after all, the point.
G / 1978 / CBS/Fox

▲ THE BLACK CAULDRON

From *Snow White* to *The Fox and the Hound,* the best thing about the Disney animated features has been their profound sense of heart. What film introduces love better than *Bambi?* This was the twenty-fifth full-length Disney cartoon, and it, too, is most affecting when it evokes affection among its characters. Its hero and heroine, Taran and Eilonwy, are a boy and girl, 14 or so, who are out to destroy a cauldron that contains a mysterious evil force. (Taken from Lloyd Alexander's *The Chronicles of Prydain,* the plot is close to the 1963 Disney film *The Sword in the Stone.*) En route they encounter the wicked Horned King, a furry creature called Gurgi (a cross between an Ewok and a cocker spaniel), a delightfully ruthless trio of witches, and the usual gnomes and fairies. Children may feel disappointed that events get taken out of Faran's and Eilonwy's hands at the end. But the animation, computer enhanced for the first time in a Disney cartoon, is impressive. In one scene a group of shimmering fairies materializes, lighting up the screen as well as the little faces watching. And when Gurgi realizes at last that he has been accepted as a friend, it is the best kind of Disney magic.
PG / 1985 / Disney

▲ THE BOY WHO COULD FLY

If your children are ready for an emotional life-isn't-easy-never-give-up-hope lesson, there isn't a better movie around. Director Nick (*The Last Starfighter*) Castle said he wanted people to feel better about themselves after seeing this movie. They should, if only by comparison with what its characters go through. Bonnie (*Heart like a Wheel*) Bedelia, terrific as always, and her two children move to a strange town after her husband has killed himself because he had cancer. There, a bunch of bullies constantly try to beat up her little boy, 9-year-old Fred Savage. Savage's dog, Maz, gets hit by a car. Bedelia's daughter, inspiringly played by Lucy ("As the World Turns") Deakins, 15, ends up in the hospital after she falls fifty feet off a bridge. Next door to Bedelia's new home lives an autistic teenager, Jan (*Desert Bloom*) Underwood, who likes to sit on his windowsill and pretend to fly. His uncle, Fred ("The Munsters") Gwynne, is a drunk. And Bedelia gets demoted at work. This is not the sort of woman who should be asked what kind of day she's having. The most touching scene occurs when Deakins tells Savage not to give up hope for his dog. In a tide of emotion amazing for such a young actor, Savage asks, "Why should I think positive? You fell on your head, Eric (Underwood) is in the loony bin, and Max is going to die." The lesson of never giving up is especially hard for Savage to learn because his dad went down without a fight. But in the end the moral isn't lost on anyone. The film's willingness to face difficult and complex issues of childhood is diminished by the ending, in which Underwood flies off into the sunset. Still *The Boy Who Could Fly* soars when it examines some of the lows in life and the resounding value of the courage that can spring from them.
PG / 1986 / Karl-Lorimar

C

▲ CANDLESHOE

A charming Walt Disney production, this warms the funnybone—and tickles the heart—as few movies do. Jodie Foster is a wise-cracking kid posing as the long-lost granddaughter of a wealthy British dowager. As Granny, Helen Hayes is simply wonderful. But the film is almost stolen by David Niven—who plays the butler, a crotchety gardener, and several other memorable characters until his ruse is finally uncovered.
G / 1977 / N/A

▲ THE CARE BEARS MOVIE

Their father was a birthday card and their mother was a cash register, but the Care Bears are a cuddly little bunch nevertheless. The warmth is surprising since the American Greeting Corp. spun off its ursine money-makers with a chilly calculation worthy of the Bears' frequent adversary, Professor Cold Heart. As this charming feature-length cartoon shows, though, the Care Bears can generate real joy in a lot of ways. In an era when most cartoon characters seem to fry the villains with laser rays or obliterate them with knockout punches, the Care Bears—Tenderheart, Love-a-Lot, Bedtime, Funshine, and friends— radiate little hearts that send the bad guys packing by loving them into submission. The do-badders in this case are an evil spirit and the teenage boy she turns into a nasty magician. If the Care Bears, who are helped out in their cause by a little boy and girl, aren't triumphant, all the caring will disappear from the world. (This is obviously not a fate creatures associated with a greeting card company would want to go out of their way to encourage.) The cartoon colors are satisfyingly bright. The animation is excellent by modern standards, if not by those of the Disney classics. The voices—including those of Mickey Rooney, Georgia Engel, and Harry Dean Stanton—are the result of real acting, not the patronizing kind of squealing and bellowing that kids too often have to put up with. And the sound track includes some spritely music written by Carol King and John Sebastian. The film may run a little long (75 minutes) for younger children, but its adorability quotient is sufficient to compensate.
G / 1985 / Vestron

▲ CARE BEARS MOVIE II: A NEW GENERATION

There's a problem with the Care Bears. They're such goody two-paws and so carey-sharey that not much can be done with them in terms of plot. About the most dastardly thing any of them is capable of is Bedtime's penchant for snoozing. That leaves most of the story line variations to the villains, and the meanie in this case, the malicious spirit Dark Heart, bears a suspicious resemblance to the malicious spirit who caused the Bears trouble in their first feature last year. The human foils are similar in both films too. In

this case they're three children who are frustrated because they're doing poorly in summer camp games. Once again the Bears are resourceful and colorful. There are some chipper songs, written by Dean and Carol Parks and sung by such people as Stephen Bishop and Debbie Allen. Children probably won't notice, or care, that the two semi-famous human big names who did voices on the original, Georgia Engel and Mickey Rooney, passed on this one. Adults will be glad that there's no real onscreen violence, and the Bears manage to convert Dark Heart within 77 minutes.
G / 1986 / Family

▲ THE CAT FROM OUTER SPACE

In the wonderful, if sometimes sterile, world of Walt Disney Productions, even a monster from another planet isn't really scary. This one, Zunar J5/90 Doric Fourseven—who becomes known as Jake the Cat—has telepathic powers. But he serves primarily as foil for a typically brainless bunch of Disney scientists played by Ken Barry, Sandy Duncan, and McLean Stevenson. The cast also includes Hans Conried, who first worked as a voice for Walt's studio in 1936. Only one human performer in a Disney film ever won an Academy Award (Julie Andrews in *Mary Poppins*). That left Rumple, the 15-month-old Abyssinian playing Jake, to gnaw on his toenails wondering if he'd get the studio's 27th Patsy—the animal kingdom's Oscar. P.S. He didn't.
G / 1978 / Disney

▲ CONDORMAN

There is plenty of invention, gimmickry, and amusement in this Bond-esque spy spoof from the Walt Disney studios. Michael Crawford plays a shleppy comic book writer who gets to live out his fantasies as one of his pulp creations, Condorman. He is recruited to help KGB agent Barbara Carrera defect. The script by Marc Stirdivant is crisp and witty, and director Charles Jarrott sustains a brisk pace. Even the smaller roles are uncommonly effective. Oliver Reed as the KGB's stern mentor and Jean-Pierre Kalfon as Condorman's devilish nemesis add especially nice touches. There is more violence than usual for a Disney product, but the movie will have you floating, just as Condorman does in his hilarious hang-glider scenes. Parents will like this one too.
PG / 1981 / Disney

418

F

▲ FANTASIA

When it was released in 1940, this Walt Disney production, which uses animation to illustrate classical music themes, was an imaginative marvel. It was critically acclaimed and won two special certificates (but no Oscar) at the 1941 Academy Awards. However, the film was poorly patronized and didn't reach the break-even point financially until 1969, by which time it was being used by psychedelic drug fanciers as a film to trip out on. Something was lost in redoing the sound track for the 1982 re-release. The idea was to take advantage of more sophisticated modern recording techniques. In the original, Leopold Stokowski conducted the Philadelphia Orchestra in fragments of such works as Tchaikovsky's *Nutcracker Suite,* Dukas's *Sorcerer's Apprentice,* and Beethoven's *Pastoral* Symphony No. 6. The animation was then drawn to fit the music. In this redubbing, veteran Hollywood conductor Irwin Kostal, using a Dolby sound system, led a 125-piece studio orchestra that had to fit its tempos to the old screen images. The result is a more faithfully reproduced but less powerful rendering of the music. This remains a wonderful way to introduce children to the classics, though. And adults who remember Mickey Mouse in the *Sorcerer's Apprentice* segment, the hippo ballerinas prancing to Ponchielli's *The Dance of the Hours,* or the dinosaurs battling to Stravinsky's *The Rite of Spring* won't mind seeing the film again.
G / 1940 / N/A

▲ FLIGHT OF THE NAVIGATOR

At the outset of this wonderful live-action Disney adventure, Joey (*Clan of the Cave Bear*) Cramer is abducted by a well-intentioned drone spacecraft from another planet so he can be studied. After being returned—eight years have passed by earth time, none by his reckoning—he finds out he's going to be held against his will by NASA. (The time confusion when he returns to earth sets up comic situations like those in *Back to the Future.*) He secretly reboards the spacecraft. But the drone, which looks like one of the menacing robots from *War of the Worlds,* has lost its star charts and can't get home without them. So it strikes a deal with Cramer, in whose brain a set of charts was stored in an experiment. If the drone drops him off at home, he'll let it "access" his brain. But the robot gets more than just navigational aid: It absorbs all the motley information in the brain of a normal 12-year-old who watches too much TV. Consequently, the robot never shuts up and talks like Pee-Wee Herman, who does the robot's voiceover. (When they fly by San Francisco, the drone sings the Rice-A-Roni jingle.) Cramer gives a spirited performance as the title character. Director Randal (*Grease*) Kleiser uses a deft touch with his material. The result is a navigator that's out-of-this-world fun for adults as well as children.
PG / 1986 / Disney

▲ FOR THE LOVE OF BENJI

Benji, the lovable mutt, returned as the star of an international thriller set in Greece. With canine cunning, the mongrel outsmarts a string of government and freelance agents. Alas, this is not the same dog that charmed the world in the original Benji film in 1975. But she is a relative—the daughter of Benji. Who says there are no good parts for females in the movies?
G / 1977 / Vestron

▲ THE FOX AND THE HOUND

The remarkable price tag on the twentieth fully animated feature from the Disney people was $12 million. Judging by the results, though, the money was well spent. The animation is marvelous, a feast of rich colors and fluid movements. The story is obvious but effective. Not realizing they are natural enemies, a baby fox and a puppy vow to remain friends for life. When they come of age, they find it's not easy to stick to youthful ideals. Some of that $12 million went to secure the "voice talents," as the credits describe them, of such talk-ons as Mickey Rooney, Pearl Bailey, and Jack Albertson. Their familiarity helps make

For the Love of Benji: No critic so far has ever been mean enough to bark out a bad word about the lovable pooch in this 1977 sequel or the 1974 *Benji* original. Go ahead, we dare you.

this a painless experience for parents. It is, in any case, a film that's sure to charm the kids.
G / 1981 / N/A

▲ **FREE SPIRIT**

There are only a few moments of drama in this British-made, imitation Disney tale about a hound named Merlin and an orphaned red fox named Tag, who are weaned together on an English estate. One such gripping moment occurs during a hunt, when dogs and riders set out after Tag, who leads them smack into an oncoming train. That enrages the estate's lead hunter, Eric Porter, who embarks on a vendetta, with Merlin—thinking it all a game—helping out. The rest of the cast—including Bill Travers as the good-guy woodsman and Rachel Roberts as Porter's wife—maintains a stiff upper lip. Though director-writer James Hill's noble lioness film, *Born Free,* worked, this time he outfoxed himself. (Disney, in fact, told a similar tale better in the animated *The Fox and the Hound* in 1981.)
PG / 1979 / N/A

G

▲ **THE GOONIES**

Nine-year-olds of every age are apt to delight in this frenzied fun house from the Steven Spielberg factory. Others watching the video in the same room are advised to supply themselves with ear-plugs and a book. *The Goonies,* from a story by Spielberg, is a visual and aural assault. Though the film is directed by Richard Donner and written by Chris Columbus, Spielberg reportedly super-

vised every detail. Don't look too hard, though, for the innocence of *E.T.*, the wonder of *Close Encounters*, or the thrills of *Jaws*. The premise is promising. A group of misfit kids (the "goonies") from Oregon are determined to save their ramshackle neighborhood from grasping realtors who want to turn the area into a country club. They find a treasure map and go underground to seek a lost pirate ship. The kid actors appear to be having a ball playing rejects who prove to be heroes. There's Sean Astin (son of John and Patty Duke Astin) as the shy kid with braces, Corey Feldman as the loudmouth, Jeff Cohen as the fat kid, and Ke Huy-Quan from *Indiana Jones* as the nerd. They're joined by Josh Brolin (son of James) as Astin's older brother, a high-on-brawn teen who can't manage to pass a driving test, Kerri Green as Brolin's sex-obsessed girlfriend, and Martha Plimpton (daughter of Shelley Plimpton and Keith Carradine) as a plain Jane. Sadly, the potential for a hip Hardy Boys in this half-pint, dirty half-dozen remains unrealized. Director Donner is stingy with the breathing space needed to develop his characters. And as soon as the goonies fall into the clutches of a family of hoods, the film degenerates into a series of chases that diminishes in impact despite some nifty special effects, including a breathtaking water slide. Ex-pro footballer John Matuszak does a delightful job as a superhumanly strong bad guy who turns good (he's really the top goonie of them all). But Disney and Spielberg clearly don't trust their audience to sit still for a quiet moment. A line in the movie describes what it's like to watch this bunch of screeching kids: "It's like babysitting without getting paid for it."
PG / 1985 / Warner

▲ THE GREAT MOUSE DETECTIVE

Full of easy humor and traditional good-vs.-evil touches, this animated Disney feature is a colorful, solid piece of entertainment for children. It's inoffensive, too, neither too violent nor too obviously designed to sell a line of toys. Its hero is not Mickey but Basil, another small rodent, who is modeled so closely on Sherlock Holmes that he is even given to fits of depression. His assistant, Dr. Dawson, is a lovable bumbler of the Watson school, and his nemesis, Professor Ratigan, makes Moriarty look like a sweetheart. Ratigan, whose voice is done with delicious ruthlessness by Vincent Price, upstages Basil at times. But he is after all a rather cheesy villain, and there's not much doubt about who is going to win the climactic fight, which is staged in and around Big Ben in London. Melissa Manchester wrote and (as a dance hall mouse) performs one tune, and Henry Mancini supplied the rest of the music, so the cartoon sounds pretty good too. This was the twenty-sixth full-length animated feature from the Disney operation. While it is clearly not the most ambitious or flamboyant, it is an engaging 72 minutes' worth of fun for kids and easy to take for their chauffeurs.
G / 1986 / Disney

▲ THE GREAT MUPPET CAPER

Here's that rare for-the-kids movie that doesn't leave adults in a stupor. It also improves on the 1979 *Muppet Movie*, whose director, James Frawley, didn't trust Jim Henson's TV creations to make the move to the big screen without a bolstering army of human guest stars. This time, with Henson himself at the helm, star cameos are kept to a minimum. *The Great Muppet Caper* also displays a flair for sassy one-liners and no-strings-attached physical comedy that keeps the wholesome proceedings from sagging into tedium. What other love story between a man and a pig could snag a G rating? The lucky fellow is Charles Grodin, who plays the playboy brother of fashion designer Diana Rigg. Tired of long-legged models with aquiline noses, Grodin falls hilariously for Miss Piggy's porky pulchritude and snouty sensuality. Kermit finally wins her back by exposing Grodin as a jewel thief, but not before Miss P has set hearts aflame with an Esther Williams water ballet and a madcap tap dance—all to Joe Raposo's catchy score. Kermit is a special joy, gasping at a swank London supper club menu: "The roast beef in this place costs as much as an Oldsmobile." But all the Muppets have their moments, from befuddled Fozzie Bear to some dancing rats. This is a troupe of performers with heart, even if it is made of felt.
G / 1981 / CBS/Fox

H

▲ HERBIE GOES TO MONTE CARLO

Disney's top money-maker of 1969, Herbie the souped-up "Love Bug," rides again—and this time he falls hood over wheels in love. Small wonder. Competing in the Trans France race, Herbie hooks bumpers with a baby-blue Lancia named Giselle. Under the bemused handling of Disney veteran Dean Jones and his bug-eyed mechanic, Don Knotts, Herbie is still the greatest clown on four wheels. This is excellent fare for the kids.

G / 1977 / Disney

I

▲ INTERNATIONAL VELVET

Elizabeth Taylor has grown up into actress Nanette Newman. (Why wasn't Taylor cast as the grown-up Velvet? Ask writer-producer-director Byron Forbes, Newman's husband.) She has settled down with a long-suffering writer of the Dashiell Hammett genre (Christopher Plummer) and her old horse Pie to make a life for herself in a beautifully scenic English countryside when her orphaned niece (Tatum O'Neal) lands on her stone doorstep. The niece is heartbroken, bratty, and aloof (did she know she'd grow up and marry John McEnroe?) until she takes an interest in a colt sired by old Pie himself. Tatum ages, learns, loves, and wins in the age-old tradition of girl-meets-horse. The picture, while a bit sappy, offers exciting sequences of a three-day Olympic competition, a combination of dressage, jumping, and steeplechase. A must-see for the horsey set and others with a good seat.

PG / 1978 / MGM/UA

J

▲ THE JUNGLE BOOK

This 1967 film, the last animated feature Walt Disney worked on before he died, was loosely based on the Mowgli stories of Rudyard Kipling. It features the voices of Phil Harris as Baloo, the scat-singing bear; Sebastian Cabot as the stuffy panther Bagheera; George Saunders as the tyrannical tiger Shere Khan; Sterling Holloway as the python Kaa; and Bruce Reitherman, son of director Wolfgang Rietherman, as Mowgli. With the movie in re-release, critic Ralph Novak and his son, Thaddeus, then 4, saw it at a northern New Jersey theater. They went home to tape the following review.

Ralph: What did you think of that movie?
Thaddeus: Fine
R: What parts did you like best?
T: I liked all of it, really. The part with Baloo and that boy was great. That's the part I'm gonna talk about. But let's do that after dinner so we don't have to talk and eat at the same time.
R (after dinner): So, how did you like the music in *The Jungle Book*?
T: The music was good, too.

R: What was your favorite song?

T: "The Bare Necessities." Baloo sang that.

R: What did you think of that tiger?

T: Not very bad.

R: Was he scary?

T: No way. I wasn't scared.

R: Did you like the little boy?

T: Very nice. Especially with the bear.

R: Was there any part of the movie you didn't like?

T: The part where the tiger tries to trick the snake into giving him the boy.

T: But he wouldn't.

R: Why didn't you like that part?

T: Because it wasn't very nice to want to eat a boy.

R: What did you think of those monkeys?

T: Very fine.

R: What did you think was the funniest part?

T: The monkeys trying to trick the boy into being a monkey.

R: If you told your friend Zachary about this movie, what would you say?

T: I would say, "Nice movie, Zack."

G / 1978 / N/A

L

▲ LABYRINTH

The best children's movies—and this is certainly one of them—challenge kids. *The Wizard of Oz, Bambi, The Black Stallion,* all in their way show respect for children's courage, imagination, and intelligence, and so does this film about a self-absorbed 13- or 14-year-old girl who one day gets her wish that the goblins would take away her infant stepbrother. There's plenty of talent involved. George Lucas was executive producer. The director is Muppet mogul Jim Henson. The writer—with uncredited help from Elaine May— is Monty Python alumnus Terry Jones, whose

Labyrinth: Jennifer Connelly and her new pal Hoggle try to maneuver their way through a tangle of fantasy and magic to rescue her baby brother from the clutches of David Bowie.

affection for the perverse removes any danger that this film will turn treacly. (The Bog of Eternal Stench seems a particularly Pythonesque touch.) The chronically enigmatic David Bowie plays the vainglorious villain, king of the goblins. Jennifer Connelly, then 15, comely and determined, is the girl who instantly regrets wishing her sibling away and pursues him into the multilevel maze of the goblins' world. As the baby, Toby Froud, the infant son of conceptual designer Brian Froud, supplies the cuteness that is wisely left out of Connelly's performance. Henson explicitly acknowledges the inspiration of children's author Maurice Sendak, whose *Where the Wild Things Are* this film resembles. There are also references to, among other things, *Snow White, Alice's Adventures in Wonderland, The Lone Ranger,* and the comedian Señor Wences. All these citations occur in the course of a journey in which Connelly meets a succession of clever Henson creatures. When she falls into a bottomless pit, for instance, she is caught by arms growing out of the pit's walls. "Who are you?" she asks. "The helping hands, of course," they answer huffily. Even Bowie's steadfastly evil allies have an appealing side. When one remarkably inefficient cannonlike device is smashed by a boulder, it lies there in a million pieces, muttering, "No problem." What children will make of the grim music Bowie wrote and performs is a question. But his final confrontation with Connelly, shot using disorienting effects that add to the tension, is scary enough to make the resolution all the more satisfying. The subtext of the movie seems embodied in a line spoken by a number of characters: "Don't take anything for granted." That lesson is taught in the most unselfconscious way, letting the wisdom work its way into the fun as best it can. Imagine a blend of *Sesame Street* and *Hamlet.* And for those of us who can't manage that kind of imagining on our own, Henson and company do it for us beautifully.

PG / 1986 / Embassy

▲ LADY AND THE TRAMP

There are splashier, more dramatic Disney animated features, but none has more charm than this canine romance, released in 1955. A lot of its appeal is supplied by the voices behind the richly drawn cartoons. Larry Roberts, a Los Angeles actor, supplied a Crosby-Sinatra nonchalance to Tramp, a free-spirited mongrel with an eye for the ladies. Barbara Luddy, a veteran actress who was then nearly 50, provided an ingenue touch to Lady, the well-born cocker spaniel. Noteworthy among the supporting cast was Peggy Lee, who wrote the songs—"We are Siamese" was the best known—and played four roles, including Peg, a floozyish Pekingese. There are enough plot problems to keep even present-day children interested. Lady needs Tramp's help to fight off a rat, some street curs, and the incursion of her owner's new baby. The action keeps Lady's and Tramp's courtship from turning to cloy.

G / 1955 / N/A

▲ THE LITTLEST HORSE THIEVES

Another Disney variation on the beloved-animals-in-peril theme, this film used ponies in an English mining town. The all-British cast (only Alastair Sim is familiar) includes the inevitable mischievous but cuddly little boy. The film otherwise avoids the virulent case of the cutes that afflicts many kiddie movies.

G / 1977 / Disney

▲ THE MAGIC OF LASSIE

With legends like Jimmy Stewart, Mickey Rooney, and Alice Faye, plus the very warp and woof of canine cinema, this could have been a real tail wagger. Unfortunately, the first Lassie movie in twenty-eight years did nothing to improve the reputation of the family film. Lassie, of course, performs impeccably, never blowing a trick as she runs away from a meanie millionaire

(Pernell Roberts) back home to Grandpa Stewart and his two grandchildren. Hitching her way across Colorado, she feigns limps, falls down mountains, rescues a kitten in distress, and otherwise acts like a director's best friend, even though she has to put up with Debby Boone singing sappy songs in the background. Stewart, Rooney, and Raye—despite their estimable credits—don't seem to have much of a way with animals. It just goes to show: You can't teach an old human new tricks.

G / 1978 / MGM/UA

▲ MATILDA

Animal movies have long been an endangered species, though every now and then a monstrous anthropoid or man-eating shark will gnaw on our fancy. But what market can there be for a scruffy-looking boxing kangaroo named Matilda with fluttering eyelashes and a flashy left jab? Especially when the title character is no more than an actor (Gary Morgan) hopping around in an unconvincing kangaroo suit. Boy, he must have felt silly. Everyone else in this punchless comedy— a thumping trashing of Paul Gallico's novel— looks and acts embarrassed. Somebody should have tied this kangaroo down, sport.

G / 1978 / Vestron

▲ THE MOUSE AND HIS CHILD

Don't be put off by the cutesy windup mouse and his little son, whose single desire is to be self-winding and free. This animated children's film is literate and delightfully sharp. Much of the credit belongs to the voices, especially Peter Ustinov as the malevolent Manny the rat, Cloris Leachman as the weary parrot Euterpe, and Andy Devine as the philosopher frog. The glimpses of dark despair amidst the typical cartoon sweetness and light give this production, backed by Japan's ambitious Sanrio Films, enough bite to keep dutiful adults entertained too.

G / 1978 / RCA/Columbia

▲ THE MUPPET MOVIE

There's charm for the kids and in-jokes for their parents (when Kermit's bicycle gets mangled, he quips, "I thought I was gone with the Schwinn"). Muppet creator Jim Henson tries to give everybody a little something. It's an on-the-road-to-Hollywood story, as Kermit the Frog collect Fozzie, Gonzo, and Co. to escape evil fast-food frogs' legs king Charles Durning and make it as a star. It gets a little mushy when Miss Piggy and Kermit meet and fall in love à la *Elvira Madigan*. Later, though he tells her, "Frankly, Miss Piggy, I don't give a hoot." The mix of Muppet and reality is wonderful, anyway. The cameos are lively—Steve Martin is a waiter, Orson Welles a movie mogul, Bob Hope an ice cream man. Paul Williams and Kenny Ascher's songs are appealing, especially "The Rainbow Connection" and a jaunty duet for Kermit and Fozzie called "Movin' Right Along." A must for any child's video collection.

G / 1979 / CBS/Fox

▲ THE MUPPETS TAKE MANHATTAN

In the Muppets' third feature, which concerns the mounting of Kermit the Frog's Broadway musical, Miss Piggy's persona takes a turn for the wurst. The wily '80s professional woman has been transformed into a '50s harridan who first and foremost will do anything to trick her fella— or, rather, frog—into marriage. It's like turning Joan Collins into Phyllis Schlafly, and it isn't very funny. This outing also highlights lots of needlessly downbeat moments (including a car accident that knocks Kermit unconscious) and little of the infectious sight and sound gags that distinguished its predecessors. The comedy only gets charged up during the climactic wedding sequence, in which the respective pink and green relatives of the bride and groom fill the pews. Directed by Frank Oz (the voice of Miss Piggy), *The Muppets Take Manhattan* is memorable in the most unfortunate way. P.S. The pig needs a new agent.

G / 1984 / CBS/Fox

N

▲ THE NEVERENDING STORY

It pokes along at times and lapses occasionally into dark moments of preachy philosophy, but this is still a charming, amusing, innocent film for kids. It focuses on a boy, Barret Oliver, whose mother has recently died, leaving him moody and listless. He happens on a book about a magic place called Fantasia and grows so absorbed in the story that he becomes one of its characters. Oliver is likable, as are little Noah Hathaway, the boy warrior and hero of the story, and Tami Stronach, eerily graceful as a troubled princess. Some of the special effects are enchanting, especially a huge, boulder-munching mountain on wheels called Rock Biter and the fiendish Gmork, which looks like a black wolf and sprouts nihilist philosophy like a Berlin coffeehouse regular. While an evil force, the Nothing, causes some good-size storms and earthquakes, by Wicked Witch of the West or Darth Vader standards, it is a pussycat. Wolfgang Petersen directed the film, shot in West Germany, with restraint. A couple of moments may be difficult for little children—when Hathaway's horse drowns in the Swamps of Sadness, for instance (though it is resurrected at the end of the film)—but there are lots of gentle lessons about the value of hope, courage, and love, and a fair share of plain old fantasy adventure.
PG / 1984 / Warner

P

▲ PETE'S DRAGON

The folks at Disney studios, which brought forth *Song of the South* and *Mary Poppins,* also produced this part-animated, part-live-action musical. *Pete's Dragon* is the story of a 9-year-old orphan who is befriended by a playful green monster. The film stars Helen Reddy, British comic and Broadway *Barnum* Jim Dale, Mickey Rooney, Red Buttons, and Shelley Winters. Sean Marshall is the boy who is rescued from evil foster parents by Elliot the Dragon. The score by Oscar winners Al Kasha and Joel Hirschhorn is appropriate if not memorable, and the production numbers choreographed by Onna White (*Oliver, The Music Man, 1776*) are lively. *Pete's Dragon* is pleasant family fare for a while, but why in the world is it 2 hours and 15 minutes long? For the sake of little attention spans, at least 30 minutes should—and easily could—have been cut.
G / 1977 / Disney

▲ PHAR LAP

The true story of an ugly duckling who was a horse, this Australian movie is about an animal so misbegotten and unpromising as a colt that even his name was an object of laughter (phar lap means "lightning" in Thai). He grew into a champion who astoundingly won thirty-seven of his fifty-one races from 1928 to 1932 before dying under suspicious circumstances in the U.S. shortly after his first North American victory. Phar Lap is still a legend in Australia—as much for his mysterious fate as for his victories—and in this beautifully photographed film he gets the mythic treatment he deserves. The acting is fine throughout. Tom Burlinson plays Tommy Woodcock, the stable hand who became Phar Lap's de facto trainer. (The real Woodcock, then 78, served as technical adviser for the film and helped coach the show jumper Towering Inferno, who had never raced, to play Phar Lap.) Burlinson and the horse shared an empathetic affection: Phar

Lap literally rips the shirts off other stable hands who try to come near him. Martin Vaughn, a veteran Australian actor with a craggy, brooding face, convincingly plays the merciless trainer who overraced the horse to cover his own runaway debts. Ron Leibman plays Phar Lap's owner, showing flash and humor playing a tough-talking transplanted American who mixes relentless cynicism with a sort of grudging generosity. Director Simon Wincer and cinematographer Russell Boyd fill the screen with slow-motion shots of thoroughbreds galloping, manes flying, muscles rippling, hooves kicking up clumps of turf. That is a treat, even if the pace begins to lag a bit in the middle of the film. Like *Black Stallion, Phar Lap* is a winner for audiences of all ages.

PG / 1984 / Playhouse

R

▲ RACE FOR YOUR LIFE, CHARLIE BROWN!

Peanuts goes to summer camp in the gang's third Mendelson/Melendez feature-length cartoon. The minimal animation is enlivened by a bluegrass score and an urbane (if sometimes precious) Charles Schulz script that entertains kids without condescending to them.

G / 1977 / Paramount

▲ RAGGEDY ANN & ANDY

Based on one of the few children's classics that escaped the Disney organization, this feature-length cartoon has sixteen original songs by Joe Raposo, "Sesame Street"'s composer-in-residence. It also has one live actor—director Richard William's daughter Claire—who plays Ann and Andy's owner. Tough sledding for anyone over the age of 5.

G / 1977 / CBS/Fox

▲ RAINBOW BRITE AND THE STAR STEALER

Rainbow, the little animated heroine, has to put up with a lot. There's the sexism of the other characters, the vanity of her horse Starlite (who refers to himself as "the most magnificent horse in the universe"), and the fact that, as Japanese animators are wont to do, the people who draw her make her so round-eyed she always looks surprised. Still, she has a dauntlessness that's appealing. She also has, in this case, an amusing adversary; a mean princess who wants to possess the planet Spectra, which generates all the light in the universe. She covets it because it is a diamond, and she has an addiction to jewels. (She also has what looks to be a poodle-sized emerald, which she walks around on a leash.) Rainbow's old enemies, Murky the colorphobe and his pal Lurky, are second-string villains in this case. Rainbow is joined by a boy named Krys—like most of her boyfriends he complains about having to put up with girls—and a robotic horse that can fly. Very young children may be confused by the plot, and parents may have trouble staying awake to sort it out for them. But the colors are indeed bright, the action relentless, and the mood one of happy spirits and affection.

G / 1985 / Warner

▲ THE RESCUERS

A Disney factory full-length cartoon, this was, happily, the kind Uncle Walt himself used to make. An adaptation of Margery Sharp's stories that took four years to produce, it includes Bob Newhart, Eva Gabor, Geraldine Page, and Jim Jordan (radio's Fibber McGee) among the voices behind the superb artwork. Meanwhile, two mice and an albatross, among others, try to save a little girl from a swamp witch. The movie should

spoil any kid's taste for the jerky stuff that usually passes for animation on Saturday morning TV.
G / 1977 / Disney

▲ RETURN FROM WITCH MOUNTAIN

The Disney kids had been seen last escaping to Witch Mountain, and in this sequel they come back with even flashier powers. For starters, they can will inanimate objects to fly. The dependably malevolent Christopher Lee and Bette Davis (who, unfortunately, isn't given anything to do) are the bad guys who try to exploit Kim Richards and Ike Eisenmann, two neo-Mouseketeer types who play the kids. But evil has never been very big with the Disney people, so while some seamlessly dazzling special effects may cause cars and buses to levitate, there never is much chance the good guys will lose.
G / 1978 / Disney

▲ RETURN TO OZ

Making this sequel was at best an exercise in futility, along the lines of adding a dormer to the Taj Mahal. Few movies have had the vitality, color, wit, or charm of 1939's *The Wizard of Oz;* few are so deservedly beloved. So this movie started out with four or five strikes against it, and it hardly needed one. It is a lackluster fantasy that picks up Dorothy's story six months after she returns from her cyclonic trip to Oz. She's propelled back there by another storm to find the Scarecrow imprisoned by a villain called the Nome King. Her partners in adventure this time are a talking chicken embodied by real-life chickens and some mechanical models (it's as lame an idea as it sounds), a roly-poly robot, a moose head, and a pumpkin character. Aairuza Balk, the California-born daughter of Turkish-Dutch parents, plays Dorothy. It's hardly fair to compare her to Judy Garland. Garland's was a rare, unique talent—when was there ever such a childhood combination of naiveté and sophistication? And in *The Wizard of Oz* she was surrounded by terrific music (Balk doesn't sing) and a charismatic cast that generated tremendous onscreen camaraderie. Balk has poise and she's very cute, but she can't carry this film. The only real impact is made by Jean Marsh who plays a wicked nurse in Kansas and a wicked witch in Oz. Nicol Williamson is a genteely mad scientist and the Nome King. Director Walter Murch is a longtime collaborator of Francis Coppola and George Lucas (he won a sound-design Oscar for *Apocalypse Now*), but he had never directed before. That may account for some of this film's lack of momentum. So might the dreary background music by David Shire. Children who aren't comparing this movie with the original might find it diverting enough. Older folks, though, will wish they were back again on the yellow brick road.
PG / 1985 / Disney

▲ ROBIN HOOD

When Disney animations are good (*Fantasia, Snow White*), they are very, very good. This 1973 re-release, however, is not good. To give most of the major *Robin Hood* characters a rural southern twang hardly seems to fit the myth of a lapsed British aristocrat who steals from the rich to give to the poor. Roger ("Dang Me") Miller plays the rooster narrator, for instance, Andy (*Wild Bill Hickok*) Devine is the badger Friar Tuck, and Pat ("Green Acres") Buttram is the wolfish Sheriff of Nottingham. More in keeping with the tale's spirit, the tyrannous Prince John, an insecure lion, is given voice by Peter Ustinov, and his flunky, the serpent Sir Hiss, gets his sibilants from Terry-Thomas. Robin is a fox, with Brian Bedford's voice, and his love for Maid Marian (Monica Evans as a vixen) is merely cloying. The entire effort, down to the too-static animation, is diffident. But the Disney approach is so comforting it can carry even mediocre material, and children too young to have seen this film in its first release may enjoy it on video in spite of its shortcomings.
G / 1973 / Disney

S

▲ SANTA CLAUS—THE MOVIE

After the New York premiere of *Santa Claus,* Patrick, the then 9-year-old son of the film's star, Dudley Moore, was asked by a TV reporter if he would have spent his allowance on the movie. "Nope," came the reply as Dudley stepped in front of the camera with a tight smile. That sums up this disaster. Only the very young, who may enjoy the bright colors and special effects, will get anything out of this extremely juvenile movie. In the opening sequence villagers huddle in a cozy hut as a blizzard rages outside. They wonder how the kindly local woodcutter, Mr. Claus, played by David Huddleston, manages to provide toys to all the children in the village. Huddleston, meanwhile, is magically transported to the North Pole. For the next couple of centuries Santa goes about making toys in a wonderfully grand set. But director Jeannot Szwarc lets the movie drag, trotting out one toy-making scene after another. As the film approaches 1985, production problems cause Santa's chief assistant, played flatly by Moore, to venture off into the uncaring world. He meets up with John Lithgow, a zanily corrupt New York toy manufacturer who begins plotting to institute a Christmas II in March. Szwarc said he wanted to make a "perennial classic like *Snow White* or *Bambi*." Ho, ho, ho.
PG / 1985 / Media

▲ THE SEA GYPSIES

An adventure movie made by the company that provided the animals for several Disney productions, this film fulfills the requirements of the genre. Beautiful Alaskan coastal scenery, vicious Kodiak bears, cuddlier species (pelican, seal, and dog), shipwreck, and romance all contribute to the neo-Swiss Family Robinson saga. A father (Robert Logan, once J. R. Hale, Kookie's successor on "77 Sunset Strip") and his two daughters (Heather Rahray and Shannon Saylor) set off on a round-the-world sail with an unwanted woman journalist (Mikki Jamison-Olsen) aboard. They discover a young stowaway (Cjon Damitri Pat-

terson), and then all are cast away on the rough Alaskan shore. There they encounter the basic inventory of lost-family perils: marauding bear, torrential rains, the threat of a cold and hungry winter, and a near drowning. All these trials, of course, only serve to draw them closer. But family friction and a realistic shortage of Crusoe-ish ingenuity make the film human and believable.
G / 1978 / Warner

▲ THE SECRET OF THE SWORD

To say He-Man is an animated hero is a vast overstatement, since he is, in the drawing (by the California company Filmation), the writing (Larry Ditillo and Bob Forward), and the voiceover (John Erwin), as animated as a redwood. This was his first feature-length do-gooding, spun off from his syndicated TV series. The plot introduces the Big H's long-lost sister, She-Ra, who has been off in another dimension acting as insufferably self-righteous as he has in Eternia. Those fans of the TV series who like the always hopeful villain, Skeletor, his henchmonster Beast Man, and their pals may be disappointed since they have only cameos in this story. Most of the time He-Man and She-Ra (he calls her "Sis" in a rare lapse into normal behavior) are battling Hordak and his Evil Horde. There is the standard He-Man quota of swordplay, laser battles, punching, and general mayhem—which is to say not much else goes on. Indeed, it's hard to fathom the appeal that He-Man's doings have for kids. Then again, once upon a time some of us thought *King of the Cowboys* and *My Pal Trigger* with Roy Rogers were hot stuff too.
G / 1985 / RCA/Columbia

▲ SESAME STREET PRESENTS: FOLLOW THAT BIRD

Instructive, charming, and gently funny as is just about everything the Children's Television Workshop turns out, this was the first "Sesame Street"

429

feature film for Jim Henson's Muppet characters and their human buddies. The pace is a little slow, especially considering that long before MTV "Sesame Street" was demonstrating the value of quick takes in maintaining young attention spans. The plot generates suspense without being too scary for little children, though, and it's involving enough. The story centers on Big Bird's move to a foster-bird family, the Dodos, in Ocean View, Ill. He soon tires of the Dodos' pastimes—hunting worms and reading *Newsbeak*—and runs off in the general direction of Sesame Street. His friends, including Bert and Ernie, Grover, Count von Count, and even Oscar the Grouch, set off to meet him (though Oscar can't resist stopping off at a diner whose neon sign advertises "Bad Eats"). There are good-natured cameos by Sandra Bernhard, John Candy, Chevy Chase, and Waylon Jennings. Most enjoyably, SCTV vets Dave Thomas and Joe Flaherty appear; they run the Sleaze Brothers carnival and don't hesitate to steal an apple from a little boy's lunch box, let alone capture Big Bird, paint him, and advertise him as the "Bluebird of Happiness." Adults will find more humor in this film than in most grown-up comedies; the Dodo family's two ditzy bird youngsters, for instance, are named Donny and Marie. While Carroll Spinney, who fills Big Bird's costume, is no canary in the singing department, he mixes vulnerability and optimism like nobody's business. The delight continues through the final credits, all 278 of them, which the Count counts off with all his usual devotion to the enumerative arts.

G / 1985 / Warner

▲ SNOW WHITE

This 1937 film was the first full-length color animation produced by the Disney studios. Adapted from the Grimm Brothers fairy tale, it was a huge success and has lost little of its charm over the years. Certainly the joyous first scenes between Snow White and the seven dwarfs who offer her sanctuary are among the most memorable in movies, animated or otherwise. There are some pleasing songs by Frank Churchill—including "Whistle While You Work" and "Someday My Prince Will Come." And the characterizations of good and evil have never been drawn more clearly than between Ms. White and her wicked stepmother, who wants the mirror to tell her she is the fairest

in the land and turns into a murderous hag when it tells her she's second to the princess. Some children may have to be gently guided through the stepmother's witchier moments—and reassured that not everyone who gives them an apple is trying to poison them—but this is still a wonderful movie for kids, and adults can always amuse themselves by memorizing the names of the dwarfs: Happy, Doc, Sleepy, uh, Grumpy, and, well, the others.

G / 1937 / Disney

▲ SONG OF THE SOUTH

This gem, the first feature film from Disney to mix live actors with animation, is guaranteed to pump some zip-a-dee-doo-dah into your family video viewing. Based on characters created by Joel Chandler Harris, a 19th-century Atlanta newspaperman, the film focuses on the character of Uncle Remus, a former slave who delighted the children on the plantation with stories of Brer Rabbit, Brer Fox, Brer Bear, and Tar Baby. These denizens of the briar patch spring to vigorous life through Wilfred Jackson's charming animation. The live-action contingent is well represented by Ruth Warrick (later a regular on the ABC soap "All My Children") whose strained relationship with husband Eric Rolf disturbs their young son, nicely played by Bobby Driscoll (who died of a heart attack in 1968 and was buried in a pauper's grave). The boy finds comfort in the fables of Uncle Remus. In this pivotal role, James Baskett—who died of a heart ailment two years after the film was released—acts with such an abundance of warmth, wisdom, and dignified delight that he won an honorary Oscar. Why he wasn't nominated for a real one remains a blot on the Academy; Baskett could not attend the film premiere in Atlanta since no local hotel would book him. Allegations over the years that the movie itself is racist in its depiction of slavery and the minstrel tradition seem off the mark. Though Disney re-releases its classics every few years, the studio pulled *Song of the South* out of circulation during the 1960s to deflect any debate on the subject. That decision may have tainted a period piece that actually undercuts stereotypical thinking. No white character in the film is possessed of anything like this former slave's principles or sense of self-worth. Uncle Remus does more than just sing and tell tales: He listens and

Song of the South: Bobby Driscoll, James Baskett, and Launa Patten provide the human foils for such animated delights as Brer Bear, Brer Fox, and the resourceful Brer Rabbit.

understands. There's a child in all of us who should not be deprived of the pleasure of his company.

G / 1946 / NYA

▲ THE SWORD IN THE STONE

Based on the legend of King Arthur in general and the T. H. White book of the same title in particular, this animated Disney feature was first released in 1963. It's colorful and wittily drawn, but it's also caught in a kind of no-child's-land: too silly in many places for older kids and too talky for the younger ones. The tale concerns Arthur only as the boy Wart—so nobody has to explain Guinevere's and Lancelot's affair to the kiddies. It's been padded with three near-identical vignettes in which Merlin turns Wart into a fish,

a squirrel, and a sparrow, largely so he can be pursued by voracious-looking predators. Then the movie zips to an abrupt ending, though it will seem none too soon for most grown-ups.

G / 1963 / Disney

▲ SYLVESTER

Sylvester is about a Texas girl who dreams of becoming a star in equestrian competition. At one point someone says, "Watching dressage is like watching cement set." This film has the same problem—it's a horse story marred by leaden pacing and enough bathos to flood the Rio Grande. Melissa Gilbert is an ornery, foul-mouthed 16-year-old orphan in filthy boots and a Stetson who breaks horses for a west Texas stockyard. She struggles to raise her two younger brothers in a rusty old trailer and fantasizes about training horses for the Olympics. When the stockyard receives an unbroken, bad-tempered, funny-looking gray gelding, Gilbert names him "Sylvester Stallone" and decides to train him to compete. But there are complications. A pesky social worker keeps trying to take Melissa's brothers, Yankton Hatten and Shane Serwin. Gilbert's gas-station-owner boyfriend, Michael Schoeffling, wants her to settle down. And the man who could help her train Sylvester, Richard Farnsworth, won't do it because he was in love with her late mother and never forgave her for marrying someone else. Director Tim Hunter takes up far too much time recounting these tribulations. In the best Hollywood half-pint tradition, Gilbert, minus her "Little House on the Prairie" pigtails or petticoats, muddles through with her stock-in-trade flashy smile, petulant pout, and trembling lower lip. She has more chemistry with Sylvester than she does with Schoeffling. He plods through the movie like Matt Dillon at his somnolent worst. Only the grizzled Farnsworth, with his quiet, wry charm, brings much to the film. When Hunter finally does let *Sylvester* become a girl-and-her-horse story, it's too late. Gilbert's sudden development into a national-class equestrienne is especially unconvincing. Sylvester's transformation is more believable (several different horses double for him throughout the film). The scenes of him daintily dancing in a four-legged sidestep or fearlessly leaping a fence are full of physical drama. *Sylvester* needed more of such images and less unlikely talk.

PG / 1985 / RCA/Columbia

▲ THE WATCHER IN THE WOODS

In the control of, say, Brian De Palma or John Carpenter, this might have been a gripping horror film. Coming as it did from Walt Disney Productions, it was a supernatural tale that was as silly as it was scary. Wholesome Lynn-Holly Johnson is a teenager who begins to "see things" after her family rents an isolated mansion from batty Bette Davis. The house is surrounded by some splendid woods where the Watcher unleashes gusts of wind and dazzling bolts of light. Director John Hough does create an atmosphere of benevolent menace, and there are several jump-out-of-your-seat frights. He utilizes his cast less well: Carroll Baker and David McCallum are wasted as Lynn-Holly's parents, and Johnson herself tends to substitute all-purpose shrieks for motion. Davis, who was in her fiftieth year in movies, is wonderfully wicked. But she can't compensate, especially for the contrived ending of this Disneyville Horror.

PG / 1980 / Disney

▲ WILDERNESS FAMILY, PART 2

In 1975's Part 1 the Robinsons decided to get away from it all permanently. They headed for the hills and built themselves a cabin near a gorgeous mountain lake. This sequel found them still there and still impossibly clean-cut but facing their first winter in the wilds. What with wolves, avalanches, cabin fever, pneumonia, and no TV, they have a pretty rough go. But it's nothing that a little Yankee ingenuity, love, and togetherness can't handle. The dialogue is simple, and the acting tends toward the one-dimensional. (Most of the original cast, headed by Robert Logan and Susan D. Shaw, returned.) But the Crested Butte, Colorado, locations are magnificent, even if the snow depth fluctuates unnervingly from scene to scene. The beauty of nature becomes a message in itself, and the movie's emotions are pure. Compared to other epics of wholesomeness it's first-rate.

G / 1979 / Media

Appendix

TWENTY-FIVE BEST AND TEN WORST BY SUBJECT

ACTION/ADVENTURE MOVIES

BEST

The African Queen (Humphrey Bogart, Katharine Hepburn)—Bogie and Kate sail to glory against the Germans in World War I Africa, riding their ramshackle steamboat and the direction of John Huston.
1951 / CBS/Fox

All Quiet on the Western Front (Lew Ayres, Louis Wolheim)—Still the best antiwar film ever made (*Platoon* can't compare), this Oscar winner of Germany in World War I hasn't lost an iota of its power to move and inspire.
1930 / MCA

Beau Geste (Gary Cooper, Ray Milland)—Foreign Legionnaires fight the desert, the Arabs, and the impossibly evil sergeant, Brian Donlevy.
1939 / N/A

Bridge on the River Kwai (Alec Guinness, William Holden)—A Japanese POW camp in Burma serves as the arena for a powerful meditation on the meaning of pride, honor, and ego.
1957 / RCA/Columbia

Butch Cassidy and the Sundance Kid (Paul Newman, Robert Redford)—Westerns have rarely come in more entertaining form, thanks to Newman and Redford at their star-shining peaks as outlaws on the run.
PG / 1969 / CBS/Fox

The Crimson Pirate (Burt Lancaster)—Pirate derring-do enjoys its finest hour as an astonishingly agile Lancaster and acrobatic sidekick Nick Craval swashbuckle across the Mediterranean.
1952 / Warner

Deliverance (Jon Voight, Burt Reynolds)—A weekend canoe trip turns into hillbilly hell for Voight, Reynolds, Ronny Cox, and Ned Beatty in this blistering version of James Dickey's bestseller.
R / 1972 / Warner

The French Connection (Gene Hackman, Roy Scheider)—Nonstop action as a New York narc cop, played by the Oscar-winning Hackman, pursues heroin smugglers. And oh, that car chase with a subway train.
R / 1971 / CBS/Fox

Goldfinger (Sean Connery)—James Bond was never more flamboyant—nor more fun—than in this chase after the goldaholic villain played by Gert Frobe and such characters as Odd Job and Pussy Galore.
PG / 1964 / CBS/Fox

The Great Escape (Steve McQueen, James Garner)—An ace cast, headed by McQueen, Garner, and Charles Bronson, finagles a breath-stopping breakout from a German POW camp in World War II. McQueen's motorcycle getaway remains an indelible movie image.
1963 / CBS/Fox

Gunga Din (Cary Grant, Douglas Fairbanks, Jr., Victor McLaglen)—Let the fireworks rip as

Her 'Majesty's soldiers battle the punjabs in Indian, with the help of water boy Gunga— Sam Jaffe.

1939 / Nostalgia Merchant

High Noon (Gary Cooper, Grace Kelly)—The ultimate Western shootout had plenty of atmosphere provided by Frankie Laine's version of the ominous title song, Kelly's pure beauty, and deft performances by such people as Lloyd Bridges, Lon Chaney, Jr., Katy Jurado, and Thomas Mitchell. Cooper, stern of jaw even by his standards, provided the reluctant heroism.

1952 / Republic

Jaws (Richard Dreyfuss, Roy Scheider, Robert Shaw)—There's this shark, see. The first and still foremost of the sea creature crop was sensationally directed by Steven Spielberg, whose failure to win an Oscar for so elegantly shattering an audience's nerves remains a shame on the Academy.

PG / 1975 / MCA

King Solomon's Mines (Stewart Granger, Deborah Kerr)—Richard Surtees' spectacular location photography supplied the color for the African treasure hunt; Granger and Kerr supplied the romance.

1950 / N/A

The Man Who Would Be King (Sean Connery, Michael Caine)—Kipling's tale of greed becomes classic John Huston filmmaking, with Connery and Caine exemplary as soldiers of fortune in Kafiristan who don't know when to stop playing god.

PG / 1975 / CBS/Fox

Mutiny on the Bounty (Clark Gable, Charles Laughton)—Some terrific actors have tried this grand tale of mutiny and revenge. Nobody has come close to the test of charisma versus power portrayed by Gable and Laughton.

1935 / MGM/UA

Northwest Passage (Spencer Tracy, Robert Young)—Tracy is the stalwart yet curiously vulnerable leader of Rogers's Rangers, Young the neophyte mapmaker he recruits to chart his explorations in pre-colonial America.

1940 / N/A

Raiders of the Lost Ark (Harrison Ford, Karen Allen)—Steven Spielberg's sophisticated update on the old-time movie serials presents a first-rate new hero in Ford's Indiana Jones and provides more thrills per second than any ride at Disneyland.

PG / 1981 / Paramount

Red River (John Wayne, Montgomery Clift)— Here is the film Wayne should have won his Oscar for, a cattle drive story of a willful, ruthless, and aging man scrapping with the rebellious young hot gun he has all but adopted—Clift, in his first movie.

1948 / Key

The Red Tent (Sean Connery, Peter Finch)— Watching this grueling saga of Antarctic exploration creates an almost tangible sense of the relentless, unforgiving cold.

1971 / Paramount

The Searchers (John Wayne, Jeffrey Hunter)— Director John Ford crafted this epic about the search for two white girls captured by Indians with extraordinary care and skill; it is as impressive in its minor details as in its stately sweep across the West.

1956 / Warner

The Three Musketeers (Gene Kelly, Lana Turner) —Kelly, in high-spirited good form, leads the all-for-one trio—Van Heflin and Alan Hale were the other two—through their colorful escapades.

1948 / MGM/UA

Treasure of the Sierra Madre (Humphrey Bogart, Walter Huston)—John Huston directed his father, Bogart, and Tim Holt as three prospectors in Mexico in what is both a rollicking good story and a treatise on the irresistible power of greed.

1948 / CBS/Fox

A Walk in the Sun (Dana Andrews, John Ireland) —No movie captured so well the enervating drudgery and terror of World War II, where the roads and the killing seemed as if they might go on forever.

1945 / Reel Images

The Wild Bunch (William Holden, Robert Ryan) —Aging cowboys fight a losing battle with the 20th century in Sam Peckinpah's brilliant and brutal elegy to the American West. A masterpiece.

R / 1969 / Warner

WORST

Airport (Burt Lancaster, Jacqueline Bisset)—It started a string of multistar potboilers that led to only one good thing: the parody *Airplane!*

G / 1970 / MCA

Billy Jack (Tom Laughlin)—An allegedly pro-peace film, this is about a half-breed who karate-kicks the bejesus out of everyone in sight. Ridiculous? You betcha.
PG / 1971 / Warners

The Bounty (Mel Gibson, Anthony Hopkins)—The famous mutiny at sea made a terrific film in 1935 with Gable and Laughton, a flawed one in 1962 with Brando and Trevor Howard, and an outright fiasco this time with a lugubrious Gibson and Hopkins.
PG / 1984 / Vestron

A Bridge Too Far (Robert Redford, Laurence Olivier)—Cornelius Ryan's finely detailed book about a disastrous 1944 Allied air drop becomes a long-winded epic with all-star cameos from a lot of actors who clearly dropped in for one thing: a paycheck.
PG / 1977 / CBS/Fox

The Conqueror (John Wayne, Susan Hayward)—Reserve a place near the top of the miscasting of all-time list for the Duke as Mongol warrior Genghis Khan. The film is good only for unintentional laughs.
G / 1956 / MCA

The Deep (Nick Nolte, Jacqueline Bisset)—Bisset's wet T-shirt was the highlight of this dopey tale of divers and smugglers.
PG / 1977 / RCA/Columbia

High Road to China (Tom Selleck, Bess Armstrong)—Better they should have taken a slow boat.
PG / 1983 / Warner

Indiana Jones and the Temple of Doom (Harrison Ford, Kate Capshaw)—Steven Spielberg ruins a perfectly entertaining lighthearted adventure spoof by using all his considerable skill to depict death, graphically, repeatedly, and in every form this side of being chopped up by a lawn mower.
PG / 1984 / Paramount

Rambo (Sylvester Stallone, Sylvester Stallone's muscles, Sylvester Stallone's weapons)—Stallone misuses the very real plight of Vietnam MIAs for yet another go at playing Master of the Universe. The only thing to say in the film's favor is that it's too dumb to be offensive.
R / 1985 / Thorn/EMI

Tarzan the Ape Man (Bo Derek, Richard Harris)—Tarz is actually a hen-pecked man around the jungle in this case, with Bo showing not much in the way of inhibitions, clothes, or Shakespearean potential.
R / 1981 / MGM/UA

CHILDREN'S MOVIES

BEST

The Adventures of Robin Hood (Errol Flynn, Olivia De Havilland)—Nobody has ever buckled his swash more dashingly than Flynn did while courting the lovely Olivia, playing Maid Marian.
1938 / CBS/Fox

An American Tail (Animated)—Don Bluth's fable about a family of oppressed Russian mice who immigrate to America stumbles a bit over its ambitions but remains a charming and tuneful delight that never talks down to its young audience.
G / 1986 / MCA

Benji, the Hunted (Benji)—Hollywood's top dog has his finest hour on film saving some baby cougars from a fierce wolf. The niftiest of animal adventures.
G / 1987 / Disney

The Black Stallion (Mickey Rooney, Kelly Reno)—A simple story of a boy (Reno) and a horse reaches the level of artistry through stunning camerawork and a lyrical appreciation of childhood.
G / 1979 / CBS/Fox

Captains Courageous (Spencer Tracy, Freddie Bartholomew)—Tracy, as a weather-worn Spanish fisherman, makes a perfect mentor for little Freddie and Mickey Rooney in this vigorous sea tale.
1937 / MGM/UA

Charlotte's Web (Animated)—The funny, enlightening, and sometimes melancholy E. B. White

story about a frightened pig and a compassionate spider gets a bright, musical treatment. Debbie Reynolds provided Charlotte's voice while Paul Lynde was Templeton the rat.
1972 / Paramount

Dr. Seuss Video Festival (Animated)—Taken from two TV specials, this captivating tape combines *Horton Hears a Who,* narrated by Hans Conreid, and *How the Grinch Stole Christmas,* the Doctor's shrewd neo-Dickensian tale about the power of faith, narrated with gleeful wickedness by Boris Karloff
1966/70 / MGM/UA

Dumbo (Animated))—Ned Washington's and Frank Churchill's songs enliven the tale of a baby elephant who learns to fly—and to have faith.
1941 / Disney

E.T. (Drew Barrymore, Henry Thomas)—Eagerly awaited on video (no date set yet), Steven Spielberg's wondrous blend of fantasy and reality stands with *The Wizard of Oz* as the best children's film ever made—for young and old alike.
G / 1982 / N/A

Follow That Bird (Carroll Spinney, Dave Thomas)—Oscar the Grouch and the other Sesame Street Muppets hit the road to liberate Big Bird, who is being billed as "The Bluebird of Happiness" in a side show.
G / 1985 / Warner

The Great Muppet Caper (The Muppets)—Tops among the three Muppet movies in terms of music, comedy, and suspense, this Jim Henson treat brings out the wildest in Kermit, Gonzo, Fozzie, and the gang, and the wickedest in Miss Piggy.
G / 1981 / CBS/Fox

The Jungle Book (Animated)—Kipling meets Disney, resulting in a cheery, tuneful version of how Mowgli the boy was raised by the forest animals. Sebastian Cabot, Sterling Holloway, and George Sanders are among those whose voices appear; Phil Harris sings "The Bare Necessities," happily.
1967 / N/A

Labyrinth (David Bowie, Jennifer Connelly)—Bowie is an eerie villain, Connelly a winning teenager trying to find the infant stepbrother she wished into goblin land.
PG / 1986 / Embassy

March of the Wooden Soldiers (Stan Laurel, Oliver Hardy)—Laurel and Hardy weave their special magic around Victor Herbert's *Babes in Toyland* operetta in a film that just gets better with repeat viewings.
1934 / Independent United Distributors

Mary Poppins (Julie Andrews, Dick Van Dyke)—Padded a bit with distracting adult pomp (the banker father's a bore), this marvelous mix of live action and animation soars when Oscar-winning Julie takes charge as a nanny with no patience for kiddie goo.
G / 1964 / Disney

Miracle on 34th Street (Edmund Gwenn, Natalie Wood)—A holiday perennial still guaranteed to melt hearts when Gwenn makes little Natalie believe in Santa Claus. Avoid the crass colorized version.
1947 / CBS/Fox

National Velvet (Elizabeth Taylor, Mickey Rooney)—Yes, Virginia, Liz Taylor was once a little girl too. This tale of her determination to win the world's toughest horse race adds up to pure enchantment.
1945 / MGM/UA

Pinocchio (Animated))—There are some scary moments for the little ones, but wishing on a star couldn't bring a better kids movie than this cartoon about a puppet who becomes a boy. Cliff Edwards gives voice to Jiminy Cricket.
1940 / Disney

Pollyanna (Hayley Mills)—Much, much better than the icky-poo title sounds as 12-year-old Hayley charms the grouches, led by Jane Wyman and Agnes Moorehead, in a New England town.
1960 / Disney

Sleeping Beauty (Animated)—Disney animation hit a post-World War II peak with this fairy tale so you can overlook the fact that the story pretty much goes over the same ground as *Snow White.*
1959 / Disney

Snow White and the Seven Dwarfs (Animated)—Snow's idyllic beauty, the witch's total wickedness, and the charm of the dwarfs combined to create a spirited version of the old German folk tale.
1937 / Disney

Treasure Island You can take your choice from two terrific versions of Robert Louis Stevenson's pirate yarn. Wallace Beery made a fine Long John Silver and so did Robert Newton.
1934 / MGM/UA   1950 / Disney

Willie Wonka and the Chocolate Factory (Gene Wilder, Jack Albertson)—Wilder, as the proprietor of the establishment in question, is pleasantly

wacky, and Peter Ostrum as young Willie is likable in this variation on the Roald Dahl tale.
G / 1971 / Warner
The Wizard of Oz (Judy Garland)—What's left to say? Just follow Garland, Ray Bolger, Jack Haley, Bert Lahr, and wicked witch Margaret Hamilton down that yellow brick road and over the rainbow at every available opportunity.
1939 / MGM/UA
The Yearling (Gregory Peck, Claude Jarman, Jr.)—Marjorie Kinnan Rawlings's story of a boy's love for a fawn his father must kill makes for an unforgettably touching family film, superbly acted by Peck, young Claude, and Jane Wyman.
1946 / MGM/UA

WORST

Care Bears II (Animated)—Tender Heart and his hench-bears can cute you into a stupor as well as into submission.
G / 1986 / RCA/Columbia
Chitty Chitty Bang Bang (Dick Van Dyke, Sally Ann Howes)—Third-rate special effects, cloying songs, and cutesy dialogue swiftly sink this concoction about Van Dyke and a flying car.
G / 1968 / CBS/Fox
The Dark Crystal (Animated)—Muppeteers Jim Henson and Frank Oz come a cropper with this murky and morose fable, allegedly a child's view of good and evil.
PG / 1983 / Thorn/EMI
Dr. Dolittle (Rex Harrison, Anthony Newley)—

Talking to the animals is all well and good, but Rex might have had a chat with director Richard Fleischer while he was at it.
G / 1967 / CBS/Fox
Gulliver's Travels (Richard Harris)—Jonathan Swift's classic story turns to mush as a hammy Harris mixes it up with some ham-handed animation.
G / 1977 / United
Pete's Dragon (Helen Reddy, Mickey Rooney)—Little Sean Marshall has to worry not only about his animated dragon pal but about being upstaged by the earnest Ms. Reddy.
G / 1977 / Disney
Return to Oz (Fairuza Balk, Nicol Williamson)—Was it Thomas Wolfe or the Good Witch of the North who said you can't go home again? Anyway, after this somber junket, you'll believe it.
G / 1985 / Disney
Robin Hood (Animated)—A rare Disney misfire, with animated animals filling the traditional roles, voiced with surprisingly little fizz by Phil Harris, Peter Ustinov, and Roger Miller.
G / 1973 / Disney
Santa Claus: The Movie (John Lithgow, Dudley Moore)—A funereally paced, big-budget bomb that begins with the deaths of Ma and Pa Claus and goes down from there. Should be used as a video holiday gift only when coal and wood are unavailable.
G / 1985 / MCA
The Secret of the Sword (Animated)—He-Man discovers he has a sis who's as obnoxiously humorless as he is; even Skeletor is more sympathetic.
G / 1985 / Magic Window

COMEDIES

BEST

Adam's Rib (Katharine Hepburn, Spencer Tracy)—The cream of the Hepburn-Tracy battles of the sexes pairs them as husband and wife lawyers on different sides of the same case.
1949 / MGM/UA

Annie Hall (Woody Allen, Diane Keaton)—Allen's largely autobiographical look at how he loved and lost Keaton took the Best Picture Oscar (over *Star Wars* yet) and still takes the cake as the screen's most comic and unexpectedly touching romance.
PG / 1977 / CBS/Fox

Dinner at Eight (Jean Harlow, Wallace Beery)— The starshine of such greats as Harlow, Beery, the Barrymore brothers, and Marie Dressler turns the Edna Ferber–George S. Kaufman play about high society into a feast of fun.
1933 / MGM/UA

Dr. Strangelove (Peter Sellers, Sterling Hayden) —Director Stanley Kubrick, his co-writers Terry Southern and Peter George, and the never-more-brilliant Sellers somehow made nuclear war darkly hilarious. The film's volcanic paranoia seems more relevant now than ever.
PG / 1964 / RCA/Columbia

Duck Soup (The Marx Brothers)—The boys' anarchic, acerbic antiwar romp derided the mindless chauvinism of ''Freedonia'' in the most enjoyable of ways.
1935 / MGM/UA

The General (Buster Keaton)—Keaton's Civil War comedy is a silent film except for the sound of laughter—your own—that can't help but bubble up each time you see it.
1927 / Budget

Ghostbusters (Bill Murray, Sigourney Weaver)— Perhaps the loosest, happiest of modern comedies, it also features Dan Aykroyd and Harold Ramis in pursuit of some reasonably evil-minded animated spirits.
PG / 1984 / RCA/Columbia

The Graduate (Dustin Hoffman, Anne Bancroft) —Age cannot wither or custom stale the infinite comic variety director Mike Nichols and his cast brought to this view of 1960s youth. Here's to you, Mrs. Robinson.
PG / 1967 / Embassy

His Girl Friday (Cary Grant, Rosalind Russell) —Grant is the manipulative editor, Russell the journalism addict he uses so deftly in this remake of *The Front Page*. Directed by Howard Hawks.
1940 / United; Silver Screen

Hold That Ghost (Bud Abbott, Lou Costello)— Perhaps the least appreciated of the great screen comics, Bud and Lou twist their clever turns of phrase around some spooks and third banana Joan Davis.
1941 / MCA

It Happened One Night (Clark Gable, Claudette Colbert)—The charm level as runaway heiress Colbert gets mixed up with news hound Gable is so high that this Frank Capra comedy became the first film to win all five major Oscars.
1934 / RCA/Columbia

Kind Hearts and Coronets (Alec Guinness)—At his most subtly devilish, Guinness plays a whole family by himself in a hilarious tale of murder— no kidding—from England's golden age of comedy.
1949 / Thorn/EMI

M*A*S*H (Elliott Gould, Donald Sutherland)— Fans of the Alan Alda TV series may need to be reminded that the black comic bite in the tale of a Korean War medical unit started with Robert Altman's classic film.
PG / 1970 / CBS/Fox

Monty Python and the Holy Grail (John Cleese, Eric Idle)—The peerless British satirical troupe proves that the shortest distance between two puns is a straight line.
PG / 1974 / RCA/Columbia

My Little Chickadee (W. C. Fields, Mae West)— Every critic has a favorite scene in this one-and-only, wholly hilarious screen teaming of Fields and West. Rent the tape and pick yours.
1940 / MCA

Ninotchka (Greta Garbo, Melvyn Douglas)—A champagne comedy from director Ernst Lubitsch finds Garbo as a Soviet envoy defecting to Paris. The result is pure enchantment, sexy and very funny.
1939 / MGM/UA

The Nutty Professor (Jerry Lewis, Stella Stevens) —Seeing Lewis's split personality—from nerd to swinger—is enough to make you appreciate the genius the French have always discerned in his movies.
1963 / Paramount

Prizzi's Honor (Jack Nicholson, Kathleen Turner)—Director John Huston's sizzling sendup of the crime business gave Nicholson and Turner the most potently funny roles of their careers as a couple of paid assassins who hit on each other.
R / 1985 / Vestron

The Producers (Gene Wilder, Zero Mostel)— The ingenious Mel Brooks's takeoff on a Broadway scam includes one of Hollywood's funniest bits: the ''Springtime for Hitler'' number, with Dick Shawn as a hippie Fuehrer.
PG / 1967 / Embassy

The Road to Utopia (Bing Crosby, Bob Hope)— The unique Crosby-Hope screen camaraderie, the Johnny Burke–Jimmy Van Heusen songs, Dorothy Lamour in a parka as well as a sarong: This is a delightful trip right down a well-beaten path.
1945 / N/A

A Shot in the Dark (Peter Sellers, Elke Sommer)—The second film in the *Pink Panther* series finds Sellers in peak lack of form as the bumbling Clouseau, and Sommer a luscious foil.
PG / 1964 / CBS/Fox

Some Like It Hot (Jack Lemmon, Marilyn Monroe, Tony Curtis)—Lemmon and Curtis in drag pursue a sumptuous Monroe in a Billy Wilder farce that belies the film's final line: "Nobody's perfect."
1958 / CBS/Fox

Tootsie (Dustin Hoffman, Jessica Lange)—Hoffman puts on the drag this time and learns to become a better man in this superbly acted, written, and directed gem of poignant humor.
PG / 1982 / RCA/Columbia

Young Frankenstein (Gene Wilder, Peter Boyle)—In another of Mel Brooks's inspired set pieces, Boyle as the monster and Wilder as Dr. Frankenstein dress up in top hats and tails to do a horribly funny rendition of "Puttin' on the Ritz."
PG / 1974 / CBS/Fox

Zelig (Woody Allen, Mia Farrow)—Strikingly original in concept, witty and cutting in execution, this Allen film about a chameleon-like man who can change into anyone he's near offered a wry comment on fame, and plenty of laughs.
PG / 1983 / Warner

WORST

Bedtime for Bonzo (Ronald Reagan, Diana Lynn)—Back then it was a chimp, and not Oliver North, who made a monkey of Mr. Reagan. But not before this insipid college comedy takes cute to the cloying point.
1951 / MCA

The Bellboy (Jerry Lewis)—Then again there are those slapsticky, out-of-control Lewis debacles that make you wonder about the French's sense of cinematic judgment.
1960 / USA

The Blues Brothers (John Belushi, Dan Aykroyd)—Aykroyd and Belushi weren't brothers, and they had nothing to do with the blues or—in this egregiously self-indulgent case—humor.
R / 1980 / MCA

Fun with Dick and Jane (Jane Fonda, George Segal)—There's a social comment in here somewhere about the pressures of modern American life, but it's lost in the nasty tone as Fonda and Segal turn from a suburban couple into a two-bit crime wave.
PG / 1977 / RCA/Columbia

Howard the Duck (Lea Thompson)—One of the most expensive flops in film history, from George Lucas no less, about a vulgar duck from outer space who can't quack the bad joke barrier.
PG / 1986 / MCA

Ishtar (Warren Beatty, Dustin Hoffman)—Trying to ape the Hope-Crosby travel comedies, Warren and Dusty got bogged down on the *Road to Egomania*.
PG-13 / 1987 / RCA/Columbia

The Main Event (Barbra Streisand, Ryan O'Neal)—Babs buys the contract of boxer O'Neal, but the biggest battle that results is between her need to be cutesy and his.
PG / 1979 / Warner

1941 (Dan Aykroyd, John Belushi)—Another expensive clunker, from Steven Spielberg no less, that tries to get yuks from Pearl Harbor.
PG / 1979 / MCA

Porky's (Don Monahan, Kim Cattrall)—A low-budget comedy about raunchy Florida high schoolers that made a box-office killing and keeps spawning sequels that bring bad taste below basement level.
R / 1981 / CBS/Fox

That's Life (Julie Andrews, Jack Lemmon)—Writer-director Blake Edwards brings wife Andrews and family together for an amateurish home movie that tries, with no success, to find the humor in impotence, crab lice, and cancer.
R / 1986 / RCA/Columbia

DRAMAS

BEST

All About Eve (Bette Davis, Anne Baxter)—Baxter's performance as an unscrupulous actress climbing her way to the top up Davis's back is a marvel of ambition; George Sanders is a model of cynicism as an unsparing critic.
1950 / CBS/Fox
Atlantic City (Burt Lancaster, Susan Sarandon)—Burt Lancaster has never been better than he is as an old man who momentarily regains love and his youth in a reborn resort town in this poignant Louis Malle film with a powerful and poetic script by John Guare. A treasure.
R / 1981 / Paramount
The Caine Mutiny (Humphrey Bogart, Van Johnson)—Bogart and his ball bearings made of the disgraced Captain Queeg not only an enduring screen character but a surprisingly sympathetic one.
1954 / RCA/Columbia
Casablanca (Humphrey Bogart, Ingrid Bergman)—As times goes by the fundamental thing still applies: this Bogie-Bergman love story (winner of the Best Picture Oscar) is as good as movies get. Play it again, Sam.
1943 / CBS/Fox
Citizen Kane (Orson Welles, Joseph Cotten)—In his first film, at 25, Welles told the story of the fall of a publishing titan and made American movies into an art form respected the world over.
1941 / Vid America
Cool Hand Luke (Paul Newman, George Kennedy)—What we have here is a triumph of communicating, with Newman glorious as a stubbornly rebellious chain gang prisoner who seems a martyr to the power of hope.
PG / 1967 / Warner
From Here to Eternity (Burt Lancaster, Montgomery Clift, Frank Sinatra)—Sinatra reclaimed his career in this convincing version of the James Jones novel about love and hate at a pre-World War II Army base near Pearl Harbor.
1953 / RCA/Columbia
The Godfather Epic (Marlon Brando, Al Pacino, Robert De Niro, Diane Keaton)—Director Francis Coppola put together a video version, with new footage, of his two Oscar-winning films about Mafia don Marlon Brando (De Niro in his younger days). The result, in 386 minutes, is the greatest crime story ever made.
R / 1972/74 / Paramount
Gone with the Wind (Clark Gable, Vivien Leigh)—Perhaps the most popular film of all time, the love story between Scarlett (Leigh) and Rhett (Gable), set against a Civil War background, hasn't lost any of its fun, fantasy, or epic sweep.
1939 / MGM/UA
The Grapes of Wrath (Henry Fonda, Jane Darwell)—John Steinbeck's novel of migrant workers in California became a dark, bitter, and often painfully moving film.
1940 / CBS/Fox
Hamlet (Laurence Olivier, Jean Simmons)—Never have the slings and arrows of outrageous fortune struck with such a penetrating, personal force, and, of course, nobody has ever graced this most gracious use of the language more than Olivier.
1948 / NA
How Green Was My Valley (Walter Pidgeon, Maureen O'Hara)—The poignant tale of Welsh coal miners suggests the warmth, travail, and love of real family life.
1941 / N/A
I Am a Fugitive from a Chain Gang (Paul Muni)—Looking hopelessly haunted, Muni portrays a man trapped in a cycle of injustice.
1932 / Key
The Killing Fields (Sam Waterston, Haing Ngor)—A monumentally moving look at Cambodia after the American evacuation benefits from an Oscar-winning performance by non-actor Ngor, who lived through this hell in real life.
R / 1984 / Warner
Kiss of the Spider Woman (William Hurt, Raul Julia)—Hurt's sensitive, sensitizing and Oscar-winning performance as a homosexual prisoner anchors this unusual, provocative, and surprisingly witty drama about life in a Latin American prison.
R / 1985 / Charter

Midnight Cowboy (Dustin Hoffman, Jon Voight)—Hoffman and Voight, never better, roam Manhattan's mean streets and develop a friendship that tears at your heart in this Best Picture Oscar winner.
R / 1969 / MGM/UA

Nashville (Lily Tomlin, Keith Carradine)—The measure of director Robert Altman's genius is taken in this masterful character study set in the country music capital but expressing the hopes and fears of all Americans.
R / 1975 / Paramount

Of Mice and Men (Lon Chaney, Jr., Burgess Meredith)—In a rare non-horror film role as John Steinbeck's pathetically retarded ranch hand Lenny, Chaney gave the performance of a career.
1939 / Prism

One Flew Over the Cuckoo's Nest (Jack Nicholson, Louise Fletcher)—Nicholson fights to beat the system, represented as an insane asylum, in this stinging film version of Ken Kesey's novel.
R / 1975 / Thorn/EMI

On the Waterfront (Marlon Brando, Rod Steiger)—Brando's line to Steiger—"I could've been somebody"—has become a cliché; the movie, about corruption on the docks, hasn't.
1954 / RCA/Columbia

A Streetcar Named Desire (Marlon Brando, Vivien Leigh)—Brando's and Leigh's portrayals of passion edged with desperation fit perfectly into Tennessee Williams' poetic vision of lost dreams.
1951 / Warner

Sunset Boulevard (Gloria Swanson, William Holden)—Writer-director Billy Wilder brilliantly bites the Hollywood hand that feeds him, with Swanson and Holden in stellar performances.
1950 / Paramount

Terms of Endearment (Debra Winger, Shirley Maclaine, Jack Nicholson)—Never has the parent-child relationship been more funny or moving than in this Best Picture Oscar winner from James Brooks and his ideal cast.
PG / 1983 / Paramount

The Way We Were (Robert Redford, Barbra Streisand)—Misfit Streisand falls for Prince Charming Redford in a heart-piercing period piece that stands close to *Casablanca* as the greatest love story in Hollywood history.
PG / 1973 / RCA/Columbia

Wuthering Heights (Laurence Olivier, Merle Oberon)—The ravishing romance of Olivier's Heathcliff calling across the moors and beyond the grave to Oberon's Cathy makes for haunting movie memories
1939 / Embassy

WORST

The Betsy (Laurence Olivier, Robert Duvall)—Harold Robbins's auto family saga demeans a talented cast, especially an aging Olivier forced to fumble with upstairs maids and a phony American accent.
R / 1978 / CBS/Fox

Cruising (Al Pacino)—Pacino hunts down a killer of homosexuals in a William Friedkin film that still holds the title as the most offensive piece of Hollywood trash ever.
R / 1980 / CBS/Fox

Daniel (Timothy Hutton, Mandy Patinkin)—It's hard to know whom to root for in this turgid melodrama of Cold War commie-baiting.
R / 1983 / Paramount

Heaven's Gate (Kris Kristofferson, Isabelle Adjani)—This bloated, incoherent Western from *Deer Hunter* director Michael Cimino has now passed into the Hall of Shame as a handy synonym for "expensive flop."
R / 1980 / MGM/UA

Interiors (Diane Keaton, Geraldine Page)—For those who think Woody Allen can do no wrong, check out this lugubrious Ingmar Bergman ripoff that even a great cast, especially Page and Maureen Stapleton, can't rescue from drowning in a sea of pretentiousness.
PG / 1978 / MGM/UA

King David (Richard Gere)—There may have been worse choices than Gere to play the biblical monarch, but then Pee-Wee Herman and Ed McMahon were probably busy.
PG-13 / 1985 / Paramount

Love Story (Ali MacGraw, Ryan O'Neal)—Love actually means never having to say, "Let's rent this tape."
PG / 1970 / Paramount

Mrs. Miniver (Greer Garson, Walter Pidgeon)—Garson, never one to underact, outdoes even herself in this relentlessly noble saga of stiff-upper-lip-hood in wartime Britain.
1942 / N/A

One from the Heart (Teri Garr, Frederic Forrest)—Also one from the ego, this phantasma-

goric mess by Francis Coppola was about a confused romance set in Las Vegas. It's a losing proposition all around.
R / 1982 / RCA/Columbia
The Sandpiper (Elizabeth Taylor, Richard Burton)—Married minister Burton has an affair with earth woman Liz in such dead earnest that it has now become a camp classic of unintentional laughs.
1965 / MGM/UA

FOREIGN MOVIES

BEST

Aguirre, The Wrath of God (Klaus Kinski)—German director Werner Herzog takes a grim look at the obsession created by greed as Kinski, a Spanish explorer, leads a hopeless search for El Dorado.
1972 / Continental
Amarcord (Magali Noel)—The fascinating, canvaslike images of Italian family life in the '30s seem to have risen—more than full blown—from the memory of director Federico Fellini.
R / 1974 / Warner
Beauty and the Beast (Jean Marais, Josette Day)—The classic fairy tale told in realistic fashion with live actors (Marais seems perfectly natural under his Beast's makeup), seems all the more touching.
1946 / Embassy
Black and White in Color (Jean Carmet, Catherine Rouvel)—The story—French and German forces fight a forlorn skirmish in World War I Africa—makes for a wryly pointed comment on European colonialism and the general tendency of humanity to embroil itself in futile struggles.
1977 / N/A
Breathless (Jean-Paul Belmondo, Jean Seberg)—If you've only seen the Richard Gere version, you've missed the point that Belmondo and Seberg convey so deftly: how easy and attractive it is to be alienated in modern society.
1959 / Various
Day for Night (Jacqueline Bisset, Jean-Pierre Léaud)—Director François Truffaut's Oscar-winning film looks at the world of movie-making with a mix of humor and heartbreak that adds up to ecstatic entertainment.
PG / 1972 / Warner

Diabolique (Simone Signoret)—You don't need to know French or even read the subtitles to get the wits scared out of you by this classic chiller about a man who has been murdered by both his wife and mistress (Vera Clouzot and Signoret) but won't stay dead.
1955 / Budget
Discreet Charm of the Bourgeoisie (Fernando Rey)—A typically abstract film by Spanish director Luis Bunuel lampoons superficiality with a meandering, bleak dinner party.
PG / 1972 / Cinémathèque
The Earrings of Madame de . . . (Danielle Darrieux, Vittorio De Sica)—A period of lost elegance, magically evoked by director Max Ophuls, becomes the setting for a duel of love and honor involving Darrieux, her husband Charles Boyer, and her lover, De Sica.
1953 / N/A
The 400 Blows (Jean-Pierre Léaud)—Nobody has ever depicted the anxieties and strength of youth better than François Truffaut did in this autobiographical tale of a boy growing up in a shattered home.
1959 / Key
Going Places (Jeanne Moreau)—Don't let the kiddies wander into the room if you're showing this brutally sexy French farce on the VCR. Bertrand Blier gets superb performances from Gerard Départieu, Patrick Dewaere, and Moreau.
R / 1974 / RCA/Columbia
Grand Illusion (Jean Gabin, Erich Von Stroheim)—The plot, about French prisoners of war in a German camp in World War I, is only a pretext for a profound confrontation between cultures.
1937 / CBS/Fox
Jules and Jim (Jeanne Moreau, Oskar Werner)

—The ultimate ménage à trois becomes both a tribute to love and a monument to its impossibility.
1961 / Key
La Dolce Vita (Anita Ekberg, Marcello Mastroianni)—Fellini at his wildest devastates the then-current idea of hip Roman society.
1960 / Republic
M (Peter Lorre)—Lorre gives an unforgettable performance as a child murderer in this German classic, directed by Fritz Lang. It's still as pertinent today as the time it was made.
1932 / Budget
A Man and a Woman (Anouk Aimée, Jean-Louis Trintigant)—Sure, it's the epitome of schmaltz, but come on, now: Who could resist hoping against hope that Anouk and Jean-Louis will end up getting back together again, plausibility not withstanding.
1966 / Warner
The Marriage of Maria Braun (Hanna Schygulla)—Rainer Werner Fassbinder paints a blistering portrait of postwar Germany with the help of Schygulla's overwhelming performance.
R / 1978 / RCA/Columbia
Persona (Liv Ullmann, Bibi Andersson)—Ullmann and Andersson, both at their peaks, merge personalities in Swedish master Ingmar Bergman's most haunting and poetic film.
1966 / Embassy
Rashomon (Tashiro Mifune, Machiko Kyo)—This Oscar-winning Japanese film from director Akira Kurosawa tells the story of a rape from differing viewpoints. A consistently compelling tale, it's from a master who proved with 1985's *Ran* that he had lost none of his powers.
1951 / Embassy
The Rules of the Game (Marcel Dalio, Nora Gregor)—A weekend house party pits servants against masters in a French tragicomedy that still stands as one of the greatest films made in any language.
1939 / Budget
Scenes from a Marriage (Liv Ullmann, Erland Josephson)—Anybody who has ever been married will recognize at least parts of the grueling tension that runs through this Bergman study of a dissolving couple; anybody who is thinking of a wedding ought to see this to make sure they want to go through with it.
PG / 1973 / RCA/Columbia
Seven Beauties (Giancarlo Giannini)—Italy's Lina Wertmuller turns this story of a low-life (a brilliant Giannini) in a World War II concentration camp into a potent parable of war.
R / 1976 / RCA/Columbia
Viridiana (Silvia Pinal)—A girl about to enter a convent enters instead the sexual and psychological madhouse of her family in Bunuel's most cutting view of his country.
1961 / Budget
Woman in the Dunes (Eiji Okada, Kyoko Kishida)—Stunning camera work makes this Japanese film about a man and woman trapped in a sand pit into one of the most effective allegories in screen history.
1964 / N/A
Z— (Yves Montand)—The Oscar-winning film from Costa-Gavras about the assassination of a peace leader in Greece uses the thriller form to make blistering political comment.
1969 / RCA/Columbia

WORST

And God Created Woman (Brigitte Bardot)—And French director Roger Vadim presumably believes it's his mission to keep woman naked. His wife number one, Bardot, was the victim this time. She looks good; the film doesn't.
1957 / Vestron
Berlin Alexanderplatz (Gunter Lamprecht, Hanna Schygulla)—Germany in the late 1920s, exhaustively rendered by director Fassbinder. Go ahead, rent the eight cassettes (running over 15 hours), and then tell us we're wrong about labeling the package a thudding bore.
1983 / MGM/UA
Fellini's Casanova (Donald Sutherland)—Of course, it's not as bad as Richard Chamberlain's TV "Casanova," but you don't expect such lethargy from the Italian master, or Sutherland, in the title role.
1976 / N/A
The Green Room (Nathalie Bayle)—Truffaut proved, like Fellini, that he too could have a bad day. The French director also stars in this endurance test as a death-obsessed journalist.
PG / 1978 / Warner
I Am Curious Yellow —This sluggish Swedish film was labeled pornography twenty years ago. Now even a grade-schooler wouldn't blush at these allegedly outrageous antics.
1967 / N/A

Le Bal (Marc Berman, Chantal Capron)—Inexplicably Oscar-nominated, this Italian film from Ettore Scola is set entirely in a dance hall and is guaranteed to produce instant tedium.
1983 / Warner

The Moon in the Gutter (Gerard Depardieu, Nastassja Kinski)—The promise French director Jean-Jacques Beineix showed in 1982's *Diva* turns to crushing disappointment in this turgid drama featuring Depardieu and Kinski's worst acting to date.
R / 1983 / RCA/Columbia

Stromboli (Ingrid Bergman)—Bergman forsook Hollywood for Italy's Roberto Rossellini in a real story far more dramatic than this bleak film they made together. It's about Bergman marrying a fisherman and settling down to a life of quiet desperation.
1950 / United

To Begin Again (Antonio Ferrandis, Encaina Paso)—This surprise Oscar winner as Best Foreign Film is no more than a cloyingly sentimental shrug of a movie about a dying professor revisiting Spain and an old love.
1982 / N/A

The Touch (Elliott Gould, Bibi Andersson)—Hey, wait a minute. What's Elliott Gould doing in an Ingmar Bergman film? Looking way, way out of his depth, that's what.
R / 1971 / CBS/Fox

MUSICALS

BEST

The Band Wagon (Fred Astaire, Cyd Charisse)—Just wait around and hope for more magical talents in one musical than Astaire, Charisse, Nanette Fabray, Oscar Levant, Jack Buchanan, director Vincente Minnelli, and composers Howard Dietz and Arthur Schwartz.
1953 / MGM/UA

Birth of the Blues (Bing Crosby, Mary Martin)—Well, all right, Bing and Mary didn't really invent the blues, but they—and Jack Teagarden, the great jazz trombonist-singer—have great fun Dixielanding up such tunes as "Wait Till the Sun Shines, Nellie."
1941 / N/A

Cabaret (Liza Minnelli, Joel Grey)—The deserving winner of eight Oscars, the musical-drama of prewar Berlin represents career peaks for its stars and director Bob Fosse.
PG / 1972 / CBS/Fox

Cabin in the Sky (Ethel Waters, Eddie Anderson)—This is much more than just an all-black musical. It has a cast of all-time great performers: the great blues singer Waters, Lena Horne, John Bubbles, Duke Ellington, and Louis Armstrong.
1943 / MGM/UA

Flashdance (Jennifer Beals)—While Beals's glory paled a bit when it was revealed a double had done a lot of her dancing, the sweaty sensuality, Giorgio Moroder's superheated music, and the fun remain. Besides, where else do you find as the heroine of a love story a welder who dances in her spare time?
R / 1983 / Paramount

Forty-second Street (Ruby Keeler, Dick Powell)—Hear the beat of clippy-cloppy feet, and you know it's Keeler doggedly tapping her way into our hearts through Busby Berkeley's typically elaborate choreography and coming back a star.
1933 / CBS/Fox

Funny Girl (Barbra Streisand, Omar Sharif)—Streisand's Oscar-winning film debut as Ziegfeld's laughing-on-the-outside, crying-on-the-inside clown Fanny Brice is still the most powerfully funny and touching musical-comedy performance on celluloid.
G / 1968 / RCA/Columbia

Gay Divorcee (Fred Astaire, Ginger Rogers)—Long before the era of explicit sex in movies, Astaire and Rogers danced to Cole Porter's "Night and Day"; there has never been a more sensuous scene in movies.
1935 / Media

Gigi (Leslie Caron, Louis Jourdan)—Charm flows like champagne in this Best Picture Oscar winner as Caron trains to be a French courtesan but settles for real love with Jourdan while Maurice Chevalier thanks heaven for little girls elsewhere.
G / 1958 / MGM/UA

A Hard Day's Night (The Beatles)—They were well on their way already, of course, yet this playful, sometimes self-mocking and cleverly directed (by Richard Lester) film confirmed the Beatles' popularity, not to mention their talent.
G / 1964 / MPI

High Society (Bing Crosby, Grace Kelly, Frank Sinatra)—Cole Porter's music, the gorgeous Kelly (in her last movie), and some cute business between Sinatra and Celeste Holm make for a high-spirited film.
1956 / MGM/UA

Jailhouse Rock (Elvis Presley)—While Elvis's movies were never very long on plausibility, the music often had a joyful élan and he rocked as enthusiastically as he sneered.
1957 / MGM/UA

Les Girls (Gene Kelly, Kay Kendall)—Three ex-show girls remember the years of struggle with mentor Kelly in a complete class act, from George Cukor's direction and Cole Porter's score to the enchanting presence of Kay Kendall.
1957 / MGM/UA

Love Me or Leave Me (Doris Day, James Cagney)—Day finds the role of a lifetime as singer Ruth Etting, whose career and life are almost ruined by her gangster husband, brilliantly played by Cagney.
1955 / N/A

Meet Me in St. Louis (Judy Garland, Margaret O'Brien)—Garland, in lovely voice ("The Boy Next Door"), and O'Brien, the next best thing to Shirley Temple, make this one of Hollywood's most lovable musicals.
1944 / MGM/UA

My Fair Lady (Audrey Hepburn, Rex Harrison)—Though Julie Andrews got *Mary Poppins* and an Oscar as compensation, it still seems criminal that she lost her Broadway role to non-singer Hepburn in this movie. Marni Nixon's dubbing of Hepburn's voice was graceful though, Harrison was wonderful, and the Lerner-Loewe tunes still seem just right.
G / 1964 / CBS/Fox

One Touch of Venus (Ava Gardner, Robert Walker)—Kurt Weill's haunting score and Gardner's staggering beauty as a statue of Venus come to life make this charmer one to search out at the video store.
1948 / Republic

Oliver (Oliver Reed, Mark Lester)—Ingratiating little Mark made an effective foil for this cynical musical that ended with most of the principals still living criminally ever after.
G / 1968 / RCA/Columbia

The Pirate (Gene Kelly, Judy Garland)—Director Vincente Minnelli's visual pyrotechnics reach their apogee as Garland imagines circus clown Kelly to be a dashing outlaw of the seas.
1948 / MGM/UA

Showboat (Ava Gardner, Howard Keel)—Okay, the plot creaks. But that Kern-Hammerstein score, from "Old Man River" to "Bill," has only gained in beauty, and if you don't cry when Ava waves good-bye at the dock, turn in your tear ducts.
1951 / MGM/UA

Singin' in the Rain (Gene Kelly, Debbie Reynolds)—Kelly, Reynolds, Donald O'Connor, and the hilarious Jean Hagen spoof the early talkies in what many consider the best musical ever made.
1952 / MGM/UA

A Star Is Born (Judy Garland, James Mason)—With thirty minutes of lost footage now restored, this Garland classic (forget the Streisand remake) about an actress on the way up while alcoholic husband Mason declines is a video must.
1954 / Warner

Sweeney Todd (Angela Lansbury)—Taped in live performance, this now legendary Stephen Sondheim musical (his peak to date) about the demon barber of Fleet Street preserves the knock-out performances of Lansbury and George Hearn.
1983 / RKO

West Side Story (Natalie Wood, Rita Moreno)—Just when you think the plot's too familiar to bear, you hear that pulsating Bernstein-Sondheim score and see Jerome Robbins's dance wizardry, and you're hooked.
1961 / CBS/Fox

Yankee Doodle Dandy (James Cagney, Walter Huston)—What an exuberant little dandy he was too, with that spasmodic, puppety dancing style, and what a joy it is to see him in this show biz fable about vaudevillian George M. Cohan.
1942 / CBS/Fox

WORST

At Long Last Love (Cybill Shepherd, Burt Reynolds)—On the bad idea list, Peter Bogdanovich's notion to let Reynolds and Shepherd sing (or, more appropriately, slaughter) the music of Cole Porter deserves a place of shame near the top.
G / 1975 / N/A

Can-Can (Shirley MacLaine, Frank Sinatra)—Everyone remembers that Soviet premier Nikita Khrushchev visited the set of this phony Hollywood claptrap with Frank and Shirl pretending to be French. Few people saw the actual movie. They're the lucky ones.
1960 / CBS/Fox

A Chorus Line (Michael Douglas, Alyson Reed)—In director Richard Attenborough's stifling translation, the singular stage sensation about an audition for a theatrical musical turns into a listless chore.
PG / 1985 / Embassy

The Jazz Singer (Neil Diamond, Laurence Olivier)—Diamond, as a cantor's son-turned-rock singer, set musicals back fifty years, and he didn't do much for his own career either. He never made another film.
PG / 1980 / Paramount

A Little Night Music (Elizabeth Taylor, Len Cariou)—Liz croaks Sondheim's "Send in the Clowns" in this laughable mess that loses every ounce of its charm (not to mention Broadway's Glynis Johns) on the way from stage to screen.
PG / 1977 / Embassy

Mame (Lucille Ball, Robert Preston)—Lucy croaks Jerry Herman's "If He Walked into My Life" in this other laughable mess that loses every ounce of its charm (not to mention Broadway's Angela Lansbury) on the way from stage to screen.
PG / 1974 / Warner

South Pacific (Mitzi Gaynor, Rozzano Brazzi)—Sure the show's a Rodgers and Hammerstein classic, but try sitting through the botch job director Joshua Logan makes of the movie version with weird colors and close-ups. Play the Mary Martin–Ezio Pinza record instead.
G / 1958 / CBS/Fox

Staying Alive (John Travolta, Finola Hughes)—The sequel to *Saturday Night Fever,* directed by Sylvester Stallone, was heavy-handed enough to seem like a Sunday morning hangover.
PG / 1983 / Paramount

Under the Cherry Moon (Prince)—Someday his movie will come; this narcissistic romance isn't it.
R / 1986 / Warner

Xanadu (Gene Kelly, Olivia Newton-John)—Too much roller skating and silly fantasy, not enough Kelly or likable music.
PG / 1980 / MCA

MYSTERY/SUSPENSE MOVIES

BEST

Anatomy of a Murder (James Stewart, Lee Remick)—Duke Ellington's score was a bonus to this hard-edged courtroom drama.
1959 / RCA/Columbia

Blue Velvet (Isabella Rossellini, Dennis Hopper)—Director David Lynch's visionary masterpiece about the dark side of Norman Rockwell America is also a bold and fiercely erotic amateur detective story.
R / 1986 / Karl-Lorimar

Blow Up (Vanessa Redgrave, David Hemmings)—A London photographer finds his life of passive hedonism abruptly altered when he discovers he may have photographed a murder in Michelangelo Antonioni's mind-twisting classic.
R / 1966 / MGM/UA

Body Heat (William Hurt, Kathleen Turner)—If beads of sweat appear on your screen when you're watching this evil gem about a murderous wife, don't be surprised; director Lawrence Kasdan set up the sultriest of moods in a hot Southern town and the Hurt-Turner misalliance is as sexually charged as they come.
R / 1981 / Warner

Chinatown (Jack Nicholson, Faye Dunaway)—It may be the slice on Nicholson's nose that everyone remembers, but this Roman Polanski thriller about corruption and incest in Los Angeles is full of intriguingly lurid corners.
R / 1974 / Paramount

The Conversation (Gene Hackman)—It's one of Francis Coppola's more modest efforts, yet this film about a professional planter of electronic bugs builds overwhelming momentum as Hackman's paranoia—an obvious occupational hazard—grows.
PG / 1974 / Paramount

Double Indemnity (Barbara Stanwyck, Fred MacMurray)—Stanwyck, at her most calculatingly seductive, lures insurance investigator MacMurray into a plot to murder her husband; then Edward G. Robinson gets on the case. Director Billy Wilder and Raymond Chandler wrote the script.
1944 / MCA

Dressed to Kill (Angie Dickinson, Michael Caine)—Brian De Palma's homage to Hitchcock is also a wickedly witty chiller in its own right as a sexually needy Dickinson gets more than she bargained for out of her sessions with psychiatrist Caine.
R / 1980 / Warner

The Friends of Eddie Coyle (Robert Mitchum, Peter Boyle)—The resignation of the lead character—a third-rate crook who turns informer to stay out of prison—is an ideal vehicle for Mitchum's natural hangdog look. Peter Yates directed from George V. Higgins's Boston-centered novel.
R / 1973 / N/A

Hound of the Baskervilles (Basil Rathbone, Nigel Bruce)—Of all the screen's Sherlock Holmes–Dr. Watson teams, Rathbone and Bruce were by far the most likable, with Rathbone's suave, icy style contrasting perfectly with Bruce's earnest bumbling.
1939 / Playhouse

In the Heat of the Night (Rod Steiger, Sidney Poitier)—The murder plot is secondary to the confrontation between Steiger, as a redneck Southern cop, and Poitier, a big-city detective. The film won the Best Picture Oscar and Best Actor (for Steiger, although it could have easily been split between him and Poitier).
1967 / CBS/Fox

Klute (Jane Fonda, Donald Sutherland)—Fonda's Oscar-winning performance as a call girl used by detective Sutherland in his search for a psycho raises this thriller way above average.
R / 1971 / Warner

Lady from Shanghai (Rita Hayworth, Orson Welles)—A masterpiece of a mystery with writer-director Welles a pawn in a murder involving a gorgeous Hayworth and a Hall of Mirrors climax guaranteed to hold you in thrall.
1948 / RCA/Columbia

Laura (Dana Andrews, Gene Tierney)—So is Tierney dead or not? Andrews, as a detective, tries to figure it out, with kibitzing by Clifton Webb and the theme they invented the word "haunting" for by David Raksin and Johnny Mercer.
1944 / Embassy

The Maltese Falcon (Humphrey Bogart, Mary Astor)—Director John Huston's film debut gives us Bogart (as Sam Spade), Sydney Greenstreet, Peter Lorre, and Astor in the detective story against which all others are still judged and found wanting.
1941 / CBS/Fox

North by Northwest (Cary Grant, Eva Marie Saint)—One of Hitchcock's most entertaining conundrums is played with style to spare by Grant and includes classic suspense sequences involving a crop duster, the U.N., and Mount Rushmore.
1959 / MGM/UA

The Postman Always Rings Twice (Lana Turner, John Garfield)—Turner, at her most impossibly beautiful, and the intense Garfield generated far more passion than Jessica Lange and Jack Nicholson did later as James M. Cain's desperate couple, doomed by their own lust and murderous instincts.
1946 / RCA/Columbia

Psycho (Anthony Perkins, Vera Miles)—Still scary and engrossing even when you've seen it nine or ten times, this Hitchcock chiller about a schizophrenic murderer blends images and sound in a startling way. Nobody who sees it ever feels quite safe in the shower again.
1960 / MCA

Song of the Thin Man (William Powell, Myrna Loy)—Escapist detective tales like this one, which

features Keenan Wynn as a comically dissolute jazz clarinetist, were a staple of '30s and '40s Hollywood, but nobody ever quite figured out how to update the concept after that.
1947 / MGM/UA
Taxi Driver (Robert De Niro, Jodie Foster)—De Niro's ex-Marine-turned-cabbie finds Manhattan's sordid underside, epitomized by Foster's child whore, tilting him over the edge in Martin Scorsese's blistering meditation on violence.
R / 1976 / RCA/Columbia
The Third Man (Orson Welles, Joseph Cotton)—Welles is mystery man Harry Lime, hiding out in postwar Vienna in Carol Reed's decadent thriller, with a first-rate script by Graham Greene.
1949 / Media
The 39 Steps (Robert Donat, Madeleine Carroll)—Just about everybody, including Hitchcock himself, recycled his notion of an innocent man dragging an unwilling (and gorgeous) accomplice on the lam with him, but nobody ever did it with more wit or suspense.
1935 / Embassy
Touch of Evil (Orson Welles, Janet Leigh)—Welles again, this time as a corrupt cop in a Mexican border town tangling with narc Charlton Heston. As writer-director, Welles had a field day with characters as bizarre as the dialogue.
1958 / MCA
Vertigo (James Stewart, Kim Novak)—Hitchcock films could have filled the mystery category, but this tale of obsession is the master's most deeply felt and unforgettable work.
1958 / MCA
Winter Kills (Jeff Bridges)—Director William Richert's cult film involving a presidential assassination is a darkly comic nightmare that deserves a wider audience on video.
R / 1980 / Embassy

WORST

Death Wish (Charles Bronson, Vera Miles)—Cheap catharsis at best, this film about an architect who turns vigilante killer after his wife is attacked spawned a loathsome new genre of revenge films.
R / 1974 / Paramount

The Fan (Lauren Bacall, James Garner)—Broadway star Bacall gets pursued by a psychotic admirer in a crude cheapie whose pretensions toward redeeming social value makes it twice as objectionable.
R / 1981 / Paramount
Gorky Park (William Hurt, Lee Marvin)—Hurt is as dour as one might suppose a Soviet cop to be and the Moscow background to this murder mystery lives down to our expectations too. This is about as much fun as asking who's buried in Lenin's tomb.
R / 1983 / Vestron
The List of Adrian Messenger (Kirk Douglas, Frank Sinatra, Burt Lancaster)—A murderer in disguise allows a lot of big stars to wear disfiguring makeup, but no gimmick can save this turkey from oblivion.
1963 / MCA
Little Drummer Girl (Diane Keaton)—The complex Le Carré novel about an actress seduced into Middle East espionage turns into *Annie Hall Goes Terrorist*.
R / 1984 / Warner
Nighthawk (Sylvester Stallone, Billy Dee Williams)—Big Apple cop Stallone pursues terrorist Rutger Hauer, who wears great designer clothes. Sly ends up in a dress. However you figure it, the movie ends up a mess.
R / 1981 / CBS/Fox
Scarface (Al Pacino, Michelle Pfeiffer)—Director Brian De Palma, forgetting his sense of humor and pace but not his penchant for graphic gore, turns Pacino into a laughably ruthless Cuban emigré-turned-mobster.
R / 1983 / MCA
Still of the Night (Meryl Streep, Roy Scheider)—Shrink Scheider falls for a woman he thinks is a killer, Streep, in her first truly awful performance. The movie's a pale Hitchcock copy.
PG / 1982 / CBS/Fox
Torn Curtain (Julie Andrews, Paul Newman)—No sparks fly between Julie and Paul in this cold war spy thriller; another pale Hitchcock copy, only this time Hitch did it to himself.
PG / 1966 / MCA
Year of the Dragon (Mickey Rourke, Ariane)—Michael Cimino directed, Oliver Stone wrote, audiences guffawed at this not-convincing-for-a-moment chop suey about organized crime in New York's Chinatown.
R / 1985 / MGM/UA

SCIENCE FICTION/HORROR MOVIES

BEST

Alien (Sigourney Weaver, Yaphet Kotto)—The slimiest, scariest, creepiest space creature flick that ever had a great performance by Weaver, though she didn't even get an Oscar nomination until the 1986 sequel.
R / 1979 / CBS/Fox
The Birds (Tippi Hedren, Rod Taylor)—Much more than just goosebumps lurk in this Daphne du Maurier story as Hitchcock reveals character through reaction to unprovoked bird attacks on a small community.
PG-13 / 1963 / MCA
The Bride of Frankenstein (Boris Karloff, Elsa Lanchester)—The monster—still the affecting Karloff—learns to say "good" and gets fixed up with the blind date of the century, the frizzy-haired, screeching Lanchester.
1935 / MCA
Carrie (Sissy Spacek, Piper Laurie)—Director Brian De Palma heightens the horror and the wit of Stephen King's story of a misfit who takes telekinetic revenge on her enemies, and Spacek's Oscar-nominated performance provides the much-needed heart.
R / 1976 / CBS/Fox
A Clockwork Orange (Malcolm McDowell)—Anthony Burgess's shocking novel of future violence finds the perfect director in Stanley Kubrick and the ideal star performance from McDowell.
R / 1971 / Warner
The Day the Earth Stood Still (Michael Rennie, Patricia Neal)—In an era of giant bug-eyed monsters, this sensible bit of sci-fi suggested that it was we humans, not beings from outer space, who were really the scary creatures.
1951 / Thorn/EMI
Dracula (Bela Lugosi, Helen Chandler)—Theretofore a serious actor, Lugosi was marked for life when he played the toothsome Transylvanian nobleman who gave new meaning to the term "necking." It was probably the most imitated characterization of all time, and the movie is still the most fun of the horror classics.
1931 / MCA
Dreamscape (Dennis Quaid, Max Von Sydow)—Quaid goes tiptoeing through the synapses in an intriguing plot about manipulation of dreams.
PG-13 / 1984 / Thorn/EMI
The Exorcist (Ellen Burstyn, Linda Blair)—The prize of the devil-made-me-do-it genre boasts a classy cast (including Jason Miller and Max Von Sydow), an Oscar-winning Bill Blatty script, and all-stops-out direction from William Friedkin.
R / 1973 / Warner
Forbidden Planet (Walter Pidgeon, Anne Francis)—A variation on Shakespeare's *The Tempest,* with a robot servant, a mad scientist, his glamour girl daughter, and space ships, this film offers a sophisticated sci-fi look at the potency and dangerous confusion of the human mind.
G / 1956 / MGM/UA
The Fury (Amy Irving, Kirk Douglas)—Another early De Palma film gives Irving the scary extra-sensory powers this time. Let's just say that when somebody hurts her feelings, she makes them go to pieces in a big way.
R / 1978 / CBS/Fox
Invasion of the Body Snatchers (Kevin McCarthy, Dana Wynter)—Directed by Don Siegel, this low-key terror about alien pods that duplicated humans was a monument to the paranoia of the '50s and it can still make you wonder why Uncle Ziggy has been acting so strange lately.
1956 / Republic
King Kong (Fay Wray)—The giant gorilla became a role model for all those misunderstood movie monsters who just wanted to settle down and raise a family. K. K. himself got reincarnated a number of times but never with more pathos than here—or, more remarkably, with substantially better special effects.
1933 / Nostalgia Merchant
Night of the Living Dead The flesh-eating zombies of George Romero's cult favorite are still the ultimate in gruesome, unless you watch the crude and unscary colorized version.
R / 1968 / United
1984 The old, grim, black and white version of George Orwell's ominous novel, not the 1985 film with the Eurythmics soundtrack. Edmond O'Brien was the terrified rebel who dared defy Big Brother.
1956 / N/A

Planet of the Apes (Charlton Heston, Kim Hunter) —Surviving astronauts, led by Charlton Heston, find a new world run by monkeys in an astonishingly clever piece of hocus-pocus.

G / 1968 / CBS/Fox

Rosemary's Baby (Mia Farrow, John Cassavetes)—Director Roman Polanski's marvelously atmospheric story of an actor who sells his soul— his wife's body, actually—to the devil is spiced by a deliciously wicked old couple of satanic cultists played by Ruth Gordon and Sidney Blackmer.

R / 1968 / Paramount

Star Wars (Alec Guinness, Harrison Ford, Mark Hamill)—Luke Skywalker, Han Solo, Princess Leia, R2D2, C-3PO, and the gang begin their trip into imaginations everywhere with this George Lucas blockbuster that just keeps spawning sequels and imitators. It's *that* good.

PG / 1977 / CBS/Fox

The Terminator (Arnold Schwarzenegger, Linda Hamilton)—Director James Cameron's look at a robotized killing machine, perfectly embodied by Schwarzenegger, is far more powerfully and provocatively realized than critics ever gave it credit for. A video store must.

R / 1984 / Thorn/EMI

Texas Chainsaw Massacre Director Tobe Hooper carried horror to its stylishly illogical extreme in creating a psychotic bunch who obviously believes that the family that slays together stays together.

R / 1974 / Media, Vestron; Wizard

Them (James Arness, James Whitmore)—Out of the salad bowl and into the fire, Arness is a good guy this time, chasing down mutated giant ants, the most fearsome of the movie creatures spawned by fear of the then-new nuclear age. Long after you've forgotten the plot you remember the weird chirp that foreshadows the insects' attacks.

1954 / Warner

The Thing from Another World (James Arness) —Arness plays a murderous walking vegetable from another world who stalks an Arctic outpost, inspiring chills in more ways than one.

1951 / Nostalgia Merchant; Vid America

2001: A Space Odyssey (Keir Dullea)—Director Stanley Kubrick's deepening on film of Arthur Clarke's milestone story is quite simply the greatest visionary film ever made. Sorry, video fanatics, the small screen just won't do it justice.

G / 1968 / MGM/UA

Village of the Damned (George Sanders)—In a small English village, Sanders finds himself teaching a class of eerie, dead-eyed children. You'll find yourself scared senseless.

1960 / MGM/UA

The Wolfman (Lon Chaney, Jr., Claude Rains)— If it's possible for a film about a werewolf to be subtle, this one is, with take-it-seriously-folks acting and Maria Ouspenskaya intoning the poem: "Even a man who is pure of heart/and says his prayers by night/Can become a wolf when the wolfbane blooms/and the autumn moon is bright." All right, so it isn't Keats; we're talking horror movies here.

1941 / Thorn/EMI

WORST

The Amityville Horror (James Brolin, Margot Kidder)—Rod Steiger's ham acting is the only real horror in this tacky film version of Jay Anson's book about a family moving into a haunted Long Island house.

R / 1979 / Warner

The Bride (Jennifer Beals, Sting)—With this cast, you'd expect the remake of *The Bride of Frankenstein* to at least include a little monster mash or some excitement, but instead it seems like a horror version of *My Fair Lady,* without the music.

R / 1985 / RCA/Columbia

Exorcist 2: The Heretic (Richard Burton, Linda Blair)—Easily the worst sequel in horror history, and that's going some. But where else can you find Burton wallowing in pure trash?

R / 1977 / Warner

Friday the 13th (Betsy Palmer)—Betsy was lucky. She lost her head over this one and (except in flashbacks) didn't have to go through the interminable series of hack-'em-up sequels.

R / 1980 / Paramount

Horror of Party Beach (Eulabelle Moore)—If the atrocious pseudo rock band doesn't get you, the ending, in which the monsters are sodiumed to death, will.

1964 / Prism

I Dismember Mama It's just what you think it is, only more so. Yuck.

R / 1982 / Video Gems

Plan 9 from Outer Space (Bela Lugosi)—This laughably cheap invaders-of-the-earth flick has won a number of awards already as the worst film ever made.

1962 / Nostalgia Merchant

They Saved Hitler's Brain Nazis flourish on a remote island listening to Adolf's still-talking head. Here is *Plan 9*'s closest competition in the Hall of Shame record books.

1964 / United

The Thing with Two Heads (Rosie Grier, Ray Milland)—No heads, in this case, would have been better than two.

R / 1972 / N/A

Tron (Jeff Bridges, Bruce Boxleitner)—Remember when video games were all the rage? Remember when this movie came along, about people who are sort of ingested into a particularly hellish game? No? Good.

PG / 1982 / Disney

INDEX

▲ CHILDREN'S VIDEOS

▲ COMEDY

▲ DRAMA

▲ FOREIGN

▲ SCIENCE FICTION/HORROR

Index